Russia and Europe

Nikolai Iakovlevich Danilevskii at the time he was writing *Russia and Europe,* circa 1867.
From the personal collection of Tatiana Vjishkina-Danilevskaya. Used by permission.

RUSSIA AND EUROPE

THE SLAVIC WORLD'S POLITICAL AND CULTURAL RELATIONS WITH THE GERMANIC-ROMAN WEST

By Nikolai Iakovlevich Danilevskii

Translated and annotated by

Stephen M. Woodburn

Bloomington, Indiana, 2013

SLAVICA

Cover: Medallion, *Miniature on the Theme of the Treaty of Tilsit.* France, 1810s. Bronze, enamel, painting. *Source:* Wikimedia Commons. The image is in the public domain. Cover design by Tracey Theriault.

Technical editor: Kelsey O'Connor

ISBN 978-0-89357-400-0

Library of Congress Control Number: 2013953394

This publication was prepared (in part) under a grant from the Kennan Institute of the Woodrow Wilson International Center for Scholars, Washington, DC. The statements and views expressed herein are those of the author and are not necessarily those of the Woodrow Wilson Center.

Slavica Publishers
Indiana University
1430 N. Willis Dr.
Bloomington, IN 47404-2146
USA

[Tel.] 1-812-856-4186
[Toll-free] 1-877-SLAVICA
[Fax] 1-812-856-4187
[Email] slavica@indiana.edu
[www] http://www.slavica.com/

Contents

   A comparison of the two years. Europe's indifference to Denmark and sympathy for Turkey. The Holstein question. The Crimean War: the significance of the key to the Bethlehem temple. The Vienna Note: Europe's political course of action transferred to the sphere of personal relations. Public opinion of Europe. Why a measurement by different standards?

   Russia is not an aggressor state. What exactly is aggression and conquest? Finland. Baltic provinces. Western Krai. Poland. Bessarabia. Caucasus. Siberia. The nature of Russia's wars. Russia does not extinguish light and freedom. The Holy Alliance. The assassination of Kotzebue. Russia's liberalism has not reduced the hostility it faces. Europe's ignorance regarding Russia. Europe does not recognize us as one of its own.

   What exactly is Europe? The artificiality of continental divisions. The historical-cultural meaning of "Europe." Russia does not belong to Europe. Russia's role, in Europe's opinion. Russia is an obstacle to the development of European civilization. The offering from the lowly for the most high: Marquis Poza. Superficial political patriotism: the Ultra-Russian party. Where is the reconciliation between national feeling and the demand for progress?

   West and East. Progress in the East: China. The death of a people. What exactly is a scientific system? A natural system. Its requirements. An appraisal of the generally accepted system in the study of world history. A new, natural grouping of historical phenomena: historical-cultural types. Their enumeration. Ethnographic material.

Austrian federation of Slavs. A thought about an Austro-Turkish federation. The idea of All-Slavdom.

The centrality of Constantinople's location. Its four names and four historical epochs. The right to Constantinople. What exactly is a historical right? Constantinople is a res nullius. To whom is the control of Constantinople all important? 1) The Achilles' heel of Russia. 2) The size of Russia. 3) The necessity of a navy, but a Black Sea navy, for Russia. 4) The expansion of Russia's moral influence from the control of Constantinople. Tsargrad must be the capital not of Russia, but of an All-Slavic union. A Slavic federation with Russia at the head, as a resolution of the Eastern question. The members of the federation must be large. Its goal is not the absorption of the Slavs by Russia. The composition of an All-Slavic union, and an enumeration of its members. The Polish question. The best resolution is by means of an All-Slavic federation.

Russia cannot be a member of the European political system. Interference never brought it any benefit. Russia must be a counterbalance to Europe. Two fates awaiting Russia. The significance of a union for the rest of its members. For Greece. For Bulgaria. What exactly is the Russian intelligentsia. For Serbia. For Czechia. For Romania. For Poland and Hungary. Russia's supposed lust for power. Three categories of subjects. The fear of world domination. The necessity of a Slavic union for humanity. The history of Europe in relation to other peoples. The system of political equilibrium. The main occasions of its disruption and preservation. An obstacle to Europe's world domination. The disastrous result of an all-human civilization. The conditions and consequences of an All-Slavic federation. The promotion of Russian as an All-Slavic language. The necessity of a struggle with Europe.

The law of preserving a store of historical strength. The rule for Russian politics. Russia has no interest in a system of equilibrium. Equilibrium is harmful for Russia, but its disruption is advantageous. Russia's relations with the main representatives of European power. With England. With France. With Prussia. The internal sources of Russia's strength. Disciplined enthusiasm. An appraisal of the wars Russia waged with Europe. The sympathy of the Slavs. The peasant allotment.

Four categories of cultural activity. Primary cultures. The single-foundation historical-cultural types. The European type. The threefold anarchy of Europe. The properties and prospects of the Slavic world. The character of Slavic religiosity. The capacity for statehood. The special nature of Russian political activity—the absence of possessions and colonies. Is the Russian people capable of freedom? Russian uprisings. Russia's social and economic structure. The obshchina and socialism. Culture in the strict sense of the word. Consuming its strength in the construction of government. The contrast between America and Russia. Indications of scientific and artistic capability. Dead Souls. Boris Godunov. War and Peace. *Ivanov's painting.* Pimenov's Transfiguration. *Mickiewicz. Slavdom — the* quadruple-foundation historical-cultural type. *Two streams of world history.*

Acknowledgments

I waited ten years for someone better qualified than me to do the work of translating this book. Eventually I concluded that the main qualification for any task is the conviction that it is worth doing, which for better or worse made me the most qualified person for the job. I am grateful for the help of so many over the course of this project. To Andy Sheppard, my sincerest thanks for encouragement and support from the very earliest stages to the end. To Bob Thurston and Carl Pletsch, Irina Goncharenko, Gretchen Ziolkowski, and Paul Mitchell, for the foundations on which it rests. To Kishimjan Bektashova, for patiently proofreading my early drafts of each chapter. To Kyrill Drezov, for his interest, encouragement, and as a source of various bits of information, including bringing some early photos of Danilevskii to my attention. To Olga Danilevskaya and Olga Tenney, descendants of the author, for their generous assistance and permission to use the rare image of Danilevskii from the time of the book's writing and the photos of the author's gravesite then and now, plus so much additional support and encouragement. To Chris Caldwell and Delilah Caldwell, who are scholars "kat' exochen." To Rex Wade, for his mentorly guidance and generous friendship. To Sharyl Corrado, David Wright, and Phil Schmidt, for various thoughtful conversations on this work. To David Ransel, for the early encouragement to make the book readable. To Melissa Stockdale, for taking an interest and writing a recommendation letter at the worst possible time. To Edith Clowes, for encouragement and helpful advice. Special thanks to Daniel Todes and Michael Gordin, for help with nineteenth-century biological arcana, and their moral support. Thanks to Vicki Polansky at Slavica for her persistence and help. And thanks to David Schimmelpenninck van der Oye for a keen eye, excellent suggestions, and the ringing endorsement.

I am grateful for institutional support, over many years, from Southwestern College, the University of Illinois's Summer Research Lab, and a short-term grant from the Kennan Institute. I would be lost without the help of an army of librarians: Jon Giullian, Veronica McAsey, Cheryl Barnett, Elise Blas, Helen Sullivan, and all the staff at the online Slavic Reference Service at the University of Illinois.

Finally I thank my wife and daughters for living with this project while it occupied so much of our lives and, at times, a good bit of the study and dining room.

This book is dedicated to my youngest daughter Ruby, whose daily afternoon naptime gave me the opportunity, and the excuse, to start.

Translator's Introduction

Rossiia i evropa (Russia and Europe) is Nikolai Iakovlevich Danilevskii's magnum opus, and it is important in two contexts. It is first a seminal work in the intellectual history of nineteenth-century Russia, condensing the Slavophile point of view articulated in the 1830s and 1840s, and recasting it in the mold of 1860s pragmatism and *Realpolitik* toward a broader, Pan-Slavic purpose. Danilevskii addressed the frustration of some Slavophiles and their sympathizers that a preoccupation with the past left them irrelevant to the present and the future. They were hung up on the reforms of Peter the Great, especially the most superficial (the adoption of Western clothing and the removal of facial hair), and prone to romanticize the distant past preserved in medieval chronicles. In this regard, Slavophilism aligned with other forms of romanticism across Europe, as an escapist refuge from the realities of modernity slowly but relentlessly transforming the continent.

The yearning for a different time—various adjectives may be applied to it: simpler, more spiritual, less turbulent, exotic, gallant, elevated, mysterious, wholesome, etc.—offered only stasis in regard to the present, and wariness toward the future. Informed by German philosophy, Slavophilism of the 1830s and 1840s constructed a romanticized notion of the ideal Russian people existing before the reforms of Peter the Great. Once the Great Reforms of the 1860s were well underway, the escapist preoccupation with an idealized, golden-hued past and native identity offered nothing concrete to meet the challenges and aspirations of the present. Danilevskii preserved the Slavophiles' reverence for the past in terms of establishing national identity and distinctness, but accepted the realities of the post-Emancipation era, not only within Russia, but across Europe.

In Russia and the U.S., the defining events of the 1860s involved the elimination of involuntary servitude. Following a humiliating defeat in the Crimean War and the death of the uncompromising Tsar Nicholas I, Russia opted for voluntary reform, beginning with the emancipation of the serfs in 1861 and expanding to the adoption of judicial reforms, greater press freedom, and local self-government. The U.S. fought a bloody civil war lasting the first half of the decade to end slavery and preserve the union of states. But in Europe, the defining events of the 1860s were the unifications of two states, Italy and Germany, where there had previously been separate kingdoms, duchies, and other sovereign entities of medieval invention, subject to conquest or swapping around among the more powerful dynastic empires on the continent. As Danilevskii was writing this book, Germany and Italy were steadily, and inexorably, taking shape, and references to these events and the leaders pursuing them are scattered throughout its chapters. Bismarck, Cavour, and Garibaldi were men of ambition and political genius whom Danilevskii could not help but admire, along with their historical antecedents, such as Philip II of Macedon or Constantine the Great, for consolidating new state entities on the basis of common identity and purpose. While this was a book for Russians, it was written with an eye on recent events in Europe. Implicit throughout the book is Danilevskii's longing for Russia to provide such a leader to unite the Slavic peoples along the same lines, along with mild but consistent criticism of its past rulers' hesitancy to pursue what Danilevskii saw as Russia's national interests abroad.

In this regard classical Slavophilism lacked ambition and goals, its adherents having a narrowly Russian focus, rooted in the past. Danilevskii crystallized the identity politics of the Slavophile movement, but gave it a broader future orientation outside Russia's borders. The Crimean War drove home the fact that Russia's rank among the Great Powers was slipping, and German unification (more than its Italian counterpart) suggested that weak states binding together would become strong. But the source of strength, for Danilevskii, lay in the alignment of peoples with polities.

Here his scientific career informed his politics. It is crucial to remember that Danilevskii the nationalist was first and foremost a naturalist (or what we now call a biologist), concerned with the proper classification of specimens by their inherent similarities or differences. His vocation provides the essential metaphor and the scientific-positivist outlook shaping the book. Its main idea is that Russia should not be classified as part of Europe, but that these two represent fundamentally different civilizational types: Europe, the Germanic-Roman civilization, and Russia, the Slavic. As a naturalist he was concerned with proper classification, grouping like organisms together on the basis of similarities. His reviews of the state of various sciences in chapters 4 and 6 are now outdated, but serve his purpose of illustrating that all sciences progress from artificial combinations and classifications of data, based on some preconceived notion, to natural systems, aligned with the observable realities of the natural world.

Assuming that politics should be as rational as the sciences, he saw the Slavs as a group of peoples that by nature belonged together, but were politically divided and, except for Russia, subject to non-Slavic rule by the Ottoman and Austrian Hapsburg Empires, which were every bit as artificial and outdated constructions as the artificial and outdated systems of science. The Slavs must be liberated from Austrian and Ottoman rule, Danilevskii believed, and Russia must act as Prussia did within the German states, to create a unified Slavdom on the basis of common Slavic identity. The book argues that the Slavs have more in common among themselves—language, history, and, in most cases, religion—than with Western Europe, which developed from the foreign principles of combined Roman and German cultural foundations. So long as the Slavs remained divided, they would be subject to predations from the West or, in the Ottoman case, the Islamic East.

Danilevskii envisioned the All-Slavic Union (chapters 14 and 15) as a protective shell around a united Slavdom, to allow Slavic civilization to come into its own and flourish, as something distinct from the Germanic-Roman civilization of the West. Danilevskii preserved the Slavophiles' mission of resisting foreign influences, updating and expanding it to encompass all of Slavdom and incorporate the realities of the 1860s: serfdom was now abolished, and the peasants had a path to small-scale landownership; multiethnic empires were in decline and the Concert of Europe had broken down; the intelligentsia of each people inclined toward liberal politics and away from the All-Slavic cause; Western scholarship increasingly led to atheist materialist conclusions; Russian nihilists revealed the harm these foreign influences could have. He saw Western civilization approaching decadence, which was all the more reason to consolidate and protect a separate space for Slavic civilization to come into its own.

The All-Slavic Union was not merely a euphemism, in his mind at least, for Russian imperialism, which set him at odds with more chauvinistic Russian nationalists of his day (some critics, according to Strakhov's essay below, considered the book "too modest").[1] Readers of Dostoevskii know Danilevskii as the suspected inspiration for the character Shatov in *The Devils*, whose tepid faith in God is an act of logical necessity and therefore of will, but not genuine conviction. The two writers shared a link to youthful revolutionism as members of the Petrashevsky circle in the late 1840s. Dostoevskii enthusiastically read the first chapters of *Russia and Europe* in the journal *Zaria*, but grew disenchanted with Danilevskii's treatment of Orthodoxy as merely the Russian national faith and not the universal truth.[2] He openly disputed with Danilevskii in the pages of his nonfiction journal *Dnevnik pisatelia* (A Writer's Diary) over chapter 14, "Tsargrad," which called for Constantinople to become an independent federal capital, like the District of Columbia in the U.S., of the All-Slavic Union. No, Dostoevskii told his readers over several installments, "Constantinople must be ours."[3] Danilevskii's vision of a Slavic United Nations headquartered in Constantinople seems liberal by comparison with Dostoevskii, who was on balance pleased with *Russia and Europe*, and

---

[1] Nikolai Strakhov, "Zhizn' i trudy N. Ia. Danilevskogo," in N. Ia. Danilevskii, *Rossiia i evropa* (1895; New York: Johnson Reprint, 1966), xxvi. For a complete translation, see pp. xxvii–xliii in the current volume.

[2] Joseph Frank, *Dostoevsky: The Miraculous Years, 1865–1871* (Princeton, NJ: Princeton University Press, 1995), 354–55, 483–84.

[3] Fyodor Dostoevsky, *A Writer's Diary*, trans. Kenneth Lantz, 2 vols. (Evanston, IL: Northwestern University Press, 1994), 527, 1206–12.

predicted that it would one day become a coffee-table or reference book (*nastol'naia kniga*)[4] for Russians, a prediction which now seems prescient.

Danilevskii believed Russia could provide leadership, drawn from its long experience with independent statehood, which the other Slavs had either never had, or not enjoyed since medieval times. But Russia's relative weakness compared to the Western powers left it ill-equipped to maintain a much larger empire. Thus Danilevskii argued that the structure of the All-Slavic Union should be a federation, preserving the dignity and autonomy of all its Slavic parts, with the smallest Slavic peoples amalgamated into viable state combinations. He assumed that because it was natural for all the Slavs to bond together, it was also essentially inevitable. This was an optimistic view, a best-case scenario, and Danilevskii only tentatively addressed the incidental things that could go wrong. After all, not all the German states had eagerly submitted to Prussian hegemony, but once accomplished in fact, they made their peace with the new reality. Danilevskii argued that the All-Slavic Union could not be created without violence, but not directed against the Slavs. Rather, Germanic-Roman Europe would never permit the rise of a strong neighbor on its eastern flank, so the Slavs would have to contend with it to claim their destiny. Just as Prussia used wars to unite Germany—the Danish War of 1864, the Austro-Prussian War of 1866, and the final stroke, after this book was written, the Franco-Prussian War of 1870—so would war provide the means to unite Slavdom, being the only measure strong enough to break the status quo and rally the Slavs behind Russia.

Danilevskii subsequently saw vindication for this view, briefly, in the Russo-Turkish War of 1877–78, when Russia secured autonomy for Greater Bulgaria and independence for Bosnia and Herzegovina, Montenegro, Serbia, and Romania, among other provisions. In Danilevskii's view, Russia won the war but lost the peace at the 1878 Congress of Berlin. As predicted, the Western powers did not welcome a large, autonomous Bulgaria friendly to Russia, or the further expansion of Russian influence in the East, and managed to reduce the gains it made in the tentative Treaty of San Stefano ending the war. At Berlin, Bulgaria was divided, half returned to Ottoman rule, with Bosnia-Herzegovina placed under Austro-Hungarian rule. Danilevskii documented his aspirations in a series of articles in the St. Petersburg newspaper *Russkii Mir* (1877–78), and his final dejection in a concluding piece for the journal

---

[4] Letter to Nikolai Strakhov, 18/30 March 1869, in F. M. Dostoevskii, *Polnoe sobranie sochinenii* (Leningrad: Nauka, 1972–), vol. 29, bk. 1, 30. Cf. "reference book," *Fyodor Dostoevsky: Complete Letters*, ed. and trans. David A. Lowe (Ann Arbor: Ardis, 1990), 3: 150; "bedside book," Frank, *Dostoevsky*, 354. Olga Maiorova perhaps renders it best as "handbook," in *From the Shadow of Empire* (Madison: University of Wisconsin Press, 2010), 184.

Russkaia Rech' in 1879.[5] But the war did bring an uptick in sales for his book, which gradually sold out its initial print run of 1200 copies. This translation includes the marginal comments Danilevskii added to several chapters of his book sometime in the early 1880s, in preparation for a new edition. In these comments, besides incidental commentary on the intervening decade of the 1870s, we see a mixture of self-congratulation and retraction: "This was proven true," or "Everything I wrote here is nonsense." Danilevskii died in 1885 before this new edition came out, with little by way of events to change his ambivalence toward his work. He left his literary estate to his friend, the literary critic Nikolai Strakhov, who eulogized the author in an introductory essay, "Zhizn i trudy N. Ia. Danilevskogo" (The Life and Works of N. Ia. Danilevskii), included in the 1888 edition and most subsequent editions. It has been translated for this edition as the most complete contemporary biographical sketch of the author; Strakhov's commentary on the book itself is limited to the promotion of Strakhov's Slavophile concerns.

The book was an important landmark in the nineteenth century, but that is not to say it was a great commercial success. The book first appeared serially in a start-up journal named *Zaria* (Dawn), which folded shortly thereafter for lack of subscribers. With a subsidy from a nationalist group, the installments were collected and published in book form, to modest sales. Subsequent editions were published only after the author's death in 1885, when Strakhov reissued the book as ammunition in an ongoing polemic with the philosopher Vladimir Solov'ev, who generally opposed the religious nationalism of the Slavophiles in favor of a form of ecumenism, and attacked the book's Pan-Slavism and advocacy of violence.[6] The controversy drove sales of the 1888 and 1889 editions. After an 1895 edition, however, the book remained out of print in Russia for almost a century.

Rossiia i evropa, as stated above, is important in two contexts, and now we come to the second. By 1991, Soviet Premier Mikhail Gorbachev's reforms had fully set in motion the forces that would dismantle the Soviet Union by the end of the year. Russians and resurgent national minorities were hounding out the regime that had hounded out the last remnants of tsarism and the Provisional Government in 1917. Soviet rule had come to Russia and its surrounding territories in a series of dramatic events, and now its end marked another dramatic and traumatic transition to an uncertain future. During this momentous year, a new edition of Danilevskii's book finally appeared in

---

[5] Collected in N. Ia. Danilevskii, *Sbornik politicheskikh i ekonomicheskikh statei* (St. Petersburg, 1890). The 1879 piece was originally called "Rossiia i vostochnyi vopros" (Russia and the Eastern Question), but was renamed by Strakhov "Gore pobediteliam!" (Woe to the Victors!).

[6] On this quarrel, see Linda Gerstein, *Nikolai Strakhov* (Cambridge, MA: Harvard University Press, 1971), 113–19; and S. A. Vaigachev, "Posleslovie," in N. Ia. Danilevskii, *Rossiia i Evropa* (Moscow: Kniga, 1991), 560–64.

print, reflecting a decision that precisely such a moment as this was the time to publish the book anew.

In this context, other aspects of the argument in the book seemed more relevant to present concerns. In general, Danilevskii's message was that Russians needed to quit trying to be something they are not (i.e., European) and concentrate on developing according to their true nature. Danilevskii's book explicitly challenged the Western European notion of Civilization (in the singular, capital-C sense) as something other peoples either lack or possess to the degree of their conformity to Western ways. He argued instead that there are multiple human civilizations, each on its own timeframe of development.

Departing from biological convention, he saw "human" as the genus, with "people" or "nation" as the species, bundled into similar groups he calls "types." Type is used in the sense of biological taxonomy (the conventions of which have remained in flux but were especially fluid in the nineteenth century), where "kingdom," "family," "order," and "class" reflect various degrees of similarity and differentiation. Although we speak of the human species, Danilevskii saw "human" as a generic (in the sense of "genus-level") term. He argues there can be no actual generic or universal human, any more than there can be a generic cat, but only humans or cats of various kinds. Without lions, panthers, housecats, or saber-toothed tigers as actual variations, the idea of "cat" becomes meaningless and dull. In the same way humanity without the various nationalities becomes a meaningless abstraction. Humanity is divided into "peoples" or nationalities identified by the distinctive civilization they produce, which unites similar peoples and separates them from others. These collective groups of peoples united by a distinctive civilization Danilevskii calls "cultural-historical types," and attempts to develop a scientific system of their analysis and classification, including laws of their "movement and development," which he validated by comparison to the systems of other natural sciences.

The 1991 edition was for 70,000 copies, and was made required reading at Russian military academies.[7] The afterword appended to the new edition sounds a warning: "In light of the events of our recent history, Danilevskii's warning that we cannot sacrifice national interests in the name of abstract goals that are falsely considered 'progress' sound, it seems, more than timely.... Danilevskii's book contains many ideas whose relevance has greatly increased in the closing of the twentieth century. One of them is the author's warning ... about the denationalization of culture. The establishment of the global hegemony of a single cultural-historical type would be harmful for all humanity, since the hegemony of a single culture, a single civilization, would deprive humanity of a necessary condition for improvement: the element of

---

[7] J. L. Black, *Russia Faces NATO Expansion* (Lanham, MD: Rowman and Littlefield, 2000), 5. I pressed Black for his source for this claim; he recalled seeing it in booksellers' advertisements but could not provide an exact reference.

diversity.... Danilevskii strongly condemned the West for imposing its own culture (under the fig leaf of 'universal values') on the rest of the world."[8] It was a warning not to abandon all the national interests of the Soviet empire to embrace the West, as Russia, deep in an identity crisis during the 1990s, mostly did. Appealing to nationalism to shore up Soviet power was not new. In World War II, or the "Great Patriotic War" as it was known in Russia, Josef Stalin promoted nationalism to bolster public morale in ways that communist ideology and intimidation by violence could not. If the release of Danilevskii's book was intended to do something similar in 1991, it came too little too late.

But the book caught on. At least seven subsequent editions of *Russia and Europe* were published in 1995, 2002, 2003, 2008, and 2010 (see appendix). The 1991 edition of 70,000 copies is a no-frills affair, printed in dense text on thin paper with a modest cloth cover, stressing utility and economy over aesthetics. A deluxe edition of 20,000 copies published in 1995, however, suggests not only a positive reception but consumer demand for a lavish, "coffee-table" edition. Bound in handsome blue tooled leather, with ornate designs and gold trim on the cover, tsarist crests on the flyleaf, and patriotic illustrations at every chapter heading, the 1995 edition is a monument to resurgent Russian nationalism.[9] Russian scholarship on Danilevskii became a veritable growth industry during this period, and new books continued to appear regularly into the new century. His book, which was only modestly successful in his lifetime, now enjoys the greatest fame and readership it has ever had — within Russia at least. Until now, only excerpts have been translated into English.

In the West, the book has been considered a seminal work in Russian intellectual history as a Pan-Slavist manifesto, and is mostly discussed in that context. Beyond that, Pitirim Sorokin, pioneer of sociology as a discipline at Harvard, was influenced by Danilevskii, Oswald Spengler, and others in the 1930s and 1940s to formulate his social-cycle theory as a rejection of the linear progress of social evolutionism rooted in the Enlightenment.[10] The only full-length monograph in English devoted to Danilevskii is Robert MacMaster's 1967 book, *Danilevsky: A Russian Totalitarian Philosopher*, which combined two hot topics of the mid-twentieth century (now rather dated), existentialism and totalitarianism, to call him an "intellectual totalitarian" and thus a philosophical forebear of Stalinism.[11] Other works addressed Danilevskii in the context

---

[8] Vaigachev, "Posleslovie," 566–67.

[9] The 1991 edition was published in Moscow by Kniga; the 1995 edition was published in St. Petersburg by Glagol, through St. Petersburg University Press.

[10] See his *Contemporary Sociological Theories* (New York: Harper, 1928) and *Social Philosophies in an Age of Crisis* (Boston: Beacon, 1950).

[11] Robert MacMaster, *Danilevsky: A Russian Totalitarian Philosopher* (Cambridge, MA: Harvard University Press, 1967). In *Social Philosophies in an Age of Crisis*, Sorokin grouped Danilevskii with several other "totalititarians" who see civilizations as the

of conservative nationalism and Pan-Slavism in the intellectual history of
Russia.[12] His importance today, and the main rationale for this translation, is
that since 1991 more Russians have been reading him than at any other time
in the past, so perhaps those who cannot read the original Russian ought to be
able to as well.

What does the book say to Russians in the post-Soviet period? For Russia,
the nineteenth century had a promising start that worked its way toward a
disappointing end, not unlike the twentieth century. Published in 1869, *Russia
and Europe* reflected the decline of Russia's fortunes from the high point of
1815, with the rout and overthrow of Napoleon, to the low point of defeat in
the "Eastern" or Crimean War of 1853–56. The defeat of Napoleon in 1815 established Russia as one of the Great Powers at the Congress of Vienna, and its
staunch defense of monarchy and legitimism under Nicholas I earned it the
reputation of "gendarme of Europe" for the first half of the nineteenth century. The image of the Russian Empire as backward and fiercely autocratic—
in its denial of press freedoms, its defense of serfdom, and its oppression of its
subject peoples—came to symbolize Europe's greatest misgivings about monarchy in general, and the tsarist juggernaut in particular. The parallels with
the Soviet era are certainly suggestive, as post-Soviet Russians are positioned
to see.

Writing the book in the middle of the tumultuous 1860s, Danilevskii
voiced the frustration of Russian nationalists: that imitation of the West never
seemed to bring the approval of the West that Russian Westernizers obviously craved. The emancipation of the serfs in 1861 began the era of Great Reforms that continued for much of that decade. These reforms, which included
the introduction of press freedoms, jury trials, and local self-government,
among other liberal initiatives, did little to improve the West's perception of
Russia. They proved no more successful in this regard than had Peter the
Great's Westernizing reforms almost two centuries prior. In the 1990s, Russian nationalist politicians attracted a following by voicing complaints in the
same vein, and average Russians had to consider not only the benefits of the
end of the Soviet Union, but also its costs and consequences.

In the first three chapters of the book, Danilevskii offers his readers an
explanation for Russia's Westernization frustration: the reason lay in the fact
that Europe, consciously or unconsciously, harbors an innate hostility to Russia that will not allow it to see Russia as part of itself. In chapter 1, he con-

---

cause behind all effects, but MacMaster prefers the political science literature of
totalitarianism and does not cite Sorokin in connection with the term (*Danilevsky*, 321–
22).

[12] See, for instance, Edward C. Thaden, *Conservative Nationalism in Nineteenth-Century
Russia* (Seattle: University of Washington Press, 1964); and Frank Fadner, *Seventy Years
of Pan-Slavism in Russia: Karazin to Danilevskii, 1800–1870* (Washington, DC: George-
town University Press, 1962).

trasted the years 1854 and 1864 to make this point. In 1854 much of Europe went to war to defend the Ottoman Empire when Russia demanded the right to protect Orthodox Christian subjects in the Balkans and the holy sites in Palestine, all under Ottoman rule. Russia's humiliating defeat in the Crimean War pleased not only the governments of Europe but also its public opinion as revealed by the Western press. Ten years later, European governments and public opinion both were strangely silent when Prussia and Austria attacked Denmark—"one of the smallest states of Europe," Danilevskii observed, "not known for being warlike, but highly enlightened, liberal, and humane"—to seize from it the provinces Schleswig and Holstein. The blatant hypocrisy of Europe's aggressive response in the Crimean War to the expansion of Russian influence, and its benign indulgence of naked German aggression against Denmark ten years later, obviously failed the test of rationality. Something irrational was afoot, and Danilevskii introduced his book as an attempt to explain what that was.[13]

Questioning why Europe is hostile to Russia in chapter 2, Danilevskii posited that it sees Russia, first, as a "colossal aggressor state, constantly expanding its borders, and thus threatening the peace and independence of Europe," and second, as "a dismal force, hostile to progress and freedom." In rebuttal, Danilevskii offered a vision of benevolent imperial expansion, incorporating the lands of scattered Finnic tribes and steppe nomads, bringing them the protection and services of an organized state (while predictably shifting the blame for the partitions of Poland to Prussia and Austria). Most of Russia's military endeavors in Europe, he argued, served European interests more than Russian interests, for which Europe never gives Russia credit. When Napoleon, on behalf of France, offered to divide all Europe between the two states, Alexander I refused and forced him into the disastrous campaign of 1812. Bearing the brunt of this invasion, Russia did not seek its own interests at the Vienna peace congress but championed the balance of powers and the restoration of Europe's toppled monarchies. True, Russia had taken up arms against the lofty principles of the French Revolution. But so had the rest of Europe, which applauded Russia's victories. Europe welcomed Russian peasant emancipation, but backed the Poles in their uprising of 1863: Polish vigilantes "become heroes, as long as their vile behavior was directed against Russia." If Russia was a dismal force and hostile to progress, Danilevskii argued, that's Russia's problem, not Europe's; in fact, Russia's enemies should rejoice to see it languish.[14]

While the victory over Napoleon may be less fresh in the minds of post-Soviet Russians, it taps the same feelings as Russia's victory over fascism in the Great Patriotic War (i.e., World War II), which remains one of the greatest sources of national pride from the entire Soviet era. The occupation and polit-

---

[13] Danilevskii, *Rossiia i evropa* (1895), 1–2, 18–19.

[14] Ibid., 20, 21, 39–42, 44–45, 49.

ical subordination of Eastern Europe, some Russians will still argue, was generally protective and paternalistic. Through the expansion of NATO and the European Union since 1991, the West seems determined to claim as many of Russia's former client states as it can. When Danilevskii was writing, European imperialism was strong and growing. Europe "looks at Russia and the Slavs in general as something foreign to it, but at the same time as something that cannot serve merely as raw material to extract for its own benefit, as it does from China, India, Africa, the greater part of America." If it is foreign, and cannot be used for Europe's advantage, then Europe can only regard it with hostility, "taking the form of distrust, Schadenfreude, hatred, or scorn, depending on the circumstances."[15]

The title of chapter 3 simply asks, "Is Russia Europe?" Geographically speaking, Danilevskii argued, Europe is an artificial designation anyway, being more a peninsula of Asia than a continent in its own right. The significance of "Europe" however is not geographical, but historical and cultural. "Europe is no more and no less than the realm of the Germanic-Roman civilization; or in the wider metaphoric sense, Europe is this Germanic-Roman civilization in itself. They are synonymous." In this respect, Danilevskii asserted Russia's dignity and worth, even while standing apart. "Neither true modesty nor true pride would allow Russia to claim to be Europe. It did nothing to deserve that honor, and if it wants to deserve a different one, it should not claim what it does not deserve. Only parvenus, having no concept of modesty or noble pride, insinuate themselves into what they consider the highest circles; people who understand their own merit consider it in no way beneath themselves to stick to their own circle and try to ennoble it, so that there is nothing to envy from anyone or anything else."[16]

Russia will never be welcomed in Europe as one of its own, so why should it keep striving for something it can never attain? This impossible infatuation with Europe, Danilevskii indicated, prevents Russia from seeing other possible alternatives: "But even those who simply cannot claim the honor of belonging to Europe are so blinded by its brilliance that they do not understand the possibility of progress beyond the path it has paved. Their fixed gaze does not allow them to see that European civilization is just as one-sided as all others on earth."[17] The critique of eurocentrism and the rise of multiculturalism is familiar ground for academics today. But in 1869 it was a marginal, and largely rejected, way of thinking. Present-day detractors find Danilevskii's notion of Russia as a defender of cultural diversity insincere.[18]

---

[15] Ibid., 49–50, 53.

[16] Ibid., 59, 61.

[17] Ibid., 71.

[18] See, for instance, Andrzej Nowak, "'Poor Empire or a Second Rome'—Temptations of Imperial Discourse in Contemporary Russian Thinking," *The Polish Foreign Affairs Digest* 3: 8 (2003): 142.

But the discourse of multiculturalism can certainly be co-opted by the power-ful, as shown, for instance, by white South Africans demanding "minority rights" and "protection of cultural diversity" with themselves in mind.

Out of print for almost a century, Danilevskii's book has elements of a time capsule of Russian nationalism. The tsars are gone, the communists are gone, but Russia remains. The 1990s brought privatization, crony capitalism, rampant inflation, and an embrace of the West in both consumer goods (at one time almost anything foreign was preferable to anything Russian) and in-ternational alignments (suddenly NATO membership seemed possible). But as Danilevskii's readership grew, so did his currency. Danilevskii's observa-tions in the 1860s fit many Russians' view of the 1990s. The essence of what Danilevskii has to say to Russians is arguably unchanged, or at least adapt-able to post-Soviet circumstances. Europe still applauds Russian reforms when they suit the West, but it protests whenever Russia seeks its own inter-ests. Just as Europe sympathized with the Polish Uprising of 1863, so the West sided with the cause of Chechen separatists in the 1990s and the anti-Russian drift of the "color revolutions" in recent years. A predictable outcry comes whenever Russia raises energy prices, plants a flag underwater at the North Pole, or contrives to keep a popular ruler in high office after the end of his term as president (although it turns out Russians were more amenable to Vladimir Putin's return to the presidency in theory, beforehand, than they have been since its occurrence in fact). The message Danilevskii would seem to have for present-day Russians is that they should neither be surprised by this, nor deterred.

Translation requires some difficult choices. One of the persistent chal-lenges in this book concerns the word *narod*, which means "people" in a gen-eral, collective sense, often rendered as "nation," a unit defined by the people constituting it, not by its government (but often used interchangeably with "government" or "state," as in the United Nations, etc.). While I have found it stylistically impossible to be completely consistent, I have preferred the often awkward "people" over the more conventional but hazy term "nation" for several reasons. At the simplest level, Danilevskii does also use the words *natsiia* and *natsional'nyi,* unambiguously signifying "nation" or "national." This does not prevent *narod* from meaning "nation" in some cases. But "na-tion" is often taken as shorthand for "nation-state," which poorly suits the ethnic mashup of nineteenth-century Eastern Europe. Danilevskii's particular grievance that so many Slavic peoples at that time lived under Ottoman or Austrian rule, makes it all the more crucial to avoid that connotation.

As a biologist Danilevskii was concerned with the study of life forms: dif-ferent kinds of living things and different stages of their development and life cycles (rejecting Darwinism, he saw the differences of species and their life

cycles as fixed).[19] Biology is not concerned with individuals except as specimens of the larger collective group. So "people" or "peoples" (*narod, narody*)
are used in the book sometimes interchangeably with "tribe" or "tribes"
(*plemia, plemena*) as collective biological terms like "herd" or "breed." He
knew and accepted the contemporary discourse of nationalism, with the nation as an often romantic abstraction rather than something concrete. There is
plenty of abstraction in Danilevskii's notions of Slavdom and Europe, and
ample romanticism in his view of history. But he strove, as a corrective, to
ground his theory in concrete, empirical reality, using historical events and
cultural phenomena as classification data for distinct peoples. His theory of
"cultural-historical types" attempted scientifically to group together similar
peoples at an intermediate level between peoples or nations, on the one hand,
and all humanity on the other. At the end of chapter 4, Danilevskii explained
that global human civilization had developed in ten distinct cultural types (a
suspiciously round number that has drawn criticism, especially since cultures
not making the list are designated mere "ethnographic material"). Each
cultural-historical type within human civilization is as distinct as the species
within the genus; so while human biology is universal, human civilization is
local and varied.

Human sciences, or social sciences, have always had difficulty bringing
the same level of rigor to the study of humanity as the natural sciences apply
to the study of the natural world. Danilevskii is no exception, though not for
lack of trying. His ideas resonate as much at the intuitive as the rational level.
At the end of the Cold War, Samuel Huntington promoted the "clash of civilizations" as the new, definitive historical narrative, to replace the discarded
narrative of a global struggle between capitalism and communism.[20] The narrative of clashing civilizations offers a compellingly simplistic, rough-and-
ready rationale with popular appeal, providing broad, intuitive justification
for the wars on Islamic terrorism or "islamofascism" of the early twenty-first
century, despite the technical merit of Huntington's critics.[21] Danilevskii
aligns easily with Huntington (preceding him at the writing, but his contemporary in present-day Russian readership), a fact highlighted in the introduction to the 2010 edition, which reviews the prominent "civilizationists" from
Danilevskii to Huntington, comparing them by their lists and tallies of civilizations, as well as the bases of civilization identified from Plato to the pres-

---

[19] See the multivolume critique he left unfinished at death, published posthumously:
N. Ia. Danilevskii, *Darvinizm* (St. Petersburg, 1885).

[20] Samuel P. Huntington, *The Clash of Civilizations and the Remaking of the World Order*
(New York: Simon & Schuster, 1996). A Russian translation was published in 2003.

[21] For an early sample, see *Samuel P. Huntington's "The Clash of Civilizations": The Debate* (New York: Council on Foreign Relations, 1996), a collection of articles from
Foreign Affairs, summer, September–October, and November–December issues, 1993.

ent.[22] Even though Russia landed on the side of the West in the "clash of civilizations," post-Soviet Russians still felt persistent tensions. In the early twenty-first century, Vladimir Putin was quick to seize the issue of antiterrorism and permitted NATO the use of Russian airspace and former Soviet bases in Central Asia, and just as quick to frame the ongoing Chechen conflict within the new narrative, as a war on terrorism. Yet making common cause with the West against terrorism did not allay Western fears of Russia's new status as an "energy superpower" or redeem its resistance to the "color revolutions" in former Soviet client states of the near abroad.

The biologist in Danilevskii was not only concerned with classification, but also with analysis of life cycles within peoples and their cultural-historical types. History, the study of change over time, viewed naturalistically, reveals apparent stages in the development of people groups. While it sounds dismissive to call cultures outside his cultural-historical types "ethnographic material," for Danilevskii this was not necessarily pejorative, but merely a way to describe the embryonic stage of tribal existence where all peoples begin the life cycle. Civilizations are organic, literally growing into existence: some to bear fruit, others not, like unpollenated blossoms left to wither. Danilevskii sometimes used *vospitanie* ("upbringing" or "breeding") in regard to peoples, but more often spoke of *razvitie* or "development" over time. The political process of state formation was one aspect of this process, but Danilevskii meant it in the broadest sense of "breeding a people," a distinct life form whose "peculiarities" (another favorite Danilevskii term) develop in response to its circumstances, just as animal breeds take on distinctive forms by selection over numerous generations. Both "upbringing" and "breeding" imply some figure guiding the process; Danilevskii saw history, sometimes divinely personified as Providence in the text, as fulfilling that role. History is an idiosyncratic guide, leading each people on a rambling tour with odd turns and chance encounters, but often enough moving in a discernible direction. "Development" is an ongoing process, and should not be taken, in Danilevskii's usage, to mean ever-rising linear Progress, but rather movement through that idiosyncratic life cycle.

All peoples have life cycles of indeterminate length, with stages of growth and decline, gauged by their cultural productivity. Danilevskii's view of history is often described as cyclical, but this should be understood in an organic, rather than mechanistic, sense. His view could be called deterministic, even material deterministic (if the matter in question is organic). But whereas Karl Marx cut the cake of human society horizontally by class hierarchy, Danilevskii cut it vertically into wedges: large wedges for civilizations or

---

[22] A. V. Repnikov and M. A. Emel'ianov-Luk'ianchikov, "Nikolai Iakovlevich Danilevskii," in N. Ia. Danilevskii, *Rossiia i evropa*, Biblioteka otechestvennoi obshchestvennoi mysli, vol. 61 (Moscow: ROSSPEN, 2010), 9–15. The authors include some civilizations Danilevskii mentioned, but did not number separately, to inflate the count to fifteen.

types, divided into smaller wedges for peoples. But the cake analogy falsely implies uniformity among the pieces; rather he saw a variety of produce coming in different seasons in a scarcely-tended, sprawling English garden. Europe in Danilevskii's day was yielding the full fruit of its civilization. But after autumn harvest comes winter defoliation and dormancy. Russia and all of Slavdom, lagging the West, he saw as a civilization still in the bud.

The book can be divided into three sections. The first, chapters 1–7, develops his theory of the biology of nations to explain the disconnect between Russia and Europe, and compares his theory to other sciences—which progress from data collection to an "artificial system" or flawed paradigm that requires a "natural system" or improved paradigm to resolve its flaws—to justify his theory of cultural-historical types as a "natural system" of this kind for the study of human history. The second section, chapters 8–11, delves deeper into history to explain a series of differences or distinctions (*razlichiia*) between the Germanic-Roman and the Slavic types: the difference in mental framework, the confessional or religious difference, and the difference in the course of historical upbringing. It concludes in an examination of Russian history diagnosing "Europeanism" (*evropeinichan'e*) as the sickness or syndrome afflicting Russia in its development, forcing its growth into an unnatural course. The last section, chapters 12–17, concerns the Eastern Question (the host of issues surrounding the decline of the Ottoman Empire and the fate of its territories and waterways), in which Danilevskii saw a coming shock that would jolt the Russian national spirit to awaken from its slumber, shake off this disease, and fulfill its historical destiny: to create a political federation of Slavic states with Russia at the head, bringing the Slavic cultural-historical type to fruition.

The second and third sections account for Danilevskii's association with the Slavophiles and the movement known as Pan-Slavism, although this requires some context. While he did quote Slavophiles in the text and epigrams throughout the work, and while his friend Strakhov called the book a "catechism or codex of Slavophilism,"[23] Danilevskii pressed the romantic nationalism of the Slavophiles into the pragmatic mold of Bismarckian *Realpolitik*. During the writing of the book, the process of Bismarck's unification of the German states under Prussian leadership was nearly complete. It is clear that, more than any Russian ruler, Danilevskii admired Bismarck for his principled ambition and pragmatic opportunism. The All-Slavic Union (*vseslavianskii soiuz*) Danilevskii envisioned as the Slavic counterpart of the Germany taking shape during the years he wrote the book (although organized more loosely in a federation of states). Only in a united federation, he believed, could Slavdom offer a counterbalance to the hegemony of Western Europe, as the Eastern Bloc in the Soviet era (its other defects and brutal legacy notwithstanding) would later demonstrate. His present-day Russian readers surely do not want

---

[23] Strakhov, "Zhizn' i trudy N. Ia. Danilevskogo," xxiii.

the Iron Curtain back, but neither do they welcome the unipolar world order dominated by an American "hyperpower," as seen since the end of the Cold War. In the twenty-first century, Russia finds support in Danilevskii's book for seeing itself as a regional power seeking its place in a multipolar world order. "We have the unique ability," says the introduction to the 2010 edition, "to look at Danilevskii's works not as 'archaic,' referring only to the distant past, but as a concept allowing us to understand the contemporary world in all its fullness, variety, and variability of development."[24]

Readers of the Russian text of this book will appreciate (though it may not be apparent to those unfamiliar with the original) the efforts made in this translation where possible to simplify Danilevskii's tortuous syntax, divide his interminable sentences, and reduce his redundancy, all without sacrificing the meaning (for a sample of more authentic nineteenth-century prose, readers are directed to the excerpt from Thomas Carlyle as the epigraph to chapter 10, or the excerpt from Alexander Kinglake's multivolume history of the Crimean War in chapter 11). This translation preserves the original division of paragraphs, however, to facilitate comparison to the original text for those motivated to do so. The result is still ponderous perhaps, but much less so than a more literal rendering would have been. Also preserved are his occasional culturally-insensitive and inflammatory statements on topics like Poland, Roman Catholicism, Islam, China, Africa, and so on. While some are products of unmasked scorn, others merely reflect ethnocentric assumptions held in the certitude of scientific observation and shared by most of his contemporaries. Explanatory annotations have been made, perhaps unnecessarily in some cases, to make Danilevskii's references clear to undergraduate or non-specialist readers.

Difficulties of style and opinion notwithstanding, it is worth persisting with this text because of its important place in Russian intellectual history of the nineteenth century, and its impact on the thinking of a growing number of twenty-first-century Russian readers. Danilevskii provides essential background for Russian Pan-Slavism and Eurasianism, the ideologies best poised to inform Russian policy over the next decades. This makes a case for calling *Russia and Europe* the most important nineteenth-century book for the post-Soviet period, and thus an object worthy of further study by specialist and non-specialist alike.

Stephen M. Woodburn
Southwestern College
Winfield, KS

---

[24] Repnikov and Emel'ianov-Luk'ianchikov, "Nikolai Iakovlevich Danilevskii," 19.

The Life and Works of N. Ia. Danilevskii[1]

Nikolai N. Strakhov

The author of this book, Nikolai Iakovlevich Danilevskii, was born on 28 November 1822. His place of birth was the village of Oberets, his mother's family estate in the Livny district of Orel province. His father, Iakov Ivanovich, commanded a regiment of hussars and rose to the rank of brigadier general. Iakov Ivanovich first entered another field, having enrolled in 1812 to study medicine at the University of Moscow; but when the French invasion began, he quit his studies and entered military service. He was wounded in the campaign abroad (possibly at Leipzig) and was treated for some time in Paris. Subsequently, he took part in the Sevastopol campaign and was the commandant of Belgrade; when an urgent request he had made was denied, he resigned in protest and retired on the Danube. At the formation of the Orel province militia, he was unanimously selected as its commander, but died of cholera on 2 August 1855, having conducted an inspection of his militia less than two hours before. Iakov Ivanovich always loved science and literature, and even wrote a comedy, which remained unpublished.

From childhood, Nikolai Iakovlevich constantly had to change places, moving around with his father's regiment. He recalled being, at age four, in Livny, then (1827) in Prokopovka (Poltava province), in Nezhin (1828), in Priluki (1830), in Pakhra[2] (1831), and in Nesvizh (1832). He was in Pastor Schwarz's *pansion* near Beppo (in Livonia) in 1833, in Pavlov's *pansion* in Moscow in 1834, and also Borgardt's *pansion* there in 1836. In 1837 he was admitted as a tuition-paying student to the lyceum at Tsarskoe Selo. From their first acquaintance at the lyceum began his friendship with Nikolai Petrovich

---

[1] This essay (with minor variations) was appended to the posthumous editions of *Russia and Europe* (1888, 1889, 1895) published by Strakhov, as executor of Danilevskii's literary estate. This is the text from the 1889, or fourth, edition (the book's serial publication in the journal *Zaria* [Dawn] in 1869 counts as the first edition; its first appearance in book form, in 1871, is technically the second edition; Strakhov's reprints were the third, fourth, and fifth editions).

[2] Possibly Krasnaia Pakhra, a small town southeast of Moscow in Podol'sk district, or a military encampment along the Pakhra river, a tributary of the Moskva River in the same area. The other locations are mostly in present-day Ukraine and Belarus.

Semenov,[3] who was his roommate and remained his closest friend for life. He graduated from the lyceum in 1842; his father came only once to visit him there, in 1840.

Nikolai Iakovlevich displayed remarkable abilities from childhood, allowing him easily to pass any course. However he made a big distinction between subjects: some he loved and studied zealously, others he stubbornly neglected, devoting only a few days to them before the exam. His memory was amazing, but had its peculiarities. He acquired languages easily and perfectly retained not only names and numbers of all kinds, but ideas as well; yet he struggled with the literal expression of an idea in a given sequence of words, loving poems and reading them excellently, but being almost at a loss to understand them.

Having completed the full lyceum curriculum, he did not consider this education sufficient for him. He felt powerfully drawn to the natural sciences, and enrolled as a free auditor in the natural sciences department of St. Petersburg University, where he studied four years (1843–47).[4] Near the end of this period I first caught sight of him in a university corridor, and even though I never saw him again and only made his acquaintance in 1868, this first meeting stuck in my memory. Suddenly students started buzzing, "Danilevskii! Danilevskii!" and I saw how a crowd gathered and grew large around a tall young man not dressed as a student. Everyone listened eagerly as he spoke, those nearest to him asking him questions, and he answering and offering explanations. They were discussing the existence of God and the system of Fourier.[5]

He was at that time a serious Fourierist. In science, he had chosen botany as his specialty, and reached the level of candidate in 1847, and in winter 1848–49 passed the exam for the master of botany degree. He spent 1847 and 1848 partly in St. Petersburg and partly in the Riazan and Orel provinces; he studied the flora of Orel province and compiled a description of this flora for his master's thesis. But in the fall of 1849, when he and fellow master's candi-

---

[3] Nikolai Petrovich Semenov (1823–1904): Official in the Ministry of Justice, member of the commission drafting the serf emancipation reform of 1861, and author of a three-volume history of the emancipation reform.

[4] [Strakhov's note]: From 1 April 1843 he was assigned to the chancellery of the Ministry of War, from which he resigned on 19 January 1847, citing poor health. During this time he twice took leave: for four months starting 1 May 1844, and from 10 June to 6 October 1846.

[5] Charles Fourier (1772–1837): French utopian socialist philosopher, whose model society was organized into collective communities called phalansteries, in which work was matched with individual passions or interests, to make work more like play.

date Petr Petrovich Semenov[6] were in Tula province (at the Krasivaia Mecha river), conducting an investigation of the black soil region of Russia and its flora for the Free Economic Society, he was unexpectedly arrested and imprisoned in the Peter-Paul Fortress. He was caught up in the Petrashevskii affair,[7] which famously led to the exile of F. M. Dostoevskii, Pal'm,[8] and others. The imprisonment, lasting a hundred days, was especially difficult at first, when books were banned. Once he was granted books and the ability to work out his thoughts, the solitude became easier for Nikolai Iakovlevich to bear. By the way, he later loved to recall that a quaint old French translation of *Don Quixote* put him into laughing fits. In the investigation he explained that he had been away from St. Petersburg for a long time, and while in Petersburg had been absorbed in preparation for his exams, which is why he had not been at Petrashevskii's for a couple of years and did not know what was going on there. Furthermore, in a lengthy statement he clearly and fully explained Fourier's system, which he was accused of teaching, and showed beyond all doubt that it does not contain anything revolutionary or antireligious, but is a purely economic teaching.

The investigative commission cleared Nikolai Iakovlevich of guilt, but he was expelled from St. Petersburg and assigned (20 May 1850) to the office of the governor of Vologda, and then (3 November 1852) by the request of Perovskii,[9] the former chief justice in the Petrashevskii affair, was transferred to the office of the governor of Samara. By 24 February 1853 he was "translator of the Samara provincial government." This was the time of his first marriage. He was married (29 September 1852) to the childless widow of a major general, Vera Nikolaevna Beklemisheva, nee Lavrova,[10] who was smart

---

[6] Petr Petrovich Semenov (Tian-Shanskii after 1906) (1827–1914): Geographer, naturalist, and memoirist, the first surveyor of the Tian-Shan mountains in Central Asia, in honor of which his surname was appended.

[7] Petrashevskii affair: The 1849 crackdown on participants in the Friday evening meetings of a literary circle meeting in the home of Mikhail Vasilievich Butashevich-Petrashevskii (1821–66), known for his eccentric habits and sizable library of forbidden works. The circle embraced French socialism, and Danilevskii gave a series of lectures explaining the system of Charles Fourier. Strakhov only hints of this above. Fourier's main appeal for Danilevskii seems to have been his rational system of organizing and categorizing humanity, which is a fundamental concern of *Russia and Europe*.

[8] Fedor Mikhailovich Dostoevskii (1821–81): Famous Russian novelist, author of *Notes from Underground, Crime and Punishment, The Idiot, The Possessed, The Brothers Karamazov*, and others. Aleksandr Ivanovich Pal'm (1823–85): Minor writer of prose, poetry, and drama, co-organizer of one of the secret circles of Petrashevtsy.

[9] Lev Alekseevich Perovskii (1792–1856): Mineralogist serving in the Ministry of Internal Affairs, founding member of the Russian Geographical Society.

[10] Vera Nikolaevna Beklemisheva, nee Lavrova (1815?–53): Very little is known of Danilevskii's first wife, to whom he was married less than a year, but whom he courted for the better part of a decade. The most complete portrait of her appears in P. P.

and very beautiful. She lived at Russkii Brod,[11] and he had loved her for several years, but only declared it to her two days before his arrest. She kept her word, and when he was exiled she journeyed to Vologda in order to marry him. But before a year had passed he lost his wife (10 July 1853); she died from cholera within the span of a few hours. By his own account, this was the cruelest loss of his life and for a whole year he was sunk into deep despair.

Meanwhile, on 18 June 1853 Nikolai Iakovlevich was "dispatched for two years as a statistician on a scientific expedition investigating the status of fisheries on the Volga and in the Caspian Sea." This assignment set the course for the rest of his life; he even died on one of his trips to study fisheries. The 1853 expedition was headed by the great naturalist Karl Ernst von Baer.[12] Over time, Baer recognized his statistician's knowledge and abilities, and came to rely on him as his main assistant. The expedition lasted more than three years, until January 1857.

On 5 October 1857 Nikolai Iakovlevich was appointed an "official in the Department of Agriculture"; 7 March 1858 he was promoted to "junior engineer" to fill a vacancy in that department, and later that year was appointed "head of an expedition to study fisheries in the White and Arctic Seas." That expedition lasted three years, and on 6 March 1861 Nikolai Iakovlevich was awarded 500 rubles for it.

The time of the great journey to the Arctic Ocean coincided with Nikolai Iakovlevich's second marriage. Back when he was exiled to Vologda from Petersburg, he became acquainted with the family of Mezhakov, the marshal of the nobility for the province and landlord of Nikol'skoe village in Kadnikovskii district. Nikolai Iakovlevich was close friends with the marshal's son, Aleksandr Pavlovich Mezhakov, who was ten years older than him and died on 2 June 1859. When the expedition was just beginning, in the winter of 1860, Nikolai Iakovlevich stayed briefly at Nikol'skoe, and on 8 February he proposed to his late friend's daughter, Ol'ga Aleksandrovna. But the marriage was put off until the end of the expedition, finally occurring on 15 October 1861. During their separation the bridegroom faithfully corresponded with his bride, telling her everything that happened to him. These letters have been preserved, and a complete picture of this difficult journey can be assembled from them.

Semenov Tian-Shanskii, *Detstvo i iunost'*, 7th ed. (Petrograd, 1917), 180–81, 207–19; Semenov mentions she was seven years older than Danilevskii (181).

[11] Near Livny, in Orel province.

[12] Karl Ernst von Baer (1792–1876): Estonian naturalist, explorer of the Russian interior, member of the Russian Academy of Sciences and a founding member of the Russian Geographical Society. He strongly influenced Danilevskii's career, including his anti-Darwinist views and ideas of biological time, the basis for much of his conclusions in *Russia and Europe*.

The first two journeys of Nikolai Iakovlevich involved the longest travels of all he made; on the first trip he went as far as Persia, at the south coast of the Caspian Sea, and on the second he visited Norway, where in 1861, he was in Trondheim from the New Year to Easter. We will briefly recount his remaining journeys to give a general sense of the external form of his life, during which there was also such abundant thought and academic writing.

The third journey was in Astrakhan. Nikolai Iakovlevich was sent there on 31 October 1861 "to attend the commission on fish and seal fisheries." Travel, by the roads of that time, through the first snows, and along the newly frozen Volga, was especially difficult and dangerous. Nikolai Iakovlevich remained in Astrakhan until June of the following year.

In November 1862 he left on the fourth assignment, "to Pskov and Chud Lakes[13] to answer complaints about fishing policies."

In the following year, 1863, Nikolai Iakovlevich began his most extensive and important work on fisheries. He was assigned as "head of an expedition for the investigation into the fisheries of the Black and Azov Seas." This expedition lasted five years. In September 1863 Nikolai Iakovlevich took his family down the Volga to Tsarina, then crossed the Don by rail and went down to the Black Sea. He tried to arrange a permanent residence for his family, first in Feodosia, then in Nikita, but finally settled in Miskhor on the South Coast [of the Crimea] on 9 March 1864. From Miskhor he made six journeys in the following order: in 1864, around the Azov Sea; in 1865, on the Dnieper; in spring 1866, on the Manych [River, tributary of the Don]; in 1867, from 19 May to 19 June, around the Black Sea; from 10 September to 17 October of the same year, to Kuban, and from 23 November to 26 December on the Danube.

The study of the fisheries predominantly occupied the season when those fisheries were in use. Thus in Miskhor, Nikolai Iakovlevich had a few quiet winters, and the fruit of this leisure was the book *Russia and Europe*, begun in the fall of 1865.

Another important circumstance relates to that time. Nikolai Iakovlevich owned no immovable property, neither of his own nor from his wife; by chance the opportunity presented itself on the South Coast to buy Mshatka, the large, working estate of Count Kushelev-Bezborodko, for a very good price. It had a huge garden, once carefully cultivated; a vineyard; the ruins of a manor house, burned by the French in the Crimean War; and a small house for the manager. The Danilevskiis scraped together all their money to buy it, and after 1 June 1867, his family lived at Mshatka.

At the beginning of 1868 (on 3 January), Danilevskii left there for St. Petersburg, where of course he often had to be at that time in the course of his duties. These trips continued to the end of his life, although he always made

---

[13] Historical name for Lake Peipus, in the shape of two lakes joined by a narrow neck, on the present-day border of Estonia and Russia. Site of Alexander Nevsky's "battle on the ice" against the Teutonic Knights in 1242.

them with great reluctance; in this essay we recall only the most important of them. Nikolai Iakovlevich spent all of his adult life and did all his work outside of the capital, and he generally did not care for city life.

On this occasion (1868) he had to remain in St. Petersburg for a longer time than any other in his term of service. Soon after his arrival, I had the good fortune of meeting him. In summer he departed for the Crimea for his family, and by 1 August they took up residence in St. Petersburg.

In the meantime, earlier in that year, in May, he fulfilled an assignment (his sixth) to Astrakhan, "to resolve questions concerning Caspian fish and seal fisheries." This time Nikolai Iakovlevich was the head of the commission, and it finalized, on the basis of all preceding studies, the policies by which they now do, or are supposed to, operate.

He began his seventh expedition in August of that year, to Arkhangelsk Province, "for a study of the status of agriculture and fisheries." The fruit of this journey was the broad and important report, "On Measures to Ensure the Food Supply in the North of Russia."

In the following year, in February 1869, Nikolai Iakovlevich was again sent to Astrakhan, "to attend the commission on Caspian fish and seal fisheries." In the fall of that year he traveled by order of the minister[14] to Nikita.

Two years, 1870 and 1871, were taken up by a longer journey, his ninth. On 9 March 1870, Nikolai Iakovlevich was sent "as head of an expedition to study fisheries in the northwestern lakes of Russia." During this expedition, in June 1870, Nikolai Iakovlevich escorted Grand Duke Aleksei Aleksandrovich[15] to Arkhangel'sk and Solovetskii Monastery. This expedition completed the study of all waters of European Russia. All current legislation on fisheries here has come from Nikolai Iakovlevich: very important work for its usefulness and first-rate in its implementation.

To give a better understanding of the hardships and deprivations Nikolai Iakovlevich endured on his journeys would require a more detailed exposition than we can do here. With extraordinary courage of mind and body, he easily overcame all manner of difficulties; boredom did not exist for him, and his mind worked unceasingly. But there was one very difficult circumstance in this life: the repeated, long absences from his family, which we can rightly call "dearly beloved," not just as a fancy expression. In September 1869, Nikolai Iakovlevich and his family left St. Petersburg and returned to Mshatka. They took me with them, and for the first time I experienced the wonders of the South Coast. When his 1870–71 expedition began, it was decided that his family should settle somewhere in the region of the expedition; the inherent attractiveness of Nikol'skoe finally won out, even though the location was not especially convenient. At the conclusion of the expedition, Nikolai Iakov-

---

[14] Presumably an official at the Ministry of State Domains.

[15] Grand Duke Aleksei Aleksandrovich (1850–1908): Fourth son of Tsar Alexander II, Russian naval officer and goodwill ambassador.

levich reached St. Petersburg on 5 December 1871, and in February 1872 he moved with his whole family to St. Petersburg and again took permanent residence here.

But by the summer of that year, Nikolai Iakovlevich was sent on his tenth mission, as the chair of "the commission to establish laws for the use of flowing waterways in the Crimea." This mission proved more agreeable to Nikolai Iakovlevich's desires than any other. Once again he moved the family to Mshatka; as it turned out, he lived the rest of his days in the Crimea, although he still had frequent absences. The matter of running waters dragged on, by no means the chair of the commission's fault. On the contrary, Nikolai Iakovlevich always skillfully stated the issues and proposed definite and decisive measures. The commission gathered the facts, conferred with landowners, and worked out the tentative bases of future legislation. In 1875 Nikolai Iakovlevich left Mshatka on 1 March for St. Petersburg (where his project was evaluated) and returned to the Crimea only at the end of June. In autumn of the following year, when everyone was agitated in anticipation of the war, Nikolai Iakovlevich again made a trip to St. Petersburg and lived there until 5 April 1877. Even before that, in the fall of 1876 a general exodus had begun among residents of the South Coast, but he remained there with his family. After his trip, his family did not leave and calmly awaited his instructions, even though since the end of December the South Coast was occupied by troops. Finally on 30 March 1877, Nikolai Iakovlevich wrote from St. Petersburg: "It's time to prepare to leave Mshatka, since war is almost here." Then all their possessions were packed up and moved to the village of Baidar; but Nikolai Iakovlevich's family continued to live in the South Coast, somehow getting by without their things. It continued thus after Nikolai Iakovlevich returned home, until news came of the Treaty of San Stefano.[16] All during the war Nikolai Iakovlevich did not want to leave and lived with his family "in bivouac." He reckoned that no one would bother bombarding a tiny hamlet like Mshatka or his little house, and in the event of an enemy landing, they could always flee beyond the mountains. But neither the bivouac life nor the personal dangers were the hard part of living in this way: Nikolai Iakovlevich was all worked up and worried from following the course of events, which made him nearly ecstatic, but everything was poisoned by the bitter conclusion.

In 1879 from mid-September through 12 December, and in 1880 from May through November, Nikolai Iakovlevich served as director of Nikitskii

---

[16] Treaty of San Stefano: Preliminary treaty concluding the Russo-Turkish War of 1877–78. The Great Powers of Western Europe considered the terms too favorable to Russia, and revised them at the 1878 Congress of Berlin (the "bitter conclusion" Strakhov mentions).

Botanical Garden, filling in for N. E. Tsabel'[17] who was then on leave. In this period, the winter of 1879, he began his work on *Darwinism*.

On 12 October 1880 Nikolai Iakovlevich discovered phylloxera[18] on the estate of Mr. Raevskii,[19] and immediately wrote to the ministry about it. The danger of phylloxera, it can be said, Nikolai Iakovlevich alone recognized and understood. During the outbreak (5 March 1873) he had demanded a complete ban on the importation of vines from abroad, and such a ban was issued by imperial command (6 April 1873). In 1880, as a result of raising the alarm, the ministry named him (6 November) the head of the Crimean phylloxera commission. Nikolai Iakovlevich at once began to destroy infected vines in Tesseli.[20] He requested to go abroad to get up to date on this issue, and left on 13 December for Switzerland and southern France, but was already back in the Crimea by 13 January 1881. From then on, each summer he inspected vineyards and tracked down phylloxera, and had those places that were infected, or at risk of becoming so, destroyed. Nikolai Iakovlevich summoned such speed and energy as won him accolades from wine researchers abroad. The destruction work required many workers, so they used soldiers. The Tsar named Baron Andrei Nikolaevich Korf[21] the overall head of the phylloxera expedition, who, once he saw how the work was going, commended Nikolai Iakovlevich and gave him full support.

Unfortunately the measures Nikolai Iakovlevich proposed at the very outset were not carried out completely, and the battle against phylloxera continues each year, to this day.[22] After Baron Korf, Nikolai Iakovlevich remained solely in charge in 1883.

In the last year of his life (1885), Nikolai Iakovlevich had to make two trips. On 3 April he was sent to Tiflis[23] for a phylloxera convention beginning

---

[17] Nikolai Egorovich Zabel (1831–1910): Botanist, director (1866–80) of the Nikitskii Botanical Garden, located in the Crimea, near Yalta. Under his direction, it opened an institute for horticultural and vinicultural advances.

[18] Phylloxera louse, or Antarctic locus fly, an aphid-like pest of commercial grapevines native to North America, causing major wine plagues of the 1850s and early 1870s across Europe.

[19] Nikolai Nikolaevich Raevskii (1839–76): Son of the lieutenant-general of the same name from the Napoleonic wars, himself a military man serving in central Asia, and Pan-Slavic polemicist who went as a volunteer to fight for Serbia in the Serbian-Ottoman War (1876–77), where he was killed.

[20] The Raevskii family estate in the Crimea.

[21] Baron Andrei Nikolaevich Korf (1831–93): Russian infantry general, subsequently named governor-general of the Primorskii Krai in the Far East.

[22] Phylloxera has never been eradicated, although its effects have been ameliorated by hybridization and grafting non-resistant varieties onto resistant rootstock native to the Americas.

[23] Tbilisi, the largest city in Georgia.

on 20 April. On the way to Tiflis he injured his leg, and suffered from this injury through the end of summer. Besides that, for more than a year he felt the onset of the heart disease destined to end his life. In spite of that, he accepted a dispatch (6 September) to investigate a decline in the fisheries of Lake Gokhche.[24] He left Mshatka on 1 October and completed the study of the lake without incident, but upon returning to Tiflis, where he intended to give a brief report, without warning he suffered a powerful attack of his illness, and died on 7 November.

His body was returned to Mshatka and buried in his garden. There, not far from the sea coast, is a narrow lane that seems to lead to a clearing in the dense thicket. But the end of this lane suddenly opens onto a large, smooth glade, surrounded on all sides by tall trees and steep cliffs, like a wall. The glade is so level and the walls are so perpendicular that this place is called "the cypress room." Now it resembles a temple, and in the middle of it is a grave, on which stands a cross, to which not only his family comes to pray, but sometimes even various simple folk from far around Mshatka who know the departed and honor his memory.

In his personal qualities, Nikolai Iakovlevich cut quite a figure. This was a man of tremendous strength in body and spirit alike, so clean and pure, such a stranger to evil or the slightest falsity, that it was impossible not to like him, and he left behind no enemies or detractors. He was too little known; he was nothing like his reputation. Only people who got to know him personally, or took a special interest in what he wrote and did, really knew him. He was one of those who can be called the salt of the Russian earth, one of the unknown righteous by whom our fatherland will be saved.

Here is the obituary which I sent to the newspapers the day after his death:

In Tiflis, at 10 a.m. on 7 November died one of the most remarkable people in Russia, Nikolai Iakovlevich Danilevskii. He held the service rank of Privy Councilor, a member of the Council of State Ministers. His labors in his field of service are incredibly vast and important. He studied fisheries throughout European Russia and created the regulations for them currently in effect. His research began under the supervision of K. E. Baer and then continued independently for decades; his last effort of this sort was a trip to Lake Gokhchke last October. Having returned to Tiflis, Nikolai Iakovlevich suffered a sudden, fatal attack of heart disease, the signs of which appeared this past year but seemed to be going away. In recent years he made two additional official contributions: establishing rules governing water rights in the Crimea and the destruction of phylloxera infecting the vineyards there.

---

[24] Lake Sevan, the largest lake in Armenia.

Nikolai Iakovlevich is a great name in literature as one of the major Slavophiles, as author of the book *Russia and Europe,* containing an original view of world history and a sort of codex of Slavophile teaching. He was an honorary member of the St. Petersburg Slavic Benevolent Society. Additionally he wrote some less broad but always excellent scholarly works on aspects of geology, political economy, the study of folk life, etc. As a naturalist, he hoped to devote the rest of his days to a broad work by the name of *Darwinism;* two volumes will soon be published of this work, which is destined to remain unfinished.

But no matter how brilliant his works, there was even more good and light in him personally than in his works. No one who knew the departed man could fail to sense the pureness of his soul, the integrity and firmness of his character, and the remarkable strength and clarity of his mind. Without any pretensions or any desire to show off, he always came across as a man of power just as soon as the topic turned to things he knew and cared about. His patriotism was boundless, but vigilant and incorruptible. There was no stain on his soul or even his thoughts. His intellect so easily and precisely combined incredible theoretical power with practical plans. Neither in his legislative work nor his intellectual constructions did he ever turn to other's examples for guidance, but was completely original. All who were close to him know what irreplaceable treasures of mind and soul he took with him to the grave.

He was sixty-three years old, and he left behind a wife and five children.

All of the preceding is nothing but the bare frames, into which must be inserted various pictures of this rich life. Perhaps with time the recollections of friends will reveal for us the details of Nikolai Iakovlevich's inner character and private life. But his intellectual and practical activity is for the most part available to all. Below, readers will find a list of everything he wrote and published, both in an official capacity and on those questions that occupied his time outside of official orders. The reports published by the Ministry of State Domains provide the material detailing his vast efforts on behalf of fisheries, but also on industry and agriculture in general, and finally on the struggle with phylloxera (although much of it remains buried in the ministry archives). Of the important works on legislation concerning flowing waters of the Crimea, virtually nothing has been published. The informal, purely literary works of our author can be divided into three main kinds: 1) natural science, the most important of which is the book *Darwinism;* 2) political-economic, a representative of which would be, "On the Low Value of Our Currency"; and finally, 3) historical or political, of which the main work is *Russia and Europe.*

To describe and characterize these broad and diverse works would require a long and careful study. All of them fully deserve such a study; in each realm, everything done by Nikolai Iakovlevich is the fruit of an unusually bright and fruitful mind. We will offer just a few words here on *Russia and Europe*.

When Nikolai Iakovlevich arrived in St. Petersburg at the very beginning of 1868, he brought a finished manuscript of this book with him, reproduced in a clean copy, corrected down to the last line. That was just how he worked: He did nothing half-way, and could not tear himself from the plan he conceived until it was carried out to the end. Thus all that was left was to print it. To publish the book by itself would mean bearing considerable expense, and at the same time consigning his work to near complete oblivion. Our public still will not buy books, and is only interested in journals. Therefore it was necessary to try to place his writing in a journal; that way the author gets paid per sheet, up front, while the essay comes to the attention of a few thousand readers, who may or may not have otherwise sought it out. But none of the journals of that day would accept something written in such a vein as *Russia and Europe*. Therefore he only attempted to find it a place in the *Journal of the Ministry of Public Enlightenment*, although there was no counting on it coming to the public's attention in that event. Fortunately just then the ardent literary enthusiast V. V. Kashpirev[25] decided to publish a new monthly journal, *Zaria*, and brought me on staff. Nikolai Iakovlevich was very pleased by this turn of events; from the very first issue of *Zaria* in 1869, successive chapters of *Russia and Europe* began to appear in it, and the whole book was published in the journal in the course of a year. It was then somewhat simpler for us to think about publishing the book separately. We had almost no publishers or booksellers for serious books, but in this case the Brotherhood of Social Welfare supported *Russia and Europe*, and the book was published under an arrangement to split the costs and profits. This 1871 edition ran 1200 copies and sold out over the course of fifteen years.[26] Our progress was obviously slow. The book had much greater demand at the height of the Turkish war, when, under the influence of military and patriotic enthusiasm, many sought to understand Russia's relationship to the Slavs and to Europe.

I will add a few more words about this book, only to repeat the appraisal I gave it when it first appeared (*Zaria*, March 1871). When Nikolai Iakovlevich read my review, he told me, "Everything you said is incredibly true and

---

[25] Vasilii Vladimirovich Kashpirev (1836–75): Founder of the short-lived conservative-nationalist monthly journal *Zaria* (Dawn; 1869–72), which folded for lack of subscribers. Besides publishing several other books, little else known about him.

[26] [Strakhov's note]: Despite convention, on the cover this is called the second edition; the discrepancy arises from the fact that the book was not actually compiled of journal articles written at different times, but was completely finished before it appeared in successive issues of the journal.

accurate; I am not talking about the praise, but your analysis of the methods and arguments of my book." Thus, I offer my observations, approved, so to speak, by the author himself.

It is certainly logical to attribute *Russia and Europe* to what is called the Slavophile school of our literature, since this book is based on the idea of the originality lying in the soul of the Slavic world. The book embraces this issue so deeply and fully that it could be called a catechism or codex of Slavophilism.

The extent to which it combines and completes Slavophile teaching is a separate question; but that it has such summative and representative significance is impossible to doubt. Perhaps with time Nikolai Iakovlevich Danilevskii will be considered a leading Slavophile, the culminating point in the development of this tendency, the writer in whom the full force of the Slavophile idea is concentrated. If the name of Khomiakov[27] will never be forgotten in the history of Russian thought, then maybe *what Danilevskii has said* will make an even more memorable, clear, and forceful impact in our minds.

But suppose that does not happen, and Danilevskii stands not higher, but merely in front of the preceding Slavophiles. In any event, *Russia and Europe* is a book from which anyone who wants to discover Slavophilism can do so. With the appearance of this book, it cannot be said that the ideas about the uniqueness of the Slavic tribes, about Europe being a foreign world to us, about Russia's future and historical purposes, and so on—that these ideas are nothing but journalistic chatter, hints, and dreams, empty phrases and allegories. No, Slavophilism now exists in a more strict, clear, defined, precise, and coherent form than almost any other school of thought among us.

Here we must consider the objection typically raised against a book like *Russia and Europe,* that it is nothing new. This question of *novelty* is incredibly difficult, and people who are not favorably inclined toward the whole matter always make use of it. What is new in Pushkin?[28] At first glance, he is no different from Zhukovskii, Batiushkov, Kozlov,[29] and others: the same language, the same forms, identical literary habits and techniques. But in its essence, the novelty is immense: the creation of Russian poetry, the foundation of Russian literature. So to grasp what is new is far from easy. A skeptic, if

---

[27] Aleksei Stepanovich Khomiakov (1804–60): Russian poet exploring spiritual themes connected with national identity, founder of the Slavophile movement, together with Ivan Vasil'evich Kireevskii (1806–56).

[28] Aleksandr Sergeevich Pushkin (1799–1837): Widely regarded as Russia's greatest poet and the founder of modern Russian literature.

[29] Vasilii Andreevich Zhukovskii (1783–1852): Leading poet of the 1810s. Konstantin Nikolaevich Batiushkov (1787–1855): Romantic poet, essayist, and translator. Ivan Ivanovich Kozlov (1779–1840): Romantic poet and translator, whose Byronic verse tale *The Monk* (1825) exceeded Pushkin's early works in popularity.

you will, might say that the first sight of a magnificent house is nothing new, since the pile of bricks from which it was built had long been a familiar sight.

But in the present case, for readers who are somewhat attentive and serious, it seems to us there can be no question or doubt. In Danilevskii's book, everything is new from the beginning to the end; it is not just a catalog and repetition of others' opinions; it contains only the author's own opinions, thoughts never uttered by anyone, anywhere, which is why he sensed the need to express them. *Russia and Europe* is an entirely original book, by no means derived from Slavophilism in the strict literary-historical sense of the term. It does not represent merely the furthest development of principles already expressed, but rather sets forth new principles, utilizing new techniques, and reaching new and more general results, which contain the Slavophile ideas as a particular case. Despite that, when we call the doctrine of *Russia and Europe* Slavophilism, we mean here Slavophilism in the abstract, general, and ideal sense; strictly speaking, it is not Slavophilism at all but Danilevskii's own doctrine, *danilevshchina* so to speak, which includes Slavophilism within it, but not the other way around.

New developments in the intellectual realm are often greeted as old, long-known to everyone: the mistake is most natural. New developments often force us to broaden and generalize the meaning of our former concepts; so with the appearance of *Russia and Europe* we must broaden and generalize the meaning of the long-used term *Slavophilism*. It turns out there is a Slavophile doctrine that is nothing like what we are accustomed to calling by this name.

What are the similarities and differences? The similarities obviously consist of the practical conclusions. It is clear that N. Ia. Danilevskii must coincide with the earlier Slavophiles to a significant degree when speaking about Russia's needs and its logical aspirations. People who vitally and deeply feel the interests of their motherland, ardently delving into its historical destiny, obviously will never diverge very far on questions of what they ought to love and ought to wish for. In this regard, as we have seen by many examples, profound insights force many to speak and act even against their own frame of mind, against the clearest principles they profess. There are occasions when, it can be said, all of Russia turns into Slavophiles.

But it is one thing to aspire according to whatever instinct, and another thing to elevate these aspirations to the level of conscious views and reconcile them with our higher principles held in common. And this is N. Ia. Danilevskii's essential distinction. If any peasant is essentially a Slavophile, and if the most ardent Westernizers sometimes join in with the peasants, and finally, if the earlier Slavophiles truly understood not only the interests but also the very spirit of the people, then Danilevskii is the writer who presents the strictest theory for these aspirations, who identified for them the higher principles held in common, and new principles not identified by anyone before him. This is the most important original contribution of *Russia and Europe*.

This book has been called too modest. But it is not at all limited to Russia and Europe, or even the broader subjects of the Slavic world and the Germanic-Roman world. It contains a new view of the whole history of humanity, a new theory of Universal History. This is not a journalistic composition, where the whole focus is borrowed from some certain practical interests; this is a strictly scientific composition, intended to discover the truth regarding fundamental principles on which the science of history must be built. Slavdom and the relations between Russia and Europe are no more than a particular case, an example illustrating a general theory.

Danilevskii's main idea is incredibly original and incredibly interesting. He provided a new formula for the construction of history, a much broader formula than earlier ones, and thus without a doubt, more correct, more scientific, and more capable of grasping the reality of the subject than previous formulas. Namely he rejected the single thread in the development of humanity, the idea that history is the progress of reason, or civilization, in general. There is no such civilization, says Danilevskii, but only individual civilizations, and the development of separate cultural-historical types.

Obviously the former view of history was artificial, forcefully shoving events into a formula borrowed from outside, subordinating them to an arbitrarily constructed order. Danilevskii's new perspective is natural, not following from a preconceived notion, but determining the forms and relations between subjects on the basis of experience and observation, and careful scrutiny of their nature. The transformation *Russia and Europe* attempts to bring to the field of history is like the introduction of natural systems into sciences where artificial systems had prevailed.

The researcher should then be guided by a certain humility before the objects of study. Theorists, especially the Germans, often rearrange nature to suit themselves, eager to see falsehood and aberration in everything that conflicts with their reasoning; but the true naturalist rejects blind faith in reason, seeking revelation and guidance not from his own thoughts, but from the objects of study. This is the belief that the world and its phenomena are much deeper, richer in content, more abundant in meaning, than the paltry and withered constructions of our minds.

For ordinary historians, something like China, for instance, is something faulty and barren, some kind of useless nonsense.[30] Therefore they do not speak of China; they relegate it to a place outside of history. According to

---

[30] The twenty-first-century reader should recall that nineteenth-century China was in full decline, confronting aggressive colonizing powers, and the attendant loss of sovereignty, while being sapped by a thriving, European-run opium trade. China's imperial government collapsed within a quarter-century of this being written.

Danilevskii's system, China is just as legitimate and worthy a topic as the Greco-Roman world, or haughty Europe.[31]

So, this is the significance, the lofty subject, and the power of Danilevskii's unique new point of departure elaborated in *Russia and Europe*. And just as original is the masterful presentation of history from this point of view. If many of the conclusions are Slavophile, they nevertheless take on a completely new guise with new supporting evidence, which they obviously lacked without the principles identified for the first time in this book.

Nowhere does the author of *Russia and Europe* rely on Slavophile doctrines as something already established and upheld. Rather, he exclusively developed his own thoughts and based them on his own principles. How he stands in regard to Slavophilism he partly indicated in the following passage:

The doctrine of the Slavophiles in its own way was colored by the humanities; it had to be, since it too had dual sources: German philosophy, which it held with greater freedom in a broader understanding than its opponents; and the study of the origins of Russian and Slavic life in its religion, history, poetics, and customs. If it emphasized the necessity of distinct national development, it was partly from understanding the great merit of Slavic principles, and from seeing through their long development the one-sidedness and irreconcilable contradiction of European principles. It considered that the Slavs were destined to complete a universal task, and that their predecessors had simply not yet managed it. Such a task, however, does not exist" (from *Russia and Europe*, chapter 6).

---

[31] [Strakhov's note]: Since the idea of cultural-historical types is suggested by the very facts of history, traces of this idea can be found in other writers; we have in mind Heinrich Rückert [1823–75, German historian and philologist, professor at Breslau], who compiled the most profound of all existing surveys of world history (*Lehrbuch der Weltgeschichte* [Leipzig, 1857]). But only N. Ia. Danilevskii grasped the full significance of this idea and articulated it in complete clarity and rigor. Rückert did not make it the basis of his survey, but speaks of it only in the appendix of his work, at the end of the second volume. [Translator's note: This off-handed mention of Rückert opened an avenue of attack to philosopher Vladimir Solov'ev (1853–1900), with whom Strakhov waged an ongoing polemic in the late 1880s, pitting a universal Christian civilization (Solov'ev) against nationalism and what would more recently be called multiculturalism (Strakhov/Danilevskii). Solov'ev dismissed Danilevskii's work as patently derivative of Rückert. In the twentieth century, Robert MacMaster investigated the question of influence, concluding there is no proof Danilevskii ever read Rückert, and despite some superficial similarities, their arguments and conclusions point in opposite directions. See Robert E. MacMaster, "The Question of Heinrich Ruckert's Influence on Danilevskij," *American Slavic and East European Review* 14: 1 (February 1955): 59–66. On Strakhov's polemic with Solov'ev, see Linda Gerstein, *Nikolai Strakhov* (Cambridge, MA: Harvard University Press, 1971), 114–19.]

So N. Ia. Danilevskii draws from another source, and his main conclusion is not a Slavophile one. N. Ia. Danilevskii is not taken with German philosophy, and does not have the same openness to it that the Slavophiles had. So he is independent to a certain extent. His philosophy can be compared to the spirit of natural science, such as the views and methods of Cuvier;[32] but this general scientific spirit cannot be considered some peculiar doctrine.

The main conclusion of *Russia and Europe* is just as independent and just as striking in its simplicity and sobriety as is the whole theory. The Slavs are not destined to renovate the whole world or find the solution for all humanity to its historical problem, but are simply a unique cultural-historical type, which has the right to exist and develop alongside other types. This resolution solved many difficulties at once, drawing the line against other impossible dreams, and setting us on the firm ground of reality. Beyond that it is obvious that this resolution is purely Slavic, representing that character of tolerance which in general we find lacking in the views of Europe, which is violent and power-loving not only in practice, but also in its mental constructions. And Danilevskii's whole theory can be regarded as an attempt to explain the place of the Slavic world in history, which for every European historian is a riddle, an anomaly, or an epicycle. Due to their exceptional place among other peoples, which really has no equal in history, the Slavs are destined to change the views of history rooted in Europe, according to which nothing can come from the Slavic world.

These are the main features of N. Ia. Danilevskii's book. The multifaceted character of this book is apparent; but we hasten to add that this is far from a complete picture of the book. The wealth of ideas, the abundance of solid contents is so great that new aspects of the issue open up on each page. In a remarkable way this essay combines the warmth of deep feelings with cold scientific rigor; it is an ardent declaration and at the same time, a precise and profoundly thought-out theory.

In the 1871 edition, the author made only one or two small additions to the text as it was printed in *Zaria*. In the previous (third) edition, we added the notes found in the margins of the author's copy.[33] These notes were written not in pencil, as was Nikolai Iakovlevich's habit, but in ink; from the sharpness of expression of some of them, we can suppose that Nikolai Iakovlevich intended to publish them, of course in expanded and enlarged form.

---

[32] Georges Cuvier (1769–1832): Pioneer in comparative anatomy, proponent of catastrophism in geology and opponent of evolutionary theories. His best-known work is *Le Règne Animal* (The Animal Kingdom; 1817).

[33] These notes added later by Danilevskii appear in chapters 10–16, where the book turns from historical argument toward current affairs, particularly the broader context of the Eastern Question. Most post-Soviet editions omit these notes. While they add little to the text, they are included in this edition for the sake of completeness, but set in italics rather than Strakhov's original bold print.

We cannot precisely determine when the notes were made, but at least no earlier than 1880 or even 1881. After the war,[34] when the book came into much greater circulation, the author began to prepare it for a new edition, and these notes obviously are part of that preparation. To distinguish them we have printed them in bold, but this also completely suits both their great import and, at the same time, brevity.

We have also preserved here an aphorism jotted on a separate sheet of paper, a partial facsimile of which appears in the preceding [i.e., third, 1888] edition. The profound and figurative thought in this aphorism does not concern the present book, but helps characterize its author. Here it is:

Beauty is the only spiritual side of matter; thus beauty is the only bond between these two basic principles of the world. That is, [beauty] is the only way that it [matter] has value and significance for the soul, the only way it responds to the needs of the soul, yet at the same time makes no difference at all to matter as matter. Conversely the demand for beauty is the only need of the soul that only matter can satisfy.

And here is the reason for the existence of matter. "God wanted to create beauty," said Nikolai Iakovlevich, "and for that he created matter."[35]

---

[34] The Russo-Turkish War of 1877–78.

[35] Following his essay, Strakhov attached a chronological list of all Danilevskii's publications. A translation of the list, updated to 1967, is already available (hence its omission here); see Robert E. MacMaster, *Danilevsky, a Russian Totalitarian Philosopher* (Cambridge: Harvard University Press, 1967), 313–19. One caveat: MacMaster wrongly included an 1846 work, *Kavkaz i ego gorskie zhiteli...*, written by a different N. Danilevskii, incorrectly attributed to this Danilevskii in American library catalogs. There were virtually no changes to MacMaster's list until 1991, when new editions of *Rossiia i evropa* started appearing regularly. For a list of works published since 1991, see the appendix to the present volume.

Figure 1. Burial site of Danilevskii and his wife, in the Cypress Hall, on the grounds of Mshatka, on the south coast of the Crimea, circa 1910. Image courtesy of Olga Danilevskaya. Used with permission.

Figure 2. Memorial on the same location, dedicated 2009. Image courtesy of Olga Danilevskaya. Used with permission.

Figure 3. The Cypress Hall, summer 2013. Image courtesy of Olga Danilevskaya. Used with permission.

ଓଃ 1 ৪০
1864 and 1854—In Place of an Introduction

The summer of 1866 had tremendous historical significance. Germany, fragmented in the course of centuries, began to unite under the leadership of the ingenious Prussian minister into a strong, single whole. The European *status quo* was obviously disrupted, and not only by what we have so recently witnessed. That skillfully assembled political machine, which was so meticulously balanced, has been thrown into disarray. Everyone knows that the events of 1866 were only a natural consequence of 1864. What happened then was the malfunction of the political-diplomatic machine, unnoticed by the machine-operators who were supposed to be monitoring it. As insignificant as the outcome of the Austro-Prussian-Danish War of 1864 turned out to be, we will not much bother with that subject.

But in the years mentioned in the chapter heading, two events occurred, separated by a decade, that are very instructive for any Russian interested in the significance of current world affairs. In short, these events were the following: In 1864 Prussia and Austria—two major states, home to about sixty million residents and capable of fielding an army of almost a million—attacked Denmark, one of the smallest states of Europe, home to no more than 2.5 million, not known for being warlike, but highly enlightened, liberal, and humane. The aggressors took away two provinces from this state, home to two-fifths of its subjects: two territories, which had been affirmed as an inextricable part of this state not thirty years ago in the [1839] Treaty of London, which the two aggressor states, among others, had signed. And this direct violation of the agreement, this assault on the weak by the strong, produced no opposition of any sort. Neither the insult to moral sensibilities, nor the violation of the so-called political equilibrium aroused the indignation of Europe, in either public opinion or in its governments. At least, it did not arouse enough to turn word into deed, so the partition of Denmark was completed in calm. Such were the events of 1864.

Eleven years before that, Russia—a large and powerful part of the political system of European states—out of its most sacred religious interests, attacked Turkey—a barbarian, conquering state, which though already weakening, still maintained its illegitimate and unjust dominion by force; a state at that time not included in the political system of Europe, the unity of which was not guaranteed by any definitive treaty. But even so, no one violated that unity. All that was needed from Turkey was to confirm its obligation and refrain from violating the religious interests of the majority of its subjects. This is not some new obligation, but was negotiated eighty years ago in the peace agreement of Küçük-Kaynarca.[1] And what of this demand, which the diplomatic collective of the leading states of Europe considered justified? The religious and other interests of millions of Christians have turned out to count for nothing; the barbarian state in the eyes of Europe has become the palladium of civilization and freedom. In 1854, exactly ten years before the partition of Denmark, about which no one had any concern, England and France declared war on Russia, Sardinia got involved, Austria adopted a menacing posture, and finally all of Europe threatened war, if Russia did not accept the disadvantageous peace terms proposed to it. This is how the governments of Europe acted; public opinion in Europe was even more hostile and tried to win over even the governments of states like Prussia and other German states, which despite the various incentives offered did not want to break with Russia. Why this indifference to liberal, humane Denmark; this sympathy toward barbaric, despotic Turkey; this indulgence even toward the unjust pretenses of Austria and Prussia; and this complete disrespect of Russia's legitimate demands? The matter deserves careful investigation. It is not just an accident, not just a journalistic escapade, not just the fervor of some faction, but a collective diplomatic posture of all Europe; that is, it is a display of the general mood not under the influence of passion, or thoughtless passing fancy. Therefore, I have chosen this as the point of departure for my investigation of the mutual relations of Europe and Russia.

We will consider first of all: Was there any kind of provocation by Denmark against Prussia and Austria, or something to excuse this oppression of the weak by the strong in the eyes of Europe; and conversely, in Russia's actions, was there any kind of insult to Europe, justifying its anger and outrage?

We will not delve into the minutiae of the Danish-German quarrel over Schleswig-Holstein, which, as is well known, spans seventeen years and in my opinion is of no interest to Russian readers. The essence of the matter is that Denmark adopted a common constitution for all its constituent parts, one of the most liberal constitutions in Europe, under which, of course, there was no hint of one nationality [natsional'nost'] being oppressed by another. But Germany would not have it: it demanded for Holstein a constitution that, although much worse, would completely separate this country from other parts of the [Danish] monarchy. It demanded not personal union, on the order of Sweden with Norway (that would have been nothing!) but some kind of state right applied to the whole province, like the Polish liberum veto [nepozvoliat'], by use of which members of Holstein could negate any resolution accepted

---

[1] The Treaty of Küçük-Kaynarca (1774) concluded the Russo-Turkish war of 1768–74, a defeat for the Ottomans. Russia claimed access to the Black Sea and the right of protection over Orthodox subjects of Ottoman rule.

for all of Denmark. Since Holstein belonged to the German Confederation,[2] the Confederation would in roundabout manner attain supremacy over the whole Danish monarchy. It considered this supremacy necessary because, besides Holstein, in the matter of which the German union had a certain right of interference, the Danish state had taken in Schleswig, a country declared by treaties to be completely outside of Germany, but populated in large part by Germans who had gradually colonized it and thoroughly Germanized its Scandinavian culture. To all politically minded Germans, Schleswig and Holstein are inseparable, but this view is not at all supported by current international treaties. To make the case, it was necessary to use Holstein as a lever to put constant pressure on all of Denmark. This would ensure that the Danish government could only rule Schleswig in a manner pleasing to Germany. Denmark evidently could not accept this, and the patriotic party (the so-called Eider Danes)[3] was ready to renounce Holstein, if only to protect the unity, wholeness, and independence of the remainder of the monarchy from continual foreign interference. We can appreciate the difficulty of such interference from personal experience. This kind of interference, based on nitpicking interpretations of certain articles of the Treaty of Vienna, brought indignation to all of Russia. It is good that the indignation of Russia, being so heavy, tilted the political balance in many diplomatic and other considerations. But who noticed the indignation of Denmark? As a matter of fact, Denmark's hands were tied by a treaty denying it the full freedom to rule Holstein as it saw fit. A battle of words[4] ensued over the true meaning of this treaty between Denmark and the German Confederation. Each side of course insisted on its own advantage; finally the German Confederation, not known for rash action, lost patience and instituted corporal punishment in Holstein. Holstein belonged to the German Confederation, and there could be no objections raised. But clearly the German Confederation, although uniting fifty million people, did not command much fear or respect: even tiny Denmark, in the face of corporal punishment, calmly maintained its position. Prussia (or, more precisely, Mr. Bismarck),[5] however, saw that there was no way this matter could end well for it. Seize upper Denmark, and all plans for Kiel Bay, the navy, Baltic Sea supremacy, and hegemony over Germany, would be lost. In short, it would mean forfeiting all German interests, of which Prussia correctly

---

[2] German Confederation: A weak association of German-speaking states created at the Congress of Vienna in 1815, increasingly dominated by the rivalry between Austria and Prussia for hegemony.

[3] Eider Danes: Danish population named for the Eider River (traditional boundary between Denmark and the Holy Roman Empire) dividing Schleswig (north) and Holstein (south).

[4] *Slovopreniia* (logomachy).

[5] Otto von Bismarck (1815–98): Prime minister of Prussia (1862–90), architect of German unification.

considers itself the main, perhaps the only, representative. Let the German Confederation triumph, and Holstein, by itself or combined with Schleswig, would become an independent state and grow stronger in an alliance with medium and small states which, as Bismarck so correctly understood, could only undermine Prussian hegemony. For the all-German, but at the same time Prussian-led, endeavor to succeed, the Confederation must not grow stronger, yet both Holstein and Schleswig must fall into its hands. From this completely correct (in the Prussian view) line of thinking, in order to secure an alliance with Austria, which in this whole matter was stoking the fires for Prussia, Mr. Bismarck stood up for the German Confederation disregarded and insulted by Denmark, and threatened war if it did not abolish the constitution ratified by its houses of parliament and shared throughout the monarchy. (Incidentally, although very liberal, this constitution was not entirely at odds with the German view, nor with the Prussian view in particular.) Technically Denmark was not completely in the right, because it could not live up to its treaty obligations, at least not in the way Germany understood them. So it decided to cut the Gordian knot of the shared constitution for the whole monarchy which, although essentially satisfying the same requirements for Schleswig as for Holstein, nevertheless completely eliminated the Confederation's interference in the matter of Schleswig and made it pointless in Holstein. Denmark, being technically in the wrong, and under threat of war from two major states, easily could have acceded to such a forthright demand. It would be absolutely imperative to announce such a renunciation in advance. The means to do that were easily found. Prussia and Austria set so short a deadline for their demands to be met, that the Danish government did not have time to summon the houses of parliament and present the demands of these states for their deliberation. Thus the Danish government had to either refuse the demands of foreign powers and bring a lopsided war upon itself, or violate its own constitution. To violate the constitution at that moment—with a weak king, newly seated on the throne, unpopular because of his German descent[6]—would have meant in all likelihood to invite revolution. So the Danish government could do no more than choose the lesser of two evils. It chose war, evidently having reason to consider it the lesser evil. In the first place, Denmark had already fought a war against Prussia and Germany not more than fifteen years ago, and emerged from it more victor than vanquished, so it might expect a similar outcome this time. This thought was perfectly good, except it did not take into account that Germany previously had a discordant parliament in Frankfurt and no Bismarck in Prussia. Furthermore, the Danish government could hope that the political system of states was founded on definitive treaties rather than empty words, and that since Europe for nearly a

---

[6] Prince Christian of Glücksborg, later Christian IX of Denmark (1818–1906): Originally not in the Danish line of succession, but chosen to rule upon the end (in 1863) of the Oldenburg dynasty, which had ruled Denmark since 1448.

hundred years had ceaselessly protested the great crime of the partition of Poland, it would never allow the partition of Denmark. Europe ought to see the knife at its throat and at least demand that the attackers allow time to think it over. But in all this it was mistaken. War broke out. The unprepared Danes of course faced defeat. To end this intolerable conflict, the European states convened in London. The neutral powers proposed a settlement that acknowledged the victory won by Prussia and Austria. But this settlement did not satisfy the members of the Confederation. They maintained their demands and Europe, its protection exhausted, left them to divide up Denmark, as they knew it would. So even if Denmark technically was not completely in the right, still Prussia and Austria did plenty wrong, not only by refusing to give Denmark a chance to retract its uncompromising stance, but by using this as the pretext to achieve their goals: stripping Denmark not only of Holstein but also Schleswig, which in their minds was part of it. Diplomatic customs, which uphold international law just as juridical forms uphold civil and domestic law, were violated not by Denmark, but by Prussia and Austria. Thus these two states, not Denmark, offended Europe.

But sometimes illegality, or that which is technically, superficially incorrect, conceals a certain internal truth, so that any dispassionate opinion or feeling takes the side of apparent incorrectness. Was there ever, for example, a more blatant direct violation of formal national law [*narodnoe pravo*] than Cavour[7] and Garibaldi's[8] formation of the Italian kingdom? The conduct of Victor Emmanuel's[9] government with the Papal States and the Kingdom of Naples could in no way be justified from a legal point of view. But any thinking and feeling human would agree that, in this case, the form must yield to the essence, and external legality must yield to internal truth. Is it not the same in the matter of Schleswig-Holstein? Would we not classify it as technically incorrect, but warranted by a hidden internal truth, and was it not that internal truth that disarmed Europe? To this we must answer no. In the first place, the national issue [*natsional'noe delo*], championed by Austria, can only be met with bitter laughter and scorn. Secondly, Europe does not officially recognize the principle of nationality [*printsip natsional'nostei*], and without various types of corroborating evidence, will not confirm anything merely by the testimony of its own eyes. Even the cause of Italy prevailed only through the reciprocal relations of the major powers, which were not inclined to defend the concern for legality. In public opinion, the principle of nationality [*nachalo natsional'nostei*] is widespread only in France and Italy,

---

[7] Camillo Benso, Count of Cavour (1810–61): Prime minister of Piedmont-Sardinia, architect of Italian unification.

[8] Giuseppe Garibaldi (1807–82): Nationalistic leader of many military campaigns of the Italian unification process.

[9] Victor Emanuel II (1820–78): King of Sardinia from 1849, named first king of united Italy in 1861.

and only because these countries consider it beneficial. Third, the last and most important reason: the principle of nationality does not completely apply to the question of Schleswig-Holstein. In 1864 the German people was not a single entity. It did not have nationality in the political sense, and so long as that had still not taken shape, [how] could it demand the partition of Holstein and Schleswig from Denmark in the name of it [nationality] without also demanding the destruction of Bavaria, Saxony, Lippe-Detmold, Saxe-Altenburg, and others as independent political entities? Granted, there existed among the various German states a weak political bond, known as the German Confederation. But Holstein was every bit a member of the Confederation, as were Bavaria, Prussia, Lippe, and Altenburg. Schleswig of course did not belong to the Confederation, but if we ignore the fact that this Danish province was colonized by Germans, and exclusively uphold the ethnographic principle, completely rejecting [the idea of] historic right, then from this point of view the furthest extent of German demands still could only be the addition of Schleswig to the German Confederation, not the complete partition of Holstein and Schleswig from Denmark. Would they say that Bavaria, Prussia, Lippe-Detmold, and Saxe-Altenburg, although independent political entities, were still completely German, but Schleswig and Holstein were somehow conjoined with the Danish nationality? But in exactly the same way Limburg and Luxembourg are conjoined with the Dutch nationality. More importantly, in exactly the same way six or seven million Austrian Germans are conjoined with thirty million Slavs, Magyars, Romanians, and Italians. If these are anomalies, then it would seem necessary to eliminate the greatest among them before becoming preoccupied with trifling cases. But these six or seven million Austrian Germans are not a subordinate nationality, like the millions in Holstein or Schleswig, but are on the contrary the ruling nationality. It cannot be denied that this circumstance has primary significance in German eyes, completely turning the matter around. But it is hard to understand what kind of significance it can have for impartial Europe, which values the German, the Scandinavian, the Italian—we will not mention the Slavic—nationalities all the same. So if the German people [narod] do not constitute a political nationality [natsional'nost'], if a significant part of it was conjoined with other nationalities under a certain government, then it could rightly demand from Denmark only that the German nationality in Schleswig and Holstein not be oppressed, but have equal rights with Danes. Yet this demand would be pointless because it had already been fulfilled without demands of any sort.

Let us imagine that the original plan of Napoleon III[10] concerning Italy had been carried out. It would consist of an Italian Confederation, like the German one, which would include the Kingdom of [Lombardy-]Venetia, even

---

[10] Louis-Napoléon Bonaparte (1808–73): President of the Second French Republic from 1848, then ruler of the Second French Empire (as Napoleon III) declared by referendum in 1852, a year after he staged a coup d'état.

though it remained conjoined with Austria. Under such conditions, could then the King of Sardinia along with the King of Naples demand the partition of Venetia from Austria, if the Italian nationality within it was in no way oppressed and the rights of Venetians in general were in no way violated? The Italians would be completely justified to consider such a state of affairs entirely unacceptable. But the main reason for the dissatisfaction would be not Austria's possession of Venetia, but the dividedness of a single Italian nationality into separate Italian states. And only by joining itself into one political whole would this nationality [narodnost'] have, if not by formal treaty then by nature, the right to demand this addition to it from Austria. We must not deny such a right to Germany, but first it would have to unite into one fully German, political whole, set apart from itself everything non-German, demand an independent national [natsional'naia] life first, and then demand its own from others. Finally from the national point of view, the restoration of a violated German national right could in any case require only a German union as it was in the beginning, but this evidently would be pushed back into the distant background, once Prussia and Austria had taken everything into their hands.

Be that as it may, the intention here is not irrefutably to show the essential injustice of Prussia and Austria's action toward Denmark. We want to show only that in the eyes of Europe there is no inherent principle to redeem the illegality in the matter of Schleswig-Holstein. For us it is less important to establish what the matter was in itself than how it was perceived by European eyes. And scarcely anyone would argue that it gained the sympathy of European governments and European (with the exception of German, of course) public opinion. In the opinion of Europe, the violation of protocols of international relations was combined with the groundlessness of Prusso-Austrian pretensions. Why then, it may be asked, did not these pretensions heed [the opinion of] Europe? The reason is obviously not the fault of Denmark, any more than the external or internal correctness of Prussia and Austria. Other explanations must be sought.

But first we will look back ten or eleven years, to a matter of greater interest to us: the Eastern Question.

By the demand of Napoleon [III], whose gains compelled him to flatter the Catholic clergy, the Turkish government violated the longstanding rights of the Orthodox Church in Holy Places, enjoyed from time immemorial. The primary offense was that the key to the main doors of the Bethlehem shrine had to be turned over to Catholics. The key in itself was an insignificant thing, but often things have value unrelated to their actual worth, stemming instead from the ideas associated with them. What real value could a piece of silk cloth fastened to a wooden pole have?[11] But this piece of silk cloth on a wooden pole is called a [regimental] standard, and dozens or hundreds of

---

[11] See the excerpt from Tolstoi's *War and Peace* in chapter 16.

people will sacrifice their lives to protect this standard or tear it from the hands of enemies. That is because the standard is a symbol, inseparably associated in the mind of a soldier with the honor of the regiment.

The Bethlehem key had exactly this kind of significance. In the eyes of all Eastern Christians, the key was associated with a notion of the primacy of the Church possessing it. Obviously the Muslim government of Turkey was not at all concerned in the question of the primacy of one Christian denomination over another. Satisfying the hopes of the Orthodox majority of its subjects would have to be the only guiding principle on which to decide such contentious issues. It is impossible to imagine that any government, on an issue that in no way affects its own profits, opinions, or prejudices, would decide its interests based not on the majority, but on an insignificant minority of its subjects, in defiance of longstanding custom needlessly antagonizing millions of people. Such a course of action would require some kind of special motivation. Fear of France's ardent demands does not explain anything, because Turkey surely knew that Russia would always defend and support it against a French attack. So would England and the other states of Europe, as they did in 1840. Obviously this concession to French demands was just the pretext Turkey had been hoping for to deliver an insult to Russia. The religious interests of millions of its subjects were violated because these millions had the misfortune to belong to the same church as the Russian people.

Could Russia really not stand up for them? The Russian government has always upheld its obligations and respected the religious feelings of its people; it would not shamefully deny the Eastern Christians the same protection it has shown them over the course of centuries. Could the Russian government be expected to let the idea take hold that the Eastern Christians' unity of faith with the Russian people is the mark of the outcast, a cause for persecution and oppression from which Russia is powerless to save them? And that real protection is only to be had from the Western states, primarily France? To any impartial observer it is clear, besides, that this demand by France was nothing but a challenge to Russia, which honor and dignity would not allow it to decline. Many people even among us consider this quarrel about the key to be insignificant, not worth the attention of those having the good fortune to live in the enlightened nineteenth century. But even from a solely political point of view, this quarrel had much more importance for Russia than any question of borders or dispute over provincial boundaries. From France's side, of course, it was no more than a tool for stirring up hostility and violating the peace. The English government even saw it that way at the time.

In response to Russia's just demand, the Turkish government promised to issue a *firman* affirming all the rights which the Orthodox Church has enjoyed from time immemorial, to be publicly read in Jerusalem. This promise has not been fulfilled even though the whole Orthodox population there was waiting for it to be read. Russia was deceived in an unworthy manner, its government reduced to a tragicomic form of powerlessness, while all the demands of

France were solemnly fulfilled. What option remained after this? Could Russia content itself with Turkey's promises? Could it trust Turkey in the slightest? The insult aside, does not it have to assume that Turkey, after making a good beginning, could on a whim deny one after another of the rights of the Orthodox Church, just to show its unfortunate followers the vanity of putting any hope in Russia? Could Russia actually fail to see what possibilities had opened for the intrigues of Latinism, which understood the value of the advantages it received and which of course would not stop there? There remained only one way to prevent this: to extract from Turkey a definite obligation in a diplomatic agreement that would forever preserve all the rights the Orthodox Church has enjoyed up to now. Could it ask for any less, when these rights had just been violated, and the promise to affirm them in a *firman* was not kept? Is it not natural to insist on a formal obligation or contract from the one who has shown that its word, its simple promise, cannot be trusted? Russia's demand for this formal obligation was called a demand for protection over the Orthodox Church in the Turkish empire, and a violation of the latter's sacred rights. Of course it was a demand of protection. But what was so new and strange about that, to arouse such general indignation against Russia? For nearly eighty years, since 1774, Russia had the formal, treaty-articulated right to [provide] this protection; what was demanded was only a clearer and more exact statement of it. The actual right of protection Russia has always had, not from a treaty but from the essence of things, and it has exercised this right ever since it was strong enough to do so. All states from time immemorial have had such a right, whenever they felt that something dear to them suffered oppression from a foreign state. Thus Protestant states often protected Protestant denominations in Catholic states. Thus Russia and Prussia rendered protection to Orthodox and Protestant dissidents oppressed by the former Polish kingdom. Thus, after the Eastern [Crimean] War, France even rendered armed protection to Syrian Christians. And in religious terms such protection has often been offered. Did not England and France grant themselves the right of protection over all the subjects of Naples, which they considered (correctly, as it were) a cruel and despotic regime, and demand reforms from the Neapolitan king in his methods and form of government? Did not France protect the Belgians against the Dutch? If in this manner this sort of protection over one state's dear interests, oppressed by another, has always existed in fact, and (being founded upon the very essence of things) will always exist, regardless of any kind of theory of nonintervention—then what is so frightening and insulting about this natural right of protection being formally expressed in a treaty? The Roman [i.e., Papal] court has its concordats with Catholic and even non-Catholic states, which diplomatically articulate the well-known rights of the Catholic Church in these states. These concordats are not thought in any way to violate the sovereignty of these states. The states concluding the Peace of Westphalia [1648] committed themselves to preserving the rights of their subjects not belonging to the dominant faith.

When the Catholic states did not uphold the agreement, Protestants intervened in the matter and enforced the treaty. Thus Frederick Wilhelm,[12] father of Frederick the Great,[13] twice provided protection for oppressed Protestants in Salzburg. It is true that in the Peace of Westphalia the obligation was reciprocal; but in Russia's relations with Turkey there was no need for reciprocity, since the Muslim subjects of Russia have never suffered any kind of oppression. So of course the treaty-established right of protection over a part of the subjects of another state cannot be applied to it, but what if it serves as the only expression of actual needs? The only way to avoid this trouble is to eliminate the cause of the need for foreign protection; as long as this cause exists, the mockery of protection by the formality of a treaty does not change anything. It can even be said that such a formal declaration of the rights of protection and intervention in certain clearly defined cases diminishes the actual chances of exercising these rights. In fact, in 1853 did not Russia interfere in Turkish affairs and take on itself the defense of the Orthodox Church without diplomatic notes or any kind of agreements (which it began to demand that year and which is apparently what bothered Europe so)? And contrarily, if such a clearly defined agreement had existed before that time, would not Turkey have used it, out of its hostility to the majority of its subjects, to preclude actual intervention by Russia? But on the issue of agreements granting one state formal rights of protection over a portion of the subjects of another state (a right which always exists, even without an actual agreement), one thing is indisputable: that an agreement, articulated in exact and definite expressions, is always more preferable than an agreement based on vague interpretations. This latter kind of agreement leads one side into the temptation of shirking its obligations, and the other into exaggerating its rights. The present case is a question of substituting the one kind of agreement for the other, in order to put off such clashes and the need for actual intervention until a future time. If such agreements infringe upon the authority of the state, then that infringement already happened eighty years ago; now it has only been given a harmless form. So the whole matter comes down to the fact that the accepted form was the most inoffensive, the most satisfying to the European states' scrupulous care for the dignity of Turkey; and in this regard Russia's compliance was boundless. It did not act with a high hand, like the German Confederation against Denmark, and when the great European powers offered their mediation, it accepted this, presenting for their consideration clear conditions by which Turkey would have to satisfy its demands. France, the instigator, composed a draft note, and the diplomatic representatives of the great Euro-

---

[12] Friedrich Wilhelm (or Frederick William) I (1688–1740): Elector of Brandenburg and king in Prussia.

[13] Friedrich II (Frederick the Great) (1712–86): Elector of Brandenburg, king *in* Prussia (1740–72), king *of* Prussia (1772–86) after the First Partition of Poland brought the lands of Polish Royal Prussia under Hohenzollern rule.

pean powers accepted and approved it. So the famous "Vienna note"[14] came to be. Russia, recognizing the intervention, unconditionally accepted the decision of the intermediaries, and it seemed the matter was resolved. If there were advantages that Russia, rightly or wrongly, could have pursued, it evidently refused to do so, accepting the decision of the collective diplomatic wisdom of Europe. Clearly its ambition was confined to what it received: in the first place, satisfaction for the violated rights of its coreligionists, by their natural protector (which, treaty or not, it has always been and always will be, by the very essence of things); in the second place, an obligation, stated delicately for Turkish vanity, but absolutely to prevent any more of such violations. And what happened? Turkey turned down this note created by the four Great Powers and accepted by Russia, making changes so as to deprive it of any significance or requirements. The changes themselves were a sign of disrespect, not only toward Russia but also the other four powers, if they took the matter seriously. Instead they seemed to view it as a trap they hoped Russia, not noticing the changes to the text, would fall into. Then they could accuse it all they like of having ulterior motives and secret ambitions and, washing their hands of the matter, put the full responsibility for the consequences on Russia. Turkey summoned the resolve from who knows where to declare war on Russia and found among the signatories of the Vienna note one secret and two open allies for itself. Only the fourth remained a neutral observer.

It is amazing how political passions can cloud the mind: the most straightforward and indisputable matter becomes doubtful and perverted in the eyes of proper judgment. Let us attempt to transfer this unprecedented form of action from the political sphere into the sphere of personal relations. The offended party demands satisfaction from the offender; but heeding mutual friends, he makes concession after concession in the form of satisfaction he demands. Finally it is agreed to leave the decision to these very friends as a tribunal of honor, like that between soldiers or students for example. This is agreed despite the fact that most of these friends are false friends; one of them was even the instigator of the offense brought upon him. He nevertheless believes in the legitimacy of the proceedings. The friends offer their decision—note, it was proposed by the instigator himself—and the offended party unconditionally submits to it, considering it entirely sufficient for himself. In addition, the offended party has more than once shown he possesses ample military force, while the offender is rather poor in this regard. Nevertheless the latter summons unexpected courage, repudiates the decision of the mediators it previously accepted, and challenges his opponent to a duel.

---

[14] The Vienna Note was drafted in July 1853 at a conference of the Great Powers—Britain, France, Austria, and Prussia—hoping to avert war after Russia occupied Moldavia and Wallachia (or the Danubian Principalities); Russia accepted the terms, but the Ottoman Empire rejected it, on the British embassy's counsel.

Of course, would not friends become indignant, declare their support for the challenged one, insist that he be granted the satisfaction they all consider fair, and force the inappropriately emboldened gentleman to grant this? Or would they not at least leave the dueling combatants to settle the matter as they see fit? But there was nothing of the sort: these friends, it turns out, have a strange notion of honor and justice. As to how poor a fighter the emboldened one is, it is as clear as "two times two is four" that he can in no way face the opponent he has challenged. Well, the duty of chivalrous honor is to stand up for the weak and defend him from attack by the strong. Unexpected fervor never grips a person so strongly as when he is under the spell of chivalry and honor compels him to play the champion. This is the course two of the friends choose. But they need some kind of reason, or if there is no reason, then at least a pretext, and a pretext, however strange, is usually found—so it is throughout history. Perhaps out of respect for the friends, or from his own good nature, or God knows why, the offended party who has been challenged offers his opponent conditions for the fight, as such: "Brother, I know you can barely fight, so I'll tell you what: if you attack, I will defend myself, and if by luck you prevail, good for you. As a small concession, stay behind this line and I won't cross it to harm you. These friends are my witnesses and your guarantors." Whether that was smart or not, I do not know. But it certainly came off as generous to the highest degree. However to the two friends, the instigator and one other, even this seemed not enough. "A line is a line, that's good, but you still need to be bound hand and foot, made to stand on one leg, and fight with only one hand, and then we will applaud while you perform these tricks. But if not, the three of us will attack you." And when the generous warrior would not submit to being bound hand and foot—well, thank God, a pretext was found, which put both friends into a serious dilemma: the choice between an all-out fight to the death, or a fight over nothing. They agreed that the third [friend] would fight alongside them, but that it would be most unseemly for him to plunge straight into the fight. After all, less than five years ago the offended party had pulled him from the water, or perhaps from the fire, when he was completely drowning or suffocating from the smoke. Simply put, he saved this third friend's life.[15] So the third friend proceeds by cunning. "The place where you intend to fight," he says, "is near me, and I will be disturbed by your fighting. So for the present I will occupy that place, and you know where that leaves you to fight. True, the place will be unfavorable to you, with the wind and sun coming straight in your eyes, from which you cannot attack and can just barely defend. But that's your problem. If you'd rather not, then while those three attack you from the front, I will

---

[15] Referring to Russia's assistance to Austria in the revolutions of 1848.

grab you from behind by the scruff of the neck." Only the fourth friend removed himself to the sidelines, saying, "This is no business of mine."[16]

I ask you, how would we even begin to judge such actions? But in that little parable there was not the slightest exaggeration or caricature, only a simple rephrasing. For "court of honor," read the Vienna Congress; for the "line," read the Danube; "bound hand and foot" refers to the Russian navy being forbidden to hinder the transport of arms to the Circassians, etc. Really, did not indeed the Battle of Sinop[17] serve as any more than a strange pretext for a declaration of war by the naval powers? Did not Austria demand the cleansing and neutralization of the Danubian Principalities, thus subjecting Russia to the blows of its enemies, without the ability to strike back by means of its land forces in addition to the naval war being waged? Who here is the insulted and offended party? Is it not perfectly evident that they were looking for any opportunity for war against Russia? Did not France from the very beginning by its excessive demands violate the peace between the rival churches and force Russia to stick up for its coreligionists? Did not Turkey deceive Russia after that, not fulfilling its promises about the *firman*? Did not France again, by advancing its fleet to the Dardanelles, force Russia into its efforts against the Danubian Principalities? Then when Russia agreed to submit the resolution of the quarrel to the mediation of the four Great Powers, and unconditionally accepted the text of the settlement proposed by them, did not the Western powers, especially England and its envoy, the always anti-Russian Lord Redcliffe,[18] incite Turkey to reject it (to break off diplomacy once there was finally a way to do so while making Russia the instigator) and declare war?

Is it even remotely imaginable that Turkey would have decided to scorn the opinion of all Europe? And having turned its back on Europe, would it then declare war against Russia from the conviction that the proposed settlement constituted the genuine, honest opinion of Europe, and not a trap? Would it have done so without being tempted by a promise of the most energetic assistance? After all that, was it not savage of the Western powers to demand that Russia, while at war with Turkey, must tolerate the delivery of arms and general assistance to the Circassians,[19] and must not use its navy,

---

[16] *Moia khata s kraiu; ia nichego ne znaiu* (I'm not from around here; I know nothing about it).

[17] Battle of Sinop, 30 November 1853, in which Russian warships sunk an Ottoman patrol.

[18] Stratford Canning, 1st Viscount Stratford de Redcliffe (1786–1880): Longtime British ambassador to the Ottoman Empire.

[19] Circassians: Residents of the northwestern Caucasus, where Russia's attempts to conquer began under Peter the Great. The Circassian War intensified in the nineteenth century, ending with the capitulation of Circassian leaders in 1864; the Ottoman Empire offered refuge to those unwilling to accept Russian rule.

but defend itself solely by means of its army? Did not these absurd demands, which Russia had to reject, serve as the pretext for war? And what can be said for the demands of Austria, which by shielding Turkey brought war to the very borders of Russia? Finally, what is there to say about little Sardinia, bless its heart, declaring war on Russia for no rhyme or reason, not only without cause but without the faintest hint of a pretext?

Does not all this really demonstrate some kind of animosity, some kind of resolution to scorn everything else, if only to satisfy the urge to humiliate Russia when a favorable opportunity presents itself? This all becomes very curious when this animosity toward Russia is compared with the indulgence toward the actions of Prussia and Austria against Denmark. Can it be chalked up solely to the Machiavellianism of the courts or governmental spheres of the European powers, seizing a favorable opportunity to gain at Russia's expense? Absolutely not! At present, intrigues such as Cardinal Alberoni[20] dreamed up are no longer possible. All the European states must now understand the climate of public opinion, and quite often are compelled by it to act. So it was with the Eastern Question. The government of England (that is, the Aberdeen Ministry)[21] was not only peaceful but was even amicably inclined toward Russia; the same must be said for the majority of German regimes. Only the power of public opinion pushed England toward war and ousted the ministry because it did not pursue war aggressively enough. Nowhere was that opinion more hostile than in Prussia, and if the rest of Germany was not drawn into war, it was only because it did not become so strong there as in England. Each small victory, not only by Western powers but even by Turks, was celebrated everywhere as the triumph of all Europe in the whole matter. It is true that the new government of France searched for the opportunity for war; but why would it choose precisely this war, which in itself offered no advantage, and even ran contrary to the political interests of France? [Louis] Napoleon, of course, understood those interests. But he knew that only a war with Russia would be most popular in Europe and help reconcile [Europe] with a Napoleonic dynasty, which it regarded with suspicion and hostility. The result entirely confirms this reckoning.

Thus in this matter the public opinion of Europe was even more hostile toward Russia than its governmental and diplomatic circles. Regarding the Schleswig-Holstein question, it was completely the opposite. Outside of Germany, public opinion—although generally disapproving the actions of Austria and Prussia, and almost everywhere standing up for Denmark—was

---

[20] Giulio Alberoni (1664–1752): Italian cardinal and statesman serving Philip V of Spain, who schemed to recover Spain's lost Italian possessions and restore Stuart kings to the English throne, uniting most of Europe in hostility to Spain.

[21] George Hamilton-Gordon, Lord Aberdeen: British prime minister (1852–55, during the Crimean War), leader of a coalition of Whigs and Peelites (the free-trade, "liberal" faction of the Conservative Party opposed to the protective tariffs of the Corn Laws).

generally cool, limp, and lacking in that impetuosity that pulls the government along with it. Thus public opinion not only left the government full freedom to act according to its discretion and prudence, but even let it speak out against war both in the press and in numerous meetings. The question again arises: Why this measurement by differing standards, when the matter concerns Russia or other European states? A thorough comparison and analysis of the Schleswig-Holstein question with the Eastern Question in their form and essence provides no answer to this riddle, as we have seen, but on the contrary, further complicates it. Has Russia in some way, by its prior conduct, treachery, or violence, provoked Europe, giving it cause for apprehension, so that Europe would seize the first available opportunity to avenge the past and safeguard itself for the future? Perhaps we will see if this really is the case!

○る 2 ○め
What Does Europe Have Against Russia?

> We hear the slander, we suffer the insults:
> Betrayal, envy, and fear of ill results.
> In the press with its Hydra-headed lies,
> Friends for our Russia nowhere arise![1]

"Look at the map," a foreigner said to me. "How can we not feel that Russia weighs down upon us with its great mass, like an ominous cloud, like some kind of fearsome menace?" Cartographically speaking, there may seem to be such a preponderance; but where, how, and when does this manifest itself in reality? France under Louis XIV and Napoleon [I],[2] Spain under Charles V and Philip II,[3] Austria under Ferdinand II[4] — these truly did weigh heavily on Europe, threatening to destroy the free and independent development of various nationalities and costing Europe great hardship to free itself from the burden of them. But has Russia ever done anything like this? Certainly it has intervened in the affairs of Europe more than once, but what was the reason for those interventions? In 1799, 1805, and 1807 the Russian army fought with some success not for Russian but for European interests. And for its trouble

---

[1] Source unknown. The editors of the 2010 edition say the author is "probably" Danilevskii himself (see 564 n. 27). This seems possible but not entirely likely, considering that all his other epigraphs come from published sources (although Danilevskii was lax about attribution), and nowhere else does Danilevskii attempt to write poetry.

[2] Louis XIV (1638–1715): Bourbon king of France, pioneer of royal absolutism, embodied in the construction of his luxury palace at Versailles. His aggressive wars for French hegemony came to naught; instead, the balance of power of the European state system was reaffirmed by the Treaty of Utrecht (1713). Napoleon Bonaparte (1769–1821) ruled France (1799–1815), after rising to prominence in France's revolutionary wars. He created a continental empire in Europe and famously led the disastrous invasion of Russia in 1812.

[3] Charles V (1500–58): Holy Roman Emperor who also ruled Spain as Charles I, including its possessions in the new world and the Philippines, nearly constantly at war with France, champion of the Counter Reformation. Philip II (1527–98): King of Spain, Portugal, Sicily, Naples, and the Netherlands, as well as England and Ireland while married to Mary I of England (1554–58), known for his religious wars against Protestantism, his defeat of the Ottoman navy at Lepanto in 1571, and his loss of the Spanish Armada, sent against England in 1588.

[4] Ferdinand II (1578–1637): Holy Roman emperor during the Thirty Years' War.

on behalf of these foreign interests it brought onto itself twenty years of calamity. When it swept [Napoleon's] army of half a million from the face of the earth (that alone, it turns out, served the cause of European freedom well enough), it did not stop there. Despite these gains (as Kutuzov[5] and all of the so-called "Russian party" saw it in 1813), for two more years it contended with Germany and Europe, and once it wrapped up the struggle with Napoleon, it protected France from the vengeance of Europe just as it had protected Europe from the oppression of France. Thirty-five years later, it again saved Austria from complete disintegration (which was hardly in its own interests), correctly or not considering it the cornerstone of the political system of European states. Everyone knows what gratitude it received for all this from both the states and the peoples of Europe, but that is beside the point. Yet this is it for Russia's active participation in European affairs up to the present, excepting its pointless intervention in the Seven Years' War. But these history lessons teach nothing to anyone. They never get tired of wailing that Russia is a colossal aggressor state, constantly expanding its borders, and thus threatening the peace and independence of Europe. This is one accusation. The other is that it is some kind of political Ahriman,[6] a dismal force, hostile to progress and freedom.

Is there any truth to all this? We will first look into the aggression of Russia. Of course Russia is not small,[7] but the main part of its territorial expanse

---

[5] Mikhail Illarionovich Kutuzov (1745–1813): Russian field marshal, career soldier, and diplomat under Catherine II, Paul I, and Alexander I, commander-in-chief for the defense against Napoleon's 1812 invasion of Russia.

[6] Ahriman: The spirit of evil in Zoroastrianism. Russia was designated as Ahriman in Henry Winter Davis, *The War of Ormuzd and Ahriman in the Nineteenth Century* (Baltimore: James Waters, 1853).

[7] [Danilevskii's note]: It is appropriate to point out here that Russia is not the largest state in the world, as is commonly believed and said. This honor indisputably belongs to Great Britain. All it takes to prove this is a thorough reckoning, with a tally sheet in hand. By the latest accounts, the expanse of Russia is nearly 375,000 square miles. Let us see how much there is in all English possessions: in Europe, 5,570; in Asia, 63,706; in Africa, 6,636; in South and Central America, 5,326; in North America—with Canada and its possessions, 64,000; the polar countries, except for Greenland (20,000) and former Russian possessions (24,000), 130,000; and finally in Australia, more than 150,000. In all, it is more than 425,000 square miles, or nearly 50,000 miles more than in all of Russia. They might say that not all of New Holland [Australia] is occupied by English colonies. This may be so. But does England let other countries place their colonies on that continent? Does it not therefore consider the whole thing its property? Or they may object that the polar lands of America are nothing but an icy wilderness, essentially belonging to no one. But could we not say the same about northern Siberia, which is nevertheless considered part of the bulk of the Russian Empire?

was occupied by the Russian people as free settlement, not as state conquest.[8] The borders attained by the Russian people constitute an entirely natural region, as natural as, say, France, but on a huge scale. It is a region that is clearly demarcated on all sides (with the exception of the west) by oceans and mountains. This region is divided in two by the Ural mountain range which, it is common knowledge, is so gently sloping at its middle that it does not constitute a natural ethnographic barrier. The western half of this region is transected by rivers running in all directions from its center—the Northern Dvina, the Neva (the outflow of all the lake systems), the Western Dvina, the Dnieper, the Don, and the Volga—just as France, on a smaller scale, has the Meuse, the Seine, the Loire, the Garonne, and the Rhone. The eastern half is transected by the parallel-running Ob, Yenisei, and Lena rivers, which likewise are not separated by mountain barriers. In all this expanse there was no kind of state entity at the time when the Russian people gradually began to leave its tribal form of existence and take on a state structure. The whole country was either wilderness or settled by the half-wild Finnic tribes and nomads. Thus nothing hindered the free settlement of the Russian people, which continued almost for the whole first millennium of its history without requiring the destruction and trampling underfoot of any historical nation in order to occupy their territory. Never did the occupation of a nation's historically destined realm cost less in blood and tears. It suffered many injustices and persecutions at the hands of Tatars, Poles, Swedes, and Livonian Brothers of the Sword,[9] but itself oppressed no one, unless we call defending oneself against unjust claims and attacks "oppression." The governmental edifice it raised was not founded on the bones of trampled nationalities. It either occupied the wilderness or over time absorbed into itself, in a completely nonviolent assimilation, such tribes as the Chud, Ves', and Meria,[10] or the present-day Zyrian [Komi], Cheremis [Mari], and Mordva,[11] which had neither the

---

[8] This is a key Slavophile doctrine, best articulated in the works and teaching of Mikhail Petrovich Pogodin (1800–75), nationalist historian at Moscow University and co-editor of the journal *Moskvitianin* (The Muscovite), which advanced Slavophile views in the 1840s; in his later career he championed Pan-Slavism.

[9] Livonian Brothers of the Sword: Military order founded in 1202 by Bishop Albert of Riga. See chap. 8, n. 25.

[10] Chud: Early Finnic peoples of northwestern Russia, Finland, and Estonia; also a mythical ancient people in these regions. Ves': Early name for the Baltic-Finnic tribes of the Veps and Karelians. Meria: An early tribe, presumed to be Volga-Finnic, settled in the broader region of Moscow. Along with the Rus', the Russian Primary Chronicle names most of these peoples among the descendants of Japheth, son of the biblical Noah.

[11] Zyrian: An ancient Komi tribe that migrated north from the region around Perm'. Cheremis: Archaic name for the Mari, a Volga-Finnic tribe of the Volga and Kama river valleys. Mordva: Uralic tribe of the middle Volga region.

rudiments of historical life nor any aspiration for it; or it ultimately gave refuge and defense to tribes surrounded by enemies that had already lost their national independence or could no longer preserve it, such as Armenians and Georgians. In all of this, conquest played such an insignificant role that in retrospect it is plain to see how easily Russia came into its western and southern borderlands, which Europe calls "conquests by Russia's insatiable greed." But first we must establish the meaning of the word *conquest*. Conquest is political murder, or at least political mutilation. Since, however, the first of these expressions is used in a completely different sense [i.e., assassination] it is better to say the murder or mutilation of a people or nation [*natsional'noe, narodnoe ubiistvo ili izuvechenie*]. Although this definition is metaphorical, it is no less correct or clear. Later on we will have occasion to express in detail our thoughts about the significance of nationalities, but for now we are content with an aphorism, which for the moment requires no special proof, since in theory at least it constitutes the belief of most thinking people: *Any nationality has the right to independent existence precisely to the extent that it has self-awareness and claims that right.* The latter condition is very important and requires some explanation. If, for example, Prussia subjugated Denmark, or France did so to Holland, it would cause real suffering by this, and would break real law. This could not be recompensed by giving some civil or political rights or privileges to the Danes or the Dutch because—beyond these individual or civil, political or so-called "constitutional" freedoms—peoples living an independent governmental and political life still feel other needs: for their achievements (industrial, intellectual, and social) to remain their own; not to be sacrificed to a foreign political body; not to disappear into it; not to be the raw materials or means by which a foreign power attains its goals. They do not want to serve another, because each historical nationality [*natsional'nost'*] has its own purpose, its own idea, its own life to live. The more unique and distinctive its purpose, idea, or life, the more the nationality itself stands apart from others in ethnographic, social, religious, and historical ways. But the necessary precondition for attaining all of this is national and political independence. Thus destroying the independence of such a nationality can rightly be called national murder, which stirs up rightful indignation against the perpetrator. This category of public events also includes what I call national mutilation. Italy, for example, genuinely suffered from the fact that a part of it—Venice—remained conjoined to a foreign political body—Austria. This did not present an insurmountable obstacle to the development of its national life, any more than cutting off a hand or foot kills a person, but still deprived it of that fullness and versatility it would have had if not maimed in this way. A historical nation that has not yet assembled all its parts or organs into one whole must be considered a political cripple. Such were the Italians, until recently, and such are, even now, the Greeks, Serbs, and even the Russians, separated from three to four million of their Galician and Ugrian fellow-countrymen. But how many nationalities now hiding under a bushel still hope for their resurrection! What has been said here, however, would be incorrectly and unreasonably applied to tribes not living an independent historical life, whether because they never had any internal resources, or because their circumstances were unfavorable, or their capacity for historical development was destroyed at such an early period of their life, when they consisted of merely ethnographic material still unable to take the form of political individuality—that is to say, before they breathed the breath of life. Such tribes as the Basques in Spain and France, Celts in the principality of Wales, and our numerous Finns, Tatars, Samoeds, Ostiaks,[12] and other tribes are destined to blend gradually and imperceptibly with the historical nationality within which they are dispersed, to become assimilated with it and to enhance the diversity of its historical manifestations. These tribes no doubt have a right to the same level of civic and social freedoms as the ruling historical nationality, but not to political independence. Not having it in their consciousness, they do not and even cannot feel the need of it. It is impossible to end the life of what has never lived; it is impossible to mutilate a body whose parts never formed a single whole. In these cases there is neither national murder nor national mutilation, so there is no conquest; regarding such tribes it is not even possible. Since they do not even show resistance, we will not apply the etymological sense of the word "conquest" to the subordination of such tribes, if in the process their personal, property, and other civil rights are not violated. Where these rights remain inviolable, there is, strictly speaking, nothing more to defend.

After this slight digression to explain our understanding of conquest, we begin our survey straightaway at the northwestern corner of the Russian state with Finland, one of the political crimes Europe reproaches us about. Was there a conquest here in this sense of national murder, having that hateful, criminal character? Without a doubt, no—since there was no nationality that would either lose its independent existence, or be mutilated by cutting off some part of it. The Finnic tribe settling Finland, like all the Finnic tribes scattered across Russia, never lived a historical life. If there is no violation of national independence, then political considerations about geographic expanse, strategic border security, etc. in themselves are not sufficient to warrant the unification of some countries as a matter of law. Russia fought a war with Sweden, which, from the very Treaty of Nystad [1721], could never get used to the concession of what by all rights belonged to Russia, and it searched for any convenient opportunity to resume this war and regain its former conquests. Russia triumphed and acquired the right to reparations, financial, territorial, or otherwise, as long as they did not extend to part of Sweden itself.

---

[12] Tatars: A Turkic tribe of central Asia, identified with the Mongol Empire, and later the khanate of the Golden Horde. Samoeds: A linguistic grouping of indigenous Siberian peoples. Ostiaks: Archaic term for the Khanty, an indigenous people of northern Siberia.

Since national territory is inalienable, then no kind of agreement can legitimize such alienation in the mind of the people, so long as the alienated part does not lose its national character. If it does, then, but only then, it must irrevocably resign itself to its fate. But it is not enough to say that Russia's annexation of Finland from Sweden did not violate existing rights: the advantages for Finland, that is, the Finnic people settling it, outweighed the advantages for Russia in demanding the transfer of dominion. A state so mighty as Russia could well enough afford not to pursue much advantage from the annexed country; a nationality [narodnost'] so mighty as the Russian could grant the Finnish nationality full ethnographic independence without harm to itself. The Russian state and the Russian nationality could be satisfied with little; for them it was enough in the northwestern corner of its territory to have a neutral country and a benevolent nationality in place of a forward post of an enemy and the dominion of the hostile Swedes. The Russian state and nationality could do without completely integrating the Finnish country and nationality into itself, whereas the weak Sweden must have aspired to do so from necessity, considering that Finland amounted to three-quarters of its territory and half its population. And in fact, only from the time of Russia's annexation of Finland did the Finnish nationality begin to awaken and finally attained what could be considered rightful parity for its language with Swedish, regarding university education, administration, and even debates in the legislative assembly. Impartial people doubtless will appreciate what Russia did for Finnish nationality, while the hostile camp of course stirs up indignation, sometimes bordering on the comical. During my time in Norway, one Swede earnestly assured me that the Russian government artfully promoted Finnish nationality out of enmity toward Sweden, and toward that end composed the epic poem *Kalevala*. It is one truly amazing government that, according to the Poles, creates the Russian language by decrees and teaches it to its Mongol subjects, while according to the Swedes, composes the national epics [of subject nationalities]!

After Finland, skipping Ingria[13] — which we do not seem to be blamed for taking from the Swedes — we come to the so-called German Ostsee Provinces: that is, the German lands along the banks of the Baltic Sea. From the name one might think of lands that Russians conquered and tore away from the Holy Roman Empire, or from its successor, the German Confederation, such as the provinces of Prussia and Pomerania, which in the present day are the only truly German provinces on the Baltic Sea — but not the expanse from Lake Chud and the Narva River to the German borders, settled by Ests and Letts,[14] which was the possession of Russia from time immemorial, where

---

[13] Ingria: Lands surrounding the Neva delta, from the Gulf of Finland coast to Lake Ladoga.

[14] Ancient Estonians and Latvians.

Iaroslav[15] founded Iuriev, later renamed Dorpat,[16] in the land where the first
bishops of Riga considered it necessary to seek permission from the Polotsk
princes. Who were the conquerors in this country? The Russians, that is, the
Slavs, who in an alliance with various Chud tribes laid the foundation of the
Russian state and peacefully introduced Christianity with the rudiments of
education to this Baltic country, just as it did in other parts making up the
single physical whole of its state territory? Or the uninvited and unbidden
German adventurers, who appeared here by fire and the sword to spread the
sacred authority of the pope, enslave the natives, and appropriate what belonged to others? Russia never recognized this intrusion of strangers! Pskov
and Novgorod, then standing guard over the Russian land in the hard times
of the Tatars, protested against it with arms in hand. When Moscow united
the lands of Rus' to itself, it took as its first duty to destroy this outpost of
crusader knights and reclaim Russia's property. At first it succeeded, but then
the lands fell into the hands of Poles and Swedes, and the struggle over it became part of the struggle for other territories these states seized from Russia.
But still this is only one side of the matter: the very annexation of the main
part of the Baltic region was not done against the will of the newly arrived
nobility, but at its request and incitement, with the helpful efforts of its representative, the hero Patkul.[17] Admittedly for the people themselves—the indigenous Est and Lett owners of the country—Russia did some, but far from all
that they could have expected from it. But of course when Europe reproaches
Russia for this, it does not look upon the annexation of the Baltic region in
this way; in its eyes, this takes the shape of hateful conquest. Completely to
the contrary, what little was done (or better to say, what is feared when coming from Russia) for the true liberation of the people and country it sees as a
usurpation by Russia, an offense to German and European civilization in
general.

Beyond the Baltic regions begins the region now known as the Northwestern and Southwestern Krais[18] but formerly called the Polish provinces.
Recently it would not have been out of place to write several pages of various
reasons why Russia never conquered this Russian krai, since it is impossible
to conquer what was already ours without conquest. So it always was, and so
it has always been considered by the whole Russian people, while in the high-

---

[15] Iaroslav I, the Wise (988–1054): Grand Prince of Rus', who briefly united the principalities of Novgorod and Kiev.

[16] Now Tartu, Estonia.

[17] Johann Patkul (1660–1707): Livonian noble and politician, allied with Peter the Great
to liberate Livonia from Sweden.

[18] Krai: Administrative region of the Russian Empire, the legal equivalent of oblast, or
"province," but typically located at the frontiers of the empire, thus sometimes
rendered "territory." The Northwestern Krai was roughly present-day Lithuania and
Belarus', while the Southwestern Krai was roughly present-day Ukraine.

est circles this vital national idea and vital national feeling has begun to falter, and as a consequence of that, many in these circles have allowed their minds to be dimmed by all that humanitarian nonsense, lacking all merit of sincerity and impartiality. The Poles and Europe, fortunately, have taken upon themselves the task of sobering up the Russians in this regard, although unfortunately, for all their efforts, have not succeeded at this so much as one might hope. This humanitarian nonsense, excused from the burden of proof and thus having accomplished what the longest and best researched discourses did not, has deeply impressed upon Russian minds the idea that the Northwestern and Southwestern Krais are exactly the same as Russia, built on the same foundations [i.e., conquest] as Moscow itself.

But in the Northwestern Krai there is a little stretch of land, Białystok, which bears some deliberation. This province along with the northern part of the present-day Kingdom of Poland—the Grand Duchy of Poznan [Posen] and western Prussia—fell to Prussia in the partition of Poland. Seven years later it went to Russia, by the Treaties of Tilsit [1807]. What a huge outcry there was in the German press on that occasion about the treachery of Russia, shamefully agreeing to take part in the plunder of its hapless former ally! All it takes is a look at the map to become convinced of the disingenuousness of such accusations.

Białystok province is adjacent to the eastern border of the Kingdom of Poland. Napoleon formed the Duchy of Warsaw from the northern part of the present-day kingdom (to which the southern part was united over two years) and Poznan province. This severed the connection between Białystok province and the Prussian estates enduring the crushing defeat. Thus, for Prussia Białystok province was lost in any case. Prussia faced two options: to let it fall into the hands of the hostile Duchy of Warsaw combined with Saxony, or let it fall into the hands of friendly Russia. Could there be any doubt about Prussia's choice here? Obviously Russia considered Białystok province not to have been taken from Prussia (because it had already been stripped from it in the formation of the Duchy of Warsaw), but from this latter state, their mutual enemy. Where is the treachery in that? Afterward, when the Kingdom of Poland was given to Russia in repayment for its service to Europe, Prussia received ample reward for the part it lost to Poland, but Białystok province could not be returned because it remained separated from Prussia by the Kingdom of Poland, just as it was earlier by the Duchy of Warsaw, which (the loss of the Grand Duchy of Poznan aside) merely changed its name.

But then could not the Kingdom of Poland be called a Russian conquest, since under the definition given above, it was evidently a case of national murder? This question deserves further investigation, because in the opinions and actions of Europe towards it there comes shining through the same, if not more of, the double standards and rigged scales by which it measures and weighs Russia compared to other states, than in the comparison of the Eastern Question to the Schleswig-Holstein Question.

The partition of Poland is in Europe's opinion the greatest crime against national rights [*narodnoe pravo*] in modern times, and the bulk of the blame for it is placed squarely on Russia. And this is not just the opinion of newspaper howlers and mobs, but the opinion of the majority of the foremost people of Europe. But where is Russia's guilt? In the reign of the Tatars, its western half was rooted in Lithuania which was soon Russified, then by means of Lithuania (at first accidentally, through a marital union, and then by force, in the Union of Lublin [1569]) was annexed to Poland. The eastern Rus' were never reconciled to such a state of affairs, as the string of ceaseless wars attests, most of which were initially fought in Poland, but from the time of Khmel'nitskii[19] and the reunification of Little Russia (*Malorossiia*; i.e., Ukraine) finally moved over to Russia. Under Aleksei Mikhailovich[20] Russia did not have the fortune of belonging to the political system of European states, and thus its hands were not tied and it was the only judge of its own affairs. That was when the first partition of Poland took place. Without asking anyone, Russia took from its own what it could—Little Russia to the left bank of the Dnieper, Kiev, and Smolensk—and would have taken more if the tsar had not had false hopes in the Polish crown, forcing the loss of a favorable opportunity. What Russia got from the partition of Poland could have been taken then, a hundred years before it actually was, with a huge benefit for Russia, of course: since at that time humanitarian ideas were not yet fermenting in Russian minds, Orthodoxy and Russian nationality could have taken hold, before the rise of the Czartoryskis[21] as the bane of the Russian cause, with their numerous followers and supporters flourishing in various guises even to this day. In any case the matter was not concluded, but just barely begun, under Tsar Alexis, and once lost, the opportunity did not return again for a century, until the time of Catherine the Great. But why should what was legal in the middle of the seventeenth century become illegal by the end of the eighteenth century? The grounds for war under Alexis were still the same: the oppression of the Orthodox population, which had appealed to its native Russia for help. And if the recovery of Smolensk and Kiev was just, then why would it be unjust to recover not only Vilnius, Podolia, Polotsk, and Minsk, but even Galicia,[22] which unfortunately was not? Well, this is all Russia got from the partition of

---

[19] The Khmel'nitskii uprising (1648–57): A Cossack rebellion in Ukraine sparked a war for liberation from the Polish-Lithuanian Commonwealth, after which Cossacks led by Bogdan Khmel'nitskii pledged loyalty to the Russian tsar.

[20] Tsar Alexis (1629–76).

[21] The Czartoryskis: A prominent Polish noble family. Adam Jerzy Czartoryski (1770–1861) headed the Polish National Government during the 1830 uprising.

[22] Galicia: A contested area once part of the lands of Kievan Rus', named for the medieval city of Galich, or Halych, on the Dniester River, in present-day eastern Ukraine and western Poland, annexed by Austria in the First Partition of Poland; inhabited by Ruthenian peasants under Polish aristocrats, and with a sizable Jewish population.

Poland! True, the form was different. In the intervening century Russia had the fortune to enter the political system of European states, and its hands were now tied. As its neighbors said, to us it's no matter whether or not you recover your ancestral possession; it's just that you are getting stronger, and we need to get stronger to the same degree. So Russia did not have the ability to recover what had by right belonged to it, without allowing at the same time Austria and Prussia to take possession of Poland proper and even part of Russia—Galicia—to which neither the one nor the other had the slightest right. It is well known that the original idea of such a partition came from Frederick [the Great]; there was no advantage for Russia in destroying the lawful boundaries of Poland itself. Completely to the contrary, Russia no doubt would have maintained influence over Poland by stripping it of its Russian territories; moreover, Poland could hope to find support only from Russia against its German neighbors, which (Prussia especially) hoped, or even depended upon, acquiring parts of Poland itself. But Russia was not about to risk war with Prussia and Austria over this! Is it not obvious that for everything unjust in the partition of Poland—the murder of Polish nationality, so to speak—Prussia and Austria are to blame, not by any means Russia, which was content to recover its property, as was not only its right but its holy obligation?! Or will those humanitarian minds say, perhaps, that generosity requires Russia sooner to refuse what had been its rightful property than agree to the destruction of Poland? Well, about the only way you can blame Russia is to take the most quixotic point of view. Such a course of action would be by all means possible, if Poland would treat its Russian and Orthodox subjects better; under current circumstances this generosity on someone else's behalf would be comical and pitiful. If a certain person lost part of his property and was compelled to reclaim it by no other means than to form an agreement with his neighbors, who openly hope to use this convenient opportunity, without the slightest right, to seize the part of the wrongful owner's property that indisputably belonged to the first person— we would have to say that these neighbors did not act in accordance with Christian morality. But making exceptions to these rules for relations between states and even peoples is a strange confusion of ideas, demonstrating only a lack of understanding of the basic foundations of the highest moral requirements. The obligation for a moral course of action is none other than an obligation for self-sacrifice, which is the highest moral law. Strictly speaking they are the same. But the only basis for self-sacrifice is immortality: the eternality of the soul. If this strict moral law of self-sacrifice is not absurd and full of internal contradictions, then obviously it must flow from the inherent nature of the one constrained to act on its foundations, as is precisely the case with all natural or divine laws. But if the present life is all there is for a person, then no doubt the laws governing his activity can come only from the requirements of this life, which constitute his essence: the requirements for calm, happiness, and the prosperity of the moment, which each individual being senses as the final, indeed the only imaginable, goal of his existence. If an entity does not have the internal obligation of our essence, which we call the soul, but contains some other inexhaustible substance of temporal earthly life, then it might put forward some other basis for its activity or basis of morality, love, and self-sacrifice. But a state and a people are transient phenomena existing only in time and thus are under obligation only to what their temporal existence provides as the basis for laws of their activity: that is, politics. This does not justify Machiavellianism, but merely affirms the idea "to each his own," that any form of existence and phenomenon has its own law. "An eye for an eye, a tooth for a tooth," is a harsh law; Bentham's[23] principle of utility, or a proper understanding of "the greater good," is a law for external politics or the relations between one state and another. There is no place here for the law of love and self-sacrifice. Wrongly applied, this high moral law takes on the character of mysticism and sentimentality, an example of which we saw in the blessed memory of the Holy Alliance.[24] On this point, we note that the properly-understood principle of the "greater good," while obviously inadequate and unsuitable as a foundation for morality, produces much better results as a political principle, for the simple reason that in that case it is properly applied. In fact, over the course of a state's long life there is a high probability that the fundamental warning in the utilitarian principle—that is, its sanction, expressed in the words, "You will be measured by the standard by which you measure others"—will have its effect. Then in the short life of a person, each has enough means, power, and cunning to hope with good reason to avoid the consequences stated in the above words.

So the part that Russia played in the partition of Poland was completely lawful and just, the fulfillment of a sacred duty before its own descendants; it avoided being confused by fits of sentimentality and false generosity, as unfortunately for both Russia and Poland it was many times confused after Catherine until the present. If there was some injustice on the part of Russia in the partition of Poland, it was only that it did not reclaim Galicia. Entirely disregarding that, Europe brought its indignation down in full force, mind you, not on the truly guilty, Prussia and Austria, but on Russia. In Europe's eyes, the whole crime of the partition of Poland was that Russia strengthened itself by reclaiming its property. If not for that sad fact, then the Germanization of the Slavic nationality [narodnost'] (despite being most obliging, but Slavic all the same) would not arouse such crying and tears. I am even convinced that, completely to the contrary, after long hypocritical condolences Europe would

---

[23] Jeremy Bentham (1748–1832): English philosopher, founder of utilitarianism, defining the good in terms of the greatest benefit for the greatest number.

[24] Holy Alliance: Mutual assistance pact between Russia, Austria, and Prussia, signed at the Congress of Paris in 1815, to contain the spread of revolutionary influences; subsequently Danilevskii blames Tsar Alexander I for being too selfless, by not demanding more territory in compensation for its service to Europe.

be secretly joyful about this longed-for victory of civilization over barbarism. Well, we know that it does not frighten Europeans and our humanitarian progressives, even when civilization appears in the form of an Austrian gendarme (see *Atenei*).[25] Really, some of the French would be sorry that they lack the same leverage against Germany. The Polish intelligentsia amply understands this direction in Europe's public opinion; it knows how to win Europe over, and does not ask for the main territory of Poland, which fell to Austria and Prussia, but for the part it had earlier taken from Russia. The foreign is dearer to Poland than its own. Anyone who has seen the repulsive but intriguing spectacle of a fight between a pair of big poisonous spiders, called "solifugae" (*falangi*), has of course noticed how often this spiteful animal, in its rage devouring one of its opponents, does not notice itself being devoured by another from behind. Are not these solifugae the true emblem of Szlachtist-Jesuit Poland, a symbol or crest that expresses its governmental character much more faithfully than a one-headed eagle?

But whatever was rightfully Russia's in the partition of Poland, now it possesses part of Poland itself, and thus must accept at least as much blame for the unjust gains as Prussia and Austria. Yes, an unfortunate acquisition! But all the same, it did not acquire it by conquest, but through that sentimental generosity we were just speaking about. If upon liberating Europe, Russia had left the rump of Poland established by Napoleon to be partitioned between Austria and Prussia, but as compensation for its priceless but undervalued service demanded for itself eastern Galicia (part of which—the Ternopil district—it already possessed at that time, and the rest had been Russian territory under Catherine) no one could blame it for this. Russia would have received significantly less in territory and slightly less in population, but its gains would have been worth so much more, since it would have increased the number of its non-hostile, non-Polish, but truly Russian subjects. What made Emperor Alexander [I] overlook this true advantage? What dazzled his vision? Not some plan for conquest, but the hope of achieving his youthful dream: to restore the Polish nationality, and thus to make amends for what seemed to him the error of his illustrious grandmother [Catherine the Great]. The proof of this is the fact that the Poles themselves saw it this way. When the hostile camp of Austria, France, and England began mounting every possible obstacle to this plan for reestablishing Poland, even threatening war, Emperor Alexander sent the Grand Prince Constantine[26] to Warsaw to appeal to the Poles to arm themselves to defend their national independence. Europe, as usual, saw this as Russian cunning—under the pretext of establishing the

---

[25] *Atenei*: Liberal journal published 1858–59.

[26] Grand Duke Constantine Pavlovich (1779–1831): Second son of Paul I, heir to the throne under Alexander I (though he secretly renounced his claim in 1823), appointed by Alexander as de facto ruler of Congress Poland (the informal name for the part of Poland ruled in personal union by the Russian tsar).

Polish nationality, hoping little by little to get its hands on those parts of the former Kingdom of Poland that had escaped its grasp—and for this reason agreed to the complete incorporation of Poland, but refused to support the independent existence of the Kingdom in personal dynastic union with Russia, as they now desire. Only when Gardenberg,[27] who as a Prussian was well acquainted with Polish and Russian affairs, explained that Russia was demanding its own harm, did the diplomats agree to the Kingdom's independence. Subsequent events showed that Russia's plans were not ambitious, but merely generous. If the Russian state had supported the Poles' hope for reunifying the Kingdom with Prussian- and Austrian-held parts of former Poland, as for instance the Marquis Velepolskii[28] later hoped, or had only turned a blind eye to the mounting intrigues, it of course would not have turned out that the uprising flared in the Kingdom of Poland but not in Poznan or Galicia, since they would have lacked the excuse of the unsatisfactory makeup of the region contributing to this uprising. Whatever is said about the constitution given to the Kingdom, the freedom it provided was in any case incomparably more important than in the aforementioned provinces that went to Prussia and Austria, in Prussia and Austria themselves, or even in the greater part of Europe of that day. The period from 1815 to 1830, in which the Kingdom enjoyed autonomous rule, had its own army, its own finances, and constitutional government, was without a doubt both materially and morally the happiest time of Polish history. The uprising can only be explained by the vexation of the Poles at the impracticality of their plans to reestablish the former greatness of Poland, albeit under the scepter of Russian sovereigns (only at first, of course). But these plans were focused not on Galicia and Poznan, but western Russia, because only there did the Polish intelligentsia have a free hand, so convenient for Polonizing and Latinizing the place. And only when the Polish intelligentsia felt there was not enough indulgence, or better to say, assistance of the Russian government (since there was indulgence aplenty) toward the Polonization of western Russia, then the indignation of the Poles flared, leading to the uprising of 1830, and again in 1863. See how aggressive and ambitious Russia's plans were, leading it to seek the reunification of the Kingdom of Poland at the Congress of Vienna!

In the southwestern corner of Russia lies Bessarabia, also recently acquired. Here the Orthodox Christian population was wrenched from the oppression of rough and wild conquerors, the Turks; it celebrated this event like deliverance from captivity. If that was conquest, then Cyrus was such a conqueror in freeing the Jews from their Babylonian captivity. It is not worth elaborating on this point.

---

[27] Prince Karl August Gardenberg (1750–1822): Prussian minister of foreign affairs, (1804–07).

[28] Margrave Aleksander Wielopolski (1803–77): Conservative nationalist Polish aristocrat, head of Poland's civil administration under Tsar Alexander II.

All the southern Russian steppes likewise were torn from the hands of the Turks. These steppes are on the Russian plain. From earliest times, in the days of Sviatoslav[29] Russian princes contended with the nomadic hordes for them, then Russian Cossacks and Russian tsars took up the fight. By what right was Turkish power brought here and maintained by predatory incursions? Also it must be said that the Crimean peninsula, though not belonging to Russia from olden days, still has served as a refuge not only for its intractable enemies but the enemies of all civilization, who at every opportunity conducted raids from there, razing by fire and hacking with the sword the lands of southern Russia all the way to Moscow itself. We can agree that here a state was conquered, and a nationality [narodnost'] lost its independence. But what kind of state and what kind of nationality are we talking about? If I classify any conquest in general as national murder, then this case would also be such a murder, which is permitted under both human and divine laws: a murder committed in self-defense and, at the same time, a just execution.[30]

All that remains is the Caucasus. Under this broad name we must distinguish for examination regions of the Transcaucasian Christians, Transcaucasian Muslims, and Caucasian highlanders.

From the time of Ivan the Terrible and Boris Godunov, the small Transcaucasian Christian kingdoms prayed for help from Russia, even offering to become Russian subjects. But only Emperor Alexander I, at the beginning of his reign and after much hesitation, finally agreed to grant this wish. He had become convinced beforehand that the Georgian kingdoms, utterly exhausted by the age-old struggle against the Turks, Persians, and Caucasian highlanders, could not maintain their independent existence and should either be allowed to perish or be united with coreligionist Russia. In taking this step, Russia knew that it was accepting a heavy burden to bear, although perhaps not guessing how heavy: that it would cost an uninterrupted sixty-year struggle. In any case, neither in form nor essence was there any conquest here, but simply providing help to the exhausted and the perishing. First of all, this drew Russia into a twofold struggle with Persia, and Russia was not the instigator. In the course of this struggle it managed to liberate some of the Christian populations from the double yoke of local sovereign khans and Persian dominion. At the same time a number of Muslim khanates were subdued: the Quba, Baku, Shirvan, Shaki, Ganja, and Talysh khanates, today comprising only so many uezds[31] and Erevan oblast [in central Armenia]. Call them conquests if you like, but as it is, the conquered came out the winners.

It is true, Russian conquests of Caucasian highlanders have not gone so well. In this case, what perished were independent tribes rather than inde-

---

[29] Sviatoslav I of Kiev (942–72): Ruler whose ten-year reign was marked by conquests from the Volga to the Balkans.

[30] This passage refers to the Crimean Tatars, defeated by Catherine the Great.

[31] Uezd: An administrative subdivision of Russian territory of variable size.

pendent states. Since the partition of Poland, no other action by Russia has aroused such universal indignation and sympathy in Europe as the war against Caucasian highlanders, especially just after the subordination of the Caucasus. Although our journalists and editorialists tried to present it as a great victory serving the cause of universal civilization, nothing helped. Europe did not like Russia undertaking this endeavor. Well, [Europe says,] on the Syr Darya [Jaxartes River], in Kokand, or in Samarkand, among the wild Kyrgyz people, we [Europe] can begrudgingly permit such a civilizing mission, come what may; those are just distractions, like Spanish flies, but unfortunately are too few in number to sap Russia's strength. But what is closer to us, in the Caucasus, we [Europe] will civilize all by ourselves. That the Caucasus highlanders—by their fanatical religion, by their way of life, by their customs, and by the very country in which they settled—are natural robbers and plunderers, who have not and cannot leave their neighbors in peace: this we do not take into account. They are fearless, blameless knights, paladins of freedom, and that is that! In the Scottish hills, a little over a hundred years ago, lived some tens or even hundreds of thousands of such knights of freedom; although they were Christian, a little more civilized, and more even-tempered (but then the hills in which they lived do not compare to those in the Caucasus), the English found that they could not abide their highlander ways, and at an opportune moment scattered them in all four directions. But Russia, unless it wants to be labeled as the persecutor and oppressor of freedom, should put up with many millions of such knights in the impassable overgrown crevices of the Caucasus, hundreds of versts from any peaceful settlement; and while waiting to win over these enemies, whom in the meantime they can expect to attack them at every turn, should with no end in sight deploy an army of two hundred thousand, to keep watch over all the paths and exits from these robbers' caves. Thus we can judge by this Caucasus Question (as with the Polish and Eastern Questions, as with anything) about the good intentions of Europe toward Russia.

About Siberia there is nothing to say. In fact, what kind of conquest is that? Where are the conquered peoples and toppled kingdoms? All it takes is to count how many Russians there are in Siberia, and how many non-Russians, in order to understand that most of it was the occupation of empty lands, achieved (as history shows) by Cossack boldness and the settlement of Russian people, almost without any government help. If we add to the number of Russian conquests the Amur region, not populated by anyone, where the Chinese government had even forbidden any settlement, is it hard to see why they [Russian settlers] consider it rightfully theirs?

And so, regarding the conquests of Russia, all that could be called by this name through various, strained interpretations is limited to Turkestan oblast, the Caucasus mountain range, five or six uezds of Transcaucasia, and if you like, the Crimean peninsula too. If we treat the matter very precisely according to conscience and strict correctness, then not one of the possessions of

Russia can be called a conquest, in the evil, anti-national, and thus hateful-toward-humanity, sense of the word. Are there many states that can say the same for themselves? England conquered the Celtic states lying alongside of it. Did it ever conquer! It stripped the people of the right to own their native land, forced them through hunger to move to America, while from nearly halfway around the world it subjugated the kingdoms and peoples of India numbering almost two hundred million souls. It seized Gibraltar from Spain, Canada from France, the Cape of Good Hope from Holland, etc. Empty lands or those populated by wild, non-historic tribes, almost 300,000 square miles in all, I do not consider conquests. France seized from Germany Alsace, Lorraine, and Franche-Comté; from Italy, Corsica and Nice; and across the sea it subjugated Algeria. But so much of it was conquered and taken away from it again! Prussia rounded out and united its scattered parts at Poland's expense, to which it had no right. Austria [i.e., the Habsburg Empire] took little or almost nothing by the sword; but its very existence is already a crime against the rights of nationalities. Spain in bygone times subjugated the Netherlands, the greater part of Italy, and toppled, then destroyed, whole civilizations in America.

If Russia cannot be reproached for the conquests it has actually made, then maybe it can still be faulted for its intentions: a criminal is not innocent just because his attempt failed. So we will examine the kind of wars it has conducted. No need to look far. Until Peter [the Great], all of Russia's wars were for its very survival, for what was torn away from it by its neighbors in unhappy times of its history. The first war it fought for a different goal than that, through which its interference in European affairs began, was against Prussia. Of course, there was no sufficient reason for Russia to take part in the Seven Years' War. Frederick [the Great]'s backbiting offended [Empress] Elizabeth, while all Europe, rightly or wrongly, considered his conduct an insolent violation of international law in general, and the laws of the Holy Roman Empire in particular. If someone deserves blame here, then Russia shares it with all Europe. Regardless, it was a chance occurrence, not consistent with the general direction of Russian policy. In the whole reign of Catherine the Great, Russia did not actively interfere in European affairs, but pursued its own goals, and as we have seen these goals were just. Russia's European wars begin with Emperor Paul. Militarily speaking, the war of 1799[32] was hardly the most glorious of those Russia has fought. It was an act of the greatest political generosity, unselfishness, and the spirit of chivalry of a crusader knight. Whether it was an act of political prudence is another question. For Russia, however, this war had a significant moral result: it demonstrated Russia's

---

[32] Early maneuvers to counter Napoleon's growing power. In 1799, Russian forces joined Austrian forces to drive the French out of Italy; a similar effort later in the year with Britain against the Netherlands failed miserably.

military capability. The wars of 1805 and 1807[33] were the same. Russia took completely foreign interests to heart, and with amazing heroism, laid its sacrifices on the altar of Europe. The Treaty of Tilsit[34] marked a brief renunciation of this policy of selflessness and a resumption of the Catherinian routine from before; but evidently Russia was not satisfied with what it could gain, seeing no alluring prospects further down that path. It held the interests of Europe, especially Germany, so close that its heart beat only for them. Russia's efforts in 1813 and 1814 were on Europe's behalf; even today impartial people agree to this, regardless of whatever political camp they belong to; but then they all praise Russia's unparalleled disinterest. Hardly anyone recognizes what the struggle of 1812, undertaken by Russia for Europe's interests, actually was. Of course, the War of 1812 was primarily a national [narodnaia] war in the full sense of the word, if you take into account how it was waged and the feelings animating the Russian people at that time. But were the causes of this famous war also national: that is, the desire to thwart Russia's interests that convinced Napoleon to undertake it? That can hardly be answered in the affirmative. The causes of this colossal struggle that had such huge consequences and toppled Napoleon were to that point so insignificant that it is impossible to understand how Napoleon could set off on such a dangerous, risky, and unnecessary undertaking, since he already had Spain. What was the actual cause for Napoleon to muster an army of 600,000 to invade a far-off country, not abundant in resources, with bad lines of communication, and fight both armies and a people whose courage was well-known? Russia's insufficient compliance with the Treaty of Tilsit (having allowed a little trade with England, when Napoleon himself allowed such deviations from the Continental System) and Russia's protest against the seizure of Oldenburg. That's all. Some think it is enough to bolster these completely insufficient reasons by citing Napoleon's insatiable ambition. Of course Napoleon was ambitious beyond all measure, but also prudent. Napoleon's true reasoning for the war he explained to Balashov[35] in these words: The [Russian] sovereign is surrounded by personal enemies, base people, as he put it—among them, the scoundrel Stein,[36] banished from his own Fatherland—which is to say, people who held German interests very dear, and who tried to steer Emperor Alexander's line of thought in the same direction. The well-understood and

---

[33] Wars of the Third and Fourth Coalitions, respectively.

[34] Treaty of Tilsit (1807): Russia allied with France and joined the Continental System, in exchange for France's backing against the Ottoman Empire.

[35] General Aleksandr Dmitrievich Balashov (1770–1837): Russian commander stationed in Vilnius in 1812, sent to deliver the tsar's communications to Napoleon during the invasion.

[36] Heinrich Friedrich Karl Reichsfreiherr vom und zum Stein, known as Baron vom Stein (1757–1831): Prussian statesman, forced to retire for criticizing Napoleon in the wake of the Treaty of Tilsit, summoned by Alexander I to Moscow in 1812.

logically-dictated meaning of these hints explains everything. Napoleon had to feel that the edifice he had constructed was very shaky, and had nothing supporting it other than his great genius. The Jérôme Bonapartes and the Joachim-Napoléon Murats[37] could offer it no support. What would remain after his death? What would he leave to his son? World dominion was beyond even his grasp, so it would be necessary to find someone with whom to divide it, and after the Treaty of Tilsit he thought he had found this ally and comrade in Russia (of course, there was nowhere else to look for any other). From a purely political perspective, he thought that Russia by its own goals and advantages would be of the same mind as him. And really, what might Russia have attained through alliance with him, if it had viewed the matter solely from its own point of view? Zealous aid in the war of 1809 would have given it all of Galicia; intensified war against Turkey would have supplied it with not only Moldavia and Wallachia but even Bulgaria, and the ability to form an independent Serbian state in union with Bosnia and Herzegovina. All Napoleon wanted was for our possessions not to extend beyond the Balkans, but Napoleon would not live forever. The Duchy of Warsaw, which he saw as the only counterbalance against Russia, he probably would have sacrificed once convinced that Russia had satisfied itself and that it was as dependent on him in pursuit of its goals as he was on it, and that Russia itself was now concerned with preserving its power. But soon after the Treaty of Tilsit Napoleon saw that he could not count on Russia, could not rely on its sincere assistance based more on political calculation than the letter of the agreement between them; he saw that Russia would formally live up to its treaty promises, but its heart was not in the alliance with him. Russia's help in the war of 1809 was only for appearances; its protection of the Duchy of Oldenburg, and even more, the influx of German patriots—which Napoleon, from his point of view, called scoundrels (entirely unjustly, of course)—showed him that Russia had taken so-called European, or more precisely German, interests to heart, more fervently than its own. What else could he do? What did the irrepressible logic of the situation in which he found himself, his personal ambition, and the very course of events draw him toward? Obviously he had the desire to secure for himself other means, independent of Russia, and to seek support for his edifice from whatever other pillar he could find, even if having less confidence in its strength. He intended to carve this pillar out of Russia itself, by restoring the Kingdom of Poland to its former size. In this he placed the hope at least of finding an ever-ready weapon against hostile Germany. Napoleon could hardly do otherwise. And without war the political edifice he had constructed would collapse, if Russia lost interest in supporting it—if not under him, then after his death. Directing a war by his genius offered at least some chance either to force Russia to provide this support, or to

---

[37] Napoleon's youngest brother, appointed as king of Westphalia, and Napoleon's brother-in-law, appointed as king of Naples, respectively.

replace it with another, less firm but more subordinate and pliable instrument. In short, if Napoleon could have counted on Russia, which he believed had its own interest in his affairs, then he never would have considered restoring Poland. Leave well enough alone; enough to eat is as good as a feast. In 1813, commanding a newly raised army, he clearly affirmed this: "It would have been much easier and wiser to take up with Emperor Alexander. I always considered Poland as a means to an end, but not important in itself. Satisfying Russia at Poland's expense would have given us the means to humble Austria and wipe it out." Could anything be clearer, more candid, and besides that, more consistent with Napoleon's true character?! Thus is it not because of Europe, specifically Germany, that Russia took upon itself the disaster of 1812? That year was technically a great political mistake, turned by the spirit of the Russian people into a great national triumph.

That Russia did not have any of its own interests in mind when opting for war with Napoleon is obvious from the fact that, having finished the first part of this war with unparalleled glory, it did not stop or use the opportunity to acquire all it could want for itself, by declaring peace and an alliance with Napoleon, as he fully sought and as many other notable people of that era, such as Kutuzov, wished. What prevented Alexander from repeating Tilsit—with the difference that this time he would have a superior, more respected role? Even for Prussia, which had already compromised itself before Napoleon, Emperor Alexander could have demanded everything that honor, in his opinion, required.

Fourteen years after the Treaty of Paris, Russia had to fight Turkey.[38] Russian troops crossed the Balkans and stood at the gates of Constantinople. Russia was friends with France, and Austria had neither troops nor money; England could not do anything, although it wanted to (at that time it did not yet have military steamships); and the Prussian government was closely allied with Russia. Europe could only entrust Turkey to Russia's generosity. So did Russia take anything for itself? One word would have been enough to annex Moldavia and Wallachia. Not even that was necessary: Turkey itself offered the principalities to Russia in lieu of its unpaid debt. Emperor Nicholas refused both the one and the other.

Then came the year 1848. The shocks taking place at that time all across Europe freed our hands for conquest and ambition. How did Russia make use of this opportune moment? It saved from destruction its neighbor [Habsburg Austria], the very one who must oppose any ambitious designs on Turkey it happened to have. And that is not all: it was possible then to combine generosity with ambition. After the Hungarian campaign, there was sufficient pretext for war with Turkey; Russian troops had occupied Wallachia and

---

[38] The Russo-Turkish War of 1828–29. Russia was provoked when the Ottomans closed the Bosporus in retaliation for the Russian navy's support for Greek independence at the Battle of Navarino (20 October 1827).

Moldavia, and the Turkish Slavs would have risen up at a word from Russia. Did Russia take advantage of all this? Finally, in 1853 itself, if Russia had made sharp, staunch demands, the way the embassy of Count Leiningen[39] did that same year, and at the slightest delay in satisfaction struck with its fleet and troops when neither Turkey nor the Western powers were at all prepared—what could it not have accomplished?

And so, the composition of the Russian state, the wars it waged, the goals it pursued, and even more, the frequent favorable circumstances it never utilized: all show that Russia is not an ambitious, aggressive power, and that in the modern period of its history it most often sacrificed its own obvious gains, which were legal and just, to European interests, often even considering that its responsibility was to act not as an independent entity (with its own significance and its own justification for all its actions and aspirations) but as a secondary power. So why, I ask, should there be such distrust, injustice, and hatred toward Russia from the governments and public opinion of Europe?

We turn now to the other main charge against Russia, that Russia is the extinguisher of light and freedom, a dark and dismal force, the political Ahriman, as I said above. The famous Rotteck[40] expressed the idea (not having his *History* at hand, I unfortunately cannot give the exact citation) that any Russian success, any increase of its resources, prosperity, and power, is a public calamity and a misfortune for all humanity. Rotteck's statement only expresses the public opinion of Europe. And again this [notion] is founded on the same shifting sand as the [notions of] Russia's ambition and aggressiveness. Whatever the form of rule in Russia, whatever the flaws of Russian administration, jurisprudence, fiscal systems, etc.—all of that, I propose, is no concern to anyone until it tries to impose all of this upon another. If all of this is so bad, then so much the worse for Russia and the better for its enemies and those who wish it ill. A difference in political principles should not be an obstacle to friendship between governments and peoples. Was not England the constant friend of Austria, despite the constitutionalism of the one and the absolutism of the other? Cannot the Russian state and Russian people gain from the sympathies of America, and vice versa? Only Russia's harmful interference in the internal politics of foreign states, or hindrance to the development of freedom in Europe, should rightly draw criticism and arouse its indignation. We must ask: What has Russia done to deserve this? How is Russia guilty in the eyes of Europe? Until the French Revolution there could be no talk of such interference or hindrance, because between the continent of Europe and Russia there was hardly any difference in political principles. On

---

[39] Count Christian Franz von Leiningen-Westerburg (1812–56): Austrian general and ambassador to Constantinople, who successfully demanded the removal of Turkish troops from Montenegro in 1853.

[40] Karl von Rotteck (1775–1840): German historian, author of a nine-volume *Allgemeine Geschichte* (General History).

the contrary, Catherine's reign was rightly considered one of the more advanced, or as we now say, progressive. It is true, by the end of her reign Catherine intended to fight against revolution, which her successor actually did. But if the French Revolution must be considered the torchbearer of freedom, then all Europe rushed to extinguish and douse that torch, with constitutional and "free" England leading the way. Russia's part in this general affair was short-lived and insignificant. But all Europe applauded the victories of Suvorov.[41] The wars against Napoleon of course were not, and were not considered, wars against freedom. When these wars ended, if defeated France then received a free form of government, it was solely due to Emperor Alexander. During the war for independence, many states promised their subjects a constitution, but none kept their promise except for Alexander, once again, in regard to Poland.

After the Congress of Vienna, it was the Russian emperor's idea for Russia, Austria, and Prussia to conclude the so-called Holy Alliance, and invite all the sovereigns of Europe to join it. This Holy Alliance constitutes the main charge against Russia and showcases an agreement among sovereigns against their peoples. But in this alliance we must strictly distinguish the idea, the original inspiration, which was Alexander's, from the practical application, which belonged to none other than Metternich.[42] Whatever the practical merits of the original idea, there was nothing oppressive in it. Emperor Alexander indisputably supported the constitutional principle everywhere that in his opinion national [narodnoe] development allowed for it. He was an enemy of charters forcefully imposed by revolt or revolution, but on the other hand was a friend of [voluntarily] granted constitutions; after recent experiences and so much harm endured by Europe, was it possible to think otherwise? And even regardless of circumstances, is this not generally the correct view? Can a conscientious agreement or an intelligent compromise really be worse than violence, on grounds of principle or consequences? Whatever has been compelled by force, if force remains behind it, rarely remains satisfied with what has been compelled; once excited by passions and intoxicated by the pride of success, is it possible to expect moderation? If, on the other hand, after the first outbreak or successful onslaught, power shifts back to the side that bowed to that challenge, can we really expect it conscientiously to fulfill the thing forced upon it? On the contrary, a concession put into effect with awareness that it is correct and beneficial, has paid a deposit to secure its own longevity. Which is the more enduring and conscientious: the [voluntarily] granted constitution of Sardinia, and of all Italy replacing it; or the imposed

---

[41] Aleksandr Vasilievich Suvorov (1729–1800): Imperial Russian generalissimo who led Russian troops against French Revolutionary armies in Italy in 1799.

[42] Prince Klemens von Metternich (1773–1859): Austrian state chancellor and foreign minister, architect of the post-Napoleonic diplomatic order in Europe known as the "Metternich system" or the "Concert of Europe."

constitution of France after 1830, and Prussia after 1848? It might be said that even the [voluntarily] granted constitution of France in 1814–15 was not fulfilled conscientiously enough, but everyone knows that constitution had only the form of a charter voluntarily granted by the Bourbons, but in essence it was a concession forced upon them by circumstances; thus its whole government bore the imprint of foreign interference, which is hateful to any self-respecting people.

In the diplomatic congresses of the 1820s the most moderate and liberal voice was Alexander's. On this point I cite Gervinus,[43] who was not favorable toward Russia or anything Russian. The source of all reactionary, retrograde measures of that time was Austria and its leader Metternich, who, ensnaring everyone (including Russia) in his nets, forced Russia to renounce its instinctive national [natsional'naia] policy of helping the Greeks and other Christians under the Turks against their oppressors; and to do so against all of its traditions, its interests, and the sympathies of its sovereign and its people. Russia was the victim of Metternichian politics. Why should the full burden of blame fall on it, and not Austria, which was guilty before the rest, and for whose benefit all this was done? Did not England itself submit to Metternichian politics in those days? Was it Russian troops that put down the uprisings in Naples and Spain, and were these uprisings and the order of things they briefly introduced such brilliant occurrences that we should feel sorry for them? Was it Russian incitements that caused all the oppression of the German press, the German universities, and the general aspirations of the German younger generation? Must not the German governments themselves, with Austria at their head, be considered guilty for all these measures, and were they not useful solely to them? Or maybe is it that all these German liberal aspirations had such force that the German governments did not dare to oppose them without hope of Russia's support? But did it really hinder the fulfillment of those aspirations in places where they really meant something? Did it keep France or tiny Belgium from giving themselves the form of government they desired? Did Russia hinder anyone even in Germany itself in 1848, or even in 1830? Are not they just making excuses for their own inability, attributing failure to some supposed influence from the dismal absolutism of the north?

The best proof, however, that Russia bears no blame for any kind of active resistance against the freedom of humanity in general or Germany in particular (the reason for the general hatred toward it) is the murder of Kotze-

---

[43] Georg Gottfried Gervinus (1805–71): German political and literary historian. Danilevskii is citing his multivolume *Geschichte des neunzehnten Jahrhunderts seit den Wiener Verträgen* (History of the Nineteenth Century since the Vienna Treaties), published 1855–66.

bue.[44] What is important here is not the act of the unfortunate student-fanatic in itself, but the general sympathy this political crime aroused not only in revolutionary circles but also in calm, sensible parts of society, for which one can hardly find another example. What was Kotzebue's crime? He informed the Russian government, they say, about the state of public opinion in Germany (primarily its university youth), which is only to say, by the way, that he did what all diplomatic agents or foreign correspondents of any newspaper do. His guilt in no way exceeded that of many Petersburg correspondents of foreign newspapers—with those *circonstances attenuantes* in Kotzebue's favor, however, that the ill-will toward Russia and the slander of Petersburg correspondents are known to all and can arouse well-founded outrage. But what Kotzebue wrote was not made public, and his whole guilt was founded on suppositions. And really, at the time of Kotzebue, were there not many people who informed the German governments (especially that of Austria) about the spirit and drift of the prevailing thinking among German youth, which of course was much more dangerous? Why such an explosion of indignation, why such an offence to national feelings that it reaches the point of sympathy for murder, if the murder is a detriment only to Russia? And this was even before the famous congresses; in no other way did Russia bring blame on itself, still fresh was the memory of deliverance from the yoke of France. Yet public opinion in Germany showed no more gratitude at this point or afterward than the Austrian government did thirty-four years later.

If they are already angry about the reciprocal advice and influence between one state and another, then of course Russia would have just as much cause, if not more, to be upset with Austria and other German domains, as Germany has with Russia. Do we not attribute the change in Emperor Alexander's line of thinking after 1822 to the influence of Metternich? Was not this influence the reason for Kapodistrias's[45] disfavor and the hostile line taken toward Greece and nationalist [*natsional'naia*] politics in general? Finally, was not this influence the reason for the whole redirection of public education in the time of Shishkov and Magnitskii?[46] But afterward, was it not for Austria's sake that any Russian moral support to the Slavs became considered almost a

---

[44] August von Kotzebue (1761–1819): German author and diplomat to Russia, who ended up in Russian civil service and returned to German lands as a Russian diplomat. His satirical works outraged German liberal nationalists, one of whom, a student, murdered him. Metternich seized this as a pretext for the Carlsbad Decrees restricting universities and the press.

[45] Count Ioannis Kapodistrias (1776–1831): Greek politician, diplomat for Russia (1809–21), after which he worked for the cause of Greek independence.

[46] Aleksandr Semenovich Shishkov (1754–1841): Russian statesman, education minister, and president of the Russian Academy. Mikhail Leontevich Magnitskii (1778–1844): Reactionary in the Education Ministry (1819–26), famous for recommending the University of Kazan be closed and ceremonially destroyed.

state crime? If European public opinion wants to be just, then let it attribute the harmful influence of Russia in German affairs to its true source—that is, to the German governments themselves, especially Austria. No, neither the actions of Kotzebue nor all such (essentially harmless) Russian interference in European affairs can explain the hatred Europe nurtures toward Russia; but the murder of Kotzebue itself, and more importantly, the attendant sympathy it aroused, can only be explained by this hatred. The reason for it lies deeper.

However, there is strong, irrefutable evidence to show that Russia's anti-liberal interference in foreign affairs is not the source or the main reason for Europe's hostility. When we think we see the reason for a given phenomenon in something, then the easiest way to confirm this supposition is if some way exists to remove the supposed reason from operation. A supposition is clearly false when the phenomenon continues despite the removal of the supposed cause. For example, the deceleration in the swing of a pendulum observed in equatorial countries was ascribed to the lengthening of the pendulum by heat. So they devised a contraption to eliminate the effect of heat; but the pendulum continued to swing slower than in the north. This made it completely obvious that heat was not the reason. Social questions almost never allow experimentation, but the subject under consideration actually was put to the test on a large scale, and what happened? It has already been a little over thirteen years since the Russian government completely changed its system,[47] in an act of such high liberalism that it is even shameful to apply to it such a vulgarized term; the Russian nobility showed disinterestedness and generosity, and the Russian masses showed unparalleled moderation and forgiveness. Since that time the state has acted in the same spirit. One liberal reform followed another. It did not exert any kind of pressure in foreign affairs. Not only that, but it used its influence to further the whole liberal cause. Both the government and public opinion sided with the Northern States [in the U.S. Civil War] more sincerely here than in the greater part of Europe. Russia was among the first to recognize the [newly united] Italian kingdom and even, as they say, "interfered" in Germany by its influence to aid an unjust cause. And what of it? Did Europe change its outlook toward Russia one bit? Yes, it certainly sympathized with the peasant reform, hoping that this would plunge Russia into unending discord, for the same reason that England sympathized with the freeing of American Negroes. We have seen much love and goodwill from their side on the topic of Polish affairs. The [Polish] lynchers and stillettists and arsonists[48] become heroes, as long as their vile behavior was directed

---

[47] Danilevskii's meaning here is uncertain; presumably written in 1868, it would refer to Alexander I's accession in 1855, but the emancipation of 1861 and the attendant reforms are clearly implied.

[48] Danilevskii is referring to the secret Fifth Department of the Polish Military Gendarmerie (in Polish, *sztyletnicy* and *żandarmi wieszający*), formed during the 1863 Polish

against Russia. The defenders of nationalities [*natsional'nosti*] fall silent on the question of defending Russian nationality [*narodnost'*], not to mention those oppressed in the western provinces, or the Bosnians, the Bulgars, the Serbs, and the Montenegrins. Will the most generous and at the same time the most genuine way of appeasing Poland, by providing the Polish peasantry with land, ever be fairly considered? Or is the English approach to the pacification of Ireland, by means of eviction through hunger, more preferable from a humane point of view? The experiment has been conducted on a large scale. The medical proverb says: *sublata causa tollitur effectus.*[49] But here, the action continues despite the elimination of the cause; therefore, the reason is something else.

It is still in fashion among us to attribute everything to our unfamiliarity with Europe, and to its ignorance concerning Russia. Our press says nothing, at least until recently, but our enemies slander us. How would poor Europe learn the truth? It is shrouded in fog and befuddled. *Risum teneatis, amici;*[50] or, as we say in Russian, it would make a chicken laugh, my friends. How could Europe—which knows everything from the Sanskrit language to the Iroquois dialects, from the laws of motion of complex solar systems to the structures of microscopic organisms—not know a thing about Russia? Is it some kind of Reuss-Greiz, Schleiz, or Bad Lobenstein,[51] unworthy of its enlightened attention? Such excuses—ignorance, naivety, and gullibility, as if we are talking about an innocent schoolgirl—are laughable coming from Europe, shrewd as a serpent. Europe does not know only because it does not want to know; or better to say, it knows what it wants to know, that is, what corresponds to its preconceived notions, passions, pride, hatred, and scorn. Also laughable are these flirtations with foreigners to try to present Russia in the best light, but thanks to these efforts to enlighten and clarify, public opinion in Europe has only become blind and gotten lost. Go ahead and satisfy a good person's curiosity; but it is useless to add optical illusions to this. There is no way to remove the blind spot from the one who has eyes but does not see; there is no treating the deafness of the one who has ears and does not listen. Enlightening public opinion by means of books, magazines, brochures, and the spoken word can be very helpful in this and all other regards, not for Europe, but for us Russians—who are accustomed to seeing through foreign eyes—and the rest of our tribe. For Europe this effort would be in vain: on its own, without our help, it will learn only what it wants, if it wants, to learn.

The point is that Europe does not recognize us for who we are. It looks at Russia and the Slavs in general as something foreign to it, but at the same

---

uprising to assassinate traitors, collaborators, and Russian military and civilian officials.

[49] Latin: "The effect ceases when the cause is removed."

[50] Latin: "How can you keep from laughing, friends."

[51] Tiny German principalities.

time as something that cannot serve merely as raw material to extract for its own benefit, as it does from China, India, Africa, the greater part of America, etc., or as material to mold by its own pattern and likeness as especially the Germans once hoped, who, despite their well-known cosmopolitanism, expect a single united German civilization to save the world. Europe therefore looks upon Rus' and Slavdom as not just a foreign, but a hostile, principle. As the uppermost stratum [of rock on a hillside]—not loose or soft, but exposed, weathered and turning to clay—all Europe understands or, more precisely, instinctively feels beneath this surface a strong, hard core not getting pounded, ground up, dissolved; and thus that it cannot be assimilated, will never become its own flesh and blood, but has both the right and the power to live its own distinctive, independent life. Rightly proud of its contributions to Europe, it is hard, though not impossible, to dismiss it. And so [Europe feels] under no circumstances, neither by fire or rain, by hook or by crook should this core be allowed to strengthen or thicken, to take root and branch out into the wide-open spaces. But is it not already too late; has not that time passed? Can there still be any thought of being impartial and proper? In a holy cause, are not all means justified? Is this not what the Jesuits and Mazzinis[52] preached to both Old and New Europe? Whether Schleswig and Holstein are Danish or German, they will at least still be European; so when there is a slight shift in the political balance, is it worth reading too much into it? When Europe does not lose any of its dominion, public opinion is not much disturbed; we should be tolerant amongst ourselves. When the scales tilt toward Athens or Sparta, that is who rules Greece. But how can we allow a foreign, hostile, barbarian world to expand its influence, even if it expands into what by all human and divine laws already belongs to it? Do not admit that the common cause of all is [based on] only what Europe feels. It can even call the Turks allies, and hang the banner of civilization on them. This is the only sufficient explanation of the double standard Europe uses to measure Russia and all the Slavic world, as well as other countries and peoples. For this injustice and animosity of Europe toward Russia—of which the comparison of the years 1864 and 1854 serves as only one of countless examples—no matter how much we search, we will not find the reason in one or another of Russia's actions. In general, we will not find an answer or explanation based on facts. It is not even a conscious thing that Europe could objectively explain. The reason lies deeper, in the unexplored depths of all tribal sympathies and antipathies, which make up the, so to speak, historical instinct of peoples, leading them (apart from, but not against, their will and consciousness) toward an unseen goal; since in broad, general outlines, history, while allowed to stray from its patterns, does not take shape according to human whim. What drove the ancient Germans to incessant attacks on Rome? They say the

---

[52] Giuseppe Mazzini (1805–72): Italian nationalist politician and journalist, champion of the cause of Italian unification.

south holds an irresistible fascination for the sons of the north. It does not take extensive ethnographic investigations to see this is completely false. Everyday experience says that each sedentary people (the Germans were already settled by the time of the wars with Rome) in primitive times at least as much as later, has an almost insurmountable attachment to its homeland: to its climate, however harsh; to the natural setting surrounding it, however bleak. The south has something deadly about it to peoples of the north. Take for example the population of Russians in the Caucasus. Do Russian people, left to their own preference, aspire to the blessed countries of the Caucasus? No, for them Siberia has vastly more appeal. Not the allure of the south, but some kind of hatred led these peoples to destroy Rome. Why such good relations between, and the gradual merging of, the German tribes with the Roman, and the Slavic tribes with the Finnic? The German and Slavic, on the contrary, repel each other, one antipathetic to the other; and where one mixes with the other, the one exterminates its predecessor, as the Germans did with the Polabian tribes and with the Baltic Pomeranian Slavs. This unconscious feeling, this historical instinct also causes Europe to dislike Russia. Impartial views, which Europe and especially Germany had not exactly excelled at in the first place, simply vanished when the matter of foreign nationalities [narodnosti] arose! It considers everything distinctly Russian and Slavic as worthy of scorn, which it is the holy responsibility and true mission of civilization to eradicate. *Bemeiner Russe, Bartrusse*[53] are terms of greatest scorn in the language of Europeans, especially Germans. In their eyes, the Russian can only aspire to human dignity when he has lost his national aspect [natsional'nyi oblik]. Read the accounts of travelers, vastly popular abroad, and you will find sympathy for the Samoeds, Koriaks, Yakuts, Tatars,[54] for whomever you like, only not for the Russian people [narod]. See how foreign managers conduct themselves with Russian peasants; pay attention to the attitude of sailors arriving in Russia toward the porters and dockworkers in general. Read articles on Russia in European newspapers, in which the opinions and passions of the enlightened part of society are expressed; finally, follow the European governments' relations with Russia. You will see the same thing prevails in all these various spheres: a spirit of hostility taking the form of distrust, Schadenfreude, hatred, or scorn, depending on the circumstances. Something touching all spheres of life, from the political to everyday life, spreading through all social strata, yet not having any kind of factual basis, can only be rooted in the general instinctive consciousness of those fundamental differences in the historical principles and historical missions of tribes. Simply put, the only sufficient explanation for this political injustice, as well

---

[53] German: "Common/vulgar Russian"; "bearded Russian."

[54] Samoed and Tatar, see n. 12 in this chapter. Koriak: indigenous people of the Bering Sea coast, north of the Kamchatka Peninsula. Yakut: Turkic people from the region of Lake Baikal and Olkhon Island near its west coast.

as this social hostility, is that Europe sees Russia and Slavdom as something foreign to itself, and not just foreign but hostile. For the impartial observer, this is an undeniable fact. The only question can be whether such a half-conscious view and half-instinctive, unconscious feeling is well-founded and correct, or only temporary prejudices and misunderstandings that disappear without leaving a trace. The following chapter is devoted to an investigation of this question.

✑ 3 ✒
Is Russia Europe?

Scattered Slavs! Again I call
To you, prepared to cry:
Join together or else we fall,
Become a mighty whole, or die!
—Ján Kollár,[1] *Slávy Dcera*

Is Europe right or not in considering us something foreign to it? To answer this question requires a clear understanding of what Europe is, in order to see whether to approach the Europe–Russia difference at the level of species or genus. The question seems strange. Who does not know the answer? Europe is one of five continents, any schoolboy will say. What exactly is a "continent," we ask further. It seems to me you will not find an answer because (presumably) it is considered so simple that it would seem like the height of pointless pedantry to define it. Whether or not that is so, we in any case need to seek this definition to answer the question we have posed. The continents are the most general geographic divisions of all the dry land on our planet, like the division of water into oceans. Is this division natural or artificial? By a natural division or natural system we mean a grouping of subjects or phenomena that considers all their characteristics, and the relative merits of these characteristics, with subjects arranged so that those put in one natural group have more affinity or a stronger degree of similarity among themselves than with the members of other groups. In contrast to this, an artificial system contents itself with one or a few characteristics, going by something blatantly obvious but completely non-essential. This kind of system can separate the most similar in essence, and combine the most heterogeneous. Looking at the continents from this point of view, we immediately come to the conclusion that this is an artificial group. In fact, the southern peninsulas of Europe—Spain, Italy, and Turkey (south of the Balkan Mountains)—are incomparably more similar to Asia Minor, Transcaucasia, and northern coastal Africa than to the rest of Europe. In the same way, Arabia is much more like Africa than Asia; the Cape of Good Hope is more like the mainland of New Holland [Australia] than central or northern Africa; the polar lands of Asia, Europe, and America are more like each other than any of them are to the mainland south of them,

---

[1] Jan Kollár (1793–1852): Slovak poet and academic, famous for the Pan-Slavic sonnet cycle *Slávy Dcera* (The Daughter of Slava; 1821), which urges the Slovaks to seek Russia's help and protection.

and so on. It cannot be otherwise because the division of land into continents was done irrespective of climate, ecology, and other physical traits that affect the character of the lands. True, distinctive characteristics sometimes correlate to the so-called continents' boundaries, but only partly so and, even then, co-incidentally. One can even say the similarity in physical character never covers the whole continent, with the only real exception being New Holland, which is relatively small. So this division is obviously artificial, established only by taking account of the strict boundaries of water and land; and although the difference between water and dry land is absolute, not only regarding human needs but in and of itself, the expanse of water very often divides parts of land that by all natural characteristics form a single, physical whole, and conversely, often fuses together completely heterogeneous parts as a continuous mainland. For example, the Crimean peninsula (surrounded on all sides by water, except for the narrow Isthmus of Perekop) is not, however, a homogenous physical whole; welded onto the Crimean steppe, the southern coast is much more distinct from it than the Crimean steppe is from other steppes of southern Russia (entirely similar to it, despite the fact that it is almost completely separated from them by the sea). If from the dawn of time the land along the coasts of the Azov and the northern Black Sea rose gradually, like the coasts of Sweden, then the Crimea would have long ago ceased to be a peninsula and would have merged with the adjoining steppe, and the distinction between the southern coast and the rest of the Crimea would be clearly delineated. The same can be said in many cases about continents, which in essence are none other than huge islands or peninsulas (it would be more precise to say, "all-but islands," as in the French rather than the German). These are more or less artificial ideas and as such cannot claim any kind of exclusive character. When we say "the Asiatic type," we mean strictly the type characterized by Central Asia, of flat high plains crossed by mountain ranges, which does not apply to the Indian, Asia Minor, Siberian, Arabian, or Chinese types. In the same way, speaking about "the African type" we have in mind strictly the type characterized by the Saharan steppes, which by no means extend to the Cape of Good Hope, the island of Madagascar, or the coast of the Mediterranean Sea, but on the contrary match the Arabian type quite well. Such expressions, strictly speaking, are metaphors by which we ascribe to the whole the character of its separate parts.

But can Europe truly be called a continent, even as an artificial division based solely on the separation of land and sea, where the liquid and solid both end? America is an island; Australia is an island; Africa is almost an island; Asia, together with Europe, would also be almost an island. Why on earth is this whole body—this huge chunk of land, surrounded like all the other chunks, on all sides or almost all sides, by water—divided into two parts for some completely different reason? The Ural mountain range sits near the half-point of this expanse. But what is so special about it that, of all the mountain ranges of earth, it alone should be given the honor of serving as the boundary between two continents, which in all other cases is reserved for oceans, or occasionally seas? In terms of height, this range is one of the most insignificant, and in terms of travel, one of the most easily crossed. At its middle, near Yekaterinburg, it is like crossing the Central Russian Upland or the Valdai Hills, where travelers ask the coachman, "Say, old chap, where are the mountains?" If the Urals divide two continents, then what of the Alps, the Caucasus, or the Himalayas? If the Urals make Europe a continent, then why is not India? After all, it is surrounded on two sides by water and on the third by mountains, for which the Urals are no match; and any physical distinctions (from the contiguous part of Asia) in India are much greater than in Europe. But the Ural mountain range is at least something; further on, the honor of serving as the boundary between two worlds falls to the Ural River, which is nothing to speak of at all. And the Uzen River is one-fourth the width of the Neva at its mouth, with banks no different on one side than the other. The only thing it is known for is good fishing, but it is hard to understand why this deserves the honor of dividing two continents. Where there is no real boundary, a division can be made a thousand different ways. So why not, instead of the Urals, give the duty of serving as the boundary between Asia and Europe to the Volga river, along with the Sarpa, Manych, and the Don? Or why not the Western Dvina and the Dnieper, as the Poles would like to think; or the Vistula and Dniester, as the Poles do not want to think? The boundary could even be shifted to the Ob. All that can be said is that there is no actual boundary; instead, it is only whatever you please: neither the one, nor the other, nor a third, fourth, or fifth has any kind of basis or harm to it. They say that the nature of Europe is distinct, even the opposite of the Asian type. But how could a part of a heterogeneous whole not have its own peculiarities? Are India and Siberia really identical types? If Asia had a general, homogenous character, but Europe alone was different, distinct from the rest of its members [the continents as a group], then that would be a different matter; the objection would make sense.

The point is that when the division of the ancient world into three parts came into use, it had a well-defined meaning in precisely that sense of big mainland masses divided by the seas, which is the only defining trait for the idea of continents. What lay to the north of the well-known ancient sea was called Europe; what lay to the south, Africa; and to the east, Asia. The very word Asia originally was used by the Greeks to refer to their original homeland, to the country lying at the northern foot of the Caucasus mountains, where according to legend the mythical Prometheus was chained to the rock, and his wife or mother[2] was called Asia; from there the name was transferred to the settlers of the peninsula known as Asia Minor, and then spread to the

---

[2] Apollodorus and Lycophron say mother; Herodotus says wife.

whole continent lying east of the Mediterranean.[3] When the outlines of the mainland became fully known, the division of Africa from Europe and Asia was confirmed, while the division of Europe from Asia seemed groundless; but the force of habit and the respect for longstanding notions was such that rather than repudiate them, new boundary lines had to be found to replace the ones disproven.

So, does Russia belong to Europe? I already answered the question. Perhaps it does, or perhaps it does not; or perhaps in part, as much as you want, however you like. In essence, in the present sense Europe itself is nothing but a peninsula of Asia, initially less sharply distinguished from it than the other Asiatic peninsulas, but becoming more split up and divided toward the end.

Is it really possible, however, that the exalted word "Europe" is a word without significance, a mere sound without definite meaning? Of course not! It has real meaning not in a geographical, but in a cultural-historical sense. And the question about belonging or not belonging to the geography of Europe does not matter in the least. But what exactly is Europe in this cultural-historical sense? The answer to that is most definite and certain. Europe is no more and no less than the realm of the Germanic-Roman civilization; or in the wider metaphoric sense, Europe is this Germanic-Roman civilization in itself. They are synonymous. But is Germanic-Roman civilization only important for the meaning of the term "Europe"? Is it not translated more precisely as "all-human civilization," or at least as the flower of it?

Did not Greek and Roman civilizations grow up on European soil? No, the realm of these civilizations was something else: the Mediterranean Sea basin, regardless of where the lands of these ancient civilizations lay, whether to the north, south, or east; the European, African, or Asian coasts of the sea. Homer, in whom lay the seed of the whole of Greek civilization that developed subsequently, was born on the Asia Minor coast of the Aegean Sea. For a long time this Asia Minor coast with the surrounding islands was the

---

[3] [Danilevskii's note]: Here is what the famous traveler, Frederic Dubois de Montpereux [1798–1849] says on this subject: "All this proves that it was a Caucasian country bearing the name Asia. Indeed, whence this ancient and strange demarcation of Europe from Asia, divided by the Tanais" [ancient Greek name for the river Don] (strange, of course! But still not so strange as the demarcation by the Urals) "if not from a country named Asia to the north of the Caucasus?

"It also proves that when Strabo [ancient Greek geographer] referred to 'Asia' he meant that a certain country near Sindica (part of the Taman peninsula) was Asia, in the strict sense of the word, and that he always used the term strictly in this sense, writing about the coast of the Maeotian [Azov] sea. It is curious to note that in Greek *ăsis* means 'alluvial mud,' which a river carries, and then deposits; *ăsios* and *ăsia* mean 'muddy' or 'boggy' like the banks at the mouth of a river, a designation so aptly applied to the Kuban River delta which is 'asia' in the strict sense of the word. From Asia proper came the Ashkenaz-Gomerites of Asia Minor, the Deucalionites, and Dardans [Trojans], and others. Probably the Ashkenazy brought with them the name of their homeland, which was in such a way transferred to Asia Minor and took root there, thus expanding to include the whole continent."

main realm of Hellenic civilization. Here was born not only the epic poetry of the Greeks, but also lyric poetry, philosophy (Thales), sculpture, history (Herodotus), and medicine (Hippocrates), and from there it crossed the sea to the other coast. True, the main center of this civilization then became Athens; but it came to an end and, so to speak bore fruit once again, not in a European country, but in Alexandria, in Egypt. Thus, in completing its development, the ancient Hellenic culture made the rounds of all three so-called continents—Asia, Europe, and Africa—and never exclusively belonged to Europe. It neither began nor ended there.

Both the Greeks and Romans formed their lands in opposition to "barbarian lands," including parts of, in the original understanding, the European, the Asiatic, and the African littorals of the Mediterranean Sea; but for them Asia encompassed the rest of the world in the same way that Germanic-Romans juxtapose Europe, or the sphere of their activity, to the rest of the world. In the cultural-historical sense, Europe is for the Germanic-Roman civilization what the whole Mediterranean basin was for the Greek and Roman civilizations. And while there are lands where it is believed, incorrectly, that Europe is the realm of human civilization in general or at least the best parts of it, it is only the realm of the great Germanic-Roman civilization that is synonymous with it; and only from the time of the development of that civilization did the word "Europe" acquire the connotation and meaning now applied to it.

In this sense, does Russia belong to Europe? Unfortunately, or perhaps thankfully, for better or worse: no, it does not. It was not fed by those roots that nurtured Europe on both beneficial and harmful juices, drawn from the soil of the ancient world it destroyed; nor was it fed by roots drawing nourishment from the depths of the German soul. It was not part of the revived Roman Empire of Charlemagne,[4] which formed a kind of common trunk, from which all the shooting branches of the European tree spread out; it did not enter into the theocratic federation that replaced the Carolingian monarchy; it had nothing to do with the single common body of the feudal-aristocratic system, which (from the time of Charles to the time of its knightly manifestation) had almost no national character, but appeared as a truly all-European institution. Then when the modern age dawned and the new order of things began, Russia likewise did not participate in the struggle against feudal constraints, which led to guarantees of civil freedom produced by this struggle; neither did it grapple with a false form of Christianity (the combination of lies, pride, and ignorance going by the name of Catholicism) and did not need the type of religious freedom known as Protestantism. Russia was

---

[4] Charles I, *Charlemagne*, i.e., "Charles the Great" (c. 742–814): King of the Franks from 768, crowned emperor of the Romans on Christmas Day, 800, after conquering Italy. The Carolingian Empire prefigured the Holy Roman Empire, founded in 962.

neither oppressed nor educated by the Scholastics,[5] and did not develop the freedom of thought that gave birth to modern Science, and did not live by the ideals embodied in Germanic-Roman art. In short, it was part of neither the European good, nor the European evil, so how could it belong to Europe? Neither true modesty nor true pride would allow Russia to claim to be Europe. It did nothing to deserve that honor, and if it wants to deserve a different one, it should not claim what it does not deserve. Only parvenus, having no concept of modesty or noble pride, insinuate themselves into what they consider the highest circles; people who understand their own merit consider it in no way beneath themselves to stick to their own circle and try to ennoble it, so that there is nothing to envy from anyone or anything else.

But some will say, although Russia does not belong to Europe by birth, it could belong to it by adoption. It has assimilated (or must try to assimilate) what Europe has produced; it has taken part (or at least, should try to take part) in its labors and triumphs. But who will adopt it? We do not exactly see parental affection in Europe's relations with Russia, but that is beside the point: Instead, [we should ask] is this kind of adoption even possible? Can an organism long nurtured on its own juices and nourished by its roots in its own soil attach suckers to another organism, become a parasite, and let its own roots and original shoots wither? If the soil is poor or if it does not provide any of the nutrients necessary for full growth, it should fertilize to add what was lacking and plow deep to turn up what it already has, so that it can be better and more easily absorbed—not become a parasite and leave its roots to wither and die. But more of this later. We will see, perhaps, just how possible is this assimilation of the foreign, but for now let's assume: If not by birth, then by adoption Russia could become Europe; or to the wild rootstock we could graft a European cutting. What kind of benefit this graft would bring, we will also see later; but for the moment we will take this change for granted. In such a case, of course, our motto must be: *Europaeus sum et nihil europaei a me alienum esse puto.*[6] All European interests must also become Russia's as well. It will be necessary to be logical and rational, to embrace European hopes and aspirations as our own, to espouse them—*il faut les épouser,* as the French so expressively put it. Being Europe, of course in one thing or another we might disagree separately with Germany, France, England, or Italy; but with Europe, that is, with our very selves, we would absolutely agree, and would have to renounce conscientiously all that Europe as a whole considers

---

[5] Scholastics: Medieval European Catholic philosophers and theologians who reconciled Christianity with the philosophy from antiquity; this tradition was codified in Thomas Aquinas's (1225–74) magnum opus, *Summa Theologica.*

[6] Latin: "I am European, and there is nothing European that is not my concern"; cf. Terence, *Heauton Timorumenos:* "homo sum: humani nil a me alienum puto" (I am human, and there is nothing human that is not my concern).

incompatible to its views and interests, in keeping with this new designation taken for ourselves.

What role does Europe grant to us on the world-historical stage? The bearer and disseminator of European civilization in the East: this is the vaunted role that falls to us which native Europe will support, grant its wholehearted blessing, and applaud our civilizing actions, to the great delight and profound gratification of our humanitarian progressivists. "To the East with you, and good luck! But pardon my asking, where exactly in the East did you have in mind?" We were thinking we would start with Turkey. Where better? That is where our brothers in flesh and spirit live under torments and sufferings, awaiting their deliverance; we would offer them our hand in assistance, as if commanded by a holy obligation. "Where?" Europe cries. "You have no business poking your nose in there. That is not your East; there are already too many kinds of Slavs there that keep multiplying, which is not at all to our liking. The noble German *Drang nach dem Osten*[7] along the German Danube is underway there. Germans have been able here and there to deal with the Slavs; they have even done a better job of Europeanizing them than you. In this regard, Europe values the holy principle of nationalities so highly that out of virtue it took Italy from the Germans, which even without them was already European by birth and nature, not by adoption or some kind of transplantation, and from necessity shut Austria out of Germany; the poor German Austrians, along with the Magyars, need something to amuse them, so let them Europeanize this East, but you head for someplace further off." So then we started toward the Caucasus, since it too is the East. The mother hen became so fretful: "Do not disturb it," she cried, "Knights, paladins of freedom, do not lay hands on such a noble tribe!" But in this case, thank God, they [Russians] did not listen and forgot their European calling. And should we not get busy spreading the seeds of civilization and Europeanism in Persia? The Germans, perhaps, would allow it; it seems they do not intend to extend their "push" so far. But as everyone knows, one hand washes the other, so out of respect for the English, they do not. [The English] already took India for themselves, and there is no denying they have done marvelously, as first-rate civilizers in lands they occupy. They are having no trouble in that vicinity, so keep going further. Does that mean China, by any chance? "No-no, there is no need for you to get in there. Is it tea you want? We will gladly ship you as much as you want. Civilization and Europeanization, like any kind of teaching, is not just a gift bestowed or an honorarium granted. China is rich and has the means to pay, so we will tutor him. And praise God, that little old guy has really come along: He smokes the Indian opium so

---

[7] German: "Push toward the East." A nationalist motto of the nineteenth century used by Slavs to refer to the political and cultural expansion of German influence into eastern and northern Europe, dating from the times of the Teutonic Knights and the Bohemian crusades.

wonderfully. No need for you here." Where in God's name is our East that we were destined to civilize? "Central Asia, that's your place. Stick to what you know. We don't have a good angle of attack on it, and the living there is poor anyway. So here's your sacred historical mission," says Europe, and our Europeanizers along with it. Here is that great role which is within Europe's interests to present to you. That and no more: Everything else has been taken by those Khlestakov's servant in [Gogol's] *Inspector General* would call "the better sort of folk."

To build itself up for a thousand years, pouring out its lifeblood to form eighty million people into a state (of which sixty million are of a single group and tribe which, apart from China, the world has never seen) — in order to dazzle the five or six million ragged residents of Kokand, Bukhara, and Khiva, plus maybe two or three million Mongol nomads, with European civilization (since this is the real meaning of those fine words about spreading civilization in the depths of the Asian mainland): this is the great significance, the world historical role offered to Russia as the bearer of European enlightenment. There is nothing to say for such an enviable role! It sure was worth it to live through all this, to build a kingdom, carry the burden of government, endure the imposition of serfdom, the Petrine reforms, the *bironovshchina*,[8] and other experiments! It would be better, in the manner of the Drevlians and Polians, Viatiches, and Radimiches,[9] to wander the steppes and forests, following tribal rule for as long as God grants legs to carry us. *Parturiunt montes, nascitur ridiculus mus.*[10] In truth, a mountain birthing a mouse, some kind of colossal historical redundancy,[11] something gigantically unnecessary is how our Russia comes across as a bearer of European civilization.

Why take such a narrow view of this topic, they ask me. The spread of civilization and Europeanism in the East means not only bringing these blessings to the Central Asian steppes, but also assimilating and spreading them across all the breadth of the Russian lands. Let those so inclined exercise their fantasy a little and imagine that on all this broad expanse there is no mighty Russian nation and kingdom, but only an expanse of forests, water, and steppes where none but Finnic hunters roam: Zyrian [Komi], Voguls [Mansi], Cheremis [Mari], Mordva, Ves', Meria, and Tatar nomads;[12] and let them thus open this country to actual European civilizers (say, Chancellor and Wil-

---

[8] *Bironovshchina*: The ascendancy of the corrupt Ernst Johann von Biron (1690–1772), the opportunistic and ruthless favorite of Empress Anna (1693–1740, r. 1730–40).

[9] Early East Slavic tribes.

[10] Latin: "The mountain labored and brought forth a ridiculous mouse." A quotation from Horace (65–68 BCE, Roman lyric poet), *The Art of Poetry*, in reference to Aesop's fable "The Mountain in Labor."

[11] Literally, *pleonazm* (pleonasm).

[12] Zyrian, Cheremis, Mordva, Ves', Meria, and Tatar, see chap. 2, nn. 10, 11, and 12. Voguls: Archaic name for the Mansi, an indigenous people of Siberia.

loughby,[13] for example). Such a picture of the true European must set their hearts racing in delight. Instead of the "sons of disobedience"[14] providing the force to nail down Europeanism (and the whole matter going poorly), pure-blood German settlers would surge in, without a doubt under the leadership of those most noble of Germans—the Anglo-Saxon races. In all this space, you see, they would establish the United States of Eastern Europe—or Western Asia, call it what you like. A wave of civilization would begin to pour in, and by now, everything would have turned out happily ages ago. God knows how many canals would have been dug; railroads of ten thousand versts built; the telegraph goes without saying; on the Volga, as on the Mississippi, not hundreds but thousands of steamships would go; and not just on the Volga—the Don would be made navigable, and the Dnieper rapids would be blown up or broken through, and how the glorious *Far East* would be opened up in a broad panorama! And oh, the speeches, how the speeches would pour out of even the smallest state (in some Mary or Betsyland[15] lying on the Neva or even on the Moscow river); I think there would be more speeches than in all the present-day [Russian] land and noble assemblies put together. There would be no trace of the *obshchinas*[16] so hateful to the highly enlightened mind, etc., etc. Without a doubt, all-human Civilization (if European civilization is the only possible, one true civilization for all humanity) would have gained immeasurably if instead of the Slavic kingdom and Slavic nation now occupying Russia, there had been (starting some three or four centuries ago) an empty expanse where some kind of barbarians would occasionally roam, as in the United States or Canada before being opened to Europeans.

And so, from supposing that Russia was not born European but adopted, we arrive at the conclusion that it is not only a gigantic non-necessity or colossal historical redundancy, but a downright insurmountable obstacle to the development and spread of the true, all-human (that is, European or Germanic-Roman) Civilization. Europe holds precisely this view of Russia. The view expressed here in a blunt form is essentially very widespread among the chorus of our public opinion and its enlightened audience. From such a point of view it becomes an understandable (and not just understandable, but in some sense proper or even noble, perhaps) sympathy and aspiration toward everything that leads to the weakening of the Russian principle along the borders of Russia; the protection (even by force) of various regions where

---

[13] Richard Chancellor (d. 1556), and Hugh Willoughby (d. 1554): Sixteenth-century English explorers of the Arctic. Willoughby and his crew died stranded in a frozen northern bay; Chancellor landed in the White Sea and traveled overland to Moscow, opening trade between England and Russia.

[14] *Synov protivleniia*: See Ephesians 2: 2.

[15] Spoofing the American colonies (Georgia, Maryland, and Virginia) named for royalty; "Betsy" as a nickname for Elizabeth I (the "Virgin Queen" of Virginia).

[16] *obshchina*: Traditional Russian peasant commune.

there are any kind of non-Russian foreign elements; the support or even the artificial strengthening of these elements, giving them a privileged position to the detriment of the Russian element. If Rus' in the sense of a distinct Slavic state is an obstacle to the work of Europeanism and humanitarianism, and if it is not possible, unfortunately, to make it a *tabula rasa* for the soonest possible development of a true, *pur sang* [pure-blooded] European culture in its place, then what remains but to weaken the national principle [*narodnoe nachalo*] giving the social and political organism its force and strength? It shall be a sacrifice on the holy altar of Europe and all humanity. Is this not an elevated and noble love for humanity, knowing none of the egoism of peoples or narrow nationalist views, as typified by Schiller's[17] ideal creation, the Marquis Posa,[18] whom we learned to revere since childhood? A native Spaniard, the noble marquis traveled around Europe rallying the enemies of his fatherland, which he considered an obstacle to the freedom and prosperity of all humanity, even urging Soliman [*sic*] to send the Turkish navy against Spain. Such an aberration, such a departure from natural human feeling, derived from a logical conclusion, is of course more pardonable in a German poet at the end of the last century than anyone else. Having been born in Württemberg [in Swabia], he did not strictly speaking have a fatherland and did not come into one until the time when, in the character of Wallenstein,[19] he recognized that this fatherland was all of Germany. But even this fatherland was only an abstract idea, not a spontaneous feeling. A Russian would be less capable of having such a state of the soul, but it can be explained as not finding reconciliation for the contradiction between *the national feeling* [*narodnoe chuvstvo*] and *the idea of the sublime offering, from the lowly to the most high* — even though in a distorted way, it expresses the characteristic of purely Slavic disinterest, the vice of Slavic virtues, so to speak. This explains why Russian patriotism only appears in critical moments. A one-sided idea can triumph over a feeling only when it is in a calm state; but as soon as something brings national feeling into an excited state, the logical conclusion loses all force, and the former humanitarian progressive, the admirer of Posa, becomes a true patriot for a while. Such flashes of patriotism, of course, are no substitute for a conscious, content-with-itself feeling of nationality [*chuvstvo narodnosti*], and it will become clear that the lands added to Russia after Peter [the Great] are not becoming Russified, despite the government's desires, and its endlessly-strengthened means of acting upon the people; whereas in olden times, with-

---

[17] Friedrich von Schiller (1759–1805): German Romantic poet, playwright, and philosopher, popular in Russia during the 1830s and 1840s.

[18] A character in Schiller's historical tragedy *Don Carlos* who voiced Schiller's liberal views on personal freedom.

[19] The hero of a trilogy of plays set during the Thirty Years' War, based on a real historical personage, the Czech generalissimo Albrecht von Wallenstein (1583–1634), who fought for the Holy Roman Empire.

out any coercion (which was neither in the spirit of the state nor in the spirit of the Russian people in general) all the acquired territories quickly became purely Russian [voluntarily].

Just as self-contradictory (being much more sympathetic, but far less logical) is the other view coming so widely into circulation in the past. It sees everything European as endlessly superior to the Russian, and unshakably believes in the salvation of a single European Civilization; it considers the very idea of there being any other civilization a ridiculous dream. But in the meantime, however, it disavows all the logical conclusions of such a view: it wants external strength and force without the internal content to justify it; it wants an empty void inside a hard shell. Obviously, here national feeling overpowered a logical conclusion, and that is why this view is more sympathetic. National feeling, of course, has no need of any kind of logical justification; like any natural human feeling it justifies itself, and thus is always sympathetic. But pitiful nonetheless is the people [*narod*] that contents itself with this, if not saying then thinking: "I love my fatherland but must recognize that there is no redeeming value in it." Such superficial political patriotism conceals bitter doubt in oneself, the awareness of pitiful bankruptcy. It is as if saying to oneself: "I am worth nothing; I need an infusion of strength and spirit from outside of me, from the West; I need to pull near to it and force my way into it—perhaps what comes out will be something like a single humanity, empty of all content." In our literature more than thirty years ago, the late Chaadaev's[20] article appeared, which made a lot of noise in its time. It expressed bitter regret that Russia, as a result of the peculiarities of its history, was deprived of those principles (such as Catholicism, for example) that in the course of their development made Europe what it is. Grieving over this, the author despaired for the future of his fatherland, neither seeing nor comprehending anything beyond Europeanism. The article had in its favor the huge advantage of inherent honesty. In essence, the same bitter consciousness lies at the very foundation of our modern, purely-superficial political patriotism; only it is less honest with itself, less sequential, hoping to reap where it has not sown. If in actual fact Europeanism contains all the vitality, then humanity, as multifaceted as it is, is essentially the same as it; if everything that does not fit its formula is rotten and false, destined for oblivion and ruin like anything pointless, should it not promptly do away with everything on foreign soil that draws upon its roots? Why worry about the shell, if there is no healthy kernel inside? Especially why worry about the increasing hardness of that shell? A strong exterior protects internal contents; any hard, dense, compact mass is harder to subject to outside influence and does not let through the life-giving rays of light, warmth, and nourishing moisture. If that outside

---

[20] Petr Iakovlevich Chaadaev (1794–1856): Russian philosopher and Westernizer. His "Philosophical Letters" criticizing Russian backwardness were forbidden from publication but circulated widely in manuscript.

influence is benevolent, then is it not better, is it not it more in keeping with its goal, to open wide the path for it, break its bonds, rally the whole mass, give free rein to the foreign external elements of the highest order, which fortunately have entered into the composition of this mass? Through this, will not the whole mass sooner be imbued with the influence of these benevolent elements? Indeed, when its borderlands take on the European stamp, will it not sooner be imbued with Europeanism, humanizing all of Rus'? The good within them is already a European leaven that—if you do not disturb it—will soon bring these borderlands into a beneficial fermentation. That fermentation will not fail to spread through the remaining mass and break down everything barbarian, Asiatic, Eastern, and render it completely westernized. Of course all this will occur only if national organisms [*narodnye organizmy*] are capable of such chemical conversions; but in such a case, you realize, there is no question of enlightened political patriotism. Why disturb a beneficial chemical process? *Corpora non agunt nisi fluida.*[21] If, for example, the political organism of the Roman Empire preserved its strength, then could those entering the composition of its people really be subject to the beneficial influence of Germanism? No, like it or not, Mr. Shedo-Ferroti[22] is correct. Also correct is the designation "ultra-Russian party," applied to this kind of purely superficial political patriotism. If Rus' is still Rus', then of course it is silly to speak of a Russian party within this Rus'. But if Rus' is at the same time Europe, then why should not there be a Russian, European, ultra-Russian, or ultra-European party? Why is it, however, that there is no such thing in other states— why could there not be, for instance, the ultra-French party in France? Because France is at the same time truly Europe, and there can be no contradiction between the interests of France and the interests of Europe, just as there cannot be (at least in the normal order of things) between the part and the whole. But in a few exceptional circumstances, however, even this can happen. So under Napoleon I there was a party, embraced by almost all the French, that wanted to enslave Europe; so there is now a party that wants to annex Belgium and the left bank of the Rhine in general. Such a party could be called ultra-French, in opposition to the European party, which does not want these seizures. But in the opinion of Europe, Russia is not flesh of its flesh and bone of its bone. In the opinion of Russian "Europeans" themselves, Russia still aspires only to become Europe, to deserve adoption by it. Does not Europe have a right to say to them: "If you truly want to be Europe, why

---

[21] Latin: "Substances do not react unless fluid."

[22] Pseudonym of Baron Fedor Ivanovich Firks (1812–72), journalist and pamphleteer. Firks published commentary in the West, in French, on issues of Russian domestic politics (read widely in Russia), advocating his subjective mix of policy goals: a gradual approach to peasant emancipation, stronger nobility as a support to autocracy, and greater autonomy for Poland (quarreling with Mikhail Katkov and the ultra-Russian press on this point during the 1863 Polish Uprising).

do you oppose the Germanization of the Baltic region? You still only want to become Europeans (and I do not know how that is going to work out for you), but here are some actual, native Europeans: why do you want to stop their actions for the good of Europe and thus of humanity? This means you are not true to your word; you hold your own Russian interests higher than European interests, and that means you are an ultra-Russian party." The same can be said in regard to the western provinces and many other questions. The conflicts of interests arising temporarily between Europe and France are constant between Russia and Europe, at least in Europe's opinion. Is not Europe right then, in a country with pretensions of belonging to Europe, to call "ultra-Russian" any party sharing that pretension, which at the same time does not want to subordinate particular Russian interests to all-European interests? How to reconcile all this to the natural and holy feeling of nationality [*narodnost'*], I do not know, but I think that on the ground of purely political patriotism, this is entirely inconceivable.

Purely political patriotism is possible for France, England, or Italy, but not possible for Russia, because Russia and these countries are entities of a different sort. They are only political units of a higher cultural-historical unit, to which Russia does not belong for many, many reasons I will try to demonstrate later. If, contrary to history, contrary to the opinion and desire of Europe, contrary to the internal consciousness and aspirations of its people, Russia still wants to become part of Europe, then according to logic and reason nothing remains for it but to renounce all political patriotism, all thoughts of strength, wholeness, and unity for its state organism, and all Russification of its borderlands, since the hardness of its external shell is only a hindrance to the Europeanization of Russia. Europe, not recognizing (as is perfectly natural) any cultural principles other than the Germanic-Roman civilization, views the matter this way. Our Shedo-Ferrotists and humanitarian progressives in general, affecting generosity á la Posa, share this view, although it must be supposed (to their pardon) not entirely consciously. Our political patriots (to the credit of their national feeling, but not their logic) want the results but reject the most prompt, easy, and sure paths leading to them.

Where will we find reconciliation between Russian national feeling and the demands of Reason for human success or Progress? Is it really in the Slavophile dream, the so-called doctrine of the special Russian or All-Slavic civilization, long mocked by everyone, still mocked even now (though not by everyone)? Has not Europe produced the final form of human culture, which only has to spread over the entire face of the earth to make all tribes and peoples everywhere happy? Have we not gone through all the transitional phases of universal human life, and has not the current of global-historical progress, so often flowing through underground caverns and crashing down waterfalls, finally found the proper channel through which it only remains to flow until the end of time, watering all peoples and generations, moistening and nurturing all the lands of earth? Disregarding the complete strangeness of such a view, which cannot cite for confirmation anything analogous in nature (where everything that has a beginning also has an end, and everything eventually exhausts its own resources), it is nevertheless something of a historical dogma believed by a huge majority of contemporary educated society. That Europe believes in it is no surprise; that is just human nature. It only takes a little fruitful activity and a true, strong feeling with no self-doubt to make us feel definitive and eternal. Does not any artist consider his own work the final word in art, which no one will transcend? Does not the academic who has produced some theory think that he has said the last word in his discipline to explain the whole truth, and that after him of course the particulars will be filled in, but his directive will remain unchanged? Does not the state official think that the system he has implemented will serve his country well for ages? Finally, does not the young lover ignore the famous poem that "love eternal is not possible,"[23] as well as the experience of the huge majority of people, to believe that his love is the exception, and will continue with the same intensity for as long as he lives? Without some kind of illusion like this, neither truly great deeds nor sincere feeling is possible. Rome was considered eternal, disregarding the fact that Memphis, Babylon, Tyre, Carthage, and Athens had already fallen; thus it only seemed so to the Romans who were making so many sacrifices on its behalf. But even those who simply cannot claim the honor of belonging to Europe are so blinded by its brilliance that they do not understand the possibility of progress beyond the path it has paved. Their fixed gaze does not allow them to see that European civilization is just as one-sided as all others on earth. But while they have understood that the political forms produced by one people are suited only to that people, they refuse to apply that idea to the other functions of a social organism.

Besides the personal feeling I just mentioned (this expectation of never-endingness), there are other reasons why the idea that a civilization other than the European or Germanic-Roman could arise seems more than a little strange to a huge majority of educated people, not just in Europe itself but even among the Slavs. These reasons, in my opinion, include most importantly a false understanding of the most common origins of historical processes; an unclear or hazy notion of the historical phenomenon known as "progress"; an incorrect understanding of the relation of the national [natsional'noe] to the universally human; and a certain prejudicial understanding about the character of what is called West and East—an axiomatic understanding, not subject to criticism. I turn first to this prejudice, though it is far from being first in importance. We can consider this in some sense the ground immediately underfoot, since so often we reject it not because the conclusion in itself seems doubtful, but because it contradicts some other conviction of ours unrelated to it.

---

[23] A line from Aleksandr Sergeevich Griboedov's play *Gore ot uma* (Woe from Wit; 1823).

❧ 4 ❧
Is European Civilization the Universal Civilization?

West and East, Europe and Asia: To our minds these seem like polar opposites. The West, or Europe, is the pole of progress, ongoing improvement, and continuous forward movement; the East, or Asia, is the pole of immobility and stagnation, so hateful to people of our times. These are historical and geographical axioms that no one doubts, and any Russian true believer in modern science trembles at the thought of being relegated to the sphere of immobility and stagnation. There is no middle here, since what is not West must be East, or if not Europe, then Asia. There is no Western-East or Eurasia, and even if there were, such an average, middling position as this would still be intolerable. Any tinge of immobility and stagnation brings harm and ruin. And so we proclaim as loudly as we can that our land is European, European, European; that progress is more dear to us than life itself; that stagnation is worse than death; that there is no salvation but the progressive European universal Civilization; that outside of it there can be no civilization, because outside of it there is no progress. To affirm anything else is foul heresy, condemning the heretic if not to burning at the stake, then to excommunication and haughty scorn from intellectual society at any rate. And this is all the most complete nonsense, superficial to the point that it is shameful even to refute it! I just explained how the division of the continents is artificial: that the only criterion it goes by is the opposition of land and sea, not all the other physical distinctions in nature (topographical, climatic, botanic, zoological, ethnographic, etc.), which we ignore; that by any one of those [other criteria], some continents do not and cannot have characteristics that distinguish one from the others; and that the expressions "European," "Asiatic," and "African" are just metaphors by which we attribute the characteristics of parts to the whole. We will introduce one more example. In Africa, the greater part of its territory shows little inclination for the development of human society, yet Egypt and the Mediterranean Sea coast in general are highly gifted in culture. I also said that Europe itself does not at all deserve to be called a continent: it is only a part of Asia, no more distinct from its other parts than they are from each other, and therefore it cannot juxtapose itself to this heterogeneous whole without violating all the laws of logic (just as Vasilevskii Island, for example, cannot on some peculiar basis juxtapose itself to all of St. Petersburg, but only to the Petersburg or Vyborg side, the Admiralty or Kolomna, and so on, each of which, like Vasilevskii Island, has its own peculiarities). We will add that any contrast not found in the lands themselves will not be found in their populations either; although almost all of Europe was settled by Aryan tribes, these tribes also settled in no lesser numbers across much of Asia. In the same way, the supposed privilege of being progressive is in no way uniquely European.

The point is on each continent there are human societies that are more capable, less capable, and completely incapable of civic development, and the European peninsula in this regard is very well endowed. The rest of Asia however is by no means deprived, but *absolutely* has lands more suitable for culture than its western peninsula, and only in a *relative* sense (to its entire expanse) should it be considered inferior to it. Everywhere that civil society and culture can develop will have the same progressive character as Europe. Let us take China as the very model of immobility and stagnation, posing the greatest contrast to progressive Europe. In this country more than 400 million people live a civilized life. If there were precise figures for China's total labor productivity, then the figures from English and American industry and trade might pale in comparison, even though Chinese trade is almost entirely domestic. Many branches of Chinese industry are even today at a level of perfection unattainable for European manufacture, such as, for example, painting, dyeing of fabric, porcelain, many silk materials, lacquerware, and so on. Chinese agriculture indisputably ranks first in the world. In the words of Liebig,[1] this is the only rational agriculture, since it gives back to the soil what it takes from it as harvest, without resorting to importing fertilizer from outside sources, which doubtless must be considered agricultural exploitation. Chinese horticulture also must rank nearly first in the world. Chinese gardeners do with plants what English farmers do with breeds of cattle, i.e., they give the plant the form they consider most advantageous or best suited to a certain goal, make it bear abundant flowers or fruit without increasing its height, and so on. In cultivating gardens the Chinese have attained remarkable results even in terms of elegance, toward which this people in general shows little inclination. According to travelers, their landscape gardens are the height of charm and variety. The Chinese mentality surely has valuable substance to it, and only from pride or a strange kind of inattentiveness has European learning to this point failed to draw upon it. Artificial pisciculture [fish-farming] has long been practiced in China and is highly productive. Hardly can any other country offer anything close to the scale of Chinese canals. In many regards the comforts of Chinese life are not inferior to the European, especially if compared not to the present, but to the first quarter of this [i.e., the nineteenth] century. Gunpowder, book-printing, the compass, and writing paper have long been known to the Chinese, and probably were

---

[1] Justus von Liebig (1803–73): German chemist specializing in agricultural chemistry, famous for discovering the role of nitrogen as a vital plant nutrient and inventing chemical fertilizer.

brought to Europe from them. The Chinese have vast literature and distinctive philosophy; they are somewhat lacking in cosmology, it is true, but show a healthy and lofty (by pagan standards) system of ethics. According to Humboldt,[2] when comets still brought superstitious fear to ancient Greeks, Chinese astronomers were already observing heavenly bodies in a scientific manner. Science and learning are nowhere on earth held in such high regard and importance as in China. Is it really possible that this high level of civil, industrial, and even in some sense scientific development—which in many ways has surpassed the civilization of the ancient Greeks and Romans, and in some ways even now could serve as a model for Europeans—could have sprung fully armed from the head of the first Chinese, like Minerva from the head of Jupiter, and then for the next four or five thousand years of its existence this people just repeated the same thing over and over and never moved forward? Were there not successes in the far east of the Asian mainland, as a result of gradual physical and intellectual accumulation, through the independent and distinctive labor of generations—just as there were in the extreme southwest of the European peninsula? And if that is not progress, then what is? True, this progress long ago ceased, and many excellent traits of Chinese civilization (such as the respect for science and knowledge, for example) turned to hollow formalism, and its vital spirit seems to have left China immobilized by the weight of the ages. But is this not the common fate of all humanity? Is the East really the only place this happens? Are not the ancient Greeks and Romans counted among the progressive Western (as they say) peoples of Europe? Does not the Byzantine Empire, however, perfectly represent the same phenomenon as China? It lived more than a thousand years after it separated from its Western Roman sister, but what kind of progress is it known for after it achieved that last great work of the Hellenic people: the establishment of Orthodox Christian dogma?

For the nation that has grown decrepit and outmoded, its business concluded, whose time has come to clear the stage, nothing will help it regardless of where it lives, either in the East or West. To all living things (as with the separate individual, so with the whole species, genus, and plant or animal order) is given only a certain span of life, and when it is finished they must die. Geology and paleontology have shown how various species, genera, and orders of living things have a time of origination, highest development, gradual decline, and finally complete extinction. How and why this occurs no one knows, although various explanations have been attempted. Essentially the aging and decline of whole species, genera, and even orders is no more remarkable than the death of each individual, the actual reasons for which may

---

[2] Alexander von Humboldt (1769–1859): Celebrated German naturalist, explorer, and author of *Kosmos*, a multivolume attempt at synthesis of all the branches of science from a holistic view of nature (a lengthy summary and review of which was one of Danilevskii's first publications).

likewise not be known or understood. History says the same about peoples: They are born, attain various degrees of development, grow old and decrepit, and die—and not only from external causes. As with the individual person, external causes usually only hasten the death of an ailing and weakened body that in the strength of youth or maturity would have very well survived the harm. External causes also assist decomposition after death: as with plants and animals, so with political organisms. But sometimes, albeit rarely, whether because the harmful external influences were weak or the organism successfully overcame them, it will die what is called a natural death or "dying of old age." China constitutes exactly this kind of rare case. The body is very homogenous and hearty, having grown up in peace and unity, amassing great powers of immunity like those old folks they say "were born in another century," or "death forgot." Vital fresh growth long ago went dormant in them, but the animal vitality or perhaps a vegetative accretion remains. Should we be surprised if in such organisms the fires of youth have grown cold and the force of progress has run low? What gives us the right to assume that they were always this way, despite the obvious evidence of productive work done by their elders of long ago? We find India these days in the same decrepitated condition as Egypt and Byzantium were for a long time before foreign invasion and general foreign influence finished them off, and started breaking down the constituent parts of their deceased body. These countries were more or less the crossroads of nations, and since they were not such huge, compact, solid masses as China, the process was completed sooner, and fresh new nations took the place of the decrepit ones. This succession of one tribe replacing another is what lends history a more progressive aspect in the West than in the East, not some special property of the soul that supposedly gives Western nations a monopoly over historical dynamism. Progress, thus, is not the exclusive privilege of the West or Europe, nor is stagnation the exclusive hallmark of the East or Asia; both are merely the characteristic signs of a nation's age, wherever it exists, wherever its civilization bloomed, to whatever tribe it belongs. Thus if Europe and Asia, East and West are actually independent distinct entities, then there can be no stigma to belonging to the East or Asia.

The second and more important point denying there is any civilization other than the Germanic-Roman or European form of culture (which is considered universal, the outcome of all prior history) consists, as I said, of an incorrect understanding of the basic principles of the historical process and a vague, hazy idea of this thing called "progress."

The level of sophistication attained by any science, the level of understanding of its subject, is precisely expressed by what the system of that science is called. By "system," I mean not a system of articulation, a mnemonic device to help commit the facts of science to memory or more clearly explain them. Systematization in this sense does not get much respect these days, for good reason, because very often it is used wrongly, with endless divisions and subdivisions only complicating the matter, often only the residue of scholastic pedantry. Rather, this system is the support beams of the scientific structure, without which it could not be built, but which must be limited to the truly necessary so as not to hide the outline of the edifice. I am speaking of the internal system of a science, i.e., the arrangement and grouping of the range of subjects or phenomena belonging to a certain science, corresponding to their actual, mutual relationship to each other. Here is an example. Astronomy, like any science, can be variously explained by one method or another to make it easier to conceive or understand more properly; it is not the manner of explanation by an external system that I have in mind, but the arrangement of the very objects of that science, that is, in the present case the heavenly bodies, which cannot be done arbitrarily but must fully correspond to the relations actually existing among them. The level of sophistication of that system will reflect the level of sophistication of the science itself. At first we imagined that the sun, moon, and planets revolved around the earth; that idea was altered so that the planets closest to the sun revolved around the sun, while those further beyond went around the earth, and later, so that not only the closest planets but all planets revolve around the sun. The first of these conceptions was complicated further by a system of epicycles. Then they became convinced the planets and earth revolved around the sun, but conceived of their orbits as concentric circles. This conception again changed and the sun was conceived as being in the focus of ellipses of different dimensions for each planet; finally these ellipses were given not a simple outline but an undulating path. Any improvement in the science—in the means of observation, in the physical explanation of phenomena, or in the methods of calculation—is reflected in the astronomical system. It is the same in any science, so that when any science begins to comprehend a true, or as it is usually expressed, a natural system for the range of its objects and phenomena, then only from that moment can it be considered worthy of the name "science" (although strictly speaking this is spurious because it is impossible to base a definition on the age or level of development at which it currently exists). All science is science—just as all people are people whether young or old—provided that it pertains to a certain range of phenomena or subjects that actually exist and are not just arbitrary abstractions.

The task of developing a natural system and demonstrating its significance and importance fell to the natural sciences in the narrowest sense of the word, that is, to botany and zoology. The overwhelmingly enormous number of subjects liable to haphazard examination led to the necessity of systematizing them, and thus to the painstaking observation of their peculiarities in the search for the signs of division. These observations led little by little to the awareness that plants and animals represent not a chaos of accidental forms to be grouped any which way just to find a way through their labyrinth, but rather they reveal a profound internal plan as if the embodiment of a creative idea, in all conceivable variety permitted, as much by external conditions, as by the internal essence of the idea itself. It turns out that all these forms arrange themselves by degrees of affinity (that is by the degrees of their similarities and differences) into groups of a defined sequence, called genera, families, orders, classes, and finally types in the plant or animal kingdoms. It turns out also that internal constructions and physiological functions vary according to these groups. In its historical development the natural system revealed the general truth that all that seems simple at first glance simply has not been given enough attention or thought. Thus the study of animals (the more accessible forms of which, such as mammals, birds, fish, or insects, reveal their internal affinity to the eye) led to a clear understanding of a natural system's requirements and how it is different from an artificial division, which is only useful for aiding memory or assigning subjects' names. This was the case for botany. Plant forms by no means reveal their affinity at first glance, but often even appear to contradict them. Raspberry and gooseberry bushes are visually more similar than the rosebush is to the wild strawberry, but the structure of their flowers and fruits shows that the latter two belong to the same family, while the first two are from completely different families. On the other hand, the strange outward forms of cactuses would appear to place them farther from ordinary deciduous plants (the plant type to which they belong) than, say, ferns, which however according to their structure belong to a completely different type. The impossibility of grouping plants by outward appearance caused a deeper investigation into their structural traits and led to a clear understanding of the conditions and requirements of a natural system. The credit for this awareness and its adoption in the field of botany belongs to Jussieu[3] who, according to Cuvier,[4] achieved by this a complete revolution in natural science. By affirming the fundamental principles of a natural system, any improvement in the study of anatomy, physiology, or embryology will necessarily be reflected as an improvement in the system, so that the words of Linnaeus[5]—"Here is a great Apollo of science, who introduced into it an entirely natural system"—remain true to this day, regardless of the increased requirements for natural science. But if the idea of a natural system is expressed in botany and zoology, it is by no means theirs alone, but a common property of all the sciences and a necessary requirement for their improvement. Comparative philology has already applied a system of natural classification to its findings; the same, no doubt, lies ahead for other sciences in the course of their improvement. However well-investigated, however well the

---

[3] Antoine Laurent de Jussieu (1748–1836): French botanist who pioneered the natural classification of flowering plants according to multiple characteristics.

[4] Georges Cuvier (1769–1832): French naturalist and zoologist who applied comparative anatomy to paleontology to classify fossilized species alongside of living species. He demonstrated extinction as a fact but rejected the idea of evolutionary adaptation.

[5] Carl Linnaeus (1707–78): Swedish botanist and zoologist, creator of the form and rules of binomial nomenclature for taxonomical classification of species.

questions of a science are explained, if the facts do not correspond to a natural affinity and do not lead to a natural system, then they will not yield correct conclusions or reveal the genuine complete sense of the matter. I will explain by an example.

The moment the false geocentric idea was replaced by the natural system of Copernicus,[6] which is to say once each heavenly body was set in its proper place in the minds of all astronomers, it then became possible to define the relative distance of these bodies from the sun: to compare the planet's distance from the sun at various points on its orbit, to compare the speed of its motion over various proven distances; and to compare the times of revolution with the distances of various planets. All resulted in Kepler's[7] three laws of planetary motion, which never by any force of intellect could have been isolated from the mass of facts, even if possessed in sufficient quantity and precision, unless they were first put in their true place by the help of the Copernican system. The application of a natural system to the study of plant and animal organisms had the same results. Without it, it would not be possible to make any kind of generalization in anatomy or physiology. Each fact acquired in these branches of knowledge would remain solitary, fruitless, and would only add to the enormous mass of collected material. The sciences of comparative anatomy and physiology themselves would be impossible. So if we are correct that this kind of scientific system is the means to reduce a science to its essential contents and determine its level of completeness, and provides the light to illuminate all its facts, then we shall see to what extent a system of history might meet the requirements of a natural system. Logic requires that we must name these requirements at the outset.

The dividing principle must encompass the entire spectrum [of material] being divided, as its most essential characteristic.

All things within a group must have a greater degree of similarity or affinity to each other than to things of another group.

Groups must be homogenous; that is, the level of affinity among a group's members must be the same as among other groups of the same designation.

The latter two requirements are self-explanatory, but the first perhaps requires some explanation. If we took the first characteristic that met our eyes

---

[6] Nicolaus Copernicus (1473–1543): Polish astronomer and Renaissance man who in *De revolutionibus orbium coelestium* (On the Revolutions of Celestial Spheres), published just before his death, set forth the heliocentric model of planetary motion foundational to modern astronomy.

[7] Johannes Kepler (1571–1630): German mathematician and astronomer who used the astronomical observations of Tycho Brahe (1546–1601) to derive his three laws of planetary motion, establishing that planetary orbits are elliptical with the sun at one of the foci; that the planets' area speed, not linear speed, is constant; and that the size of the orbit and distance from the sun are proportional.

as the principle of division and characterized one group by it and all the others by its absence, then in this way each characteristic could of course be called a principle that embraces the entire spectrum under division. But a negative manner of characterization like this is not a natural system, and fails the simple test of common sense. For instance, animals can be divided into a group having four legs and a group not having four legs. The first group would suit any kind of four-legged animal, but the second group would place humans and chickens, as two-legged creatures; beetles, which have six; crabs, which have ten legs; and the oysters, which have none—all in the same category. There would be two mistakes in such a ludicrous division: first, that it takes a non-essential characteristic as the principle of division, and second, that one of the groups is not characterized by anything positive, but only a certain common absence. The second mistake alone is enough to make the system worthless. And so, for example, the possession of an internal skeleton is a perfectly essential characteristic, and in itself defines a very natural group of the animal kingdom, but all the animals not having a skeleton are so diverse that the lack of a skeleton provides no basis for making a single group of them in opposition to the first. Likewise, in the plant kingdom the group Cryptogamia is characterized only by the lack of a true flower, a negative characteristic combining pulpy mushrooms, branchy ferns, and delicate moss—completely diverse plants by visual appearance and by internal structure, and thus this group could never be allowed as a sensible classification.[8] Neither the skeleton in animals nor the flower in plants is important or essential enough to be thought to encompass the whole spectrum under division by their presence or absence in the plant or animal kingdom.

I turn now to an evaluation of a generally accepted system in the study of world history.

The most common way of grouping historical facts and phenomena is to assign them to periods of ancient, medieval, and modern history. How well does this division satisfy the aforementioned requirements of a natural system? The basis for separating ancient from medieval and modern history is the fall of the Western Roman Empire. More recent works of history, however, no longer present it as the curtain falling on one historical scene in the year 476, after which a new play was ready to begin; but the essence of the matter has gained little from this improvement to the account. However slowly and gradually the curtain came down, to the extent the curtain did fall, and however much the plot of the new play intertwined with the old, the question remains: Was this curtain big enough by itself to partition off the entire scene, and can another curtain big enough be found? What does the fall of the Western Roman Empire have to do with China or India? Even in the neighboring countries of the Euphrates basin, was not the fall of the Parthian

---

[8] This category was first proposed by Linnaeus, but soon became obsolete.

and the rise of the Sassanid Empire[9] much more important than the fall of the Western Roman Empire? Whether this empire fell or not, would there not have been the same religious revolution that had such huge consequences in Arabia? Above all, why would the fall of this empire lump into another group of phenomena (opposed to the first) the fates of ancient Egypt and Greece, which were already defunct, and the fates of India and China, which continued to exist by themselves as if there had been no Rome? Simply put, does the fall of the Western Roman Empire, which in itself was not so significant, constitute this kind of dividing principle encompassing the entire spectrum under division? The answer has to be negative. It is just as obvious that this is not because the principle was badly chosen (actually, the best possible one was chosen), but because there generally are no such events that could divide the fate of all humanity into sections of any kind. Strictly speaking, to the present there has been no simultaneous universal event, and there probably never will be. Even Christianity itself—the phenomenon having the most enormous influence on the fate of humanity to the present, and which in time will encompass it entirely[10]—appears on the historical horizon of each people at a different time. If we take Christianity as a major historical boundary, then the history of Rome, concerning the life of that one people, would be divided into two parts; while the second is obviously further developed than the first, the introduction of the Christian idea into Roman life could not change it in an essential way and could not revive its obsolete principles. So the division of history into the ancient (on one hand) and the medieval and modern (on the other) does not satisfy the first requirement of a natural system, any more than would the division of plants into phanero-gametes (or visible-breeding) and crypto-gametes (or hidden-breeding), or animals into vertebrates and invertebrates, regardless of whatever event we might take as the historical boundary. Ancient history really is like Linnaeus's Cryptogamia category, where (just as ferns are grouped with mushrooms, because they both lack flowers) the Greeks are lumped with the Egyptians and Chinese only because they lived before the fall of the Western Roman Empire.

The second requirement, that the phenomena of one group have more affinity among themselves than with phenomena belonging to other groups, is not fulfilled any better. Is it really possible that the history of Greece and Rome is more analogous and connected with the history of Egypt and even

---

[9] Parthian Empire: A major power in Persia from the third century BCE to the third century CE. Sassanid (or Sassanian) Empire: Successor state in Persia to the Parthian Empire, enduring until the seventh century CE.

[10] Danilevskii takes for granted the eventual universal acceptance of Christianity. Here and elsewhere he rests on the notion of Providence, the force by which God gradually (rather than suddenly and miraculously) accomplishes his will on earth. For Danilevskii, divine agency is patient and passive, rather than aggressive and interventionist, allowing Danilevskii to reconcile God, as Providence in history, with biological time.

India and China, than with the history of modern Europe? This is quite
doubtful. But the worst error and distortion of this system of world history is
clearest regarding the third requirement: that the level of similarity must be
the same in equivalent groups or other groups of the same order. While
"ancient history" combined Egypt, India, China, Babylonia and Assyria, Iran,
Greece, and Rome, which all reached various stages of development, we see
that the Germanic-Roman tribe's stages of development are divided into different groupings—so-called medieval and modern history (which obviously
contain identical phenomena, since modern history is either just a continuation of medieval development, or is its negation and rejection produced by
the same surroundings, to the extent that many historical figures began their
activity in the medieval period and finished in the modern). While on the one
hand not only are Cato and Emperor Constantine,[11] Pericles and Theodosius
the Great,[12] but also Emperor Phocas, Pharaoh Ramses, and King Solomon,[13]
along with Epaminondas and the Gracchi,[14] all lumped together in one group;
on the other hand we find any old Rudolph of Habsburg put together with
the Emperor Maximilian,[15] someone like Philip IV ("the Fair") put with Louis

---

[11] Presumably Cato the Elder (234–139 BCE), Roman statesman, famous for ending
speeches, regardless of topic, with the words "Carthage must be destroyed." Constantine I, "the Great" (272–337 CE): Founder of Constantinople, who converted to Christianity and proclaimed religious toleration throughout the empire in the Edict of Milan
(313).

[12] Pericles (495–429 BCE): Athenian statesman and orator, spokesman (in Thucydides)
for the Greek Golden Age between the Persian and Peloponnesian Wars. Theodosius I,
"the Great" (347–95 CE): Last Roman emperor to rule both western and eastern halves
of the Roman Empire, who made Christianity the official state religion of Rome.

[13] Phocas (d. 610 CE): Byzantine emperor (602–10), a usurper, soon overthrown, in
whose brief reign the empire's frontiers began to collapse. Eleven pharaohs of the later
New Kingdom were named Ramses (or Ramesses) (1290–1077 BCE); for contrast with
Phocas, Danilevskii presumably has in mind Ramesses II, "the Great" (1303–1213
BCE), the greatest ruler of ancient Egypt. Solomon: Biblical king of Israel fabled for his
wisdom, son and successor of David, and builder of the First Temple in Jerusalem
(destroyed by Nebuchadnezzar II in 587 BCE).

[14] Epaminondas (418–362 BCE): General and statesman who led the rise of Thebes to
defeat Sparta and become the dominant power in Greece; praised by some, blamed by
others for making Greece weak and easily conquered by Alexander the Great. The
Gracchi brothers (Tiberius Gracchus [d. 133 BCE] and Gaius Gracchus [d. 121 BCE]):
Plebeian politicians who promoted land redistribution and reforms to help the masses;
forerunners of populism, socialism, and political martyrdom, as both were
assassinated.

[15] Rudolf I, of Habsburg (1218–91): King of the Romans (i.e., king of Germany), increased Habsburg power locally, at the expense of the Hohenstaufen and Premyslid
dynasties. Maximilian I (1459–1519): Holy Roman emperor, spread Habsburg influence to include a dynasty in Spain and possessions in the Netherlands.

XI and Richelieu,[16] and even Sultan Bayezid with Sultan Suleiman I[17]—all grouped together for performing the same function, the way a plough always makes the same furrow, across different eras of history or even at various ages of humanity so to speak. Is this not like grouping the raven with the oyster because neither one has four legs?[18]

Obviously the reason for such an incongruous grouping of phenomena is a mistaken perspective. The difference in the character of events in medieval and modern times inevitably seems so important and essential to historians closer to those events (both in terms of time and the tribe among which the events occurred) that the rest of humanity and all preceding ages seem to them like a distant landscape where all distinguishing features blur, serving only as a backdrop for the picture in the foreground. But science is not concerned with the seeming and apparent, but the essential and real. Taking this view of history led to the mistake of putting the whole gamut of distinctive developmental phases of several tribes, existing concurrently or sequentially, under the name of "ancient history" and lining them up on the same level with each of two developmental phases of one tribe alone, like the third original phase of that tribe's development. In short, the fate of Europe or the Germanic-Roman tribe was equated with the fate of all humanity. No wonder that this violation of the laws of a natural system produced a complete distortion of the historical edifice, its lines having lost all proportionality and harmony.

Strictly speaking, Rome, Greece, India, Egypt, and all historical tribes have their own ancient, medieval, and modern history; that is, like all organic things they have their phases of development, but of course not necessarily always three. Just as in the life of a human one can discern three stages (minority, majority, and seniority—as used for civil purposes, for example) or four stages (childhood, youth, maturity, and old age), or even seven (infancy, childhood, puberty, young or first adulthood, maturity, old age, and senility), so it is possible to discern various numbers of developmental stages in the life of historical tribes, depending partly on the perspective of the historian, and partly on the nature of their development, subject to frequent or fewer

---

[16] Philip IV, "the Fair" (1268–1314): King of France, known for being inflexible, a spendthrift, and reliant on bureaucrats to enact unpopular measures. Louis XI, "the Prudent" (1423–83): King of France, known for his intrigues to fend off many powerful rivals for the throne. Cardinal Richelieu (1585–1642): French clergyman and statesman, chief minister of Louis XIII, arguably more powerful than the king himself; promoted French interests above all others, laying the groundwork for Louis XIV's absolutism.

[17] Presumably Bayezid I (1354–1403): Ottoman sultan captured in battle and held captive by Tamerlane. Suleiman I (1494–1566): Longest reigning Ottoman sultan, presiding over the height of his empire's power.

[18] The last line in the paragraph expresses the main idea, not always clear in these comparisons: that an arbitrary distinction creates groups of dissimilar things.

changes. So it is no trick of perspective: the history of Europe has its own true ancient phase, in the times before Charlemagne when the new nationalities and states separated and formed out of chaos following the migration of peoples. They then contained only the embryo of the principles whose development and elaboration comprise the main contents of the medieval era, and the negation and rejection of which comprise the main contents of the modern era.

It can be argued that this mistake of perspective is not essential, and that only slight changes to the dividing lines between main groups of historical phenomena would fix it: for example, putting the ancient peoples of the East into one group under the name ancient or earliest history, and separating the history of Greece and Rome into a special group called middle history, and putting the outcome of Europe into another group under the name of recent history. Of course this would be much tidier, but even so, ancient history would still be a strange combination, since in the absence of truly universal events (in the full sense of the word), the first requirement of a natural system (that the principle of division should encompass the whole spectrum under division) would still be unmet, and the fundamental problem of the initial system of history unsolved. A deceptive perspective is only the most obvious reason or circumstance leading to a false grouping and thus a false understanding of historical phenomena. The very falsity of this grouping, the false understanding to which the faulty perspective merely leads, is something completely different and incomparably more important and essential.

I resort once again to a comparison with science, where the idea of a natural system has its most broad and full development and application; in regard to botany and zoology, the same kind of deceptive perspective led to the same kind of mistake and for a long time the system suffered from it. The deception of perspective in this case came from the fact that the higher plants and animals attract incomparably more of observers' attention and (concerning animals, at least) can be considered closer to them, most like humans in their structure. All the so-called cryptogamous plants, along with the lower animals like worms, are considered in some way supplemental, like an appendix, to the visibly-flowering (phanerogamous) plants and vertebrate animals, as if deserving no more attention than the doorstep to the proper edifice of botany and zoology. We have seen that a conscientious natural system began strictly in botany. Groups of plants similar enough to be called families were already sufficiently outlined by the young Jussieu; but the arrangement of the families themselves remained completely artificial—most importantly the forms of plant life at that time were presented as a ladder of gradual development and perfection, indicated by one or a few characteristics that served as the standard of perfection, and correspondingly the families were arrayed in linear order, thus undermining the fundamental principle of a natural system which pursues an all-encompassing investigation and the evaluation of the total aggregate of characteristics. What started with botany was completed in zoology, when by a stroke of genius Cuvier distinguished what he called "types" of organizations while investigating lower life forms. These types are not levels of development in a ladder of gradual perfection (levels of hierarchical subordination, so to speak) but a completely different kind of arrangement in which these creatures reach a wide variety of recognizable forms by their own unique paths; an arrangement which does not have a common standard against which the various types of creatures are measured to determine their level of perfection. It is strictly speaking an "incommensurable magnitude."[19] To turn to a more familiar set of subjects and explain the significance of their structures by means of comparison, we say they correspond not to the parts of some building in a certain style (plinth, colonnade, architrave, turret, cupola, steeple), but to completely different architectural styles (Gothic, Greek, Egyptian, Byzantine, etc.). Although not all these styles are capable of the same levels of complexity, and although some of them correspond to a rudimentary state of the art, it is nevertheless impossible to say that they serve as stages in the development of architecture and rank them in order so that any subsequent addition would have to be more developed and complex than its predecessor. There are those architectural styles about which one can only say that each is excellent in its own way and all of them express some capacity for art, not only to improve by successive levels of development but to diversify and take various types to the level of excellence. In the same way, if among the types of animals there are the absolute lowest, such as the protoplasmic (infusoria, sponge) and radial (coral, hydra, starfish), and there are the absolute higher, such as the vertebral (mammals, birds, fish), then there are also things like mollusks (clams) and arthropods (insects, shellfish, segmented worms), among which it is hard to say which among them represents the higher level of organization. One aspect of an organism is more developed in some and another in others. This idea of the types of organizations was then applied to plants; and in general, without the change from groups defined by level of development and perfection of organization, to groups determined by peculiarity of design and by type of development, there could be no natural system in either zoology or botany.

Without this distinction—the level of development versus the type of development—there could also be no natural grouping of historical phenomena. The absence of this distinction is also the fundamental problem of the historical systems just mentioned. The division of history into ancient, medieval, and modern, even adding "most ancient" and "most recent," does not cover all its contents. The forms of historical life of humanity, like the forms of the plant or animal world, like the forms of human art (styles of architecture, schools of painting), like the forms of languages (monosyllabic, prefixed,

---

[19] A term from Euclidian geometry for quantities inexpressible in whole number ratios (subsequently known as "irrational numbers").

inflected), like the manifestations of the soul itself, striving to accomplish forms of good, truth, and beauty (which are entirely independent; one cannot be considered an outgrowth of another), not only change and improve over time, but also vary by cultural-historical types. Therefore, strictly speaking, only within a single type, or civilization as they say, is it even possible to distinguish those patterns of historical movement signified by the words ancient, medieval, and modern history. This division [into periods] is only subordinate; the main one must be the distinction of cultural-historical types, which is to say the independent, distinctive timelines of religious, social, customary, industrial, political, scientific, and artistic—in short, historical—development. In fact, for all the influence of Rome on the Germanic-Roman and purely German states arising from its ruins, is the history of Europe really just the furthest development of the principles of the vanished Roman world? Wherever you look in the categories of historical phenomena just listed, you will find other principles. The Christian religion takes on a papist character, and although the Roman bishop previously bore the title of pope, the papacy, as we now understand it, was formed only in the Germanic-Roman era, and thus it cannot belong to the original sense and significance [of Rome]. Relations between social classes have completely changed since the society was formed on principles of feudalism, which in no way corresponded to the ancient world. Manners, customs, attire, way of life, individual and public amusements: all changed completely from Roman times. Three hundred years after the fall of the Western Roman Empire, it was restored in the form of Charlemagne's monarchy. Despite the new Roman emperor's intention to create it in the form and likeness of its ancient counterpart, the effort turned out completely different, taking the character of a feudal suzerain to whom in worldly regards all heads in the new society must bow, just as in spiritual regards they bow to the pope. But this ideal (in Catholic understanding, accepting obligation is the earthly reflection of the heavenly kingdom) was never realized after Charles, and despite their claims, the Germanic emperors were essentially the same kind of feudal monarchs as the French and English kings, and soon became their inferiors in power. Science, having gradually declined over the course of several centuries, took the form of scholasticism, which cannot be considered a continuation of either ancient philosophy or ancient theological thought, as manifested by the great Fathers of the ecumenical Church. Then European science turned to the positive investigation into nature, for which the ancient world offered virtually no model. The majority of the arts— namely, architecture, music, and letters—took on a completely distinct character, from antiquity; painting in the Middle Ages also pursued completely new goals, having an idealized character and unjustly disparaged forms of beauty. Even if they had tried to assimilate ancient forms of perfection, we still could not judge how much it did or did not continue in the direction of ancient painting, of which almost nothing has survived to our time. Only sculpture has an imitative character and endeavors to follow the path the ancients trod; but then this art itself not only failed to advance or establish anything new, but even doubtless fell behind its prototypes. In all regards the foundations of Roman life completed the cycle of their development, yielded all the results they could, and finally ended; there was no way for it to develop further. There was nowhere to go from where Rome left off: it had already reached the end of its own path and could not go beyond it. In order to go anywhere, it would have to head in a new direction, toward new lands with a broader expanse lying open to it. But even this was not boundless, and this procession would have a limit it could not cross. So it has always been, so it shall always be. Whoever is determined to go anew will also head in a new direction toward new lands. Progress consists not of everyone going in the same direction, but in the whole field of humanity's historical activity proceeding in different directions, since up to now it has revealed itself in exactly this way. But more about that later.

Subordinating levels of development to types of development in the historical system has one more advantage: it releases us from having to resort to some groundless hypothesis about where humanity is on the path at any given moment. By examining the history of a separate cultural type, if its cycle of development lies entirely in the past, we can precisely and accurately determine the level of its development. We can say, here concludes its childhood, its youth, its maturity; here begins its old age, here, its senility—or in other words, we can identify the early ancient, ancient, medieval, early modern, fully modern, and so on. We can do this with some degree of probability, by the help of analogy, even for cultural types that have yet to complete their run. But what can be said for the path of development of humanity in general, and how can we determine the stage of the history of the whole world? Is there any basis to ascribe the life of some peoples or some group of historical phenomena to ancient, medieval, or modern history (that is, to the childhood, youth, maturity, or senility of all humanity)? Does this not make the terms *ancient, medieval,* and *modern* (even if applied more judiciously than they currently are) meaningless, senseless words, if applied not to the history of individual civilizations but to the history of the world? In this regard historians are in the same position as astronomers. Astronomers can determine with all desired precision all points of the orbits of the planets under their observation; they can even approximate the paths of comets which fall only partly under their observation; but what can they really say about the movement of the whole galaxy, except that it does move, and perhaps, a few conjectures about the direction it is moving? And so, a natural system of history must rest on the distinction of cultural-historical types of development as the main basis for distinguishing the levels of development, which can only be used to divide these types (and not the whole entirety of human history).

The identification and enumeration of these types is no difficult task, because they are so well known. They are not merely identified for their paramount importance, which, in spite of the laws of a natural system and basic common sense, is subject to the arbitrary and, as we have seen, completely irrational division by levels of development. These cultural-historical types or distinct civilizations, ranked in chronological order, are the following: 1) Egyptian; 2) Chinese; 3) Assyrian-Babylonian-Phoenician, Chaldean, or ancient Semite; 4) Indian; 5) Iranian; 6) Jewish; 7) Greek; 8) Roman; 9) neo-Semitic or Arab; 10) Germanic-Roman or European. To those can be added, perhaps, two American types: the Mexican and the Peruvian, which died a violent death and did not manage to complete their development. Only the people groups comprising these cultural-historical types were positive agents in the history of humanity; they all independently developed a principle consisting of both the peculiarities of their spiritual nature and the special living conditions under which they emerged, by which they made their contribution to the common treasury of humanity. Among them we must distinguish the isolated types from the sequential types, the fruit of whose activity passed from one to another as fodder or fertilizer (that is, enrichment by various absorbable, nourishing substances) to the soil on which the subsequent type developed. The successive types were the Egyptian, the Assyrian-Babylonian-Phoenician, the Greek, the Roman, the Jewish, and the Germanic-Roman or European. Since none of these cultural-historical types was granted the privilege of endless progress, and since each people eventually becomes obsolete, then it is clear that the results attained by the successive efforts of these five or six civilizations—eventually replacing one another and furthermore receiving the supernatural gift of Christianity—far surpasses the completely secluded civilizations, such as the Chinese or Indian, even though the continuous lifespan of these latter two equals them all. This in my opinion is the simplest and most natural explanation for Western progress and Eastern stagnation. However even these secluded cultural-historical types developed certain aspects of life which their more fortunate rivals did not experience to the same degree, and by which they contributed to the multifaceted manifestation of the human spirit which is the essence of progress. Not to mention the discoveries and inventions (such as the decimal system, the compass, silk-making, gunpowder and engraving, for example) that were transmitted to Europe from the East by way of the Arabs. And must we not acknowledge that Indian poetry and architecture enriched world art? Humboldt, in the second part of his *Cosmos*[20] noted that Indian scholars' discoveries in algebra could have contributed to European science if they had become known a little earlier. But in other realms of knowledge European science is actually much indebted to Indian science; Indian grammarians produced the idea of root words playing such an important role in linguistics. And Chinese agriculture

[20] Alexander von Humboldt, *Kosmos*, vols. 1 and 2 were published 1845–47. Danilevskii published three summary/review articles of the work in *Otechestvennye zapiski* in 1848.

constitutes the highest level attained to this point in this most useful of the arts.

But these cultural-historical types we have called positive agents in the history of humanity do not exhaust the whole spectrum of human phenomena. The solar system has not only planets but also comets appearing from time to time then disappearing for centuries into the void, and cosmic matter revealed to us as falling stars, aerolites, and zodiacal light. In the same way, besides the positive-acting cultural types or distinct civilizations, the world of human affairs has temporarily-appearing phenomena that trouble their contemporaries, like the Huns, Mongols, or Turks, which, having completed their destructive feat in delivering the deathblow to civilizations gasping for life and scattering their remnants, fade away into their former nothingness. We may call them the negative agents of humanity. Sometimes, however, those tribes play both a creative and a destructive role, as was the case with the Germanic and Arabian tribes. Finally, there are those tribes that are not accorded creative or destructive greatness (whether because their distinctiveness ceased extremely early in their development or for some other reason), and thus played neither a positive nor a negative role. They constitute mere ethnographic material, which is to say, a sort of inorganic substance entering into the makeup of historical organisms or historical-cultural types. Without a doubt they enrich them with their diversity and wealth, but do not themselves attain historical individuality. The Finnic tribes are like that, as are many others having even less significance.

Sometimes a dead or decaying cultural-historical type descends to the level of ethnographic material, waiting for a new structuring or forming principle to unite it again along with other elements into a new historical organism—to call it to independent historical life in the form of a new cultural-historical type. For example, this is what happened with the peoples constituting the Western Roman Empire, which even in their new form, having been exposed to the Germanic forming principle, still took the name Roman.

And so either the positive activity of a distinct cultural-historical type, or the destructive activity of the so-called "scourges of God," bringing death to decrepit civilizations languishing in death throes, or serving foreign goals as ethnographic material: these are the [only] three roles a people can end up playing.

We will now delve a little deeper into the properties and character of the various cultural-historical types. Will there turn out to be common characteristics or generalizations that could be considered laws of cultural-historical movement, and which, as conclusions drawn from the past, could serve as rules governing the future? If the grouping of historical phenomena according to cultural-historical types truly satisfies the requirements of a natural system concerning history, then such general conclusions and generalizations will surely, in a manner of speaking, prove themselves. They must arise from the very disposition of the facts once the historical phenomena stand in proper relation to each other, without being forced to fit some kind of preconceived notion not proceeding from the facts themselves. That is what we consider the idea of arranging the phenomena of global history by levels of development, leading to its irrational division into ancient, medieval, and modern, ostensibly constituting three evolutionary phases of development for humanity as a whole, which completely loses sight of the qualitative distinction between the tribes in the human family.

Ꮺᏸ 5 ᏸ
Cultural-Historical Types and Some Laws of Their Movement and Development

Out past the waves
Of the seas of your mind
Is a land, on which shines
Full of beauty most glorious
An empire of new ideas.
—Khomiakov[1]

I will start right off by explaining some general conclusions or laws of histori-cal development, derived from the grouping of historical phenomena into cultural-historical types.

Law 1. Any tribe or family of peoples characterized by a separate lan-guage or group of languages with similarities that can be readily detected without deep philological investigation constitutes a distinct cultural-histori-cal type, if it has already grown out of its infancy and is inclined toward and generally capable of historical development.

Law 2. For the civilization of a distinct cultural-historical type to be born and develop, the peoples belonging to it must have political independence.

Law 3. The principles of civilization for one cultural-historical type are not transferable to the peoples of another type. Each type produces its own, influ-enced more or less by foreign civilizations preceding or contemporary to it.

Law 4. The civilization of each cultural-historical type only attains full-ness, diversity, and richness when its diverse ethnographic elements, inde-pendent but not combined into a political whole, form a federation or political system of states.

Law 5. The course of development for cultural-historical types closely re-sembles that of perennial plants that bear fruit only once, whose period of growth is indefinitely long, but whose period of flowering and bearing fruit is relatively short and exhausts its vitality once and for all.[2]

The first two conclusions cannot be doubted and do not require much explanation. In fact, of the ten cultural-historical types whose development makes up the content of world history, three belong to tribes of the Semitic

---

[1] Khomiakov, see Strakhov's preface, n. 27. From the 1848 poem "K I. V. Kireev-skomu" (To I. V. Kireevskii).

[2] Danilevskii is describing monocarpic plants, like bamboo and agave.

races, and each tribe characterized by one of the three Semitic languages—Chaldean, Hebrew, and Arabic—had its own distinct civilization. The Aryan languages, as is well known, subdivide into seven main linguistic families: Sanskrit, Iranian, Hellenic, Latin, Celtic, German, and Slavic. Of the tribes corresponding to these seven language families, five (Indian, Persian, Greek, Roman or ancient-Italian, and German) were, or are, distinct cultural-historical types, developed within distinct civilizations. True, one tribe, the Celtic, did not constitute an independent type, but (combined with the decomposing elements of Roman civilization and under the influence of the German formative principles) ended up as ethnographic material within the Germanic-Roman cultural-historical type. But the Celts lost their political independence at an early stage. Although the Gauls and Britons had the instincts for distinctive development—both in peculiarities of national character and in an independent religious and artistic worldview, as well as favorable conditions of the lands where they resided—all these instincts were crushed by Roman conquest. No civilization can be born and develop without political independence, although once having attained a certain strength, a civilization can continue for some time after losing its independence, as we see in the example of the Greeks. This phenomenon from which there is not a single exception in history is perfectly clear in itself. What hinders the development of the person in slavery also hinders the development of a nationality lacking political independence, since in both cases individuality, having its own goals, is turned into a servile instrument, the means for attaining the goals of others. If an individual or nationality falls into such circumstances at an early stage of development, then obviously its distinctiveness will die. Thus the Celts seem to present an exception from the first law of cultural-historical movement only because of what the second law requires.

Outside the Semitic and Aryan tribes, two other distinct tribes—the Hamitic or Egyptian, and the Chinese—also formed distinctive cultural-historical types. All other tribes of any significance did not form distinct civilizations, either because like the Celts they were absorbed by other tribes and subordinated to other cultural-historical types (such as the Finnic tribes, for example), or because from living in lands unsuitable for culture they did not leave the state of savagery or nomadism (such as the whole black race, and the Mongol and Turkish tribes). These tribes remained at the level of ethnographic material, which is to say they did not at all take part in [constructive] historical life, or they rose only to the level of destructive historical elements.

The third law of cultural-historical development requires a more detailed investigation and explanation. We know too few details of the history of the most ancient cultural-historical types—Egypt, China, India, Iran, Assyria, and Babylon—to scrutinize events of their history from our perspective. But the results of this history entirely bear out [the third law]. It is uncertain whether any people of non-Egyptian extraction adopted Egyptian culture. Indian civilization was confined to the peoples who spoke Sanskrit-based languages.

True, the Phoenicians and Carthaginians belonged to the ancient Semitic cultural type, but the former were descended from the same roots as the Babylonians, and the latter were Phoenician colonists. The civilization of Carthage was not passed on to the Numidians or other aboriginal Africans. Chinese civilization was spread between the Chinese and Japanese—who were, of course, originally settlers from China. The Jews did not pass on their culture to a single people living around them or concurrently with them.

With Greece we enter more familiar ground. While Greece's civilization was so wealthy, politically it was too impoverished even to think about spreading Hellenism to other peoples until the Macedonians—a people of Hellenic extraction, or Hellenized at an earlier ethnographic stage of its life— took its civilization and gave it political strength. The representative of Hellenism, Alexander, undertook not only to subdue the East but also to spread Greek civilization within it, which according to the theories now prevailing should be considered the universal [civilization] of the fourth century before Christ. For the lofty humanitarian goal of Alexandrian conquests, in the eyes of history he lost his intentions as a conqueror and assumed the dimensions of a hero of humanity. In practice, these civilizing intentions panned out less than his conquest plans, which at least for a time succeeded. In the eastern part of Alexander's domain, aided by Parthians and Scyths over the course of seventy or eighty years, the cultural type of Iran was established, which continued in the new Parthian empire and later in the Sassanid empire. In the western regions this side of the Euphrates, Greek culture was better accepted. In Syria of Asia Minor kings of Greek extraction reigned; the court, capital, and large cities adopted Greek customs and fashions. Greek architects, sculptors, engravers, goldsmiths, etc., did brisk business and their products sold profitably, as do French modistes in Russia of our time. In Egypt it was even more so. In Alexandria libraries, museums, and academies were formed; philosophy and positive science flourished. But who were the philosophers, who were the scientists, and in which language did they write? All were native Greeks and everything was written in Greek. In all this, Egypt itself was neither hot nor cold, as they say. Educated Alexandria was a Greek colony. The Ptolemies[3] generously patronized Greek scholars, supplying them with everything they needed for their work, and the Greeks gathered there from all around. With abundant support, Greeks generated more fruitful results than they would have by their own means, each in his own village, during the disturbances that tore through Greece as it fell and decayed. And we have the Ptolemies to thank for their enlightened generosity, which greatly benefited Greek science. But this Greek civilization was no better transferred to Egypt

---

[3] Ptolemaic dynasty: The last ruling dynasty of ancient Egypt, in which all the male rulers took the name Ptolemy; Hellenistic rulers of Egypt following its conquest by Alexander the Great, until its conquest by Rome (330–305 BCE); and more broadly, the Macedonian Greeks who formed a powerful upper class running Egypt's affairs.

than the East in general, just as nowadays the English took many active and productive scholars to Calcutta, but still have not in the least transferred European civilization to India. To transfer civilization to another people obviously means to make that people assimilate all cultural elements (religious, social, political, academic, and creative) so that they completely penetrate it and continue to operate in the spirit they were imparted with at least some success, so that, although separate from it, [the recipient] can be on a level with the giver, to be at once its rival and the perpetuator of its line.

Nothing like this was accomplished, however, under the Hellenization of the East begun by Alexander of Macedonia.[4] Were not the Greeks happier in the West? I am not talking about Greek culture in Sicily and southern Italy: Pythagoras and Archimedes were just as Greek as Plato and Aristotle,[5] the way Franklin is just as English as Locke or Newton.[6] But since the Greeks failed to transfer their civilization by conquest, did they not make up for this by transferring it to the Romans who conquered them? In some sense they did, despite the objections of Roman Latinophiles. What fruits Roman civilization would have borne if it had let original circumstances work themselves out, no one can say. But there can hardly be any doubt that Cato was right,[7] that his party standing for distinctive development was correct (that is, as the only possible course of progress), that taking in foreign Greek elements either poisoned or at least struck barren all aspects of life in which they penetrated. Only in the ways Romans remained Roman did they produce anything great.

---

[4] Alexander III of Macedon, known as "Alexander the Great" (356–323 BCE), son of Philip II. Tutored by Aristotle and experienced in combat, he assumed control of his father's kingdom and battle-tested troops, which he used to conquer as far as Egypt in the south and Persia in the east. Invading India, his troops refused to go further, and he died in Babylon under mysterious circumstances. The sprawling empire of his conquests dissolved rapidly into civil war, and many cities he founded were abandoned, but some endured, particularly Alexandria in Egypt. Danilevskii faults Alexander for subjugating other peoples instead of consolidating a state to protect his own people, which is the same grievance he has against the Austrian and Ottoman Empires in the nineteenth century.

[5] Pythagoras (6th century BCE): Philosopher and mathematician living in Croton, a Greek colony on the south coast of the Italian peninsula. Archimedes (third century BCE): Mathematician, engineer, inventor, from the Greek colony at Syracuse, Sicily. Plato and Aristotle hailed from Greece proper, but traveled widely.

[6] Benjamin Franklin (1706–90): Colonial American polymath, a founding father of the United States. John Locke (1632–1704): English philosopher of the Enlightenment, advocate of social contract theory and the liberal political tradition. Isaac Newton (1642–1727): English physicist and mathematician.

[7] Cato the Elder (234–149 BCE) finished his political career as Censor, technically charged with keeping the census, but also with overseeing public morality. Cato famously disapproved of Greek culture's growing influence, which he believed undermined traditional Roman values and simplicity. Also see chap. 4, n. 11.

In morals and in lifestyle, luxury, delicacy, passion for pleasure—all moderated in the Greeks by their aesthetic nature, to show balance and harmony in all things—the Romans turned into outright debauchery, the like of which (except for Babylon) there never was, nor will be again. In science and philosophy it turned out completely barren. What little was done in this regard during Roman times, even outside of Alexandria, was done by the Greeks. The speculative, metaphysical inclination of the Greek mind evidently did not suit the people of the Latin race, and they were struck barren when they ventured into this area, imitating Greece. But it would hardly be correct to say that ancient Italian tribes lacked the spirit of academic investigation. The few traces of original Italian (Etruscan) civilization seem to suggest that the Etruscans successfully engaged in the observation of nature. There is reason to suppose, for instance, that they knew about lightning rods. What we know of their observations of birds' flight or animal entrails, although used for religious purposes of divining the fortunes of the state and individual persons, in light of Greek and especially Aristotelian philosophy could have led to physiological and biological investigations in general, just as astrology and alchemy led to astronomy and chemistry. If the descendants of the Etruscans had continued to follow their own tribe's path perhaps Roman science would not have been so insignificant and barren. In the plastic arts, there was only the imitation of Greek forms, mostly produced by Greeks, while in this regard Etruscan production preserved few traces of original creativity trampled by imitativeness. In drama and epic literature, Latin civilization left to posterity only a few flowers of imitative poesy, having conceded much to the original, distinguished only by the virtue of form but lacking distinctive content. Thus even here a direct transmission did not succeed. It was tried but failed because it remained fruitless.

We see completely opposite results where Romans remained true to original principles. Fidelity to the principles of its national-state structure made Rome, in relative terms, the strongest political entity of all time. The rules governing civil relations among Roman citizens, adapted from legal customs and turned into a structured system, laid the foundations of jurisprudence and became the basis for a civil code that is a marvel among jurists the world over. Romans dared to remain distinctive in architecture, using their arches and cupolas to create the Coliseum and the Pantheon, on par with the best works of Greek architecture. Finally, the Romans broadened the field in poetry, which reflected Roman life in the odes of Horace, elegies, and satire. The same must be said about the reflection of state life in academics, in history, where Tacitus stands on the level of Thucydides, not as an imitator, but a worthy rival.

Having conquered the world, as is commonly said, but more accurately the Mediterranean basin and the Atlantic coast of Europe, the Romans themselves forcefully transferred their civilization to conquered peoples. They destroyed the rudiments of distinctive culture where they were (as in druidic

Gaul, for example), and in their place put cities as colonial outposts of Roman life and Roman customs. But nowhere were civilizations that had a national language and had arisen from national elements (Gallic, Iberian, Illyrian, Numidian, and others) induced to take on Roman form and Roman spirit. The ancient supremacy of Rome and the dissemination of Roman civilization only stunted the first shoots of distinctive development. The few scholars, artists, and writers that were born and lived outside of Roman native soil, were either descendants of Roman colonists or Latinized natives from the highest social classes (such as our Polonized intelligentsia of the Western Krai) who did not, and could not, have any influence on the masses of their fellow countrymen.

This outcome could be attributed to the fact that Roman culture was not transferred by means of the free exchange of civilization and its benefits, but by forceful subjugation that destroyed both political independence and all national initiative. There is doubtless some degree of truth to this, but it is far from completely true, as the examples already mentioned and others show. Of the Germanic tribes that dismantled the Roman Empire, the most gifted and most capable of civilization was of course the Goths. They penetrated into Italy and formed a mighty kingdom at the head of which was Theodoric, one of the wisest and most devoted rulers ever to reign.[8] He apparently set himself the noblest and most humane goal: to merge the conquerors with the conquered and implant Roman civilization into the former. And what happened? The Goths could no longer develop their national principles, which from close contact with the civilization of Rome were stifled by its magnificence, and by imitating the foreign but not assimilating it they lost their political strength along with their nationality. For nearly three centuries the gloom of barbarism intensified and in its shade the distinctive principles managed to grow and strengthen, until a cultural-historical type again sprung up that could safely begin to make use of the fruits of the vanished civilization. From the distance of the past it was less seductive than it had been at close proximity. Obviously the great law-giver of the Jews understood better than Theodoric the laws of historical motion when he commanded his nation, crude and unlearned but preserving the promise of distinctive development, not to enter into close relations with the other peoples surrounding it (standing at the height of culture) so as not to lose their distinctiveness by borrowing customs and morals. The example of the Goths excellently demonstrates that the principles within the people of one cultural-historical type (which by their distinctive development necessarily bear the most abundant fruit) can be distorted or destroyed, but cannot be replaced by principles belonging to another cultural-historical type without destroying the people itself (that is, turning it

---

[8] Theodoric the Great (454–526): Ostrogoth king who invaded Italy in 488 and conquered the whole peninsula by 493, ruling it from his capital at Ravenna until his death.

from an independent historical actor into ethnographic material, to be absorbed into the newly arising nationality).

Is it really possible that historical activity—the results attained over the life of one cultural-historical type—will bear no fruit for all other types living at that time or coming afterward? Must these types really remain as foreign to each other as, for example, China is to the rest of the world? Of course not. It was already noted above that overlapping cultural-historical types have a natural advantage over isolated ones. What does this advantage come from? All history shows that civilization is not transferred from one cultural-historical type to another; but that is not to say that they do not influence each other. But influence is not transference; the means by which civilization is disseminated must be more precisely explained.

The simplest means of dissemination is transplantation from one place to another, by means of colonization. In this way the Phoenicians spread their civilization to Carthage; the Greeks, to southern Italy and Sicily; and the English to North America and Australia. If there ever were to be a universal civilization, then for its sake we would have to hope it used this means of dissemination everywhere, so that there would no longer be any other peoples besides those who produced this universal civilization, just as, for example, for the sake of agriculture it would be highly desirable for there to no longer be any weeds. And just as it is for the farmer, if you will, all means of destroying [weeds] are permitted, so the disseminators of the one universal civilization would be permitted to destroy other peoples, which are only more or less a hindrance to it. Since the ones who produced this [universal] civilization in its purest form could both preserve and spread it across the face of the earth, that would be the simplest, most direct and certain method of making progress. This method has been used successfully more than once in America and other places. But if this seems too radical, it would at least make sense to strip the peoples and states outside the universal cultural type of the power to oppose it, that is, their political independence (whether by means of cannons or opium—as they say, by hook or by crook), and over time to make them servants of the highest goals, an ethnographic element soft as wax or clay, without resistance taking any form seen fit to impose on it.

Another form of disseminating civilization is grafting, which is usually what is meant by "transferring civilization." But unfortunately, it is typically used in a mysterious, mystical sense by people unacquainted with physiological theory or practical gardening. In this sense, a transplanted cutting or grafted scion makes the wild rootstock noble and fruitful, or even turns the apple tree into a pear, plum, or apricot tree, and back again. But this mystical, even magical, sense is neither true among plants nor among cultural-historical types, as examples have sufficiently demonstrated. A bud inserted into a cut in the bark of a tree branch, or the cutting attached to a fresh slice in a trunk, in no way changes the character of the plant to which it is attached. The wild rootstock remains as wild as before, the apple tree remains an apple tree, the pear tree, a pear tree. The grafted cutting or scion also retains its character, drawing from its host plant only the sap it needs for growth and development and converting it according to its specific traits. The wild root-stock becomes the means or servile instrument for the cultivated cutting or scion, like an artificial parasitic growth for which all the branches from the top to the base are cut off so they will not crowd it out. This is the true mean-ing of grafting. Alexandria was exactly this kind of Greek cutting or bud grafted to the trunk of Egypt, just as Caesar grafted Roman culture to Celtic roots. The great benefit of this for Egypt or the Celtic tribes my readers can judge for themselves. One must be deeply convinced that the plant itself is worthless to opt for such an operation, to put it in service of foreign goals and strip it of all possibility to produce its own (*sui generis*) flowers and fruit. One must firmly believe that these flowers and fruits had no redeeming value and will never amount to anything. In any case, grafting brings no benefit to the rootstock grafted upon, neither in a physiological nor in a cultural-historical sense.

Finally there remains the method of one civilization influencing another. This is the method by which Egypt and Phoenicia acted upon Greece, Greece acted upon Rome (as far as was helpful and fruitful), and both Greece and Rome on Germanic-Roman Europe. This action we compare to the influence of soil fertilization on plant life, or similarly, the influence of improved nutri-tion on animal life. The organism retains its specific traits; if the material from which it takes its organic structure is supplied in great quantity and high quality, the results will be magnificent. Results like this always bring variety to the field of human development, rather than the useless repetition of the old that inevitably happens wherever one cultural-historical type is sacrificed to another through grafting, which to be successful requires frequent pruning of the branches that continue to grow from the original trunk, in spite of the graft. Only through the free interaction of peoples of one type with what is produced by another, in which the former preserve their own characteristic political and social structure, morals and way of life, religious views, and intellectual and emotional framework—put simply, only by preserving their full distinctiveness—can a newly arisen civilization truly benefit from the in-fluence of a fully developed or more advanced civilization. Only in this way should the peoples of a certain cultural type become acquainted with the products of foreign experience, taking from them and applying to itself what-ever stands outside the realm of nationality, so to speak, such as the methods and conclusions of natural science, technical devices, and refinements in art and manufacturing. All the rest, especially everything concerning knowledge of humans and society, not to mention its practical applications, cannot at all be borrowed, but can only be taken strictly as information, as an element of comparison for one reason or another, because to solve a problem of some sort, one civilization cannot have another's social principles in mind, so that its solution will be individualized, sufficient for it alone, not universally applicable.

The fourth general conclusion drawn from grouping historical phenomena according to cultural-historical types concerns civilization, i.e., the unfolding of principles residing in the peculiarities of the spiritual nature of the peoples making up a cultural-historical type, under the influence of the distinctive external conditions to which they were exposed in the course of their lives: it says, the more rich and diverse these conditions, the more diverse and independent will be its constituent elements, that is, the nationalities produced as the type is formed. The richest and fullest civilizations of all those in existence up until now belong of course to the Greek and European worlds.

By the way, one of the reasons for this fullness and wealth has to be seen in the fact that these worlds were made up of more or less independent political entities, and by the general character of the Greek and European types, each could freely develop its own peculiarities, producing the political subdivisions into which these worlds were broken. These roughly corresponded to the Dorian, Ionian, and Aeolian tribes for the Greek world;[9] and for the European world, the Anglo-Saxon, the High German (predominating in Germany itself), the Low German (independently developing in Holland), the Norman or Scandinavian, as well as the French, Italian, and Spanish, which all came from the decomposing elements of the Roman and Celtic [tribes], altered by the influence of German principles. All other cultural-historical types lacked this kind of vital diversity, and produced incomparably poorer results. Thus it seems we can rightly conclude that this kind of diverse composition is one of the conditions for the fullness of life and development in cultural-historical types. Although this diversity of course cannot be created artificially where there is no ethnographic basis for it, it is undoubtedly necessary for the proper development of a cultural-historical type that has this complex character by nature. However, political fractiousness within a cultural-historical type has its harmful side, in that it lacks political strength and thus the ability to resist external coercion. The example of this is Greece, in which not only were all ethnic differences slight, but often the bases of independent political entities were completely circumstantial. This enabled them to manifest all kinds of peculiarities, but this was also the reason for the short-lived political independence of Greece, so that it had to finish its development under a foreign yoke. The political system of Europe in this regard was incomparably better structured, because it took shape under conditions requiring diversity and strength. Only in two constituent groups, Italy and Germany, did this political fractiousness far exceed the necessary limits, and the harmful consequences of this soon appeared, not only in the political strength but also in the very culture of these countries. Not only did they more than others lack civil

---

[9] Dorian, Ionian, and Aeolian were the main linguistic divisions of early Greeks, and by extension the tribes who spoke them.

and political freedoms, but even the development of literature and learning, initially accelerated by conducive circumstances, were held back in these countries precisely as a consequence of political weakness and the disturbances that come from it, so that only in the last half-century has strong and independent development begun in Germany. Often it is said that this political fragmentation in Germany served as a guarantee of the free development of learning and literature. But it seems permissible to think that if the German peoples had constituted one great political whole, there would have been no need of such pitiful guarantees.

From this the question arises: Where is the boundary line between the demands of national distinctiveness [*natsional'naia samobytnost'*], to ensure the free development of all peculiar inclinations and diversity in the living manifestations of a cultural-historical type—its internal independence, so to speak—and the demands of national unity [*natsional'noe edinstvo*], to manifest its political strength and external independence? This line, it seems, is made very clear by nature itself. People speaking a single language, the dialects and accents of which are so similar that in everyday social, economic, and political life mutual understanding is no difficulty, must constitute a single political whole. The Russian people, regardless of the difference in dialects of the Great Russians, Little Russians, and White Russians;[10] or the German people, regardless of the even greater difference of High- and Low-German dialects, must form independent homogenous political wholes, which we call states. Conversely for whole peoples speaking separate languages within a linguistic family corresponding to a distinct cultural-historical type, instead of merging into a single whole state without diversity of cultural life, a looser bond must be preferable, requiring more or less close association between them, depending on circumstances. This could take the form either of a legal federation based on an articulated law code, or only a type of political system (such as, for example, the European system based on incidental treaties, the frequent revision of which formed close relations and a kind of customary international law).

This kind of a flexible bond, whether a federation or only a political system of states, can only exist among members of a single cultural-historical type. To spread it further than the boundaries of that type could only be done artificially and to the common detriment, since a necessary condition for a social bond is the sublimation of particular interests (individual, social, territorial, even state interests) to the common interests of the higher group. Thus if this bond crosses the boundary of a cultural-historical type as the highest historical entity, it loses the necessary independence for attaining its goals. There can be no objection that the concept of the cultural-historical type itself is subordinate in relation to humanity, and therefore must subordinate its interests

---

[10] Conventional terms of Danilevskii's time for Russians, Ukrainians, and Belorussians.

and aspirations to the common interests of humanity. Humanity does not set
out any real, conscious goals pointing in any particular direction, but is only
an abstraction from the concept of the rights of the individual person applied
to all. That is why everything that is said about obligations in regard to humanity leads precisely to obligations in regard to the individual person, whatever their race or tribe, whereas apart from these obligations, there exist particular obligations not only to the state but also to that higher entity we call
the cultural-historical type. So the Greeks not only had obligations to the
republic of Athens, Sparta, or Thebes, wherever their citizenship lay, but also
to the whole of Greece. Phocion,[11] speaking of the necessity of submitting to
either Philip or Alexander, could not be considered a bad citizen, although in
this regard the particular interests of Athens evidently did not coincide with
the interests of Greece. But the Athenian who advocated submission to the
Persians or later the Romans must be considered a traitor in the full sense of
the word. And this is not because Greece as Greece had some common institution, such as for example the Amphictyonic League[12] or the Oracle at
Delphi,[13] etc., but Greece had its common interests rooted in the very nature
of things, in the essence of Hellenism, which any true and good Greek, as
even Phocion certainly was, must have understood. The same goes for Europe
in its present, natural borders — the Germanic-Roman world understands itself as this cultural-historical entity. The expression "European interest" is not
a simple expression for the Frenchman, the German, or the Englishman, but
has a meaning understood by all of them apart from the interests of England,
Germany, or France, which understood properly cannot contradict the more
general interests of Europe. This however would be completely distorted if
the true borders of the cultural-historical type were violated.

What exactly is the interest of humanity? Who could know it besides God,
who is thus the only one to take up this matter? Without a doubt it was in the
interest of humanity for Rome to fall and for barbarism to rule in place of its
civilization temporarily. But of course not a single Roman nor a single German knew or could have known that this was required by the interest of humanity. Each of them, if he did not know, at least felt what was required by
the interest of the tribe to which he belonged. Could it have been even faintly
perceived that the interests of humanity required the Germans to remain in
their forests and not concern themselves about the fall of the vessels of world

---

[11] Phocion (4th century BCE): Athenian statesman and strategos (military commander
and tribunal, elected annually) for an unprecedented 45 terms, known for his principled opposition to the majority opinion.

[12] Amphictyonic League: A somewhat legendary defensive association among tribes
in Archaic Greece.

[13] Oracle at Delphi: Also called the Pythia, the priestess at the temple of Apollo at Delphi, known for inspired prophecies; probably the most highly regarded religious institution of ancient Greece.

civilization and progress of their day? It goes without saying what a great service would have been rendered to humanity if some ancient German wise man or chief, convicted by a humanitarian idea, had enough influence to convince his countrymen to act in accordance with the interests of all humanity. But on the other hand, understanding the benefit for humanity of the barbarian invasion (if it were possible) could of course never oblige a Roman citizen to work toward that outcome for the good of humanity, nor absolve him from guilt of treason for any effort toward this end. Thus if the group we call the cultural-historical type is not the absolute highest, then in any case it is higher than the others. A person can understand its interests, and it constitutes the final extent to which lower interests can be subordinated to higher, or the individual good sacrificed to the common good.

The indistinguishableness of this close bond among members of a cultural-historical type from other, completely external and incidental relations between peoples of various types, has produced one of the characteristic distinctions of modern history from ancient: that peoples of the ancient world developed separately from one another, but in the modern world relations between peoples are so close that the history of one people is inseparable from the history of another. Of course the bond of history for the peoples of the Germanic-Roman type is very close, but this is because it is the history of a single whole, presenting the same kind of bond of history as among the [city-] states of Greece. Just as no one would think of the history of Athens or Sparta separately, so there can be no talk of the history of France, Italy, or Germany; strictly speaking, there can be no such history, but only the history of Europe from a French, Italian, English, or German point of view, by focusing attention on the events of each of these countries. Once we go beyond the borders of a cultural type, whether in ancient or modern times, then a common history of different types becomes impossible in both cases without dividing into periods by the most strained interpretation, under which events of one type are completely arbitrarily torn apart according to the course of events in another. As in the ancient world the history of Greece and the history of Persia, for example, remained completely separate except for the foreign wars bringing them temporarily into purely superficial contact, just as in modern times the history of Russia or the Muslim East essentially has only temporary, incidental points of contact with the history of Europe. Any attempt to connect the historical life of Russia by an internal, organic bond with the life of Europe gradually leads only to the sacrifice of Russia's most vital interests. One can only say that in modern times, as the result of improved sea-travel and the means of communication in general, the interactions among peoples of various types have become much more frequent, but have not become any closer from this. China and India are still as foreign to the world of Europe as they were to Greece and Rome, even though ships sail continually between them now, while in earlier times, it took a full year to complete an exchange of goods between the Mediterranean basin and South Asia through Alexandria.

The fifth law of cultural-historical movement is that the period of civilization of each type is comparatively very short; it exhausts its strength and does not return a second time. By "period of civilization," I mean the time in which the peoples comprising a type have left the unconscious, purely-ethnographic ways of life (which strictly speaking must correspond to so-called ancient history); when they have created, strengthened, and protected its outward existence as a distinct political entity (which strictly speaking is what constitutes medieval history); and when primarily they reveal their spiritual activity in all areas that indicate their spiritual nature, not only science and art but the practical realization of their ideals of truth, freedom, social improvement, and personal well-being. This period ends in the time when the creative activity of the peoples of this type runs dry. They either rest content with what they have accomplished, considering the legacy of posterity an eternal ideal for the future, and grow decrepit in *the apathy of self-satisfaction* (such as, for example, China); or they reach an insoluble, to their minds, antinomy or contradiction (such as humanitarian universalism, for example) that proves their ideal was incomplete, one-sided, or mistaken; or they find unfavorable circumstances have obstructed the path of development. In this case disappointment sets in, and these peoples fall into *the apathy of despair*. So it was in the Roman world during the expansion of Christianity. However the example of Byzantium shows that this second form cannot last; it turns into the first if, once the moral principle of life has dried up, these peoples are not swept away by storms from outside, or do not return again to the original ethnographic ways of life from which historical life can arise anew. The period of civilization for the Roman world can be considered to last from the end of the Punic Wars and the subjugation of Greece[14] to the third century CE, or approximately 400 years. For Greece, it runs from the third century BCE to the decline of the Alexandrian schools, also in the third century, or for approximately six centuries. But with the destruction of Greece's independence, this civilization was limited to the single sphere of knowledge, the most abstract and most able to survive the longest, once removed from its native soil. The period of Indian civilization likewise continued only a few centuries. For the Jews it could be considered from the time of Samuel to the time of Ezra and the later prophets,[15] that is, five or six centuries.

If the period of civilization is relatively short, then the time preceding it, especially the ancient or ethnographic period beginning at the very moment

---

[14] The Punic Wars from 264 to 146 BCE; Rome conquered Greece by 146 BCE, in a series of Macedonian Wars.

[15] Samuel (11th century BCE): Last of the judges of Israel's pre-kingdom period and first of the biblical major prophets. Ezra (6th century BCE): Priest and leader of the Jews returning to Jerusalem from Babylonian captivity.

of the cultural-historical tribe's separation from its ancestral tribes, is extremely long. In this long preparatory period lasting for millennia, reserves of strength are collected for future conscious activity, and peculiarities of the frame of mind, will, and emotions accumulate, comprising the full distinctiveness of the tribes. This gives it the imprint of a special type of human development and prepares it for distinctive activity, without which the tribe would be a commonplace, useless, superfluous, pointless historical redundancy among other human tribes. These tribal peculiarities, regardless of their original cause, reveal themselves in language (one of the things produced in this long period of time), mythological worldview, epic traditions, basic patterns of daily life—that is, in the tribe's relations both within itself, and with the surrounding world as the source of its material existence. If a tribe did not produce a unique psychological outlook, then how could it produce such an essential distinction as the logical construction of language? Why does one tribe worry about distinguishing all the nuances of verb tense, while another (such as the Slavic) almost entirely ignores this, but focuses attention on the quality of action [i.e., perfective or imperfective]? One uses the verb *to have* as an auxiliary means of conjugation, while the other uses the verb *to be*, etc. Comparative philology could provide a basis for the comparative psychology of tribes if one could read into grammatical differences the difference in psychological processes and worldviews from which they originated.

If the ethnographic period is a time of gathering and building up reserves for future activity, then the period of civilization is a time of spending. Spending is a useful, salutary goal, the very reason for accumulating, but it is still spending; and however great the reserve of strength, it cannot avoid growing scarcer and eventually exhausting itself, all the more so in the time leading up to the birth of civilization, which then soon runs its course. Each peculiarity formed in the course of the ethnographic period and revealed in the period of civilization must certainly reach its limit, beyond which it cannot go, or at least from which point further forward movement slows, limited to particular gains or refinements. Then comes stagnation, because progress stops; endless progress or development in one or another direction (not to mention in all directions at once) is obviously impossible. Really, how could a finite existence, such as a human's, endlessly develop and perfect itself, without at the same time changing its nature—that is, eventually becoming no longer human? I know that to those who think events from the *Thousand and One Arabian Nights* or Ovid's *Metamorphosis* already occurred once with the apes (which, no match for the onslaught of progress, were turned into people), and that humans after all are nothing more than a perfected fungus or protozoan, it does not seem strange for the human form, which is hard to improve upon, to be changed as if by its own volition into something even better.[16] But I draw

---

[16] Darwinism clashed with Danilevskii's scientific outlook, shaped by both Humboldt and Karl Ernst von Baer. Anti-Darwinism preoccupied him in his later life, but the

the conclusion that whatever is based on a false foundation (whether in history or zoology) leads to a false conclusion, and among the greatest falsehoods ever to enter the human mind is the idea of endless development and endless progress. No one can say whether Cuvier had a sharper mind than Aristotle; whether Laplace[17] was more insightful than Archimedes; whether Kant[18] was a better thinker than Plato; whether Frederick the Great and Napoleon I had a better grasp of military tactics and strategy than Hannibal and Caesar; still less can anyone say whether Canova and Thorvaldsen[19] understood beauty better than Phidias or Praxiteles.[20] But without a doubt the mass of scientific material and the complexity of international matters of war and peace have become immeasurably greater, so that for the academic to solve his problem or for the state official to govern costs much more time and effort now than it did back then. While Aristotle could successfully study zoology, botany, physics, logic, metaphysics, politics, and aesthetics, Cuvier could only study zoology, and this science had already become too complicated for all of its branches to be mastered by any one person. Therefore to the extent that the scope of academic inquiry has narrowed, discoveries must become more and more detailed. They try to alleviate this by the division of labor and the systematic combination of forces of separate individuals: by means of academic societies, conferences, and congresses, etc. But this artificial combination, well suited for the factory and having some use for scientific relations, is no substitute however for the natural accumulation of multifaceted materials in the mind of one person. Thus complexity, inseparable from advancement, limits material progress in those branches of human authority (or human endeavor in general) to which over time much attention and effort has been devoted. To keep forward movement from ceasing in the life of all humanity, once it has reached a certain point of improvement in one direction it must begin a new point of departure and go by another path; that is, it takes other psychological peculiarities, or another cast of mind, will, and emotions to take up the pursuit, which only peoples of another cultural-historical type possess.

---

lengthy treatise he envisioned was left unfinished at his death. See Linda Gerstein, *Nikolai Strakhov*, 155–162. On Darwin's reception in Russia generally, see Daniel P. Todes, *Darwin Without Malthus* (New York: Oxford University Press, 1989).

[17] Pierre-Simon Laplace (1749–1827): French mathematician and astronomer.

[18] Immanuel Kant (1724–1804): German philosopher, famous for his synthesis of rationalism and empiricism.

[19] Antonio Canova (1757–1822): Italian sculptor famed for his Neoclassical marble nudes. Bertel Thorvaldsen (1770–1844): Danish Neoclassical sculptor of heroic reliefs, statues, and busts, frequently compared to Canova.

[20] Phidias (5th century BCE): Regarded as one of the best sculptors of Classical Greece. Praxiteles (4th century BCE): Famed Classic Greek sculptor, first of his era to depict a full-size female nude, the Aphrodite of Cnidus.

As we said above, progress consists not of everything going in one direction (if that were the case, it would soon cease), but of pursuing the whole realm of humanity's historical activity, in all directions. Therefore no one civilization can boast of being the highest point of development in all fields compared to its predecessors and contemporaries. So in regard to the idea of beauty, one might say the Greek world reached the limits of perfection, and modern European civilization has not produced anything to compare to, not to mention eclipse, Greek achievements in the plastic arts, which can be called the equal of nature itself as the fullest and best interpretation of it. Greek art became the property of all humanity, the heritage of subsequent civilizations, but only this: a heritage which they can enjoy and take pleasure in, which they can understand but cannot acquire anew as the Greeks acquired it, but can only take further in that direction. Thus the people of the European cultural type went in another direction by the path of analytical investigation into nature and created the natural sciences, the like of which no other civilization had ever produced. Of course the spiritual gifts of the peoples of each type are not so limited as to pursue only one aspect of life—the Greeks to achieve only the elegant and beautiful, and the Europeans only positive knowledge. The Greeks accomplished much in the sciences, even bringing forward one genius, Aristotle, who was the harbinger in the Greek world of the direction Europe would take. Likewise the Europeans did much in art, and even if they did not go further, they did broaden its domain. In the realm of pure beauty—that is, in beauty of form and full harmony of formal composition—the peoples of the Germanic-Roman world of course never produced anything like the poems of Homer,[21] the statues of Phidias, or the tragedies of Sophocles,[22] even though they went deeper into psychological analysis in the depiction of characters, and in rendering the passions in paintings, though not without violating the harmony of forms. Where they intended to follow in the footsteps of the ancients, as in French pseudo-classical tragedy, they produced only caricatures. Likewise, the Semitic tribes produced the highest religious ideas. I would not think of denying that the Jews received supernatural revelation in this case, since only the Semitic tribes (no doubt according to the peculiarities of their psychological nature) could accept and preserve their belief in the truth of monotheism. The same also applies to the more personal realms. The system of civil law produced by Roman life is the model unsurpassed to this day. There is also nothing like the great political edifice created by the smallish Roman people which, sacrificing all it bore in its soul to the ideal of the eternal state, was able to graft onto itself completely foreign nationalities and force them to worship its idols and

---

[21] Homer (dates uncertain): Traditional author of ancient Greek epic poems *The Iliad* and *The Odyssey*, attributed to the eighth century BCE.

[22] Sophocles (5th century BCE): Ancient Greek tragedian, most famous for *Oedipus Rex* and *Antigone*.

even take them as their own. Rome is often compared to England in this regard, but nothing could be less apt. England could not even force its own colonies settled by English people to share its sense of state greatness, not to mention graft this feeling onto other nationalities. I say this not as a reproach: on its merits as much as its faults, England is another story altogether. France comes closer to this Roman spirit, although on a much smaller scale; the desire to imitate it fully on a greater scale (in the time of Charlemagne, as well as Louis XIV and Napoleon) again produced the same kind of caricatures ending in complete fiascoes.

This duality in the life of cultural-historical tribes produced over a long period of formation—unconsciously acquiring material and laying foundations of future activity, then in a comparatively short developmental or active period of expending these reserves in the creation of civilization—has an intermediate stage when the peoples prepare the ground for their activity, so to speak. They build a state and preserve its political independence, without which, as we have seen, civilization can neither begin, nor develop, nor strengthen. The move from the ethnographic to the state phase, as from the state phase to the civilization or cultural phase, depends on a stimulus or series of stimuli from external events, producing and supporting a people's activity in a certain direction. So the Dorian invasion[23] served to begin the formation of the Greek state, while an acquaintance with Eastern wisdom and even more so the Persian Wars,[24] which exerted the spirit of the people, mark Greece's entrance into the civilizational period. The founding of the ancient Italian state and the struggle that gave supremacy to Rome are not known to us, but the rule of the aristocratic patricians over the plebeians characterized the state period of Rome; its Punic Wars[25] and acquaintance with Greece, arousing the national spirit, led Rome into the civilizational period. The German peoples' clashes with Rome brought the Germans out of their ethnographic existence; the increase of their acquaintance with Greco-Roman civilization through Byzantine emigrants, naval exploration, and early inventions opened up the period of civilization. The struggle with Canaanite peoples[26] led the Jews to construct a state; the divided kingdoms and conflicting cul-

---

[23] Dorian invasion: A notional migration of early Greeks, known in legend as the "Heracleidae" or descendants of Heracles/Hercules, into lands of Mycenean Greek civilization, sometimes held as the cause of its collapse and the ensuing "Dark Ages" of Ancient Greece, 1200–900 BCE.

[24] Persian Wars: The Greek city-states fought repeatedly with the Achaemenid Empire of Persia (499–449 BCE).

[25] Punic Wars: Rome's three wars against Carthage, its rival in North Africa (264–146 BCE).

[26] After the Exodus and nomadic wilderness period, the Israelites fought to claim the land of Canaan, promised to them by God, from its inhabitants.

tural principles of Assyria, Babylonia, and Phoenicia[27] stimulated the development of Israel's prophetic civilization. India's state began with the struggle between invading Aryans and local natives.[28] The civilizational period of India appears to begin with the Buddhist movement.[29] Of course it should not be expected that this was accomplished in some correct form according to a certain scheme. Phenomena become intertwined and increasingly complex; often, complementary phenomena of one kind or another are separated by long intervals of time, and phenomena of one period continue to operate in the next. And not all cultural types manage to complete all phases of this development; either they are destroyed by external storms, or their stores of strength are insufficient, or their endeavors are too narrow for full development. Iran is one such cultural type, prompted to take on state form as a consequence of struggles with Caspian tribes but never crossing to the level of civilization. This was because on the one hand, in the greatest period of its state under Cyrus and Darius,[30] it lost its distinctive character by incorporating the ancient Semitic civilizations of Assyria, Babylonia, and Phoenicia (which had the same harmful influence on it that Greece had on Rome, without the redeeming aspects of the latter case). And also, on the other hand, the repeatedly revived state of Iran was subsequently destroyed by the Macedonians, Arabs, and Mongols. Concerning the history of ancient cultural types, the record is so fragmentary and incomplete that we have lost all sense of its events. However, judging by the history of certain cultural-historical types, one may determine how common a characteristic of the state period of development was the relative loss of their original tribal independence (their tribal will, in one form or another), and how common a characteristic of the civilizational period was the desire to liberate themselves from this subjugation and replace the lost ancient tribal will with true freedom (a desire which

---

[27] After Solomon's reign, Israel divided into the Northern Kingdom (Israel) and the Southern Kingdom (Judah). In the eighth century BCE, Assyria conquered and forced the ten tribes of Israel into exile, with no official return, hence the "lost tribes of Israel"; in the sixth century BCE, the Babylonian empire exiled the people of Judah (the Babylonian Captivity), who were permitted to return when Persia defeated Babylon. Phoenicians are the biblical Philistines, Israel's opponents in frequent local clashes.

[28] Aryan invasions: A contested theory of migrations of Aryan linguistic groups into the Indus River valley in the middle to late Bronze Age, supported by linguistic but not by archaeological evidence.

[29] Buddhist movement: Buddhism originated in India during the fifth century BCE and rose to prominence by the third century BCE, when the Mauryan emperor Ashoka the Great (r. 273–232 BCE) converted and promoted the faith.

[30] Cyrus II, "the Great" (6th century BCE): Persian ruler, founder of the Achaemenid Empire, conqueror of the Neo-Babylonian Empire, who returned the Jews to Palestine, ending their Babylonian exile. Darius I, "the Great" (550–486 BCE), ruled at the peak of the Achaemenid Empire; his invasion of Greece (the first of the Persian Wars) was famously repulsed at the Battle of Marathon in 490 BCE.

was never once attained, however). For the present I will limit myself to this brief summary, while proposing to develop these thoughts later on. But now I turn to the matter of sorting out the prevailing opinions about the relationship of the national [*natsional'noe*] to the universal.

Above I tried to show that a correct grouping of historical phenomena, corresponding to the laws of natural systems, leads us to the conclusion that the development of humanity has proceeded by means of none other than distinct cultural-historical types corresponding to the great tribes—that is, by means of distinct national groups. What remains to be shown, is that it could not proceed by any other way.

∝ 6 ∽
How What Is National Relates to What Is Universally Human

$$a + b > a$$
— from simple algebra

Usually the relationship of the national to the universal is presented as the opposition of the contingent (basic, narrow, and limited) to the boundless and free, like a cocoon or shrouding chrysalis that one must break through to enter the light, or like a line of courtyards and fenced enclosures surrounding a broad square, that can only be entered by breaking through these partitions. The universal genius is considered someone who manages by the force of his own spirit to break free from nationality, and bring himself and his contemporaries (in whatever field of activity) into the sphere of the universal. The civilizational process of national development consists precisely of the gradual rejection of national contingency and limitation, to gain entry into the realm of vital universality. So the contribution of Peter the Great was precisely that he brought us out of the captivity of national limitation and ushered this child of humanity into freedom, or at least showed it the way. This idea developed among us in the 1830s and 1840s, up to the literary pogrom of 1848.[1] Its main representatives and champions were Belinskii and Granovskii;[2] its followers were the so-called Westernizers, which included almost all intellectuals and merely educated people of that time; its organs were *Otechestvennye zapiski* and *Sovremennik*;[3] its inspirations were German philosophy and French socialism; its only opponents were the outnumbered Slavophiles,

---

[1] In response to the Revolutions of 1848 cropping up across Europe, Tsar Nicholas I launched an aggressive crackdown on all forms of apparent subversion within Russia, including debates of political and social questions. Danilevskii himself was imprisoned and exiled for his participation in the Petrashevskii circle, even though technically cleared of wrongdoing. Rigid censorship, for both Slavophiles and Westernizers alike, remained in place until the 1860s.

[2] Vissarion Grigorievich Belinskii (1811–48): Russian literary critic championing "social literature," or fiction exploring social problems. Timofei Nikolaevich Granovskii (1813–55): Moscow University lecturer on medieval European history, proponent of Western ideas and values.

[3] *Otechestvennye zapiski* (Notes of the Fatherland) and *Sovremennik* (The Contemporary): Literary journals popular with the Russian intelligentsia. *Sovremennik* became more radical in the 1850s and 1860s, until shut down by the state in 1866, after which *Otechestvennye zapiski* continued that line, until shuttered in 1884.

standing alone, the objects of laughter and scorn. This was completely understandable. "National" meant not something general, but something specifically Russian-national, so poor and insignificant, especially if seen from a foreign point of view. And how could people not take a foreign point of view,
when their whole education was drawn from foreign sources? It took more
than the normal degree of courage, independence, and sagacity to see in the
poor, beggarly guise of Russia and Slavdom a hidden unique treasure, and to
say to Russia:

> *Revive the past in your heart,*
> *And from its hidden depths*
> *Seek out the spirit of life!*[4]

"Universal" referred to what had developed so broadly in the West,
namely the European, or the Germanic-Roman, in contrast to what was narrowly Russian. There were two reasons for confusing the European for the
universal. First, the universal was considered neither German nor French (not
to mention English), which likewise bore the imprint of narrow nationalism,
but something transcending national limitations and seeming all-European.
Thus a generalization had been made, and from it followed a universaliza-
tion. Besides, it was essentially this already, and had not only spread everywhere superficially, but must inevitably be completed by means of steamship,
railroad, telegraph, the press, free trade, and so on. Here it was not understood that France, England, and Germany were individual political entities,
but Europe as a whole was always a single cultural entity; that therefore there
could be no further outbreak of national divisiveness; and that Germanic-
Roman civilization had always been the common property of all the tribes,
and so it would remain. Secondly, and more importantly, the recent products
of European civilization (German philosophy and French socialism, starting
with the Declaration of the Rights of Man)[5] had broken the fetters of nationalism, even all-European nationalism, and in both scientific theory and social
policy aspired to concern themselves with nothing less than the most-univer-
sally-human (*naiobshchechelovechneishee*). German philosophy, disdaining everything contingent and relative, set out to wrestle with the very Absolute and
seemed to overcome it. In the same way socialism intended to uncover the
general forms of society, also absolute in their own way, capable of bringing
happiness to all humanity regardless of time, place, or tribe. In a certain frame
of mind this passion for the universal was understandable. The doctrine of
the Slavophiles in its own way was colored by the humanities; it had to be,

---

[4] From A. S. Khomiakov's 1840 poem "Rossii" (To Russia).

[5] Declaration of the Rights of Man and Citizen: A body of resolutions adopted in 1789
by the National Constituent Assembly as precursor to writing a constitution for
France, emphasizing individual rights and accountable government.

since it too had dual sources: German philosophy, which it held to more loosely within a broader context than its opponents; and the study of the origins of Russian and Slavic life in its religion, history, poetics, and customs. If it emphasized the necessity of distinct national development, it was partly from understanding the great merit of Slavic principles, and from seeing through their long development the one-sidedness and irreconcilable contradiction of European principles. It considered that the Slavs were destined to complete a universal task, and that their predecessors had simply not yet managed it. Such a [universal] task, however, did not exist—at least in the sense that it might at some point be concretely completed, that sometime, some cultural-historical group would achieve this for itself and the rest of humanity. The task of humanity, however, consists solely of the manifestation in various times and in various tribes of all facets and peculiar tendencies that reside virtually (in possibility, *in potentia*) in the idea of humanity. If, when humanity completes its path (or more correctly, all its paths), someone were capable of surveying all that has occurred and all the multifaceted types of development in all their phases, that person could assemble an understanding of the idea which humanity existed to realize—and thus complete the task of humanity. But this "completion" would only be accomplished in the ideal realm, not something accomplished in reality. What form of plant completely fulfills the pattern for the idea, or the task if you will, of the plant kingdom? The palm, cypress, oak, laurel, or rose? Obviously, such forms do not fit the bill; mosses reveal a certain side of plant life better than more developed forms. The idea of plants, fully realized, consists only of the complete diversity of all possible types and varieties of plants at all levels of complexity and development. It can only be grasped in the ideal, not accomplished in reality. The animal kingdom is no different. Humans seem to be the highest realization of the animal idea. Not at all! The human as an animal in many respects ranks below other animals. Freedom of movement is one aspect of the animal idea, but humans move less freely than fish in water, birds in air, horses, deer, or dogs on land, monkeys or squirrels in trees, and so on. Despite the artificial means they have created, such as steam power, locomotives, hot air balloons, etc., they are still inferior. The ability to digest foreign matter within one's body is another aspect, and in this regard the digestive organs of horses and cows are much better developed, since they can chemically extract necessary nutrients from matter so non-nourishing (or so poor in these nutrients) as grass. The ability to survey the surrounding world is another aspect, but humans see poorly compared to eagles and falcons, which can see telescopically up close and far away. A dog's sense of smell far exceeds a human's; a bat's hearing or sensitivity of touch is like a sixth sense, apprising them of the presence of things they neither touch nor see. The distinction of humans as animals consists solely of the fact that they are much less animal than all other animals and thus able to be indwelled with a spirit, which further subdues residual animal traits. Thus even the animal idea is fully realized not in one form or another, but in all the variety and levels of complexity in the animal kingdom. Take an individual person: How well has he developed all aspects of his nature? When did one develop all [human] characteristics to the fullest? Never. In some regards he may be, so to speak, a full human only at maturity; in others, only as a youth; in another, such as experience, only at a ripe old age; in another, such as memory, in childhood. But when we say a complete person, we mean one who reveals the full variety of human nature in all phases of its development. Thus even the idea of a person can be understood only by combining all these moments of his development; but such a thing cannot exist at any moment in reality. There is, however, the essential differ- ence that a person remains conscious of his individuality while going through each stage; thus this could be considered the real achievement of that ideal comprehension to fulfill the task. But if that person fulfills his task in one phase (or at one moment) of his existence, this partial realization—stemming from his single consciousness—could still be considered only a consolation for his inability to bring together all moments of his life completely. Neither humanity as a collective whole, nor any individual human, can have con- sciousness of all humanity. Therefore, what good would it do to fulfill the task of humanity completely at one or another moment of its history? What would be the point of a civilization that itself embodied (if such were possi- ble) all separate aspects revealed by various cultural-historical types up to that time—Europe's mastery of the positive sciences; ancient Greece's achievements in the realm of higher ideas; the vital religious feelings and con- sciousness of the Jews and the first Christian centuries; India's fertile imagina- tion; China's prosaic striving for the practical and functional; the greatness of the Roman state; and so on—all developed to their highest degree, with the addition of the ideal social structure? What sense could be made of a few cen- turies or even a millennium of an ongoing golden age, in comparison with all the millennia that passed before? To acquire that sense, one has to accept [Pierre] Leroux, *On Humanity* [*De l'humanité*, 1840] or [Maximilian] Perty, *Mystical Phenomena in Human Nature* [*Die mystischen Erscheinungen in der menschlichen Natur*, 1861], on the existence of some kind of demiurge or world spirit that is conscious of the whole collective life of humanity as its own indi- vidual life.[6] Otherwise all the efforts of the separate civilizations, each reveal- ing a certain side of the idea of humanity (though not all equally significant) would turn out not as vital contributions to the common treasury, but only a pitiful pile of lumber not worthy of special attention; childish attempts that

---

[6] Pierre Leroux (1797–1871): French socialist philosopher, advocate of pantheism. He was elected to the National Assembly in 1849, but forced to flee France after Louis Napoleon seized power in 1851. Josef Anton Maximilian Perty (1804–84): German entomologist and professor of natural history at the University of Bern, a critic of Darwinism. The work cited here attempted to treat the magical, spiritual, and divine realms as areas for scientific observation and scrutiny.

exhausted their potential, and ceased to matter. The individual person can fulfill his task, or realize his destiny, because he is immortal and was destined to do so from above, regardless of time, place, or tribe; but that destiny lies beyond the boundaries of this world. For the collective, ultimate existence of humanity there is no other purpose than the expression of the full diversity of living activity in all times and places (that is, in all peoples), the whole spectrum of often incompatible human potential, as much for a single person as for a cultural-historical type.

No one believes, or at least not many believe, that German philosophy actually brought the Absolute down into human consciousness, or that French socialism discovered the transcendental formula to solve all social problems. But despite this, Europe is still mistaken for all humanity and supposedly has transcended the narrow-national sphere to the universally-human sphere. I attribute this to confusing the notion of a cultural type's levels of civilizational development for a notion of universal development based on the assumption that civilization always aspires to overcome peculiar forms of dependence on tribal will in the transition of peoples in a cultural type from the ethnographic to the governmental form of existence, and to replace them with certain forms of freedom. These forms of dependence are considered national, but the forms of freedom are considered human (following an ahistorical view that confuses levels of development for patterns or blueprints, and posits a new history in which the civilizational stage of Germanic-Roman peoples becomes the highest level of development of all humanity); however, their forms of development and corresponding forms of freedom are both equally national and mutually dependent. For example, the religious despotism of Roman Catholicism is considered the national heritage of European peoples, but the anarchistic freedom of Protestantism is considered the universally human form of Christianity. Or religious intolerance and church interference in matters of state, society, and family relations are considered narrow-national behaviors, corresponding to medieval times or the national stage in the life of European peoples, while religious indifference and state atheism (with civil marriage and other things) are considered the universally human way. Monarchical feudalism is a German-national phenomenon, but the English form of constitutionalism is the universal model. The same kind of opposition is set between feudal serfdom and unbounded personal economic freedom—that is, collective slavery on one hand and the modern proletariat on the other—between guilds and corporations [in the protective, regulatory sense], and the *laissez faire* economy; between mercantilism and colonial exploitation on the one hand, and free trade on the other. For whatever reason, the European-national has been taken for the universally human. But we must examine whether it is possible in general to juxtapose the national with the universal.

The whole of humanity and a certain people (a nation or tribe) relate to each other like the genus to the species; thus the relations between them must be analogous. Take some well-known examples: the raspberry from the plant kingdom, and cats from the animal kingdom. I do not mean to imply an unflattering comparison for humans, but to explain the relation of the genus to the species by example. The genus consists of everything common to all species. The raspberry is characterized by small flowers resembling a small rose with a calyx of five sepals (not ten, as in strawberries), with fruit composed of small individual berries or simply stony little balls stuck together and set like a cap on the convex-semicircular end of the stem. The cat is characterized by a round head and blunt snout, a distinctive shape, an array of numerous teeth, five-toed forepaws and four-toed paws on hind legs, ending in claws. Obviously neither raspberries nor cats can we fully understand at the genus level. It is something abstract, incomplete; to have actual existence and take familiar forms, it must be further elaborated. The flower and fruit of a certain form must have a certain color, as well as certain leaves and stalks, and all of it must be on a certain bush or cane. By elaborating on the generic characteristics of the raspberry we get more distinct conceptions: the cultivated raspberry, blackberry, cloudberry, arctic raspberry, and so on, all pertaining to the genus raspberry [or *Rubus*]. In the same way, in addition to the cat's distinctive line of teeth, paws, and snout must be added various body sizes, various tail lengths, the presence [or absence] of a mane, round or slitted pupils, ears with or without tassels at the ends, single-colored, bi-colored, or multicolored coats, and so on, that distinguish the forms of lion, tiger, panther, lynx, housecat, and so on, which all belong to the genus cat.[7] Genus understood in this way is only an abstraction, arrived at by excluding all that is peculiar to species. It is the sum of all characteristics of all species, minus everything not common to all, and thus genus is something impossible in reality. By its incompleteness it is something poorer than each species individually, which adds the peculiar to what is generic, although the peculiar is less essential, less important than what is common.

But we can understand the genus in another way. Namely that what is common within it must be joined with what is peculiar, not all possible peculiarities, but only those peculiarities that correspond to it. Common raspberry features must be joined with peculiar plant forms: with wide round simple leaves, white flowers, and orange fruit to form cloudberries; or with bushy vegetation, compound five-bladed leaves, and black fruit to form blackberries. But they cannot be joined with woody vegetation, long pointed leaves, yellow flowers, white fruit, etc. In the same way, common cat features are joined with medium height, a smooth single-colored coat of coarse, dense fur, a tail ending in a clump, a mane, and round pupils to form a lion; or with short height, a soft coat, and longitudinally slitted pupils to form a housecat;

---

[7] This analogy reflects the state of nineteenth-century biological taxonomy. "Cat" is no longer a genus, but the family *Felidae* with over a dozen living, and several extinct, genera (plural of genus) of cats.

but cannot be joined with a hair tail like a horse's, a bushy tail like a squirrel's, flapping ears like an elephant's, a deer's diametrically-opposed pupils, etc. Thus each generic conception includes, in addition to the aggregate of abstract characteristics, the ability to take only certain forms in reality. This is theoretically indefinable; it can only be empirically validated. Combining this capability lying in the essence, or the idea, of the genus, with the abstract conception of the genus, means that the genus is made up not only of what is common to all its species, but of what is common plus all its possible manifestations. In this sense genus is not an abstraction, but corresponds to something actual, existing not in one place or time but in various places and times simultaneously. The raspberry genus is not what is *common* between the cultivated raspberry, the blackberry, stone berry, cloudberry, arctic raspberry, etc. but is the aggregate of all of these types. The cat genus is not the abstract *common* features of lions, tigers, panthers, lynxes, and housecats, but all of them collectively. In the first sense, genus is only *generic,* and in this sense is something less than any individual species; but in the second sense, genus is *all-specific,* and thus broader and higher than any particular species. To avoid misunderstanding, it is necessary to add that the genus relates to species independently of any genetic conception we bring to the idea of species: that is, independently of whether we conceive of species as something genetically original, spontaneously created, or evolved and differentiated over the course of time under the influence of external circumstances. Since we have been discussing actual genera and species in a natural-historical context, it fully applies to breeding or variation (in which there is no genetic distinctiveness) in regards to species. Our understanding of horses, in a non-systematic or scientific sense, is the same kind of abstraction as the zoological notion of the cat, inadequate as a full representation of reality because any given horse belongs to one breed or another. In fact there is never a *basic horse* (we have no idea what it would look like), but only breeds like Arabian, or the light, fast, lean English horses, or massive German draft horses, or unstately but tireless nags, etc.

We now apply these analogies to the relationship between peoples (nations [*natsii*] or tribes) and humanity. A tribe does not have to be a genetically unique entity, but may evolve over the course of millennia into a group not just with a characteristic visual appearance but with a unique mental framework. This makes humanity in the abstract much broader than its other meaning, as it essentially is in the conception of peoples and tribes as species, in relation to humanity as the genus. Thus the conception of the universally human not only is nothing real, but is actually narrower and lower than the conception of the tribal or national, since the latter necessarily includes the former and to that adds something special and additional. And this must be protected and cultivated, so that the generic (in its second, true meaning) conception of humanity could realize its full capacity for variety and richness. Thus not only does the *universally human* not exist in reality, but to wish for it means to be satisfied with the generic level, colorless unoriginality, or simply a nonexistent, incomplete form. The *all-human* [*vsechelovecheskoe*] is another matter, which must be distinguished from the *inter-human* [*obshchechelove-cheskoe*]: it is without a doubt higher than anything narrowly human, or national. But this consists only of the aggregate of everything national, existing in all places and times. It is non-coincident and not realized within one or another nationality; it can only exist in multiple places and multiple times. The universal genius is not the one who expresses in any given sphere of activity something generically human, devoid of anything distinctively national (such a person would indeed be a genius, but a vulgarity in the fullest sense of the word), but rather the one who fully expresses something above the generically human and its full national peculiarity, by adding to it still other angles or facets belonging to other nationalities, from acquiring some level of proximity to and understanding of them, although never so much as their own people. The English may well laugh at Germans pretending to have a better understanding of Shakespeare than they do, as will the Greeks about such claims regarding Homer or Sophocles. There are no thinkers so Baconian as the English, and none so Hegelian as the Germans.[8] [Yet] such richly gifted thinkers would be correctly called not just inter-human geniuses but all-human geniuses, although strictly speaking there was only one All-human — and He was God.[9]

So to turn to the comparison I made at the beginning of this chapter, it turns out that the relationship of the national to the universal does not at all resemble crowded courtyards or enclosures surrounding a broad square, but can be compared to intersecting streets, forming at their intersection a square, which is no more than a part of each street and belongs equally to all of them, but is therefore narrower and less than each of them individually. In order to form a city, which is all humanity in our comparison, there is nothing to do but finish building your own street according to your own plan, and not crowd into the common square or try to extend some other street (the character and building plan of which is known only to its original residents, who

---

[8] Referring to the philosophies of Francis Bacon (1561–1626), emphasizing empirical observation, inductive reasoning, and scientific inventiveness; and of Georg Wilhelm Friedrich Hegel (1770–1831), regarding all being as an integrated whole, from the individual to the absolute, in an ideal unity of mind, spirit, and the universe unfolding through history.

[9] Danilevskii is referring to Jesus Christ, emphasizing his dual nature as fully divine and fully human. The Council of Chalcedon, in 451, established the doctrine that both natures were equal and separate, joined by "hypostatic union" as expressed in the doctrine of the Trinity, one God in three persons. Oriental Orthodox Churches (in Armenia, Syria, Egypt, and Ethiopia) rejected the Council of Chalcedon, insisting that Christ had only one nature, that was either divine only, or both human and divine. See chap. 8, n. 18.

have all they need to keep building). Thus the city will not lack for diversity and growth in all directions.

We now apply everything said in this and the two preceding chapters to the relations of Russia, or more precisely, all Slavdom (of which Russia is only the representative) with Europe.

An all-human civilization does not and cannot exist, because it would only be this impossible and undesirable incompleteness. Some all-human civilization one might wish to join does not and cannot exist also because it is an unattainable ideal or, to put it differently, an ideal attainable only by the consecutive or concurrent development of all cultural-historical types, whose self-directed activity unfolds the historical life of humanity in the past, present, and future. Cultural-historical types correspond to the great linguistic-ethnographic families or tribes of humanity. Seven of these tribes or families of peoples pertain to the Aryan race. Five of them produced more or less complete, totally independent civilizations; the sixth, the Celtic, lacking political independence and still in its ethnographic period of existence, does not constitute a distinct cultural historical type and does not have its own civilization, but became ethnographic material for the Roman [civilization] and later, along with the remnants of its collapse, for the European cultural-historical types and the civilization produced by them. The Slavic tribe is the seventh of these Aryan families of peoples. The greater part of the Slavs (no less, if no more, than two-thirds) constitute a politically independent whole—the Great Russian Empire. The remaining Slavs, while not being an independent political entity, have borne all the storms that have befallen them, and which—the German, the Hungarian, and the Turkish—continue to this day. But they have not lost their distinctiveness, preserving the language, morals, and (for the most part) the original form of Christianity they received—Orthodoxy. Proto-national and all-Slavic consciousness was awakened among the Turkish[-ruled] and the Austrian[-ruled] Slavs, which only lack favorable circumstances to attain political independence. Thus by all historical analogies the Slavs, like their Aryan brothers further along the path of development, can and must form their own distinct civilization. "Slavdom" is a term of the same sort as Hellenism, Latinism, Europeanism, and is the cultural-historical type in which Russia, Czechia, Serbia, and Bulgaria are analogous to France, England, Germany, and Spain within Europe; or Athens, Sparta and Thebes within Greece. Furthermore world history says that if there is no such thing as Slavdom, then its whole thousand-year ethnographic preparation, the centuries of its national-state existence and struggle, and all its political might achieved by so many sacrifices by certain Slavic peoples is just a soap bubble, a form without contents, a pointless existence, a sprout killed by frost, since civilization is not transferred (in the only true and meaningful sense of the word) from people of one cultural-historical type to another. If for external and internal reasons they are not capable of producing a distinct civilization—that is, developing to the level of a cultural-historical type, of a vital and productive organ of humanity—then there is nothing left for them to do but dissipate and dissolve into ethnographic material, the means for foreign ends; lose their formation or organizing principle; and take on nobler foreign graftings to nourish by their labors, and then their flesh and blood. And the sooner the better. What is the point of supporting what is useless, or in any case, doomed to perdition? Above were given examples of civilization supposedly transmitted from one cultural-historical type to the peoples of another (examples of the so-called *Kulturträger*[10] and the results of these frequently repeated attempts) from the Greek, Roman, and German worlds. There is also no lack of such examples in the relations of the Germanic peoples with the Slavic, which are especially instructive for us.

The principles of the Germanic-Roman type were imposed more or less by force upon the Poles and Czechs. And what did Czech and Polish civilization produce? The form so uncharacteristic of the Slavic soul in which European peoples assimilated Christianity—Catholicism, especially in Poland (where, due to the circumstances, it was assimilated most sincerely) it became a complete caricature and had the most corrosive effect, incomparably more harmful than in Spain itself (where despite its most extreme results, Catholicism did not distort the national character). The distortion of Slavic democratism by German aristocratism and chivalry produced *szlachtists*.[11] Despite their long influence, European science and art did not take root on Polish soil enough to make Poland a distinctive contributor in this regard. The Czechs fortunately were not so passive toward principles foreign to their national character and tried to throw off their yoke; and only these independent Czech impulses, these "anti-German, anti-European" feats, as Europe considered and considers them (namely, the Orthodox manner of religious reform, and the resulting struggle with Europe in the time of Hus and Žižka,[12] and the Pan-Slavist movement begun by them in the current [i.e., the nineteenth] century) can and must be considered world-historical feats of the Czech people, their legacy to posterity. Following the European or Germanic-Roman spirit and direction, the Czechs were as fruitless as the Poles. Is it necessary to add that Russia would be too? Peter the Great wanted to graft European civilization onto the wild Russian rootstock, in that mysterious sense of the word "graft" that implies changing the very nature of the rootstock. But no matter what you think, even though Peter himself thought so, this did not change the essence of things: the graft remained a graft, and did not achieve

---

[10] German: "Culture-bearer."

[11] From *szlachta* (Polish aristocracy).

[12] Jan Hus (c. 1369–1415): Bohemian religious reformer, excommunicated and martyred. Jan Žižka (c. 1360–1424): Follower of Hus, Bohemian general in the Hussite Wars, who defeated Western forces in 1422 to end the Second Anti-Hussite Crusade.

an Ovidian metamorphosis.[13] The people continued to preserve their distinctiveness; often it was necessary to prune off new wild shoots growing up beneath, so that the graft would not be choked out. But the results were obvious: from these operations, the original culture did not grow on the Russian soil, but neither did it assimilate the foreign, so the superficiality of elite society never penetrated deeper. The foreign element in this society produced mongrels of the most rotten sort: nihilism, absenteeism, Shedo-Ferrotism, separatism, bureaucratism, restricted democratism, and—the latest offshoot—this new-fangled aristocratism *a la Vest'*,[14] the most harmful "-ism" of all.

Thank God that at least the wild rootstock survived and preserved its vegetative force. Attaching foreign principles of a foreign civilization to the Slavic tribes generally and Russia specifically was just as unsuccessful as all other such attempts. But it was all the more inappropriate for lacking the justifications that could be claimed in other cases, such as the Hellenism of Alexandria. In that case, on the one hand was [Greece,] a well-endowed cultural-historical type that, due to weaknesses in political organization at the state level (too much effort spent cultivating the variety, too little concern for the unity and strength, of the culture), had decayed on its native soil, having failed to complete its development and bear the fruit of which it was capable; on the other hand, the Egyptian nationality onto which Hellenism was grafted had already completed its cycle, borne its own flower and fruit, and long since entered into stagnation and would inevitably descend to the ethnographic level of development. Therefore what was of no use for Egypt could be, and actually was, useful in a broader human sense. But why sacrifice the youth and distinctiveness of the Slavic tribes, which have potential for their own development and results, when European civilization moreover is in a completely different situation than that of the Greeks in the Macedonian era? It is strong from its own soil and can fulfill its own destiny upon it, with no need to take on a foreign parasite. Sacrificing it not only is too costly, but would be completely pointless as well.

And so, *for any Slav—a Russian, Czech, Serb, Croat, Slovene, Slovak, Bulgar (and I would like to add, Pole) following God and His Holy Church—the idea of Slavdom must be the highest idea above freedom, above science, above enlightenment, above any earthly good,* since not one of these can be attained without it, that is, without a spiritually, nationally, and politically independent and distinct Slavdom. In fact, all these other desirable goals will be necessary results of this independence and distinctiveness.

---

[13] A reference to the Latin mock-epic poem by Ovid (43 BCE–18 CE), recounting the history of the world in a series of stories emphasizing transformation, often with ironic results.

[14] *Vest'*: Reactionary newspaper published in St. Petersburg (1863–70), representing aristocratic opposition to the reforms of that era.

All the preceding elaboration of the question facing us has led to this conclusion. Of course it is nothing new to those who already subscribed to the so-called Slavophile idea. But putting myself in the place of the reader to whom this is an unfamiliar idea, the question arises: What will this new Slavic civilization be? Against the brilliant backdrop of European civilization, its rudiments are not so discernible to our bedazzled eyes. Does advanced science, with its wealth of practical results bringing nature under human dominion, really require fundamental reforms? Have those who achieved so much in the field of science for so long really grown tired and worn out, ready for some obscure newcomers to take over? If I have made myself clear to this point, then it seems to me such doubts should not trouble anyone. The peoples of each cultural-historical type do not labor in vain; the results of their work belong to all peoples reaching the civilizational period of their development, and this work will never be duplicated. But this activity is always one-sided and predominantly generates a certain kind of results. The development of positive science in the study of nature is the most evident result of the Germanic-Roman civilization and the fruit of the European cultural-historical type, in the same way as excellence in the arts and the realm of ideas were the main fruit of Greek civilization; law and political organization of the state were the fruit of the Roman civilization; and the development of the idea of the one true God is the fruit of the Jewish civilization. Thus it is not at all likely for the primary task of the Slavic cultural-historical type to be the further development of the analytical, positive science of nature. In the first place, experience shows that the European peoples have not yet exhausted their potential in the field of science, and better than any other people can continue the work they began and have conducted so long. In this the Slavic and all other peoples can only emulate them and be their assistants. In the second place, the necessity of a change in direction (to a new field of activity) for the continuation of progress constitutes the internal reason why new peoples must appear on the stage of history with a different mental framework—the peoples of a new, distinct cultural-historical type. This does not mean that the different civilizational type cannot achieve the same level of success as others in those fields, but such activity cannot be its main task.

Modern science is such a majestic phenomenon that it causes all other aspects of life somehow to lose their significance. Do not many people think of art as more of an amusement or diversion from something else one needs to do, a suitable pastime for slackers, but strictly speaking, unworthy of an age like ours, so well-endowed with practical sense? There is no need to mention what role this one-sided view relegates to religion. Religion reverts to nothing more than a superstition, suitable for eras of darkness and ignorance, not only superfluous in an age of enlightenment and progress but even an outright impediment to further development and achievement. All the inadequacies of the social order (or what appear to be such things) in the same way seem to be products of ignorance, and not the necessary consequence of the underlying conditions of historical development. Thus it seems as though they can be eliminated by the application of a social theory worked out by some scholar or utopian thinker. In such a view, of course, science (specifically a positive science of nature) can somehow swallow up the whole civilization and become a synonym for it. And what is more, everything that is not part of science is a drag, a burden, a dead weight that slows down the procession on the path of progress. The one-sidedness of such a view does not need to be demonstrated. Civilization is a much broader concept than just science, art, religion, political, civil, economic, or social development taken in isolation, because civilization includes all of these within itself. I state that even religion is a concept within a civilization. This is correct of course only in regard to states or human societies in general, not to individual persons for whom religion doubtlessly has incomparably greater significance than the other things we mean by the word "civilization," and is not contained by civilization, because its very essence transcends earthly boundaries. From this it follows that a civilization, or a cultural-historical type, can be considered not only new and original, but also having great significance in the general development of humanity, even if it produced nothing new or original in the field of positive science, but only followed the timeworn path. Rome is an example of a cultural-historical type that was not the lowest-ranking within humanity, even though it was almost fruitless in scientific pursuits. Although art and science (especially science) are a valuable heritage left behind by cultural-historical types, and although they constitute the most essential contributions to the common treasury of humanity, they do not however provide the basis of national life. In this regard religion (as the moral basis for all actions), and the political, civil, economic, and social structure have much greater significance. If to us Homer, Phidias, Praxiteles, Pindar,[15] Sophocles, Plato, and Aristotle are the essence of Hellenism and most interesting for having enlightened the life of Greece two thousand years ago, to the Greeks themselves that interest was primarily expressed for and concentrated upon Lycurgus, Solon, Themistocles, Pericles, Epaminondas, and Demosthenes,[16] who served the practical life of Greece or ruled over it. Science and art as products of the national life are more like the finer extractions of vegetative organisms (balsam, essential oils, or dye pigment) which give fragrance and shine to the flowers and fruits; or they are more like starch, supplies kept in reserve to

---

[15] Phidias and Praxiteles, see chap. 5, n. 20. Pindar (c. 522–443 BCE): Greek lyric poet, known for his lofty style; the best preserved of the major ancient Greek poets.

[16] Lycurgus (8th century BCE): Legendary founding lawgiver of Sparta. Solon (6th century BCE): Athenian statesman regarded as the founder of Athenian democracy. Themistocles: Fifth-century Athenian military populist statesman, hero of the second Persian War. Pericles and Epaminondas: See chap. 4, nn. 12 and 14. Demosthenes: Famed orator of fourth-century Athens.

nourish future growth, than the cells of leaves and trunk which hold the very origin of life and growth of the plant.

Thus, if we must not deny the existence of distinct cultural-historical types capable of important contributions to the life of humanity, even without scientific or artistic initiative, nevertheless we must not fail to mention that such a life is poor and one-sided, that in the eyes of posterity even mighty Rome must yield before not only the peoples of the Germanic-Roman type, for having surpassed Rome in absolute political power, but also the politically-insignificant Hellas [classical Greece]. Of course we could not rightly expect such a colorless future for the Slavic peoples. That they may have their art is not widely disputed, and it would be hard to do so when its beautiful beginnings in various fields are there for all to see. But what exactly is uniquely Slavic science? Is there a place for it, and is [such a thing as] national science possible in general? However out of date this question is (once serving as the pretext for a lively quarrel in our literature), I cannot let it pass without an investigation in this chapter, which covers the topic of how the national relates to the universal.

All the arguments I know against the possibility of science having a national character come down to the following three: 1) Truth is singular, and thus science, having the truth as its goal, is also singular. 2) Science is successive, and what is produced by a certain people at a certain time passes as a legacy to other times and other peoples, which can continue building science only on the prior foundation. This cannot be said (at least, not so strongly) of the arts, since any artistic production is a distinct whole and cannot be continued. The art of other ages and peoples advances the course of general progress, either by producing new technical methods or providing material to study, examples of embellishment conveying nature itself. Any true artist creates originally and, so to speak, begins anew. Shakespeare could write his tragedies even if Aeschylus[17] and Sophocles had not gone before him; but Newton is inconceivable without Euclid, Copernicus, and Kepler. 3) The common language of the poet and his fellow countrymen makes the artist dependent upon his audience, which explains the national character of literary production; in translation it always loses its beauty. Meanwhile language has no great significance in scientific matters; any language can be employed, so long as it is known to the majority of educated or academic people—even a dead language, such as Latin.

The two latter arguments attempt to explain why nationality, acknowledged by everyone in the arts, cannot pertain to science, and they certainly may have a point. But what they say about the influence of language infusing national character into artistic production only relates to poetry. Meanwhile the other forms of art—music, painting, sculpture, architecture—are em-

---

[17] Aeschylus (5th century BCE): Eleusinian playwright, considered the father of Greek tragedy.

ployed by all peoples as a universal language of sounds and forms, despite having a national character (in fact, the best works have this national character).

A great capacity for transmission and continuity is the inherent property of science, but this by no means contradicts the fact that each independently working people draws from its heritage (just as it draws from the data of its investigations into nature itself) what is especially relevant to its inclinations and capabilities, and transforms them into techniques and habits of thought to suit itself.

The first argument, that truth is singular and thus science is singular, is based on a complete misunderstanding. What is truth exactly? The simplest but at the same time most precise possible definition seems to me the following: *Truth is knowledge of what exists precisely as it exists.* This conveys two elements. An external element—not truth, but reality, which of course is independent not only of nationality, but of all things human in general; and an internal element—the reflection of that reality in our own consciousness. If this reflection is completely precise and wholly complete (that is, if not a single trait or nuance of reality is lost, overlooked, or added) then such a complete truth will of course bear no imprint of nationality or subjectivity. But such a reflection of reality in human consciousness is impossible, at least in the majority of cases, just as a reflection of an object in a mirror bears not the qualities of the reflected object, but of the reflecting mirror. Therefore all (or almost all) of our truths are either one-sided or contain an admixture of falsehood— or both at the same time. If that were not the case, then everyone's conception of well-known things would have to be identical. But they are different, in two ways. In the first, various lines of truth interest various people to varying degrees, so that each remains more or less indifferent toward some branches of knowledge (or categories of truth), while taking the deepest interest in other branches. In the second, the scholars pursuing those branches of knowledge have an equally adequate grasp of their subjects but take completely different views of them. For instance, Cuvier and Geoffroy Saint-Hilaire, or Cuvier and Oken[18] lived at the same time and studied the same branch of science, but had completely different views not only of the world in general, but of the specific topic of their pursuits, the animal kingdom, which, however, remained the same regardless of who investigated it—Cuvier, Geoffroy Saint-Hilaire, or Oken. But each of them added to it the reflection it had to have in his own consciousness, with a certain one-sided character and even certain subjective traits added to it. So now we ask: Were these peculiar habits of thought and methods of investigation all scattered haphazardly among all

---

[18] Cuvier, see chap. 4, n. 4. Étienne Geoffroy Saint-Hilaire (1772–1844): French naturalist and proto-evolutionist. Lorenz Oken (1779–1851): German naturalist, pioneer of animal classification according to evolutionary stages tied to sensory organs. The contrast with Cuvier implied here stems from Cuvier's rejection of evolutionary theory.

peoples, or can they be grouped by nationality, the same as moral behaviors and aesthetic sensibilities? Of the latter, there can hardly be any doubt; but if that is the case, then science must necessarily bear the imprint of nationality, in exactly the same way as do art, political and social life, indeed all human phenomena. Of course that does not mean that one or another scholar cannot stand closer (by his perspective, views, habits of thought, and research methods) to a foreign nationality than his own, not at all from imitativeness but simply according to the peculiarities of his mental nature. Accordingly Geoffroy Saint-Hilaire was more German than French, inclining toward the school of *Naturphilosophie*; Aristotle was more a European of modern times than an ancient Greek; but such examples always remain exceptions.

It can be inferred that a one-sided perspective, or an admixture of falsehood, is inherent in everything human, and constitutes precisely the realm of the national within science. This is partly the case, but not entirely. Truth is like the noble metals, which we can only extract by first alloying them with base metals. This admixture with base metal, of course, decreases their value; but do we not have to be reconciled with this, if admixture is the only way to acquire them; if in its pure form it is not to be had, and a certain kind of admixture is the precondition for the extraction of this precious metal? Does not the admixture itself in that case become valuable in our eyes as the tool, the condition, the *sine qua non* for the greatest success in the revelation of truth? It is true that in the course of time, from the variety of national perspectives (and more importantly, through that variety) these admixtures are refined and eliminated, leaving the pure noble metal of truth. However the role of nationality (that is, of certain individual peculiarities, grouped by nationalities) in science is not reduced or weakened by this, since science opens newer and newer horizons which require the same work, it cannot produce anything except by means of admixing individual, and thus also national, traits to the reflections of reality in the mirror of our consciousness.

But this is only one side of the subject. A peculiar mental framework characterizing each nationality (especially each cultural-historical type) is revealed not only in some subjective taint brought to any scientific truth discovered, but also (from a slightly different point of view) in what compels each people to look at a subject of scientific inquiry. Thus even the reflections of this inquiry in the soul of various peoples are not exactly identical, but each bears something that suits their respective one-sidedness. It is very strange that those who deny there is nationality in science because truth is singular will still admit that science is different things at different times. They have not given up the words *contemporary science* and *modern science*. If science has different eras according to what stage popular consciousness has reached, why can it not differ by place, according to the mental framework that distinguishes any people at all stages of its development? If we want to gain a complete, exact idea of some complex subject—for example, a mountain—it is not enough to climb higher and higher just to survey it from various heights; we must also go around to various sides. The necessity is all the greater for a highly complicated subject of investigation. If instead of a mountain we take a pyramid or column, of course, a survey from whatever point of view is enough to gain a clear understanding of its form, since it is simple and follows a simple rule easily discerned, which saves us from having to survey it from multiple viewpoints.

Besides the specific subjective admixture and inevitable one-sidedness that depend on the peculiarities of various nationalities' mental frameworks, science takes on a national character by the preference or predilection that each people has for certain branches of knowledge, which likewise comes from none other than a certain correspondence between the various categories into which a subject of scientific inquiry is divided, and the inclinations (and therefore, the capabilities) of various peoples. Just as an individual person may feel an inclination toward mathematics, natural science, philology, history, or the social sciences, so whole peoples can be inclined predominantly toward math, philology, and so on. For example, in the love (and therefore, ability) for pure and applied mathematics, first place doubtless goes to the French. They have brought forward in this field more first-class scholars than all the other European peoples combined: Pascal, Descartes, Clairaut, D'Alembert, Monge, Laplace, Fourier, Legendre, Lagrange, Poisson, Cauchy, and Le Verrier[19]—all French. Germany, so advanced in many fields of scientific activity, can only offer three or four mathematicians against this constellation of stars: namely, Leibniz, Euler, and Gauss.[20] To a greater degree Germany takes first place in linguistics and comparative philology, which Germany practically created and developed the furthest. Against such figures as Bopp, Pott, Wilhelm Humboldt, Grimm, Lassen, Schleicher, and Max Müller,[21] France can offer few worthy rivals. The Germans' indisputable primacy in the field of linguistics is all the more notable for the fact that it cannot be attributed to some accidental cause. The study of classical philology, clearly the closest preparation for comparative philology, was not a German specialty. In French and especially English schools, Latin and Greek are taught

[19] The French mathematicians listed here are Blaise Pascal (1623–62); René Descartes (1596–1650); Alexis Clairaut (1713–65); Jean-Baptiste le Rond d'Alembert (1717–83); Gaspard Monge (1746–1818); Pierre-Simon Laplace (1749–1827); Joseph Fourier (1768–1830), not to be confused with the utopian socialist Charles, of Danilevskii's youthful enthusiasm; Adrien-Marie Legendre (1752–1833); Joseph-Louis Lagrange (1736–1813); Siméon Denis Poisson (1781–1840); Augustin-Louis Cauchy (1789–1857); and Urbain Le Verrier (1811–77).

[20] The German mathematicians listed here are Gottfried Wilhelm Leibniz (1646–1716); Leonhard Euler (1707–83); and Carl Friedrich Gauss (1777–1855).

[21] The German linguists listed here are Franz Bopp (1791–1867); August Friedrich Pott (1802–87); Wilhelm von Humboldt (1767–1835), brother of the naturalist Alexander; Jacob Grimm (1785–1863); Christian Lassen (1800–76); August Schleicher (1821–68); and Max Müller (1823–1900).

with the same or possibly more zeal than in German schools. On the other hand, English scholars have much greater opportunity and convenience for studying the Sanskrit language, which obviously served as a starting point for the field of comparative linguistics. The first German linguists had to be sent to London to study Sanskrit, since at the start of the present [i.e., the nineteenth] century only that city offered the means to study it. I will not go into such subjects as practical astronomy, in which England has long held first place, which can be attributed to the fact that the British government constructed an outstanding observatory and in general provided the resources, in view of the practical applications this science has for a predominantly sea-going nation. But also England has a favorite science: geology, the most important discoveries of which were made by Englishmen.

Thus we find three reasons why science, the same as other aspects of civilization, must necessarily bear the imprint of nationality, despite the fact that in scientific matters the influence of one people upon another, and the past upon the present, is stronger than in other aspects of cultural historical life. The reasons are: 1) the preference shown by different peoples for different branches of knowledge; 2) the natural one-sidedness of each people's distinctive abilities and worldview that cause it to see reality from a unique point of view; 3) a certain admixture of objective truth with individual, subjective peculiarities that (like all other moral qualities and traits) are not randomly distributed among all peoples, but grouped by nationality and, taken collectively, constitute what we call the national character.

The two latter reasons are not uniformly applied to all branches of scientific investigation. The simpler the subject, the less important is the point of view from which we look at it, the acquisition of a correct understanding of it—as the foregoing examples of a mountain, column, or pyramid show. But the influence is proportional to the level of complexity within a science. Namely if the development of some branch of knowledge reaches the point that its investigation rests on a certain definitive method, then to a large extent that will remove the one-sidedness of personal and national views, along with the subjective admixture. An exact method of investigation manages to survey the subject from all points of view, and in a manner of speaking, improves the mirror of the soul that reflects reality, constituting what we call Truth. To demonstrate the influence that method can have, ask a few people to draw a circle by hand. One would make it elongated, forming an oval; one would make it more linear, like a square with rounded corners; a third's would turn out like some kind of polygon. With a little practice one could determine who drew which circle. But give a compass to those who are drawing (that is, show them an exact method of drawing circles) and the individual distinctions will disappear, with no one being able to tell who drew one circle or another. With enough practice they might be able to come close even without using the compass. In this example, individuality was eliminated due to the simplicity of the task and the application of an exact method. But let us consider a more complex subject. Let some people draw a forest, a colonnade, bridge, the vault of a church, etc. If they all knew exact rules of perspective, they would draw the horizon, designate vanishing points, and by that approach draw the various lines to their respective points. By joining the intersecting lines according to the rules of perspective, all the draftsmen will present us with perspectival views as identical as two drops of water. But let them from sight draw a flower (not to mention a whole landscape, portrait, or group of people on some occasion) and this flower will reflect the individuality of the artist; and since nationality [*natsional'nost'*] is part of that individuality, then it will always be possible to distinguish the national [*natsional'nyi*] character of the artist, even where no national or other kind of school of drawing exists. There can be no conceivable reason why the same would not apply to the sciences. Some sciences develop exact and usually very simple methods of investigation. For example, all practical astronomy comes down to determining where light shines in the sky: that is, in technical terms determining its declination and right ascension,[22] which can be done again and again by strictly following the established method. All further considerations and calculations are based on this, and in their own way follow an established method of computation, limiting the role of subjective will or views. Or consider organic chemistry. The matter under investigation is subjected to various tests, under which it its known that one substance dissolves one sort of material, another dissolves others, and in this way any contaminants are divided out. The substance attained in a purified form (*substance immediate*) is tested by fire and the by-products collected and weighed—and in this way the substance's makeup is defined. The investigation of substances is none other than the reduction of them through contact with various substances under various conditions and the results produced by this form of analysis. Of course these facts are obtained through combinations made by the mind, and even at the highest levels, sciences like chemistry and astronomy remain simple enough for peculiarities of the individual to creep in; but in proportion to a science's complexity, that simplicity decreases. Even in these exact sciences governed by a strict method, the character of various nationalities appears all the more in the choice of method and means of expressing results of scientific investigation.

What could be more exact than pure mathematics? Where would national character reveal itself in that? Yet it does appear there, and in the most acute form. It is well known that Greek mathematicians made use of the so-called geometrical method, while scholars of modern Europe predominantly use the analytical method. This difference in methods of investigation is not acciden-

---

[22] Declination and right ascension are the equivalents of celestial latitude and longitude, respectively. Declination is measured in degrees above (+) or below (-) the celestial equator; right ascension is measured in time, by converting 360 degrees into 24 hours.

tal, but may be best explained by the mental peculiarities of those peoples—of the Hellenic and Germanic-Roman cultural types. The geometric method requires studying the characteristics of a geometrical figure and continually imagining all of its distinctiveness, which with more complex figures (such as those in three dimensions, in solid geometry or descriptive geometry, for example) requires great force of imagination, and this is one of the pedagogical benefits of this method. The analytical method, on the contrary, puts the scrutiny of a figure into an equation based on the connection between certain essential characteristics, and subjects this equation to a dialectical process while completely disregarding the appearance of the figure itself. If this dialectical process is done correctly, conclusions will generate themselves to explain the characteristics of the figure. Rousseau[23] observed in his *Confessions* that he could never really master mathematical analysis, always feeling an overwhelming disgust for it. It always seemed to me, Rousseau said, that some kind of formula is put into a barrel organ: turn the handle, and out pop new mathematical truths.[24] What Rousseau said of himself applies to almost all people with artistic inclinations, that is, people with strong creative abilities, which is not to say lacking in fine dialectical reasoning. Take for example Pushkin,[25] whose lack of ability in mathematics is legendary among those in the lyceum. But the Greeks were a predominantly artistic people. One relationship between subjects and understanding was not enough for them; they also needed a vivid pictorial representation of these subjects. The Greeks' preference for the geometric method must not be explained by their weak level of development in mathematics, for which this difficult method served their purposes, just because it is completely insufficient for the level of scientific development of present times. We know that another people standing at the same level of development as the Greeks, but having more inclination for abstract thought, would take the analytical method in mathematics much further. Such were the Indians, who invented algebra and, as Humboldt said, made discoveries in this field that European mathematicians would have put to use, if only they had known about them earlier.[26] This example might be falsely taken against my explanation of the Greeks' preference for the geometric method. Namely, the Indians are said to be a people with powerful fantasy or an especially fertile imagination. But the characteristic imagination or fan-

---

[23] Jean-Jacques Rousseau (1712–78): Swiss philosopher of the late Enlightenment and early Romantic period. His *Confessions* departed from tradition by focusing on personal feelings and everyday matters.

[24] From *Confessions*, Book VI: "Resolving geometrical problems by the help of equations seemed like playing a tune by turning round a handle" (Aldus Society, 1903).

[25] Aleksandr Sergeevich Pushkin (1799–1837) is widely regarded as Russia's greatest poet and the founder of modern Russian literature.

[26] Danilevskii makes the same point in chap. 4; see Alexander von Humboldt, *Cosmos*, part II, chap. 5.

tasy of the Indians is completely different than that of the Greeks. The Indians' imagination combines and piles up the strangest, but at the same time, most obscure and ambiguous, fantastical forms; but I have in mind the specificity, definiteness, or—so to speak—plasticity of representations that characterize the Greeks' imagination and which are precisely what is required for geometric representations. But this is nowhere to be found in the compositions of Indian art and the metaphysical constructions of Indian philosophy, which, on the contrary, are characterized by daring, far-reaching dialectical conclusions.

In proportion to the complexity of the subject of a science and the lack of a strictly defined method of scientific investigation, the presence of the individual (and thus the national) element becomes more and more palpable within them. During the quarrel in our literature about nationality in science,[27] its defenders in my opinion produced some very successful examples in support of it. But there are much stronger examples that would be even harder to refute. Imagine a whole line of theory that bore the unmistakable imprint of the distinctive character of the nationality that produced it. I think all will agree with me that the essential, predominant trait in the English national character is the love of individual initiative [samodeiatel'nost'], and of the multifaceted development of one's personality and individuality, which becomes apparent in the struggle against all obstructions and hindrances both in the world of nature and in human society. Struggle and free competition is an Englishman's life: he accepts them with all their consequences, and demands them as his right; he does not abide restrictions, even those designed for his comfort or enjoyment. An Englishman takes up the struggle from his school days on, and where life does not present sufficient opportunities for it, he creates them artificially. He runs, swims, races by sail, boxes one on one (not as we prefer to fistfight in Russia, in large groups, where victory in the national pastime only gladdens us when attained through mutual, cooperative effort). For the Englishman, struggle enters into all social institutions as well. In the courts or in Parliament, there is individual competition everywhere. In imitation of parliamentary struggle, they set up debating societies where a proposed issue is deliberated and the winner is determined by the majority of votes. Any of the Englishman's pastimes is enlivened with betting, which is a form of struggle by opinion. This betting is organized into a regular system. The English have a club of mountain climbers, not as a learned pursuit (what little there is, is beside the point) but only for the pleasure of overcoming difficulty and danger, not only by oneself, but in competition with others. So struggle and competition constitute the basis of the English

---

[27] For a view of this quarrel in regard to the Imperial Geographical Society, which supported Danilevskii's early research, see Nathaniel Knight, "Science, Empire, and Nationality," in *Imperial Russia: New Histories for the Empire*, ed. Jane Burbank and David Ransel (Bloomington: Indiana University Press, 1998), 109–16.

national character, and if three notable scholars create three theories in different fields of knowledge, all will be founded on this fundamental trait of the English national character.

In the mid-seventeenth century the Englishman Hobbes[28] created a political theory of the formation of human society on the basis of universal struggle, the "war of all against all" (*bellum omnium contra omnes*).

At the end of the eighteenth century the Scotsman Adam Smith[29] created an economic theory of free competition—between producers and consumers (which constitutes the price of an object), and between producers (to reduce prices and improve production)—and the theory that constant struggle and competition must produce economic harmony.

Finally we see in the field of physiology the Englishman Darwin devised the theory of "struggle for existence" to explain the origin of plant and animal species, and produce biological harmony.

These three theories have had very different fates. Hobbes's theory is completely forgotten. Smith's theory grew into the whole science of political economy, providing its most essential contents. Darwin's theory has been widely disseminated and informs contemporary views in botany and zoology. This is not the place to quarrel with these ideas.[30] In my opinion, all of them are one-sided and bear the same character of exaggeration as their common foundation in the English national character. In any case, for us what is important is that it lies beyond all doubt that they all bear the imprint of nationality.

Obviously the opposite idea of the necessity of state guardianship over individual will and the individual person is deeply rooted in the French national character. And the three French schools of economic thought—the mercantilists, the physiocrats, and "right to work" socialists—all demand state protection: one, of industrial manufacturing; the next, of agricultural produc-

---

[28] Thomas Hobbes (1588–1679): English philosopher, theorist of the social contract and the rights and equality of individuals, expressed in the book *Leviathan* (1651).

[29] [Danilevskii's note]: Scottish is only a minor tribal designation within the Anglo-Saxon tribes, just like Great Russian, Little Russian, and White Russian for us. Thus Adam Smith is an English scholar, just as Walter Scott is an English novelist. [Translator's note: Adam Smith (1723–90): Scottish philosopher, best-known for his treatise *The Wealth of Nations* (1776), detailing the theory of capitalism and political economy, the basis of modern economics. Sir Walter Scott (1771–1832): Scottish poet and historical novelist, famous for *Ivanhoe*, *The Lady of the Lake*, *Rob Roy*, and the *Waverly* novels, which popularized and romanticized Scottish culture, blunting Danilevskii's point here.]

[30] Danilevskii did so elsewhere. His critique of Darwinism, unfinished at his death, was published posthumously (1885, 1889), and several articles on economics from the 1880s were gathered in the 1890 *Sbornik politicheskikh i ekonomicheskikh statei* (Collected Political and Economic articles). We see a hint of his critique of Adam Smith and political economy near the end of this chapter.

tion; and the third, of artificially providing paying jobs to workers, even when there is no need for the products of their labor. The French Saint-Simon[31] and his school even created a whole theory of social and political organization in which the state (in the person of the so-called "father of humanity" and his assistants) rules over all social labor, distributing the wealth to each according to his abilities and matching the abilities of each to his work. Again, without debating the merits of these theories, can we not rightly affirm that they all bear the imprint of the French national character? Do we still need to demonstrate [nationality's] impact on the practical direction of Baconian philosophy, so excellently displayed in Macaulay's[32] biographical study of the great English philosopher, or on the utilitarianism of Bentham?

It seems to me these examples are strong and persuasive enough, but it is possible to present something that is even more persuasive because it is more general. It shows us that when certain periods or phases in the development of science belong to certain nationalities, then other nationalities, whose general activity in the field of science is much more broad and fruitful, do not at all take part in scientific communication of these levels of development. To show this requires a fairly lengthy preliminary argument.

Accounts of the history of the sciences, enumerating their gradual improvements amid the helpful and harmful external influences that hastened or slowed their path, usually pay too little attention to their internal growth and thus often attach to external influences the same importance as the evolutionary phases of their development, and take these external influences as the basis for dividing the history of science into periods. Thus the path of their development is presented as more or less accidental, with no way to compare the level of development of one science to others. In other words, they either present only the external history of science (for example, the famous history of the natural sciences compiled from Cuvier's lectures), or a mixture of the internal and external history. Meanwhile, if even political history requires that the internal process of society's development occupy the center of attention, then it is all the more necessary for the history of science, in the development of which everything external can only play a secondary role, since a science is the logical, investigative development and the construction of the truth concerning a certain sphere or category of subjects.

To search out a common path of internal development for all sciences, we must take science out of the single-national context, since in the multinational

---

[31] Claude Henri de Rouvroy, comte de Saint-Simon (1760–1825): French aristocratic socialist, inspired by British industrialism and American society to envision a new political and social order based on scientific principles, most influential posthumously.
[32] Thomas Babington Macaulay (1800–59): British historian and Whig politician, identified with (and derided for) the Whig view of history, in which the past serves mainly to validate the present; his study of Bacon mentioned here was published in the *Edinburgh Review* in 1837. Bentham: See chap. 2, n. 23.

context one part of a science might advance far ahead, while other parts fall significantly behind, having become entangled and obstructing the common path of development. Besides that, our investigation also requires a kind of science that has already attained a significant level of sophistication, or has gone through a significant number of phases of development. Astronomy meets all our requirements.

As with the subject of astronomy itself, so with the course of its development: it is so simple that there can be no doubt when in its development to locate the turning points, leading to its modern stage of sophistication. These turning points are indicated by four great names: the Greek Hipparchus; the Slav-Pole Copernicus; the German Kepler; and the English Newton.

Up to the time of Hipparchus,[33] all the work of astronomers consisted of collecting the facts, the building blocks for the future scientific edifice. Even if they did know the laws by which heavenly phenomena such as eclipses can be predicted beforehand, then strictly speaking these could not have been laws in the true sense of the word, but more recipes or formulas, just like those used in factory production. Recipes instruct us to take so much of this, mix it with that, boil for three hours, and so on; they do not distinguish the rules from the essence of the process, but only have derived them from a long, thoughtless process of trial and error. Thus this would be the *period of gathering materials*.

But the mass of facts accumulates to the point it becomes impossible to survey it all. Thus it becomes essential to arrange them into some kind of system, based on a certain connection between them. This is usually some principle that is especially eye-catching or convenient for one reason or another. It is highly unlikely that this chosen principle of systematization directly corresponds to the very nature of the assembled facts, or embraces the whole collection of data. More likely, the first attempt at systematization gives us only an artificial system. That is what happened with astronomy; Hipparchus's system was completely artificial. It did not correspond to or express the essence of the phenomena, but only presented an auxiliary mnemonic device to help navigate the mass of details. To that end it gave some satisfaction to the mind's inquisitiveness, presenting a harmonious connection among a multitude of complex phenomena. Any system, even an artificial one, offers the invaluable benefit of allowing each new fact to be set in its place. It does not remain isolated, but by being placed into a system must be harmonized with it. And if it truly does harmonize, this supports it all the more; if it does not

---

[33] Hipparchus (2nd century BCE): Greek astronomer, considered greatest of antiquity, pioneer of trigonometry, known for detailed observations of eccentric solar and lunar movement. Most of his work is known only through references in subsequent works, notably Claudius Ptolemy (2nd century CE), Egyptian astronomer known for his namesake geocentric model of the solar system, with circular planetary orbits augmented with complex epicycles.

harmonize, that reveals the need to refine the system. The facts already known to Alexandrian scholars harmonized poorly with the geocentric system. To make them fit into this system required further complication, and they came up with epicycles, or circles made by planets around imaginary centers. These centers move in a circle around the earth, the planets move in circles around the imaginary centers, following them around the earth. As the accuracy of observation increased, they piled up epicycles upon epicycles. Thus the Hipparchan period must be called the *period of the artificial system.*

This extreme complexity led the brilliant Slavic mind of Copernicus to doubt it, and he replaced the Hipparchan or (as it is usually called) the Ptolemaic artificial system[34] with a more natural system, in which any heavenly body could be given precisely the same place within science as it occupied in reality. Thus this great individual led astronomy into the *period of the natural system.*

The presentation of scientific facts in their actual correspondence lends the ability to seek out the dependence they have between them. So the acceptance of the Copernican system opened the possibility of calculating the distance of the planets from one another and the varying distances of one planet from a central body at various points along its path. These distances were not accidental, it turned out, but connected, along with the speed of rotation, to certain simple relationships which have come to be called Kepler's Laws of Planetary Motion, named for their great discoverer.[35] But the laws themselves remained disconnected, seemingly accidental, not proceeding from a single, common, clear, and understandable principle. Therefore laws of this type, which only connect certain phenomena but cannot explain them, are called individual, empirical laws. Thus we can call the Keplerian period in the development of astronomy the *period of individual empirical laws.*

Finally Newton discovered the common principle which could not only incorporate all those individual laws (so that they proceed from it, as individual deductions or conclusions), but by being comprehensible, could give them an explanation. In fact, in Newtonian law the only thing not explained is the very essence of gravity. But in and of itself it is clear that its force must be stronger when the number (or mass) of attractive particles is greater, and it must weaken in proportion to the distance of attractive bodies, at the rate of this distance squared (since the force going out from a body radiates equally in all directions, and thus, just as with the surfaces of spheres with varying diameters, the surfaces increase as the squares of their diameters). Thus the Newtonian period of astronomy must be called the *period of the general, rational law.*

He completed the science; there is nowhere further to go. Of course it is still possible to broaden and enrich the science with new factual discoveries

---

[34] See previous note.

[35] Kepler's Laws: See chap. 4, n. 7.

(new planets, comets, etc.), improve methods of calculation, extend a fundamental law to the minutest detail, broaden its domain in other systems, and
so on. But no revolution is necessary or possible in any science that has
attained this degree of sophistication.[36] The only possible, philosophically-
significant, forward step is this kind of generalization of a common, rational
law, which in its own way would connect with a common, rational law regu-
lating another category of phenomena in another area of science.

So we can all agree the history of astronomy divides into these five designated states or phases of internal development (*gathering materials; artificial
system; natural system; individual empirical laws; general rational law*) which for
short could be called the *pre-Hipparchan, Hipparchan, Copernican, Keplerian,* and
Newtonian periods. This shows that the levels of development are not accidental but necessary. That is to say, they are required by the most natural path of
scientific development; thus we must expect them to be repeated in any other
science. Before we test what is shown by astronomy (a natural logical path of
development, independent of favorable or unfavorable external influences)
for other sciences, we note that we cannot go far while still holding to the external history of science, or confusing the external for the internal. In this case
we would have to talk about the history of astronomy among the Chaldeans,
Egyptians, and Greeks; the influence of the Arabs; the significance of advances in optics; the improvements of English astronomers' observation
methods; and so on. In this way it is easy to overlook the predominating influence of the great reformers of science, or at least to treat incidental circumstances as equal in importance to their contributions. In astronomy, to be sure,
the role of these architects of science is so obvious that it would be almost
impossible to deny them proper significance; but in other sciences this is easier to do.

Another science that has not yet attained such a level of sophistication as
astronomy, but which has gone through most phases of development and, by
its lack of complexity, very clearly reveals the main phases of its development, is chemistry. And without straining the interpretation one bit, it shows
us exactly the same course of development.

---

[36] These statements reflect certain assumptions of nineteenth-century science, that sciences have an end point, when a complete set of empirical truths has been discovered
in Nature (we cannot blame Danilevskii for failing to anticipate Einstein and the
breakthroughs of the twentieth century). Hereafter Danilevskii consciously, but im-
plicitly, builds the case that he has made the same kind of final breakthrough in the
"science" of history, seeing his own theory of cultural-historical types as a "natural
system." It is ironic in light of his warning, at the end of chapter 3, about the hubris of
"the academic, who has produced some theory, think[ing] that he has said the last
word in his discipline to explain the whole truth, and that after him of course the particulars will be filled in, but his directive will remain unchanged." This statement
makes clear that Danilevskii's positivism was still tempered by the persistent awareness of science as a human activity, subject to human fallibility.

In ancient and medieval times, chemical facts were collected, partly through various manufacturing processes and partly through the influence of fantastical and mystical ideas. They were not grouped together in any way, artificially or naturally, reasonably or foolishly. From the time of Aristotle, the idea of the four elements had no chemical basis, but more of a biological character, since water, wind, earth, and fire (the last referring to heat, light, and everything then called weightless) could only be regarded as the source from which organic bodies are formed and to which they revert. These elements, as something brought from outside, could not serve as a unifying thread in the chemical phenomena of the alchemists, so the idea of the four elements could not serve, even nominally, as an artificial system.

The artificial-system period of chemistry was ushered in by the German Stahl,[37] who therefore can be called the Hipparchus of chemistry. He came up with the idea of phlogiston, which supposedly was released from a body upon burning, so that the products of burning or oxidation (rust, lime, alkali, oxides) are simple bodies, but their combination with phlogiston produces metals. This system was as artificial as Hipparchus's; just like his, it joined all then-known chemical phenomena by a common thread, and gave an account of the interaction of substances with each other and allowed newly discovered facts to be introduced within this framework. So newly discovered chlorine was called dephlogisticated hydrochloric acid, and so on. The collection of facts came into harmonious order, all phenomena lost their separateness (or accidentalness), and without fail had to either support the system and be harmonized with it, or if not, refute it or at least complicate it with newly introduced provisions. In this way Stahl's theory took on its own variety of "epicycles,"[38] even stranger than the ones that disfigured Hipparchus's system. When it turned out that upon the supposed extraction of phlogiston, the weight of the products of this process actually increased (that is, the body without phlogiston came to weigh more than it did with it), then the Ptolemy of this system—the French chemist Guyton de Morveau[39]—ascribed to phlogiston a special, undemonstrated quality of negative weight.

The ingenious Frenchman Lavoisier[40] disproved all of that (in its time, incredibly useful) confusion by giving central importance to actually-existing

[37] Georg Ernst Stahl (1660–1734): German chemist and physician, known for the phlogiston theory as described here.

[38] Ptolemaic astronomy assumed planetary orbits were circular, even though observations pointed to the contrary. The discrepancy was accounted for by the further assumption that planets moved in epicycles, like the movement of reflectors on the spokes of bicycle wheels. So "epicycles" here describes a second false assumption to rescue an initial false assumption from being disproven.

[39] Louis Bernard Guyton de Morveau (1737–1816): French chemist who developed the first system of chemical nomenclature.

[40] Antoine Lavoisier (1743–94): French chemist considered the father of modern chemistry, who named oxygen and hydrogen and described the process of combustion.

oxygen, instead of supposed phlogiston, and by this put everything into a more desirable place, better corresponding to reality. Lavoisier thus introduced a natural system to chemistry, becoming its Copernicus.

And so again in the same way as astronomy, the result of the natural system was to hasten the search for individual connecting principles bringing chemical phenomena into mutual dependence. The German Wenzel [Karl Friedrich, c. 1740–93] discovered laws for the formation of salts, and the French Gay-Lussac [Joseph Louis, 1778–1850], the laws for formation of gases in simple relationship to volume; the French Proust [Joseph Louis, 1754–1826] discovered the most fruitful chemical law, known as the law of definite proportions or shares, according to which bodies contain not all possible combinations, but only certain, simple quantities of elements determined by weight; Dulong [Pierre Louis, 1785–1838] and Petit [Alexis Thérèse, 1791–1820] discovered the ratios of these proportional weights to specific heat capacity. All these discoveries are like Kepler's laws, what might be called individual empirical laws of chemistry. In this Keplerian period, advances were introduced not by one ingenious chemist, but by several more or less talented or ingenious scholars. A general rational law for chemistry has yet to be discovered. Dalton's atomic theory,[41] fully explaining the laws of proportional weights and volumes, is not completely free of objections, but most importantly does not at all explain chemical affinities (the level of which can only be described empirically), and does not show any certain dependency between atomic weight and other characteristics ascribed to atoms. To do this, the so-called electrochemical theory was proposed, which has also turned out insufficient. So we must acknowledge that chemistry has not left the Keplerian period of development, the period of individual empirical laws.

One part of chemistry—namely, organic chemistry—has long trailed behind its older sister. Although Lavoisier's system influenced its development, oxygen is much less significant here than for inorganic chemistry. Thus the classification of bodies and reactions in organic chemistry has long relied on purely superficial guidelines (by chemical standards) such as their origin and other external qualities. They have formed interpretations of plant bodies (as tri-elemental), of animal bodies (as tetra-elemental), as well as of acids, alkalis, resins, fatty oils and essential oils, even dyes and extracts. Such a system, like the Aristotelian notion of the four elements, cannot even be called artificial, since it neither explains anything nor leads to any connections or correspondence. The credit for introducing an artificial system to organic chemistry goes to the Swede Berzelius [Jöns Jacob, 1779–1848] and the German Liebig [Justus von, 1803–73]. Guided by the analogy of ammonia and cyanogen, they

---

[41] John Dalton (1766–1844): English chemist and physicist who set forth the atomic theory of matter, that elements are composed of indivisible, identical atoms which can be neither created nor destroyed and which combine with other elements in simple ratios to form chemical compounds.

conceived of a series of bodies called "complex radicals," or complex bodies that play the same role in compounds as simple bodies. Leibig called organic chemistry itself "complex radical chemistry," in distinction to inorganic chemistry, "simple element chemistry." These complex radicals are for the most part hypothetical, never yet seen by anyone, yet very well explained. However there were still many exceptions. They thought this was the result of unfamiliarity with the reactions of these bodies, and they hoped with time everything would come to fit under the system of complex radicals. Instead chemists had to renounce this theory and switch to a system of chemical types and substitutions, predominantly developed in France by Dumas [Jean-Baptiste, 1800–84], Laurent [Auguste, 1807–53], and Gerhardt [Charles Frédéric, 1816–56]. This system evidently resembles a natural system; whether in fact it is remains to be seen.[42]

Turning to physics, we find that this science long ago attained a high level of sophistication, and in distinction to astronomy and chemistry, has an extraordinary heterogeneity. Not only have its different parts always stood at various levels of development, but it is even hard to find a definition to express clearly and precisely what its contents are. It must sooner be attributed to scholars' happy instinct than conscious thought that this whole heterogeneous assortment of facts and learning remained under the arch of physics as a single science. Only discoveries of modern times have confirmed this (more or less) scientific instinct. Thanks to these discoveries we can give physics a short and simple, but also clear and precise, definition. It is the science of the motion of substances, considering each case of motion in equilibrium — parallel if not opposed to chemistry, which is the science of substance in and of itself. Motion is two-fold: either it consists of discernible movement through space or vibratory movement of the particles within a body, revealed to our senses as heat, light, and, probably, electricity. Spanning both these types of motion is the wavelike motion of sound and drops of liquid, since the nature of their motion is often called weightless; the movement pertains not just to the innermost particles of a body but is also accompanied by discernible movement, such as, for example, in a quivering string. The first type of motion is the focus of the first branch of physics (as it is called by the conventions of this science) and consists of the application of mathematical analysis to separate observations of certain characteristics of bodies, and the application of theory developed in other sciences (such as gravitational theory or chemical theory). Since it does not stand on its own, this field of study cannot clearly be shown to follow the path of development proposed here. In the study of weightless phenomena, optics holds first place, and the development of this particular science clearly demonstrates that path.

---

[42] These passages illustrate just how much scientific theory was still in flux in the nineteenth century. For economy's sake, in this section only names and dates are added to what information Danilevskii provides.

The collection of facts, some of which came under a certain mathematical formulation (such as the reflection and refraction of light), followed from their artificial systematization by Newton under the theory of emanation. At almost the same time the Dutch Huygens [Christiaan, 1629–95] applied a natural system to phenomena of light, known as the wave theory of light. Many laws discovered by Malus [Etienne, 1775–1812], Fresnel [Augustin-Jean, 1788–1827], Young [Thomas, 1773–1829], and Fraunhofer [Joseph von, 1787–1826] made up the period of individual empirical laws that supported this natural system. The study of heat followed upon the successes of optics: the majority of optical phenomena and laws (even interference) were also discovered in phenomena of heat, mainly by the Italian Melloni [Macedonio, 1798–1854]. On another front, a connection between what was called electricity, galvanism, and magnetism was shown by Ørsted [Hans Christian, 1777–1851], Arago [François, 1786–1853], and Ampère [André-Marie, 1775–1836], and also a connection between heat and light by Melloni and Faraday [Michael, 1791–1867]. Finally the forefront of development, long held by optics, was overtaken by the study of heat. By the preliminary efforts of [Count] Rumford [Benjamin Thomas, 1753–1814] and most importantly the ingenious notions of the German Doctor Mayer [Julius Robert von, 1814–78] and the experiments of the English Joule [James Prescott, 1818–89], the study of the relationship of heat and light was brought to the Newtonian level of a general rational law: the *conservation of motion* [*sic*; the law described here is the conservation of *energy*] according to which the distinctiveness of so-called weightless substances was explained as the conversion of motion from the movement of a body through space to the internal vibration of its particles, which in its own way is capable of conversion back into motion in the narrow, commonly accepted meaning of the word. Here (as with the force of gravity in Newton's laws) only one thing eludes our understanding: the hypothetical ether that serves as the driving mechanism for this motion. It remains only to be developed and applied with equal success to the phenomena and conversion of electricity. In this way the study of the special subject of weightless phenomena within physics ranks just behind astronomy at the highest phase of scientific development.

In botany, attempts to establish a system began in the sixteenth or seventeenth century, and the great Swede Linnaeus [Carl, 1707–78] succeeded pretty well. His system was almost completely artificial, a near perfect example of an artificial system's merits (its great convenience and simplicity of classification under its headings) and at the same time its incredible unnaturalness (grouping the dissimilar, dividing the similar; in short, headings not based on the connections actually existing between things in reality). But here too the artificial system had its helpful influence, as it always does, on the development of a science. With the newfound ability to group facts together, incorporate the labors of predecessors, and relate their own labors to others in a common connection with all matters of a given science—the results turned

out the same. The framework of the artificial system quickly proved too con-
strictive; the facts squeezed into it broke it apart by themselves. The ingenious
French Adanson [Michel, 1707–1826] and the two Jussieus, uncle [Bernard,
1699–1777] and nephew [Antoine, 1748–1836], introduced a natural system to
botany, and by this not only ushered their science into the modern, Copernican stage of development but (in the words of Cuvier) achieved a revolution in all natural science, because a natural system for plants served not only
as an example for zoology, but enabled generalization to the extent of all anatomical and physiological observations of plants and animals. Without a natural system, neither comparative anatomy nor comparative physiology (one
for plants, the other for animals) would be possible. Besides that, since in the
plant kingdom visual appearance hardly corresponds to the essential morphology of the plant, the establishment of a natural system could not be some
sort of accident or lucky guess, but was demanded by the articulation of the
very theory of a natural system (considering all traits of the subjects, weigh-
ing the relative merits of these traits, and so on). This was done in botany,
then perfected in zoology (by the establishment of organizational types) as an
example to guide all other sciences.

Linnaeus also introduced an artificial system to zoology. Here it must be
noted that, by the very essence of the matter, there can be numerous artificial
systems, existing simultaneously or one replacing the other. In astronomy besides the Hipparchan system perfected by Ptolemy, there was an Egyptian
system, and even after Copernicus the artificial system of Tycho Brahe [1546–
1601] appeared, hoping to reconcile the customary falsehood (which was hard
to renounce) with the truth.[43] So in both botany and zoology there were a few
artificial systems, but here I take as the divider between the two periods of
development only the one that more completely than the others expressed the
idea and goal of an artificial system, and which thus had the strongest influence on the development of the science, which is characteristic of an artificial
system in general.

For the introduction of a natural system, zoology has Cuvier to thank. As
opposed to artificial systems, a natural system (like anything true) can only be
singular, but it can be continually improved, drawing closer and closer to an
expression of the correlation between its subjects and the phenomena as existing in nature. In speaking of a natural system, it is necessary to make a useful observation. Namely, Linnaeus's zoological system was not entirely artificial. The higher divisions of the animal kingdom Linnaeus made were entirely natural. But this was due to the fact that the characteristics of the main,
upper-level, natural groups of animals are so sharply distinguished by nature
itself that they are impossible to miss. These groups were accurately identified by Aristotle; it could even be said they were never actually declared by

---

[43] The "customary falsehood" was geo-centrism; in Tycho's model, all other planets
orbit the sun, but the sun itself (as well as the moon) orbits the earth.

anyone, but were always apparent even to the simple, nonscientific person. Mammals, birds, fish—is it possible to confuse the nature of these groups? It is more possible with things that crawl, like snakes, lizards, turtles, and frogs; in fact, in their case Linnaeus did make a mistake. If the different traits of lower animals were so clearly revealed in the external form as it is in the higher animals, then an artificial system would have been impossible by the very nature of things. Therefore it could happen that another science could skip the stage of the artificial system in its development. We soon will see an example of this.

Mineralogy is strictly the morphology of inorganic phenomena. It does not have its own physiology since it coincides with chemistry and, in part, physics. The first attempt at anything close to a system of classifying mineral forms came from the great German scholar Werner [Abraham Gottlob, 1749–1817], and his system too was artificial and had the same influence on this branch of knowledge as Linnaeus had on botanical and zoological classification, attracting a great deal of scholarly attention. The French Abbé Haüy [1743–1842] holds the honor of establishing a natural morphology of minerals. After him, some German scholars—Mohs [Friedrich, 1773–1839], Rose [Gustav, 1798–1873], and especially Mitscherlich [Eilhard, 1794–1863]—discovered separate empirical laws determining the forms of crystals, and specifically Mitscherlich, with the discovery of isomorphism, showed the connection between the forms of crystals and their chemical composition. But a general principle for the formation of crystals and the rational dependence of the outward form upon the inner arrangement of particles remains unknown.

The same Werner presented the first scientific system of geology, the phenomena of which to that time were cited only as confirmation or refutation of biblical references to the days of creation, or provided the basis of various fantastical-imaginary cosmogonies. Werner's system, in which everything was produced by water [Neptunism] turned out to be artificial; but the influence of that system on the development of the science was so great that many terms introduced by Werner (primitive series, flotz series; primary, secondary, or transitional formations) have remained in use for that science ever since. The Scottish Hutton [James, 1726–97] and his followers stood fire and water, Vulcan and Neptune, in their proper place in the formation of the earth's core, and by this brought the science into its period of the natural system, where it now stands.

We have thus surveyed the whole spectrum of the natural sciences and, it seems to me, without straining the interpretation in the slightest, placed all the sciences regarded here under the single common pattern of development so clearly displayed in astronomy. From the other sciences, only one—comparative philology, or linguistics, which some include among the natural sciences—has reached a sufficient level of sophistication to point to any evolutionary phases it has gone through.

Before the end of the past century, the whole realm of linguistics presented only a mass of academic material, with no mutual connections. Just as in geology, some theoreticians subjected the facts to a principle drawn from elsewhere: a narrow theological view that the Hebrew language must have been the first language of humanity, from which the rest sprang forth (which of course brought arbitrariness and strained interpretation to the whole field).

The discovery of the Sanskrit language revolutionized this science. It produced the same effect as I described for the zoological system of Linnaeus in regard to the higher animals. The first Sanskrit expert was the English Wilson [Horace Hayman, 1786–1860], who knew both Greek and Latin besides his native tongue (an outgrowth from Germanic roots), and could not fail to notice the affinity between them, expressing it definitively. Thus the first systematization of languages turned out to be the natural one, skipping the step of the artificial system in this case, so that linguistics went straight from the stage of collecting materials to the stage of the natural system. But because of its simplicity and obviousness this natural system could not long remain the center of attention, and right on the heels of the English Sanskritologists, the German philologists Bopp [Franz, 1791–1867] and Grimm [Jacob, 1785–1863] (concerning the German language) ushered their science into the period of individual empirical laws, with laws of phonetic alteration of sounds through the etymological derivation of languages. In the family of Romance languages (derived from Latin or ancient Italian speech) there was likewise no place for an artificial system; here again, the natural system came directly to light. Other language families also followed the scientific path, beginning with the family of Aryan languages.

In other sciences, logic and pure mathematics (which have no external object and consist of more or less pure thought) not only do not display these phases of development derived from the history of other sciences, but by their very nature cannot undergo any kind of revolutions in their path of progress. Whereas objective sciences proceed from the data of the visible world in all its complexity and fragmentation, and lead toward broader and simpler principles by gradual grouping, the point of departure for subjective sciences is the simplest principle inherent (so to speak) in our mind, from which the furthest development proceeds as a consequence. Thus these sciences are derivative, deductive sciences. So the rest of the sciences are either unoriginal, applied sciences (such as therapy, agronomy, technology, etc.) which borrow their principles and materials from other branches of knowledge, and apply them only toward certain goals; or are still either in the period of collecting materials or in the period of continually replacing one artificial system with another (such as the philosophical, historical, and social sciences).

It is remarkable that for four of the five periods of development, the results attained in the preceding period preserve their full significance in the subsequent periods, so that the body of the science only grows. The only exception is the second period, of the artificial system. It resembles the transient organs of animals, such as the Wolffian body,[44] which plays only a temporary role, disappearing after the embryonic stage and leaving no trace of itself. In fact, Kepler's laws did not eliminate Newton's laws from astronomy, nor did either eliminate Copernicus's system; even the observations of Alexandrian and Chaldean astronomers retained their scientific validity and usefulness. But regarding the systems of Hipparchus, Ptolemy, and Tycho Brahe, science now acts as if they never existed; they are merely a part of its history and are studied only in this context. It is the same with the systems of Stahl, Werner, Linnaeus, and Newton's theory of emanation.[45] It seems to me this is how we must understand the proposition that in science the facts stay the same while theories come and go. Not all theories change; only those that belong to the period of the artificial system, which is like the scaffolding of scientific knowledge: now removed, but without which the edifice could never have been built. On the other hand, the artificial system is perhaps in some sense the most useful and fruitful step in the development of science itself. It lends unity to the collected material, and brings it out into the open, without the secrecy, individual methods, or formulas of the so-called "adepts," making the mass of facts available to anyone wishing to devote his efforts and abilities to this branch of knowledge. Although this system necessarily adds something false to the facts accumulated, it also provides the means to refute and remove this false proposition by its own contradictions. Thus only with the introduction of the artificial system does knowledge become science. But at that stage science risks falling into a cycle of falsehood, replacing one artificial system with another, not moving forward in an essential way. Only the introduction of a natural system eliminates this risk, at which point science takes the correct course.

After this long digression I can finally draw some conclusions about the influence of the peculiarities of the national mental framework on science. We have examined the development of nine sciences and noted within them a total of 33 stages of development, distinguished by 24 scientific reforms. We have deliberately noted the nationality of the scholar or group of scholars who raised their science to the highest level of development in each case. This allows us to construct the (very enlightening) table on the following page grouping the great figures of science by nationality.

This table shows that those who helped advance a science from one period of development to another were:

Germans in	10 cases	Dutch in	1 case
French in	7 cases	Slav in	1 case
English in	6 cases	Greek in	1 case
Swedes in	3 cases		

---

[44] Wolffian body: Also called *mesonephros*, an embryonic renal organ in vertebrates.

[45] Also known as the corpuscular, or particle, theory of light.

Period of Development

Science	Artificial system	Natural system	Individual empirical laws	General rational law
Astronomy	Greek	Slav	German	English
Inorganic chemistry	German	French	German and French	---
Organic chemistry	Swede and German	French	---	---
Study of weightless phenomena	English	Dutch	French, English, and German	German and English
Botany	Swede	French	---	---
Zoology	Swede	French	---	---
Mineralogy	German	French	German	---
Geology	German	English	---	---
Linguistics	---	English	German	---

Thus first place in moving science productively forward indisputably belongs to the Germans. But this progressive activity of various nationalities varies widely among periods of scientific development. Namely if we look at those peoples that have been the main contributors to science—the Germans, French, and English—we see that the English have advanced the sciences at all four levels of development, while the Germans primarily raise sciences to the level of individual empirical laws, having more or less served this purpose for all the sciences that have reached this developmental stage. With the English they [Germans] share the distinction of raising sciences to their highest level of perfection: In four of eight cases they were the solitary actors or main contributors to the artificial systematization of knowledge—but *did not advance a single science to the stage of a natural system.* On the contrary, the French are the main agents taking sciences into the period of a natural system, doing so in five of nine cases while never once giving a science its artificial system.

From this we see first of all that the role of each of the three nationalities in the general advancement of science corresponds precisely to the level of distinction of their national character: in this case, the French and the Germans are complete opposites, but the English, who connect the French and Germans ethnographically and linguistically, here function as the same kind of connecting link. Secondly and most importantly, the Germans' strong record of establishing artificial systems despite never establishing a science's natural system, alongside the French's prevalence in the natural-system period of scientific development and absence from the artificial-system period, can be marvelously explained by widely-recognized peculiarities of the mental framework of these two richly endowed peoples.

We have seen that the artificial system almost always precedes the natural. This comes from the fact that it is highly unlikely to take a disorderly pile of material and directly grasp within it all the similarities and distinctions, as well as the right way to consider and evaluate each of them. It is much more likely that at first what catches the eye is some kind of sign, which for one reason or another seems predominant. So in astronomy this initial predominant sign was the deceptive appearance of things; in chemistry, it was also the deceptive appearance of *something* in fire, what Stahl called phlogiston. But that was only one of the reasons for the artificiality of the system: the objective reason, so to speak, came from the very grouping of the data. But there is another reason, the subjective reason that depends on the mental framework of the classifier. If he is gifted with primarily speculative abilities, then the complexity of relations between subjects will hardly satisfy him, but will seem to him only irrational coincidence. He will certainly seek out some pervasive principle, what the Germans call *ein durchgreifendes Princip*, and once he thinks he has found it, he will modify it by a dialectical process of development, derive all variations of the theme, and place everything being classified under these variations of his main principle. Therefore when the natural system was established in botany and zoology, so that it only required further refinement, speculative minds were not satisfied and tried to do it all over in their own way, to force it into their own logical categories, into a framework of some dialectically-developed pervasive principle. So Oken [Lorenz, 1779–1851], following the principle that the animal kingdom must be differentiated or partitioned according to the parts of the individual (and thus fully complete) animal organism, established groups of head, chest, and abdominal animals guided by some kind of head, chest, or abdominal characteristics. According to Oken's system, each of these groups could be separate types or could cross with other groups, so that there were animals that were head-head, head-abdominal, head-chest, abdominal-abdominal, abdominal-chest, abdominal-head, and so on. Within the last thirty years another German scholar, Reichenbach [Ludwig, 1793–1879], this time a botanist, thought he had found this pervasive principle of division in the dialectical method of Hegelian logic. He first distinguished forms in which the rudiments of future development lay in a state of indifference, or what is called the *prothesis*. He developed the prothesis into the typical form of *thesis* and its opposite *antithesis*, which then reconcile themselves into a higher entity, the *synthesis*. Each group of plants allegedly had members corresponding to the prothesis, thesis, antithesis, and synthesis, mirroring the dialectical process itself.

Leaving aside all that is strange and exaggerated in these examples, does not writing a long treatise according to a strict outline fall into the same category? In this case it is no detriment, because the idea proposed as the basis of division may actually pervade throughout the whole treatise. But for this idea truly to have the same character when applied to all of nature—to vary exactly when it varies and develop dialectically the way nature's taxonomy develops—is not at all likely.

It is clear that the mental inclination of most Germans is not at all suited for grasping and evaluating signs, objects, and phenomena without some preconceived notion. On the contrary the French, less expert at dialectics and profound thinking, have minds more open to direct perception of external impressions and their combination according to the degree of relationships actually existing between them (and not bothered by the absence of some all-pervading principle). Notice that the natural system in botany was established where it was least likely to do so. Bernard Jussieu was the keeper of the king's garden; that is, a gardener. He sought those forms that coordinated by physiognomic appearance and set them close by one another, gradually correcting his mistakes; and his kinsman established the scientific groupings achieved by this physiognomic method. But if a speculative frame of mind and its ability to apprehend some kind of all-encompassing idea poorly suit the establishment of a natural system in any field of knowledge, they are truly valuable for the discovery of both peculiar and general laws of nature, which almost always come from speculation. Kepler was completely guided by the notion that the planets took their paths according to some kind of harmonic combination, and he tried to associate the relations between the distances and times of planetary movement with the relations between the different sizes of geometric solids and the laws of musical harmony, and only then, under the influence of these prevailing notions, did he try to find his eternal laws.

It seems as the result of all these examples we must accept that the fruits of science are truly the property of all humanity, rather than just aspects of a civilization, which cannot be transmitted so completely from one people to another, especially from the people of one cultural-historical type to another. But the very production of these fruits, that is, the development and refinement of the sciences, bears no less of the national character than art, customs, and politics. For the nationalities that have developed these sciences, however, the difference in subjective characteristics (in mental framework) is not the only reason the development of science bears the imprint of nationality. For some sciences, the very subject of study is essentially national. Such is the case with all the social sciences.

To prove that the sciences' national character comes from the peculiarities of the mental frameworks pertaining to various nationalities, we have resorted to tracing the path of their historical development. To prove the high degree of nationality of certain sciences—nationality revealed not only in the subjective, but also in the objective sense—we will resort to classifying the sciences, not taking it so far, but only to the extent that suits our particular purposes.

It seems to me the main division of the sciences is between those with a subjective or objective character. By subjective sciences we mean those that do not have an external subject but essentially trace the very path of human thought, such as mathematics and logic. All other sciences have their contents in the external world.

Some of these sciences can be called general or theoretical, because their subject is the general essences of the world, set apart from the special forms in which they are enshrouded. There are three such general world essences: matter, motion, and spirit. The study of matter in and of itself is the subject of chemistry; the study of motion is the subject of physics; the study of spirit in isolation from its particular revelations must be the concern of metaphysics. However it is entirely doubtful that there is, or even could be, a science [of metaphysics]. For the study of the laws of spirit in general to be possible would require there to be at least some spiritual beings [to study], and the ability to distinguish what is accidental about them (that which depends on the form of union of the spirit with matter, and the organization of that matter) from what pertains to the pure essence of spirit as spirit. But we know only one spiritual being, which is the human; therefore it seems more prudent to replace metaphysics with psychology. Whether or not metaphysics is possible as the science (parallel with chemistry) of the spirit in isolation from its manifestation in union with certain forms, the important thing for us now is only the fact that psychology presents an example of something that does not fall under the laws of matter and of its motion. Therefore, all the primary, original laws that support the whole realm of human knowledge are drawn only from these three sciences: chemistry, physics, and psychology. If astronomical investigation has led to the discovery of the law of gravity, then that is still a law of physics, and not a specifically astronomical law.

All the remaining sciences have as their subjects only the modifications of material and spiritual forces and laws, following a morphological principle, about which we can only note that it no more results from the properties of matter and its motion than a steam engine results from the force of steam in the open air. The morphological principle is ideal in nature, but this is not the place to develop that idea. For us what is important is the resulting distinction for the character of sciences taking as their subject the general essences of the world—matter, motion, and spirit—from those that examine only the diverse manifestations of these things under the influence of the morphological principle. This distinction consists in that only the first sciences can produce general theories, and the rest can seek out only individual laws which may apply to a wider or narrower group of subjects or beings arranged by a natural system, but cannot in any case explain all of them by itself. For illustration we will compare some chemical laws on the one hand with some physiological laws on the other.

Chemistry tells us that bodies form only in the way determined for each body according to the weight of quantities known as chemical proportions or atomic weights. And we are fully convinced that these formations proceed in exactly the same way on the moon, the sun, Jupiter, Sirius, and in the furthest corners of the universe. In the same way we believe that light going through a transparent medium is refracted, that from polished surfaces it is reflected at the same angle going out as the angle coming in, wherever this reflection takes place—on earth or in the stars of the Big Dipper—and whatever the light comes from—a lamp, the sun, or a star. But the physiological laws common to all plants and animals are only those that depend on the common chemical or physical properties for all of them, such as, for example, weight. There seems to be a general law that the reproduction of living things comes from mating like creatures; then the so-called alternation of generations (*Generations-wechsel*) shows us that there are many living creatures for which there is no resemblance between parents and children, but between grandparents and grandchildren, or even great-grandparents and great-grandchildren. In the same way, there seems to be a general law that under sexual reproduction there must be two elements, the male and the female, either in two individuals or conjoined into one; but then the phenomenon of parthenogenesis or "virgin-birth" shows us that completely virginal butterflies lay eggs, from which fully-formed creatures develop. Thus even these laws seemingly common to all living things apply only to some, certain-sized groups. If other laws did not produce such broad generalizations, it was because from the very outset physiological investigations concerned sufficiently diverse creatures. But imagine that we did not know of any aquatic animals; without a doubt, we would believe that any living creature immersed in water would certainly suffocate, since it could not breathe in water. We would think that lung air-pipes (tracheas) are the only possible breathing organs, and of course would never imagine gills as even a theoretical possibility.

These examples are sufficient to show that only chemistry, physics, and a science of the spirit can be theoretical sciences, and that there cannot be theoretical physiology or anatomy, but only comparative physiology and anatomy. The same goes for philological sciences, historical sciences, and of course, social sciences. Social phenomena are not subject to any special type of forces, thus they are not governed by any special kind of laws, except general spiritual laws. These laws act in a special way, under the influence of a morphological principle of social formation. But since these principles are different for different societies, there can be no theoretical, but only a comparative, science of "social-ology" [*obshchestvoslovie*] and its parts, such as politics, political economy, and so on.

It has long been recognized that a general theory of civil and political structures of societies is impossible, and there are few doctrinaires who would think, for example, that the English political structure is some kind of ideal that everyone should aspire to imitate, or that there is no qualitative difference among states (or societies in general) other than age. But one small corner of the social sciences stubbornly preserves this doctrinaire attitude, and that is political economy. It says that any idea prevailing within it applies to all kingdoms and peoples, and that, for example, since there are no agricultural communes [*obshchiny*] in the societies where this science is studied, from which their theories are drawn, there must be no communes anywhere, and such a phenomenon is abnormal. Political economy holds that so-called free trade, which is the most profitable form of exchange for England (where this science studies commerce and manufacturing), must certainly apply to America and to Russia as well. In my opinion, this is the same as saying that it is possible to breathe only by lungs (or gills), without looking at the fact that animals do live in the water (or air). Theoretical politics or economy is just as impossible as theoretical physiology or anatomy. All these sciences, in fact all sciences except for the three exceptions listed above, can only be comparative sciences. Thus from the lack of a theoretical foundation or any kind of original, not contrived, economic or political forces and laws, all phenomena in the social world are national phenomena and can only be studied and examined as such. However they can and must be compared among themselves and this comparison may yield a rule for some large or small group of political societies. But never can a political or economic phenomenon observed among one people, for whom it is appropriate and beneficial, be automatically considered appropriate and beneficial for another. It may be, but it may not be. Thus social sciences are national by the very object of their study.

So we can conclude that science too can be national, but the level of nationality is different in various sciences. Nationality appears least of all in the sciences that are simple in their contents, advanced in their level of development, and adhering to strict methods of investigation. These methods to some degree are hindrances to nationality and individuality in general. Here the role of nationality is restricted almost solely to the means of communication and the choice of research methods, if there is a choice of methods. The role of nationality in the sciences increases in proportion to the complexity of the subject, and the relative absence of a strict, exact method. If the sciences are not social sciences, they take on a national character by dint of the peculiarities of the mental framework of each nationality, and especially of each cultural-historical type. The social sciences take on all the more national character (or at least need it for their successful development), since here the very object under investigation is itself national [*natsional'nyi*]. This clearly relates also to linguistic and literary sciences, but there is nothing to say about them since no one anywhere believes that rules of German grammar apply to Russian language, and so on.

⚛ 7 ✥
Is the West Decaying?

> O, never on earth, from the days of creation,
> Was seen such brilliant illumination!
> But woe, the age passed, and a deathly shroud
> Covered the whole West in dark profound...
> Hear the voice of fate take a new cadence:
> Awake, slumbering East, into new radiance!
> —Khomiakov[1]

In the preceding chapters, I have tried to show that the classification and comparison of historical events as developmental stages, or steps toward perfection, contradicts the laws of natural systems, since it does not encompass the full gamut of phenomena, and as in zoology or botany, leads to an artificial system in the construction of a science. To the division into ancient, medieval, and modern, or more numerous periods as levels of development, a qualitative distinction must be added by introducing the dividing principle of cultural-historical types as the highest principle of division. I attempted to define the indicators for grouping historical phenomena, and from those I found the major ethnographic distinctions by which humanity is divided into several large groups. One of these groups consists of the Slavic family of peoples, which are just as distinct as the Sanskrit, Iranian, Hellenic, Latin, and Germanic peoples. Thus the family of Slavic peoples forms an original cultural-historical type, just like the other tribes named here. If the Slavic type is denied the independent development of its principles, then it must be denied all historical significance and reduced to the level of mere ethnographic material, to serve foreign goals—and the sooner, the better. To clarify, a digression seems necessary to explain the relationship of the national to the universally human, both in general and particularly concerning scientific development, which usually resists [the influence of] nationality all the more. I will rely on external, formal evidence. I do not address the essence of the Slavic character nor the essence of the character of other cultural-historical types, but only try to show that if the Slavic family has the same degree of difference from other ethnographic families of humanity in general, and the families of Aryan extraction in particular, as they have from each other, then the root difference in historical-cultural development must also be the same. The only argument

---

[1] From the 1834 poem "Mechta" (The Dream).

against this seems to be the following. The analogy assumes an original Slavic civilization, but the Slavic tribe might be an exception, not unique enough to develop or produce a distinctive culture. This argument often comes with a categorical challenge to explain what exactly this new civilization will consist of, what its science, art, civil and social order, etc., will be like. In my view this is completely absurd, since if it were possible to give a satisfactory answer, there would be no reason for this civilization to develop. In general terms, I can only give a tentative answer to this difficult question by comparing its beginnings, in the character of civilizations that have managed to reveal themselves to this point in the Slavic cultural-historical type. But a firmer answer to this question is a long way off. For now we must turn to an investigation, not into the more or less likely future results of this development from time immemorial, but into those fundamental distinctions between the Slavic type and the Germanic-Roman or European type, since the whole question rests on this distinction. I do not hope to settle the whole matter of this difference, but would wish to present some of its characteristics, the foundations of which were already articulated by the Slavophiles to which I have taken the liberty of making a few additions. But before we begin with this, I would like to clear up one essentially inconsequential formal concern which must be resolved before we enter into another line of thought and evidence.

Many in the past have wrangled over this question: If Slavs have the right to historical-cultural distinctiveness, then it must be acknowledged that they have unfortunately chosen an unwelcome time to present themselves and their demands. The West, or Europe, finds itself at the apogee of its civilizational greatness. Its splendor shines to all corners of the globe; the world is enlightened and warmed by the light and heat coming forth from it. Is this any time for the modest beginnings of a new culture or a new civilization to appear? And why this one, when the other is obviously so powerful and finds itself at the height of its strength, and when there is no sign of it weakening enough to feel any need to take note of another new culture? But Europe is neither imperial Rome nor Byzantium. Could it be possible to say in all seriousness, as Khomiakov and Kireevskii[2] once did, that the West is decaying? If Slavophiles themselves dismissed this extravagance, is it not *plus royaliste que le roi*[3] to uphold such paradoxes?

I have called this argument essentially inconsequential, for I have already said several times that in the time of one culture's brilliance, a new one is born. Did not Rome's steady march begin when Greece was lit up in full civilizational brilliance and trying (however unsuccessfully) to spread itself to

---

[2] Aleksei Stepanovich Khomiakov (1804–60): Russian poet exploring spiritual themes connected with national identity, around whom the Slavophile movement took shape, along with Ivan Vasil'evich Kireevskii (1806–56), through literary disputes with Westernizers like Aleksandr Herzen (1812–70) and Timofei Granovskii (1813–55).

[3] French: "More royalist than the king."

the furthest peoples of the East? Strictly speaking, the most ideal order of things would be if all the great ethnographic groups into which humanity is divided simultaneously developed their own distinctiveness to the level of cultural efflorescence. If the cultures of ancient China, India, Iran, emergent Europe, young Slavdom, and especially young America were to reveal their fullness and variety in full force simultaneously, this would only intensify their fruitful interactions with each other. Such a condition of universal culture would have only one drawback from a universal-historical point of view: whatever it would gain by encompassing so much territory, it would lose in temporal succession, which would contradict the demands of economy that nature always observes. No culture can be eternal. If all flared up in their brilliance at once, then also all would fade at once (or almost at once), and the dark night of barbarism would spread over all lands with nothing left to light the lamp of new cultural life. As in earliest times, it would be necessary once again to obtain the fire of civilization the hard and slow way, by rubbing sticks together. Therefore, although we see no reason why two original civilizations could not exist simultaneously side-by-side, we are more inclined to think, however, that if a new historical type is called to life, then the old one must be dying out. Does this not explain the instinctive enmity the former historical actor feels toward the new—as the predecessor feels toward the successor? The Slavophiles' idea about the decay of the West seems fully correct to me, but some exaggerations crept in from being expressed in the heat of argument, in too bitter a quarrel [with the Westernizers in the 1830s and 1840s].

Decay is the complete breakdown of the structure of an organic body, accompanied by a distinctive, offensive odor. The idea of this whiff of decay concerned our Westernizers as if it insulted them most profoundly. The polemical articles of that time sarcastically spoke of "chemists" incapable of distinguishing decay from the ferment of life.

The ignorance here was not on the part of these "chemists," but of the sharp-wits who saw a real difference between decay and any kind of "ferment of life" which, obviously, does not exist in nature. Fermentation is always decomposition—that is, a change from a complex form of matter to a simpler form, producing inorganic compounds. Thus in our examination, decay or ferment is the same thing. Ferment is the decomposition of forms, whether chemical combinations or social ways of life. For elemental decomposition to yield a new organic form would require the presence of an organizing principle, under the influence of which these elements could form a new whole endowed with an internal, life-giving source. This source was not identified, but it is the essence of the matter. However we are going to make further concessions. Sincerely and gladly we admit that there is no sign of the complete decomposition of European life, whether in the sense of decay complete with the release of putrid gases, or without that, in the sense of fermentation. But that is not the point. Having given up all exaggeration, the real question is, in what period of their development do we find European societies? Where are they on the path: are they still rising by the winding path of social development; have they attained the culmination point; or have they already passed it and started heading toward the twilight of life? In the lives of separate individuals it is easy to answer this question because for each of them there are numerous points of comparison. When the hair starts turning white, the posture stoops, and the face wrinkles, we know what these signs mean from having seen them countless times before. Regarding whole societies, this is not the case. True, history reveals some cultural types that have gone through the whole cycle of their evolution, but the circumstances of this evolution for the most part remain unknown to us. Strictly speaking, only Greece and Rome preserved adequate records of themselves for us to use as the basis of comparison. And of these two, Rome was far from completing its own life, being extremely distorted by the powerful influence of Greece. India in some ways fits the bill. But this is not enough. We must, of course, make use of these comparisons, but with an insufficient amount of data we must instead turn to analogies with other phenomena. Although not the same as civilizations, they all demonstrate the process of evolution under influence of causes regularly and gradually diminishing in intensity.

For the first example, take the change in daily temperature, which depends on the visible movement of the sun through the sky. The sun attains its highest point, or culmination, at noon, but the result of that movement—namely heat—continues to increase for two or three hours after that, even as the cause producing it has already started to decline.

Next, we turn to the analogy with processes of life on earth, which are conditioned by an annual cycle. The summer solstice, corresponding to the longest day and highest position of the sun, falls in the month of June, but the temperatures resulting from this seasonal movement reach their greatest height only in July or August. At that time or later, the results for plant life manifest themselves. At the end of summer or the start of fall, the time when the promises of spring are fulfilled begins, as the days have already shortened and the sun goes lower in the sky.

Turning now to the life of individual persons: the fullness of moral and physical abilities is reached by age thirty. For some time they stay at a certain level, then after forty they begin to weaken visibly. When do these forces give their best, most abundant results? Not before age forty. In one of his exemplary critical or biographical studies—unfortunately I cannot recall where—[British historian Thomas Babington] Macaulay notes that not one truly first-class creation of the human spirit, either in the field of science or art, has been produced by anyone under the age of forty (although without a doubt the original idea may have been born in the mind at a much earlier age). Even if exceptions to this rule can be found in English history, there will in any case be very few of them.

The evolution of languages also demonstrates this. Philologists unanimously affirm that all the most complete languages, including ancient

tongues—such as Sanskrit, Avestan [*zendskii*], Greek, Latin, and Hebrew—
reached their height in the period just before all trace of their existence ends,
and were already in the condition of degeneration and decline at those long
distant times when they first became known to us. In Müller's[4] very persuasive explanation, which includes a principle for genetic classification of
languages by Aryan roots, the development of this family of languages culminated at the time when all the languages of Aryan roots still had not separated into their respective branches. But when did the force that shapes languages—that is, the flowering and fruit of literature—give its greatest results?
In an incomparably later period, [and] for some languages, such as for example the Slavic, it has yet to come.

From all these phenomena it indisputably follows that the high point of
the forces causing all kinds of well-known phenomena does not coincide with
the high point of results arising from those forces' gradual development, but
the latter always comes significantly later than the first. Comparison is not
evidence—*comparaison n'est pas raison*, says the French proverb. This is so. But
if it is possible to detect a common factor in all cases under comparison, and if
that common factor is a necessary part of the phenomenon these comparisons
demonstrate, or if comparisons gain the force of evidence because the action
of a particular cause determines the unfolding course of a process and requires comparisons to explain it, then it follows that this law must pertain to
that whole category of causes and must be identical with these causes acting
in analogous phenomena under comparison. The common factor in the four
phenomena chosen by us (the course of daily temperatures, the course of annual temperatures and with it the cyclical phenomena of vegetative life, the
development of individual persons, and the development of languages) is
that the culmination point of the causative force does not come at the point of
its greatest results, but always precedes it, so that at this latter moment, the
cause of these results has already more or less weakened and already begun
the downward slope of its trajectory. This is explained by the following simple, obvious comparison. The results of a cause accumulate more and more—
capitalize, if you will—until their expenditure surpasses their income; and
even if the income declines relative to the past, the profits still accrue so long
as it exceeds expenses. This is perfectly understood with days and years. And
is it not really the same with the development of a person? If we accept that
from age thirty onward one's strengths begin to weaken, still the mass of
knowledge, experience, and ability to combine intellectual material might increase; the analytical method and the mental gymnastics improve. These
gains can thus for a long time counterbalance the weakening of the immediate
strengths. The same takes place in the evolution of whole societies, of course

---

[4] Friedrich Max Müller (1823–1900): German philologist settled in Britain, pioneer in
India studies and comparative religion. Presumably Danilevskii is referring to his 1864
Lectures on the Science of Language, published in Russian translation in 1866.

in a somewhat less apparent manner. In the evolution of art, for example, the immediate creative forces can decrease, but the manufacturing technology, the influence of examples, the rise of traditions, cautions against mistakes to avoid, and labor-saving shortcuts all create a legacy so that art will continue to flourish for a long time and even attain a higher degree of perfection. A decline in an individual person's strengths seems reasonable, or at least so familiar that it is not source of wonder. But how the creative forces of a whole society can weaken defies explanation, since society consists of continually renewing elements—that is, individual people. However history undeniably shows that it does happen, and not necessarily from external causes, but from internal causes. After Justinian,[5] for example, the Greek people did not produce any more truly great figures in any field over the course of the almost thousand-year existence of its empire.

I said above that the deterioration of an individual person was understood. This is not quite correct: in essence, it is understood just as poorly as the deterioration of societies. The individual person also consists of continually renewing elements. The cells of the body are consumed by it, forming and dividing themselves in various ways, to combine into the new. Why are these new cells worse than the old? Why do they form worse combinations, or hold together more weakly, so that they have less of a beneficial effect for the whole? This is no easier to explain than why, with the continual renewal of the individuals forming the body of society, these entities lose their superior qualities. When once among the Greeks were born figures like Pericles and Epaminondas, Aeschylus and Sophocles, Phidias,[6] Plato and Aristotle, and even in later times, Belisarius, Tribonian, Anthemius of Tralles, and John Chrysostom,[7] why are they now entirely replaced with insignificant people? As with the human or the animal, so with the societal, body—in both cases, the very principle that produces and contains these elements gets old. Whatever the case, the analogies introduced for comparison make it extremely likely that the very successes of European civilization in the nineteenth century are the signs that the creative force producing them has run its course and already begun to fall off.

---

[5] Justinian I, "the Great" (482–565 CE): Byzantine emperor heralded as the "restorer of the empire," who updated the civil law code and reconquered much of the former territory of the Western Roman Empire.

[6] Pericles and Epaminondas: See chap. 4, nn. 12 and 14. Phidias and Sophocles: See chap. 5, nn. 20 and 22. Aeschylus: See chap. 6, n. 17.

[7] Belisarius (d. 565 CE): Byzantine commander under Justinian the Great, responsible for the territorial gains of that era. Tribonian (d. 547): Byzantine jurist overseeing the revision of the law code under Justinian. Anthemius of Tralles (5th–6th century CE): Byzantine architect who collaborated with Isidore of Miletus to construct the Hagia Sophia for Justinian. John Chrysostom (d. 407): Archbishop of Constantinople and Early Church Father, known for his eloquence.

Let us turn to the analogies of other cultural-historical types that have already run their course. When did Greek civilization's creative powers come into bloom? Without a doubt, the age of Pericles [461–429 BCE] marked the end of this period. By that point the flower had already fallen in the arts, philosophic analysis, and the scientific inquiry that characterized Greek learning. By the Peloponnesian War [431–404 BCE], Greece was obviously heading for its fall. The age of Aristotle [384–322 BCE] marked the time of outright decline, even though that time bore the full fruit of philosophy and even art; only later, in what can be called the time of complete breakdown, or (less politely) of decay did positive science achieve its full development in Alexandria [c. 300 BCE–300 CE]. In the same way, the Roman people were in full force at the close of the Punic and Macedonian Wars [264–146 BCE, 214–148 BCE], yet starting with the Gracchi [133–122 BCE], the illness plaguing the body of Rome's society had become very clear, requiring the strong palliatives of the Caesars. But Roman civilization flourished and started bearing its best fruits in the reign of Augustus [27 BCE–14 CE]. Even under the Antonian dynasty[8] [96–180 CE], just before the time of final breakdown, the fruits of Roman civilization appeared in full brilliance. Rome produced almost nothing original in philosophic thought or in scientific inquiry. The only exception to this is in the practical field of law, and its academic formulation came at a very late time in Roman life—beginning with the Antonians, but the greatest period of that law outlived the Western Roman state that produced it and was transplanted to Byzantine soil. From what little we know of the history of Indian culture, the time of its creative period must be considered when Brahmin civilization developed after the subjugation of the Gangetic plain, when its chauvinism prompted Buddhist protests. But this culture's most brilliant results appeared in the pre-modern period, in the time of Vikramaditya,[9] when Kalidasa[10] lived, when the splendid pagodas of Ellora and Varanasi[11] were built, and the fields of philosophy and mathematics flourished. Does it not follow from these three examples that the culmination point of creative social forces that give rise to civilization coincides with the flowering of the arts and encyclopedic knowledge, which chart the course of future academic development; and the high point of science, especially practical, applied sciences, comes at

---

[8] The "Five Good Emperors": Nerva, Trajan, Hadrian, Antoninus Pius, and Marcus Aurelius.

[9] Chandra Gupta II (r. 375–413 CE).

[10] Kalidasa (dates uncertain): Sanskrit poet, possibly Gupta era.

[11] Ellora: Complex of monumental Buddhist caves, constructed in the fifth–seventh centuries; Hindu caves, in the sixth–eighth centuries; and Jain caves, in the ninth–tenth centuries. Varanasi: One of the oldest cities in the world, supposedly built by the deity Shiva, thus a major pilgrimage destination; its temples have been frequently built and rebuilt, so it is unclear what era Danilevskii has in mind.

the time when creative social forces have already gone far past the solstice point?

What epochs in the history of European civilization correspond to this high point of creative forces and the greatest culmination of their results, as seen in the vanished cultures of India, Greece, and Rome? The analogy is so striking that it would be hard to deny. The first corresponds to the sixteenth and seventeenth centuries, when St. Peter's Basilica [in Rome] was raised; Raphael, Michelangelo, and Correggio painted; Shakespeare composed his dramas; and Kepler, Galileo, Bacon, and Descartes laid the foundation for the new rationality and the new methods of scientific investigation. And the second corresponds to the abundant theoretical and practical results of the nineteenth century. In the first epoch everything original in European arts and science was established, so that in the following period it only continued to evolve on the same path. Fruit is predominantly the gift of early fall, but the flower is predominantly the gift of late spring. Just as the formation of the fruit in the bud is completed in the blossom, striking in form and brilliant in color, so the budding fruit of new philosophy and scientific thought is enveloped by the blossom of poetry and the splendor of art. The moment of flowering presents us with the final onset of new life for a plant, but also must be considered its highest moment of creative vegetative forces, after which a certain ripening follows. After that it continues even though the leaves, its main feeding organ, wither; it continues sometimes when the very fruit is torn from where it grew on the plant; it could even be said to persist as it sits on a shelf in the pantry. In the same way, the highest moment of creative social forces must be the appearance at last of the ideas that will support and maintain all further cultural development. The effects of that impulse might still increase and bear splendid, abundant fruits of civilization, but already the forces propagating it will weaken and start heading for collapse. Such is the general character of all gradual development; we understand to some degree the path of this cycle running its course in all civilizations. If the cultural-historical type of Europe is going to be an exception to this trend, then some reason must be demonstrated for such a singular type of exception. But it is obvious we will not be seeing any such thing.

Thus we must not lose sight of the following: Rome's cultural type was simple, operating within one state. The Greek type was more complex, but that complexity bore the consequence that the various stages of its development could not be completely simultaneous. When the life of Athens had already faded to a glorious memory, the Achaean and Aetolian Leagues[12] preserved the vitality of the Greek idea for a time. It was preserved longer and extended further in the Alexandrian conquest, and then further in Tsargrad

---

[12] Achaean and Aetolian Leagues: Hellenistic Greek confederations, to the south and north of the Gulf of Corinth, respectively, that contended with each other, with the declining power of Macedon, and with the rising power of Rome.

[Constantinople]. The dual basis of the European type is even more complex, so it is only natural that if any of its constituent nations found the path of development blocked by unfavorable circumstances, the full development of the creative principle and its results would appear later than other nations. This is what happened in Germany, where 300 years of devastating internecine war blocked the development of high culture that had begun in the time of the Reformation. Thus only in the middle of the past century did its highest poetic creativity begin, and after that came the development of original German philosophic thought, and finally also positive science, in which it did not occupy a preeminent place until late in the first quarter of the nineteenth century. To our view this poses no contradiction of the general course of European civilization, that nearly 150 or 200 years ago its creative forces entered the descending part of their path. The time of bearing fruit has already begun. Is this the harvest time, the gathering of fruit? Is it late summer? Early, or late, fall? It is hard to say. But in any case, the sun that brings forth fruit has already crossed the meridian and is headed for the West. This would become more clear and evident if we could examine the very character of the creative forces underlying and nurturing European civilization, as Khomiakov and Kireevskii did. I will allow myself to explain my thoughts about this in the following exposition of distinctions between the Slavic and the Germanic-Roman type, which without further delay I will begin. For now I will conclude that the development of an original Slavic culture is not only necessary in general, but more precisely, its time has now come.

❧ 8 ❧
The Difference in Mental Framework

> The Merciful Lord has provided our kind with
> such gentleness and good-heartedness as other
> peoples can only envy, and which other peoples
> could only attain, with great effort, through a long
> process of civilization.
> —Galician satirical journal *Scarecrow* (*Strakhopud*)

> Oh Rus'—like the man of wisdom,
> Whom conscience keeps from falling,
> With a noble soul untroubled—
> We follow a divine calling!
> —Khomiakov[1]

The differences among peoples of separate cultural-historical types form the basis for the difference in the very civilizations that are the essential contents and fruit of their vital activity. They fall under the following categories: 1) ethnographic differences, or the tribal qualities that express themselves in the peculiarities of the mental framework of peoples; 2) differences of guiding moral principles, the only possible basis for the fruitful development of civilization, in scientific and artistic as well as social and political terms; 3) differences of the course and conditions of the historical upbringing of peoples. From these three points of view we also will examine the peculiarities of the Slavic, especially the Russian, character, since only the Russian people has attained and preserved its political autonomy—the condition without which, as history shows, civilization never begins or exists, because it cannot do so. The goal of this examination is to evaluate whether these differences are great enough to enable and require the Slavic peoples to produce their own original culture, from fear of losing their significance as a historical tribe in the highest sense of the word.

In defining essential ethnographic differences between the Slavic and Germanic peoples, we find first of all the physiological difference, which some anthropologists consider a stark contrast between the Slavic and Germanic-Roman tribes, which to our mind ought to serve our purpose. But instead, this physiological difference relegates us to the lower order of human

---

[1] From the 1854 poem "Raskaiavsheisia Rossii" (To a Repentant Russia).

tribes, thus eliminating our claim to a high degree of cultural development, as if condemning us to serve as ethnographic material. I have in mind here Retzius's[2] division of the human tribes into the long-headed and short-headed, or dolichocephalic and brachycephalic. It goes without saying that our many "well-wishers" strongly emphasize this allegedly degrading difference for the Slavs. As if in lockstep, the German historian Weber[3] applied his rhymed division of classes, states, and societies in general into *Lehr-, Wehr-,* and *Nährstand* [scholarly, military, and agriculturalist classes] also to the very peoples populating Europe[4] (in the commonly understood sense of this word) and of course put the Slavs among the agriculturalists and the Germans among the scholars: that is, consigning the Slavs to material labor in service to the higher tribes. Let us examine the famous division of Retzius. Where does it lead us?

Besides long-headedness, in which the head's diameter from the forehead to the back exceeds the transverse by a ratio of at least 9:7, and short-headedness, in which this ratio is 8:7, Retzius takes one other sign as the basis of his division: the direction of the front teeth and dental protrusions at the front parts of the jaws. The teeth and dental protrusions can stand vertically in straight-jawed fashion (*orthognathy*); or they can slant in a forward, protruding direction (*prognathy*). These two directions of teeth and jaws combined with long-headedness and short-headedness, create four categories into which the tribes of humanity can be placed in the following way:

Long-headed straight-jawed. Indians (of Aryan descent), Iranians, Germans, Celts, Greeks, Romans, Jews, Arabs, Nubians, Abyssinians, Berbers, Finns, the eastern American Indian tribes settling the plains of North and South America (called "American Semites" by Latham).[5]

Long-headed slant-jawed. Negroes, Kaffirs, Hottentots, Copts, New Zealanders, Eskimos, and Greenlanders.

Short-headed straight-jawed. Slavs, Latvians, Turks, Laplanders, Basques, Raetians, Albanians, ancient Etruscans.

---

[2] Anders Retzius (1796–1860): Swedish comparative anatomist and anthropologist who defined the cephalic index, or ratio of the head's length to width, the variations of which among different populations supported his belief in polygenism, that different races had separate origins.

[3] Georg Weber (1808–88): Historian and director of the high school in Heidelberg, prolific textbook author.

[4] Weber associated the three castes with Germans, Romans, and Slavs; see *Allgemeine Weltgeschichte für die gebildeten Stände,* 4: 861.

[5] Robert Gordon Latham (1812–88): English ethnologist and philologist.

Short-headed slant-jawed. Chinese, Japanese, Mongols, Malaysians, Polynesians, Papuans, peoples of the American Cordillera, including the ancient Peruvians ("American Mongols," according to Latham).

First of all, we must not fail to note that such a division has a completely artificial character. Here there is one pervasive principle exhibited which, as is usually the case, puts disparate things together and divides similar things in other ways. So, for example, by strictly following these divisions, northern and southern Germans would be scattered among various classes of humanity, since the former are long-headed and the latter are short-headed.

How can we reconcile this kind of division with other division schemes: by skin color, kinds of hair, the "facial angle" of Camper,[6] or finally, a linguistic division? Here everything is subordinated to a single trait that is given primary significance. If the Slavs, despite speaking an Aryan language, have a particular shape of skull, then one must accept that they borrowed their Aryan language from some long-headed Aryan tribe (a tribe speaking a Slavic language, of course, and sufficiently numerous and strong to pass on their language to such a major part of humanity; probably of Turkic origins since, in the vicinity of those places where the Slavs have lived or do live now, only certain Turkic tribes combine short-heads and straight-jaws). How come no trace remains of this original proto-Slavic tribe? From this, it would seem more reasonable to conclude that, although it can and should be grouped with other anthropological traits distinguishing various groups of humans, the ratio between the lengthwise and crosswise diameters of the skull cannot bear such primary significance as it has been given. However, for the time being we will preserve its primary significance and see what kind of conclusions come from this.

The peoples attaining such high culture as the Aryan or Semitic tribes, in both ancient and modern times, are all long-headed; thus the Slavs are not among the higher tribes of humanity. Sir Duchinski[7] would have welcomed such a conclusion, but unfortunately if Russians are Turks then so are Poles, since like it or not they must share the same fate with Russia as with all the Slavs. But if a certain phenomenon can be legitimately interpreted two different ways, then of course each has full right to accept the interpretation that seems most pleasing.

From the idea that to this point only long-headed tribes have attained a high level of culture, the conclusion can be drawn of course that short-head-

---

[6] Pieter Camper (1722–89): Dutch anatomist famous for his "facial angle" theory, comparing the races by lines from nostril to ear and upper jaw to forehead, originally in the context of portraiture.

[7] Franciszek Henryk Duchinski (1816–93): Polish historian and ethnographer, emigrated to Paris after the 1831 Polish uprising; argued that Great Russians were neither Aryan nor Slavic, but Turanian (from Central Asia, like the Turks).

edness is some kind of hindrance to it, indicating less ability for higher development. But one can also conclude that this happened only because the short-
headed Slavs came into circumstances favorable for culture later, started to
develop later, and have not yet produced the culture of which they are capable by natural instincts. One can also conclude that since history is not yet
ended, in accordance with general laws of nature the highest developed
forms are typically not only a higher, but a later, development. The first interpretation would have a certain advantage, if the Slavic tribe not yet having
reached a high level of culture had shown no individual examples of a high
degree of giftedness. But the Slavs brought forth such ingenious scholars as
Copernicus; such religious reformers as Hus; such statesmen as Ivan III and
Peter the Great; such poets as Pushkin, Gogol, and Mickiewicz; such military
leaders as Suvorov; such models of enlightenment as Lomonosov.[8] Thus the
Slavic tribes have no lack of instincts for the highest human development. So
to validate the first interpretation requires proof that short-headedness in and
of itself is an indicator of lesser development, and that the aforementioned examples of highly-gifted, short-headed individuals are only exceptions, perhaps the product of some kind of inter-tribal crossbreeding. But the intrinsic
reason why the predominantly long-headed would be at a higher level than
those with skulls of more proportionate diameters (front to back and side to
side) has not been found. Thus we must turn to the most systematic arrangement for classifying tribes. It will show us that of the two traits we have considered as principles of division, one—the angle of the jaw and teeth—can
serve as an indisputable indicator of the levels of perfection among human
tribes: namely, straight-jawed peoples are indisputably more advanced than
slant-jawed peoples. This trait establishes a horizontal division of the human
species. The question is, can we ascribe the same hierarchical character to the
other principle of division—based on the ratio of skull diameters? If we grant
this proposition, then we will see that among the lower, slant-jawed tribes of
the human species the round-headed are superior, since the Chinese,[9] Mon-

---

[8] Copernicus: See chap. 4, n. 6. Hus: See chap. 6, n. 12. Suvorov: See chap. 2, n. 41.
Pushkin: See chap. 6, n. 25. Ivan III, "the Great" (1440–1505): Moscow prince, crowned
Grand Prince of all Rus', who ended Mongol rule and "gathered the Russian lands"
under Moscow's sovereignty. Nikolai Vasilievich Gogol' (1809–52): Ukrainian-born
naturalist-realist Russian author, Pushkin's contemporary and rival in popularity.
Adam Bernard Mickiewicz (1798–1855): Widely regarded as Poland's greatest poet,
known for the epic *Pan Tadeusz* and political-nationalist works. Mikhail Vasilievich
Lomonosov (1711–65): Renaissance man of the Russian Enlightenment era, accomplished in the natural sciences, art, and literature, especially poetry.

[9] [Danilevskii's note]: If we consider the Chinese medium-headed (*Mesocephali*), whose
skulls are an intermediate form between long- and short-headed, then they must of
course be left out of any resolution of the present question. But even after excluding
them, the mental superiority among the slant jawed tribes indisputably remains on the
side of the round-headed.

gols, Malaysians, and Polynesians stand much higher than the Negroes, Kaffirs, Hottentots, and residents of New Holland [i.e., Australian aborigines], which constitute the lowest of the human races. But if that is so, then the obvious analogy forces us to recognize that short-headedness must preserve that predominance even among the slant-jawed tribes, so that the ascending order of human tribes would look like this:

> *Slant-jawed, long-headed tribes* (Negroes and others)
> *Slant-jawed, short-headed tribes* (Mongols and others)
> *Straight-jawed, long-headed tribes* (Europeans and others)
> *Straight-jawed, short-headed tribes* (Slavs and others)

If one does not want to accept this outcome, which is the most simple and natural conclusion—in fact the inevitable outcome, if long-headedness and short-headedness are considered hierarchically—then one must recognize that the ratio between different diameters of the skull in general cannot provide a horizontal [i.e., hierarchical] division, but only a vertical [i.e., categorical] division of humanity. That is, it cannot establish superior and inferior groups, but only two groups that are parallel, side-by-side in their development: right and left, so to speak.

For this reason, Retzius's division logically leads to one of the following three conclusions which, from the standpoint of national pride, we can accept equally: 1) This is only an artificial division, not having such predominant significance as some ascribe to it, and the traits it is based on can only serve alongside others to characterize the breeds, races, or general groups into which the human species is divided. This seems to me the only reasonable and well-founded conclusion. 2) Both principles of division (the angle of front teeth and the ratio of skull diameters) are hierarchical principles, determining the degree of racial perfection. In this case, the highest rank goes to the short-headed, straight-jawed—that is, to the Slavs. 3) Only the angle of teeth indicates the degree of perfection among tribes; the ratio between skull diameters only produces a vertical division into various tribes, but not into higher and lower tribes. In this final view, just like zoological divisions into types and classes, we would have two different systematizing principles: one establishing ethnographic types, not ranked higher or lower but only distinguished as different from one another; and the other establishing ethnographic classes signifying the level of perfection of the organism. Having concluded this brief digression, I will now turn to the actual topic of this chapter.

It is very difficult to grasp accurately and definitively, and clearly articulate, the difference in mental frameworks of various nationalities. Differences of this kind, between individual persons and whole peoples alike, are only quantitative, not qualitative. It is hardly possible to find some trait of the national character that another nation completely lacks; the difference lies in how common or rare it is from one people to another. In the majority of people of one tribe it is pronounced; in the majority of another it is hardly found. But these degrees of frequency or rarity are inexpressible in numbers; such statistics do not exist. And that is why any description of the national character will resemble those meaningless collections of epithets used to characterize historical figures in poorly written history books; and that is why these descriptions of the national character by various travelers are sometimes so different, even though they are equally observant and conscientious. One finds certain characteristics, the other finds others, but in what proportion they exist among the whole population necessarily remains undefined and unknown to both.

Tracking down the characteristics that could be considered true traits of the national character, and thus of essential importance, requires taking a different path than a simple descriptive account of individual observations. If we succeed in finding such traits of the national character expressed in all historical activity, in the whole historical lives of the peoples under comparison, then that would solve the problem. That is because if some trait of the national character is revealed in the whole history of a people, then one must conclude, in the first place, that it is a trait common to the whole people, and only by exception might one or another individual person lack it; secondly, that this trait is constant, independent of accidental and temporary circumstances of one or another situation in which the people finds itself, of one or another stage of development through which it has passed; and finally, in the third place, that this trait must be of essential importance if it can imprint its character upon the whole of its historical activity. Thus we could properly take such a trait as the moral and ethnographic sign of a people, an expression of the essential peculiarities of its whole mental framework. One of the traits common to all the peoples of the Germanic-Roman type is *violence* (*Gewaltsamkeit*). Violence in turn is nothing but an over-developed sense of personality and individuality, by which the afflicted person holds his interests and his way of thinking so high that any other interests or way of thinking must, voluntarily or involuntarily, seem to him inferior or not equally valid. From the perspective of over-developed individualism and an exaggerated sense of one's own merit, imposing one's own way of thinking onto others and subjecting everything to one's own interests does not even seem in any way wrong. It only seems like the natural subjection of the lower to the higher, even as if in some sense the lower should be thankful. Depending on the circumstances, such a framework of the mind, feelings, and will leads in politics and social life to aristocratism, the oppression of other nationalities, boundless freedom unrestrained by anything, or extreme political fracturing; in religion, to intolerance or the rejection of any and all authority. Of course it also has its good sides, as a basis for persistence, a strong defense of one's rights, and so on. We will trace the course of events in European history to see whether violence truly is the root characteristic of all the Germanic-Roman peoples.

This violent European character appeared earliest of all in the religious sphere, since it was long the predominant interest over all others. Religious violence—that is, intolerance—reveals itself just as much in the Roman tribes as in the tribes of Germanic stock. It is well known that the first blood of heretics was shed in the West, even though the prevalence of heresies was much greater in the East. In the year 385, the Spanish heretic Priscillian[10] and six of his followers were tortured and executed in Bordeaux, after being condemned by synods at Saragossa, Bordeaux, and Trier. The orthodox Church, in the persons of Ambrose of Milan and Martin of Tours,[11] was horrified and opposed further persecution. This execution, this religious violence—committed still during the time of the Roman Empire and while general orthodoxy still prevailed—served as the beginning of the intolerance Catholicism subsequently revealed. But if we consider the execution of Priscillian as an isolated event, then it is possible to attribute all the religious intolerance and violence of the centuries that followed precisely to the influence of Catholicism, and not to the influence of the national character of the Germanic-Roman peoples upon the religious belief and activity of the medieval and early modern eras. But what is Catholicism but Christian teaching subjected to the influence of the Germanic-Roman character? Christian teaching in itself does not contain any hint of intolerance, so one cannot say that it gave a violent character to the peoples professing faith in it (as can be said in all truth concerning the influence of Islam, for example). Thus if Catholicism displays the characteristics of intolerance and violence, it must have adopted them from no other source than the character of the peoples professing it.

Christianity in the pure orthodox form was adapted to the traits of the Germanic-Roman character, and from this Catholicism was formed. Catholicism was born in the time of Charlemagne, when by his own patronage he affirmed the power of the Bishop of Rome over all his lands, the borders of which almost matched what we now call Europe. Up to that time the Roman pontiffs only enjoyed the respect associated with the name of Rome, and also what they secured for themselves in the eyes of the peoples conquered by

---

[10] Priscillian (d. 384): Bishop of Avila, taught a strict asceticism and celibacy, arousing suspicions of Manichaeism (a Gnostic ascetic tradition that associated evil with matter, to be overcome by the mind, where good resides), and welcomed women as equals with men, arousing suspicions of impropriety. The Western Roman Emperor-usurper Magnus Maximus ordered his execution, arousing protests against civil authorities governing ecclesiastical affairs.

[11] Ambrose (d. 397): Bishop of Milan, one of the Four Doctors of the Western Church. Martin (316–97): Bishop of Tours, widely venerated throughout Christendom.

In the original text, Orthodox Church (*Pravoslavnaia tserkov'*) is capitalized as the first word in the sentence, but is rendered lower-case here (meaning "correct" or "consistent with traditional practice") to avoid anachronism. Believers tend to associate their own tradition with the side of the right by deliberate anachronism, and such is possibly the case here.

Romans in Italy, Gaul, and Spain, by their faithfulness to the orthodoxy these peoples professed before their conquest by barbarians, at which point they, like their barbarian-conquerors, for the most part accepted Arianism.[12] For similar reasons, they began to enjoy the same respect in the East as well, during the time of persecution of the emergent iconoclasts. If the popes had remained true to orthodox dogmas, then it is very likely they would have been granted not supremacy, of course, but predominant influence and reverence in the East as in the West, since the Eastern Christians would come to consider them a refuge against the frequent despotism of Byzantine emperors in churchly affairs. The role of the mediator as the high arbiter of churchly matters obviously comes close to a position of predominance. The popes could not fail to see these vistas opening before them, which provided a suitable goal for their ambition at that time, before the forgery of the Pseudo-Isidorean Decretals,[13] when they were still under attack from the Lombards.[14] At this time they could foresee neither the secular dominion that lay ahead of them, nor the establishment in Europe of feudal-theocratic monarchies half full of pagans and threatened by Muslims, as in the bloody disorders of Merovingian France.[15] Obviously the doctrinal dispute with the East could not have been a part of their plan, nor was it. The popes did not instigate a doctrinal schism in the Church, as Khomiakov superbly demonstrated in a well-known brochure; they merely accepted it after long denying it, and once they had accepted it, of course, they began to take advantage of it.

The doctrinal difference between the Eastern and Western Churches arose for no other reason than the ignorance prevailing in the West during the first centuries of the medieval period, as well as the violent character that undergirds all despotism: the violence that considers a personal, subjective opinion to be sanctified and confirmed by the fact that it is *ours*. The conference with

---

[12] Arianism: The doctrine taught by Arius (see chap. 9, n. 31) that Jesus, as Son of God, did not exist eternally but was created at his birth, thus not equal with God the Father, but the highest of all created beings. It was ruled heretical by the First Council of Nicaea in 325, but this was reversed (under duress) by the First Synod of Tyre in 335, then finally ruled heretical again at the First Council of Constantinople of 381.

[13] Pseudo-Isidorean Decretals: A large collection of ninth-century forged documents (including the infamous Donation of Constantine), which generally sought to free bishops from secular authorities and supervision by archbishops, and promoted papal power toward that end.

[14] Lombards: Germanic tribe ruling a pagan and Arian-Christian kingdom in Italy in the sixth to eighth centuries, viewed as a threat to the Roman Catholic Church, subsequently conquered by Charlemagne, which secured him the Church's favor.

[15] Merovingian France: Dynasty founded by Childeric I, son of Merovech (hence the name) in the mid-fifth century, ruling France for three centuries, succeeded by the Carolingian dynasty (named for Charles Martel, 676–741).

the East[16] was an embarrassment in the Western clergy's own eyes. Through this, by an act of force, the part (the Western Church) hijacked and usurped the rights of the whole (the universal Church). In this the popes personally were innocent.

A second case of force was revealed in the way this particular opinion gained the sanction of accepted dogma in the West. This was done by the Council of Aachen in 809,[17] which the Catholics themselves understood was no more than a local council, the outcome of which did not even have to its credit the sanction of papal authority. Charlemagne interceded for this [papal sanction] on the Council's behalf, following the example of many Eastern emperors in this case, with the essential difference however that they [Byzantine emperors] often used their power and influence to gain acceptance for some orthodox or heretical opinion they personally believed in, which could not have been the case for Charles. In fact, doctrine about the procession of the Holy Spirit from the Father only, or from the Father and the Son, is just one of a number of teachings that, by themselves, are not at all clear to the average mind. Both are equally incomprehensible, mysterious teachings beyond the grasp of reason. The teaching of Arius could seem more comprehensible, simpler, less lofty and mysterious than the orthodox doctrine of the Trinity, and thus more appealing to those inclined toward rationalism. The same could be said for Nestorianism, Monophysitism, and Monothelitism; to a great extent it still applies to iconoclasm.[18] Other teachings, Gnosticism[19] for example, could

---

[16] Presumably the Synod of Gentilly in 767, at which the procession of the Holy Spirit (the root of the *filioque* controversy) and use of images in worship were discussed, though records of the outcome were lost.

[17] Council of Aachen (809): The Frankish Church approved the addition of *filioque* to the Nicene Creed, so that the Holy Spirit proceeds from the Father "*and the Son*" (Latin: *qui ex Patre Filioque procedit*). This and the issue of papal primacy later became the grounds for the formal split between the Church East and West. Pope Leo III (in office 795–816) rejected the change, and the Roman Catholic Church did not approve it until 1014.

[18] Nestorianism: The doctrine, ruled heretical, that Jesus has separate human and divine natures, rather than one nature fully human and fully divine. The Nestorian Church, of the Syrian rite, was spread by the Sassanid and Mongol empires to India and China. Monophysitism: The heretical doctrine that Jesus had only a single, divine nature, attributed to the Oriental Orthodox Churches who rejected the Council of Chalcedon. These churches prefer the term miaphysitism, to express that Christ's single nature was both human and divine, thus rebutting the charge of heresy. Monothelitism: The doctrine, ruled heretical, that Jesus had two natures but only a single divine will, preserved in the Maronite Church of Syria. Iconoclasm: The rejection (and destruction) of all images associated with worship, from a very literal interpretation of the Ten Commandments, in the eighth-century Byzantine Empire.

[19] Gnosticism: Syncretic religion of esoteric, mystical knowledge revealed only to a privileged few.

on the contrary have a mystical attraction for people rich in imagination. The teaching about the procession of the Holy Spirit could be a genuine conviction for the refined mind of a Scholastic who has arrived at it by the path of narrow dialectical conclusions and fine distinctions, or the erudite and the exegetes, who come to it through an incomplete, subjective examination of the scriptures and the writings of the Church Fathers. But how could it be a matter of deep conviction for such a practical mind as Charlemagne, especially when the most knowledgeable authority of that day (not only in the eyes of his contemporaries, but also in the eyes of Charles), Alcuin,[20] held the opposite, that is, the orthodox, view? It is obvious that Charles had to have another, less ideal reason impelling him to demand Leo III's assent to a change of the Nicene-Constantinopolitan Creed. In my opinion, this reason is not hard to find. Everything Charles did was for the sake of his cherished ideal: the creation of a universal Christian state in which all high authority, both secular and sacred, would be combined in the person of the Emperor, the ideal of Caesaropapism that foreigners like to attribute to Russia. He sought to elevate his own power and significance by elevating the significance of everything indebted and obliged to him, or protected by him against the papacy's many enemies. To achieve this goal required that both church and state be free of any outside influences and interference. But how could this be, so long as the pope was only one of the five universal patriarchs,[21] so long as any change not only in articles of faith but in the common liturgical norms and canonical order of the church required the authority of the ecumenical councils (which to that time had always met in the East) or at least the assent of the highest Eastern hierarchs? Stated simply, Charles needed what we now call a state church, and he made use of a doctrinal difference born in the West to establish it, just as Henry VIII[22] later separated the Anglican Church from the Roman. Catholicism, which in its very name claims a universal character, has its true origin however in Charles's desire to create for his dominion an independent state church by breaking it off from the universal Church. Whether from a sincere conviction that changing the Creed was impermissible or from the desire to preserve his autonomy from the emperor's power, Leo III, as we know, did not agree to Charles's ambassadors' urgent demands. Despite the pope's opposition, however, the new false doctrine became firmly established, something that could not have happened if in the Western priesthood—that is, in all the educated strata of the society of that day—there

---

[20] Alcuin of York (735–804): English cleric and renowned scholar, invited to serve at Charlemagne's court.

[21] The Pentarchy: A division of Christendom into five patriarchal, apostolic sees— Jerusalem, Rome, Constantinople, Alexandria, and Antioch.

[22] Henry VIII (1491–1547): Tudor king of England, famously separated from the Roman Catholic Church to secure a divorce the Pope refused to grant, creating the national Anglican Church.

had not prevailed that spirit of violence which wants to know nothing beyond one's own convictions, even if by the nature of things, one's conviction on that subject cannot be competent.

We see the same thing in the time when Christianity was preached to the Slavs by the apostles Saint Cyril and Saint Methodius in the state of Moravia.[23] And here the opposition to the Slavic mission came not from the pope, but from the German bishops. The popes repeatedly resisted the use of *filioque*, and even after Nicholas I[24] permitted the reading of the Creed without it. Finally the outright fabrication of the Pseudo-Isidorean Decretals, which laid the foundation of the future Catholic edifice, did not come from the popes or even under their influence, but was done without their knowledge to strengthen bishops against their regional archbishops. I bring this as evidence that Catholicism arose and became well established not so much as the result of papal ambition but from the violent character of the Western priesthood, seeing itself as all-important, and outside itself, nothing worth knowing. The popes, of course, made use of this advantageous development and used it to try to subordinate the East.

The subsequent religious history of Europe confirms this. If not for the common violent character among the Germanic-Roman peoples, why would they undertake such an uncharacteristic form of Christian proselytism, using fire and the sword to force conversion on the tribes of eastern Germany under Charlemagne, and under later emperors upon the Slavic tribes of the northwest? Why these chivalrous orders of Teutonic Knights and Livonian Brothers of the Sword,[25] bringing violent preaching to Lithuania, Latvia, and Estonia, and placing the persons and possessions of these peoples in feudal bondage to themselves? Where did the popes get the means for the bloody suppression of the Albigensians and Waldensians?[26] How did Catherine de'

---

[23] Cyril and Methodius: Ninth-century Byzantine missionary ambassadors sent in 862 to Great Moravia at the invitation of Prince Ratislav, who had expelled representatives of the Roman Church. They are credited with creating the Glagolitic alphabet, the basis for Cyrillic.

[24] Pope Nicholas I (r. 858–67): Champion of papal supremacy, heightened the confrontation with the East and was excommunicated by the (local) Council of Constantinople of 867.

[25] Teutonic Knights: German military monastic order, formed during the Crusades in Acre (until its collapse), defended Hungary from Turkish invaders until expelled, then instrumental in the Prussian Crusade, where they established a Teutonic kingdom. The Livonian Brothers of the Sword were founded separately but were merged with the Teutons in 1237 as a separate branch, the Livonian Order, forming a crusader state on the Baltic Coast.

[26] Albigensians were Cathars (a protest movement against Church corruption with a number of heretical beliefs) in the Languedoc region of France, against whom Pope Innocent III declared a Crusade in 1209; warfare continued until 1255. Waldensians rejected the authority of the clergy and preached according to their own interpretations

Medici recruit the murderers of St. Bartholomew's night?[27] Without violence in the national character how could there be more ardent defenders of the papacy than the popes themselves, who have spread and defended its dominion through the subtle force of Jesuitism and the brute force of the Inquisition? But it is not Catholicism that imposes the character of violence, as if from the outside, upon the religious life of European peoples; the best proof of this is that, in places where Catholicism has been displaced by Protestantism, which claims to teach freedom of conscience, we see no great tolerance among its followers either. Calvin burned at the stake his adversary Miguel Servet,[28] who was no worse than anyone at the Council of Constance;[29] the Anglicans burned Catholics and Presbyterians alike; the Puritans presented themselves as models of religious intolerance. But that is all long in the past, some will say, the result of crudeness and barbarism; but these days does not Europe set an example not only of Protestant, but also Catholic, religious tolerance and complete non-interference in matters of human conscience? True. But when did this redeeming conversion occur? Not before religious interest in general was relegated to second, third, or fourth place—to put it simply, was shoved into the background—and faded behind other present-day interests preoccupying European society. When religion lost the bulk of its significance or its social character, in a manner of speaking, when it ceased to be *res publica*,[30] when it was left in the depth of personal, family life—then it became easy to be not only tolerant in regards to it, but essentially indifferent, as the saying goes: "Give to God what you can live without."[31]

---

of scripture, for which they were anathematized at the Fourth Lateran Council of 1215. They were eventually incorporated within Protestantism in the Reformation era.

[27] St. Bartholomew's Night: Massacre of Huguenot (French Protestant) leaders starting 23 August 1572, after King Charles IX's sister married the Protestant Henry III of Navarre (later Henry IV of France). The violence ran for weeks and killed thousands. The instigation of Catherine de' Medici (1519–89), mother of Charles IX, was widely believed but unsubstantiated.

[28] Miguel Servet (1511–53): Spanish theologian and Renaissance man, condemned by both Catholics and Protestants alike, sentenced by the government council of Geneva, with the approval of John Calvin, to be burned at the stake for rejecting both the doctrine of the Trinity and the practice of infant baptism. John Calvin (1509–64): French Protestant pastor and theologian based in Geneva, Switzerland, author of the *Institutio Christianae religionis* (Institutes of the Christian Religion; 1536). The doctrine of predestination is associated with his name (Calvinism), and Reformed and Presbyterian churches are based on his theology.

[29] Council of Constance (1414–18): Summoned to resolve the Three Popes' Controversy (alternately known as the Western Schism, in which two rival popes were elected by the same group of cardinals, then a third was elected when neither backed down), and which also condemned to death Jan Hus (see chap. 6, n. 12).

[30] Latin: "A public matter."

[31] *Na tebe, Bozhe, chto nam negozhe.*

But this did not eradicate violence as a basic trait of the European character. Shut nature out the door, and it will come in the window. When something new attracts society's attention, it will necessarily reveal the predominant traits of the national character. While religion had not yet lost its primary significance for European society, its attention turned to distant, newly discovered lands overseas that promised wide open, profitable opportunities for all enterprising people willing to go there. Colonial conquests and colonial politics were the main issues for the peoples of Europe during the Reformation and for a long time after. The world appeared too small for the ambitions of both Spain and Portugal, so it seemed necessary to divide it between them with a demarcation line.[32] The feats of conquistadors are so well known there is no reason to go on about them; their actions were attributed to coarseness and greed, as adventure-seekers mostly from the rabble of human society. But this is not what I would like to bring into view. For my purposes I must confine myself to the main, most common characteristics interwoven into the whole society, so to speak. And the fact of the Negro slave trade would seem to be substantial enough: hunting down humans, packing them up for sale, throwing them overboard by the dozen, and enslaving them by the million! Despite Negroes' strong nature and being bred like livestock, they could not endure the burden of involuntary, never-ending work and thus had to be continually replenished from Africa as an inexhaustible source. There is nothing like it in the history of the world. To find something remotely similar, albeit on a microscopic scale, we would have to look at those pirate states in certain cities of Sicily and southern Italy during the struggle of the Greeks [sic; Rome] with Carthage at the beginning of the Punic Wars.

Well, if this is not from the distant past, it is in the past nonetheless. The main thing is that evil was eradicated, or at least greatly reduced, by the philanthropists of Europe itself. I do not intend to diminish in any way the service of those great individuals like Wilberforce and Buxton[33] who devoted their whole lives to the opposition and struggle against the deep-rooted evil, nor the service of England in general to curtail the despicable trade. I consider groundless all the accusations that try to cast a shadow of doubt on the unselfishness of England in its efforts and sacrifices toward that end, and I readily acknowledge that the very strength of the evil summoned a hearty reaction against it. But the fact of an incomparable, centuries-long act of violence remains, and can be explained by nothing other than violence of character,

---

[32] Referring to the pope-sponsored Treaty of Tordesillas (1494), which established zones in the New World and the lands of the Pacific Ocean for Spain and Portugal to colonize without fighting over territory.

[33] William Wilberforce (1759–1833): English Member of Parliament, evangelical Christian abolitionist and humanitarian reformist. Sir Thomas Buxton (1786–1845): English member of Parliament, Quaker-influenced social reformer and opponent of capital punishment.

since this trade was not some legal or political action imposed by force on the people [of Europe], but a matter in which a significant part of society, everyone who had any interest in it, took part voluntarily. However, even though the Negro slave trade has ceased, or almost ceased, and even though the Negroes have been freed in most of the colonies and colonial states, is not the same trade in human beings still visible in the voluntary hiring of "coolies"?[34]

After colonial fever passed, the European peoples' main interest turned to questions of civil and political freedom. And again their violence of character was revealed to no less degree than in religion and colonial politics. The continual operation of the guillotine, the Lyons grapeshot executions, the sinkings [of barges of counterrevolutionaries] in Nantes, the foreign wars by which they preached liberty, fraternity, and equality with sword in hand,[35] just as Charlemagne and the crusader knights once did for Christianity: What is this but intolerance, the violent imposition of one's ideas and interests in every way? And is not the governing principle here (the same as the Jesuits', that the end justifies the means) the true formulation of violence?

But the revolutionary spirit also subsided, interest in politics diminished, although not so much as in religion, and once again material interests of production and trade played the primary role. By their very essence these interests are personal, and would not seem to have any use for violence. And yet even in such an enlightened and humane age as ours the global transmitter of civilization, European trade, provides an example of such singular violence as the trade of Negro slaves. At the beginning of the 1840s [in the First Opium War, 1839–42], England used guns to open up China [to the sale of opium], to its detriment. Are not conquistadors, counter-reformation warriors, inquisitors, or terrorists only a hair worse, a hair more violent than civilized traders forcing an entire people, peaceable and worthy of respect for its antiquity, to become poisoned morally and physically [i.e., the opium trade] in their pursuit of commercial profits? The "great and holy interests" in whose name those traders committed their acts of brutality might be counted as mitigating factors for them, if there could be any excuse for such uses of force.

Toward the Slavic peoples oppressed by Turkey, are not the Western states violent in the same way? A false understanding of egotistical self-interest forces them to oppose the liberation of these unfortunate peoples by all manner of terrible injustices, even with weapons drawn. The interests of religion once demanded [the massacre of] St. Bartholomew's Night; the interests of liberty demanded the Septembrist massacres and continuous operation of the guillotine; and now the interests of political equality and civilization (threatened by who knows what) demand the defense of Turkish barbarism

---

[34] Coolies: Low-cost manual laborers from Asia, primarily India and China, supplied by brokers. They became the alternative colonial labor supply after the abolition of the slave trade.

[35] Events from the radical phases of the French Revolution (1792–95).

and the sacrifice of the freedom, life, and honor of the Slavs and Greeks to this new Moloch.

What parallel to the violence of European history, revealing itself in any kind of predominant interest, can be found in the history of Russia? Religion has been a prevalent interest for the Russian people over the course of its existence. But it did not need the teachings of the Encyclopedists[36] to become tolerant. Tolerance is the distinguishing characteristic of Russia, even in the worst times. They say [Eastern] Orthodoxy gave it this character. Of course. But Orthodoxy was also the original religion of the West, after all; as we have seen, however, it became distorted precisely under the influence of the violence of the Germanic-Roman character. If it did not undergo the same kind of distortion among the Russian people and the Slavic peoples in general, then that means their own natural behaviors lack the instincts for this kind of distortion, or if it had such instincts, they were at least so weak that not only could they not overpower the gentle spirit emanating from Christianity, but on the contrary were completely absorbed into it and healed by it. Moreover even those Slavic tribes like the Czechs who renounced Orthodoxy for Catholicism as a result of Germanic violence never embraced religious intolerance. They were forced to suffer it, but did not force such suffering onto others. Steeped in their blood were those Orthodox principles so powerfully displayed in the glorious days of Hus and Žižka.[37] One of the Slavic peoples presents a true and lamentable exception: the Poles. Their history has been marked by violence and intolerance. But the comparatively small part of the Polish people that bears the blame for this, the nobility,[38] could assimilate European violence only by completely distorting and denying its whole Slavic character, breaking ranks with Slavdom in all regards, to such a degree that it became a tool for Turkey to use to oppress the Slavs. In Russia's own history, the characteristic of religious intolerance does appear every so often, namely in regard to Old Believers.[39] Not to make excuses, but for one thing, it must be said that our persecutions pale in comparison to European persecutions, and for another, to be precise we must distinguish two very different kinds of persecution: those before and after Peter the Great. Only in the first, rather short, period did they have a truly religious character; doubtless they acquired it from the influences beginning to appear at that time in western Russia among

---

[36] Encyclopedists: The *philosophes* of the French Enlightenment who contributed articles to the *Encyclopédie* edited by Denis Diderot (1713–84) and Jean le Rond d'Alembert (1717–83). Articles in the *Encyclopédie* frequently editorialized against the religious intolerance of Catholic France from an "enlightened" point of view.

[37] Hus and Žižka: See chap. 6, n. 12.

[38] *Shliakhetstvo*, from Polish *szlachta*, the hereditary noble, landowning class of Poland.

[39] Old Believers: Minority Russian faith community that rejected mid-seventeenth-century reforms to align the Russian Orthodox liturgy and worship practices with original Greek sources, adhering instead to the "old belief."

the Kievan clergy. Under continual persecution from Latin Christendom, they unintentionally became infected with some degree of Catholic intolerance, which then spread so successfully to the government in Moscow that it affected the eastern Russian clergy. In the second period, the persecution was strictly political, and it targeted the Old Believers as the most powerful protest of Russian life against foreign domination; at its height under Biron,[40] it even targeted Orthodoxy itself. Besides this, we must recall that the Russian people never supported the persecution of Old Believers, and even less took part in it: it was done by the police, a force outside of it [the people]. We must also note that, having undertaken this alien endeavor, the government showed itself completely ham-handed. Concerning Russian religious persecution, we can echo the words of a disappointed briber: "When it comes to that, they won't even do it for money."

The Russian people also had a period of broad and extensive conquest, or rather, settlement. As in the time of the Spanish conquistadores, these conquests were accomplished almost without any government participation, by adventure-seekers and even bandit chiefs. But what a difference! Not only were the poor, half- or completely-wild foreigners not exterminated and wiped off the face of the earth, but they were not even deprived of their liberty or property, nor were they enslaved by their conquerors.

So this is one essential difference. By their very nature the Slavic peoples have been spared from that violence of character that the Germanic-Roman peoples, throughout the age-old process of civilization, managed to spread from one sphere of activity to another. Is it really possible for this kind of native humanity not to be reflected as the distinct defining characteristic of the civilization it created? It is reflected in many others, for example in Russian jurisprudence concerning the death penalty. From the time of Vladimir's acceptance of Christianity [c. 988],[41] he felt it [the death penalty] was completely incompatible with the highest principles he had been taught, and by that proved that he was more filled with the Christian spirit than were his teachers and instructors, who used their sophistry to remove the ample doubts of the saintly prince. Monomakh[42] felt the same about the death penalty, and this was at the height of medieval barbarism in Europe. After the re-

---

[40] Ernst Johann von Biron (1690–1772): Opportunistic and ruthless favorite of Empress Anna, who held considerable sway over state policy, known as the *bironovshchina* (see chap. 3, n. 8) during her reign in the 1730s.

[41] Vladimir I, "the Great" (958–1015): Grand Prince of Kievan Rus' who converted to Christianity in 988, baptized all his people, and built many churches as part of an alliance with the Byzantine Empire, sealed by his marriage to Anna (963–1012), the sister of Emperor Basil II (958–1025).

[42] Vladimir II, "Monomakh" (1053–1125): Grand Prince of Kievan Rus' near the end of its Golden Age, namesake of the crown ("Monomakh's Cap") symbolizing the power of ancient Russian grand princes.

forms of Peter the Great, when Russian life began gradually to turn back to its former ways, the Empress Elizabeth,[43] a woman with a true Russian heart, again abolished the death penalty much earlier than Europe came out against it even in theory. Her Russian heart did not need theorists like Beccaria.[44] If this gracious law was not always put into practice, then again, just as with religious persecution, it was from none other than European influence, to which we are unfortunately so accommodating. In principle at least, in our jurisprudence to this day the death penalty is considered only a necessary defense, but not a just punishment, as is evident from the fact that, for example, it applies in the case of violating quarantine, and it certainly applies in other cases to courts-martial. In the same way, the whole society regards the criminal in a completely humane and truly Christian manner. We also find an absence of violence in the relations of the Russian people and the Russian state to its subject peoples: absent to the extent that they are often incorrectly treated as fully indigenous Russian people. All of Russia's foreign relations have this same character, often to its detriment. Its too-generous policies often have undesirable consequences for those who are more entitled to our help and sympathy. But these very mistakes nevertheless originate from the same lack of a violent character that prompts us to put foreign interests ahead of our own.

Another common trait of the Russian character, it seems, can be discerned from the way all major transformations in the life of the Russian people have taken place, compared to how they take place in the lives of other peoples. Without going into every defining moment in Russian history, I would simply like to discern from them some traits of the psychology of the Russian people. The late Konstantin Aksakov[45] said the history of the Russian people can be called its life, and this is profoundly true. How do great moments typically occur in the lives of not only European peoples, but others too? Some powerful interest arises, either from historical circumstances or as the result of ideas from some great historical figure. This interest gradually grows, then contends with the basic order of things which it challenges to some degree, is defeated, arises again and resumes its challenge, finally ends up triumphant and starts to persecute those formerly ruling interests, which revive occasionally but gradually yield to their opponent, until at last, completely vanquished, they exit the stage of history. Was this not the way of the Protestant

---

[43] Elizaveta Petrovna (1709–62): Russian empress, daughter of Peter the Great, known for her humane policies and lavish court life.

[44] Cesare Beccaria (1738–94): Italian political philosopher, author of *Dei delitti e delle pene* (On Crimes and Punishments; 1764), which called for a reformed justice system without torture or the death penalty.

[45] Konstantin Sergeevich Aksakov (1817–60): Russian writer and prominent Slavophile who distinguished the life of the Russian people, tied to the soil, from the culture of the Russian state, borrowed from foreign examples.

Reformation, the French Revolution, and, on a lesser scale, the Parliamentary reforms or the repeal of the Corn Laws[46] in England? Did not the new Parliamentary reforms there and the abolition of slavery in America occur in the same way? Each interest forms its party, and the struggle of these parties is what makes up historical life, for modern Europe the same as ancient Greece and Rome, in my opinion.

The process of historical development in Russia is completely different. It is as if all the great moments in the life of the Russian people have no precursors, or at least they are insignificant and unimportant compared to what they foretell. But neither does the change occur by *deus ex machina*. The only process preceding it is purely internal, invisible and unheard, taking place in the depths of the soul of the people [*narodnyi dukh*]. The old order of things, or one aspect of it, no longer satisfies the soul of the people; its deficiencies become ever more clear to an internal consciousness, until it finds the thing loathsome. The people inwardly renounce what needs to be changed; the struggle takes place within the people's consciousness, and when the time comes to replace the old with the new, it happens unbelievably quickly with no outward sign of struggle, to the complete amazement of those who think it has to happen in a certain normal way. Within the people's consciousness, the process of internal rebirth is the same as what happens in the soul of an individual undergoing a conversion to a higher moral framework, who has become disgusted with the former way of life. This psychological process, to which the lives of the saints attest and which turned Saint Mary of Egypt[47] from a harlot into a paragon of holiness and chastity, is a process of which each of us has heard and seen examples, and which is frequently encountered in the lives of Russians.

The first historical act of the Russian people—the creation of the Russian state—has this character. The Novgorod Slavs threw off the yoke of foreigners, but internal quarrels soon inspired their revulsion for the existing order of things. The representative of the people's consciousness [*narodnooe soznanie*] appeared in the figure of Gostomysl[48] (whether a historical person or just

---

[46] The combined effect of the Reform Act of 1832 and the repeal of the Corn Laws was to reduce the power of British landlords and aristocrats by reducing their representation in Parliament (eliminating pocket-boroughs and expanding the franchise) and their relative wealth (eliminating protective tariffs on grains).

[47] Mary of Egypt (4th–5th century CE, according to Sophronius, 7th-century patriarch of Jerusalem): The patron saint of penitents, she renounced a life of prostitution and embraced Christian asceticism after a pilgrimage to Jerusalem.

[48] Gostomysl appears in later rather than earlier sources and appears to be borrowed from the Western Slavs, or Wends. Some sources attribute the "calling of the Varangians" to his wise counsel, as Danilevskii does here. In this legend, the people of Rus' agreed they needed a ruler to mediate their disputes, and they invited powerful

the personification of the national idea [*narodnaia ideia*] is inconsequential). Without any partisan struggle, by some kind of peaceful unanimous decision, they sent ambassadors across the sea to invite the [Varangian] prince to rule them, and once chosen, this form of power has faithfully served the people over the course of its historical life. This event is so unusual that it seems either unbelievable, or that this "true" story from the chronicler is just a revision, adapted to national pride, of the story of the Norman Conquest. That event allegedly occurred the same way, according to a French historian of modern times, brushing aside the defeat of the great army [at the Battle of Hastings], etc.

A clearer example of this characteristic, from an event we know much more about, is the Russian people's acceptance of the Christian faith. We know many examples of how peoples convert to the new faith, usually in one of the following ways. Apostles or missionaries, through their long ministry of continual efforts and even martyrdom, clear the way for the new teaching, which gradually gains adherents and through a shorter or longer period of struggle between parties, finally wins the victory. This is how Christianity overtook the Roman Empire. Alternately, the victors may impose their creed on the vanquished, as the Arabs did to the peoples they conquered in Asia and Africa, as Charlemagne did to the Saxons, and as the Livonian Brothers of the Sword did to the Balts. Or finally, the conquerors may accept the faith of those they conquer, as the Franks did from the Romanized Gauls. But Russia's case was none of these. What little missionary activity there was could in no way account for the rapidity and effortlessness of Christianity's dissemination. A single person who provides the very personification of the Slavic nature comes to represent his people. Happy, sociable, and hospitable, not to mention enthusiastic and thoroughly imbued with Slavic good nature— Prince Vladimir [I of Kiev] began to sense the emptiness in what paganism offered and an aspiration for something new and better able to satisfy his spiritual thirst, even though he did not know what that might be. At his invitation, missionaries from various religions gathered; he freely considered each of them, consulting with their delegations about the teachings they presented to him, sent trustworthy people to investigate the character of the religion where it was practiced, and having become convinced of the superiority of Orthodoxy by this type of free investigation, accepted it. Through him, with almost no opposition, the whole Russian people also accepted it. This process, which continued in the same spirit as the prince displayed, was only a more definite and conscious repetition of the change of heart all Rus' had gone through in those days. That is the only possible explanation for the lack of opposition toward an innovation like this in such a fundamental thing. It all occurred without any outward struggle, because it was only the outer mani-

---

Varangians, or Vikings, as neutral outsiders, to take the job. This brought the dynasty of Riurik to power, as the founders of Rus' and by extension, Russia.

festation of an inner struggle that had already taken place: the renunciation of the old and outmoded, the inner thirst for the new and better suited. The story of Vladimir's acceptance of Christianity is considered a legend. If it is a legend, that is because it tells about much more than a simple historical event, which could be merely accidental. As a legend it serves as the expression of how, in the mind of the Russian people, the conversion from paganism to Christianity must have taken place. There are also those who doubt the accuracy, or at least the completeness, of the chronicler's account of the spread of Christianity. And they want to see some manuscript accounts, for example about the sorcerers in Rostov,[49] as proof of a prolonged struggle between the old and new religions. But if the new religion had to wage a mighty struggle with paganism, then consider: With the weakness of state power in those days, the lack of roads, and the endless forests dividing region from region and district from district, how would any power be capable of imposing Christianity against the will of the people? And more importantly, consider the chronicler monks, for whom all other events and accomplishments were insignificant compared to the feats of the apostles and martyrs (those who would have accomplished the dissemination of Christianity, had the people seriously opposed it): How could the chronicler monks fail to mention these great feats of faith? Further proof of the peaceful and unhindered spread of Christianity in Russia is the oft-cited fact that pagan ideas and practices long persisted among the people (and even today are far from completely eradicated). The content of Christianity, measured by its high moral ideals, is infinite and is hardly ever achieved completely even by individuals of the highest moral character, not to mention by the whole mass of the people. But the full realization of the Christian ideal in all of life and all human activity is one thing; the more or less clear acknowledgement of its primacy and its dominion over the soul is quite another, which is all I am talking about.

Minin's feat[50] has a similar character, and he seems to represent the thoughts and sentiments of the whole Russian people; he only grasped these things more clearly, or was momentarily more inspired by them than the rest of the people.

---

[49] In the Russian Primary Chronicle for the year 1071, traveling sorcerers or pagan priests (*volkhvy*) in Rostov "proved" by conjury that prominent women were to blame for a famine in the land, and killed them for plunder. For an analysis of this episode in light of later practices, see Russell Zguta, "The Pagan Priests of Early Russia: Some New Insights," *Slavic Review* 33: 2 (June 1974): 259–66.

[50] Kuz'ma Minin (d. 1616): Prominent meat merchant from Nizhnii Novgorod turned national hero during the Time of Troubles, who raised a volunteer army (placed under the command of Prince Dmitrii Pozharskii, 1577–1642) to drive out the Polish forces occupying Moscow. Danilevskii emphasizes his commoner status, as a representative of the people, but his status was probably comparable to a wealthy guild leader.

But the peculiarity of the Russian people's [*narodnyi*] character under consideration here is even more evident in an event we all have witnessed. In the emancipation of the serfs—as in the calling of the Varangians, the acceptance of Christianity, and the liberation from the Poles—the thoughts and sentiments of the whole Russian people was expressed in a single person, the Emperor Alexander II.[51] Everyone knows full well there was no agitation for the emancipation of the serfs, no verbal or printed propaganda. Everything was unprepared for it; the interests of the only educated classes in the government were opposed, even openly hostile, to it. Yet everything happened quickly, with unbelievable success. The serfs were not merely emancipated in the European manner, but were also apportioned land, without any struggle or opposition from any side, without any partisanship besides the ugly and insignificant pretense of a party represented by the newspaper *Vest'*.[52] Everyone who knows anything about Russia is convinced that everything turned out well for the people. But many people's confidence in the redeeming outcome of the matter wavered, I think, when it came out that the reform's implementation was entrusted to certain nobles designated by the marshals of the nobility and supported by the governors, without the participation of peasant deputies or any influence over the decision by their intermediaries. In the European way of looking at things (which is so hard for us to renounce entirely), it must be supposed that peasant interests, placed in the hands of the noble interests opposed to them, would be violated to the extent allowed by the letter of the law (and we well know how far that means). It seemed that the fulfillment and application of the law stripped away its essential significance. And such fears proved very well founded where the intermediaries and executors were not the Russian nobility but the Polish *szlachta*. In Russia the reform was accomplished in a way that not only Europe but even most of us could not imagine. The Russian people, peasantry and nobility alike, comported itself in such a way that, to characterize adequately how they acted during that time, we must use the language of the people for whom everything lofty and virtuous has a civic character [i.e., Latin]. This is *virtus*[53] in the full sense of the word. If we go mentally a few centuries into the future and imagine what few traces from our times are left, like we have from the founding of the Russian state or the conversion to Christianity; and imagine also that over these centuries we have not lost the habit of judging the phenomena

---

[51] Danilevskii's theory of autocracy draws analogies from biological anatomy, in which a few cells or a single organ can govern, but also reflect the will of, the entire organism. The tsar is typically that governing organ, but in time of crisis others, like Minin, may channel the will of the whole being. In this analogy, disturbances such as the Kazan uprising mentioned further on in this passage are like passing involuntary spasms.

[52] *Vest'*, see chap. 6, n. 14.

[53] Latin: "Civic virtue."

of Russian life from a European point of view; and then if the archives of the history of this occurrence in the backwaters of Kazan[54] and a few other such places were discovered, how those Europeanizing historians would then rejoice! Factual evidence of a struggle of classes and interests would come to light; individual examples of insignificant exceptions, or not even exceptions but just pitiful misunderstandings, would be blown up to a whole system, according to which peculiar events from Russian history would take on the common, normal, only-possible character of the European course of development. In the present, of course, it is impossible to settle for that interpretation. It can be explained various ways: by the pressures of power, the lack of an energetic defense of its interests, or the influence of bureaucratic elements. Of course, state power in Russia has great material, and even greater moral, power, but we know full well that in this matter it did not need to use it at all. We also know that it would not take active opposition to render all of its power ineffectual; passive resistance or an unscrupulous approach to the matter would be entirely sufficient to accomplish that. The *szlachta* of the western provinces provides an example of how this works; and if not for the happy accident of a popular uprising, the peasant reform in the western provinces not only would not have had the desired results, but actually would have brought the most harmful consequences. If the Russian nobility was afflicted by such a narrow, egotistical view, and if its main motive was self-interest, then regardless of any strong power (whose agents would necessarily share the narrow view of that class), things would have gone no better than under the Polish arbitrators in the western provinces.

It would likewise be wrong to conclude from the common character of all the major transformations in the life of the Russian people that it lacks energy or initiative, or is so pliable it could be molded into any form. We will see other examples that show the great efforts of the state have not been directed toward any goals the people opposed or about which it was completely ambivalent. Old Belief proves the first point, an example of so many actions, reforms, and innovations that became a dead letter, an empty form without contents, even though there was neither active nor passive opposition toward them, but only complete ambivalence or apathy, which sufficiently proves the second point.

---

[54] In Bezdna, a small village in Kazan Province, five thousand peasants from surrounding areas rebelled against the terms of the 1861 Emancipation reform, convinced they were being deceived, and that the actual terms were surely more favorable, thus demanding more land without redemption payments. Hence Danilevskii's characterization as "pitiful misunderstandings." The uprising was violently put down, with dozens killed and hundreds wounded, adding to the pity. The tone of contempt here is directed toward Western *Schadenfreude* at the event, more than the event itself; however, the event does undermine Danilevskii's notion of the organic unity of the people.

The trait of the Russian people's character, demonstrated here in the most important triumphant moments of its life, supports the conclusion that the mainspring or main motive force of the Russian people is not self-interest but its inner moral consciousness: incubated slowly within its spiritual faculties but completely enveloping it when the time comes to reveal it and put it into practice. And since self-interest is the basis of what we call parties, there is nothing in the historical life of Russia that corresponds to this primarily Western European or Germanic-Roman phenomenon. All that could be called parties in Russia comes from the intrusion of foreign and heterogeneous influences into Russian life. Thus when they talk about an aristocratic or democratic, a conservative or progressive party in Russia, everyone knows full well that these are empty words with nothing lying behind them. On the contrary, everyone understands the idea of a German or Polish party, in opposition to a Russian party, which is not and cannot be a party by virtue of the name they give it. We also know that behind the names of these parties there lies some actual, more or less powerful, force. Of course we have a difference of opinion about this or that aspect of public life, but because they are only opinions, they do not represent any certain interest. Statistical data about the subscribers to all our political magazines would clearly bear this out: that all differences in coloration and opinion among the periodicals do not correspond to any particular class or other interest among their subscribers. Only one periodical, without a doubt, would present an exception: that is the newspaper *Vest'*, which can only be called a party organ [for restoring aristocratic power]; but just like the German and Polish parties with which this party sympathizes, it did not grow up on Russian soil. This is sometimes called the Boyar Party, but these days it can be called pseudo-aristocratic. Its animating principle, of course in a more healthful and national [*narodnoe*] form, has adapted itself to the life of the peoples in which it has its roots, gaining power and prosperity in England, preserving and fortifying the Magyar subjects of the overextended Kingdom of Hungary, and attaining, if not freedom and prosperity, at least the power and might of the Venetian Republic over the course of many centuries. Being less harmonious with the character of the French nation, it brought it great harm and led to a horrible catastrophe, but at least it imparted much splendor to a long period of its history. But on the completely foreign soil of Slavdom, this principle could only take the phoniest form and have the most disastrous consequences. Imbibing it along with Catholicism and various German customs, the Polish upper classes eventually poisoned all of Poland, which not only brought it to ruin but reduced its whole history to a slogan. In Serbia it bowed its head to the Muslim yoke; in Bohemia it was Germanized; and in western Russia it was Polonized. In Russia where (thank God) it [the aristocratic party] never had any great force or meaning, it conspired during the childhood and youth of Ivan IV,[55] kissed the cross of Prince

---

[55] Ivan IV, "the Terrible" (1530–85): Russian tsar, overshadowed in childhood and

Vladislav,[56] and, being defeated by the commoner Minin and the prince Pozharskii, then crushed by the might of Peter the Great, in its last gasp it
brought upon Russia the ten-year punishment of the *bironovshchina*,[57] and
would have had much worse results if it had not been cut off at the root by
the Russian nobility. It is no surprise that such an anti-Russian and anti-Slavic
principle takes on the foreign guise of a party, with the party of the Polish
szlachta, and more recently the German *junkers*,[58] as its model and ideal,
though it still retains warm sympathies for its original prototype.[59]

Another conclusion from the above-described historical peculiarities of
the most important moments in the development of the Russian people is the
huge preponderance within any Russian person of the all-Russian element,
over the individual, personal element. And for that reason, whereas one who
becomes conscious of being English, German, or French still preserves
enough moral principles to retain a splendid individuality in one regard or
another, one who becomes conscious of being Russian becomes nothing, a
useless rag, of which doubtless there are so many examples that there is no
need to point out any one in particular.[60]

Besides those characteristics we have noted as being revealed in the special character of a people's history, the peculiarities of a people's mental

---

youth by powerful boyar families, whom he suspected of foul play in the deaths of his
mother, acting as his regent, and later his first wife. His suspicions affected his reign;
the *oprichnina* was intended to break the boyars' power and influence.

[56] Vladislav IV Vasa (1595–1648): Son of Sigismund III Vasa and heir to the Polish-
Lithuanian throne; the Seven Boyars (*semiboiarshchina*) who deposed Tsar Vasilii Shui-
skii in 1610, during the Time of Troubles, named Vladislav tsar ("kissing the cross"
was a making pledge of loyalty), but he never claimed the throne. The Seven Boyars'
power faded when the Poles invaded later that year.

[57] *Bironovshchina*: See chap. 3, n. 8.

[58] Junkers: Landed aristocrats of Prussia and eastern Germany who collectively owned
most of the land but generally ranked as lesser nobility and hence were usually very
conservative and protective of their rights.

[59] The "original prototype" is presumably the Polish szlachtists, Danilevskii's perennial villain, but of the examples he has cited, the boyars of Ivan's childhood and youth
would be the earliest.

[60] By the mid-twentieth century, it would be hard not to interpret the idea of a paragraph like this as essentially fascist or totalitarian, as in Robert MacMaster's biographical study *Danilevsky: A Russian Totalitarian Philosopher* (Cambridge, MA: Harvard University Press, 1967)—although MacMaster himself called Danilevskii's political theory
Slavophile and Rousseauist, with the tsar as the incarnation of the popular will (see p.
349), beside which a single individual was insignificant. In patriotic thinking, the individual was nothing beside the greater, national good, especially when this was threatened, as in the Time of Troubles or 1812. And the Slavophiles cherished the idea of *so-
bornost'*, or transcendent community, in which unity was more spiritually meaningful
than individuality.

framework can also be determined through a natural classification of moral qualities according to species, genus, family, and class. These qualities would be arranged into groups further and further apart from each other, according to their inherent incompatibility with each other. Obviously under this arrangement, the higher the group of qualities (in a systematic order) characterizing different peoples (of course setting aside individual exceptions, which cannot be considered), the greater the essential difference must be between them, and the less their patterns of activity will have in common.

It seems to me that moral qualities (I am not speaking of virtues, because not only their deficiency, but even their excess, can be a vice) can be very naturally divided into three groups: the qualities of kindness, fairness, and purity. The last category cannot sustain any kind of national characterization, because it concerns resisting various types of material temptations and pertains to the realm of a person's obligation to oneself. It is the crown of individual human virtue, so to speak. Both of the remaining categories are social qualities, since they stipulate a certain kind of mutual relations between people. It does not take great powers of observation to recognize that the first is a predominantly Slavic attribute, and the second is an attribute of the German national [*narodnyi*] character. Of course it is very good to adopt other good qualities less akin to us, to the extent that they do not hinder the cultivation of our personal or national [*narodnye*] virtues, which is of course possible to some extent. But nevertheless the fact that we can accurately classify the two national [*narodnye*] characters not by any peculiar traits, but by a whole grouping of the higher-level moral qualities separating one from another, has to indicate the essential difference in the whole mental framework between Slavic peoples and Germanic peoples.

In intellectual attributes, the characteristic peculiarities of the Slavic tribes, if not harder to observe than those of the moral realm, are however more difficult to prove. Owing to the narrow and brief development among Slavic peoples of the sciences, where the peculiarities of intellectual attributes are more clearly reflected (see the examples in chapter 6), the materials necessary for comparison are lacking.

This would be easier to do in regard to the aesthetic traits of the Slavic soul, since there is much greater material for this kind of study. But a deeper investigation would require comparative study of Slavic literature with the literatures of other peoples. I have neither the requisite knowledge nor abilities for this; therefore anything I could say in this regard would be insufficiently supported by facts. For another thing, it would depart too far from the true goals of this book, which have little to do with aesthetics.

○⟨ 9 ⟩○
The Difference in Religious Beliefs

> Le romanisme, en remplacant l'unité de la foi
> universelle, par l'indépendance de l'opinion indi-
> viduelle ou diocésaine a été la premiére hérésie
> contre le dogme de la nature de l'Eglise ou de sa
> foi en elle même. La Réforme n'a été qu'une con-
> tinuation de cette même hérésie sous une appar-
> ence différente.
> —A. S. Khomiakov, "Quelques mots par un chré-
> tien orthodoxe sur les communions occidentales"[1]

In terms of spiritual principles, the basic distinction is that Russia and the majority of the other Slavic nations practice Orthodoxy, and the Germanic-Roman nations, Roman Catholicism or Protestantism. Is the distinction between these two confessional traditions great enough to form the basis for a cultural-historical distinction between the Slavic and the Germanic-Roman cultural types? Is it not simply a trivial distinction, paling in the light of a general concept of Christian civilization? And on the other hand is not the difference between Catholicism and Protestantism more important than that between Catholicism and Orthodoxy, which seem similar since both are founded on authority, whereas Protestantism is founded on free investigation? There is a short answer to this: namely, that the difference between truth and falsehood is infinite, and that two falsehoods are more like each other than either is to the truth. But such a reply would satisfy only those who were already convinced. For those who see no more than a formal distinction between these three forms of Christianity, corresponding to different levels of development in religious consciousness, such a reply says nothing at all, and thus I allow myself to devote some time to this vitally important subject.

The essence of Christian dogma is set forth in the [Nicene-Constantino-plan] Creed, and all of us—Orthodox, Catholics, and Protestants—read this creed almost the same. We attach completely different meanings, however, to

---

[1] "Roman Catholicism, by replacing the unity of the universal faith with the independence of individual or diocesan opinion, has committed the first heresy against the natural dogma of the Church and of its faith. The Reformation is nothing but a continuation of this same heresy under a different guise." A. S. Khomiakov, "A Few Words by an Orthodox Christian on the Western Faiths" (Paris: A. Franck, 1853).

the words "I believe in the one holy catholic and apostolic Church." The meanings are so different that Khomiakov, in his famous brochures, could call all of Western Christianity a heresy *against the Church*, whereas those unorthodox communities in the East[2] that have fallen away from the true Church, by incorrectly interpreting or understanding various other dogmas in the creed, have nevertheless preserved a proper understanding of the essence of the Church itself. The importance of a proper understanding of the Church is such that, whereas a false teaching about even the most fundamental truth of Christianity confines its harmful influence to a certain set of ideas pertaining to it (leaving everything else unharmed and true), a false concept of the Church inevitably leads, by a slow but inescapable logical process, to the undermining of all Christian teaching, stripping it of any foundation or support.

The Christian Church and all those Christian communities calling themselves churches claim Divine Revelation as their foundation, and any teaching that rejects Revelation is no longer considered Christian. Thus the necessity of Revelation serves as a point of departure for our discussion of the different forms of Christianity. The necessity of Revelation acknowledges that it alone can provide an entirely reliable, unshakeable foundation for faith and morality. Revelation—that is, communication made as an act of Divine will—can present itself either by directly acting upon the will (that is, acting by force, as an irresistible instinct), or by indirectly influencing it through consciousness and understanding. Obviously in regards to human beings endowed with a free nature, only the second type of Revelation is possible. But everything that presents itself to our understanding can be taken either in all its objective truth, or in a completely distorted form, or in a partially correct way; indeed, this last manner of understanding is the most probable, almost the only possible, way. Thus Revelation understood as such necessarily loses its reliability; thus it loses its power and significance, its very essence and reason for existence, and becomes pointless. So it is obvious this kind of Revelation is completely useless and utterly fails its purpose, unless it is accompanied by some means of preserving its reliability, true meaning, and correct application in every given case. This means is what we call the Church, which by necessity is as infallible as Revelation itself, being the only possible guarantee for Revelation's infallibility, not in the Church itself, but in its understanding of Revelation. The relation of the Church to Revelation is exactly like the relation of the court to civil law, of course with the difference that internal reliability is replaced by external obligation. Imagine the perfect civil code: for all its perfection, it would be useless coming only from a book, without judicial power for its interpretation and application. Two litigants, of course, would never settle their lawsuit if they both were left to consult the law about which of them is in the right. But if all the litigants were wise enough and free enough from personal egotism to settle their lawsuit in this way, then the law would

---

[2] Nestorianism, Monophysitism, and Monothelitism, see chap. 8, n. 18.

be superfluous for them, since they would already carry it in all fullness and perfection in their hearts and minds. And so, finally, the very significance of Revelation depends upon the significance given to the concept of the Church (and inseparably from it, the concept of its infallibility).

In the Christian world, as we all know, there are four main concepts of the Church and its infallibility: 1) the Orthodox concept, which affirms that the Church is the assembly of all believers of all times and all nations, under the supremacy of Jesus Christ and the direction of the Holy Spirit, and ascribes infallibility (understood in this manner) to the Church; 2) the Catholic concept, which concentrates this concept of the Church into the person of the pope and thus ascribes infallibility to him; 3) the Protestant concept, which transfers to each member of the Church the right to interpret Revelation, and thus transfers infallibility to each, but of course only as regards himself personally—which is to say, it rejects infallibility altogether. 4) finally, the concept of what might be called the mystical sects (for example, Quakers, Methodists,[3] and so on), for which infallibility depends upon the direct illumination of each individual by the Holy Spirit, and this illumination exhibits itself in the personal consciousness of each one considering himself inspired or illuminated. Of these four concepts, all except the third—the Protestant— are theoretically possible; they are not self-contradictory (if they can show their views to be correct). The Protestant concept, on the contrary, by rejecting infallibility altogether and leaving all to the mercy of personal interpretation, deprives Revelation itself of any actual significance. Instead it sets it aside like any other philosophical notion (however, with the disadvantage for Revelation that it lacks that force of proof inherent in a systematized approach, since its truth is proposed in specific instances without proof, and not as the conclusion of a general principle derived from a logical process). Therefore in the Protestant view, the whole essence of religion necessarily comes down to only a personal, subjective feeling. But subjective religion—that is, the belief in whatever you want, or if you will, in whatever you believe—is to deny any positive Revelation, or to deprive it of any binding force, which is to say, of any reliability. So it is a denial of religion in general, which becomes meaningless without the complete reliability that subordinates the human spirit to itself in the same way that logical reliability subordinates a single human mind. It seems to me, the following example from the life of President [Thomas] Jefferson of the United States may serve as a very clear emblem or symbol of the Protestant view. Jefferson was what is called a freethinker or *esprit fort*, so he did not recognize the divinity of Christianity, but still respected many of its

---

[3] While few Methodists today would consider themselves a mystical sect, John Wesley did entrust the understanding of scripture to the illumination of the Holy Spirit. Also, nineteenth-century Methodism, especially in America, was known for raucous tent meetings and revival services, with mystical experiences of ecstatic worship, from which the holiness movement, and later, Pentecostalism, emerged.

truths. Wishing to separate the true from what he considered false, he took two copies of the Gospels and cut out the parts he thought corresponded to a healthy understanding of morality, or to put it more simply, whatever parts he liked. He pasted his clippings in a special notebook and in this manner compiled a code of moral teachings for himself, or if you will, a religious system for his own use.[4] Each adherent to Protestant teaching in essence is doing the exact same thing, and as a matter of fact cannot do otherwise. Under this approach, of course, each collects a notebook with particular contents, which obviously will reflect the preferences of its owner. The mystic would not include those excerpts that seemed too simple or naturalistic, nor the rationalist what seemed too mysterious or supernatural. It would be odd if the scissors did not take a certain direction from those inclined toward vengeance, or ambition, or vainglory, or self-interest, or sensuality, and so on.

Protestants eliminate, to the extent possible, the inevitable consequences of such a view by establishing agreed-upon, arbitrary, artificial orthodoxies known by the names of Anglican, Lutheran, Reformed, Presbyterian, etc. These obviously can have no authority among their thinking congregants, because they do not acknowledge the inspired authority of Henry VIII, Luther, Calvin, or Zwingli,[5] nor do they attribute conciliar authority to their clerical assemblies, such as that of Augsburg.[6] Thus all these "orthodoxies" are merely different clipping systems. Rejecting Church tradition, Luther cut out the words of the apostle Paul which mandate being governed by tradition; rejecting certain sacraments, he also cut out texts by which the apostle Jacob [i.e., James] established extreme unction [*eleosviashchenie*], or by which the apostle Paul avowed that marriage is a great mystery,[7] and so on. Calvin went further in his excerpting: for example, from the Gospel of John cutting Jesus Christ's whole talk with the disciples about the significance of celebrating the Lord's Supper. Switching from one pattern of clipping to another, it seems to me hard to distinguish between the clippings establishing arbitrary

---

[4] This was eventually published, after Jefferson's death in 1826, as *The Life and Morals of Jesus of Nazareth*, known more commonly as "the Jefferson Bible." The original cut-and-paste text can be viewed online at the Smithsonian Museum of American History website.

[5] Henry VIII: See chap. 8, n. 22. Martin Luther (1483–1546): German priest and Protestant theologian, namesake of the Lutheran Church, famous for confronting the Roman Catholic Church's sale of indulgences in ninety-five theses for doctrinal debate. John Calvin: See chap. 8, n. 28. Huldrich Zwingli (1484–1531): Swiss reformer based in Zurich, led political and military battles of the Reformation in Switzerland, debated theology with Luther and others, but no distinct theological tradition of "Zwinglianism" has endured.

[6] The Diet of Augsburg (1530) produced the Augsburg Confession, a foundational document of Lutheranism, explaining its position on twenty-eight doctrinal points.

[7] Cf. *taina* (mystery) and *tainstvo* (sacrament).

orthodoxies and the clippings of Renan,[8] who saw fit to cut out everything having any kind of supernatural character, even the resurrection itself. At which step of this staircase does it stop; on what foundation does it rest; and is there really any possibility of halting before you reach the very bottom, at which point there is nowhere left to go?

The mystical view among the Quakers, Methodists, and other sectarians can be set aside, since the teachings of these sects are not part of the intellectual origins of European nations, instead being only an insignificant exception to the predominant religious views among them.

It cannot be said the Catholic concept of the Church includes the same kind of internal contradictions as the Protestant concept. It is reasonable, if only it could be proven. But in this case, all that can be proven is its impossibility. There is no need to go into all the facts of church history, since this type of evidence only persuades the one who actually investigates it from the sources. For others, who must accept the word of the investigator as truth, it is hard to take one side or the other with complete impartiality, due to the prevailing quarrels among investigators partial to one doctrine or the other. But that is entirely unnecessary. The impossibility of papal primacy and infallibility seems easy to demonstrate from a few of the best-known facts and claims, acknowledged by Catholics themselves. But the defenders of Catholicism, often consciously unscrupulous, are like slippery serpents, sliding from your grasp when you think you will catch them. Therefore for each of their distinctive dogmas they have several opinions in their polemical arsenal to draw upon as needed. So concerning the primacy and infallibility of the popes, and the relation of their power to the power of the ecumenical councils, there are a variety of opinions among Catholics themselves. Some consider the pope higher than any council; others subordinate the pope to the councils' authority. It is evident that only the ultramontanist[9] view, which holds papal authority higher than, or at least equal to, conciliar authority, can be defended from the Catholic point of view, which considers the pope as the deputy of Jesus Christ. If the pope does not possess complete authority over the church, then how can he establish new doctrines without calling an ecu-

---

[8] Ernest Renan (1823–92): French scholar best known for his critical approach to the history of Christianity. His 1863 book *Vie de Jésus* (Life of Jesus) approached the subject as a historical biography and challenged the supernatural claims in source documents.

[9] Ultramontanism: Label applied in Fránce and Germany over time to defenders of papal power and prerogatives (literally, the point of view from "beyond the mountains," i.e., the Alps). Ultramontanism peaked at the First Vatican Council of 1868, which doctrinally defined long-accepted notions of papal supremacy and papal infallibility, even as Italian unification was depriving the pope of temporal power (as the Kingdom of Italy absorbed the Papal States in 1860 and annexed Rome in 1870).

menical council?[10] If he is not granted full authority, then on what is all Catholic teaching based? Who established all the differences observed between present-day Catholicism and ecumenical Orthodoxy of former times? No ecumenical council was ever summoned for this purpose. Who made an addition to the ecumenical creed?[11] After all, this could only be done with conciliar authority, or something equal to it. But there was no ecumenical council concerning this issue; one council, with John's ambassadors among its members even condemned this innovation—a judgment which subsequently the pope alone refused to ratify, since it did not fulfill the hope for which he had made so many concessions.[12] Thus, changing the creed can only make sense from the Catholic point of view if the pope has authority at least equal to that of the ecumenical council. But if popes have such authority, and infallibility along with it, then someone must have conferred this authority, this high degree of clerical blessing, upon them. Catholics avow that it was given to them by the apostle Peter. Accepting the primacy of the apostle Peter over the other apostles in this Catholic sense, agreeing that Peter was the bishop of Rome, ignoring for the moment that the first two bishops of Rome, Linus and Anacletus, were appointed by Paul, not Peter[13]—still it has yet to be revealed when and by means of what official act did the apostle Peter confer his primacy over the Church upon his alleged successor? As is well known, the apostle Peter did not name anyone pope after himself. He appointed a few bishops, but infallibility was not conferred upon a single one of them, according to Catholics themselves. Obviously, that takes a much higher degree of blessing than that of a bishop: it requires the blessing incumbent in the whole Church to be concentrated into one person who will be its visible apex. Since logically it does not follow that a person could be ordained a bishop among priests without the special ordination to that office by the bishop ordaining him, likewise it does not follow that one of several bishops ordained by the apostle Peter

---

[10] After the Seventh Ecumenical Council of 787, Western councils did not include Eastern Orthodox representatives, and thus were no longer "ecumenical."

[11] I.e., the controversial *filioque*.

[12] It is not certain, but most likely, that Danilevskii has in mind what the Orthodox call the Fourth Council of Constantinople (879–80), sometimes called the Eighth Ecumenical Council, which reinstated Photius as patriarch of Constantinople, and condemned Roman claims of papal primacy and the use of *filioque*. It was attended by representatives of Pope John VIII (r. 872–82), who approved the proceedings. Subsequently, as the dispute between East and West deepened, Catholics rejected this council in favor of the preceding council that had removed Photius (although forced to accept his reinstatement in fact), to preserve their commitment to *filioque*. Both sides later claimed proof that John VIII had, or had not, accepted the council's decisions. See Edward Siencienski, *The Filioque: History of a Doctrinal Controversy* (New York: Oxford University Press, 2010), 100–04.

[13] Sources on these early popes are scant and contradictory.

could take possession of all fullness of churchly authority without a new, special declaration of this blessing by that apostle. Otherwise we would have to accept that all the bishops ordained by the apostle Peter received this fullness of authority that resided in his apostolic person, and thus, so did all the bishops they ordained. Either the primacy of the apostle Peter was not transferred to anyone, since he personally did not name anyone pope, or it was transferred to all of them, and the number of these people continued growing over the course of centuries. Finally, if we are agreed that the apostle Peter by a special act appointed his successor over the Roman Church and declared for him all fullness of churchly authority, which he himself possessed, then this same transfer must be demonstrated for each passing of the mantle to the new pope. But everyone knows full well that no such transfer was ever made, and thus each new pope does not receive primacy over the Church and everything connected with it, including infallibility, from his predecessor, who is of course the only one in the whole world possessing these things. It may be asked, where is it gotten from, where is the source of this high degree of blessing which popes allegedly possess? This is the question that so perplexed our Old Believers, until the agreement with Amvrosii disabused them of it.[14] But who will disabuse the pope of it? There are only two possible outcomes. One is, if it is recognized that the power of the pope is not higher than, but equal to, the power of the ecumenical council, then of course such a council assembled at the accession of each new pope could confer on him all the power and authority that is attributed to him. But no ecumenical council is assembled after the death of each pope: Catholics count only twenty of their own councils, but the number of past popes is much greater than that. That leaves only one last way: that popes gain their authority directly from the same source as the disciples themselves; that is, for the selection of each new pope they ought to reconvene that high assembly that took place in Jerusalem fifty days after the resurrection of Christ, with the coming of the Holy Spirit.[15] Since Catholics themselves will not agree to this, it must be recognized that no source exists from which papal power could come; thus it is self-proclaimed, which even every sensible Catholic must recognize.

There is still another simple and obvious way to prove the groundlessness of papal pretensions, and thus of the whole Catholic concept of the Church. Again taking the Catholic point of view and granting the primacy of the apostle Peter over the other apostles in the sense that Catholics understand it, consider: Who had this high authority in the Church after the apostle Peter? Obviously, the other apostles. After the death of the apostle Peter, the apostle John lived more than thirty years, yet he did not take the Roman bishopric and in fact was not summoned. Thus, if it is held that popes have

---

[14] The 1840s suppression of Old Believers, or Russian Orthodox schismatics, culminated in the exile of their leader, Metropolitan Amvrosii Popovich (1791–1863).

[15] Acts 1: 15–26.

primacy over the Church because they are the heirs of the apostle Peter in the Roman pulpit, a strong objection can be raised that since the highest churchly authority after the death of Peter was not summoned to that office, then it must be that in the first Christians' understanding, supreme churchly authority was not necessarily attached to the Roman bishopric. Or it means either the popes Linus, Anacletus, and Clement had power and authority over the apostle John himself, or in those days there were two equivalent authorities in the Church, each of which had full authority. For clarification, assume you had to settle the following historical question. In the capital of a certain state there was some significant and important post, the exact significance of which we do not precisely know. We do not know if it has full autocratic, royal power, or if it was just a high and respected post without actual supremacy. But we do know the following things: 1) the first person having this post had royal power; and 2) there is a law of succession for this power—for example, it is transferred from father to eldest son as a birthright, so that in the eyes of the people the son has the highest authority after his father. These things are certain, but things go as follows: The father dies. Yet it is not the son who accedes to the post he occupied, but somebody else who was selected not by the father, but by election. Then in the public mind, the accession to this post (the power of which remains in question) resumes its rightful form, and the occupant considers himself its rightful holder. Eventually the one who by birthright ought to have held it, as in a royal succession, also considers the one selected instead of him to be the rightful holder. At that time, however, both the people setting up this post and the heir realize that the royal power (or in our case, the highest churchly authority) indubitably belongs to none other than the heir. If in all this we discover that this post of indeterminate significance is in fact a royal post, then we come to the following irresolvable contradiction: all the people (that is, all the first Christians), the very ones occupying the post in question (Linus, Anacletus, and Clement), and even the legal heir to the throne (the apostle John)—all recognized the ones who for more than thirty years occupied this quasi-royal post as both integral, rightful rulers and usurpers of the throne. To escape this contradiction we have to accept that the post in and of itself did not have royal significance, and that if the first of its occupants was also a royal ruler, it was only coincidental, such as for example, the Roman emperors who often also claimed for themselves the title of consul. The objection must not be raised that circumstances or a personal disinclination prevented the apostle John from taking office in Rome, since it should have been offered to him all the same; in fact he should have claimed it in order to clarify its significance for successive generations, after which he could have stepped down for whatever reason. The Jesuit fathers did not think about this beforehand, or they certainly would have searched out some kind of evidence of such events, without which it must be recognized that neither the first Christians, nor the first popes, nor the apostle John himself attached to the Roman bishopric any notion of churchly primacy, and thus not even Jesus Christ had in mind this kind of primacy for a single individual.

Regardless of whether Catholics themselves come to see the utter groundlessness of papal pretensions, the most practical consequences of the power and significance given to popes are such that the Catholic nations cannot bear the burden of them and try by various types of inconsistencies to free themselves from them. For example, they restrict the infallibility of the pope to a certain spiritual realm on the basis of the words "My kingdom is not of this world" and "Render unto Caesar the things that are Caesar's, and to God the things that are God's."[16] Such a demarcation is no doubt correct, but how can the boundaries of this world be determined, where the things of Caesar end and where the things of God begin? Obviously neither the world nor Caesar can decide this, since they are fallible and will likely draw the boundaries incorrectly; they can exceed their limits just as Pilate did, to whom the first of these words were spoken; just as the Roman Caesars certainly exceeded them, as they were generally not inclined toward intolerance and the persecution of faith, but thought that they were only demanding things that were Caesar's: compelling Christians to make sacrifices to the gods of the Roman state and burn incense on the altar erected to Caesar, the representative of the deified state. If the pope is Christ's deputy, then obviously no one but him could undertake the demarcation of the things that are God's from the things that are Caesar's. Pius IX promulgated his famous encyclical.[17] Even from an impartial point of view, it cannot be said that its many paragraphs do not concern the realm of things that are God's, such as the question of religious tolerance. What objection can be raised to that? Only that it contradicts the spirit of the times, and the pope is urged to agree with this spirit if he wants to preserve his power and significance. How perplexing and insignificant such objections must seem to a true Catholic! The great importance is actually how the spirit of the times compares to the one who in the Catholic concept is imbued with the power of the Spirit of eternity! If the spirit of the times contradicts him, it would not be the first time; this spirit of the times is the spirit of the one who is called the king of this world [i.e., Satan]. Is not the pope invited to worship him to preserve his power, in the same way as was tempted in the wilderness the One whom Catholics believe the pope represents?[18] The longstanding practical difficulties for states and peoples that call themselves Catholic have now been elevated to a degree of irreconcilable contradiction by Pius's "*non*

---

[16] John 18: 36; Mark 12: 17.

[17] Pius IX (r. 1846–72) issued thirty-eight encyclicals during his reign as pope; probably Danilevskii has in mind *Quanta cura* (1864), famous for its "Syllabus of Errors," condemning the nineteenth-century revolutionary ideologies socialism and communism, but also liberal democracy, freedom of speech and religion, rationalism, secret societies, and even Bible societies.

[18] I.e., Jesus Christ. See Luke 4: 5–8.

possumus,"[19] which nevertheless one must respect as an expression of intrepid thoughtfulness and deep personal conviction. To our eyes, if this does not increase these contradictions, it at least gives them an indelible imprint by the assent of Rome's pseudo-ecumenical council. In general, the role of Pius IX consists of severely formulizing and revealing in full clarity the pretenses and claims of Catholicism, so that the contradictions pop out alongside of the completely legitimate claims in other realms of life and thought, so that even the most shortsighted, the most dimwitted people will see the gap between the one and the other, removing all possibility of an uncertain, equivocal relationship between Catholicism and European civilization. Catholic nations have one of three choices: either reject the fruits borne of many ages of blood, struggle, and toil to return to the times of Gregory VII and Urban II;[20] reject the Catholic understanding of the Church and thus choose either to take the slippery path of Protestantism or return to the bosom of Orthodoxy; or finally renounce Catholicism and all Christianity along with it. Considering the intolerable burden lain upon them by Catholicism, it comes as no surprise that the peoples and states of Europe are apparently turning toward the last alternative. As Cavour[21] was famous for saying: "A free Church in a free state," or more completely and exactly, a Church freed from the state in a state freed from the Church. What exactly does that mean? The Church, in our Orthodox concept, is the assembly of believers of all times and peoples under the supremacy of Jesus Christ and under the direction of the Holy Spirit. In what manner could a state be free of it, or free from Christ? Of course, in no other way than ceasing to be Christian. For example, we can without a doubt affirm that Turkey is a state freed from the Church (that is, from the Christian Church). Is that what the advocates of Cavour's famous formula want? Of course not, at least not all of them. And actually from the Catholic point of view the question is not so radical. The Church, in the Catholic concept, is concentrated into a hierarchy, and the hierarchy is concentrated in the pope, so that strictly speaking, a state free of the Church means nothing more than a state free of the pope, which so far is not that extreme. But although the Church in the Catholic concept is concentrated in the pope, its internal content is more than just papal power. The denomination, although Catholic, is still Christian. Therefore, not everything in Catholicism is false; much truth of the genuine Church is in it, so the state that declares itself free of the Church thus declares itself outside the Church and inevitably divides itself from the core of Christianity.

---

[19] "We cannot": General term for Pius IX's foreign policy, especially his refusal of concessions offered in exchange for his loss of territory in the process of Italian unification.

[20] I.e., the eleventh century, time of the Investiture Controversy and the launch of the Crusades.

[21] Cavour, see chap. 1, n. 7.

In many respects, the state cannot and must not interfere with what is essentially Christian, since its activity is restricted from that sphere. But often both spheres of church and state are so closely connected that they permeate each other like spirit and body. For example, one such case is marital union, both sacramental and civil at the same time. Declaring itself free of the Church, a state necessarily violates that unbreakable bond: it must see marriage as an exclusively civil institution and thus deprive it of any moral foundation. Not to mention how it offends moral sensibilities to subordinate love—the most free, most shy, most sheltered from rough handling of all human relations—to the jurisdiction of a district magistrate (one would rather leave relations between the sexes to natural inclinations than subject them to inappropriate administrative interference), we turn our attention to the necessary logical consequence to which so-called civil marriage leads. These consequences are not just contrary to Christianity and morality, but are also absurd. When I say this, I have in mind precisely the kind of civil marriage introduced or being practiced in various European states, pretending to be more or less free of the Church, and not civil marriage as it is understood by some of our intellectuals [i.e., cohabitation]. Even though this last sense is also contrary to Christianity, from their point of view it is not absurd; that is, its defenders do not end up contradicting themselves.

If marriage is solely a civil institution, then it can be no different than any other contract between two persons sworn before a governmental authority, which takes upon itself the guarantee that each party will uphold it as much as the other party requires, but no more than that. If subsequently both sides wish to dissolve this agreement, or somehow change it by a mutual consent, the civil authority can in no way oppose it, from fear of inconsistency or exceeding its power, since it does not have the slightest right or basis to do so. Thus, civil marriage can be dissolved *ad libitum*.[22] True, such a dissolution can injure a third party—children. But similar consequences often accompany the dissolution of other types of contracts, which do not give the state any right to demand their preservation. For example two people form a contract by which they pledge a mutual account to build a factory. But some time later, by mutual agreement they decide to close their factory and dissolve their binding agreement. The factory workers could lose their means of earning a living and end up in a very dire situation from this, which would force the state itself to be concerned with their plight. But that is not a reason to refuse their request by mutual consent to dissolve their freely made agreement. In the same way, concerning a marriage agreement, the state can take measures for the security of children by laying requirements on their parents, designating guardianship over the children, etc. After all, it rushes to provide these kinds of security for

---

[22] Latin: "at one's pleasure." The twenty-first century reader is reminded that, although divorce is now relatively easy and common, in the nineteenth century it was rare and hard to come by. So at the time of writing this idea seemed shocking indeed.

children in the case of dissolution of marriage by death or for other reasons allowed by the Church. So, civil marriage can be dissolved and undertaken anew every week or month. The only possible limitation from this point of view would be the excessive burden on public officials concerned with such matters, under such frequent dissolutions and formations of marriages.

But a free agreement not only can be dissolved by mutual consent, it can also revise its terms in the same way. For example, if a wife is not at all jealous, then why would she not agree to admit into the marital union a third person—another wife with rights equal to hers? There would be no reason for a state official, from his own convictions, to refuse such a revision to the marital agreement. Should he concern himself with morality? If so, what kind— Christian? A state freed from the Church must be freed from all such churchly things. What about some universal human [morality]? Even if such an elusive, indeterminate principle were recognized, polygamy can in no way be considered against it, since it is practiced and considered moral in Turkey, Persia, China, and India, the residents of which have every right to call themselves humans, and thus to claim that what they consider moral is part of this concept of universal human morality. Polygamy was practiced by the kings and even the patriarchs of the Hebrews, who are considered fully moral humans. Of course, the reverse case could also occur: there could be a permissive husband who agrees to a revision of the marital contract to permit polyandry, and if the state official likewise opposed it on some basis of universal human morality, the husband could offer the example of Tibetans, or even better, the example of the noble race of Guanches, the ancient inhabitants of the Canary Islands wiped out by the Spaniards. Based on these irrefutable facts, from the standpoint of universal human morality, the whole company of permissive wives, and whatever permissive husbands there might be, could march down the path of progress with irrefutable logical consistency, seeking to live in harmony with universal human morality according to the Turkish, Persian, Chinese, Indian, as well as the Tibetan and Guanchan concept, on the principle of shared wives and husbands. Furthermore, we must not fail to note the difficulties of the same state official, approached by a brother and sister who wish to enter into a marital agreement, and all his protestations of things contrary to nature and the immorality of such a union. They would triumphantly object that, in the first place, they themselves are the judges of what is natural or unnatural about the union they wish to enter, and that, although it is considered unnatural to feed on spoiled meat or rotten eggs, no administrative authority, however, can consider itself authorized to change the dinner menu of a person with such unnatural tastes. And in the second place, they would offer the triumphant example that Zoroastrians did not consider marriage between brothers and sisters contrary to universal human morality, so in the eyes of the officials serving a state freed from the Church, fire-worship and Christianity must have the same value. The unfortunate administrative official appointed for marital affairs would have no

other choice but to rely on a law of morality drawn from horse-breeding practices, if such could be considered sufficient to regulate interpersonal relations.
Of course it could be objected that no administrative official has any business
overseeing the principles of universal human morality or other such abstractions; he should content himself with existing laws. It is just not allowed, period. Of course that is true, but we are permitted to think, however, that the
law itself should not merely express what someone dreamed up; the law itself
must be based on something.

With the liberation of the state from the Church and the adoption of the
formula a famous statesman[23] once uttered, that the law is atheistic (*la loi est
athée*), all Christian foundation for the law is denied, if not immediately upon
the acceptance of this formula, then with the passage of time. Society has its
own type of inertia or lethargy, by which it continues moving in a given
direction long after the motive force has ceased to act. But irrefutable logic
finally has its way regardless. Consider the example of the Roman state, in
which civil marriage operated essentially under the same conditions as in the
Christian Church. The example is partly correct, because Roman marriage
should not really be called civil marriage. Not only was the Roman state not
free of its pagan church, but on the contrary, was in closest union with it, so
that the Roman state was at the same time "churchly." The Roman emperor
was at the same time *pontifex maximus*[24] as well. It is well known that the
Emperor Gratian [r. 367–83 CE] was even killed by the pagan camp because,
as a Christian, he did not want to don the robes of the pagan high priest. Perhaps on the other hand the United States might be offered as an example
where the state is free from the Church without any harmful consequences
from it. But the example of the United States points only to that false situation
in which a state accepting a false principle inevitably ends up, where extreme
inconsistency is the only possible outcome. On the banks of the Salt Lake in
the Utah territory is a community of Mormons that, as everyone knows, con-
dones polygamy.[25] And the United States, while declaring its state free from
the Church and its Church free from the state, refuses to grant Mormons the
right to form an independent state.[26] On what basis, one might ask. And also

---

[23] Odilon Barrot (1791–1873): French lawyer and politician.

[24] Latin: "highest priest." It was the highest religious office during the Roman Republic, but Caesar Augustus (founder of the Roman Empire, r. 27 BCE–14 CE) claimed the
title, and thenceforth it was conjoined with the title of Emperor, until dropped by Gratian (r. 375–83 CE).

[25] Mormons taught polygamy, or "plural marriage," for much of the nineteenth century and openly practiced it from 1852 to 1890. It was outlawed by the 1862 Morrill
Act, and upheld by the United States Supreme Court in 1879, on the basis that laws
may not regulate religious beliefs, but may regulate religious practices.

[26] *Shtat*: Territorial state, as opposed to *gosudarstvo*, governmental state, as in "church
and state."

one might ask, what if the Chinese (of whom there are already a great many in California) got more than 40,000 together and settled in some unsettled place (which are still plentiful in the United States) and demanded their region be recognized as a state [*shtat*]—it would be interesting to know, what would the federal government say to that? If it allowed a Chinese state, then by its authority it would allow and officially consecrate polygamy, and would not have any basis to deny the same thing to Mormons (and in fact, for any and all who wanted to live in that form of marital union). But by continuing to refuse to recognize it for Mormons and other citizens of the Union, it would show that it is not at all free from the church, but rather has its own state church, a conventionally established state religion, and state morals founded upon it—as even now the United States indubitably has. And this state religion, *impliciter* recognized by the United States, is distinguished from other Protestant state religions only by the very limited capacity of the note-book in which, by Jefferson's example, they have pasted their clippings.

From this it follows that the Protestant and the Catholic concepts of Christianity have sprung from the same roots, and do not stand up to the simplest criticism but only persist from one era to the next by inertia or lethargy prevailing in the moral realm. If the shakiness of the foundations is clearer in the consciousness of the Protestant world than the Catholic world, it is only because the practical consequences of Catholic views have already lain so heavy upon the peoples of this religious persuasion [Protestantism], and the heaviness became for them unbearable. This state of internal contradiction no longer touches only certain dogmas of Christian teaching—which in a utilitarian view of religion would not amount to great harm—but has permeated its very fruits, that is, the ethical and moral sides of Christianity. Given enough time this was inevitable, according to the faster or slower pace of deriving practical conclusions from a given starting point, which varies from one people to the next.

The Orthodox concept of the Church and its infallibility has neither theoretical contradictions nor unbearable practical difficulties. This concept does not deny the firm unshakeable ground of Revelation for religion, as Protestantism does, and does not exceed the boundaries acknowledged in scripture itself, "I will build My Church, and the gates of hell shall not overcome it"[27] by arbitrary additions to it not founded on scripture or tradition, as Catholicism does, which concentrates the insuperability of the Church in the person of the pope, ascribing infallibility to him in spite of history. The Orthodox concept of the infallibility of the Church does not lay heavy burdens on the mind, even though it is correctly considered miraculous, as all manifestations of the direct action of divine Providence must be. Both the established orders of nature and history are infallible; the infallibility of the Church only exhibits divine Providence more straightforwardly and directly. This infallibility is ex-

---

[27] Matthew 16: 18, omitting the preceding words: "You are Peter and on this rock...."

pressed in all that constitutes the voice of the whole Church: most evidently and directly, in the ecumenical councils. But calling an ecumenical council is not within the power of any tsar or patriarch, nor any isolated individual for that matter. A council can be called ecumenical only when it is affirmed by divine Providence, since there are no outward characteristics by which a council can be classified as ecumenical. By the same token, this classification only pertains to those councils which are consciously recognized by the whole Church as such: that is, if I may say so, those that were ratified by the very Head of the Church [i.e., Jesus Christ] and the Holy Spirit, by means of the whole Church.

While history repeatedly undercuts the infallibility of the pope, the infallibility of the councils, on the other hand, placed its imprint upon history with wonderworking power. All Christian historians see the dissemination of Christianity as a miraculous occurrence and have offered it as one of the proofs of the divinity of Christian teaching. But the actions of the ecumenical councils bear the exact same miraculous imprint. Whenever the council thundered its proclamation of anathema, the banned teaching lost its vitality and withered like the cursed fig tree,[28] even though in many cases all the external factors, all forces of worldly power, were on the side of the teaching cast out and ruled heretical. After the death of Constantine, Arianism[29] prevailed in the East and West, and a whole line of emperors promoted it with all their might, just as before Constantine a whole line of pagan emperors like Julian the Apostate[30] supported paganism with all their might. Besides the Empire, the most capable peoples of the time—the Goths, occupying the lands of the Balkans, the Danube, Elyria, Italy, southern France, and Spain; the Burgunds, occupying southwestern Germany; and the Vandals, based in Africa—zealously followed Arius.[31] Compared to such power, Orthodoxy seemed persecuted and pitiful! But the council pronounced its anathema, and all that power lost its importance; within three centuries, the last followers of Arius were gone. The same happened again with Iconoclasm. While the Nestorian, Monophysite, and Monothelitist heresies[32] (also often supported by emperors) have not yet completely disappeared, their paltry followers linger on only in overgrown and out-of-the-way places in Asia and Africa, outside of any historical and religious movement, like the slowly dying remnants of tribes amounting to ethnographical curiosities in the untraveled mountain

---

[28] In Matthew 21 and Mark 11.

[29] Constantine: See chap. 4, n. 11. Arianism: See chap. 8, n. 12.

[30] Julian, "the Apostate" (r. 361–63 CE): Western Roman Emperor, attempted to revive paganism during his short reign.

[31] Arius (250?–336 CE): Christian elder and theologian in Alexandria. His rejection of the Trinity spread throughout the Church, prompting the First Council of Nicaea to resolve the dispute, but Arianism continued to spread after his death.

[32] Iconoclasm, Monophysitism, Monothelitism, and Nestorianism: See chap. 8, n. 18.

hollows of the Caucasus or the Pyrenees. The word of the councils was a word endowed with power. Can the same be said for papal actions and anathemas, backed by the raised sword and all the might of emperors and kings?[33]

The Church's practical influence on civil society, or the question of church-state relations so important among the nations of Europe, is simply not an issue on Orthodox soil. The boundary between the things of God and things of Caesar, between kingdoms of both worlds, is inviolable, because in everything that concerns it the Church itself is infallible, and can never be infringed upon. A case of state infringement upon it is nothing but partial and temporary coercion, which of course can bring harm or suffering to individual Christians, hierarchies, or even whole peoples, but has no power over the Church in general. Its freedom is inviolable for the simple reason that it is unattainable by any earthly power. The Church remained free under the persecutions of the Neros and Diocletians,[34] under the heretical emperors of Byzantium, and under the oppression of the Turks. Emperor Constantius forcing Pope Liberius to recognize the semi-Arian creed and disown St. Athanasius[35] not only would have infringed but also would have destroyed the freedom of the Church, if at that time the Christian Church existed in the way Catholics think of it. Upon conferring the title *ecumenical* upon the Patriarch of Constan-

---

[33] [Danilevskii's note]: One of the few comments made upon our work took issue with this view of the effects of conciliar decisions, as a sign of very superficial understanding of historical events. Evidently the author of this comment took our words to mean this: The council's anathema was proclaimed, and in some magical way, by some hocus-pocus or abracadabra the discredited teaching loses its power, influence, and vitality. But yet I had already mentioned above in what way the infallibility of the Church was, in our opinion, miraculous. Why could they not understand our words this way: Anathema means excommunication, and so the teaching banned by anathema means a teaching recognized as inherently false, incompatible with the creeds, doomed to death and destruction, despite whatever external patronage it enjoys. So if the Church and its highest expression, the ecumenical council, have the ability to distinguish indisputably truth from falsehood, then for that very reason, *ipso facto* as they say, the councils' decisions will be endowed with the ability to pronounce the death sentence upon the teachings they condemn, with such force and power that one way or another the sentence will certainly be fulfilled.

[34] Nero (r. 54–68 CE): Last Roman emperor of the Julio-Claudian dynasty, blamed for the great fire of Rome in 64 CE; he in turn blamed it on Christians. Diocletian (r. 284–305 CE): Roman emperor, responsible for the last and most extensive persecution campaign against Christians under Rome.

[35] Emperor Constantius II (r. 337–61 CE): Son of Constantine, co-ruler with his brothers, forced the messenger of Pope Liberius (352–66 CE) to denounce Athanasius (bishop of Alexandria, d. 373 CE). Danilevskii's point is that the pope being subject to coercion undermines the Catholic conception of papal authority, although Catholic definitions of infallibility specify that it does not apply under conditions of duress.

tinople, Pope Gregory the Great [r. 590–604] wrote to the Patriarch of Antioch: "You must agree that if a bishop is called ecumenical, then the whole church would collapse if *what is ecumenical* should fall." But what could be accomplished by all the persecutions of Leo III the Isaurian, or Constantine V Copronymus?[36] What did all these apostasies mean to one or another patriarch under the Orthodox concept of the Church? They only increased the number of martyrs, or gave new examples of human weakness.

From all this, the lack of understanding or carelessness of Western writers in all matters concerning Slavdom or Orthodoxy is perfectly clear, as if it is just not possible for the enlightened minds of one cultural-historical type to understand aspects of another type they regard with hostility. Historians writing about the Byzantine Empire never fail to talk about the so-called "courtly Orthodoxy" (*Hoforthodoxie*) that was supposedly established by imperial will. They forget however that whatever religious beliefs the emperors tried to impose on their subjects, Orthodoxy always remained the same, and what existed in the Byzantine Empire was the same as what existed in the West at that time, over which the emperors either did not have power, or had it only in a few places, or only for a short time at that. If Orthodoxy was what Theodosius, Justinian, Theodora, or Irene[37] professed, then why should it not also be what Constantius, Valentinian, Heraclius,[38] Leo III, or Constantine Copronymus professed? Does this not mean that only when emperors believed what the Church avowed as Orthodox did their religious zeal leave behind permanent results, and when they followed their own personal instincts, their efforts and strivings disappeared without a trace? Did the churchly or the courtly Orthodoxy prevail over Byzantium after this? Did Orthodoxy give force and significance to the emperors ruling it, or did it derive its force from their personal beliefs and views?

---

[36] Leo III, "the Isaurian" (717–41), and Constantine V, "Copronymus" (741–75): Eighth-century Byzantine emperors who were iconoclasts, forbidding the use of images in worship, thus violating centuries of tradition.

[37] Theodosius: See chap. 4, n. 12. Justinian: See chap. 7, n. 5. Theodora: Byzantine empress (d. 548), wife of Justinian I, powerful woman venerated as an Orthodox saint, praised publicly by Procopius (6th-century historian) but lambasted in his *Secret History*. Irene of Athens (r. 775–802): Byzantine empress regnant, consort, and dowager, restored the veneration of icons to end the iconoclasm controversy of her predecessors' reigns. To that end, she summoned the Second Council of Nicaea in 787, the last of the seven councils recognized as ecumenical by both churches East and West.

[38] Valentinian I, "the Great" (r. 364–75 CE): Roman emperor, considered the "last great Western emperor" for campaigns on all frontiers. Though a Christian, he promoted religious freedom and toleration. Heraclius (r. 610–41): Byzantine emperor, reconquered Asia Minor from the Persian Sassanid Empire, which brought Monophysite Christians back into the fold; thus he promoted Monothelitism as a theological compromise, but this was resisted by both sides, and he was deemed a heretical ruler.

This brief review of the Orthodox, Catholic, and Protestant concepts of the Church's significance has sufficiently distinguished the differences between the spiritual principles the Russian and the majority of Slavic nations profess, and those upon which European civilization is based. There can be no talk of a general Christian civilization because European civilization, while it has borne many truly Christian fruits, has intentionally and unintentionally distorted the correct understanding of the Church, through the inevitable course of development of a germ of Western falsehood that was confused for an ecumenical truth. It has reached a point of irreconcilable theoretical and practical contradiction with both Western forms of Christianity, the Protestant as much as the Catholic, which Europe identifies with Christianity itself. Thus in the realm of convictions it tries to replace it with more or less radical rationalism, and in the practical realm it tries to eliminate the contradictions by separating church and state, that is, separating the body and the spirit. In other words, it wants to shake it off like a mortal illness. This replacement and separation are not yet fully complete, but the latter is occurring in more and more states, fast approaching a crisis point. The former penetrates more deeply into the layers of society in which rationalism—including the whole spectrum from deism to nihilism, with a huge preponderance for the latter, depending on the development and level of education in those layers of society—is no longer just a philosophical conviction, but accepted as truth, a predominantly atheistic truth and thus, from a utilitarian point of view, lacking any ethical significance. This contradiction appeared earlier in Catholic countries, because the practical contradiction between the Catholic view and the new civil society became apparent much sooner under Catholic oppression. But following the initial outbursts there was a tentative, superficial reconciliation, because only at the highest levels was the contradiction detected, and the opening abyss seemed too terrible. Since the Catholic principle was not flawed throughout by an inescapable internal contradiction, it seemed expedient to avert the eyes and not look too closely at its rotten roots and cracking supports, in order to achieve whatever temporary and external reconciliation could be made. By contrast, the contradiction in the Protestant view appeared later, when all hope had disappeared of discovering positive religious truth by means of criticism based on rationalism—criticism that had already started its work with the preconceived notion, formed consciously or not, of rejecting everything that departed from the order of things conceived in the narrowest scope of reality. It penetrated deeper because it had begun later, and by the fundamental principle of Protestantism could not stop at any point. It will not help to look away; the contradiction is obvious to the internal gaze, which cannot be averted. What can be done? Elevate Luther, Calvin, Zwingli, Henry VIII, Schleiermacher,[39] or some such person to the level of a prophet who has

---

[39] Friedrich Schleiermacher (1768–1834): German liberal theologian and biblical scholar, pioneer of historical or "higher" criticism, rationalist skeptic who rejected

come to proclaim the law, or else go straight to Büchner,[40] or cling to the narrow and slippery edge of the slope leading to him. On the other hand, it turns out a prolonged reconciliation with Rome, even a superficial one, was impossible, for just when you think you can rest easy, the papal troops launch their attack with an unflagging persistence worthy of some better goal than the gradual, imperceptible turning back toward the order of the Gregories, Urbans, and Bonifaces.[41] Now what is to be done? Is there a way out? For individual people, hungry for the truth—yes; the doors of Orthodoxy are always open. For whole nations, there is probably no straight or direct way out; they would have to retrace all the steps leading to decrepitude, sickness, death, and decay, in order to assemble from the decayed elements a new ethnographical whole, a new cultural-historical type. For nations, as for individual people, there is no living water or fountain of youth. The saying "There is no resurrection without death" also applies to nations.

Orthodox teaching considers the Orthodox Church the only way to salvation. This is not the place to go into what this means regarding individual people. But the significance of this teaching in regard to whole nations seems to me the following: a non-Orthodox view of the Church deprives Revelation itself of its reliability and unshakeability in the eyes of those adhering to it, and thus, by a slow but inevitable path of logical development, destroys the very essence of Christianity in their minds. And without Christianity there is no true civilization; that is, there is no salvation even in the earthly sense of the word.

---

orthodox doctrines, emphasizing the subjective experience of religion instead.

[40] Ludwig Büchner (1824–99): German philosopher, author of *Kraft und Stoff* (Force and Matter), a forceful statement of atheistic materialism.

[41] Generic pope names; there have been sixteen popes (and two anti-popes) named Gregory, eight named Urban, and nine named Boniface.

C₃ 10 ₂₀
The Difference in the Course of Historical Upbringing

"Or better, I might call them two boundless, and
indeed unexampled Electric Machines (turned by
the 'Machinery of Society'), with batteries of opposite quality; Drudgism the Negative, Dandyism
the Positive; one attracts hourly towards it and
appropriates all the Positive Electricity of the
nation (namely, the Money thereof); the other is
equally busy with the Negative (that is to say the
Hunger), which is equally potent. Hitherto you
see only partial transient sparkles and sputters:
but wait a little, till the entire nation is in an electric state: till your whole vital Electricity, no
longer healthfully Neutral, is cut into two isolated
portions of Positive and Negative (of Money and
of Hunger); and stands there bottled up in two
World-Batteries! The stirring of a child's finger
brings the two together; and then — What then?
The Earth is but shivered into impalpable smoke
by that Doom's thunder-peal; the Sun misses one
of his Planets in Space, and thenceforth there are
no eclipses of the Moon."

— Thomas Carlyle, *Sartor Resartus* (Chap. X, Book
III)

Another essential, typal distinction between the Germanic-Roman (or European) world and the Slavic world consists of the course of historical upbringing each received. Before describing this difference, we need to define some
theoretical concepts of the state. What is the state exactly, and what is its process of formation and development? Setting aside all mystical definitions that
do not clarify anything (such as, for example, when we were taught in school
that the state is the highest expression of the law of truth and justice on earth),
it seems we must instead take as most satisfactory the English concept, that
the state is the form or condition of society that protects its members' property and individuality, understood as life, honor, and freedom. This definition
seems right to me, if the life, honor, and freedom of the individual are understood in the broadest sense of the words: that is, not just the individual life,

honor, and freedom, but also the national life, honor, and freedom, which are the essential part of these blessings. Without that, the concepts of personal honor and freedom presented by states would not fulfill the definition. Indeed, why combine millions and millions of people into huge political entities with no other purpose for their combined power than to protect life, property, and personal honor and freedom? It would seem the Swiss cantons or the average German dukedom would be adequate for that. If the state exists only for these personal rights, then why, for example, should the peoples of Germany have resisted the power of Napoleon in 1813? His power was enlightened enough to guarantee all these rights at least as much as they had been under German rule. The Confederation of the Rhine[1] benefited German nationality more than the Holy Roman Empire, or after it, the German Confederation.[2] For example the Napoleonic Code and its standardized system of jurisprudence were gifts of Napoleon's dominion, often sorely missed after his overthrow. And why should we [Russians] have sacrificed hundreds of thousands in lives, hundreds of millions in funds, and burn city and village alike, if it was only a matter of defending individual life, property, honor, and freedom? Doubtless if we had submitted to his power, not only would Napoleon not have violated these rights, but he might even have given them such a guarantee as could not have been imagined under the conditions of Russian civil society of that day. But it was just as obvious to the Germans as to us, that all these rights were trifling compared to national honor and freedom. If we look at the sacrifices each state demands from its subjects as fees for membership and obligations for service, we will see that at least four-fifths of these sacrifices go to preserve the good of the nation, not the individual. This includes nearly the entire navy (after all, how many courts of law protect personal property from pirates?) and almost the whole army (likewise, it takes few troops to preserve the peace domestically). Almost all states borrow to cover expenditures, and all this government debt is devoted to the defense of national honor and freedom, or the national interest, not the defense of such things for individual people. It's the same with financial administration: the size of expenditures can only be explained by the size of the funds that must be collected for the upkeep of the army, navy, and payment on the national debt. Without these obligations even the administration itself could be much simpler and less costly.

People groups and nationalities [*narodnosti, natsional'nosti*] are the organs of humanity, allowing the idea contained within them to be expressed in space and time, in all possible diversity, in a full multifaceted manifestation,

---

[1] Confederation of the Rhine: A union of sixteen German client states loyal to Napoleon's French Empire, formed by the Treaty of Pressburg (1805), lasting 1806–13. Prussia and Austria were excluded.

[2] German Confederation: Created in 1815 at the Congress of Vienna, it included Prussia and Austria with most of the members of the Confederation of the Rhine.

as has been shown in previous chapters. Thus the sacrifices required for the defense of nationality are the most essential and imperative, even the most sacred. Nationality therefore constitutes the essential basis of the state, the very reason for its existence; and its main purpose is the defense of that nationality. From this definition of the state it follows that the state without a national basis has no living principle, and in general has no reason to exist. If a state is actually a random mix of nationalities, then what kind of national honor or national freedom can it preserve and defend, when the honor and freedom [of multiple nationalities] may be (or in the majority of cases, must be) opposed to each other? What do the millions spent on the navy, army, financial administration, and government debt all go for? Nothing but the insult and deprivation of national honor and freedom for the nationalities squeezed into its artificial frame. What is the meaning of the honor and freedom of Turkey, Austria, or the former Poland? Nothing but the oppression and insult to the true feeling of the people and the true national freedom of the peoples making up these states: Greeks, Serbs, Bulgars, Czechs, Russians, Romanians, and until recently, even Italians. These states can only be dear to the hearts of those with the power to insult and oppress: the Turkish horde in Turkey; a small clique of Germans, and more recently, also Magyars, in Austria; the Catholic clergy and the Polish *szlachta,* cut off from its Slavic roots and its own nationality [in Poland].

From the national significance of states, it follows that each nationality that has acquired and not lost the consciousness of its own original historical national significance must take the form of a state, and for one nationality there must be only one state. These propositions have many apparent exceptions, but they are only apparent.

The first proposition, affirming that any nationality has the right to statehood, necessarily is limited by the consciousness of that right, since for people, the same as for individuals, it is impossible to be unaware of one's own existence, or to take existence away from one who does not have it. A people can be unconscious of its national existence for various reasons: a fundamental inability to rise above its wild condition and tribal dislocation, or merely from failing to reach a sufficient state of maturity. It is very likely that both these reasons essentially combine into one. Nevertheless if a tribe at an unconscious level of development is taken into another that has already begun its political growth, the former will be absorbed by the latter, since the mightier, more developed tribe cannot cease its growth just because it encounters these nascent tribes in its path. When a foreign object comes between the wood and the bark, the tree grows around it and makes it part of itself. But with peoples it is different. In the tribal, ethnographic, prehistoric period of existence, people groups are very flexible and supple organisms. Without yet experiencing the influence of their own peculiar formative principle, they maintain the ability to conjoin with other people-groups [*narodnosti*], just as many chemical substances can combine among themselves only in their nascent state (*in statu nascenti*). These ethnographic elements produce a mixed type if they are of equal strength, or a few may become major types if one of the conjoined tribes overwhelms the other by its numerical strength or moral persuasion. If these absorbed tribes were allowed to continue their independent existence, or if the [foreign] influence on their tribes acted from a distance while they furthered their development, then their existence might reach a historic moment when they would form independent states. But lacking this good fortune, or being incapable of it, they would become part of the predominant tribe destined for historical existence. The process of absorption is not sudden; the slower the process, the more natural and less violent. This is what happened to the Finnic tribes, scattered across the expanse of Russia. From the beginning of history the Slavs never subdued them, but their tribes came into a friendly union with the Slavic tribes and jointly laid the foundation of the state. But a stronger tribe absorbs them by a natural process of assimilation. This process is still not complete and thus far we have seen the Finnic tribe at all stages of integration—from just a few remaining traces of the former difference (in a batch of Finnish-sounding names) to fully preserved tribal appearance (in the Ests), not to mention those who would eagerly become Russians if we ourselves did not prevent them. It is clear that the Ves', Karelians, Zyrians [Komi], Mordva, Cheremis [Mari], and Chuvash,[3] the same as the Ostiaks, Voguls [Mansi], and Samoeds,[4] cannot form [their own] states nor have any pretensions of it; their nationalities have neither historical consciousness nor political character, and therefore it cannot be. It is the same, for example, with the Basques in France and Spain.

Other peoples lost their political existence, but still preserved their ethnographic distinctiveness. The Jews serve as an example of this type of people, nowhere showing the slightest inclination for political reunification.[5] In the same way as the different sides of a person, so the national character's different sides are revealed only gradually, and only gradually fade away. Similar to the Jews (regarding the loss of the political, and thus the historical, side of its national character) are the Armenians, who want to preserve the peculiarities of their language, religious practice, and customs, while showing no aspiration for political life. Meanwhile, the Greeks oppressed in Turkey never cease demonstrating their political vitality. Finally, as with individual persons, so there are peoples who are servile (both in relation to themselves and to neighboring peoples), and deprived of their freedom, which they always

---

[3] Ves', Zyrians, Mordva, and Cheremis: See chap. 2, nn. 10 and 11. Karelians: Baltic-Finnic ethnic group of northwestern Russia and eastern Finland. Chuvash: Turkic ethnic group of uncertain origin, settled from the Volga region to Siberia.

[4] Ostiaks, Voguls, and Samoeds: See chap. 2, n. 12 and chap. 3, n. 12.

[5] So it seemed in the 1860s. Jewish immigration to Palestine became significant in the 1880s and especially after Theodore Herzl's (1860–1904) 1896 book *Der Judenstaat* (The Jewish State) articulated Zionism as an ideology.

abused. Such are the Poles. The incorrigible behavior of the upper classes toward the lower; their inability to preserve their own nationality [*narodnost'*];
their continual efforts to oppress other nationalities and deprive them not
only of political existence but also religious freedom and their whole way of
life; rebellions fostered in neighboring states; and finally the betrayal of their
own tribe: all these are ample proof of the Poles' incapability of responsible
statehood. Although each individual person has the indisputable right to develop his own personality, no one would refuse to take away that freedom
from a person guilty of all the Poles have done (that is, the upper classes of
Polish society). So it is hard to see why a whole people group should be allowed to abuse its privileges with impunity. Russia alone had the right to
punish Poland and render it harmless, since Poland has constantly offended it
and all of Slavdom. By what right Austria and Prussia could do this is another
question.

If the primary purpose of the state is to defend and preserve the life,
honor, and freedom of the nation [*narod*], and since there can only be one life,
honor, and freedom for an individual nation, then thus understood, the second proposition is also correct. That is, a single nationality can comprise only
one state. If any part of a nationality becomes part of another state, this would
violate its freedom and honor. If a part of a nationality formed another separate state, the purpose of both states cannot be attained by either; as a matter
of fact, the purpose no longer exists, or at least does not exist fully. Thus
neither state attains true consciousness of its national individuality; their purpose can only be something temporary or accidental. The existence of the
United States, which by nationality is English, apparently contradicts such an
understanding. But just as the fleeting existence of the Finnic tribes within the
Russian state only shows the incomplete, unfinished process of their assimilation, so the existence of the United States as an independent state indicates,
conversely, the birth of a newly-formed nationality, completely different from
the English. Although hardly aware of it (since any process of a new formation is so subtle, so imperceptible), we are now witnessing by the migration of
peoples exactly what it was like when the present-day European or
Germanic-Roman cultural-historical type was born. The reasons for this migration of peoples are identical to those that produced the so-called Great
Migration [of Germanic peoples into Europe]: in both cases the means of subsistence in the emigrants' homelands were insufficient. The scale of the new
migration is no less, if not more, than what occurred in the first centuries of
the Christian era. Hundreds of thousands, even up to half a million people,
cross the ocean every year. The results of the migration are the same: the
blending of peoples arriving on new soil, not in the form of a compact state,
but as more free, or in a manner of speaking, diluted, ethnographic elements.
It would indeed be strange if this mixture of Dutch, English, Germans, Celts,
French, Spaniards, and even Slavs (Czechs), under the completely unique
moral and physical conditions of the country did not produce a new nation-

ality, or new nationalities—just as the mixture of various Germanic, Gallic, Roman, partly Slavic, and Arab elements produced the new nationalities of English, German, French, Italian, and Spanish. These elements, in mixtures of various proportions occupying the western part of the Roman Empire and Germany, were not completely wild at that time, and thus must have had some kind of social or even state structure, especially those under the influence of the Roman cultural element. Settled onto new soil, they were not politically disconnected tribes like the American natives, for example; but the political connection between them could not be a state founded on the people's national character [*na narodnom natsional'nom kharaktere*], since no such thing had been created yet. The ancient world of Romans, Gauls, and Britons was destroyed, and a new (predominantly but not exclusively) Germanic one had not yet managed to form a new entity or entities. Therefore the first states emerging after the fall of the Roman Empire had a temporary, provisional character, providing, in a manner of speaking, the shelter under which new nationalities could be produced. The Lombard, Ostrogoth, Visigoth, Suebi, Burgundian, and Merovingian Frankish states did not produce well-defined nationalities. Even before that an all-German element predominated within them, so that they could still form a unified whole under the scepter of Charlemagne, which was the true birth moment of modern nationalities: the French, Italian, and especially German [nationalities] were correctly designated by the Treaty of Verdun,[6] concluded almost 400 years after barbarians occupied their modern homelands. The same temporary, provisional character can be seen in the United States. Their instincts for statehood are very strong (as the energy displayed in their recent Civil War attests), but they have still not revealed a special national character, or have done so very weakly. I am by no means trying to say that the United States are headed for their downfall, to be replaced by new states founded each on their own independent nationality. There is no basis to extend the analogy so far, and the analogy itself does not require it. If the ruins of the Goth empire became part of several states, then in the strictest sense of the word, the Frankish monarchy continued to exist from the time of Clovis or Merovech[7] to the present. It continues to exist because under the shelter of the old, not yet national French monarchy, a special French nationality developed. I am only trying to make the point that the present form of the United States is provisional, under the shelter of which one or several nationalities must take shape, and depending upon [the outcome of] that, will become one or several states.

---

[6] The Treaty of Verdun, in 843, ended the war between the three sons of Charlemagne's successor, Louis the Pious, and divided the lands of the Carolingian Empire into three separate kingdoms.

[7] Merovech (d. 457): Legendary founder of the Merovingian dynasty in what became the dominant Frankish tribe. Clovis I (d. 511): First Merovingian king of the Franks, who united all the Frankish tribes under his rule.

If the most essential purpose of the state is the preservation of nationality, then it is apparent that the force and strength of the national armor must adjust to the strength of the danger with which it has contended and must contend. Therefore the state must take the form of a single, centralized political whole where that danger is great, but can take a more or less weak form, such as a united federation of separate parts, where the danger is small.

Nationality [*natsional'nost'*] is not, however, such an extreme concept that everyone not belonging to it would be equally foreign to it. Even concerning individual personality, there is not such extreme delineation. Both individuality and nationality have a more or less close kindred bond, which can be so close that the freedom and honor of one's relations can be as dear as one's own, and completely inseparable from them. Such groups form families of individuals and peoples; and peoples belonging to such a family cannot remain completely separate from each other. No matter how close this connection, however, it cannot completely erase either national or personal boundaries. Thus while peoples may be very close, if they consider themselves distinct political entities, they cannot easily be combined into one state. But for purposes of mutual defense, the glory of each individual nationality, or strengthening their natural bonds, they can form a federation, with a bond of varying force and strength (depending on how great the danger it must face), which can take the form of: a united state [*soiuznoe gosudarstvo*], a union of states [*soiuz gosudarstv*], or just a political system. The first can take place when all the political activity of the union is concentrated into the hands of a single power, but the members of the union are given broad administrative autonomy. The second is when politically independent parts are connected by an inviolable agreement of coordinated external relations, both defensively and offensively. The third is when the mutual activity is based only upon a certain moral consciousness, without any definite, positive obligations. In the first two cases, the bond is secured not only by a common legislative authority, encompassing a more or less broad range of the members' activity, but also judicial authority, resolving issues that arise from the application of laws to individual cases, and executive authority, having to put judicial decisions into practice. By way of contrast, for the political system there is neither judicial nor executive authority for the union; and the legislative authority for the union, expressed in international treaties, only applies to individual cases, and is valid only concerning those particular cases, with no obligation, not even a moral one, to obey even the most natural, logically necessary conclusions resulting from it. Of course it can be said that in a union of states there cannot possibly be any compulsory authority, as we saw not long ago in the example of Prussia disregarding the union's decision.[8] But such a case is also possible within a single state, if the recalcitrant has enough

---

[8] Danilevskii has in mind the 1866 Austro-Prussian War, in which the German Confederation mostly sided with Austria.

power to oppose state law. The system of states, on the other hand, by default has no force of compulsion for its judicial or executive authority, but essentially the complete absence of either, which is why any violation of the interests of one or a few of the members by the others can be only be resolved by force, that is, by war, or by voluntary reconciliation.

And so these forms—a politically-centralized state, a union of states, and the political system—are conditioned upon, on the one hand, the individual identity and mutual affinity of the peoples comprising them, and on the other hand, the level of danger threatening the national honor and freedom the state must defend and protect. A false understanding of these relations never goes unpunished and leads to the most fatal consequences. For example, all the Greek tribes could have made up a single state on the basis of national affinity, since they had the same language, the same religion, the same traditions, etc. But living in a country with such excellent natural defenses, separating them from enemy nationalities by mountains and sea, they long existed without any external danger, and thus could easily have formed themselves into a unified state, or a union of states even, for which there was some basis in common institutions: the Amphictyonic League, the common treasury of the Delian League, the common Games,[9] and so on. But the Greek states bristled at any bonds between them and only formed themselves into a political system. An external danger approached, but even that could not compel them to unite more closely together. And their discord having gone on so long, they rejected the anchor of their salvation: the great Macedonian sovereign Philip.[10] Only by force would they submit to the saving unity, and they only maintained it so long as that force acted upon them. Thus the Greeks died as a nation long before the vital force of Hellenism ran out. Greek culture had to live out its days in foreign quarters, lingering in Egypt and Pergamum [Turkey], before finally having to submit to a total stranger, Rome.

If nationality is the true basis of the state, the reason and purpose of its existence, then of course the origin of the state depends on the consciousness of that nationality as something original and unique that must summon all its strength to establish and protect it. And any event that causes this consciousness to arise, any juxtaposition with other nationalities, will serve as the cause for the formation of the state, in the same way that the feeling of the external world juxtaposed to the internal world leads to the consciousness of individual personality. Nobody believes anymore in some kind of precondi-

---

[9] Amphictyonic League: See chap. 5, n. 12. Delian League (477–404 BCE): A defensive association of Greek city-states under the leadership of Athens. The Olympic Games (776 BCE–394 CE): Prestigious athletic competitions held every four years in Olympia in honor of Zeus, the temple statue of which was one of the seven wonders of the ancient world.

[10] Philip II, king of Macedon (382–336 BCE), conquered and united all of Greece except for Sparta. His son and heir was Alexander the Great.

tion, agreement, or [social] contract serving as the basis of the state, just as nobody believes in such a basis for language. You cannot even claim a basis in some innate human social instinct, which would only lead to cohabitation in society (as a group, tribe, or commune) but not in a state. It takes something more, some necessary external stimulus, to lead a tribe to a clear awareness of their national individuality, and thus of the need to defend and preserve it. At the very least, we do not know of an example of any state that formed without some kind of external stimulus: one or several, spontaneously or gradually fostering national consciousness within a tribe. Whether it would be possible to develop a state without it is hard to say. In any case, to form a state on the basis of internal motivations would require an impossible confluence of circumstances: namely, it would require the total absence of any disturbing external or internal influences over an incredibly long time, so that inherent human development, having led to complications in relations with nature and with each other, could summon all by itself all the required strength from within itself under the influence of certain obstacles presented by nature.

In all likelihood, a state formed under such ideal conditions would take the form of a federation, but one completely unlike all those we know. State supremacy would not reside in the whole, but in the most elementary social union—in the rural (or *volost'*) district community [*obshchina*]—and the mutual bond and dependence would become weaker at each higher level of these communities: there would be stronger and closer bonds at the local level than the district level, the district than the territory level, the territory than the regional level, the regional than the state level.

This division into communities must certainly come before all further development, because sedentary living requires it. Sedentary civilization is only possible in a land offering physical impediments to mass migration. Nomads are incapable of development, and although pastoral life constitutes obvious progress over hunting, that progress is deceptive because it is a dead end. Nomadism offers too many conveniences, too much security in large herds, and too much reward for laziness. But the only physical obstacles to nomadic life are mountains, forest, or periodic river floods, such as in Egypt. However the last example is too great an obstacle; it demands from a wild tribe too much vigilance to derive the benefits from it. Mountains completely divide people, locking them into valleys and hollows, well preserving their ethnographic distinctions, offering little chance to develop a first-rate original civilization. Thus only forest remains as a sufficient impediment to the development of nomadic life while not presenting an insurmountable barrier to sedentary life, and thus to the development of a first-class culture by the weak means of a tribe forced by necessity to leave its original savage existence. Forest thus has tremendous significance for fostering culture. It also has another influence: Its mysterious depths and semidarkness cast a poetic mood upon the soul of the people living within reach of its shadows.[11] I do not think an original culture *untouched by any outside influence* could develop any place but in a forested land. But how would such forest settlements occur? In the same way as separate islands. Just pay attention while crossing a wide forested land (such as northern Russia, for example), and you will see how this occurs. At first small, widely-scattered settlements form rare "islands" within the forest "sea." Settlements, farmsteads, and clearings open new places not far from established centers. The wooded barriers separating them diminish, and a rural locality [*volost'*] is formed from a few villages that the woods no longer separate. Near the bigger island of settlement are smaller islands. A number of localities are separated by wide forest expanses; the number of localities increases and the forest in which rare settlements were sprinkled turns from an ocean into a network of intersecting strands. But other obstacles, such as large swamps, prevent this forest network from being further reduced by settlements. Wide forest expanses still remain like watersheds, or portages [*voloki*] as we call them in the north, that divide one group of settlements from another. As the population grows, the network is broken up, rural localities combine and eventually form a continuous network in which remnants of the forest are now scattered, just as settlements had been scattered in the forest network. The forest remnants diminish, and a continuous sea appears, or perhaps more aptly lakes, of human settlements in which are scattered islands of forest. These lakes do not combine into one big sea, however, having been separated for so long from each other by watersheds. The development of societies must follow the same pattern as the settlement of wooded land. Long isolated from their neighbors, localities form their own unique, sovereign social entities; these are essentially small, independent political centers. When they come into contact with other localities, their uniqueness has already been fortified by time. Of course, as more and more people come into contact, and more complex relations form between them, it brings to light certain needs that the locality cannot satisfy, and thus it becomes necessary for all those localities that have formed such close relations to give up part of their power—and so on, and so on, from the smallest to the largest kind of group. But each group surrenders part of its power to the higher group it joins—of course, only a small part of its power, concerning only those issues and interests that cannot be administered within the smaller group. A federative relationship forms naturally from this; not the kind in which power spills over from the top down, but rather comes up from below. It seems to me this accounts for the federative structure of all peoples living in forest regions, which history first finds in the ethnographic stage of life (such as the Germans and Slavs, for example). This also accounts for the federative structure of the United States, where due to the peculiarities of its position, the influence of external disturbances must be, and until very recently was,

---

[11] A rare dash of romanticism seasons Danilevskii's prose.

comparatively weak. But would a people influenced only by the local features of the land surrounding its course of settlement attain an awareness of its own nationality by that means—in however long a time, during which that influence was continuous—and thus give rise to a true bond of statehood, which actually satisfies all their needs? That is quite doubtful. Even more doubtful is the possibility of the continued lack of any disturbing influence, either from outside tribes or from passions arising within the tribes, or most importantly, the forceful personality rising above the level of the people's common ideas, and striving to subject his fellow tribesmen to his influence. It was only my intention to demonstrate that a tribe left to develop on its own, removed from all disturbing influences, but subjected to the conditions that prompted it to take on sedentary life, would likely assume a federative structure.

In reality, of course, it does not go like that. Different tribes clash with each other, and this clash clarifies their national consciousness and creates a sense of the need to protect their nationality's freedom and honor; if it was violated, to restore it; or to defend its predominance over other nationalities once acquired. If under the influence of nature alone, undisturbed by others, it had managed to form a weak federative bond, it would have to let stronger bonds take over in order to emerge from the struggle victorious. But the necessity of protecting nationality born of tribal struggle is not enough to bring a people into statehood. Struggle is temporary: for its objectives a temporary strengthening and centralization of power are enough, such as for example in Cossack societies accepting the power of atamans only in wartime, or in the tribes of Israel accepting dictatorial power of the judges only in an era of great dangers. The lessons of the past are generally soon forgotten, and even sooner in the primitive or even tribal stage of a people's existence. The ungovernable tribal will so well suits the primitive individual that he will renounce it only under the pressure of causes acting gradually. *Struggle is not enough for this; it requires dependence.*

The condition of dependence summons the strength of peoples or tribes to shrug it off, and gradually leads to an understanding of national freedom and honor, training the individual to submit his will to common goals. Not just the subjection, but the actual domination of one people over another also acts to rally the dominating people, since it forms a solid bond between the individuals who constitute that people, the gradual submission of individual will to common goals, to protect the dominion it has acquired. In the life of a people, dependence plays the same role as, in the life of the individual, an academic discipline or even an ascetic moral order, which teaches the person to submit his will to higher goals. It is by no means necessary for an academic discipline to limit its demands only to what is required to attain academic goals, or for the ascetic order to place only those restrictions and deprivations which seem necessary for moral goals. Not only is it unnecessary, but in most cases it is insufficient. Fasting, taking vows, the period of training as a novice, living in the desert (which the great Christian ascetics, not only the purely contemplative but even those devoted to practical living, undertook for a time): these have no significance in and of themselves; they have no distinct moral virtue, but instead serve as moral gymnastics for the will, making it more flexible and ready for any great deed. There is also a kind of historical or political asceticism that has the same character, consisting of various forms of dependence that sustain a people and destine them for some secret historical purpose. This dependence is undertaken to subordinate one's personal will to some other (even an incorrect one) so that the individual will is always able to be subjected to that other will striving for the common good, and it has the distinction of taking a people from *the tribal will* to *the existence of civil freedom* [*grazhdanskaia svoboda*]. Thus only the forms of historical dependence that serve this purpose can be said to correspond to the goals of a people. And however oppressive they seem to that people, they must be considered beneficial. But neither academic discipline that completely stifles the initiative, merit, and originality of one's personality, nor religious asceticism that turns a living person into a dead corpse in the hands of a Jesuit father superior, could be said to correspond to one's interests. In the same way, the dependence that carries a people into its historical stage of life must only be considered useful and necessary when it leaves the moral virtue of a people intact, and preserves the conditions allowing civil freedom to replace the tribal will (conditions without which civil freedom cannot even exist). It is this wandering in the wilderness, through which a people passes from the existence of the tribal will into the promised land of civil freedom by the path of various forms of dependence, that I call the historical upbringing of a people. And this upbringing was fundamentally different for the Germanic-Roman peoples and for the Russian people, as well as for others of its fellow tribesmen. It must not be forgotten that parts of this thorny path traveled by them and by others are far from similar.

History in general presents three forms of national dependence, constituting the historical discipline and asceticism of peoples: *slavery, tributary obligation*, and *feudalism*.

As history shows, slavery (that is, the complete subjugation of one person to another, by which that person becomes an object in his owner's possession) is a form of dependence that will never attain one's goals. It debases both slaves and masters to the same degree and, continuing long enough, ruins all possibility of establishing true civil freedom in states founded upon slavery. This is sufficiently proven by the examples of Rome, Greece, and the cultural-historical types preceding them, in all of which there existed slavery—except for China, the long continuous existence of which might be partly attributable to this fact.

Tributary obligation occurs when a people has placed another in dependence, but is so distinct from it either in terms of national [*narodnyi*] or even racial [*porodnyi*] character, level of development, or way of life that it cannot combine or blend with the one it has placed in dependence. Not even wanting to settle on its land (the better to preserve its cultural uniqueness) it places it in collective slavery, but leaves its internal life more or less as it was. Therefore tributary obligation is burdensome to widely varying degrees. Russia under the Tatar yoke and the Slavic states under Turkish rule are examples of this kind of dependence. The effect of tributary obligation on national self-consciousness is obvious, but no matter how long it continues, peoples subjected to it remain fully capable of attaining civil freedom.

The word feudalism I take in its broadest sense, meaning the relationship between a predominant tribe and a subjugated tribe, in which the first does not remain separate but settles among the conquered people. Individuals from the conquering people seize the possessions of the conquered, but the latter retain, if not legally then in actual fact, the use of part of their former property in exchange for certain tax, labor, or service obligations.

This last form of dependence set in among the peoples joining the Roman Empire after it was taken over by Germanic tribes; then those peoples, having grown stronger and having attained some degree of statehood under the influence of Roman principles, introduced it into their original homeland, Germania. Usually it is taken as a fact that feudalism was the order introduced by Charlemagne, by which he distributed his royal lands on the condition of fulfilling certain obligations to the state. But this was only the formal legitimization of the order of things that emerged from the conquest, done in order to revive and support it once it was breaking down—as a consequence of which the Frankish landlords, who had completely crushed all opposition of the subjugated people, felt the need for reciprocal bonds and hierarchical subordination to preserve their dominance. Thus Charles's reform only broadened the realm of feudalism, spreading it also to royal lands. Under a strong ruler, even those landlords who were not royal beneficiaries [who owned or inherited their lands] acquired the same relationship to the sovereign as the beneficiary landlords [who received their lands by grant of the king]. On the other hand, the beneficiary landlords, under the weak descendants of Charles, in their turn acquired the hereditary rights of the former, so that everything took on a more or less uniform character.

To the burden of feudalism were added two other kinds, one of which counterbalanced it to some degree. This was the burden of thought under the unconditional authority of ancient thinkers (primarily Aristotle) poorly understood; and the burden of conscience under papal despotism, which they helped lay upon themselves: both the peoples, by the violent elevation of their particular opinion to the level of universal dogma, and the rulers, by wanting to substitute the state church for the universal church.[12] Medieval

---

[12] Danilevskii does not say which of these counterbalanced feudalism. Perhaps he saw some salutary effect in ancient learning, however limited; more likely, he meant the

development proceeded under these three burdens of thought, conscience, and life.

After the heroic era of the Crusades had summoned the full forces of medieval society and led them into contact with Arabic civilization, the thirteenth century began: a period when medieval theocratic and aristocratic culture was in full bloom; a period of the harmonious development of all the forces within it, under which the lower social classes were, in the fullest sense of the word, what the Germans call *Nährstand*,[13] taking the place of Athenian and Roman slaves, like Atlas bearing the sphere of culture on their shoulders, wheezing and buckling [under the weight]. The romanticists idealize this first flowering of European culture. But upper-class society itself, especially the thinking people within it, felt the weight of the burden upon it when the confluence of several inventions, discoveries, and political revolutions acquainted them more closely with ancient thought and aroused their own independent thought. The first to be felt and shrugged off was the burden of authority in the realm of thought, in what is called the Renaissance, corresponding to the fifteenth century. After that, with the help of this independent thought, the religious burden was shrugged off in the time of the Reformation, corresponding to the sixteenth century.

The highest social classes could be satisfied with this. The burden laid on them by the indirect influence of the vanquished Roman element was shrugged off, but the one they themselves laid upon those they vanquished remained in full force, and had not come into the full, clear, and definite awareness of those burdened by it. From this state of things emerged the second blooming of European culture, which was also the height of its creative powers, providing internal security to the development of the European cultural-historical type. This corresponds to the seventeenth century, which is actually the ideal of what is now called the retrograde tendency: the ideal time for European conservatism, to which all of its adherents would like to return, with the exception of a small party of romanticists and ultramontanists, whose ideal age is even longer ago.

But even that age was only a pause in the general movement of Europe. The wheel of European movement (in the expression of K. S. Aksakov)[14] turns once a century; however, the beginning of a new cycle comes not at the beginning of each century, but at the middle. The eighteenth century came, and that turning sloughed off the third burden, feudalism. The French Revolution accomplished this. After that had to come a third period of harmonious development, the third flowering of European culture, which would seem to have no end in sight, according to those going by the name of liberals, but more

---

validation of their beliefs and vicarious sense of shared triumph through the rising power of the papacy.

[13] See chap. 8, n. 4.

[14] Aksakov: See chap. 8, n. 45.

accurately would be called neoconservatives [*neokonservatory*]. The nineteenth century is their ideal, which (like the thirteenth and sixteenth centuries) truly represents the character of the third flowering of European culture. This is the age of industrial development, and the age of the achievement and dissemination of what are called the great principles of 1789.

But the wheel of European motion keeps turning every hundred years. European culture's path of development can be symbolized by the medieval city or castle, consisting of several walls enclosing one after the other. As the life of that city grows, these walls begin to constrain it. One by one they fall, and wide boulevards take their place, increasing the ease of interaction and bringing into the city more daylight and fresh air. The last wall was broken in the eighteenth century. But by the mid-nineteenth century it turns out that the very dwellings laid out and built up according to the needs and demands of the old European society are no longer comfortable, constraining those living within them all the more. Boulevards can replace walls, but what can replace the buildings themselves? And where is there to live until new ones can be built? Where will the materials for new buildings come, and most importantly, where is the plan for the new structures? Will they not have to live in bivouacs, under the cold rain and hot sun of the open sky? In 1848 for the first time the solemn demands for the general demolition came forward. Never in earlier times had demands for the destruction of the outer walls come with such callous zeal as they came now for the very dwelling places of European civilization and culture. Neither the storming of the Bastille nor the seizure of the Tuileries presents such an example of street carnage as the July Days of 1848.[15] Then came the days of Marius, as the new Cimbri and Teutons[16] held the gates of Italy. The beginning of the end had come.[17]

---

[15] The Bastille, a Paris castle used as a military prison, was stormed by the mob on 14 July 1789; the Tuileries was a palace in Paris which housed both the royal family and the National Assembly after the 1789 "March of the Women" demanded their return to Paris. The mob stormed the Tuileries on 10 August 1792 and placed the royal family under arrest. Danilevskii appears to be conflating the July Revolution of 1830 ("July Days") with the "June Days" uprising of 1848, the latter of which saw tens of thousands of demonstrators and barricades in the streets, and thousands killed as government forces put down the uprising.

[16] Gaius Marius (156–86 BCE): Roman general and seven-time consul, known as the "third founder of Rome" for defending Rome from the Teutones, Ambrones, and Cimbri, Germanic tribes invading Italy from Gaul in 102 BCE.

[17] [Danilevskii's marginalia, published posthumously]: *Twenty-three years later came the second act, the second call for general demolition — the even more horrible days of the Paris Commune. The third act will not be long, when the goal of destruction will be accomplished.* [Translator's note: In a bloody week of fighting in late May 1871, tens of thousands were killed, and later, thousands more executed, as royalist armies put down the Paris Commune, which arose in the aftermath of France's defeat in the Franco-Prussian War. Among the buildings destroyed was the Tuileries Palace.]

European peoples passed through the crucible of the feudal forms of dependence and yet did not lose their moral qualities or consciousness of their rights; but in the course of their difficult development they lost one of the necessary conditions under which civil freedom can and must replace the tribal will: they lost the very soil of freedom, the earth on which they live. They try to make up for this loss by all kinds of palliatives: They even came up with the absurd notion of the "right to work,"[18] which no one knows how it would be paid for, in order to avoid saying the fearful words, *right to land*, which however have still been loudly proclaimed. If even this demand must be fulfilled, if even this last trace of the conquest must be effaced, then the entire basis of the community would be given such a shock that the whole community would lose its meaning, a shock that the culture itself or the very civilization undergoing such a dreadful operation could scarcely survive. Yet it must inevitably go through it. Of course the social forces of Europe are tenacious, strong, and evidently able to withstand the assault of barbarians, from outside or from within. After all, fourth- and fifth-century Rome was not weakened or exhausted. And Europe would perhaps successfully resist it, if not for the inherent irreconcilable contradiction that immobilizes it and, like all irreconcilable contradictions, possesses irresistible force.

The moral virtue [*nravstvennoe dostoinstvo*] of European peoples survived many trials and matured in the course of the long struggle they waged. Moreover, the political structure of the European peoples and the events of their history alike have favored the excessive development of the individual. Individual freedom constitutes the principle of European civilization; refusing all external restraints, it can only restrain itself. From this arises the principle of popular sovereignty, which becomes more and more significant not only in theory but also in the practice of European state rights. Its application irrepressibly leads to the democratic constitution of states, founded on universal suffrage. Even though democracy and universal suffrage means the rule of everyone, it also essentially means the rule of [only] some, just like aristocracy—that is, the rule of the numerically largest and (according to the social structure of European states) completely indigent classes of society, and certainly by that part of it which from high concentration will always have the force of numbers on its side. This means the rule of big centers of working-class populations—capitals and manufacturing cities.

Has it even occurred to anyone that the ruling class will use the power placed at its disposal to improve its material condition, even in essentially phony ways? Did not Bright[19] tell the workers that their situation would improve only when they gained proportional representation in Parliament, and did not the workers put more trust in him than in all the economists' ideas?

---

[18] "Right to work" socialism is attributed to Louis Blanc (1811–82), and was a popular slogan in the Revolution of 1848 in France.

[19] John Bright (1811–89): British Liberal politician and famed orator.

Let them become the aristocracy, with power in their hands but having taken a vow of voluntary poverty; then it could be possible to trust that the starving people are capable of self-control while surrounded by all the temptations that come with the office of supreme ruler. If the principle of popular sovereignty must be fulfilled in reality, then it is also necessary to be prepared for the power-holder to demand a proper upkeep, annual stipends,[20] and various subsidies. During the English Parliament's debates on reform at the beginning of the 1830s, one of its champions, the famous Macaulay,[21] in one of his speeches full of clear thinking, said that he rejected universal suffrage because it could only lead to communism or military dictatorship. No more than twenty years later events in France confirmed the prediction of the famous English historian. Military dictatorship, even christened with the mighty name of Caesarism, was introduced in theory; the one who established it [Louis Napoleon] sought the name "savior of society," and I think correctly received it.

But, some will say, France is not all of Europe. No, France is precisely Europe in miniature, its fullest expression. From the very time of Clovis,[22] the history of France is nearly the history of Europe, with one exception (which however can be fully explained and proves the rule). Everything France does not take part in constitutes [only] the peculiar phenomena in the life of individual European states, but everything that is truly all-European (even if not universal, or all-human, as they like to proclaim) is without fail also a predominantly French phenomenon. It is possible to know superbly the history of England, Italy, or Germany, and still not know the history of Europe; but being acquainted with the history of France means knowing essentially the whole history of Europe as well. France was always the tuning fork of Europe, to which events in the lives of other European peoples are attuned.

Clovis's conversion to the Roman form of Christianity was the external cause for the triumph of Catholicism (which was still Orthodox then) over Arianism, paving the way for its supremacy in Europe. The service and defense of the French kings laid the foundation of papal power. The empire of Charlemagne constituted a common kernel from which what is called the European order of things grew. When the part of the Frankish Empire that constitutes France proper had weakened under the last Carolingian and first Capetian[23] kings, there were no common, truly-European events in the history of Europe, regardless of what German historians proclaim about the time

---

[20] *Tsivil'nyi list* (civil list): The annual budget approved by the British Parliament for the expenses of the royal family.

[21] Macaulay: See chap. 6, n. 32.

[22] I.e., fourth to fifth centuries CE. Clovis: See n. 7 in this chapter.

[23] The House of Capet: Rulers of France (987–1328) following the Carolingian dynasty; "the Capetian dynasty" refers to the House of Capet plus its cadet branches, which spread across Europe and has survived to the present.

of their Ottos and Henries.[24] Only when the French-descended Pope Urban II [d. 1099], heeding the voice of the French Peter the Hermit of Amiens [d. 1115], in the French town of Clermont proclaimed the First Crusade [1095], in which the French kings, vassals, and knights played the most important role, did events again take on an all-European character. And over the course of more than two centuries this movement maintained, with a few exceptions, a predominantly French character. The Crusades were begun by the French, and were ended by the French. Customs of chivalry bear a primarily French character; French chivalry served as the example and pattern for other peoples. France set the example of state centralization, the alliance of kings with towns, and the whole struggle against feudalism, and completed them earlier than other states. Even though the so-called Renaissance took place in Italy, it gained its general significance for everyone after being reworked by the French. Then came the Reformation, and thus appears the exception I mentioned. The primary role here unquestionably was played by Germany; but for this reason that phenomenon does not have an all-European character, but was limited strictly to those peoples of German roots and produced only weak echoes in Romanic countries, of which however this movement was most strongly developed in France. France gave the first impulse toward the political relationships known as the political equilibrium of states. When the storms of the Reformation subsided, the whole political life of Europe revolved around Louis XIV. Court etiquette, all outward trappings of civilization, and high fashion from that time to the present day are set by France. The French language has displaced Latin to become the language of diplomacy and high society for all Europe. French literature has become the model for all Europe, which is all the more surprising since this predominance is not justified by its internal merits. It even takes the lead in countries such as England, despite having Milton and Shakespeare;[25] Italy, despite having Dante;[26] and Spain, despite having Cervantes and Calderon[27]—the literatures of which, by internal merits and significance, infinitely surpass French literature (I have in mind here belles-lettres). When French literature traded its pseudo-classical character for the philosophical, this new direction not only preserved

---

[24] I.e., the tenth to thirteenth centuries, when there were four emperors named Otto and six named Henry.

[25] John Milton (1608–74): Poet and author of *Paradise Lost*. William Shakespeare (1564–1616): England's greatest playwright, famous for *Romeo and Juliet, Hamlet, A Midsummer Night's Dream*, etc.

[26] Dante Alighieri (d. 1321): Greatest Italian Renaissance poet, famous for *The Divine Comedy*.

[27] Miguel de Cervantes (1547–1616): Famous for the mock-epic novel *Don Quixote*. Pedro Calderón de la Barca (1600–81): Poet and dramatist of the Golden Age of Spanish baroque theater.

but even strengthened its supremacy. Voltaire[28] presented an example not seen before, nor since, of literary hegemony over public opinion. Even the vices of French society are highly infectious. Whereas the decadence of English society under Charles II[29] was confined to England, the decadence of the Regency and the reign of Louis XV[30] was imparted to all of Europe. In exactly the same way the French Revolution enflamed all Europe (setting aside the fact that in terms of actual benefits introduced, the English Revolution[31] far surpasses it). To an even greater degree than Louis XIV, Napoleon I was the center of the political life of Europe over the course of fifteen years. Victorious France reclaimed the supremacy of its political tribune and the new direction of its literature, even though borrowed from Germany and England, and even though in those places that tendency bore incomparably greater fruit. The July Revolution [of 1830] produced a series of flashes across the whole continent, and the Revolution of 1848 had even greater influence; and as did philosophical and political propaganda before, so now socialist propaganda in France rocked all of Europe. Finally Napoleon III[32] for the third time made France the center of the political life of Europe, providing its tone and direction.[33]

France's significance in this regard is well understood. The people of France is where both ethnographic elements making up the European cultural-historical type [i.e., Romanic and Germanic] most fully overlap, and is itself the result of their mutual interpenetration. Thus everything that makes a splash in France and ripples out from it necessarily produces an echo in both the Germanic and the Romanic worlds as its own native thing; and while it is difficult for these worlds, being too different, to have a direct impact on one another, everything produced by them passes through France, and only in the French revision will it become all-European. This mutual neutralization of the

---

[28] Voltaire: Pen name of François-Marie Arouet (1694–1778), prolific writer, philosophe, leading figure of the French Enlightenment.

[29] Charles II (1630–85): King of England, Scotland, and Ireland whose reign is known as the Restoration, marked by permissiveness and ostentation, after Oliver Cromwell's Puritan Commonwealth in the interregnum of 1649–60.

[30] Louis XV (1710–74): Bourbon king of France, known for his decadent court, uncontrolled spending, and defeat in the Seven Years' War (1756–63).

[31] English Revolution: The so-called "Glorious Revolution" of 1688 was relatively nonviolent, established constitutional monarchy and religious tolerance, and granted citizens a Bill of Rights.

[32] Louis-Napoléon Bonaparte: See chap. 1, n. 10.

[33] [Danilevskii's marginalia, published posthumously]: *And his conqueror, Germany, with the genius Bismarck at its head, can in no way hold this central, predominant position. All it amounts to is merely Bismarck's purely political influence and the high regard inspired by Germany's exceptional military organization, which other states have not yet fully managed to imitate.*

Germanic and Romanic elements in the French people is the reason why everything it produces is less original and has less inherent value than the work of the geniuses in the Germanic and Romanic peoples, who have preserved more of their distinctiveness and originality. The only exception, at any rate, is natural science, in which the French are second to none. But this science is also for the most part a European phenomenon, the most characteristic fruit of the European type of development, so it is no surprise that the true (or standard) representative of Europe, France, holds so high a place precisely in that regard. Everything that is French-national is comparatively weak, having a rather average character, but still has the greatest ability to spread throughout the whole realm of European culture. Therefore even the internal contradiction revealed in the political freedom and economic bondage of the lower classes of European society (only halfway emerged from the [feudal] dependence laid upon them at the very founding of the European order of things, and unable to fully extricate themselves without wrecking the whole order) would have to appear first of all in France, but would also have to spread to the rest of Europe.

The same causes must certainly produce the same effect, and this dissemination was powerfully apparent in other countries further down the path of political advancement. In England, this contradiction [political freedom, economic bondage] in itself is much stronger than in France, and if it has not advanced to the same degree or reached the point of crisis, it is only the result of [the following] particularly favorable circumstances.

1) In the first place, the result of the fortunate absence of strict logical consistency in the English frame of mind, concerning itself more with the practicality than the logicality of its activity. In everything they make compromises that neither the French (in reality) nor the Germans (in theory) can bear. The best example of this is the English religious reform, which stopped at the halfway point. Taking enough from Protestantism to get free of papal power, the English replaced it with the infallibility of the state in churchly matters (which of course is beyond absurdity), but in practice avoided the consequences of the new inconsistency, by ascribing a purely formal character to the infallibility and supremacy of the state, and in reality going so far as full religious freedom. The English founded the pretensions of their Church's ecumenical significance on a purely superficial apostolic succession somehow existing within its episcopacy, without realizing that by calling Catholicism (through which this succession passed to the Anglican Church) a heresy, they created a chasm which true apostolic succession could never cross. But the happy gift of sacrificing logical consistency to practical usefulness is nevertheless only a palliative. And so the Anglican Church, not feeling solid ground beneath it, is divided into currents striving either to go further into the chasm of consistent Protestantism, or to return to the falsehood of Catholicism, or even (a subtler current) to the truth of Orthodoxy. These currents go further and further from their common center and will probably tear off from each other; knowing the

English, it would be no surprise at some point to see the spectacle of a ruling state Church that has (like an army at peacetime) only a few cadres of bishops, deacons, vicars, and so on, with great material means but no flock at all.

This inconsistency [in the national frame of mind] allows England to proceed slowly down the path of parliamentary reform, and permits the famous Macaulay to make every effort to secure the victory of this reform, leading the English constitution along the slippery slope of democratism—in the full assurance that continuing in such a way leads to communism or military dictatorship. The English hope that history will stop the logical progression of their development for them, just as the sun stopped in its path for the biblical Joshua.[34] But scarcely more than thirty years later comes the time to take another step on the path toward communism or Caesarism. Will it be that many years before the time comes, willingly or unwillingly, to take the next step? If not hindered, one of these steps will lead to what Macaulay feared.

2) It must be considered a particularly fortunate circumstance for England that the most radical, and thus the most consistent, part of its population—the Puritans—saw fit to cross the ocean, the sooner to put their ideals into practice. This departure of democratic elements shored up England for a long time.

3) The conquest of India, giving England a huge chunk of wealth (as a support to its industrial and commercial enterprises as well as an allotment of high-paying positions for the younger sons of the aristocracy), makes up for the many inadequacies of the English social structure and gives an artificial strength to the aristocratic element in its struggle with other classes. The structure of the Anglican Church also has a similar effect.

4) But the greatest palliative is the abnormal concentration of world trade in English hands. The mass of wealth flowing into England from this acts as a kind of oil, abundantly greasing all the axles, pistons, propellers, and gears of the English social machine, and preventing excessive friction from which they would otherwise overheat or break down. The benefits England derives from this concentration of world trade in its hands are incalculable. What does it earn on freight, from foreign consumers of products that not only are not produced on English soil, but are not even made by English labor? What does it make in commissions from brokering global trade? Finally what does it get for processing raw materials, which could be done by those very peoples from whose lands they come, or by those who consume the materials in processed form? The wealth flows very disproportionately into England, but the mass of wealth is so great that a considerable amount still reaches the poorer classes.

Such a state of affairs must not be considered normal, however natural it may be, just the same as many other monopolies, however naturally formed, still are not normal. Based on England's advancement in manufacturing, the

---

[34] Joshua 10: 1–15.

concentration of global trade is natural because it is the result of many favorable conditions of its situation, the most important of which is being an island, which from the time of William the Conqueror[35] has protected it from enemy invasion and allowed it to accumulate capital. Also, being an island boosted the English navy, commercial and military, so that in time of war (such as in the Wars of the Spanish [1701–14] and Austrian [1740–48] Successions, the Seven Years' [1756–63] and Napoleonic Wars [1803–15], for example) it could destroy the trade and seize the colonies of Holland, France, and Spain, thus securing England's predominance in world trade, and even, indirectly, in manufacturing as well. Nevertheless this condition is not normal, because the normal course of trade and industry would be for each state to produce everything it could profitably produce by processing its own raw materials, and only trade its surpluses for what it cannot itself produce, due to climatic and other factors, but only trading directly, without intermediaries. Such a normal condition of world trade and industry, which Napoleon's Continental System[36] was intended to bring about artificially and by force, to weaken England, inevitably must follow the path of natural industrial development, if the state's trade policy can profitably and appropriately use both means within its grasp: fostering competition by free trade, and guaranteeing internal markets through patronage wherever competition would be fatal, due to the weakness of the industry. Both Genoa and Venice in their day enjoyed a natural but abnormal trade monopoly: It was taken away from them by the opening of sea lanes and the expansion of merchant navigation beyond the bounds of the Mediterranean Sea, and the industrial development of other countries. The more favorable position of England took away this natural but abnormal monopoly from Holland. Could England possibly hang onto it forever? The opening of the Suez Canal[37] will certainly reverse the benefit of opening sea lanes around Africa, and partly restore the old routes of world trade, in regard to which many countries are situated more favorably than England.

With the weakening of all these numerous palliatives, the logical development of the contradiction between democratic aspirations in the political realm and aristocratic structures of the social and economic order must inevitably lead England into the same crisis that has by all appearances come to France.

---

[35] William I, "the Conqueror" (d. 1087): First Norman king of England, invaded England in 1066 and won the throne at the Battle of Hastings.

[36] The Continental System: a trade embargo against Britain that France imposed on most of its client states and allies, but found nearly impossible to enforce. Russia's withdrawal from the Continental System partly prompted the decision to invade in 1812.

[37] The Suez Canal opened in November 1869; note the use of future tense here.

But in reality, even for France the dreaded moment of crisis has still not begun; we have only seen its harbingers. In the course of centuries through which Europe consistently freed itself from the three burdens laid on it at birth (the burdens of scholasticism, religious despotism, and feudalism), imperceptibly its peoples became fettered and entangled in a new snare, finding a new burden laid upon them: the burden of the abstract State upon living nationalities. When the foundations of European society were laid, the different nationalities making up Europe had not yet formed; of necessity, the states constituting the order of things of that time had a temporary, provisional character. All the German and Roman tribes *in statu nascenti*[38] united around the principle of the divine state, serving as the continuation of Roman tradition realized under Charlemagne, then later the principle of hierarchical unity realized under Gregory VII.[39] Furthermore they wove a network of all-European aristocracy, since the landholdings of the vassals of Charles's empire did not correlate to the boundaries of the states, or to put it more correctly, the pieces into which the empire broke apart. This general European character of the aristocracy was maintained by the institution of chivalry even after the separation of European nobility according to nationality. The undertaking of Crusades common to all European peoples likewise supported this unity. Meanwhile there proceeded a slow ethnographic process of the formation of separate nationalities from tribal chaos, following from the migration of peoples.

It was completely natural that the results of this process long remained unnoticed and imperceptible, so that compared with aforementioned unifying principles of a seemingly higher order, there was no great significance attached to these newly risen national distinctions. What actual importance could the peculiarities of language, customs, or any kind of national communities have in comparison to the unity of the Church, Empire, and chivalry?! This would be a good place to note one more distinction between the Germanic-Roman world and the Slavic world. While the unity of the former is rooted in the overarching (so to speak, conjoining) circles of the church and civil hierarchies and in the aristocratic institution of chivalry, yet the people becomes more and more isolated, the unity of the latter [Slavic world] is rooted in the internal similarity (at first only felt instinctively but more and more consciously) of the masses of the people, divided artificially by acci-

---

[38] Latin: "In the state of (or from the moment of) birth."

[39] Pope Gregory VII (r. 1073–85): Famous for asserting papal primacy in his dispute with Holy Roman Emperor Henry IV, known as the Investiture Controversy, in which he asserted the papal right to depose an emperor and twice excommunicated Henry, who had appointed his own bishops and in turn, attempted to depose him as pope.

dents of history, the intrigues of Catholic clergy, and the lawless ambitions of the *szlachta*.[40]

But in the course of time the power of the hierarchy, the concept of the empire (as a continuation of the Roman universal state), and an all-European chivalry have all disappeared or lost their significance; the consciousness of nationality as the principle of the state has still not become fully clear. Even in more recent times, the idea of political freedom has taken on a cosmopolitan tinge. Evidently in this situation dynastic rights receive predominant significance, and the only counterbalance against them is the concept of the equilibrium of parts, which prevents the accidental accumulation of territories and their populations under a single monarch (as happened, for example, under Emperor Charles V).[41] But this equilibrium does not quite correct for the artificial, accidental order of things. As the principle of dynastic inheritance unites the most diverse, so the principle of equilibrium breaks apart the most similar, cutting the ties that bind. So in the second era of the harmonious development of European cultural forces after the end of the Thirty Years' War, in place of the ideas of the divine state of Charlemagne and the sovereignty of the representative of Jesus Christ over earthly powers, the idea of the abstract State came to the fore. Congresses are its councils [i.e., Church councils], diplomats are its priests, and political equilibrium is its regulatory principle. In its name Louis XIV made his famous declaration, *"L'etat c'est moi."*[42] But as in the realm of science, where the artificial system sometimes coincides with the natural order, the image of which serves as evidence for the system, so it is with the artificial political system: the importance of states founded on an abstract principle sometimes coincides (under the influence of predominant forces of natural conditions) with their natural importance, founded on the principle of nationality. So even under Louis XIV France was (then as now) an entirely natural, national state. But such happy coincidences did not happen everywhere, and an opposite case may be seen in the Austrian [Habsburg] state. There are a great many intermediate degrees between these two extremes. Consciousness of the importance of nationality as the root principle on which the state must be founded, Europe attained only in the nineteenth century.

I have already pointed out that the century, a hundred-year interval, has the most obvious essential significance in the course of Europe's development, at least in the latter part of its history; but the predominant character of a century only reveals itself around the chronological midpoint. Of course the origin of the new direction can be detected much earlier; but among the many facets of social life, it is hard to discern which of these aspects or directions

---

[40] [Danilevskii's marginalia, published posthumously]: *And now by the feeble-mindedness of the so-called intelligentsia, seeing its ideal in the absurdities of liberalism.*

[41] Charles V: See chap. 2, n. 3.

[42] French: "I am the state."

will provide the predominant character for which an era is known. So only at the midpoint of the fifteenth century did the printing press, Portuguese naval discoveries, the resettlement of Byzantine scholars after the fall of Constantinople, and the weakening of feudalism supporting the power of monarchy all launch the intellectual movement and practical activity that characterize the transition to so-called modern history. This was an era of Renaissance in more than the usual sense of the word. At the midpoint of the sixteenth century religious interests enveloped all of Europe, and the storms of the Reformation finally passed only at the midpoint of the following century (in the year 1648). From the midpoint of the seventeenth century to the midpoint of the eighteenth century extended the era known as the age of Louis XIV. The age of revolution, with the subsequent reaction and restoration, and political revolution triumphing anew, continued until the midpoint of the nineteenth century. From that time on, concerning the nineteenth century, it would be hard to say which of the various aspects of social movements will make the lasting imprint by which it will be known to posterity. The powerful development of the speculative idealist philosophical direction in Germany, the opposite of the materialist direction of the eighteenth century, caused some to think this would be called the Philosophical Age. But in the 1840s positivist science gained indisputable dominance and, having developed from materialism, it is no less potent than its predecessor. However we must not consider the positivist-science direction to be the predominant character of the nineteenth century, because it is not exclusive to it, but is the general character of European science; the ages of Galileo, Bacon, Newton, and Lavoisier were no less positivist in this sense. Also, for a significant part of the nineteenth century, science departed from this direction. The development of industry could rightly characterize our age, but it too only furthers a general direction from past centuries of European life. Similarly trade and colonial policy—material interests as well—also played a predominant role in earlier periods of European history. Finally, it turned out that social and economic questions bested them all, both in the realm of theory and as the direction prevailing over popular movements, and toward the end of the 1840s seemed to have started becoming a reality.[43] To the general horror, it seemed a dreadful crisis had arrived. But since then it has grown clear that its time has not yet come. It was as if minds had taken another direction, but the change was only apparent. What became the prevalent direction had begun much earlier, only little noticed; under the influence of ideas of another sort, they deliberately and inadvertently mixed nationalist movements with political movements. In reality these nationalist movements have been the prevailing phenomena in the life of peoples from the very beginning of the century.

Napoleon I provided the shock that brought the nationalist question to the consciousness of European peoples. Prompted by ambition as much as the

---

[43] [Danilevskii's marginalia, published posthumously]: *This was repeated in 1871.*

fortuitous position in which he found himself, he went from victory to victory to reestablish the empire of Charlemagne. But in the thousand years since Charles, the peoples emerging from under his reign had already fully separated themselves into national groups. The principles of unification that Charles relied on had long ceased to exist; the modern principle of political freedom, supposedly represented by Napoleon, could only in jest be laid as the foundation for the edifice raised by the French emperor. Thus instead of the new unification of the peoples of Europe, the ventures of Napoleon could only cause them to feel their national distinctions and national affinities more strongly. Where Napoleon intervened in a political body founded on the principle of the abstract state, victory came easily. Having used his military artistry to gain strategic and tactical preponderance over his enemies, there remained nothing more for him to overcome. But victory was not so easy where he had to contend with living national entities, even so weak as Spain. From Spain a national movement began to repulse the French conqueror. In 1809 came the first outbreak of the German national spirit, which by 1813 had turned into a powerful national movement. The Russian national movement of 1812 was not exactly the awakening of the national spirit, because among the Russian people it had never even gone to sleep, in national-political terms. The national uprising in Serbia also falls within the first years of our [i.e., the nineteenth] century. After peace came, the Congress of Vienna paid just as little or even less attention to nationality than its predecessor, the Congress of Westphalia,[44] and by prompting a reaction against it, also raised consciousness of the principles of nationality. The Italian movement that started in the 1820s, while tinged with political revolution, was still essentially a nationalist movement continuing with a few gaps up to the present time, leading to the unification and political independence of the Italian people. The Greek Revolution took up almost three decades of the nineteenth century and was recently resumed in Crete. Only malicious intent could confuse this movement with political revolutions. The Belgian Revolution had an essentially national character. Just as in the time of some epidemic all other illnesses take on a special urgency, so both Polish uprisings led by szlachtists and Catholic clergy took on a nationalist coloration, even though it essentially had (like everything Polish) an anti-national character. The Eastern [Crimean] War was conducted by Western powers against Russia's national policy toward the peoples of the Balkan peninsula, but the Italian War was to assist the national policy of Piedmont. The war over Schleswig-Holstein, and the subsequent Prussian-Austrian war[45] also served the interests of German nationality and served as the coronation of the German movement, which had a consistently

---

[44] The Congress of Westphalia produced the Peace of Westphalia in 1648, to end the Thirty Years' War.

[45] [Danilevskii's marginalia, published posthumously]: *And the Franco-Prussian [War] as well.*

national character from 1848 or even from 1813, which prevailed everywhere in the clash of interests of political freedom, something the Jacobin[46] sort of abstract democrats cannot understand. The same became apparent in Italy. All the Magyar movements have been full of national spirit, and proceed solely from it; a dash of the political-revolutionary element was only a temporary chance occurrence that drew no popular sympathy to its side. The Slavic movement, having begun in the 1820s in the realm of science and ideas, had almost no political taint to it, and is exclusively concerned with the interests of nationality. Under the influence of national ideas, Napoleon III undertook his ill-fated Mexican expedition [of 1862–66].[47]

The inherently national character of all nineteenth-century aspirations caught the observant eye of Napoleon III, and his skillful hand used them [national aspirations] for his own purposes: that is, to divert attention from social questions. This goal was attained and the danger was averted for a time, while a whole series of movements inspired by nationality failed to come full circle; the clashes they provoked, long captivating the peoples' attention, did not reveal their full consequences, which of course Napoleon III himself did not suspect when he espoused it [nationality] as his new political principle. In Napoleon's mind, of course, this new principle was only a pretext for attaining his own personal goals. He hoped to impose his own will and, besides diverting the national attention from questions he considered more dangerous, intended to derive additional benefits. However egotistical, insincere, shortsighted, and, perhaps, trifling the calculations by which the sovereign of France ruled, he deserves full credit for proclaiming nationality as the highest political principle,[48] bringing this principle out from hiding (where it was confused with various underground revolutionary machinations) and into the light of day.

Both Napoleons were fated to bring into the foreground, consciously or unconsciously, the question of the political significance of nationality, although under the second Napoleon it probably did as little good for France as under the first. From the point of view of French interests, it cannot be denied

---

[46] Jacobin: A reference to the most radical political faction of the French Revolution of 1789 and after.

[47] [Danilevskii's marginalia, published posthumously]: *The last Russo-Turkish War and the Serbian- and Montenegrin-Turkish wars preceding it were purely national; the suddenly-aroused national-Slavic interest on Russia's part overcame all purely political considerations, which prevailed only after the end of the war at the Congress of Berlin; one must be blind not to see that those national questions call for Russia in the near future to make war on Austria, and perhaps with Germany as well.*

[48] [Danilevskii's marginalia, published posthumously]: *When all was said and done, having destroyed it.*

that Thiers's[49] criticism was correct. France, being a fully national state, enjoyed the benefit at that time of being considered by all European states, a necessary member of the system founded on the principle of political equilibrium. Obviously French politics had to rely on the principle that promised it the greatest benefit. Relying on political equilibrium, of course, France could hinder the unification of Italy as well as Germany, and if it would gain nothing for itself, neither would it lose anything. By relying on the principle of nationality, granted, it gained Savoy and could lay claim to the French part of Belgium and even Switzerland perhaps, but it would have to admit to itself that it had acquired Nice and Corsica alike in violation of that right. But setting that aside, was it not also evident that [the benefits of gaining] the few surrounding French territories could not compare with the disadvantages presented by the unification of Germany, which threatened the concentration of forty-five million people into a single state entity, on this very foundation of the principle of nationality. Moreover, since in the European point of view the Slavs have no legal standing [*pravosposobnost'*], the German state may well grow to fifty-five million, through union with the whole non-Hungarian part of Austria, as some orators in the Prussian diet have already advocated. Finally regarding the Eastern Question, the principle of nationality places France in most scandalous contradiction with itself.

To neutralize some of the unfavorable consequences the principle of nationality would have for France, they gave it a minor role and devised a strange and completely ridiculous means of using it: a universal vote [i.e., a national referendum]. In reality, any vote proposes to subject the will of the minority to the will of the majority, and on the basis of what? Evidently, on the basis that there is another interest (at least they proposed the existence of a higher interest), above the interests over which the majority and minority are divided, on which both the majority and the minority agree. And treating this very agreement on the higher interest as more important than the disagreement forces the minority to submit to the majority, even if the latter did not have a preponderance on its side. The French people elected the president of the Republic [in December 1848]; the majority voted for Napoleon; a significant minority voted for Lamartine, Cavaignac, and Ledru-Rollin.[50] On

---

[49] Adolphe Thiers (1797–1877): French historian of the French Revolution turned statesman, prime minister three times under King Louis-Philippe (r. 1830–48), vocal critic of Napoleon III's expansionist foreign policy.

[50] Alphonse de Lamartine (1790–1869): French author and politician, helped found the Second Republic (1848–51), worked to abolish slavery and the death penalty, created the "right to work" national workshops. Louis-Eugène Cavaignac (1802–57): French general who suppressed the June Days uprising (1848) in three days of bloody street fighting and summary justice for the rebels. Alexandre Auguste Ledru-Rollin (1807–74): Champion of the working classes, compromised by his law and order stance in

what basis did these admirers of various republics (sentimental, ideal, and social) submit to the Bonapartist republic, which was obviously the empire in masquerade? They submitted because their followers considered the principle of the unity of France highest of all, and they had to submit to the decision of the majority so as not to violate it, and they submitted of their own free will. The opposite occurred following the selection of Lincoln in the United States. The system Lincoln represented was more contrary to the South than the very collapse of the Union, and they rose up. There was no higher principle uniting the minority with the majority, and it did not submit, but relied instead on its own strength. For any country holding a vote on the fate of the nation, what kind of higher principle could acknowledge both the will of the majority and the minority? It is none other than a completely free predetermination that whatever the outcome, the country holding the vote will remain an indivisible and irreducible whole. In Savoy they might be asked, do you want to belong to Italy, or to France? But Savoy itself, never mind why, is considered a kind of indivisible political atom. Obviously the outcome of the vote would depend most importantly on what kind of boundaries will be determined for the country being asked to express its popular will. If, for example, we take Poland in its 1772 boundaries as a unit, then there cannot be the slightest doubt that all of it would fall to the Russian empire—although the majority of the people in the Polish Kingdom would vote, some western provinces and eastern Galicia would be enough to tilt the majority toward the Russian side. But districts could be divided so that significant parts of the western provinces would have to separate from Russia. If the principle of expressing the popular will were strictly enforced, we would be forced to divide it in some unthinkable stripe-pattern. On the other hand, what would be the meaning of such a farce of a vote in Venice, for instance, compared to fifty years of its continual declaration that it wants to belong to Italy? Nationality is not only a right, but is also an obligation. One people not only can, but must, constitute one state. Do we even need to take a vote on this?

And so the course of European peoples' historical upbringing and the characteristics of the school of dependence they went through had the result that, although these peoples did not lose the moral qualities that enable them to replace the primitive tribal will with civil freedom, while going through feudalism they all had the misfortune of the majority losing the grounds for this freedom—the right to the land on which they live. They won back their personal rights in full measure from their conquerors, but the land remained under the latter's control. And this contradiction inevitably leads to that collision that threatens wholesale ruin and destruction. Lacking the material basis of civil freedom, they at the same time lack the moral basis, not just for this freedom but for life in general, from having set their religious faith either

summer 1848. He was the Socialist candidate for the presidential election, then an opposition leader against Louis-Napoleon, exiled to London 1849–70.

upon the crumbling pillar of papal infallibility or the individual tyranny of Protestantism. The consequences of those religious falsehoods have unfolded continually and irrepressibly, but still have not reached their furthest point in the peoples' general consciousness. The consequences of the contradictions in the political realm have already been revealed in the first clash, but their further development was prevented by diverting attention toward national questions. On western European soil these national issues in and of themselves have no great significance and have declined in importance before other issues (scientific, religious, political, socio-economic) working themselves out in the history of Germanic-Roman peoples. They have even almost exhausted their full potential and must soon give way to other aspects of public life. But their true importance lies in being wrapped up in the knot tying the European world to the Slavic world, the knot fraught with events destined over a long period of time to mark and define the history of both these clashing cultural-historical types: the Germanic-Roman and the Slavic.

The political events proceeding from these other aspects of European development did not directly concern the Slavs. Slavs took no active part in the scientific question, the liberation of thought from the authority oppressing it. The results of this must be, and are, of great benefit to the Slavs (as to all peoples in general) but only because these results built upon the heritage of Greeks and Romans. The religious question is of no interest whatsoever to the huge majority of Slavs; those that were unfortunately drawn into it played only a passive role, being oppressed, hampered, and violently deprived of the truth to which they all were originally predisposed. The only active part taken by Slavs in the religious life of Europe was the great Hussite movement,[51] which rejected the European understanding of the faith, and aspired to return to Orthodoxy. The Slavic world's involvement in the political struggles of Europe was likewise either involuntary, as for the [Slavic] peoples under Austria, or if voluntary, it was founded upon a misunderstanding, as for Russia. The storm of the French Revolution summoned Russia's prolonged (and decisive) involvement. But from a purely Russian and Slavic point of view, there can only be regret for the tremendous efforts Russia made to take control in some sense of that struggle which essentially concerned Russia about as little as the Taiping Rebellion [1850–64] in China, and as a matter of complete indifference to it, should not have called forth either Russia's so-called conservative instincts or so-called progressive sympathies. It remains a pity that these outsize efforts were not applied (at so opportune a moment)

---

[51] Hussite movement: Followers of Jan Hus (see chap. 6, n. 12) divided into a number of groups. Here and elsewhere, Danilevskii identifies the Hussite movement as Orthodox, primarily because the Czechs of Bohemia were converted to Orthodoxy (9th century) before being Catholicized (10th century). Protestants typically view Hus and his followers as proto-Protestants, like the English reformer John Wycliffe (1328–84), who preceded and influenced Hus. The Hussites' anti-Roman views support both claims.

toward resolving purely-Slavic concerns, for which the Treaty of Tilsit[52] offered a prime opportunity. Of course, this is stating the matter from the purely Slavic point of view. Russia's involvement was of course necessary from the general historical point of view, which Russia itself heeded. Like nature, history derives all possible results from each form it has created. Europe was set to complete a vast cycle of development; the predominance of France threw it off the correct path; and Russia was summoned to rescue Europe. Russia's role was by all appearances tsarist, but was actually merely a servile role. Now Europe, particularly France, proclaims the principle of nationality (which not only does not mean much, but is even harmful) by which it repays Russia and Slavdom, which also submits to it, imagining that it is acting in accord with its own interests.

Therefore the question of nationality, having now taken first place in the life and activity of peoples and connected the Germanic-Roman and Slavic worlds, is the most natural point to address the peculiarities of the historical upbringing Russia received while building its state structure, and the peculiarities of the forms of dependence the Russian people underwent in the transition from tribal will to civil freedom, which it is just beginning to enjoy.

The first impulse, setting off the thousand-year process of the Russian state's formation and upbringing, was the calling of the Varangians by the Slavic tribes scattered across the expanse of Russia of those days. The very fact that for Russia it was a calling, instead of a conquest, has essential importance for the psychological characteristics of Slavdom, but does not have great significance as concerns us here and now. The Anglo-Saxons were likewise called by the Britons to defend them from raids of the Picts and Scots;[53] but even so, the order of things they introduced in England was not substantially different from what was introduced into other European countries, and judging by its consequences, the calling was tantamount to conquest in that case. Of course, the same could have happened with the Russian Slavs as well, if the newcomers summoned to deliver them from internal discord had been great in number. But fortunately the summoned tribe was small in number, as is proven by the fact that even today we can argue over who exactly the Varangians were. If their numbers had been greater, they could not have disappeared practically without a trace into the mass of the Slavic population, so that Riurik's own grandson had a Slavic name, and his great-grandson, Vladimir,[54] became a model in the public mind of the purely-Slavic character. If

---

[52] Treaty of Tilsit: See chap. 2, n. 34.

[53] Picts and Scots were tribal peoples inhabiting present-day Scotland starting in the late Iron Age; Britons in the same era occupied present-day England and Wales. The Anglo-Saxons were Germanic tribes arriving in Britain during the fifth century CE.

[54] Riurik (d. 879): Semi-legendary founder of the dynasty ruling Kievan Rus', and later Russia, from the ninth to the end of the sixteenth century. His grandson was Sviato-

there were not any kind of manuscript evidence about who were the Angles, Saxons, Franks, or Normans under William the Conqueror, then that question would have to be resolved by an investigation into language and institutions bearing the imprint of the conquerors' national character. Despite being called, the Varangians' small numbers did not allow them to introduce a new order of things into Russia, as resulted in other places from a dominant nationality ruling over a subject nationality. Therefore the Varangians served only as the leaven or yeast stimulating the movement toward statehood within the mass of the Slavs, still living in a single ethnographic, tribal existence— but could not lay the foundations of either feudalism or any other form of one people's dependence upon another. The relationship between the first impulse bringing a statist tendency to the life of the Russian Slavs, on the one hand, and the Germanic conquests laying the basis of European history on the other, is the same (if I may be allowed to make this comparison) as that between the smallpox vaccine and smallpox. The latter acts powerfully on an organism, producing an organic cataclysm within it, and for the most part, even in the best outcome leaves permanent traces behind. It causes deep pockmarks on the face, marring and disfiguring it, often affecting vision and other vital organs. The smallpox vaccine, on the contrary, has only one (beneficial) consequence: protecting the organism from future infections, without marring or disfiguring it. On the other hand, however, the protection it gives for the future is less complete than having had the actual disease. The weaker-acting vaccine, to maintain its effectiveness, must be repeated time and again. Lacking the support of feudalism, the original state system of Russia either could not be transmitted from Kiev and Novgorod to the broader lands where Slavic and Finnic peoples settled, whose tribal will remained protected behind boundless expanses of woods, swamp, and steppe; or would have had to have a sort of tributary relationship between the smaller core and the broad peripheral regions, like the metropolis to its colonies, in which the equal rights of all parts of Russia would be subsumed by the governmental center. And the appanage system [*udel'naia sistema*] only exacerbated this: By means of it, on the one hand, the state system became widespread; but on the other hand, each part retained its equal rights as a special, independent principality. This process could be likened to the physiological process called *proborozh-denie*,[55] which gives reproductive capability to the entire contents of an egg.

slav I, "the Great" (d. 972), son of Igor I (d. 945); his great-grandson was Vladimir I, "the Great" (958–1015).

[55] A neologism, not found in dictionaries, a combination of *proba*, "trial, try-out" (in the preliminary sense) with *rozhdenie*, "birth." The word is close to *devorozhdeniia* (mentioned in chap. 6), "parthenogenesis" or "apomixes," asexual reproduction among mature females ("virgin birth"). Here Danilevskii has in mind the very recent and controversial discovery of larval reproduction (i.e., among sexually *immature* insects), observed by the Russian zoologist Nikolai Petrovich Vagner (1829–1909) in

Relations between members of princely houses preserved their connection as parts of the state; but as the princely clan grew and the bonds between its members weakened in the succession of generations, a single grand-ducal center became inadequate. Not only did the number of princedoms increase, but proportionally to the increase, there also formed new grand-ducal centers. This process did not reach extreme limits, but one comes involuntarily to the conclusion that, had it continued, there could only be two outcomes. If the state element became predominant in the form of princes and their troops, then the appanage system would end up being reborn as an extreme form of outright feudalism (an example of which would be medieval Germany, but without the unifying power of the emperor or the pope) and national freedom would be crushed under the weight of minor tyrants. [Or] under the predominance of the people's tribal origins, as in Russia, the state system itself would end up in ruins from princes turning into petty tribal chiefs without any bonds between them; the people's will would be preserved but the tribes would not combine into one people under the protection of a single state. To avoid this required a new dose of the state system, and it was administered to Russia by the Tatar invasion.

The calling of the Varangians that took the place of Western-style conquest, not only turned out too weak to impress a permanent state character upon Russian life, but created the need for another form of dependence— namely, tribute. But this tribute system had just as weak an inoculating effect as the calling of the Varangians. When we read the accounts of the Tatar invasion,[56] it strikes us as terrible and crushing. Without a doubt it was, for a huge number of individual people who lost their lives, honor, or property from it; but for the whole people collectively, even the paying of tribute to the Tatars must be seen as a very mild form of dependence. Tatar raids were painful and devastating, but Tatar rule was light compared to other examples of tributary dominance offered by history (such as the Greeks and Slavs under Turkey). The levels of culture and ways of life of the settled Russian Slavs and the nomadic Tatars were so different that not only was there no possible mixing between them, but even the power of the latter over the former could not penetrate deeply, but only gripped the surface. The character of the landscape

---

1861, which Danilevskii's mentor Karl Ernst von Baer termed *paedogenesis* in an 1865 article. *Proborozhdenie* may have been an alternate term in trial circulation, or may be Danilevskii's attempt to recall the name, or provide a name. See Michael D. Gordin, "Seeing Is Believing: Professor Vagner's Wonderful World," in *Histories of Scientific Observation*, ed. Lorraine Daston and Elizabeth Lunbeck (Chicago: University of Chicago Press, 2011), 135–40. The prospect of permanent immaturity, larva begetting larva, was not a happy thought, considering Danilevskii's concern for Slavic civilization to complete its development and reach full fruition.

[56] The Mongol-Tatar Golden Horde invaded Russia in the thirteenth century, establishing control in a series of raids that destroyed many Russian cities and towns. Muscovy broke free from Tatar rule in 1480.

also helped, allowing our conquerors to preserve their customary and preferred way of life on the steppe across the Don and Volga Rivers. The whole
storm might even have blown over leaving hardly a trace (with neither ongoing harm nor benefit) if the budding genius of Moscow had not been able
to adapt to circumstances and extract all the advantages from the relations between the subjugators and the subjugated. Seeing resistance was futile and
grasping the need to stave off devastating raids by timely payment of tribute,
the subjugated realized they had to place the people into a stricter condition
of dependence in regard to the state. To the people, paying tribute is always
an incomprehensible imposition, the emblem of dependency imposed on it,
and the main source of its hostility toward state power. People oppose it as
much as they can, requiring force to compel them to pay it. To guard against
excessive requisitions, the people demands representation in one form or another, expecting that dividing [the state's] interests will prevent it from au-
thorizing any requisitions not justified by the most vital necessity. The Moscow princes had in their favor the advantage that all the hateful aspects of the
ordeal fell upon the [Tatar] horde; the horde constituted the threat of force to
compel the people to pay the tribute. Moscow appeared, if not as the deliverance, then as the easing of the burden the people were forced to bear under
the foreign yoke. Besides the understanding of state power rooted in the soul
of the Slavic peoples, it was the Moscow princes' mediation freeing the people
from direct interaction with the Tatars that no doubt accounts for the feeling
of complete trust and love that the Russian people feels for its rulers. So the
Moscow princes, and later the tsars, became invested with the fullness of
power that the Tatars acquired by conquest, leaving them in the position
where any power they held came as a burden for the people, especially a people unaccustomed to civil order, having preserved the full tradition of tribal
will. The Moscow rulers, in a manner of speaking, played the role of the
mother of the family, who while carrying out the will of a strict father, also
guards against his anger, and thus to the extent they held the authority of
power over the children, they did so with tenderness and love.

But when the foreign yoke was thrown off, the horror of submissively
having to bear the full weight of state power vanished, as did the force enabling the Moscow sovereigns to bring state unity to the Russian people. They
had to find their own means of doing so. There were few such means available, and very many obstacles to overcome. The main obstacle, once again,
was the wide expanse and the characteristics of the Russian land. What need
is there to submit to the harsh demands of the state order, individual service,
and monetary payments, when the woods offers such an impenetrable refuge
that even today there are occasionally discovered whole populations manag-
ing to hide in it from the sharp eyes of police chiefs and local bosses; when the
wide steppe free of powerful plunderers offers so much open space and freedom; and when the rivers and seas teeming with abundant fish offer easy
subsistence and even profitable trade? What means did the state have, with-

out standing armies, without a battalion of bureaucrats, without an organized feudal hierarchy, with little industrial development and insignificant urbanization, and no funds to create or maintain any of it? Actually in Russia the state system was still so weak that when the end of the tsarist dynasty[57] broke the bonds of affection and habit formed over the course of centuries, the state collapsed under the weak attacks of Poles—not even the Polish state, but just roving Polish gangs. This aroused the national spirit, which no state can govern. The 750 years from the founding of the Russian state to the time of [Kuz'ma] Minin[58] had created a single whole national organism, bound by a moral and spiritual connection, but had still not managed to form a strong state body. Obviously, resorting to the refuge of national life only under threat was risky and could not be considered the normal order of things. Without the national spirit, any state system is dust and dirt; but since most importantly of all, a state exists precisely to protect it, so being animated by it will provide strength and unity to the form it takes in order to defend nationality. Without that strength and unity, even the heartiest national spirit would turn out to be inadequate for a struggle with more concentrated and better guided forces than those of the Polish state. But how did the state tap into this force? Under the circumstances of the time, there was only one way to consolidate the whole people into the strength of the state. Boris Godunov[59] anticipated the need of this, Peter the Great completed it. For the consolidation of the Russian state, which could not be achieved by voluntarily calling foreigners to rule, nor by the violent extraction of tribute (both being weak inoculations), it was necessary to resort to serfdom, that is, a form of feudalism, yet distinct from the actual, original feudalism, just as a disease introduced artificially in a vaccine is different from the natural disease.

There can be no doubt that serfdom is a form of feudalism (in the broad sense of the word given above), since it shows all the basic signs: members of the privileged class are given almost boundless power over some of the people, in exchange for service to the state. Even though it was not that way at the beginning of serfdom in Russia, it became so once fully developed under Peter the Great. For those of us who have seen serfdom abolished, and have seen all the evil that goes along with it, it seems that an excessive burden, hard to call a mild form of dependency, was laid upon the people. But everything is relative, and similar phenomena allow a comparison. If we compare

---

[57] The interregnum known as the Time of Troubles (1598–1613) began with the end of the Riurik dynasty, was marked by famine, foreign invasions, and political instability, and resolved gradually with the election of Mikhail Romanov as tsar in 1613, thus establishing the Romanov Dynasty, which ruled Russia until 1917.

[58] Kuz'ma Minin: See chap. 8, n. 50.

[59] Boris Godunov (d. 1605): Regent for Ivan IV's son Fedor until his death in 1598, then ruled as Russia's first non-Riurikid tsar until his death. His son and successor ruled only a few months before being murdered by boyar rivals.

our serfdom with European feudalism, the mildest form of which can be seen among the Letts and Ests of the Baltic provinces, then of course the dependence of serfdom seems mild. Lord and peasants being of the same tribe and having the same faith, coupled with the typical Russian's characteristic gentleness and good-nature, eased the burden of serf dependence at every stage of its development; but beyond that, due to its special character serfdom presented special conditions at each stage, easing the burden. The first stage can be considered to last from the establishment of serfdom to its final affirmation by the revisions Peter introduced. At that time the free movement of serfs from landlord to landlord had not yet been restricted, and besides that, the weakness of state power and the disturbances marking the beginning of this period prevented serfdom from taking on its full weight. With the revisions brought by Peter, all this changed: peasants were placed in full dependence upon their landlords, who were obliged to provide without reimbursement a set number of military recruits, and tax payments. But this was strictly a burden imposed by the state, not by the arbitrary will of individuals, which had almost no chance of appearing, since the nobility itself was bound to the state and obliged to spend their whole life in state service. The third stage of serfdom began with the nobility's release from obligatory service, which took away the reason for its existence. In theory, it turned into pure and simple exploitation, since the state was able to pay its servitors and maintain them solely by granting them the right to the peasants' obligatory labor; in practice, the burden for the peasants had to increase once the nobility got the right to retire from service and live off their estates. But if we consider the prevalence of the natural economy at that time, and the fact that landlords for the most part lived well off their lands—had great stores of bread (which for lack of markets, they fed to their numerous servants), had great stores of oats (which they fed to the horses of neighbors traveling to visit them for whole weeks), distilled their own wine drawn from berries out of their own gardens and woods, sweetening these liqueurs with honey from their own hives, and in general lived quite well from the produce of their estates, having neither the option nor the need to make more money from it to spend on various comforts of life—then we will see that the landlords had no reason to overburden their peasants with work. House-serfs suffered under personal arbitrary rule, from angry outbursts, from the cruelty of character, or the debauchery of other landlords, but this was the exception, and most importantly did not apply to the whole lot of the peasant class. Often even cruel owners and insufferable tyrants over their servants, were very good landlords to their peasants (such as, for example, Kurolesov in the *Family Chronicle* of S. T. Aksakov),[60] of

---

[60] Mikhail Maksimovich Kurolesov, in section 2 of Aksakov's book. Sergei Timofeevich Aksakov (1791–1859): Russian memoirist. The *Family Chronicle* was written in installments beginning in 1840, and finally collected and published in a single volume in

which one finds more than one example within living memory. The last and worst stage of serfdom arrived when awareness of luxuries and European comforts spread from the capital to the provinces and townships, and burgeoning industry and trade replaced the natural economy with the monetized economy. Any product not for direct consumption soon reaches a limit, beyond which not even the most extravagant person feels any need to have more; but for money such a limit or saturation point does not exist. Therefore, setting aside the general softening of tempers, the decrease of examples of wild abuse of personal power, and the many laws restricting the arbitrary rule of landowners over the people under their power—the most recent time of serfdom's existence could hardly fail to be the most burdensome, as can be amply demonstrated by the very manifesto proclaiming the end of dependency from serfdom in Russia. Therefore it seems I have the right to say that serfdom—this Russian form of feudalism (just as the calling of the Varangians is the Russian form of conquest, and the submission to the Tatars is the Russian form of tributary dependence) used by the Moscow sovereigns for the political centralization of Rus'—had a comparatively mild character.

Serfdom finally disappeared, the last of the scaffolding assembled for the construction of our state system. The Russian people passed through various forms of dependence, which were needed to unite it into a single body, wean it off individual tribal egoism, teach it to submit its will to higher, common goals, and attain these goals. The state was founded on the unshakeable foundation of the people, and while in the course of this thousand-year process tribal egoism was not replaced with class egoism, the Russian people, having preserved its moral virtues, preserved the substantial foundation for its highest development, since it preserved the [people's] ownership of land to an incomparably greater degree than any other European people. And not only did it preserve that ownership, but it safeguarded it for itself by the peasant-commune form of landownership. It is fully prepared to accept civil freedom in exchange for tribal will which (like any historical people) it had to forfeit during the growth of its state. The dose of freedom it can take is, on the one hand, greater than any other people, because by owning land, it is endowed with a high degree of conservative instincts, since its current situation is not in contradiction with its political future; but on the other hand, its political demands (or better to say, hopes) are quite moderate, since due to the lack throughout its existence of a history of civil strife between the various classes of Russian society, it does not regard power as an enemy (against which a feeling of self-preservation would impel it to take all possible means of precaution) but regards it with the most complete trust.

<hr>

1856. His sons Konstantin (1817–60; see chap. 8, n. 45) and Ivan (1823–86) became prominent Slavophiles, and their circle gathered at the family house in Moscow.

Europeanism: The Sickness of Russian Life

> Gripped by the stupor of arrogance,
> Drunk from the "wisdom" of earth,
> You renounced all things held in reverence
> In the land of your native birth.
> —Khomiakov[1]

So the Russian people and the Russian state are characterized by spiritual and political health. Meanwhile Europe in spiritual terms has gradually shaken off the keen religious understanding it substituted for ecumenical truth and broken through the Pillars of Hercules,[2] from which it can either set out into the boundless sea of denial and doubt or return to the light-bearing East. And in political terms, it has reached the irreconcilable contradiction between producing ongoing demands for personal freedom and upholding the rights preserving the distribution of property. If we look at Russian life, however, we quickly see that it is not in complete health. True, it is not suffering from some incurable ailment leading inevitably to ethnographic decomposition, but still has a very serious illness, gradually draining the organism of its productive forces, which can eventually be fatal. This illness is the more frightening because (like old age for a dog) it gives the youthful, lively manner of the Russian social body the appearance of senility, and threatens it with something worse than death: a sterile and impotent existence.

Besides the three phases of state development which the Russian people completed fairly easily, resulting in the formation and consolidation of the Russian state without depriving the people of a single necessary condition for replacing tribal will with civil freedom—Russia still had to undergo a difficult operation known as the Petrine reforms. By that time European civilization had already taken on its practical character to a significant degree, and thus its distinct openness and inventiveness in science and industry became part of its governmental and civil makeup. The ignorant and strictly agricultural Rome, coming into conflict with the mercantile, industrial, and vastly more enlightened Carthage, was able, solely through patriotism and devotion to the common good, to battle it victoriously even at sea, which until then had been a foreign element to Rome. At that time, combat tactics were very simple, not

---

[1] From the 1844 poem "Ne govorite: to byloe..." (Do not say: "The past...").
[2] I.e., the Strait of Gibraltar.

only on land but also at sea. But by the eighteenth century, and even earlier, no kind of devotion to fatherland or patriotism could take the place of technical advances in shipbuilding, navigation, artillery, fortifications, etc., all of which have become very complex sciences. On the other hand, the state's need of such complex weapons of war created a need for a special class of people completely devoted to military purposes; the costs of maintaining this sizable class were so great that the state would never have the means to do it without promoting industry. Thus the most essential goal of the state (the defense of nationality against external enemies) demanded a high degree of technical organization, which has only increased proportionally ever since, especially in the second quarter of the nineteenth century.

By the beginning of the eighteenth century Russia had almost finished the victorious struggle with its eastern neighbors. The spirit of the Russian people, awakened by events, under the leadership of two unforgettable figures, Minin and Khmel'nitskii,[3] also won a victory over the Polish *szlachta*, which had betrayed Slavic national principles and wanted to force the Russian people into the same betrayal. Not far ahead in the future doubtlessly lay a struggle with one or another of the peoples of Europe which, with the enterprise and ambition characteristic of all strong historical actors, always aspire to expand their power and influence in all directions: across the sea to the West, and likewise to the East. *Der Drang nach Osten*[4] [the push toward the East] was not just dreamed up yesterday. For this inevitable struggle it was necessary to strengthen the Russian state by borrowing from the cultural treasury and scientific and industrial achievements of the West, and do so rapidly, without waiting for Russia to attain the practical results of enlightenment the state needed by the slow, natural process of deriving enlightenment from its own native principles. Peter saw this need clearly, but (like most great historical figures) he did not calmly follow a deliberate plan, acting instead with passion and enthusiasm. Having acquainted himself with Europe, he fell in love with it, in a manner of speaking, and wanted to make Russia Europe by any means possible. Seeing the fruits borne by the European tree, he concluded the plant itself was superior to the still fruitless, wild Russian variety (disregarding the difference in age, and not considering that maybe the wild tree's fruitful time had not yet come), and thus he wanted to cut it down to the stump and replace it with the other. Such a replacement is possible with dead subjects, formed under the influence of foreign ideas. It is possible, while still living in the house, to replace the façade, each stone and brick it was built from, with other bricks and other stones. But regarding a way of life

---

[3] Kuz'ma Minin: See chap. 8, n. 50. Bogdan Khmel'nitskii (d. 1657): Cossack hetman whose military victories liberated Ukraine from rule by the Polish-Lithuanian Commonwealth, briefly established an independent state, then allied with Russia.

[4] *Der Drang nach Osten*: See chap. 3, n. 7.

formed by an internal, original organizing principle, such substitutions are not possible: they can only cripple it.

While Europe inspired Peter's passionate love and enthusiasm, toward Russia he was ambivalent. He both loved and hated it. He loved it strictly for its power and might, which he not only anticipated but recognized. He loved it as the instrument of his will and his plans, as building materials which he intended to erect in a form and likeness of an idea that arose in him, influenced by European models. But he hated the very principles of Russian life, as much for its merits as its shortcomings. If he did not hate it with the passion of his soul, he would have treated it more cautiously, more guardedly, more lovingly. So it is necessary to distinguish two sides to Peter's activity: his state activity, or all the military, naval, administrative, and industrial disseminations; and his reform activity in the narrow sense of the word, or the changes in lifestyle, manners, customs, and ideas that he tried to introduce to the Russian people. The first type of activity deserves eternally grateful, reverential memory and blessed posterity. However difficult for the people of that time were his recruiting efforts (by which he not only replenished his troops but built cities and settled countries); the ruthless financial system of monopolies he introduced; the strengthening of serfdom; simply put, placing the whole nation into the harness of the state—however difficult all this was, that was what earned him the title "the Great" and the reputation as founder of the greatness of the Russian state. But in his second realm of activity, he not only did great harm for the future of Russia (harm that drove its roots in deeply and to the present has eaten away at the body of the Russian nation) but even needlessly hampered his own efforts. By arousing the indignation of his subjects and troubling their consciences, he complicated his mission and set up obstacles for himself, the overcoming of which had to put a great drain on his excessive energy, which could have been put to better use. Why shave beards, don German clothes [*nemetskie kaftany*], compel to attend balls, force to smoke tobacco, introduce drinking binges (in which even vice and debauchery had to be done in a German way), pervert the language, introduce foreign etiquette in court and high society, reform the calendar, and limit the freedom of clergy? Why give foreign ways of life the most honored position, and by doing so, cast all things Russian as low and ignoble, as they used to say? Could this really strengthen national consciousness? Of course, certain state innovations (in the strict sense of this word) were not enough: Russia needed to develop what gives strength and power to everyone, that is, enlightenment; but what did all these distortions to the national appearance and character have to do with true enlightenment? Moreover, enlightenment is not spread by act of will like changing a style of dress, or introduced by one or another administrative arrangement. It follows not to implant it from the outside, but to cultivate it from inside. This path would be slower, yet more reliable and fruitful.

In any event, Russian life was forcefully changed to match a foreign pattern. At first it succeeded only in the highest layers of society, on which the government could act forcefully and directly, and which is generally more susceptible to temptation always and everywhere. But little by little the distortion of Russian life became more deep and widespread; that is, it dispersed from the upper classes to a more modest place in the social hierarchy, and these reforms designed to strip away nationality [*obeznarodovaiushchaia reforma*] penetrated from the surface into the thoughts and feelings of those exposed. After Peter came reigns in which the ruler had not this dualistic love-hate character, but only the hatred, the scorn toward all things Slavic, especially anything Russian, with which Germans are so well endowed. After this a difficult period continued for a long time, even to this day, of wavering between preference for the Russian (as under Catherine the Great) and the foreign (as under Peter III or Paul).[5] But from the influence of the jolt delivered by Peter, the very notion of what is truly Russian was distorted, so that even in happier periods of national politics (internally and externally) what was considered Russian were often things completely undeserving of the name. In saying this I mean not the government alone, but the whole mood of society, which, although occasionally electrified by Russian patriotic feelings, lost its nationality [*obeznarodovalos'*] more and more under the influence of European temptations, and took on some kind of all-European coloration. Sometimes the French, the German, or the English coloring prevails, depending on the circumstances of the times, and the levels and circles into which society is divided.

This illness—having infected Russia, spread and embedded itself for a century and a half, the signs of relief[6] only appearing in most recent times— seems most appropriately called *Europeanism* [*evropeinichan'e*]. And the root question, the answer to which will determine the whole future not only of Russia but of all Slavdom, is this: Will this illness have as benign an impact as the introduction of foreign rule over the Russian Slavs, the payment of tribute to the Tatars, and the Russian form of feudalism; or will this illness act more like an inoculation that puts the organism through a beneficial revolution and is shaken off without any lasting harmful effects, but giving a boost to the very foundations of national vitality? First we will examine the symptoms of this disease, at least the most important ones, then we will look back to see if some medicine was prepared for it or some axe was taken to its roots.

---

[5] Peter III (1728–62): Unpopular Russian tsar who reigned for less than a year, known for his pro-Prussian stance; his wife usurped his throne after conspiring with his murderers and became known as Catherine the Great. Paul I (1754–1801): Son of Catherine and Peter III, pro-Prussian tsar from 1796, murdered in a conspiracy that brought Alexander I to the throne.

[6] [Danilevskii's marginalia, published posthumously]: *I recognize this as a grievous mistake on my part.*

All the forms of Europeanism with which Russia is so richly endowed can be placed into one of the following three categories:

1. the distortion of the national way of life and substitution of its forms with foreign, non-native forms—distortion and substitution which, once started at the surface, will inevitably penetrate into the internal thoughts and life of the uppermost layers of society, then deeper and deeper;
2.. the borrowing of various foreign institutions and their transplantation onto Russian soil, with the idea that if they are better elsewhere, they must be good everywhere;
3. the viewing of internal and external issues of Russian life from a non-native, European perspective, through European glasses or lenses polarized to a European angle, through which things that ought to appear surrounded by rays of the most brilliant light, often look like complete dark and gloom, and vice versa.

The distortion by foreign manners of all internal ways of life—dress, home construction, household utensils—seem to many to be nonessential and inconsequential. But due to the close connection between the external and the internal, it can hardly be so. The Slavophiles, first going in for Russian national dress, acted completely reasonably in my opinion; the only unfounded part unfortunately was the idea that their example would be universally imitated. What kind of imitation could there be when the distortion of Russian ways even had police support on its side! We will, however, see what we were missing, what was lacking from the national conditions of our life.

First of all we were lacking, or at least extraordinarily hampered in, the ability to birth and develop national arts, especially the plastic arts. The history of Greece's development, as with any national arts in general, shows us that it has two roots: forms of liturgy and national ways of life in general, such as national dress and national architecture. If not for the simple and noble forms of Greek tunics (which so majestically draped the form of the body, without hiding it or deforming it), could Greek sculpture have attained the perfection it did in Athens during the age of Pericles and for a long time afterward? The significant and majestic forms of our liturgy (equally remote from Protestant aridity and from Catholic fanciful theatricality) could, besides its religious merits, be an outstanding aesthetic school if while acquiring perfected technical methods we had preserved the other root of the arts: independence of our ways of life.

Among all modern nations, sculpture is not an original art, but only drags along in an imitative rut: either by working on foreign mythological subjects so that nudity is permitted, or dressing their monumental heroes in Greek or Roman clothing. It could not be otherwise, since all European varieties of costume are either completely ugly (like the coats, robes, and caftans from the time of Louis XIV) or, though pretty, are fanciful enough to be picturesque but not elegant (like Spanish costume, with poufy sleeves and pant legs, or Tyrolean pointed hats, or various kinds of lace). Only Russian national attire is sufficiently simple and majestic to deserve being called elegant. All it takes to become convinced of this is to take a critical look at the various costumes seen on monuments. Minin stands in Russian dress on Red Square in Moscow; Susanin[7] stands in Kostroma before the bust of Mikhail Fedorovich,[8] whom he saved. There are many statues depicting little boys or young people playing games.[9] Without getting into the inherent merits of these sculptural works, however, it can easily be affirmed that the attire of these figures satisfies all the demands of art. In modern times, it is true, both here and in Europe they have begun *faisant bonne mine à mauvais jeu*,[10] to disregard the demands of elegant attire for statues, sacrificing artistry to historical truth, and some of these attempts succeeded—but which? The figure of Napoleon in a drab frock-coat or overcoat and an ugly tri-cornered hat seems majestic. But this is only symbolic grandeur. The overcoat and hat, in our eyes, are symbols of dozens of victories, the emblem of unconquerable will and military genius. To someone having artistic taste and aesthetic sense but no knowledge of modern history, this short man in a hat and overcoat would simply look deformed. Whereas to admire the statues of Roman emperors that have come down to us from posterity, there is no need to see Caesar or Trajan, or to know the epic stories of their lives: any Didius Julianus[11] or even Caligula would produce the same impression. I had the opportunity to see the colossal statue erected not long ago in Sevastopol in honor of Admiral Lazarev.[12] The colossal figure, over three fathoms tall on a huge pedestal among the ruins on a high steep bank over the harbor, produces a striking effect from a distance. But upon examining the details of the figure—its dress-uniform topcoat with little tails, close-fitting trousers, the short scabbard of a naval dagger—it is only by recalling the hardships suffered by the famous admiral during the construction of the Black Sea fleet, and considering the dismal fate that befell his creation only four years after his death,[13] that one can use these serious

---

[7] Ivan Susanin (d. 1613): According to legend, saved the tsar-elect by misguiding a roaming band of Polish soldiers intent on killing him.

[8] Mikhail Fedorovich Romanov (1596–1645): Founder of the Romanov dynasty, whose reign as Tsar Mikhail I, starting in 1613, ended the Time of Troubles.

[9] Literally, *babki* and *svaika*, "knucklebones" and "spike."

[10] French: "To make the best of a bum deal."

[11] Didius Julianus (d. 193), reigned as Caesar for only three months.

[12] Mikhail Petrovich Lazarev (1788–1851): Russian admiral and explorer who discovered Antarctica, later a commander of Baltic and Black Sea fleets, who signed the Treaty of Hünkâr İskelesi in 1833.

[13] The Crimean War, after which the Black Sea was demilitarized by the Treaty of Paris.

and sad thoughts to drive away an involuntary smile. In colossal dimensions, the contemporary European dress that fate has cast upon us looks like a colossal joke. Meanwhile everything that depended on the artist—the pose, the casting, the wrinkles in the uniform, and the finishing little details—all were masterly. The ugliness of European attire was not some peculiarity of the naval uniform; an army uniform, or even worse, a state official's tailcoat or overcoat, no doubt would look just as ridiculous and ugly. A great man sculpted in marble or cast in bronze, three fathoms high, in a coat of the latest style with a shirtfront and starched collar points, would be such a laughable figure that even the most audacious sculptor could hardly make such a thing. But what can be done for languishing arts? Dress up the monumental heroes of the nineteenth century in tunics and togas? But would that not mean avoiding the ugly by embracing the absurd? Between the two hazards of the laughable and the nonsensical, like the Scylla and Charybdis, lies one very narrow path of concealing

... this oddity, 'gainst reason
in spite of all the elements, the changing season[14]

with an overcoat or cloak thrown on like a toga. Art would die off, if constrained to such a narrow place!

The influence of foreign attire, foreign forms of architecture, and foreign lifestyles was not limited to the deadening influence of a single sculpture. All the native-grown arts suffered. Khomiakov, in his article on Ivanov's picture, said the only ideal kind of painting worthy of being called great artistic production is iconography. Iconography is to painting what epics are to poetry, which is a representation not of individuals but of the ideals produced by a whole people, merely handled in various ways (within the constraints of the epic form) in individual artistic works. In this manner, the face of Greek tragedy as much as the forms of Greek sculpture were panhellenic, national-epic, and typal representations, which merely occurred to the artistic imagination of Sophocles or Phidias with greater vitality and fullness than to other Greeks, and were executed by them with a perfection others lacked. Greek sculpture was icon-sculpture; Greek drama was icon-drama. Originally even these immortal forms doubtlessly lived as rough and rudimentary representations of the people. In order to attain that refinement as embodied by great artists of the age of Pericles, it was necessary for the Greeks to produce or borrow the various perfected technical methods from more advanced peoples. This technical borrowing was done from the Phoenicians, from whom the Greeks learned molding and casting in the sculptural arts. But having borrowed tech-

---

[14] Chatskii, in Griboedov's *Woe from Wit*, Act III, scene 22 (*Aleksandr Griboedov's "Woe from Wit": A Commentary and Translation*, trans. Mary Hobson [Lewiston, NY: Edwin Mellen Press, 2005]).

niques, they did not borrow foreign ideals or ways of rendering them in visual form. Their ideals remained the people's [narodnye]; the outward forms in which they were rendered were taken from the people's own way of life [narodnyi zhe byt], taking on all the trappings in which the Greeks adorned their artistic production.

For us, there have existed and do now exist the kinds of icons that render the Russian people's religious ideas. To bring them to a state of artistic perfection, we would need in the same way to develop our own perfected technical methods, or borrow them—but them only—from more advanced peoples. The first requires too much time, and besides that repeating work done by peoples of various other cultural-historical types would be completely pointless. The difficulty remains: How should we students, who usually regard teachers with reverence (especially such teachers as the great masters of Italian art), limit ourselves only to the assimilation of the technical methods and material techniques of art through which these teachers fulfilled their ideals without being captivated by those ideals themselves, without giving in to imitativeness and sacrificing the rough and rudimentary religious art forms that national creativity [narodnoe tvorchestvo] produced or at least assimilated to itself. To the artists given these powers, the problem is insoluble: they must be forced to solve it by inexorable social demands. If the Old Russian way of life were preserved in all its trappings among us, not only in the lower but also the upper classes, then how could the artist, captivated in any way by Italian modes of painting, create a work of a religious content to adorn the sanctuary that does not conform to strict Orthodox requirements? How could he bare the female body and give the Holy Virgin a coquettish demeanor and look, or dress in a fashionable, elegant, and slightly ostentatious way, as they now do, such youthful, venerated warriors as Saint George, Alexander Nevsky, the Archangel Michael, etc.? All these characteristics, so foreign to the national representation [narodnoe predstavlenie] of the aforementioned figures, are also foreign to the habits of the people's lifestyle [narodnyi byt] and thus, appearing in a picture or in the artist infected with foreign ideas, they would be jarring to the eyes of those unaccustomed to seeing them in everyday life. If the artist wants his picture or statue to be well received, then he must reconcile the acquisition of technique (anatomy, drawing, perspective, coloration, arrangement of shadow and light, etc.) with the demands of his public, through acquaintance with its ways of life, which must be imprinted upon the ideas originating elsewhere.

The same applies to architecture or music. We have begun to develop a natural and very diverse style of church construction and, even though they are built by foreigners, they absolutely must conform to national demands; they would never be built otherwise. If our churches cannot compare in size and architectural splendor with the Gothic cathedrals in northern Europe or the basilicas of Italy, then it is merely from a lack of technical expertise, and even the lack of material means to raise such a huge edifice. But if through the acquisition of these things, we had preserved the traditional ways of life in the upper classes of the Russian people, and thus those tastes and requirements, then of course our cities and towns would not be dotted with miniature caricatures of St. Peter's Basilica in Rome, but we would have raised churches in the shape and richness of detail of the original Russian style, fortified by financial and borrowed-technical means. If the old ways of life still endured, we likewise would not allow bravura arias or concerts sounding like abbreviated operas during the worship service, since (thanks to an unequivocal church resolution) organs would not be allowed in churches. In all these ways we would be essentially Old Believers, but Old Believers equipped with all the technical means of Western art, and from the *old* would come something truly new.

Fancy architecture, like the ornamentation of houses and household utensils, was not highly developed in Old Russia, due to the simple demands of the time, but also because most of the structures were wooden. But with the development of more complicated tastes and demands (this is not the privilege of European peoples only), and with the accumulation of material means to gratify them, inevitably the courts of our tsars and the mansions of the rich would have arisen and been decorated, but would have done so according to our peculiar demands, to our notions of comfort, to our taste. These days they sometimes try to reproduce it artificially. But if this works in the architecture and ornamentation of churches, it is because that tradition has not yet died out. All the efforts in the realm of everyday architecture and ornamentation have been unsuccessful attempts, because art is based on life; archeology can only be a support to it.

It is the same with national attire [*narodnaia odezhda*]. It is often heard that the lovely, universally-pleasing Russian women's attire is nothing but theatrical costume, hardly resembling anything so elegant as what the people actually wear. As if the national attire is a uniform, a form determined with pedantic precision! It is a type which changes, varies, and is decorated accordingly, depending on social position, status, taste, and the vanity of the wearer. It exists only in its essential characteristics. National attire is not intended to remain in absolute monotony and permanence; it changes according to fashions, even in the belongings of the common people, obviously changing more often regarding the belongings of all classes. If the fashions of the people [*narodnye mody*] change less often than the fashions of high society, it is not because of some special characteristics of the national dress (as opposed to the European), but because the idleness and frivolousness of high society, especially the female half of it, constantly changes the most important elements of its frivolous life. This changeableness often depends on the fact that control over fashion usually falls to the French, a superficial and for the most part changeable people.

By changing our national ways of life, we also lost our originality in manufacturing. We have heated quarrels about free trade and protection of industry. I believe in the latter idea with all my heart, because originality in politics, culture, and industry constitutes the ideal to which all historic peoples must aspire. But where originality is unattainable, independence at the very least must be preserved. One must not agree with those who say that it is a sad thing to support this independence by any sort of artificial means. We would not need to resort to artificial means had we preserved our independent ways of life (the demands of which industry satisfies, after all). The way of life among Eastern nations demands large quantities of carpets. In Persia, a rug is not a luxury; it is an essential item even for the poorest classes. Thus the production of carpets there has attained such perfection that of course the carpet industry there needs no kind of tariffs to protect it. The same applies to Indian shawls, or Chinese silk, porcelain, lacquer items, and dyes. So with us, the unique forms and requirements of our liturgical and priestly vestments required improvements in engraving metals, the preparation of brocades, the casting of bells—and in all these ways we were completely independent of foreigners. The degree of sophistication in a branch of industry corresponds to the degree of uniqueness in lifestyle, of which a small example is our samovars, which the French government saw fit to place tariffs upon, to restrict imports as well as enrich itself. In short, since the original always outranks the imitation, distinctiveness of lifestyle fosters originality of manufacturing, and leads to more daring industrial and trade policy. But when manufacturing lacks this character, as a result of the distortion of lifestyle by foreign models, then nothing remains but at the very least to guard its independence by means of patronage. Contemporary fashions, for example, are applications of French taste and notions of elegance to the demands of life; therefore, in the so-called *articles de Paris* and in fashionable wares in general, France will have the advantage over other countries, not because these products of French manufacturing really are any better (they may be, or may not) but only because everywhere they are considered the best for being French.

As a consequence of changing its ways of life, the Russian people divided into two strata, which may be readily distinguished by outward appearance. The lower stratum remained Russian, and the upper became European—indistinguishably European. But the wealthier and more educated upper estate always has a magnetic pull on the lower orders, which involuntarily aspire to resemble them and be as much like them as they can. Therefore the people involuntarily form the idea that their Russianness (in its very essence) is something inferior or lower. Anyone can tell, I believe, that when we use the word *Russian* in various expressions it means something lesser or poorer: a Russian nag, a Russian ewe, a Russian hen, a Russian dish, a Russian song, a Russian story, Russian clothes, etc. Everything with the designation "Russian" is considered somehow only suitable for simple folk, not deserving attention from wealthier, more educated people. Will not such an idea lead to the humiliation of the national spirit, and suppress the feelings of national dignity? And this self-abasement, by the way, is obviously rooted in the fact that all who rise from the ranks of the masses (in education, wealth, and social standing) always put on foreign trappings.

But the abasement of the national spirit [*narodnyi dukh*] resulting from this bifurcation of the people in its most outward appearances is probably a lesser evil than the distrust engendered among the people preserving the original ways of life toward those who have changed. In Arkhangelsk province, where it is well-known they never had serfdom, their mistrust and suspicion toward the foreign-looking classes of society cannot be explained by that. During my time there[15] I happened to have the following conversation with one of the coastal proprietors. I was curious to find out the understanding of cholera among the coast-dwellers, who have developed far beyond our peasant masses. My interlocutor did not hide from me that the majority of them attributed this illness to poisoning. But who, I asked, did they think did this poisoning? The lords, he replied. But you do not have any kind of landlords among you, except state officials, I argued. Did he really suppose that the officials serving the tsar were poisoning the people? Of course, he answered, the simpletons among us think that the tsar knows nothing about it, but the lord was bribed by "Germans" (by which he meant, as the word itself[16] implies, foreigners or Europeans in general). But why would foreigners poison you? Why not, he exclaimed. Everyone knows that foreigners don't like Russian people. The people instinctively understand Europe's contempt for Russia, and thus any ordinary passing calamity befalling them they ascribe to this hostility, although of course they exaggerate its appearance. But how would they have the judicious capacity to discern what this hostility might or might not do? After all, a significant part of European public opinion defends the printing of phony money, if it will harm Russian national or political interests; it defended the "stillettists" and "hanging gendarmes";[17] after all, it turned deaf ears and blind eyes toward the clear evidence of political arson; after all, Europe not only tolerates but lends moral support, and if necessary material force, to Turkish violence (robbery, rape, and murder) against the Greeks and Slavs solely out of enmity toward Russia and Slavdom. After all of that, can the Russian people be judged harshly if it does not so precisely draw the line to which that hostility is allowed to go? But that is not the point, so much as the foreign attire of our Europeanized classes leads the people astray, inducing the people to consider them capable of joining the hostile-to-Russia camp. "We become acquainted by appearance, but take our leave

[15] Danilevskii's seventh expedition; see Strakhov's introduction. His report, "O merakh k obezpecheniiu narodnogo prodovol'stviia na krainem severe Rossii," in *Pravitel'stvennyi Vestnik*, nos. 90–93 (1868), is reprinted in N. Ia. Danilevskii, *Sbornik politicheskikh i ekonomicheskikh statei* (St. Petersburg: Izd. N. Strakhova, 1890).

[16] *Nemtsy* means "Germans," but in earlier usage meant foreigners in general.

[17] Danilevskii is referring here to the secret Fifth Department of the Polish Military Gendarmerie. See chap. 2, n. 48.

knowing their heart,"[18] as the saying goes. What is strange is that the people often judge even the sentiments by the clothes. One must dig down to find the true sentiments, to make them somehow reveal themselves, but clothing is evident at first glance. And is it not natural to take for an enemy someone who wears the enemy's livery? If similarity of lifestyle could unite the supposedly aristocratic party of *Vest'*[19] with the remaining mass of the Russian people, then would this party ever consider Polish magnates[20] closer to its heart than the completely foreign Russian peasants of the western provinces?

It is also a well-known fact that military attire, as opposed to civilian national attire, is considered necessary because it separates the soldiers from the people, and in the event of an uprising prevents them from joining it. In the eyes of these politicians [the *Vest'* aristocrats], attire and appearance are more significant than others believe, although the significance they ascribe to it in this opinion is wrong. They say that the people's attire everywhere differs from the clothes of the upper classes; it may differ, of course, yet it may remain true to the same type. In essence, the European suits, robes, and overcoats are the same as the camisoles and coats[21] worn by the peasantry in European states, only more carefully sewn, of better fabric, in a slightly better style; and these distinctions are very gradual, depending on the level of prosperity of various classes. Are we really talking about differences of type or genus, or just differences as variations on the same theme?

Finally the character of attire and all trappings of everyday life have an important influence on the blending of subject nationalities with the ruling nationality. Many small nationalities have entered into the makeup of the Russian state, which it did not conquer or subordinate by force, but took under its protection. These nationalities (such as, for example, Georgians and Armenians) had no reason to be hostile to Russia, and actually were not. Without exception, they have preserved en masse their national way of life. But individual members, entering the freedom of general public life, will always try to imitate the lifestyle and trappings of the upper class of the ruling nationality. At the same time, especially among these foremost individuals, there forms either a certain regret about the former political independence of their nation [*natsiia*] being irretrievably lost with the passage of time, or dreams of its future rebirth. Both of these aspirations conflict with each other, and since the latter has no internal basis, it crumbles under the power of the first, more concrete aspiration and vanishes like an impractical dream. But if this first aspiration does not find resistance, or even finds support, then the national formation of these (necessarily lacking political independence) nationalities leads not to their blending with the nationality ruling the state, but

---

[18] *Po plat'iu vstrechaiut, po umu provozhaiut.*

[19] *Vest'*, see chap. 6, n. 14.

[20] Magnates: Members of the Upper House of the Diet.

[21] *Vamsy*; cf. German *Wams*, "jerkin, waistcoat."

to separation from it, which brings mutual harm. In the past, various Tatar lords, Circassian princes, and German immigrants turned voluntarily toward the Russian nobility, since there was no other option but to remain in their tribal estrangement or merge with the Russian nation. But now that the lifestyle of the upper classes of Russian society has lost its national character and become European, such an option is now closed. In order to enter the arena of general Russian public life, there is no need to become Russian in one's manners or customs—there is not even the possibility of doing so!—but instead one must take on a European look. But this all-European character, which in its essence is hostile to the Russian-Slavic character, does not weaken but rather reinforces that element of estrangement which is more or less characteristic of any non-Russian, and from this very blending arises such things as "Young Armenia" or "Young Georgia," of which we were just speaking, but perhaps also even a "Young Mordva," "Young Chuvashia," "Young Yakutia," or "Young Yukaghiria," which we should not be shocked eventually to hear about.

The second form of Europeanism, I said, consists of the aspiration to transplant foreign institutions onto Russian soil, under the idea that everything good in the West will certainly also be good for us here. Thus a number of German bureaucratic procedures, municipal structures, etc. were transplanted here. To investigate all these transplantations and their harmful influence on Russian life would fill up a whole book, which I am not in the slightest inclined to do. But there is no great need for such a work, since experience has amply shown that they have not taken root but have withered, and must be continually replenished. And on the contrary, experience also says elegantly enough that those changes to our social and political life which proceed from the internal needs of the people take root uncommonly well and grow so quickly that they choke out the sickly transplants. So the great historical reform of the present reign [i.e., the emancipation of the serfs], restoring to the Russian people its original freedom (in the novelty of which our Old Believers heard what they had known from olden times), were not carried out in a Western or Baltic pattern, but according to [our own] original plan, and have secured the national good for many, many ages.

But it can be shown that another reform, of the judiciary, rivaling it in beneficial influence, is something different, like a transplant from Western judicial systems. However, in the first place, it has changed or is changing a form of justice borrowed from the West, and this change will be for the better, not worse. Secondly, from an examination of the elements making up the new judicial system, it is not hard to believe that within it the Western elements play a completely secondary role.[22] Namely, these elements are: oral, public

---

[22] [Danilevskii's marginalia, published posthumously]: *Everything I wrote here is nonsense. The reform had only just begun, and I wanted to believe, then did believe, that it would*

judicial proceedings; independence from the [tsarist state] administration; the absence of the class system in court; and finally, the adversarial system of advocacy by professional lawyers. Oral and public was the original form of our trials. Independence from the administration is a necessary consequence of the complications of civil life. Traces of it are evident in the old Russian trial by the elders of the *guba*:[23] traces which could not develop, because the thread of judicial tradition was broken when the complication of civil life began. Taking sworn testimony at trial[24] is for the most part a Slavic principle, related to the Slavic spirit and character, so that on the question of its basis, Khomiakov posited Slavic origins for the Anglo-Saxons, who, if German by descent, then by place of residence must have come under continuous Slavic influence. Thus we have only brought back what was once our own. Estate trials[25] or trial by peers, the same as paternity trials and also the subjection of the lower classes to trial by the upper class—these are all purely Western principles. Some of them were transplanted here, and we are only just beginning to be free of them. Concerning the adversarial system, on the one hand, it places an impossible requirement of complete impartiality on human nature. Strictly speaking, instead of an adversarial proceedings between a plaintiff and defendant, it would be much better to introduce an impartial, sworn deposition, in which would be laid out the full force of evidence for and against the accused, with no exaggeration or understatement. But such impartiality is scarcely attainable; just try to play a game of chess with yourself. There seems to be no reason one should favor black or white, but once you are engrossed, you will certainly notice that eventually you take one side, and play worse for the other. Therefore it is necessary to separate the defense from the prosecution.

It is true, on the other hand, that lawyerly prosecution and lawyerly defense have a purely Western character: the character of struggle, which has penetrated throughout all of European life. Where everything is divided into hostile parties, social strata, and corporations, even trials must take the form of a duel: guilt or acquittal at all costs. And thus this character of the trial as a verbal duel is what our attorneys of the bar must by all means avoid, so that our new form of trials does not descend into chaos.[26] Our lawyers find themselves in exactly the same place as our artists who have studied under Western masters. For our trials to have an original Russian character, our lawyers

---

take on a rational character; but in fact it turned into a foreign caricature. From a more sober-minded perspective, this could and ought to have been foreseen.

[23] Court of old Muscovy.

[24] [Danilevskii's marginalia, published posthumously]: *This is nonsense. The form corresponds only to the primeval, epic form of nationality, but not to the complexity of statehood.*

[25] *Soslovnost'*, a court ruling on one's claim to belong to a class or estate (*soslovie*).

[26] [Danilevskii's marginalia, published posthumously]: *They did not avoid it, but once again took it to the point of caricature.*

must in the same way be able to borrow from their teachers only the technique, but not the spirit of European adversarial justice. It is the same kind of difficult problem for them as for our artists, and just as hard for them to solve it without society's assistance. It may be in this case society has preserved more originality in its requirements than in its ways and trappings of life, because judicial truth constitutes a more vital necessity for all layers of our society (including those still non-Europeanized) than aesthetic requirements. Besides, regarding justice, no one can be an Old Believer the way it is possible regarding churchly grandeur and rituals. Therefore there is hope that concerted pressure of the whole society or (in this case, more correctly) the consensus of popular opinion will compel the adversarial system to stick to a national track. Perhaps it will, or not; who knows?[27]

We will now examine the third great reform of the present reign: the liberation of the printed word from censorship. Free speech is not a political privilege, but a natural right. Thus, by the very essence of the matter, in liberating it from censorship there cannot be any kind of imitation or borrowing from the West; otherwise, even walking on two legs instead of four could be considered an imitation of somebody else. Censorship itself was a result of our imitative life, a result no one asked for; its cessation was a restoration of the natural order of social life. But censorship was not simply abolished, it was replaced (for the periodical press, at least) with a new warning system. Is this system an original occurrence (that is, an occurrence prompted by internal requirements of Russian national and political life) or only a transplant, like the guild and shop system for towns; a transplant based on the principle that anything in the countries of the enlightened West is *ipso facto* already healthy, beneficial, enlightened, and necessary for Russia? To answer this question, we must analyze the nature of the power of the periodical press, and the ways in which the warning system is different from the criminal justice system formulating laws about the press. There is no doubt that the warning system is not based on the principle of judicial fairness, according to which the penalty must always correspond to the crime, since even if we assume complete impartiality for an administrative office or personage in charge of press affairs, three warnings will still almost always go easier on the publisher, who may lack all status, than the most strict judicial penalty he might face. By the way, the very necessity of resorting to warnings, instead of putting the offending periodical on trial, shows that the publisher's offense is so doubtful, so uncertain, that in all likelihood a trial would not produce any reason to convict him. Thus the warning system must be based on the principle of self-defense, which neither society nor the government can deny, and under which the state sometimes resorts to the most strict, even severe, measures to prevent acts that are not so much criminal (if looked at from a purely judicial standpoint) as threatening great harm to society. So, for example, sim-

---

[27] [Danilevskii's marginalia, published posthumously]: *It turns out, not.*

ple thoughtlessness could cause a person to violate quarantine, but this would deserve the death penalty, in view of the horrible consequences this thoughtless and careless crime would have. So the warning system is entirely justified, if the evil to which it has given a warning beforehand, might have consequences as grave as a violation of quarantine.

It is usually thought that the press is either useful or harmful, by exposing its readers to certain beliefs they do not hold, or by changing the beliefs they do hold. But belief is a harmonious system of logically interconnected thoughts and thus it presupposes a high level of mental development and significant mental work. Therefore, even in the most educated countries, the mass of the public, strictly speaking, does not have independent beliefs and scarcely could have them; what are called the beliefs of the masses are simply the result of habits, communicated and accepted through one's upbringing or surroundings. Therefore these beliefs are always distinguished by uncommon firmness, formed and changed over nothing less than ages of invisible labors by a whole host of generations. It is nearly impossible for an individual writer or periodical to communicate new beliefs, or change the old beliefs of the bulk of even the most advanced social class. It is harder than drilling into the rocky face of a cliff. Most people, having neither the time, nor inclination, nor capacity for prolonged deep thought, are adept, so to speak, at deflecting the force of the most logical, most eloquently expressed opinions. Even if the mind is briefly amused, it will still hold to *its own*, to what has been passed down from the ages, to what is acclimated to the ways of its social surroundings. As proof of what I have said, any thinking person who claims to be persuasive should only remember: How many people has he managed to convince of something, or actually change their minds? How often has he himself become convinced of something [new] or had his mind changed by others? But if the mass (the majority) is barely pliable in their beliefs generally, then it is incomparably rarer to find new beliefs posing a moral principle of action that would outweigh the opposition of self-interest, apathy, and routine. After all, this is the only kind of belief that has practical significance; only this kind of belief can be evaluated whether it is useful and beneficial, or something to be truly feared, something to be opposed, as harmful and pernicious.

But however rare or frequent are beliefs in general, and living convictions in particular, the very worst transmitter of belief has to be the periodical press, especially daily newspapers. The variety of topics discussed by them hinders the concentration of attention, which is the main prerequisite for acquiring any kind of belief. Today they are talking about the Eastern Question, tomorrow about Luxembourg, the day after that about the improvement of the clergy's living conditions, then about a system of public childcare, the Russification of the Western Krai, judicial reform, then again returning to the Eastern Question, etc. etc. And all of this is lightly read, by the way, among thousands of routine news reports, all diverting attention to themselves. How could this kind of reading shape beliefs, not to mention change them? Regarding beliefs, more serious compositions have a vastly greater, though often indirect, influence. Only a few people have the time, inclination, and ability to contemplate them, and thus to adopt the new or change their old beliefs. These few people slowly communicate them to others, primarily through schools (in which young minds not yet preoccupied by the cares of life, still pliant by nature, feed on and assimilate them) or through small circles of thoughtful people, sharing new beliefs they have worked out, from which something little by little enters into general consciousness.

This impotence of the periodical press, especially the dailies, to spread or change beliefs is entirely borne out by experience. For example, in the 1820s the teaching of Saint-Simonism appeared in France. The works of Saint-Simon[28] were assimilated by a few followers. They searched with great effort for new adherents, and finally a small circle of admirers formed a new school. To promote it they launched the journal *Le Globe*. Did it attract many followers? Almost none. The Fourierist organ *Democratie Pacifique* had the same negligible result. They say that these teachings did not spread because the public's good sense rejected these eccentric theories. However, by way of independent treatises and personal recruitment they gained new, highly talented followers.[29] Let us take a different subject, a doctrine that has become very widespread and won acceptance by many states: the doctrine of free trade. It continues making inroads into the beliefs of the public through [academic] departments and courses on political economy, debates in state chambers, and personal recruitment, but where is the daily periodical to which it owes its success?

Is it really possible that the periodical press, considered one of the most important social forces of our time, has essentially negligible influence? Can it be prejudice only that lays on it such hope and arouses such opposition against it? No, the periodical press, especially the daily papers, truly constitutes a huge force, but that force is founded not on the dissemination of belief, but on arousing and explaining interests, and arousing awareness within these interests of their own strength. A newspaper, noticing some interest existing in society and appraising its significance, features a series of leading articles explaining it. From reading the articles, the reader sees the exposition of what he thinks. "Those are my thoughts exactly!" he exclaims, not without some pleasure, feeling flattered that this high journalistic authority seconds his ideas. However, for the most part, the reader will be mistaken; what he considers his own thoughts were only unclear, vague, fragmentary sensations — and only after having read the account in the newspaper are they explained to him. As with the one reader, so with other readers into the thousands. Each hopes to share these interests newly clarified to him with others,

---

[28] Saint-Simon: See chap. 6, n. 31â.

[29] Presumably Danilevskii has himself in mind, having been captivated by Fourier's theories when he was a student.

and discover that they are not his only, but represent the opinion of the majority of his acquaintances. Thus the public's interests are not only explained but are given consciousness of their strength, by being elevated to the level of public opinion. Thus the newspapers that have actual social significance are like the midwives of public opinion, helping it to come into the light of day. This is also not hard to prove by its own persuasive examples. The newspaper having the most social influence is without a doubt the London *Times*. But even it does not advocate its own opinions, but tries only to skillfully explain those which prevail in English society about one or another question—to notice English social interests, explain them, and thus raise them to the level of a social force. I allow myself to introduce a small excerpt from Kinglake's history of the Crimean War[30] in which, concerning the influence of that newspaper on the character of the Eastern War, he tells the history of the origin of that famous newspaper and the method by which it acquired its influence. In England there had long existed a company that collected all kinds of news, advertisements, and announcements, printing them in a list it published. "But many years ago," says Kinglake,

> it had occurred to the managers of this Company that there was one important article of news which had not been effectually supplied. It seemed likely that, without moving from his fireside, an Englishman would be glad to know what the bulk of his fellow-countrymen thought upon the uppermost questions of the day. The letters received from correspondents furnished some means of acquiring this knowledge, and it seemed to the managers of the Company that, at some pains and at a moderate cost, it would be possible to ascertain the opinions which were coming into vogue, and see the direction in which the current would flow. It is said that with this intent they many years ago employed a shrewd, idle clergyman, who made it his duty to loiter about in places of common resort and find out what people thought upon the principal subjects of the time. He was not to listen very much to extreme foolishness, and still less was he to hearken to clever people. His duty was to wait and wait until he observed that some common and obvious thought was repeated in many places, and by numbers of men who had probably never seen one another. That one common thought was the prize he sought for, and he carried it home to his employers. He became so skilled in his peculiar calling that, as long as he served them, the Company was rarely misled; and although in later times they were frequently baf-

---

[30] Alexander William Kinglake, *The Invasion of the Crimea*, 8 vols. (Edinburgh and London: W. Blackwood and Sons, 1863–88); only vols. 1 and 2 were published at the time of writing.

fled in their pursuit of this kind of knowledge, they never neglected to do what they could to search the heart of the nation.

When the managers had armed themselves with the knowledge thus gathered, they prepared to disseminate it, but they did not state baldly what they had ascertained to be the opinion of the country. Their method was as follows: they employed able writers to argue in support of the opinion which, as they believed, the country was already adopting, and, supposing that they had been well informed, their arguments of course fell upon willing ears. Those who had already formed a judgment saw their own notions stated and pressed with an ability greater than they could themselves command; and those who had not yet come to an opinion were strongly moved to do so when they saw the path taken by a Company which notoriously strove to follow the changes of the public mind. The report which the paper gave of the opinion formed by the public was so closely blended with arguments in support of that same opinion, that he who looked at the paper merely to know what other people thought, was seized as he read by the cogency of the reasoning; and, on the other hand, he who imagined that he was being governed by the force of sheer logic, was merely obeying a guide who, by telling him that the world was already agreed, made him go and flock along with his fellows; for, as the utterance of a prophecy is sometimes a main step toward its fulfillment, so a rumor asserting that multitudes have already adopted a given opinion will often generate that very concurrence of thought which was prematurely declared to exist. From the operation of this double process it resulted of course that the opinion of the English public was generally in accord with the writings of the Company; and the more the paper came to be regarded as the true exponent of the national mind, the more vast was the publicity which it obtained.

Plainly then this printing Company wielded a great power; and if I have written with sufficient clearness, I have made it apparent that this was a power of more vast dimensions than that which men describe when they speak of the "power of the Press." It is one thing, for instance, to denounce a public man by printed arguments and invectives which are believed to utter nothing more than the opinion of the writers, and it is another and a graver thing to denounce him in writings which, though having the form of arguments, are (rightly or wrongly) regarded as manifestoes—as manifestoes declaring the judgment of the English people. In the one case the man is only accused, in the other he seems to stand already condemned.

But though the Company held all this power, their tenure of it was of such a kind that they could not exercise it perversely or whimsically without doing a great harm to their singular trade; for the whole scheme of their existence went to make them—not autocratic, but—representative in their character, and they were obliged by the law of their being to keep themselves as closely as they could in accord with the nation at large.[31]

And we have a similar example. The newspaper with the greatest number of subscribers and the greatest influence is without a doubt *Moskovskie Vedomosti*.[32] Does it preach any kind of new teaching; does it impose its convictions on the public? In the majority of cases, no. It only with reliable tact seizes that interest that already exists in society, although in all probability it does not even have to its credit a single penetrating intellect who could advise it on the status of public opinion. Even such a person would be of little help to it, because among us it is impossible to eavesdrop on public opinion: it must first be awakened. *Moskovskie Vedomosti* owes its success in the Polish question, and in the question of classical methods of education in secondary schools, to this kind of skill at perceiving social interests. But *Moskovskie Vedomosti* itself shows that where it departs from that method which provides its force and significance, it loses its influence. In trade policy *Moskovskie Vedomosti* defends the system of free trade, the theory of surplus currency, etc. and despite the broad circle of its readership, these theories it advances have not caught on. On the contrary, everything shows that "free traderism" and its offshoots[33] are losing more and more ground, that public opinion, so inclined toward "free trade" seven years ago, is gradually turning toward a more healthy [i.e., protectionist] view of the economic interests of Russia.

Thus where our *Times* differs from its prototype, its activity comes to nothing. A daily newspaper will not produce new convictions or a change in the old ones. Thus, the power of the periodical press is not independent and original, but only conditional, existing in strictest dependency upon the interests existing in the public around it. If these interests are not observed by the press, if the personal convictions of the editors exclude the interests of the majority, the activity of the paper will amount to nothing. If it resolves to advance ideas contradicting the public interests, it will amount to even less. All the power of the periodical press comes from conformity to them.

If therefore society's interests stand in contradiction to the interests of the government, there can be no doubt that the government by necessity must resort to restricting the press, in order to keep it from raising these antisocial interests, explaining them to the public, and showing to the public the power of these interests. This form of action is completely appropriate here; to punish simple thoughtlessness with extreme strictness is appropriate if it might

---

[31] Kinglake, *The Invasion of the Crimea*, 4th ed. (1863), 1: 361–63.

[32] *The Moscow Gazette*, edited by prominent conservative journalist Mikhail N. Katkov (1818–87).

[33] *Fritrederstvo so svoimi sukkursaliami*; cf. French *succursale*, "branch."

cause incalculable harm to the country. But consider a country closed off in quarantine against a plague, inhabited by peoples not predisposed to the prevailing epidemic illness of a given time. Is it appropriate solely for the sake of preserving a generally accepted rule, for monotony and symmetry, out of imitation of quarantines imposed by foreigners, to execute by shooting those found guilty of violating the rule of quarantine? Would it not be sufficient in this case to subject the violators to punishment based on common law—punishment proportional to the guilt of the offender? Moreover is it not obvious to any conscientious person that, in Russian society, antisocial and antigovernmental interests simply do not exist, and thus the Russian periodical press (by its very situation, independent of its good will) is quite potent for good but completely powerless for evil? Thus in regards to it, there is no instance of self-defense or necessary protection. And if any magazine commits an offense against some resolution about the press, then this offense can in no way threaten any social harm, even in the slightest measure, neither now nor in the foreseeable future. So, depending on the level of Russian social morale, the usual prosecution imposing due penalties on any violator of press restrictions is usually sufficient for its goals, and thus a system of administrative warnings is not rooted in national needs and demands, but is a product of other circumstances and living conditions, brought to us from strangers.

These examples are sufficient to illustrate what must be understood by "Europeanization" in institutions and in governmental measures.

The third form of Europeanization (the most harmful and ruinous of all) consists of looking at both internal and external issues of Russian life from a European perspective, as if through European lenses. This perspective, which tries in every way to align Russian issues with European norms, either unconsciously (from the original wellsprings of Russian thought having run dry) or even consciously (from the desire to give these issues the honor and merit they lacked by not being European) caused much puzzlement and all kinds of confusion in the realm of learning, and incalculable harm in practice. We will not examine the consequences of the first type, but will turn our attention to only a few examples which reveal (or must inevitably reveal) the harmful influence of this type of Europeanization on Russia's internal and external life.

In the United States the two main political parties there bear the names of Republicans and Democrats. These names are borrowed from the European order of things, foreign to America, and thus do not express the essence of the aspirations of either party bearing these names. What does "Republican Party" mean in a country where there is no monarchy, and where no one within it even strives for one? What does "Democratic Party" mean in a place where the entire society was built on democratic foundations? Strictly speaking, American Republicans are defenders of political centralization, and Democrats are defenders of the political autonomy of the states. Here the borrowing from the foreign European world goes no farther than the names, and thus presents merely a confusion of nomenclature, to the extent that American Democrats are actually the representatives of aristocratic tendencies of that society. But this confusion of nomenclature has no practical influence because Americans are used to living their own life. For us, unfortunately, the borrowing of nomenclature has produced much greater confusion, because our uppermost social classes, accustomed to living an intellectually foreign life, involuntarily import into real life the European ideals they have seen or read about, giving European names to our social phenomena of the day, on the basis of the most superficial comparison. This is how "aristocracy" and "democracy" appeared in Russia.

The very word "aristocrat" came to us recently, at the same time as stories of high society entered into our literature and the hearts of provincial madams beat faster with the hope of living up to this flattering name, having assimilated themselves, their lifestyle, and the prevailing tone of their households to the notion they associated with the word "aristocracy." Aristocracy or aristocratism, applied to Russia and Russian society, meant then and means now nothing but the genteel tone and polish prevailing in the wealthy households of the capital, which is nothing more than people in the course of a few generations almost completely changing their manners to those of the old French marquises or present-day English lords. There is no other notion of Russian aristocratism or Russian aristocracy. But where there is nothing inside, the outside appearance, the name, and the designation becomes all important. And so there appeared among us outlets of public opinion with aristocratic tendencies.

How ridiculous, and at the same time harmful, are such borrowed foreign views, can be seen from the conclusions to which they lead. Western aristocracy is not unique or proprietary to any one particular European state, but is by its provenance an all-European institution in the full sense of the word. It only takes on national coloration afterwards, when peoples stand out dramatically, like those making up the unified French monarchy, as discussed above. It is only natural that commonality of provenance would lead to solidarity with all European aristocratic interests. Therefore when the French Revolution declared a war to the death on aristocratic-feudal institutions within its own house, all aristocracies felt wounded. Even England, enjoying institutions of freedom in its house, considered it necessary to muster its forces to defend the aristocratic principle. Knowing the spirit that always governs English politics, it is impossible to suppose that only a certain disinterested indignation (aroused by the madness, fury, and criminality that distinguished the French Revolution) was the incentive prompting England to throw itself into the memorable twenty-year struggle with France—a struggle ending in the apparent defeat of France, but which had essentially toppled the aristocratic principle not only on the Continent, but in England itself. The solidarity of all European aristocracies was the true motivating cause of that struggle, which was the main historical event of the end of the eighteenth and beginning of the nineteenth centuries, and even caused French democrats to speak of the alliance of aristocracy and monarchy against the freedom and welfare of nations.

Accordingly, our imitative aristocratism—*Vest'*[34] and its party—could do nothing but cling to this universal aristocratic solidarity, and start demanding an alliance between the imaginary Russian aristocracy and the not-at-all imaginary Polish nobility and Baltic barons. Whatever one's opinion of the latter group, the Polish nobility is doubtless the most evil, longstanding, fundamental enemy of the Russian nation. So then, the French democrats' accusation that the alliance of European aristocracies was seeking the end of freedom and welfare of nations—does this not this fully conform to the party standing as the defender and patron of the Polish nobility, which said that the Polish landowner was nearer to its heart than the western Russian peasant? Did it not actually preach the destruction of the Russian nation by posing as the intercessor and defender of its most evil enemy? This is where imitativeness leads; these are the results of transferring European views and tendencies onto Russian soil.

But if we have Europeanizing aristocrats, we also have Europeanizing democrats. We recall articles written from our democratic camp (along the lines of our "national tactlessness"); we recall the alliance of our democrats with the Polish Right; and we shall see that democratic Europeanization was also prepared to sacrifice the Russian nation to its most evil enemy, taking on the aristocratic and democratic guise in order more certainly to harm it.

Since both aristocracy and democracy constitute real elements and forces of European society, then in line with their most extreme manifestations (having in mind the Junkers[35] and the demagogues known as "Reds") from the one side or the other, it is possible not only to identify truly robust manifestations of these elements of European life (phenomena like the aristocratism of Count Bismarck and democratism of Count Cavour or Garibaldi),[36] but to show that these robust parts are the main force within both parties. Our aristocratic and democratic Europeanization, on the contrary, for lack of internal support must necessarily present something of a caricature. Hardly anyone but the newspaper *Vest'* doubts that our Junkers are an alien, hybrid, crossbred phenomenon. It would take a long time inhaling the miasmas of chivalry and Polish nobility to become infused with them. We would need to fill our spiritual and intellectual void with them, so to speak, bringing to light something monstrous like the notion of cross-breeding the hardy aristocracy of our borderlands with the stillborn aristocracy at the core of our state to jointly rule the people, and to unify the state in this devious, impossible way, when the people of the state borderlands either form one ethnographic and organic whole with the people of the state core, or wish only to blend with them into

---

[34] *Vest'*: See chap. 6, n. 14.

[35] Junkers: See chap. 8, n. 58.

[36] Bismarck, Cavour, and Garibaldi: See chap. 1, nn. 5, 7, and 8, respectively.

such a unity, with the aristocracy of these borderlands as the only obstacle. Through such an impossible alliance there would be nothing left for the aristocracy of the state core (if such a thing even existed) to do but to promote the divisive goals of their allies.

But if the non-Russian provenance of this pseudo-aristocratism is obvious and not disputed by anyone, then some will on the other hand go to any length to ascribe a Russian home-bred provenance to our pseudo-democratism, or our starkest manifestation of it—known by the name of nihilism. It is little wonder when our European friends keep chanting in unison that Russian society and the Russian people are corroded by socialistic, materialistic, and democratic teachings of the most pernicious kind; when by their accounts Russian democratism threatens the well-being of Europe, just as formerly Russian absolutism threatened it—that is just the way things are: *à la guerre comme à la guerre.*[37] But what is surprising is the way a newspaper like *Moskovskie Vedomosti* (which usually takes such a sensible view of things), influenced by its displeasure (however justified) over our system of public education, turns nihilism into a product of the Russian soil! This is completely incomprehensible. Nihilism is nothing more nor less than one of the forms of our Europeanization, and however poor our gymnasia and universities may be, they did not cause this plague, and however useful a classical system of education may be, it will not cure us of it.[38]

What exactly is nihilism? Nihilism is consistent materialism and nothing more. Materialism has already enjoyed wide circulation several times in European society: in the seventeenth century it prevailed in England, in the eighteenth, in France, from which it spread among the upper classes of other states, including Russia. The reaction against this materialism was German idealism, which now in its turn, under the combined influences of Protestantism (having rejected any positive religious content of Christianity), Hegelianism (taken to its most extreme logical development), and finally the successes of positive science, has also reached the uttermost point of materialism and atheism. Meanwhile, for as slow on the uptake as official Russia has been, France has long stood as the embodiment of everything antisocial, antireligious, and contrary to moral teachings; while modest and serious Germany styled itself as counteracting this pernicious trend with its saving idealism. So it is no surprise our system of public education was given an exclusively German character. Not so long ago, young people sent abroad were strictly for-

[37] French: "In war as in war." Idiomatically, "so it goes" or "take it as it comes."

[38] [Danilevskii's marginalia, published posthumously]: *And it did not cure us; nihilism continues to grow. Now they attribute it to the university reform of 1863, and this again is piling a great evil on a completely insignificant foundation.*

bidden from going to France as if to a morally plague-ridden country; then as the plague long ago left French soil, it spread into Germany.[39]

Without independent development, accustomed to trusting our foreign tutors, and more recently learning exclusively German teachings, we have been infected with the most modern and most fashionable of [Europe's] trends, which encounter neither internal nor external opposition. To what nation do Vogt, Moleschott, Feuerbach, Bruno Bauer, [Ludwig] Büchner, and Max Stirner[40]—these coryphaei[41] of modern materialism—belong? Are they really Russians, or schoolboys at Russian gymnasia, made nihilists by insufficient instruction in Greek and Latin classics? Did Russia produce those teachings which, although they could not be called purely materialistic, still served as necessary supports of materialism—such as Darwin's teaching of the origin of the species, Huxley's[42] conclusions about the similarity of humans to apes, and Buckle's[43] dismissal of human freedom on the basis of statistical results? What did Russians contribute to this treasure-house of materialist teachings? Nothing. The very term "nihilism," although apparently coined in Russia, is obviously based on Max Stirner's "I Rest My Case on Nothing" book,[44] dedicated with philistine cynicism to *"meinem Liebchen."*[45]

We have repeated foreign words and thoughts like parrots: as our grandfathers parroted the teachings of the Encyclopedists and occasionally mystics, so did our fathers the teachings of German transcendental idealism. If these teachings, having spread somewhat in Russian society in earlier times, cannot be considered Russian phenomena, then why should nihilism, which has such an obviously foreign origin? Or can it be that with the imitators' characteristic

---

[39] [Danilevskii's marginalia, published posthumously]: *As it turned out, however, it did not leave France. But everything in Germany takes on the most radical and most highly infectious form.*

[40] Danilevskii's implication is that all are Germans (a stretch in some cases). Karl Vogt (1817–95): German scientist, materialist, evolutionist, and left-wing politician. Jakob Moleschott (1822–93): Dutch anatomist, professor at Heidelberg and Zurich, famous for the statement that "the brain secretes thought like the liver secretes bile." Ludwig Andreas Feuerbach (1804–72): German Left Hegelian philosopher, atheist, materialist. Bruno Bauer (1809–82): German philosopher and historian, shrewd rationalist critic of early Christianity. Ludwig Büchner: See chap. 9, n. 40. Max Stirner: German materialist nihilist philosopher, author of *Der Einzige und sein Eigentum* (The Ego and Its Own, 1844).

[41] Leaders of the chorus, in ancient Greek theater.

[42] Thomas Henry Huxley (1825–95): English biologist and aggressive proponent of Darwinism.

[43] Henry Thomas Buckle (1821–62): English historian. He made this claim in *The History of Civilization in England* (1857), chap. 1.

[44] Paraphrasing the opening and closing line of *The Ego and Its Own*.

[45] German: "My sweetheart."

penchant for exaggeration, we went overboard with our borrowed teachings? Fortunately or unfortunately, there is no longer any apparent difference between our teachers and ourselves. When they say that humans are direct descendents of gorillas or orangutans, that "the brain secretes thought as the liver secretes bile" [quoting Moleschott], that to consider anything holy is as ridiculous a custom as the *taboo* of the Polynesian islanders—then is there anything left to exaggerate?[46]

But if there is something Russian in nihilism, then it is the sheer caricature of it. But this property distinguishes it from Russian aristocratism, from Russian democratism, from Russian constitutionalism—put simply, from all Russian Europeanization. No matter how crude or unrefined these teachings are, if they (like modern materialism, communism, or Caesarism) seem the result of a long development gone down a false path, or the result of irreconcilable contradiction reaching the point of negating various aspects of life, then these teachings and social phenomena—the fruit of the despair of whole generations—have a grand, tragic character. When these teachings arise not from the internal life of a society but for no reason at all, then this tragic greatness becomes deformity and caricature. After all this, how do we make sense of the strange justification for living abroad, so that children can be educated in foreign schools away from the plague of nihilism, when it is these very schools that bred the pure strain of nihilism compared to which our nihilism is only a pale copy, a poor knockoff?

But nihilism, aristocratism, democratism, and constitutionalism are very particular manifestations of our Europeanization; its most common form, seemingly less pernicious, but actually most dangerous of all, is our balance in the scales of European public opinion, which we consider our judge, before whom we tremble, whose mercy we seek. Such a relationship with foreign public opinion, even if it were not radically hostile toward all things Russian, cannot help but deprive us of our freedom of thought and of all spontaneous action. We become like those dandies who love society functions, but lack confidence in the gentility of their manners. Constantly under the weight of their worries over whether their poses, gestures, movements, gait, costume, opinions, conversation are properly *bon ton* and *comme il faut*, these naturally bright and dexterous people only end up acting clumsy and speaking nothing but nonsense. Is it not the same with our public figures, incessantly looking around and listening in on what Europe says? Do their actions deserve to be called enlightened Europeanism? Famusov [in *Woe from Wit*], in light of his daughters' dishonor, exclaims, "What will Princess Maria Alexeevna say!" and by this reveals the full depth of his moral insignificance. We have raised Europe to the dignity of our Maria Alexeevna, the high judge of the worthi-

---

[46] [Danilevskii's marginalia, published posthumously]: *Unfortunately, exaggeration proved possible; but even this was not without the help of our "well-wishers," and secondly, due to the stupidity of our policies.*

ness of our deeds. Instead of the approval of the national conscience, we let our actions be motivated by cowardly fear of the verdicts of Europe, taking humiliatingly vain pleasure in its praise.

Take a certain example everyone knows. Europe accuses us of greedily eyeing Constantinople, and we blush at the accusation as if it is indeed some kind of evil thing. England has already taken possession of nearly all straits around the globe; why on earth it seized the Spanish coast commanding the entrance to the Mediterranean Sea is not entirely clear; but in regards to us, striving for free passage within our own house is considered an impermissible appropriation, the possession of which would besides lay upon us the attendant moral obligation to drive the Turks from the Slavic and Greek lands. We of course can attest to the fact that at the present moment we have no intention of that: just as we definitely did not before the Eastern [Crimean] War, so, unfortunately, we doubtless do not, even now; but to take the European point of view is to see in the very hope of taking possession of Tsargrad, driving out the Turks, and freeing the Slavs—to see this as some kind of infringement on the rights of Europe, which is an unforgiveable moral humiliation. I am not speaking here about the language of diplomacy (it has its own conventional language and political morality, which is: if you want to live with the wolves, you had better howl like one), but I merely have in mind the expression of Russian public opinion. French diplomats do not speak of extending the border to the Rhine, but that does not prevent French public opinion from freely expressing its thoughts and hopes on this subject, even though the legality for them is in much greater doubt than the legality of Russia's hopes.

In the same way we shun the charge of Pan-Slavism [*obvineniia v panslavisme*], as if any honorable Russian who understands the word could never be a Pan-Slavist [*panslavist*], that is, could never put one's whole heart into the cause of freeing one's Slavic brothers from their yoke and uniting with them into a single whole, governed solely by Slavic interests, even if they were a hundred times opposed to the interests of Europe and the rest of the world, which are not and must never be of any concern to us.

Among those whom Americans consider their greatest people is one who did not free them from the foreign yoke (like Washington), proclaim their civil and political freedoms (like Franklin, Adams, and Jefferson), or free the negroes (like Lincoln), but who simply declared from the height of the presidential office that America belongs to Americans, and that any interference by foreigners in American affairs would be considered an insult to the United States. This simple and unpretentious edict is known as the famous Monroe Doctrine,[47] and constitutes the highest principle in the foreign affairs of the

---

[47] Monroe Doctrine: An 1823 policy statement from President James Monroe (1758–1831) that Latin America should be off limits to further European colonization, as it had gained or was gaining independence from Portugal and Spain. In a larger sense, it declared the western hemisphere an American sphere of influence, although the orig-

United States. The Slavic world must advance such a doctrine, and no fear of any Maria Alexeevna must keep us from proclaiming it loudly where all who yearn to hear it, will.

But in certain foreign matters, is not the influence of hostile Europe always and everywhere hanging over our frame of mind and our actions? Having believed what Europe says, that Catherine the Great committed a great political crime by adding lands to Russia that were originally Russian from time immemorial, fulfilling the agonized hopes of millions of Russians, we just barely avoided committing a real crime against the Russian people for the sake of these humane goals and intentions. Afraid of being reproached by Europe for our religious intolerance, we started to side with "tolerant" pastors and barons against Orthodox-trained Latvians and Estonians, who had already proved their deep desire to merge with the Russian people, as their ancestors and kinsmen once laid the foundations of the Russian state. But it is better to stop at these first examples of how the fear of Europe influences our internal politics, and turn to foreign history, where there is nothing to hide, where the reckoning is clearer and it is much clearer what we have gained and what we have lost, from taking the European point of view and looking at our affairs and interests through European glasses.

After the great national policy of Empress Catherine reuniting western with eastern Russia, extending Russia to the Black and Azov Seas into the expanse from the Dnieper to the Kuban, we fell into an unselfish fear of the brutality of the French Revolution after it had already run its course, and no-less unselfish sympathy for the misfortunes of unselfish Austria. And thus the great Suvorov[48] was adorned with the title of Prince of Italy, and Russian arms shone with everlasting glory. The 1799 war brought tremendous moral results, showing how capable Russian forces are under the leadership of a Russian military genius; but in terms of practical or useful results it not only did not, but could not bring any kind of positive outcome. Even without us, Napoleon subdued the revolution and appeared as the protector and restorer of order. His ambition had not yet become apparent, to reveal the urgency of taking timely measures against him. The historical struggle between England and France, in which the latter was stripped of all of its colonies, naturally led to the one [i.e., Napoleon] who stood as the bearer and representative of all its fortunes and aspirations, in the hope of outmatching its rival. The nonfulfillment of the Treaty of Amiens[49] provided the sufficient pretext. The coast of England was threatened with invasion. France's finances and Austria's nat-

---

inal declaration would not have been viable without the assent of Britain, the predominant naval power.

[48] Suvorov: See chap. 2, n. 41.

[49] Signed in March 1802 between Britain and France, a reprieve marked by distrust, lasting a year.

ural hope to try to reclaim what it had lost[50] distracted France from this final thrust intended for England. What was our concern in all this? But we took the European point of view and, knowing already how Austria and England repay the unselfish desire to help them, nevertheless we entered into a new alliance with these unselfish powers. The war of 1805 did not have the same moral results as 1799. The war of 1807 was its necessary continuation. This time, Russia's honor truly required war.[51] Concluding the war in the Treaty of Tilsit was not the most glorious moment for Russia; however it was perhaps the most advantageous of any treaty Russia ever signed. It gave [Russia] possession of the Białystok region, Finland, and Bessarabia, and the only reason it did not acquire Galicia, Moldavia, and Wallachia, nor support Serbian independence, was because Russia was looking at everything from the European point of view and did not want it. The height of Europeanism led it to prefer the independence of Oldenburg to independence for Serbia and Slavdom. Following from this view, the War of 1812 again had great moral results for Russia, and also could have had great practical results, if only we had made peace with Napoleon and left Germany and Europe to face their own fate.

After 1815 Russia seemingly held the dominant role in Europe; but by following idealistic, all-European goals, with the political center of its activity located outside itself rather than within, Russia served the politics of Metternich[52] and (like a lightning rod) drew the hatred he deserved away from him and onto itself. Metternich managed to exploit Russia's European point of view to pull the wool over its eyes twice over: first, by striking fear in its heart of Carbonari[53] plots and democratic agitations which (I repeat once more) essentially concerned Russia about as much as the Taiping Rebellion; and second, by forcing it to see the sacred uprising of the Greeks as a democratic revolution. By this the Austrian minister managed to rip from Russia's hands the honor it attained as the sole helpmate and participant in the struggle of its co-religionists. This glory was divided between Austria and the other hypocritical friends of the Greeks, having filched what they could of useful results from this sacred struggle.

Instead of being the standard-bearer of the Cross and freedom for truly oppressed peoples, we became knights of legitimism, paladins of conservatism, and defenders of the sacred tradition of Versailles *bon ton*, as is fitting

---

[50] In 1805, Austria invaded Bavaria, which had sided with France, and was defeated by France at the Battle of Ulm. This diverted a massive French army from Boulogne, where they were preparing for the invasion of England.

[51] The War of the Fourth Coalition (1806–07) became all the more vital when France rapidly defeated Prussia and advanced on the Russian frontier.

[52] Metternich: See chap. 2, n. 42.

[53] Carbonari: Italian secret societies of the nineteenth century with a vague revolutionary cast. The name derives from the charcoal trade (akin to Freemasonry's nominal association with brick and mortar construction).

for the pupils of French emigrants. The more sincerely and disinterestedly we assimilated one of the European points of view, the more deeply Europe hated us, refusing to trust our sincerity and seeing deeply-hidden, power-loving designs where there was only sincere devotion to European legitimism and conservatism. This hatred did not disturb our conservatives; they were proud of it, and considered it completely natural. How indeed could Russia, the awesome defender and preserver of the community and order, not be hated by the rabble of democrats and revolutionaries of all stripes? They did not in the least doubt that they had the sympathies of the friends of order and all conservative forces everywhere. Our progressives also were not disturbed by the hatred of European public opinion, likewise considering it natural; however they were not proud, but rather ashamed, of it as a deserved punishment for our anti-progressive aspirations.

But then the Eastern [Crimean] War began. Its beneficial effects for us were extolled in the saying: "Only when it thunders does the Russian peasant cross himself." But perhaps it is more correct to credit not the military defeat but those beneficial internal reforms that came after the Treaty of Paris, the uniquely good initiative of Emperor Alexander II, who doubtless would have launched them all the same, no matter what the outcome of the Eastern War. However, the war was not without beneficial consequences. It revealed to us that we were hated not by any certain European party, but on the contrary, however Europe was divided by particular interests, they all were united by a common feeling of hostility toward Russia. In this the clerics joined hands with the liberals; Catholics with Protestants; conservatives with progressives; aristocrats with democrats; monarchists with anarchists; Reds with Whites; legitimists and Orleanists with Bonapartists. Listen, though, to the arguments in the French legislative assembly on the foreign policy of the Empire. One or another opposition party finds words of condemnation for the French government's Italian, American, or German policy, but all parties agree among themselves, and with the imperial government, in the appraisal of its Eastern policy—so long as it is hostile to Russia.[54] This general hatred toward Russia (crossing the lines of all parties and interests) which Europe reveals in both words and deeds finally became apparent to our eyes. Unfortunately this sobering effect of the Eastern War was not strong enough, because it has not helped, even with a greater degree of free speech.[55]

We refused to hear any insulting word about Russia, in the same way that all crudity or obscenity would break the virginal purity and delicacy of a

[54] [Danilevskii's marginalia, published posthumously]: *Even now, France, insulted by Germany, shuns Russia.* [Translator's note: A Franco-Russian Alliance was finally created in 1894, lasting until 1917.]

[55] [Danilevskii's marginalia, published posthumously]: *Not even the Congress of Berlin opened our eyes; meanwhile [even with freer speech] the number of times anyone has said something reasonable you can count on one hand.*

young girl's ears. From the official defense of Russian interest, everything still continued to flow with the conventionalism from which we suffer. We are so used to official falsehoods that even the one holy truth looked and sounded like falsehood to us. The majority of educated people still cannot give up the old habit of seeing all of our affairs with European eyes, and considers itself very shrewd, thinking to itself that Europe has taken up arms against us to punish our unbearable arrogance. *Our arrogance*—how fascinating it would be to catch sight of such a marvel as that! When, where, and how does it ever reveal itself? Even after the Eastern War, there passed from hand to hand a manuscript, rightly or wrongly attributed to Professor Granovskii,[56] in which the Eastern War was presented precisely as just retribution for our political arrogance, even though it was essentially carried out in political humility and modesty exceeding all bounds. I do not make bold to claim the aforementioned manuscript was actually the work of the famous professor; but if it were counterfeit, and public opinion were to take a more national direction, of course no one would even think to ascribe views of this type to the pen of one so widely admired.

It took another event to open Russian eyes even further to the true attitude of European public opinion toward Russia: Europe's interference in Polish affairs [in the 1863 uprising]. What the Eastern War could not accomplish, Europe's interference in Polish affairs did,[57] in spite of the fact that this interference did not have the insulting character or harsh consequences of the events of 1853–56. But these eye-opening events helped generate publicity and public opinion.[58]

All the types of Europeanism here enumerated and demonstrated by examples are of course only symptoms of the disease, which can be called the weakness and sickliness of the national spirit in the upper, educated layers of Russian society. But while being symptoms of the disease, they are at the same time the inborn cause of the disease, from which it originates and draws continual support. This disease as a whole hampers the realization of the great destiny of the Russian people and, having dried up the wellspring of the national spirit, it may finally (in spite of all the appearances of a capable state) deprive the Russian people's historical life of its internal creative force, thus making its very existence useless and superfluous, since anything without internal contents is just historical rubbish, to be swept up and burned in the fire on the Judgment Day of history. What will cure us of the ailment that has befallen us, and, once we have eradicated all distortion of our national appearance, what will turn illness into growth, as we already turned around our

---

[56] Granovskii, see chap. 6, n. 2. The pamphlet in question is "The Eastern Question from the Russian Point of View," written by Boris Chicherin and circulated anonymously; Granovskii praised it, hence the confusion.

[57] [Danilevskii's marginalia, published posthumously]: *For all too short of a time!*

[58] [Danilevskii's marginalia, published posthumously]: *Alas, a flimsy support!*

burden of tribute and slavery to the Tatars? Both the direct application of power and the force of words to us seem insufficient for this. The impoverishment of the spirit can only be shaken off by arousing and invigorating the spirit, which would begin to rouse all layers of Russian society, bring them into living contact, and fill in the gaps of the spirit precisely where it lapses into imitativeness and blind veneration of foreign ideals, by drawing from that concealed wellspring that has often spouted from the deep, as it did in the days of Minin, and was starting to do in the more recent times of trial in 1812 and 1863.[59] Deliverance from the captivity and slavery of the spirit requires a close bond among all captive and enslaved brothers; it requires a struggle which, once it has torn off all masks, will finally bring us face to face with our enemies, and bring us to hate our own idolatry and worship of our openly-declared enemies and opponents. This can only be done by the school of hard knocks, the fearsome experience of history. These curative events, from which (whether we want to or not) we will learn our saving lessons, have already appeared on the horizon of history, and are called: *The Eastern Question.*

---

[59] [Danilevskii's marginalia, published posthumously]: *And 1876 and 1877.*

৫ 12 ৪০
The Eastern Question

The Voice divine: "Peoples of earth, go East,
For the righteous judge, prepare!"
And blindly, to their destined fare,
The peoples plow through stormy seas
And by earthen paths rush there.
—Khomiakov[1]

The Eastern Question is not one that will be resolved by diplomacy. History consigns the day-to-day jumble of minor events to the bureaucratic mechanisms of diplomacy, but proclaims its great universal decrees governing the life of peoples for entire ages without any intermediaries, accompanied by thunder and lightning like the Lord of Hosts atop Mount Sinai. There is no need to prove this. Everyone understands that the importance of the Eastern Question is so great that no one would even think to squeeze it into the narrow framework of diplomacy; it would never enter anyone's mind to propose a conference to resolve it. Diplomacy, despite undertaking a great deal, senses it is not up to the task, and only tries to stall the rush toward its resolution to give time for everyone to make use of the dreadful historical crisis ahead, which will long absorb the peoples' attention and efforts, and push all other matters and concerns into the background. In this manner it of course fulfills its obligation to smooth, as much as it can, the paths of historical movement and if not to prevent, then to reduce and minimize, the clashes.

The relative impotence of diplomacy, this inability to resolve the most important international questions by means of peace talks, is considered by many a sign of the imperfection of all human societies. The natural and lawful aspiration for peaceful development increasingly draws all peoples to prefer the stock exchange view of politics. But if storms and lightning are required within the physical order of nature, then no less necessary are the direct clashes of peoples that wrest their fate out of the sphere of the narrow-minded rationality of the politicians (who of necessity judge the needs of historical movement from the standpoint of momentary interests, without a complete understanding of its full essence) and place it under the direct guidance of historical Providence that governs the world. If the great questions

---

[1] From the 1854 poem "Sud Bozhii" (literally: The Court of God; figuratively: trial by ordeal).

that caused the deepest and stormiest historical crises had been resolved by talks between the most expert and astute politicians and diplomats of the day, how pathetic would have been the historical results of these well-meaning efforts which (for all the good intentions and human wisdom guiding them) could not discern the needs of the future, nor the fruitful and productive influence of events that, from the perspective of the moment, could only be considered harmful and disastrous. On the contrary, the fact that the peaceful resolutions of the fate of humanity are almost completely beyond the influence of the narrow, petty wisdom of the political actors in times of great historical upheaval, must be seen as one of the most beneficial laws guiding the movement of history.

But if everyone recognizes that the Eastern Question has outgrown the dimensions of a diplomatic question, then on the other hand there have been those who have falsely widened its scope but denied the profound depth of its historical meaning. I refer to the opinion of our famous historian Solov'ev,[2] who sees the Eastern Question as one of the phases of the age-old struggle between Europe and Asia, in which the former personifies the salutary and life-giving influence of the sea, and the latter, the lethal, ruinous influence of the steppe. Both are a kind of historical Ormuzd and Ahriman,[3] the eternal struggle of which constitutes the most essential stuff of history. To apply this view to the Eastern Question, of course, required Europe-as-Ormuzd to betray its own goals, repeating on a larger scale Sparta's betrayal of the common Greek cause [by allying with Persia], which led to the Peace of Antalcidas [ending the Corinthian War in 387 BCE]. It seems to me this is not solely the opinion of Professor Solov'ev: it is shared, more or less, by those who want to reconcile the original historical role of Russia and Slavdom with their European character, in contrast to the fundamental opposition between the interests of the Slavic and the Germanic-Roman world, and in contrast to the very consciousness (revealed in word and deed) of Europe, in the narrow and only precise meaning of the word.

Against this view, it seems possible to me to raise a few completely irrefutable arguments:

1.	There has never been and can never be a struggle between Europe and Asia, because Europe, and Asia even more so, has never conceived of itself as any kind of whole, capable of undertaking some struggle, the way not only contending states but even whole groups of states and peoples bound into political and cultural-historical entities have conceived of themselves.

---

[2] Sergei Solov'ev (1820–79): Russian historian at Moscow University, author of the multivolume *Istoriia Rossii c drevneishikh vremen* (History of Russia From Ancient Times; 1851–79).

[3] The Zoroastrian spirits of good and evil, respectively.

2. There has never been a war in which, even accidentally or unconsciously, all the peoples of Europe took up arms against all the peoples of Asia, or vice versa.

3. Europe and Asia are either geographic, or ethnographic, or cultural-historical conceptions. As geographical conceptions, very artificial ones at that, they could not enter into any kind of struggle between themselves. As ethnographic conceptions, they could correspond only as follows: Europe to the Aryan tribes, and Asia to the Turkish, Semitic, and others. But besides the fact that this ethnographic division does not coincide with the geographic division (which can be neither widened or narrowed), in the ethnographic sense of the concepts of *Europe* and *Asia*, the same tribe might be deemed either Europe or Asia, depending on whomever it ends up fighting against. So if we take the Iranian tribe as the representative of Asia in its struggle with Greece, we would also have to see it as the representative of Europe in the struggle against Turan[4] and the Scyths, true representatives of the steppe.[5] As cultural-historical conceptions, Europe as defined above (with which the author whose opinion we are now picking apart could scarcely agree) genuinely consists of an independent, cultural-historical whole, but Asia does not correspond to anything of the sort, with no kind of unity in this sense, and thus cannot enter into any kind of struggle with Europe. It takes a more definite opponent of some kind for such a conflict to proceed.

4. Many wars that, geographically speaking, could be counted as part of the struggle between Europe and Asia, are in other regards indistinguishable from many other wars undertaken by the peoples of Europe amongst themselves, or by the peoples of Asia amongst themselves. This becomes abundantly clear from an unbiased examination of the examples Mr. Solov'ev offered to support his ideas about the struggle between Europe and Asia, between the influences of sea and steppe. The first example offered is the two-hundred-some years of almost constantly continuing warfare between the Greeks and Persians, very well fitting the general conception of struggle between Europe and Asia, disregarding the fact that the expression is no more than a metaphor that takes a part for the whole, not to mention the fact that part of Asia (at least in the geographic sense) took the side of Europe: namely, the Greek colonies of Asia Minor. But forcing this isolated example of struggle between Asia and Europe to be

---

[4] Turan: Persian term for Central Asia.

[5] [Danilevskii's marginalia, published posthumously]: *If you consider the Scyths and Turanians Turkish tribes, then this is wrong.*

repeated in another great historical struggle made it necessary to reckon Carthage as Asia, geography notwithstanding. To consider it Asia because of its Phoenician descent would mean that Rome likewise would seem to be Asia, as a consequence of the Aryan, which is to say Asiatic, descent of the Italian tribes. But if the influence of the steppe is the historical characteristic of Asia in its struggle with Europe, then the representative of the sea, despite its proximity to the Sahara, would in any case seem to be Carthage, not Rome. After the Punic Wars the Romans indeed fought a whole series of wars against states situated in Asia; but these states, according to the prevailing cultural element within them, were Hellenistic states, and thus predominantly European, so a war with them is a struggle of Europe against Europe, not in any sense against Asia. Therefore, out of all of Rome's wars, only the war with the Parthians[6] has all the necessary characteristics to be considered a struggle between Europe and Asia. But clearly these wars were events of completely secondary historical importance, having decisive influence neither for the fate of the Roman nor the Parthian state. The time of the great migrations of peoples ensued, and if Rome happened to battle in part against arrivals from Asia—Huns, Avars, and so on—nevertheless, its major opponents appear to have been Germanic peoples, which is to say, Europeans. True, the Arab Muslim advances would seem to be a case of true representatives of the steppe battling with Europe; but in the same way they also battled with both Africa and Asia, and their hostility toward Europe had the same nature as their hostility toward Persia, with the difference that the former seemed more vulnerable than the latter, and was not so easily acquired.

5. Finally, if the Eastern Question were actually just one phase of the struggle between Europe and Asia, then it is not worth discussing, since not only the small part of Asia that belongs to Turkey but even the whole continent could not mount any kind of serious opposition, not only to a big push from all of Europe, but even to a single powerful European state, as is demonstrated by the incursions of Russia in Persia and Turkestan; England in India; and England and France in China.

---

[6] In the years 66 BCE–217 CE, Rome fought a series of wars with the Parthian Empire, which ruled Persia from the third century BCE to the third century CE. In 114 CE, Roman Emperor Trajan (r. 98–117 CE) annexed Armenia, intensifying the conflict for a century.

This generally mistaken view of the Eastern Question is not helped by the comparison of Germanic-Roman Europe's actions with Sparta's actions in the Peace of Antalcidas. In that case, Sparta, betraying the common Greek cause, asked the Persians for help and, having gained with their aid a victory over the Athenians, helped conclude the shameful Peace. But in the present case, Europe, not threatened by anyone, itself offers and provides help to impotent Turkey for the oppression of the Christians under its power. In those days, Sparta's betrayal was an exception to the common character of Greek behavior in their struggle with the Persians, a betrayal in which Sparta sought to smooth the way in Asia Minor for Agesilaus II;[7] these days, Europe remains consistent with the general character of its mode of action since the very beginning of its historical existence, as I now hope to demonstrate, which is why this mode of action, being neither violent nor improper, does not deserve to be called "betrayal." It would only be a betrayal if Europe acknowledged Slavdom and Russia as essential constituent parts of itself; but because it has never done that, of the two equally foreign elements to itself, the Slavic-Christian and the Turkish-Muslim, it could direct its protection and encouragement to the one it considers closer to itself, and choose the more advantageous course of action without deserving blame for betrayal.

All these anomalies and contradictions sort themselves out if, instead of artificially assembling them under the general category of struggle between Europe and Asia, they are left as scattered historical phenomena, conforming to the requirements of a natural grouping of historical events according to cultural-historical types. Then it will turn out that the peoples of one cultural-historical type have a natural inclination to expand their activity and influence as much as their strength and means allow, the same as an individual person does. This natural ambition necessarily leads to a clash of the peoples of one cultural-historical type with the peoples of another, regardless of whether their boundaries coincide with arbitrarily-drawn geographic boundaries of the continents (which can of course happen sometimes) or not. The first case was an incorrect generalization, leading to the idea of an imaginary struggle between Europe and Asia, instead of the actual struggles taking place between Hellenic and Persian, Roman and Ancient Semitic, Roman and Hellenic, Roman and German, and finally, Germanic-Roman and Slavic, types. This last struggle consists of what is known as the "Eastern Question," which is merely the continuation of an ancient Eastern question, consisting of the struggle of the Roman type with the Greek. We must take a brief look at this twofold, roughly two-thousand-year struggle to gain a full understanding of the history of the Eastern Question, its essence, historical significance, and only possible final solution.

---

[7] Agesilaus II (444–360 BCE): Spartan king and military commander. The treaty in question gave Sparta a free hand in Greece, with the backing of Persian military might.

The peoples of the Hellenic cultural-historical type, so richly gifted in many regards, had one basic deficiency, however: they lacked political instincts, with which the Roman people, on the contrary, was gifted to the highest degree. The Greeks, having resisted the Persian invasion (with the help of the patriotic enthusiasm they summoned), exhausted themselves with pointless internecine strife because they could not find a political form to provide the kind of mutual bond between them that would correspond to the relative strength of the political units into which they divided. The sought-after form was none other than what is called "political equilibrium." Instead of that, the strongest of the Greek states (originally Athens and Sparta, and later Thebes) sought exclusive hegemony, for which none of them had sufficient strength. Therefore, during most of the original existence of the Greek federation or the political system of Greek states, there was dualism: first between Sparta and Athens, later between Sparta and Thebes. Dualism is nothing more than a temporary truce between those seeking exclusive state supremacy; it cannot create anything durable. Meanwhile in this disastrous time of civil strife, the Greek people still had not fulfilled the great task history had laid upon it. Art and philosophy had already brought forth their best fruits, but their cycle of development was still not complete; it remained for them to lay the foundations of positive science, and apply philosophy to the religious truth yet to be revealed to humanity, to create Christian theology. Greece lost its political strength before its genius had exhausted its potential.

Then in the country neighboring Greece, populated by Greeks or Hellenized tribes who had not, however, taken part in the general life of Greece to this point, there appeared a man of genius who had not only strength, but the desire and ability to supply the political instincts that the Greeks lacked. This was Philip of Macedon.[8] The best and most noble of the Greeks of that day, Phocion[9], understood that submission to Philip was the only means of rescue from internal quarrels, and the only way to preserve and guarantee the independence of Greece (just as in our times, for example, the most enlightened minds in Italy understood the necessity of submission to Victor Emmanuel,[10] or the best minds of Germany, submission to Prussia). But the shortsighted democrats led by Demosthenes[11] did not think so. Philip crushed their opposition, however. Greece was given the unity it lacked. The young, energetic, but still unrefined peoples from the Balkan Peninsula (perhaps even Slavs among them) all the way to the Danube were made to submit to the power of Philip. With these forces he intended to launch a war against Greece's traditional enemy, the Persians. Knowing Philip's character—both passionate and

---

[8] Philip of Macedon: See chap. 10, n. 10.

[9] Phocion: See chap. 5, n. 11.

[10] Victor Emmanuel II (1820–78): King of Sardinia (1849–61); then the first king of a united Italy until his death.

[11] Demosthenes: See chap. 6, n. 16.

prudent, decisive and cautious—we must not think that under him the Asian campaign degenerated into that civilizing mission, with no limits or bounds, that his brilliant son[12] sought to accomplish. By all accounts, Philip would not have extended his conquest any further than the peninsula of Asia Minor and the Syrian coast. In this form the Greco-Macedonian state, approximately in the borders later held by the Byzantine Empire, would have had all the conditions of internal strength: the enlightenment of Greece; the military art of Macedonia; the untapped potential of such young, energetic peoples as Thrace, Epirus, Mysia, and Illyria; and the wealth of Syria and Asia Minor, where the Greek element already predominated. Such a state would have had all the necessary elements to mount successful resistance against even the devastating power of Roman arms. Philip could have established firm principles for the political independence of a Hellenic state for centuries to come, and the ancient Eastern question would have been resolved in a just and truly beneficial way for all humanity. But the brilliant genius of Alexander, whose political dreams knew no limit or measure, stripped the actual center of gravity from the structure begun by his father. Once scattered across the vast expanse of the East, spread from the Danube to the Indus, Hellenic enlightenment and Macedonian power no longer had sufficient concentration and stability to withstand the elements of corruption, which upon the death of the conqueror destroyed what he had built. Its remnants either returned to the Iranian type of development or fell to the power of Rome, which took many centuries to build the kind of worldwide monarchy that took Alexander only years.

But great historical ideas do not go away. While a person may exercise his freedom against the general historical plan of events inscribed (unbeknownst to him) by the hand of Providence, to slow it down and temporarily alter its course, this plan will still be completed, although by other, more roundabout paths. One of the unfinished tasks of Greek life—laying the foundation for positive science—was completed in one of the fragments of Alexander's empire, under the aegis of the science-loving Ptolemies.[13] But still the destiny of Greece was not completed. And so six and a half centuries after Philip, a kindred spirit by character and frame of mind took the throne as emperor of Rome. Constantine,[14] both passionate and prudent, decisive and cautious, moved the capital to the coast of the Bosporus and lay the foundation there for a neo-Greek monarchy in which the cultural life of the Greek people completed the application of philosophical thought to the establishment of Orthodox doctrine, and Hellenic artistry to the establishment of the forms of Orthodox worship and liturgy.

---

[12] Alexander the Great: See chap. 5, n. 4.

[13] Ptolemaic dynasty: See chap. 5, n. 3.

[14] Constantine I: See chap. 4, n. 11.

But both Rome and Byzantium exhausted their creative forces and had to leave their legacies to other peoples. The inheritors of Rome were the Germans, and the inheritors of Byzantium were the Slavs; and these peoples had to revive the age-old struggle, waged with all available weapons, between Greece and Rome.

The inheritance in each case occurred in different ways. Germans occupied the very lands of the Roman culture and became closely associated with their conquerors, and thus quickly developed their state system. The Slavs remained for a long time at the tribal stage of development, and the Greek influence on them was only inductive, so to speak, transferred much more gradually and much less completely. Little more than three hundred years after the fall of Rome, the main aspects of the ethnographic process forming the new Germanic-Roman peoples had been completed, and Charlemagne[15] united them into a single state body, which from that time on always preserved a vital political life in one part or another. But both historical tribes preparing to undertake the struggle were still united by a common enlightening principle—the one Universal Orthodox Church. As the opposition between them increased, even this bond had to be broken. The same Charlemagne who laid the first foundations of the European state system also established the principle of the West's secession from ecumenical unity and the principle of the religious disagreement that has divided the Germanic-Roman world from the Slavic-Greek world since that time.

Here we encounter one of those great examples of historical synchronism which all the more clearly and strikingly reveals the reasonableness of history's world governance. When studying the phenomena of nature or history, we gradually go from particular facts to more general truths, which is what first causes are. Individual phenomena appear like radiant beams all meeting at a few central points, which in turn unite at other centers of the highest order, and so on. This going from particularity to the more general principle is also what we call the explanation of phenomena, which our mind irrepressibly seeks. Ascending in this way from the particular to the general, we will reach a few general categories of phenomena, which not only remain separate from each other, however, but from which the highest ascent toward a single real cause is even entirely inconceivable. But we cannot stop at that separation, so all we can do is either willfully ignore the inevitable demands of the highest unity, deny it, and attribute everything to chance, or recognize the necessity of ideal unity, which brings together various categories of phenomena that have no real common cause.

Take a few examples. All matter compresses and thickens when cooling. The only exception is water: cooled to 3.12° Reaumur,[16] it expands to the

---

[15] Charlemagne: See chap. 3, n. 4.

[16] This would be 3.9° Celsius. On the Reaumur scale, 0° is freezing and 80° is boiling for water.

greatest point before freezing, so that ice floats on the surface of water. This is why lakes and rivers do not freeze from the bottom up, which allows organic life [to survive]. Of course, such a property of water is no miracle in the strict sense of the word, and is explained by this body's peculiar crystallization. But why should this peculiarity fall precisely upon water? The real common cause from which all this proceeds—not only the peculiar crystallization of water, but also the necessity of no other fluid than water for organic life on earth, as well as the universality of its distribution—is inconceivable. Thus all we can do is either attribute it to chance, or from these phenomena of diverse categories derive a common ideal center; that is, a certain reasonableness behind the construction and governance of the natural world.[17] (I see no reason why the significance should be diminished by the fact that not only water, but also molten silver, has the characteristic mentioned.)

The flowers in certain plant families are constructed in such a way that makes direct fertilization by their own pollen impossible. But these plants have a receptacle of sweet juice that some insects drink, with no way to get at it except by raising the little flaps enclosing the pollen; the fertilizing pollen grains stick to the little hairs covering the insect's body, then randomly fall on the stigmas of other flowers and fertilize them. The morphological laws of the structure of plant and animal organisms are completely unknown to us.[18] Since Aristotle it has been known, for instance, that mammals cannot have horns without also having a cloven hoof, and cannot have a cloven hoof without missing the upper front teeth; that insects cannot have tail stingers without having at the same time four wings, and that with two wings the stinger, if there is one, must be in front; and so on. But what these requirements between organs depend upon is completely unknown. From all this it is entirely natural to propose the existence of a real cause for this connection, and that these anatomical peculiarities of flowers are necessarily connected with the whole organization of the plants exhibiting them. But what causes this harmonious correspondence between the instincts and anatomy of the insects, and the anatomy of the flowers? For this again, as for the crystallization of water, only an ideal cause is conceivable, or else coincidence.

The synchronism of many historical events leads perfectly to this conclusion; without this synchronism these events in and of themselves would lose most of their significance. Let us take the best known example. The invention of the printing press, the fall of Constantinople to the Turks, and the discovery of America—occurring almost simultaneously[19]—had such important influence that their confluence was deemed sufficient to mark a new era in the life of humanity. And even though such a notion of them does not meet the

---

[17] "Attribute it to chance" is Danilevskii's hint at an explanation by evolutionary theory, which he opposed.

[18] At the time of writing, DNA research was in its earliest infancy.

[19] Circa 1440, 1453, and 1492, respectively.

proper requirements of a historical system, in any case the aggregate of these events divides history into two essentially distinct periods, if not for all history in general, at least for the history of the Germanic-Roman cultural type. But most of the force and significance of these events comes precisely from their totality, their influence upon each other, infinitely intensifying the influence each had on the development of enlightenment, and the expansion of European peoples' activity.

Without the stores of ancient knowledge pouring out from the land of the Greeks to be disseminated, book-printing would have only been concerned with the reproduction of Catholic breviaries and prayer-books, just as, without the help of the printing press, Greek learning scattered across the face of Europe would have died under the mass of general ignorance, the way the remnants of Roman enlightenment were lost to the barbarism sweeping over them. Without the discovery of America, both the printing-press and the dissemination of the Greeks' knowledge would probably have led to a purely imitative civilization, content with mere commentaries on the ancient authors, and glosses on grammar and other matters. Things we are used to from childhood do not attract special attention, or present special problems and challenges, but already seem completely self-explanatory. Only a genius, or a mind devoted to the advancement of science, can shrug off the dulling influence of the everyday world. The originality and distinctiveness of nature in tropical America, on the contrary, could not fail to foster originality in peoples' minds. The mountains, rivers, air currents, plants, animals, and people — all were completely new in America and could not help but spark curiosity and experimentation. On the other hand, Aristotle, Theophrastus, Dioscorides, or Pliny[20] could not be of any use for answering the challenges and problems presenting themselves in America at every step. One would have to turn away from the commentaries on such figures to conduct original research and investigations. Therefore it occurs to me that one of the main reasons that science in the Germanic-Roman world took the direction that it did — the positive investigation of nature — had to come from the fact that from the start of cultural development in Europe, the main participants' attention was turned by the startling new natural phenomena of America toward the observation and investigation of nature in general, and thus aroused independent thinking in awakening minds. But again, if the discoveries of the New World had not been publicized to the masses by the printing press, but

---

[20] Theophrastus (4th century BCE): Greek philosopher and naturalist, studied under Plato and Aristotle and wrote many works on a variety of topics, now lost, but his pioneering works on botanical classification were preserved. Pedanius Dioscorides (1st century CE): Greek physician and herbalist, author of a multivolume catalog of herbal medicine. Pliny the Elder, or Gaius Plinius Secundus (23–79 CE): Roman naturalist and military commander who published a multivolume *Naturalis Historia* (Natural History).

remained the possession of the few, then they could never have achieved general influence over the direction of this civilization's awakening activity. In the same way, without scientific training imparted by the spread of classical education, America would have presented only mildly interesting curiosities which, having fallen on uncultivated ground, would not have caused any kind of mental life to grow.

Of course for each of these three events marking the beginning of a new direction in the life of Europe, a completely satisfactory explanation can be found. But what can explain their convergence, which is the main determinant of their transformative power? Where is the common root that would have consequences like not only the invention of the printing press, the fall of Constantinople, and the discovery of America, but that would also deliver the impetus to launch a historical movement that would yield consequences of such diverse kinds of phenomena coming into existence at the very same historical moment? Obviously, we should not search for it in any actual past event, nor in any embryonic moral or material conditions in the formative historical life of peoples. Where is the force that led the Altai barbarians[21] to the Bosporus coast at precisely the time when the inquisitiveness of German inventors uncovered the secret of moveable type, and when Spain's and Portugal's competition in overseas ventures provided a favorable reception to the Genoese sailor's [i.e., Columbus's] bold idea? Of course we must not hope to find reasons for the synchronous connections between events so diverse anywhere nearer than the realm of world-governing Providence, according to which the historical life of humanity unfolds.

To all the other distinctions between the Germanic-Roman and Slavic-Greek worlds was added, in the middle of the eighth century, the religious distinction through the separation of the Roman Church from Universal Orthodoxy. But at the same time the Slavic peoples were taking up spiritual arms through their own system of writing, which gave them the means to protect and preserve their principles, as a people, from the religious ambitions of the West. In material regards for the most part still not having emerged from the tribal stage of development, the Slavic peoples, of course, could not pose a serious hindrance to the West, which Charles had already fitted with the armor of the state system. But in that remarkable time, in the far northeast were amassing great reserves of governmental strength, on which the western Slavs could rely when their own strength was exhausted in the struggle, and when all the outer protection enabling them to preserve their history until that time had been lost.

By this time, the first stage of the Eastern Question had ended: the stage of storing up and preparing. It lasted from the time of Philip of Macedon to the time of Charlemagne, the division of the Church, the Slavic mission of

---

[21] I.e., the Turks, in reference to the Altai Mountains in Central Asia. Not to be confused with the Turkic-Mongol Altai people who live there now.

Saints Cyril and Methodius, and the foundation of the Russian state. In this period Philip, as if prompted by prophetic instincts, strove to secure an independent political future for the Greek people and Greek culture; Constantine brought his unsuccessful attempt to fruition when the vital strength of Greece and Rome had run out. Their legacy was inherited by two different tribes, the Slavic and the Germanic, and to the ethnographic differences between them was added a difference in the very method of transmitting the culture they had inherited, as well as, finally, the religious difference.

At the beginning of the modern period there also began the struggle between the Germanic-Roman and the Slavic-Greek worlds: a struggle fought by all manner of spiritual and material weapons. It was an unequal struggle in which the opponents are, on the one side, an energetic, fresh, ambitious youth, combining the youthfulness of a tribe only just having arrived on the historical field with the strength of a state apparatus; and on the other side, a decrepit old-timer and his child, who has not yet left the sphere of tribal existence. Could there be any doubt in the results of the struggle?

From the very beginning the Illyrian Slavs, residing at the eastern end of the Alps and the northern Adriatic coast, became vassals of the Frankish monarchy. Over the course of several centuries a more persistent struggle dragged on in the north; it ended however not only in complete political submission, but almost the complete destruction and Germanization of the Slavs of the Elbe and White Sea coast. In between them, victoriously resisting Germanic pressure, Svatopluk I[22] of Great Moravia summoned the help and spiritual weaponry from Orthodox Byzantium, brought by Slavic missionaries. The Magyar invasion[23] destroyed the power of the Slavic sovereign. However it would seem to be wrong to consider the Magyar intrusion (subsequently doing great harm to the Slavic cause) the main factor undermining Slavic strength in the central Danube countries. Even before the Ugric invasion, the strength of the German priesthood managed to strip the Moravian state of its religious independence. Methodius and his pupils had to leave Moravia and Pannonia and seek refuge in Bulgaria, as a consequence of the intrigues of the bishops of Salzburg and Passau controlling the mind of the aged Slavic prince [Svatopluk]. Without this spiritual support, the Latinization and Germanization of the western Slavs would have been inevitable. It may even be that the Hungarian invasion prevented this occurrence, blocking Germany from making a systematic push against the Moravian and Pannonian Slavs, thus protecting them from the fate of their northern brethren.

---

[22] Svatopluk I (c. 840–94): King of Great Moravia at the peak of its territorial expansion, asked the Byzantine emperor to send Slavic-speaking missionaries to Bohemia, resulting in the 863 mission of Constantine (later, Cyril) and Methodius. After various religious intrigues, he placed his kingdom under the pope's protection in 880 and expelled Methodius's disciples in 886.

[23] Magyars settled in the Carpathian Basin starting in 895.

In the mountains of Czechia, Slavic independence was preserved longer, but even there it submitted to Latinism and became the vassal of the German empire. But the memory of Orthodoxy lived on in it more strongly than in other western Slavic countries, and broke out with irrepressible force in the famous Hussite rebellion which, having strengthened the national principles of the Czechs for a long time, allowed them to be resurrected once again after their complete external repression.

In contrast, of all the Slavic countries, only Poland, despite remaining materially independent from German dominion, accepted western religious principles without a fight and assimilated itself to them. For this reason, it has been for most of its history not only a useless but a downright harmful member of the Slavic family, for having replaced Slavic principles and aspiring to spread, by force and by guile, the principles harmful to the Slavic world, of Catholicism and szlachtist-aristocratism, even into the very heart of Russia.

And so, the assault of the Germanic world upon the Slavic, of Latinism upon Orthodoxy, ran from the Adriatic Sea and the central Danube to the Baltic Sea coast, and from the Elbe to the Dvina and Dnieper, marked by more or less complete success. Fortunately it went differently in the southeast, where the boundaries of the Turkish Empire now lie.

Here we encounter the enigmatic phenomenon of Islam. It has already completed the full cycle of its development and, without a doubt, now finds itself in a stage of complete exhaustion and decay. Its general idea, like a completely finished event from which nothing new is expected, may thus be fully understood. I do not attach any mystical significance to this general "idea" as a historical fact, but I mean only the most general result which holds the most essential contents of the fact—just as from the general idea underlying a whole series of natural phenomena, the law of nature applying to all of them becomes clear.

Does the religious process that humanity has undertaken include the general idea of Islam within itself? After all it appeared six centuries after the absolute, universal religious truth was already revealed. After Christianity, what possible purpose could Muslim doctrine have? Some contend that it constitutes a form of religious consciousness, the teaching of which ranks below Christianity but is better suited to the ardent passions of the peoples of the East. Besides the fact that such an understanding insults Christianity (which is either a delusion, like the other religions of humanity, or is the universal truth, applying to all ages and all peoples), we see that such a view contradicts history. Christianity came into being in that very same East that produced Islam, and spread within it with great success. Syria, Asia Minor, Egypt, and Africa produced the greatest thinkers and ascetics of Christianity. Its whole intellectual movement was concentrated there, the greatest deviation from Christian truth [i.e., Arianism] was produced there, and the ceremonial voice of the ecumenical councils was restored there. The following were born and worked there: Origen, Athanasius of Alexandria, Ephrem the

Syrian, John Chrysostom, Cyril of Alexandria, Cyprian of Carthage, and Augustine of Hippo.[24] Here the Theban desert presented to the world the highest example of the strictest ascetic life and the height of Christian self-denial. How could the countries where Christianity became so widespread and so flourishing feel any need of a teaching less lofty and more indulgent of human nature's emotional impulses? The main realm of Islamic life and activity was not countries full of pagans, too crude to grasp the lofty teachings of Christ, but on the contrary, countries long enlightened by Christian teaching, who had interpreted it and borne fruit no less abundant or less perfect than that of countries lying under grayer clouds in cooler climates.

Equally unfounded is the view that the teachings of Islam are easier to understand and its requirements easier to fulfill, and so it was somehow intended to serve as a preparatory step toward the acceptance of Christianity. The facts say the exact opposite. The peoples who have accepted Islam stagnate within it; and whereas the paganism of Greece and Rome fell before the force of Christian belief, the fire worship [Zoroastrianism] of the Persians only began to crumble little by little. Whereas Christianity conquered the crude paganism of the Germanic and Slavic peoples and now continually triumphs over the even cruder paganism among the natives of Asia, Africa, America, and Australia;[25] and whereas Christianity has attracted numerous followers in China and Japan, Islam nowhere succumbs to the influence of Christianity. It thus presents an obstacle to its spread, not a preparation for its acceptance. So from the religious point of view, the teaching of the Arab prophet is an obvious step backwards, an inexplicable historical anomaly.

Is it redeemed by rich manifestations of other aspects of human civilization? Even this we must answer in the negative. True, one of the peoples having accepted Islam, its original disseminator, was distinguished by its love of science and enlightenment. But what, however, has it produced? It preserved some works of the Greek philosophers and scholars, in mostly distorted translation; but they would have been much more faithfully and completely preserved if the countries taken over by Arabs had remained part of the Greek empire. Arabs also conveyed to Europe some discoveries and inventions from

---

[24] Origen (184–254): Alexandrian theologian and Church Father. Athanasius of Alexandria (c. 296–373): Bishop of Alexandria, theologian, and Church Father, lead opponent of Arianism. Ephrem the Syrian (c. 306–73): venerated theologian and hymnographer, in Catholic tradition a Doctor of the Church. John Chrysostom: See chap. 7, n. 7. Cyril of Alexandria (376–444): Patriarch of Alexandria, Church Father, Doctor of the Church, opponent of Nestorius. Cyprian of Carthage (d. 258): Bishop of Carthage, opposed the reinstatement of Church members who lapsed in the face of persecution. Augustine of Hippo (354–430): Influential philosopher and theologian, best known for his *Confessions* and *The City of God*.

[25] [Danilevskii's marginalia, published posthumously]: *And the even more ancient religion of Japan.*

China and India; but in this regard their services had a completely negative character. Occupying the countries in between and making them inaccessible to Europeans, they were probably not so insurmountable a barrier, not so impenetrable a curtain, as the Mongol and Tatar tribes would have been. But if these countries separating the West from the Far East and storing the fruit of ancient cultures had continued to be the home of Christianity and Greek learning (even in decline), would not the commercial enterprise of Venice, Genoa, and other Italian republics have done the same thing?

Concerning art, the religion of Muhammad was completely hostile to it. The only refinements the Muslim peoples set forth were in architecture. But do the mosques of Cairo and Damascus, and the patterned marbles of Alhambra, really convey the true sense and significance of the Islamic movement, or redeem the rivers of blood it has spilled, the piles of ashes, the ruin and enduring barbarism for which it is known? Would it not be enough if the results of the influx of barbarians into the educated countries of the Greco-Roman world were limited to Gothic cathedrals, battlements, and castle towers?

However much we search, we will not find a justification for Islam in its internal cultural results. From this point of view it will always represent a mysterious, incomprehensible step of history. Not finding justification for this historical occurrence based on its own positive results, it is necessary to investigate its external, supportive relationship to foreign goals. And we actually do see that the general, essential result of the whole history of Islam consists of the rebuff it gave to the Germanic-Roman world's aspirations in the East, aspirations which still live on to this day in the peoples of Europe. They are a necessary aspect of the expansive force and natural ambition of any vital cultural-historical type, which instinctively aspires to put its imprint on everything around it. This ambition took the Greeks to the coast of India and the mouth of the Dnieper, the Don, and the Kuban. It also took the Roman legions to the Atlantic seacoast and the plains of Mesopotamia, to the forests of Germania and the Numidian steppe.

The general idea or essential meaning of Islam thus lies in its involuntary and unintentional service to Orthodoxy and Slavdom, protecting the first from the pressure of Latinism, and saving the second from absorption into Germanic-Latindom, when their natural defenders lay in the grip of senility or the diapers of infancy.[26] It did this unconsciously of course, but nevertheless it did it, and thus protected the embryo of a new life, a new type of development, another side of the multifaceted life of humanity in general, which seemed about to be crushed and suppressed by the mighty stature of Germanic-Roman Europe. This idea, strictly in regard to Orthodoxy, was expressed at the start of the Greek uprising by the Patriarch of Constantinople Anthimus III [r. 1822–24]: "Providence chose subjugation to the Ottomans in

---

[26] Danilevskii has in mind the Byzantine Empire in the former case (senility), and Russia in the latter (infancy).

substitution for the Byzantine Empire (strictly speaking, it would have to be called an emperorship), wavering in its Orthodoxy, as a defense against the Western heresy."

This idea seems barbaric to the German historian Gervinus,[27] from whom I borrowed this fact, but it is profoundly true. Let us imagine that Jerusalem and all the holy sites were added to the spiritual jurisdiction of the pope by the Crusader forces, so that from the north, south, east, and west, Western feudal states gradually surrounded the core of the Byzantine Empire. What would become of Orthodoxy, lying exhausted in the northeast before triumphant Catholicism gaining strength and renown from its sovereignty over the places where Christianity was born? It would seem like nothing more than one of the archaic sects of Christianity, like Nestorianism and the various remnants of Monophysitism and Monothelitism[28] still existing in the East. Likewise, what would become of Slavdom? Would not the Slavs of the Balkan Peninsula share the same fate as the Slav domains falling under the dominion of Germany? Could the Serbs and Bulgars stand against the simultaneous threats of political oppression, religious persecution, and the everyday, customary temptations of European culture? The result cannot be in doubt.

The same fate threatening Orthodoxy would overtake Slavdom. Preserved by mountain refuges or the inhospitable climate of the North, it would merely present material for ethnographic studies, like the disappearing tribes of Basques in the Pyrenees or Gaelic peoples in the Scottish highlands and Wales. Would not the fate of Russia itself, everywhere surrounded by the advance of Germanic-Roman forces (not only from the west but the south as well), be completely changed by this? If part of it preserved its political independence, what would it represent to the world? What kind of name would its bearers have? All the great significance for Russia would reside in the fact that it is a refuge and a saving anchor for the broader Slavic world, which is pressed but not crushed, not abolished altogether. Except for that, it would be some kind of introduction to the past, an intrusion from the land of the dead into the realm of the living, and in order to become a participant in life, it would really have no other choice but to cast off its Slavic guise at once. That would be an existence without point or significance, and thus, essentially impossible.

The significance here attributed to Islam might prove false, since the very idea of the conquest of Jerusalem was aroused in the peoples of Europe precisely because these holy sites of Christianity had fallen under Muslim control. But if this were not the case, could there be any doubt that the conquering spirit of Catholicism would never leave them in declining Byzantium's

---

[27] Gervinus: See chap. 2, n. 43. His history of the Greek uprising comprises volumes 5 and 6 of the source mentioned in the other note, and appeared separately in a two-volume French translation in 1863.

[28] Nestorianism, Monophysitism, and Monothelitism: See chap. 8, n. 18.

possession, especially after its [Catholicism's] own power and significance was shaken by the Reformation? Do we not see a whole series of continual papal demands to subdue the East? Is not the fate of the Russian people under the dominion of the Kingdom of Poland[29] a sign of what would have happened to other Orthodox peoples if the Ottoman terror had not caused Europe to shudder about its own fate? Would the ambition and political arts of the Venetian aristocracy and the Habsburg dynasty really have been more restrained, considering the plunder lying in the Balkan countries, the Danube region, and the Aegean coast, than the ambition of the [Crusader] knights laying a fifty-year siege to the Bosporan capital [i.e., the so-called Latin Empire, of the Fourth Crusade]?[30]

Having laid its chilling hand upon the peoples of the Balkan Peninsula, having starved out their vital development, Islam nevertheless preserved them by pouring this cup of suffering upon them against the threat of a greater spiritual evil—the loss of their moral and national autonomy.[31] And this influence was not confined to the peoples who came under the Turkish yoke. The southern Slavs bordering Turkey owe their national and cultural independence to that age-old struggle they have conducted not only for their own defense but also for the defense of the German Empire against Ottoman might. When they were the main dam against the Turkish flood threatening to overtake the hereditary lands of the Austrian house there was no time to think about Germanizing them, which is the goal they always have in mind for all German districts and regions.

Europe's relations with the Turks have never been disinterested. For five centuries it has seen, and still does see, Ottoman power as the means of spreading its own power and influence over the peoples of the Greek and Slavic world. Like Satan the Tempter, it said to declining Byzantium: "Behold the kingdoms of earth; bow down and worship me, and all shall be yours."[32] In view of the threat from Islam, it summoned the Council of Florence [1439–45] and agreed to extend a helpful hand to those who were perishing, only on

---

[29] Danilevskii views the peasants of Poland as Russian people under Western-leaning Catholic aristocratic domination ("szlachtism"). The Kingdom of Poland was separate from Russia, but ruled in personal union by the Russian tsar, an arrangement created at the Congress of Vienna in 1815 and enduring until 1917.

[30] Latin Empire: Byzantine lands from the Bosporus to the Dardanelles occupied by Catholic Crusaders after the sack of Constantinople, from 1204 until 1261, when Byzantine rule was re-established by Mikhail VIII Palaeologus, founder of the dynasty bearing his name.

[31] [Danilevskii's marginalia, published posthumously]: *Even now we see that this icy hand was more beneficial for the Serbs than their liberation. Russia did not maintain its rightful influence over them, having declined—of course we hope temporarily, halfheartedly—to fight for the Slavic idea.*

[32] Matt. 4: 1–11; Luke 4: 1–13.

the condition that they renounce their spiritual treasure and reject Orthodoxy. Decrepit Byzantium showed the world an unparalleled example of spiritual heroism. It chose political death and all the horrors of barbarian invasion in exchange for faith, the price of which was its survival. The same understanding of the significance of the Turkish pogrom also lives in the heart of the Serbian people. The epic tale of the Battle of Kosovo [1389] tells of the vision of Prince Lazar, who was given the choice between victory and an earthly crown, and a heavenly crown bought at the price of death and defeat. The instinctively prophetic, national-poetic soul somehow saw, in victory over the Ottoman force, the loss of the people's spiritual autonomy. And to this day the Slavs prefer the heavy Muslim yoke of Turkey to the civilized dominion of Austria.[33]

Just as five centuries ago the Muslim threat gave Europe a very convenient pretext for subordinating the Slavs and Greeks to itself, so today it pursues precisely the same goal, using all its power to preserve Turkish dominion and elevating this as the highest political principle. It fears that on the ruins of Turkey, independent Slavic life would develop; it hopes that a long languor will finally lead to the result it sought from the Council of Florence. As it did then, so now it says to the Christian peoples of Turkey: "Become the spiritual vassals of the Germanic-Roman world, and prove the sincerity of your surrender by apostasy, and you will break the bonds you have forged."

From this it is clear how false is Mr. Solov'ev's comparison between Europe's course of action regarding Turkey and Sparta's course of action regarding the Persian Empire, ending in the Peace of Antalcidas; and how falsely he rebuked it for betraying all-European interests in its phony struggle with Asia. Europe has not changed, but with steely consistency aspires toward the same goal, whether in the Council of Florence or the Congress of Paris [1856].[34] This goal is the subjugation of the Slavic-Greek Orthodox world to itself at any price. Ottoman power, in Europe's eyes (whether battling with it or propping it up), constitutes nothing but the means for attaining this goal.

Thus, however great the significance of Islam in the development of the Eastern Question, it nevertheless constitutes only an episode in the great historical drama known by this name. At first Europe battled it in the name of Christianity, as much for its own protection as for the spreading of its dominion over the Holy Lands and adjacent countries. In this struggle known as "The Crusades," it deserves complete sympathy, although from the point of view of Orthodoxy and Slavdom, its failure must be considered a great bit of

---

[33] [Danilevskii's marginalia, published posthumously]: *Bosnia and Herzegovina are proving this now by their heroic uprising.* [Translator's note: Presumably the Bosnian-Herzegovinian Uprising of January–April 1882, a mostly peasant resistance movement against Austrian rule.]

[34] [Danilevskii's marginalia, published posthumously]: *And at [the Congress of] Berlin, we should add.*

good fortune. Then it sought to use the new Muslim threat spiritually to subjugate the Orthodox peoples to itself, which constitutes yet another instance of Europe's continual pressure on the Slavic world—and in this case, of course, it deserves no sympathy at all. Then with Ottoman power sweeping into Europe it again battled for its own safety. In that struggle the main actors would appear to be the Slavs themselves, who by this were saved from spiritual and cultural subjugation to Europe. Then when Turkish power weakened and the danger passed, Europe continued to pursue its egotistical goals, and it again wanted to enlist Ottoman power, which had threatened it from olden times (but which it now tries to support), as the means for its ends. It wants to use it to undermine Slavic strength, to force the Slavs to rush into its embrace, and thus avert the formation of a new, independent cultural and political force. It does not want to grant it a portion of its global influence, but wants to preserve it entirely as its indivisible possession. Acting in this way and finding an ally in the southeast in Turkey, which it supports *per fas et nefas*,[35] it finds in the northeast another ally in Poland, the age-old adultress of Slavdom, and likewise *per fas et nefas* strives to establish the *szlachta*'s dominion over millions of Russians and even the Polish people itself, not quite adhering to the principle of nationality it so boldly proclaims, and shamelessly distorting incontrovertible facts.

Of all the Slavic countries only Poland enjoys its favor, because it is the example and pattern of how Europe would like to mold the other Slavs, for their complete enslavement to itself—even to the extent that it would grant them purely superficial political independence, which true Slavs have always valued less than their internal spiritual and cultural autonomy.

The third ally and beloved offspring of Europe is the young but ambitious and politically advanced Hungarian people, which, like the Turks and the Poles, enjoys its full sympathies, again despite the hypocritically-proclaimed principle of nationality. But to Hungary, as to Poland, we will return later.

Europe's turn away from struggling with the Turks to defending and protecting them is completely logical and does not quite deserve to be called treachery, coinciding as it does with two facts that were clear by the middle of the past century. First, the decline of the Turkish state's strength and energy took away its significance as a threat to the calm of Europe itself, but also took away its protective function, unconsciously and involuntarily serving Orthodoxy and Slavdom. Second, this turn of events coincided with the maturity of the true, rightful, and conscious defender of Orthodoxy and Slavdom prepared by the ages—Russia.

With the rise of independent Slavic power, Turkish dominion lost its purpose, and Islam had finished playing its historical role. The empire of Philip and Constantine was reborn on the wide plains of Russia. Charlemagne's restoration of the Western Roman Empire of the Germanic nationality, which

---

[35] French: "Through right or wrong."

in our day corresponds to the political system of European states, gave rise to and received its counterweight in the restoration, by Ivan the Great, Ivan the Terrible, Peter the Great, and Catherine the Great, of the Eastern Roman Empire of the Slavic nationality, which has not yet attained its full stature and conveyed to Europe the message, *suum cuique*.[36]

The idea of Russia having such significance, already sensed long ago in Moscow and in Tsargrad [Constantinople], was revealed and defined in the genius of the Russian Empress [*monarkhine*] and the genius of her plenipotentiary minister Potemkin of Tauride.[37] From that time on, Turkish power became the rubbish of history.[38] This power, which heretofore could be characterized by the words of Goethe, "*Die Kraft die stets das Bose will und stets das Gute Schafft*,"[39] lost its ability to do anything good, even involuntarily and unconsciously, but preserved its capability for a certain type of evil, for senseless and pointless oppression. And that is when Turkey began gradually courting the favor of Europe to strengthen itself, and the injustice, self-interest, and illegality of its Eastern policy attests precisely to this.

Here concludes the second period of the development of the Eastern Question, the period of Western pressure upon the East, or more precisely, the period of the Germanic-Roman, Catholic and Protestant world's pressure upon the Orthodox, Slavic-Greek world—a period lasting from the time of Charlemagne to the time of Catherine the Great.

The third period of Eastern Question, which began with the birth of the idea of reviving the Eastern Empire, must be called a time of pressure of the East upon the West, of the Slavic-Greek world upon the Germanic-Roman: pressure which began at all points on the boundary line between them upon the accession of the empress to the throne, but so far only in the north has been crowned with complete success.

This period of development of the Eastern Question has a new, distinct characteristic trait. Just as previously the pressure of the Germanic world against Slavdom took the form of the struggle against Islam, so in this period

---

[36] Latin: "To each his own."

[37] Grigorii Aleksandrovich Potemkin (1739–91): Military hero, favorite (sometime lover and advisor) of Catherine the Great, governor-general of the southern provinces, received the honorific Tavricheskii ("Tauride") for his role in the annexation of Tauris province (i.e., Crimea) in 1783, and built the namesake Tauride Palace in St. Petersburg.

[38] The Khanate of Crimea long enjoyed Ottoman protection, but after the Ottomans' defeat in the Russo-Turkish War of 1768–74, the Treaty of Küçük Kaynarca (1774) made it nominally independent but subject to Russian control. By the same treaty, the Ottoman Empire also lost control of the Black Sea and granted Russia free passage through the Bosporus Straits and Dardanelles.

[39] German: "That force which, always willing evil, always produces good." Goethe's Mephistopheles thus describes himself to Doctor Faust.

Slavic-Greek pressure takes the same form of a struggle against Islam. That struggle, having masked the true contenders, did not let the historical enemies stand face to face and recognize each other. Obscured by the temporary struggle with Islam, Europe at first saw Russia as an ally in the cause, and public opinion applauded all its successes. Even Austria, ruled by the anti-Austrian Emperor Joseph II,[40] whose intention was to shake the foundations of his artificial monarchy and act against its true interests, formed a genuine alliance with Catherine to crush Turkey. Only a few men—experts at politics, such as the French Minister Choiseul[41] or the English leaders, and occasionally Prussian and Austrian politicians who were more sagacious about public opinion in Europe—opposed Catherine's plans by all measures, and finally drove Europe into its true role. However the very alliance of Catherine with Austria shows that at that time the historic task she had undertaken was not entirely clear in her great mind.

Meanwhile, the Slavic world's resurgence on Russia's western border had an almost satisfactory outcome in the reign of Catherine herself, through the return of Russia's ancient property, with the sole exception of Galicia, sacrificed until now to Polonization and Germanization.[42] But the successes of Russian arms and policy were far from decisive in the struggle with Turkey, despite waging five victorious wars against it. One can find a particular explanation for each individual case of this relative failure. For example, the results of the second Turkish War under Catherine would of course have been very different if the main Russian forces had been entrusted to the great Suvorov, who had already managed by then to demonstrate his genius in particular victories he won. In the same way, if in the six-year war under Alexander [1806–12] the main Russian forces had been dispatched where the main Russian interests were involved (instead of their continual distraction by far less near and dear goals), then its victory would not have been limited to the annexation of Bessarabia only. But besides these particular reasons, there were (as always) general reasons that explain them. There were two such general reasons: a lack of clarity about the goals they hoped to attain, and the absence of policies at once liberal and national [*natsional'naia*], the combination of qualities needed for a successful resolution of the Eastern Question in favor of Russia and Slavdom.

---

[40] Joseph II, Holy Roman Emperor (1765–90), Habsburg ruler (1780–90), attempted to be the model of enlightened despotism, but his modernizing reforms alienated all major groups among his subjects.

[41] Étienne-François, duc de Choiseul (1719–85): French foreign minister responsible for France's losses in the Seven Years' War.

[42] [Danilevskii's marginalia, published posthumously]: *And furthermore Ugric Russia was subjected to Magyarization (but there had not yet been sufficient cause to add it to the list [by the time of writing in 1869]).*

As in the days of Catherine, so afterward it turned out there could only be three outcomes Russia could hope for in its wars with Turkey: the partition of Turkey between Austria and Russia; the complete annexation of all of Turkey to Russia; and the so-called Greek Project, which is the revival of the Greek Byzantine Empire. We must have had the first outcome, or a combination of the first and the last, in mind for the alliance of Russia with Austria against Turkey during the second of Catherine's wars [the Russo-Turkish War of 1787–92]. There is now no need to prove that the concession of any part of Slavic lands to Austria is a real crime against Slavdom and completely against Russia's interests.[43] The second outcome has hardly entered the imagination of the Russian government; the notion of annexing any significant portion of Turkey (for example, Moldavia and Wallachia) to Russia, if it ever even came to mind, has always scared off Russian politicians by the many drawbacks of bringing many millions of foreign populations into the empire. It is well known that when Turkey proposed that Emperor Nicholas should take the Danubian Principalities [Moldavia and Wallachia] in lieu of a heavy war indemnity, not only did he not accept this offer, but even preferred to forgive a significant part of the Turkish debt. This unselfish course of action was hardly the most helpful for Russia. Concerning the Greek Project, this without a doubt would be the most harmful resolution to the Turkish part of the Eastern Question, for the interests of Russia and Slavdom. Russia would create by its own hands a new Austria on the Balkan Peninsula, in which the Greek element would play the same role in regard to the Slavic, as the German element plays in present-day Austria; due to its weakness, this element would in all probability resort to a Greco-Romanian dualism for the complete moral enslavement of Slavdom, just as Austria resorted to German-Hungarian dualism to the same end. Here Russia would either have to cherish its enemy, or refuse to create it with its own hands. But how hard this last course of action is, the example of France makes clear, which had to *volens-nolens*[44] endure the unification of Italy, the construction of which proceeded against its wishes. If Russia decided on this course of action, then without a doubt the new Byzantium would find other patrons and allies who would support and reinforce this yoke laid upon the neck of the Slavs, just as from jealousy they now support the Turkish yoke, and would have even more plausible pretexts for doing so than in their current Turkophile policy.

Concerning the combination of the liberal and national [*natsional'noe*] directions in politics for the favorable development of the Eastern Question, it must be noted first of all that, in using these terms, I am bowing to widely accepted usage, since strictly speaking the liberal policy is completely impossible if it is not nationalistic, since liberalism consists of the free development of

---

[43] [Danilevskii's marginalia, published posthumously]: *A crime committed after this most recent, victorious war by the apostasy at [the Congress of] Berlin.*

[44] French: "Willingly or unwillingly."

all the healthy aspects of the national life, among which national aspirations occupy the most important place.

The necessity of a national policy [*natsional'naia politika*], that is, the preference of one's people's interests [*narodnye interesy*] over all others (however lofty and unselfish they may be), is self-evident for the resolution of the Eastern Question, since these so-called "higher" European interests constitute the only obstacle to the liberation of the Slavs and Greeks, through the banishment of the Turks from their conquests on the Balkan Peninsula. If during the Greek Uprising[45] Emperor Alexander I did not listen to his generous, freedom-loving heart, it was only because he thought it necessary to subordinate the national interests and goals of Russia to the interests of peace and the European world: the hazy higher goals of counteracting the revolutionary aspirations threatening once again to overtake European society—which Russia itself had neither grounds nor cause to fear. As long as Russian decision-making is influenced by these or similarly foreign ideas, such as maintaining political equilibrium and so on, there can be no thought of a satisfactory resolution of the Eastern Question that does not violate if not its legal rights and interests, then at least its own understanding of its rights and interests, both in reality and in the general consciousness of Europe.

The necessity of a liberal policy for the resolution of the Eastern Question follows from the fact that it is a policy of liberation. And would not its concern for the freedom of peoples have to seem like hypocrisy not only to Russia's enemies, but also to its friends, when domestically it governed itself according to completely opposite principles? Empress Catherine's policy was without a doubt national and at the same time as liberal as possible, but only to the extent possible, because there could not be true liberalism so long as serfdom existed. Was not the great empress herself obliged by logical consistency (with the general condition of Russia) to extend serfdom into Little Russia [Malorossiia: Ukraine], where it had not previously been? Would not the Slavic peoples have to feel an involuntary distrust toward Russia fighting for their liberation but at the same time preserving widespread slavery at home? Would not this chill the sympathy of its fellow tribesmen and co-religionists, and give its enemies the right to say, "Physician, heal thyself"? How much has that sympathy grown in our eyes, disregarding the setback of the Crimean War, just as soon as the yoke of serfdom was taken off the back of the Russian people! Did not this internal liberation give Russia the ability

---

[45] The Greek War of Independence (1821–32). Initially Alexander I attempted to stifle the uprising, then issued an ultimatum to Constantinople in the summer of 1821, and the Western powers convinced the sultan to make concessions. Public opinion gradually forced the Western powers to support full independence for Greece. Tsar Nicholas I, succeeding Alexander in December 1825, took a more aggressive stance, sending a fleet to the 1827 Battle of Navarino, after which the Sultan closed the Straits to Russian ships, provoking the Russo-Turkish War of 1828–29.

to resolve to its advantage the dispute with Poland, still persisting in spite of its outward subordination; and did not this give a final, beneficial direction to the Polish part of the Eastern Question? Only from the great day of 19 February[46] and only by the annually commemorated holy act of liberation did Russia gain the means and the tools to perform the great task laid upon it in the Eastern Question, which is the complete liberation of all Slavic peoples. That great day fulfilled the Gospel promise that "the last shall be first." Roles are reversed. The preachers of freedom in theory become the defenders of slavery in fact, but the alleged champions of slavery and oppression can with a clear conscience carry forward the name of freedom.[47]

All that remains for complete success is to eliminate the other obstacle: the lack of clarity in our goals and aspirations. But even in this regard, consciousness has spread to all spheres of society. The example of recent events in Italy and Germany showed Russia the path that it must follow. The events themselves will do the rest, forcing it to cast off (even if unwillingly) that customary and habitual deference to existing, time-honored interests that are actually harmful and illegitimate, as did Prussia in view of the natural, truly legitimate, and honorable interests that German nationality presented to it.[48]

The Eastern Question's course of development, since the great Empress gave it a direction, has gradually dispelled the haze obscuring it. After three wars, ending with the peace treaties of Küçük-Kaynarca, Jassy, and Bucharest,[49] had completely broken Turkish power, European public opinion still was not concerned by Russia's successes, and was ready to applaud the victories of Russian arms during the Greek uprising,[50] if raised to defend the birthplace of Homer and Plato. From the other side, Russia was even less inclined to see the general opposition not only of Europe's governments, but also its public opinion, as a major obstacle to the liberation of Christians subject to the Turks. Their hostility gathered significant force, however, after the Battle of Navarino,[51] especially in England; and even more after the march of Russians across the Balkan peninsula and the conclusion of the illustrious, if nearly useless, Treaty of Adrianople.[52] Agitation on behalf of Poland greatly

---

[46] 19 February (Julian calendar) 1861, date of the Emancipation Manifesto.

[47] [Danilevskii's marginalia, published posthumously]: *So it was in the Serbian, and later the Turkish, wars; and so it continues even now.*

[48] [Danilevskii's marginalia, published posthumously]: *Unfortunately, even now our eyes have not seen the light, and still, perhaps even more than before, are plagued by leukomas [white opacity in the eye].*

[49] Russo-Turkish Wars of 1768–74, 1787–92, and 1806–12.

[50] The Russo-Turkish War of 1828–29.

[51] At the Battle of Navarino, 1827, the combined British, French, and Russian fleets destroyed a combined Turkish, Egyptian, and Algerian fleet.

[52] The Treaty of Adrianople (1829) opened the Dardanelles to commercial shipping, gave Russia access to the mouth of the Danube and the territories of Moldovia and

increased the hostile disposition toward Russia. And the awakening of Slavic consciousness, together with the appearance of the first signs of the idea of Pan-Slavism, revived the longstanding hostility (primarily in Germany) against all of Slavdom, considering it dead, buried, and condemned through decomposition to nourish and strengthen the growth of the German body. Fallmerayer's study,[53] showing that the current residents of Greece have in their veins the blood of Slavic barbarians, not the sons of Ancient Hellas, caused the sympathies for a resurrected Greece that had been stirred by classical remembrances to fall silent. The Treaty of Hünkâr İskelesi[54] had a similar influence, especially in the highest political spheres. The Slavs, not just in fact but also in theory, were made pariahs of Europe and denied all the blessings of freedom and the fruits of civilization.

Hostility toward a rival just beginning to recognize its rights and its strength blurred any feeling of truth and justice in Europe, until Europe not only began to shut its eyes to the suffering of Turkish Christians, who had the misfortune of being Slavic and Orthodox, but even fell in love with the Turks, in whom it saw the only element capable of conveying to the East the principles of true European civilization. In place of Philhellenes, Europe (England, in particular) became full of Turkophiles.

They all began to conclude that the enemies of Europe and its culture were neither Islam nor the Turks, but the Slavs, and their representative, Russia. This view became even stronger and firmer when in 1849 the Austrian Slavs rose up against phony Magyar liberalism (a close relative of Polish liberalism) and the Russian Slavs, coming to the aid of Austria while not seeking their own advantage, broke it up. The new emperor of the French could make use of this frame of mind for his own purposes, but 1853 and the years following opened wide the eyes of both Europe and Russia.

The ancient struggle of the Germanic-Roman and the Slavic worlds was resumed, moving from the realm of words and theory into the realm of facts and historical events. The Muslim-Turkish episode in the development of the Eastern Question ended: the haze dispersed, and the opponents stood face to face in expectation of dreadful events, the fear of which forced both sides to back down and postpone the inevitable conflict as long as possible, or while God allows. Henceforth a war between Russia and Turkey has become impossible and useless; but a struggle of Slavdom with Europe is both possible and

---

Wallachia in lieu of indemnity payments, and recognized Russia's possession of Georgia and the territories ceded by Persia.

[53] Jakob Philipp Fallmerayer, *Geschichte des Kaisertums von Trapezunt* (History of the Empire of Trebizond), 1827.

[54] The Treaty of Hünkâr İskelesi (1833) amended the Treaty of Adrianople, reducing Turkey's indemnity payments and creating a defensive alliance for mutual assistance should either Russia or Turkey be attacked, which aroused the Western powers' distrust.

necessary—a struggle which of course will not be resolved in a single year or in a single campaign, but will occupy a whole historical period.[55] The third period of the Eastern Question ended with the Crimean War, and a fourth and final period of the resolution of the Question has begun, which will reveal whether the Slavic tribe is only great in terms of its number and the extent of the lands it occupies, or in terms of its internal significance; whether its members possess the same fundamental rights as the family of Aryan peoples; whether it has the potential to play the role of a world power alongside its older brothers; and whether it is destined to form one of the independent cultural types of world history, or fated to the second-rate status of a vassal tribe, obliged to serve and sustain its proud sovereigns and rulers [in Europe]. The analogy of all history[56] convinces us this is not so, and compels us to use all means, all strength, and all energy in the decisive dispute which cannot be postponed for long.

---

[55] [Danilevskii's marginalia, published posthumously]: *And this became even clearer after the last Turkish war and the Berlin treaty.*

[56] [Danilevskii's marginalia, published posthumously]: *Although at the present moment the matter is in flux, the analogy of all history and so on....*

ﾃ 13 ﾎ
The Place of Austria in the Eastern Question

From the preceding chapter it is clear that the Eastern Question is the development of one of those great, world-historical ideas that put their imprint
on a whole period in the general life of humanity. It is a series of events, the
likes of which have not been seen since the fall of the Western Roman Empire
and the Great Migration of peoples, laying the foundation of life for the
Germanic-Roman cultural-historical type. Not one of the events of the so-
called New [i.e., modern] history can compare with it in terms of world historical importance, since all of them—the founding of Charlemagne's monarchy, the development of papal power, the Reformation, and the [French]
Revolution—were only manifestations of the internal development of a single
cultural-historical type, whereas the Eastern Question is a struggle between
two different types. The probable outcome of it must amount to something
completely new in the life of humanity, every bit as exceptional as what came
from the life of the Ancient Greeks, comparable to the lives of ancient Egypt,
India, Babylon and Assyria, Persia, and Judea, or to the life of Rome and all
that can be called Europe. What is this hoped-for Slavic solution, the possibility and necessity of which is ensured by all historical analogy and the true
meaning of history? That the peoples of the Balkan Peninsula—Serbs, Bulgars, Greeks, and Romanians—must attain complete national and political
independence, and that the Turks should have no presence north of the Dardanelles, the Bosporus, and the Sea of Marmara. Of this there can be no
doubt, but this is far from enough to resolve the problem the Eastern Question poses to the world.

The Eastern Question affects all of Slavdom, all the peoples of the European peninsula that are not part of the Germanic and Germanic-Roman tribes
(thus, not belonging to Europe in the cultural-historical sense of the word, not
living an active historical European life, but only being captured by it and
from time to time passively serving foreign goals and aspirations). Besides
Russia and Turkey, these peoples constitute the majority of the population of
Austria, and so it is necessary for us to include this state in our examination of
the Eastern Question before we can present a satisfactory solution to it, according to the demands of history.

It is fitting at this point to review briefly the history of the formation of
the Austrian state, that is, the history of cobbling together various escheated

landholdings,[1] lands given as dowry, passed from owner to owner, and finally concentrated in the hands of the most fortunate heirs.

There is a well-known Latin phrase: *Tu felix Austria, nube!*[2] But originally this was not the happy fate of Austria (that is, the Austrian archdukedom), but of Czechia [Bohemia], which was long the nucleus of political crystallization from which the Austrian center itself split off and took various remnants, until it was finally absorbed by its more fortunate rival. Besides Czechia and Moravia, the Czech king Otakar II [Ottokar II, r. 1253–78] even held the Austrian archdukedom [1251–78]. During the crusade against the pagan Lithuanians [1254–55], he counted Rudolph of Habsburg[3] among his vassals. When Rudolph was made emperor, Otakar did not want to submit to him. Using the German power now lodged in his hands, Rudolph defeated Otakar, took the Austrian archduchy from him, and gave it to his son Albert in 1278. Twenty years later, Albert ascended the imperial throne and ruled ten years, until 1308. He villainously ordered the murder of Otakar's grandson and last descendant, Viacheslav [sic; Viacheslav III, or Wenceslas III, d. 1306], in 1301 with the idea of taking his lands, but was himself killed by his nephew [1308], after which the imperial crown left the House of Habsburg for 130 years, during which six emperors reigned, four of whom, from the House of Luxembourg, were at the same time kings of the Czechs. But during that time the House of Habsburg continued accumulating inheritances.

In 1308 Henry VII of Luxembourg [1275–1313] was chosen as emperor, who also inherited the Czech crown after the line of Czech kings ended with the killing of Viacheslav [III/Wenceslas III]. After the death of Henry, poisoned while taking communion in Florence in 1313, his son John [the Blind, of Bohemia, 1296–1346] inherited only the Czech, but not the imperial, crown. He took part in the campaigns of the Teutonic Knights, acquired Silesia by purchase from the Polish king, and was killed at the Battle of Crécy in 1346. Under John, Czech possessions temporarily increased significantly. The Count of Tyrol, also named John [sic; actually Henry VI of Carinthia, 1265–1335], who besides Tyrol also held Styria and Carinthia, challenged John of Bohemia's claim to the Czech throne on the basis of having married Viacheslav's aunt. From 1308 to 1329 he considered himself King of Bohemia. A peace between both pretenders was concluded when the daughter and only heir of the Count of Tyrol, Margarete Maultasch [1318–69] was given in marriage to John of Bohemia's elder son [John-Henry of Luxembourg, 1322–75].

---

[1] Landholdings ceded to the state for lack of an heir.

[2] Preceded by *Bella gerant alii*: "Others go to war—You, happy Austria, marry!" For economy's sake, in this section names and dates are added to the information Danilevskii provides in the text, with footnotes for clarification only.

[3] Rudolph I, of Habsburg (1218–91), king of the Romans after 1273, the first Habsburg to possess the duchy of Austria.

Thus it turned out that almost all of present-day Cisleithania,[4] with Silesia in place of Galicia, was brought under the power of Czech kings. But Margarete had no children. After eleven years of marriage she left her husband and in 1342 married Louis the Brandenburger [1315–61], son of the German emperor Louis IV of Bavaria [1282–1347] who, after the conflict with Frederick the Fair [c. 1289–1330] (the son of Albert of Austria)[5] ended in the latter's defeat at the Battle of Mühldorf [1322], took the imperial throne in 1322 and ruled until 1347.

John, angry at his son for not having children with Margarete, which caused Czechia to lose Tyrol, Styria, and Carinthia, stripped his primogeniture rights and made him Margrave of Moravia. John-Henry married a second time and this time had children. From her second marriage, Margarete also had a son, but he died while still a minor in 1363, so she conferred her rich inheritance on the Austrian archdukes, the children of her maternal aunt, and died herself in 1369. Thus, from that time on Austria consisted of the Archduchy, Styria, Carinthia, and Tyrol.

While [Emperor] Louis IV of Bavaria [1282–1347] was still living, following the death of John of Bohemia [in 1346], the pope proclaimed his other son Emperor Charles IV,[6] to whom the right of primogeniture was transferred after his older brother's banishment to Moravia for his politically-detrimental infertility. This German emperor and king of Czechia lived permanently in Prague, founded Karlovy Vary [Carlsbad], and was known for his affection and justice toward Slavdom, for which Germans hated him and called him *Pfaffen-Kaiser*.[7] He ruled 1347–78 and for 200,000 talers bought Brandenburg, which he first designated an electorate for his son Viacheslav,[8] but in 1373 he completely incorporated Brandenburg into the Kingdom of Czechia which, if it had kept all its holdings ceded to the Austrian royal house, almost would have extended slantwise from the coast of the Baltic to the coast of the Adriatic seas.

His son Viacheslav, as king of Czechia, elector of Brandenburg, and German emperor, held the imperial throne from 1378 to 1400. He [Viacheslav] gave Brandenburg to his two brothers Sigismund and John [Jobst]; had his wife's confessor, John of Nepomuk [1345–93] (a Catholic saint), thrown into

---

[4] Cisleithania: A name for the Austrian lands in the north and west of the Dual Monarchy, Austria-Hungary; derived from Latin, "on this side" of the Leitha River (a tributary of the Danube), in contrast to Transleithania.

[5] Albert I of Habsburg (1255–1308): Duke of Austria, king of the Romans.

[6] Charles IV (1316–78): Elected king of the Romans in 1346, king of Bohemia after 1347, crowned king of Italy and Holy Roman emperor in 1355.

[7] German: "The priest's emperor," i.e., chosen by the pope.

[8] Wenceslas IV of Bohemia (1361–1419): Elected German king (formally Viacheslav, King of the Romans) in 1376, succeeding Charles IV; deposed as German king in 1400, continued as king of Bohemia until death.

the Vltava river; was thrown into prison by the Czechs, and escaped with the help of a boatman's daughter. The Germans deposed him as emperor, but he remained the Czech king until 1419 when he died of an attack of apoplexy from fear of the name Žižka.[9]

For ten years Rupert, elector of Palatine, called the Vise [1352–1410], wore the imperial crown, after which came Sigismund, elector of Brandenburg from 1378, king of Hungary from 1387, German emperor from 1410, and king of Czechia from 1419. He was pledged to marry the daughter of Frederick V, burgrave of Nuremberg [c. 1333–1398], of the Prussian Hohenzollerns, but actually married the daughter [Mary, 1371–95] of the King of Hungary [Louis the Great, 1326–82], and at his death inherited his kingdom.

So Czechia was the mightiest state of its time, not much smaller than the Austrian Empire of today, since its Austrian possessions and Galicia had been replaced by Silesia and Brandenburg.

When Sigismund was emperor, Jan Hus was burned at the stake by the Council of Constance on 15 June 1415, and a little earlier in the same year Brandenburg was sold to Frederick VI, burgrave of Nuremberg [1371–1440, later Frederick I of Brandenburg], for 400,000 golden guilders. And so both states subsequently ruling over Germany jointly—Prussia and Austria—are offshoots of the Kingdom of Czechia. Soon even Czechia itself became a part of Austria. After himself Sigismund left only a daughter [Elizabeth of Luxembourg, 1409–42], who married Albert [V of Austria, b. 1397, r. 1404–39], the Austrian archduke. In 1438 he received the Czech, Hungarian, and Imperial crowns as Albert II, and having united all the Austrian lands together, died the following year. Then, as is well known, Austria lost Silesia, but in exchange, through the three partitions of Poland, acquired Galicia and the southern part of the Kingdom of Poland (later breaking off as the Duchy of Warsaw, then being joined in 1815 to Russia), and also the Venetian Republic through the Treaty of Campo Formio,[10] and Lombardy at the Congress of Vienna, which we have seen it forfeit,[11] but it has retained its Venetian legacy of Dalmatia. From that time on, all the German-Roman Emperors, with the exception of Charles VII (1742–45) belonged to the House of Habsburg.

Such was the formative principle of the Austrian monarchy. But the accidental coincidence of so many inheritances cannot provide the sole bond between such diverse elements, so it was necessary to find some kind of unifying idea. There were two such unifying ideas, contained within temporary, external goals: 1) the defense of the fragmented, disconnected Germany against the pressure of centralized France from the west; and 2) the defense of

---

[9] Žižka: See chap. 6, n. 12. By other accounts, it was news of the First Defenestration of Prague, a Hussite uprising, that gave Viacheslav/Wenceslas a fatal shock.

[10] The Treaty of Campo Formio (1797) concluded Napoleon's Italian campaigns. By the treaty, Austria ceded Belgium to France, but retained Venice, Dalmatia, and Istria.

[11] Lombardy was annexed to the Kingdom of Italy in 1859.

the lands united under the Austrian scepter, as well as all Europe in general, against the pressure of the Turks surging across the Balkan peninsula. Both of these roles fell primarily upon the various Slavs constituting the bulk of the Austrian peoples and the main strength of the Habsburg monarchy, not only in terms of their numbers but also by their fighting spirit.

It would not hurt the Germans to recall that they owe not only the order and tranquility that allowed them to develop their culture but their very existence as an independent people now unified into a strong political body to the Slavs—both those who became bound to their state, and those independent Slav states contending with them over the course of many centuries. The German Empire, after its period of strength and weakness during the reigns of the Frankish, Saxon, and Hohenstaufen royal houses, entered a period of complete chaos and weakness so that it had no internal strength. An emperor chosen from a family without vast hereditary lands had no means of forcing into obedience the numerous sovereigns of small- and medium-sized lands, each of whom pursued his own goals, even to the point of allying with the enemies of the empire for his own selfish aims. Therefore, over the course of many centuries the electoral crown was given to the Czech sovereigns initially, and later to those from the Austrian royal family whose hereditary lands provided the means to bear the weight of imperial obligations and defend the empire from external enemies. The empire's own troops, never on time, badly trained, badly armed (in the full sense *die elende Reichsarmee*, as it was christened by a typographical error,[12] while hastily assembling against Frederick the Great) proved its inability to defend the interests of Germany in the days of Louis XIV and Napoleon, as well as in our times under the German Confederation that has replaced the empire. But the main strength of the Austrian royal house, which shouldered the defense of Germany for four hundred years from the French and Turkish enemies of the empire, was its Slavic strength. Regarding the struggle against the Turks, there is nothing to say: the predominant role of the Slavs in it is all too clear and obvious, but the strictly Slavic interest here was deeply hurt. But without the strength of the Slavs, the French conquests would not have been limited to Alsace, Lorraine, and Franche-Comté. If the Germans can still sing,

Sie sollen ihn nicht haben,
Den alten deutschen Rhein[13]

---

[12] German: "The miserable Imperial army," instead of *eilende Reichsarmee*, "rushing" or "rapidly mobilizing Imperial army." Danilevskii's source may have been Thomas Carlyle, *History of Friedrich II of Prussia, Called Frederick the Great* (1858), book XVIII, chap. 1; cf. Carlyle's *Sartor Resartus* in the epigraph for chap. 10.

[13] German: "They shall never have him, / The old German Rhine."

then it is only because more than once the waves of that old German Rhine and the surrounding plains were stained with Slavic blood, shed for German property and German honor.

When Slavic forces from within Germany were not enough, Slavic help appeared from without. When the Turks besieged Vienna, the Polish and Russian troops of John III Sobieski[14] came to its rescue. When revolutionary France and the genius Napoleon attacked and enslaved Germany, Russians came to the rescue three times, and the fourth time, were the main participants in the liberation of Germany, despite the fact that wounded German pride does not want to recognize that Russia's great service to Germany was done without the slightest advantage in doing so, and was even done against its interests.

That Russians were the main participants in the so-called *Befreiungskriege*[15] is incontrovertibly proven by the numbers. Here are some figures taken from Mr. Bogdanovich's[16] work measuring the participation of Russians in the war of 1813:

Battle of Lützen:	54,000 Russians	38,000 Prussians
Battle of Bautzen:	65,000 Russians	28,000 Prussians
Battle of Katzbach:	56,000 Russians	38,000 Prussians

At the Battle of Kulm, on the first day it was Russians alone: at first 12,000, then 16,000, who took out 7,002 French men. At strongholds under siege: Danzig—13,000 Russians; Küstrin—4,000 Russians; Glogau—5,000 Russians and 3,000 Prussians. At the Battle of Leipzig, it was Russians, 127,000; Prussians 71,000; Austrians 89,500; Swedes 18,000: in all, 160,000 Germans of all types to 127,000 Russians, and the number of casualties were 21,000 Russians to 21,300 Prussians and Austrians. But among the Austrian troops, how many were Slavs? And thus, what is the total Slavic contribution to the Great War of Liberation, *im grossen Befreiungskriege*? What do the Germans ever say about the great service shown to them by the Slavic world, and Russians in particular?! It is not hard to reckon who stands in debt to whom.[17]

Therefore, according to the Czech historican Palacký,[18] the concept of the Austrian conglomerate of peoples, the idea of the Austrian state, lies in the

---

[14] John III Sobieski (1629–96): Ruler of the Polish-Lithuanian Commonwealth, celebrated for his victory over the Turks at the Battle of Vienna (1683).

[15] German: "War of Liberation," alternately called the War of the Sixth Coalition.

[16] Modest Ivanovich Bogdanovich (1805–82): Russian lieutenant general and military historian, author of several works on the Napoleonic wars, including a two-volume history of the 1813 war for German independence (1863).

[17] [Danilevskii's marginalia, published posthumously]: *And were not these services of Russia to Germany repeated in 1870 and 1871? And repaid by the Congress of Berlin.*

[18] František Palacký, *Idea státu Rakouského* (The Idea of the Austrian State, 1865).

defense of weakened and fragmented Germany against pressure from the French and Turks, a defense to which the Slavs made the main contribution. This idea came about due to accidental, external circumstances, and once they ceased, it obviously canceled this idea itself, that is, the need for and the whole point of the existence of the Austrian state. Having served its purpose for that time, it turned into precisely the same kind of historical rubbish as Turkey itself, once Orthodoxy and Slavdom no longer had any need of its protection from outside forces. The intentional or unintentional, conscious or unconscious, benefit from both Turkey and Austria alike ceased; what remained was only oppression, an obstacle to the development of peoples; and now it is time these peoples were freed from this heavy guardianship.

Here again we encounter one of those great historical synchronisms that proves that historical processes do not occur accidentally, but both their outer form and inner contents exist in mysterious interdependence, so that what is accidental in history occurs in harmony with and in submission to its inner content. The Austrian lands were conjoined into a single whole by means of a series of inheritances and marriage contracts right when it was time to mount a defense against Turkish power and the French unification then underway. This formal basis of the Austrian state was destroyed and the dynastic right of inheritance ceased, once again, at the same moment (to the very year) as the cessation of the very reason necessitating this artificial bond to unite so many peoples of southeastern Germany and southwestern Slavdom into a single whole.

In 1740 Charles VI[19] died without a male heir, which by itself canceled the formal bond that united the country known as the hereditary lands of the Austrian royal house. And in the very same year was the cancellation of the second reason why that bond existed, providing its purpose and meaning.

According to an ancient German legend, in a cave in the mountains of Salzburg, sunk in the slumber of many centuries, lies the representative of Germany's vanished greatness, Frederick Barbarossa.[20] He is supposed to awaken and emerge from his cave when breaks the dawn of new glory and greatness for the German people. In 1740 he supposedly emerged from his cave and revealed himself under that very name,[21] and laid the foundation of the new German kingdom. This plain Prussian king was the direct perpetuator and reviver of the edifice that had started to go to pieces after the mighty Barbarossa.

---

[19] Charles VI (1685–1740): Holy Roman emperor; his claim to the throne of Spain triggered the War of the Spanish Succession (1701–14). His daughter, Maria Theresa (1717–80), was the last Habsburg ruler of the Habsburg Empire.

[20] Frederick Barbarossa (1122–90): Holy Roman emperor and ambitious medieval conqueror, known for multiple Italian campaigns, who died en route to the Third Crusade.

[21] I.e., Frederick the Great (r. 1740–86).

From that time on, Prussia took the fate of all Germany into its own hands, and before our very eyes has led almost to its glorious completion.[22] For more than a hundred years after this, Austria was considered the leader of Germany, and only recently has that been taken away from it. But for a long time it has had no business being in that position anyway. It only interfered, and continued its role solely on the strength of an impulse it received once, which has not yet been eliminated by the friction of events. From the side of France, Germany no longer needs Austria or Slavdom in general to give it any more protection. Prussia, which is to say Germany proper, can defend itself.[23] Thus the Slavs too shall gain freedom of action by the ending of their servile historical role.

In the same year 1740, the Russian Empress Anna died, and after a brief disturbance, Elizabeth ascended the throne of her great father. What is the connection between this event and the fate of Austria? The state reforms that Russia underwent, although completely necessary from the state point of view and within the framework of the state system, went beyond all necessary proportion and knocked Russia off the national path. While the great reformer [Peter the Great] lived, he governed the whole Russian interest, at least in the political sphere. But with the death of Peter the German influence, which was already so hugely preponderant, never stopped growing, so that by the time of Anna it could be wondered: Will the Russian national character disappear and be completely eradicated from the Russian (in name only) state? Will the Russian people become a tool, the material means for German goals?

History has examples of this. All states emerging from the ruins of the Alexandrian Empire (Egypt, Syria, Pontus, and others) were Greek in spirit and by the prevalent culture within them. But the peoples themselves making up those states had already lost their independence and their character, so that if we did not have other sources of information, for example, of the Bosporan Kingdom,[24] besides those dug out from the ruins and tombs of Panticapaean and Phanagorian antiquity,[25] then we would have to assume that the lands of the Azov coast were settled exclusively by Greeks. If in distant

---

[22] [Danilevskii's marginalia, published posthumously]: *And soon after the writing of these words it was entirely completed.*

[23] [Danilevskii's marginalia, published posthumously]: *And this was proven true.*

[24] The Bosporan Kingdom *was* formed of Greek colonists, mixed with local peoples, but in the nineteenth century, following Herodotus, it was common to place the ancient nomadic Cimmerians on the coasts of the Crimean and Taman peninsulas, called the Cimmerian Bosporus, prior to Greek settlement. Archeologists now place the Cimmerians in the south Caucasus.

[25] Pertaining to sixth-century BCE port cities Panticapaeum, on the Kerch Strait, and Phanagoria, across the strait on the Taman Peninsula, settled by Greek colonists from Asia Minor.

centuries fragmentary tales have survived about the times of Anna and the actions of Biron,[26] then without a knowledge of the events preceding and following that time, future historians would certainly conclude an invasion of German people from some mighty country of Courland[27] had taken place and brought all Russia into submission; true, they subsequently were driven out, but their domination left behind deep traces that took a long time to vanish. The very calling of Anna [by the Supreme Privy Council], the restrictions they wanted to place on her, her rejection of them, and so on, would surely seem to shrewd observers like fables concocted from national vanity to conceal its enslavement by foreigners. Of course we know, fortunately, that this was not the case; but undoubtedly, after such harsh reforms, the Russian character of the history of the Russian state was secured only by the ascension of the Empress Elizabeth, and became crystal clear only in the reign of Catherine the Great. Thus only with the accession of Empress Elizabeth did the Russian state combine the ability for strong external state activity, acquired by means of the reforms, with the ability to have a true Russian policy and to pursue Russian state goals.

The most important goal of Russian state policy, which it must never renounce, is the liberation of the Slavs from the Turkish yoke, and the destruction of Ottoman power and the Turkish state itself. Thus once the Slavic matter can be entrusted to Slavic hands, then the other reason for the existence of the Austrian conglomerate of peoples will have been completely abolished. In this manner the Austrian state will have been simultaneously deprived by history of both its formative principle and its inherent reason for its existence; that is, stripped *of the excuse* for the artificial accumulation of diverse elements *by reason of external necessity.*

In place of the one and the other Charles VI intended to substitute a piece of parchment, known as the Pragmatic Sanction of 1713.[28] But however strong and durable parchment made in the ancient way from animal hide may be, a sheet of it still makes too simple and wishful a basis upon which to raise a mighty state structure that can withstand the ravages of time while lacking any inherent unifying concept and not even justified by external necessity.

In 1740 Austria actually finished its historical existence. From then on it began to fall: It lost Silesia, plundered from Germany by Napoleon I; later it

---

[26] Biron: See chap. 8, n. 40.

[27] I.e., Latvia; Empress Anna had married Frederick Wilhelm, the Duke of Courland (1692–1711). She distrusted Russian nobles and preferred to put Baltic Germans in positions of power.

[28] Pragmatic Sanction of 1713: Charles VI's attempt to secure approval for a female to rule the Archduchy of Austria, due to the lack of a male Habsburg heir. The Great Powers approved the compromise, but France, Prussia, and Bavaria reneged after Charles died, resulting in the War of Austrian Succession (1740–48), in which Charles's oldest daughter Maria Theresa secured her rule, at the cost of ceding Silesia to Prussia.

[Austria] was formed into a special kind of empire, attained temporary predominance over Germany and Italy, but in the end was kicked out of both
and was ready to collapse under blows from a minor revolution [in 1848] and
the Hungarians' little people-group [*narodets*], but was saved by Russia and
its own Slavs; however, it had lost its inherent reason for existence, and went
chasing after any possible remedies to extend its life, with no soul animating
it at that point, only continuing by historical inertia.[29]

With the reign of Maria Theresa [1740–80] the fall and dissolution of Austria began. Joseph II [r. 1765–90] gave it the most powerful shock by his attempted reforms. Understanding that Austria lacked any internal cohesion,
that it was only a rabble of tribes and peoples brought together by chance and
external necessity, he intended to give it internal unity and consistency
through the Germanization of its parts. Joseph II first introduced to Austrian
politics the system of centralization, which Bach and Schmerling[30] subsequently pursued so unsuccessfully. In doing so, Joseph awakened the sleeping spirit of nationality in the Slavs and also other peoples of Austria. He was
the original, involuntary founder of what would become Pan-Slavism. Subsequent wars with the French Republic, and then Empire, weakened the structural integrity of the state, but then there appeared a man of genius in the full
sense of the word to shore it up.

For more than thirty years Prince Metternich[31] was able to slow the collapse of the worn-out structure. The defensive character of his actions was the
complete opposite of the character of Joseph's actions. By his liberal reforms,
Joseph carelessly injected a spirit of life where there had been no room for
one. For a time, Metternich wore down, or at least put into a deep swoon, this
carelessly awakened spirit of life. Metternich was not a centralist, not a dual-
ist, and not a federalist. He was—how to express it?—a sort of druggist, or
hypnotist, who knew full well that Austria faced only two alternatives: either
to sleep in a deep sleep, sunk in lethargy; or to disintegrate and vanish from
the face of the earth. And so he hummed a sweet, sleep-inducing lullaby;
sedated, using all the comforts of the carefree, affordable, happy life; closed
all the curtains so no light could get in; and closed out all sound from outside.
However outside light could be made bright enough and outside noise could
be made loud enough to wake those who sleep. So Metternich used all the
tricks in his wily mind to extinguish the light flaring up from outside, or at
least cover it with a wide, dark shade, to bring peace and quiet everywhere.

---

[29] [Danilevskii's marginalia, published posthumously]: *Now it is pushed by Germany to
enslave the rest of Turkish Slavdom: that is, from being useless, it has become absolutely
harmful.*

[30] Baron Alexander von Bach (1813–93): Austrian minister of the interior (1852–59).
Anton von Schmerling (1805–93): Austrian minister of the interior (1860–65).

[31] Metternich: See chap. 2, n. 42.

First of all it was necessary to bring this quiet to those three expanses directly opening onto Austria: Germany, Italy, and the Turkish lands. In fact, any movement in Germany could not fail to penetrate into the German provinces in Austria, and through them into all of Austria, since the German fibers spread out from there. Any movement in Italy would awaken Lombardy and Venice, and through them all the other parts. Finally, any movement where it would apparently be least of all be expected, in the Balkan Peninsula (if only at its terminus, in Greece) could spread among the Slavic peoples of Turkey, and through them to their fellow Slavs in Austria. And of these three sides, it was from there that the movement actually began. He had to squelch it at any cost, and squelch it without any conflict, without too evident a show of force, since conflict and a show of force are means of awakening. Everything had to be done by certain sleep-inducing manipulations, bringing in a soporific fog or haze. This was done, even under very difficult circumstances!

The conflict with Napoleon awoke all the forces of Germany. This awakening gave great advantages to Prussia. Prompted by all its interests and enabled by all its policies to stand as the head of the Germanic nation, by the natural course of things and by the natural ambition of this state, it had to support this movement. None of the people failed to understand this necessity. Metternich however was able to frighten it by imaginary dangers, and managed to turn the constant rival of Austria into a serviceable tool for its goals. Not only the peoples of Germany, but also many of its sovereigns opposed the predominance of Austrian influence. The liberal inclination of the one [the German peoples] and the despotism of the other [the sovereigns] were simultaneously opposed to the Austrian system, and both the one and the other had to bow before the inimitable artistry of the Chancellor [i.e., Metternich].

Italy presented obstacles both in terms of peoples and rulers. Sardinia played the same role there as Prussia in Germany, but nevertheless, everything in this case went Austria's way.

It was much harder to resolve matters with Greece. It was already noted that for Metternich it was not enough to destroy any opposition to his system, but he had to do it on the sly, without any noise or conflict; if forced by necessity to take up arms, then he had to assemble such overwhelming force that any thought of opposition would vanish. Thus he did with Italy, when rebellions broke out in Naples and Piedmont. To pacify the pathetic bands of Carbonari[32] required not only a powerful Austrian army but also the fearsome specter of the Russian force deployed under the command of Ermolov.[33]

---

[32] Carbonari: See chap. 11, n. 53. The Carbonari rose up in Naples and Piedmont in 1820, and Austria intervened to put them down.

[33] Aleksei Petrovich Ermolov (1777–1861): Russian general, won fame and honors in the Napoleonic Wars, then was given command of the Georgia corps in the Caucasus

But in the matter of Greece, everything conspired to ensure that this time the fearsome power of Russia would not be on the side of peace and quiet at all costs. This was the honorable fight for the independence of a Christian people of the same faith as Russia against the insufferable Muslim yoke. This time there was no fear of revolutionary, liberal contagion, nor was it frightening in general for Russia. Just as the uprising was to the Greeks, so in the eyes of all Russia, helping them seemed like a sacred obligation, something like a crusade, having nothing to do with political agitations. Thus not even the most suspicious policeman could suspect this uprising would result in liberal-political propaganda. All the traditions of Russian politics supported the same view. Had not Catherine the Great taken up the cause of Christians oppressed by Turkey, and did she not summon the Greeks to rise up? Did not Emperor Alexander himself assist the Serbs' uprising? Finally, the personal character of the Russian sovereign—liberal, seeking popularity, religiously mystical—also led him to propose that Russia lend all its power to the help of its fellow believers, as the liberator of Europe wanted to win himself the even more glorious crown of liberator of the East. If Metternich's ability to force Russia to act in European affairs against its interests and against the personal inclinations of its monarch can be called a wonder of the political arts, then his success in the matter of the Greeks must be considered a veritable master-piece. Besides the Chancellor's primary, direct objectives—preserving Austria's serene sleep, and the hypnotism of Europe required for that—by involving Russia in his policy, he accomplished a different, secondary objective. On the one hand, concerning Italy, Spain, and Germany, he put the full weight of Europe's outrage and indignation onto Russia, and on the other hand, concerning the East, he weakened the sympathy for it among its fellow Orthodox and fellow Slavs, who to Austria's great advantage, could not outwit the master of their fate.

In this manner, by the apparent subjugation of Napoleon's main conqueror—Russia—the House of Habsburg under Metternich's tutelage attained great political influence, such as it had not enjoyed since the days of Charles V [r. 1519–58]. Germany and Italy were vassals of Austria in the full sense of the word. In Spain and Portugal, the same system was implemented by the French. Having hijacked the generous but impractical concept of the Holy Alliance for its own benefit, Austria turned Russia into the executor of its plans. England itself played the unaccustomed role of supporting freedom, if not of the East, then in the central and western Mediterranean peninsulas.

The 1830s shook Metternich's system in many ways, but his artistry continued in all its brilliance, since he proved himself able not only to run his system and protect it, but also to renew and repair it as much as possible, whenever a foreign blunder or truly unavoidable course of events caused a big

---

in 1816, where he earned a reputation for ruthlessness in suppressing resistance. He was not actually deployed against the Carbonari.

breach in it. If that is not genius in the realm of politics, then I do not know what would deserve the name.

It is common not to give Metternich credit as a highly gifted statesman, but merely to call him a clever diplomat like any old Kaunitz or Talleyrand,[34] on the basis that he allegedly could not gauge the spirit of the times and did not understand the power of ideas, and thus engaged in an unequal struggle with them, ending a thirty-three-year triumph with the complete collapse of his system (during his lifetime) and the near-ruination of Austria. Actually, there can be no truly great politician without a good grasp of the spirit of the times and the direction events are taking, but there are very many clever diplomats. Thus it would be correct to reproach Metternich if he, being the ruler of England, France, Prussia, Russia, or any other state, had acted according to his own system—but not Austria, which could only preserve its existence by going into a condition like hibernation. The fact that he could extend that sleep for a whole thirty years in the middle of the nineteenth century proves that he understood both the spirit of the times and the power of ideas, since without such a good understanding of his enemy, he never could have fought it off for so long and so successfully. But it was necessary either to contend with it or to renounce the calling of an Austrian statesman altogether. He was in the position of a physician dealing with an incurable disease, performing miracles just to extend the life of his patient. Should a doctor up against an incurable illness really deny all treatment to the patient? Or it might be more precise to say he was in the position of a fortress commander: He laid mines and countermines, dug trenches and counter-trenches, carried out sorties, demolished the enemy's siege works, and withstood fire from installations outside. The fortress was eventually taken, since no fortress is impregnable. But is it right to judge this commander the same as a commander on the open field, who despite his skillful strategic maneuvers was still beaten in general combat? It can be said in accusation: "Why did he enter into battle without comparing his forces to the enemy's? His hands weren't tied; he had full freedom of action." But to the fortress commander the accusation does not apply, since the coming of the siege was beyond his control. Was the defense really in vain if, when all is said and done, surrender was inevitable? If it could be shown that by leaving the fortress and assembling his army on the open field, the commander could have won the war, then that is a different matter. So anyone who believes this can of course blame Metternich, but it seems to me that the only possible proof here is to the contrary. To preserve a

---

[34] Wenzel Anton Kaunitz (1711–94): Diplomat and foreign minister of the Holy Roman Empire under Maria Theresa. Charles Maurice de Talleyrand-Périgord (1754–1838): French diplomat whose career spanned from the reigns of Louis XVI to Louis-Philippe, who supported the French Revolution, aided Austria and Russia against Napoleon after 1807, and was instrumental in the Restoration.

non-living organic substance, there is nothing to do but hermetically seal it in a solid vessel to keep out all air and moisture, or else freeze it solid.

Despite his indisputable genius, the last protector of Austria could not however arouse anyone's sympathy. To determine his enigmatic significance among the notables of history, whose actions or legacy had decisive influence on the fate of the kingdoms and peoples they belong to, we must examine the categories and ranks where we could find a place for the Austrian Chancellor.

The first category of politicians consists of those who in full measure deserve the name of great statesmen: people combining a precise understanding of their surrounding circumstances with the ability to utilize the means within their hands, or the more rare gift of being able to create their own means, with the unwavering will to attain the goals animating them, and almost prophetic intuition in the service of these goals, in a mostly instinctive consciousness of their alignment with the general direction of historical movement. This last gift of Providence exists almost in opposition to other, more prosaic characteristics such as practical rational abilities—but without it there is no truly great political action. Statesmen earning the designation "great" (like Caesar, Constantine, Charlemagne, Peter, Frederick II, and Catherine) seemingly give direction to a whole period in the history of their peoples. But without a doubt, the course of historical development does not depend upon the will of the mightiest genius. No one can determine it; one can only align with it, and that requires a certain ability to foresee it, to have a more or less conscious presentiment of it. The gift of intuition, foresight, or practical prophecy thus constitutes a necessary precondition of truly productive political action. But this precondition takes shape not by the individual, personal means of the historical actor, but also according to the position in which Providence places him, the side he is on in the struggle of the world's interests. Great statesmen are not just appointed by nature showering them with abundant gifts; there must also be good fortune, combining their fate with the fate of their peoples and with those historical interests that destine them for success and victory.

Therefore there is a different type of person who can bear comparison with the Caesar, Charles, or Peter, in terms of the strength of spirit, but whose actions history has judged as fruitless failures. With irresistible force they can draw all our sympathy toward the great struggle they have undertaken, but at the same time serve as a lesson in human insignificance. Theirs is a tragic personality. Two Carthaginian heroes, father and son, stand as unattainable models of tragic greatness; two human individuals combine into a single historical form. Obliged by the unconquerable force of their spirit, they showed how much one person can do, and at the same time, how insignificant is all human activity. Unsupported by their homeland, Hamilcar Barca and Hannibal[35] entered of their own accord into all-out war with Rome. Their contemporary Archimedes[36] had said, "Give me a fulcrum [and a lever long enough] and I will move the earth"; they created not only a lever, but the very fulcrum itself, and by leaning upon it, they intended to overturn the fate of the world. Using gifts to bribe the rulers of Carthage not to interfere with them seeking global dominion for their homeland, they subdued and organized Spain in order, by leaning upon it, to overthrow the odious power of Rome. A titan in the full sense of the word, Hannibal piled the Alps on top of the Pyrenees to grasp the book of fate, but barely managed to tear off a few of its most significant pages. The hero of a drama beyond the powers of Shakespeare himself, he was not struggling against the fate hanging over him by the will of the gods from a curse on his family or birth (like the descendants of Laius and Atreus in the works of Aeschylus and Sophocles),[37] but entered into battle to determine the fate of the world, and for sixteen years forced the scales of world history to tilt his way. Mithridates VI and Widukind[38] reprised his tragic historical role.

Judging his political artistry, Metternich could be ranked among the great statesmen; but the fate compelling him to act on behalf of a doomed historical mission lends him the tragic character of one defeated in battle. But can we call his struggle tragic, meaning it has an essential, inherent character of greatness? Hannibal, Mithridates, and Widukind had the misfortune of pursuing a doomed historical mission; but nevertheless they were representatives of great nationalities [narodnosti] and serious historical interests. What nationality, what interest does Austria itself represent? Such a contradiction between the greatness of the means and the insignificance of the goals for which they are required, as in the fable of the mountain giving birth to a mouse,[39] is

---

[35] Hamilcar Barca (275–228 BCE): Carthaginian general and statesman, commander of land forces in Sicily in the First Punic War (264–241 BCE), and conqueror of territory in Spain, father of Hannibal (248–183 or 182 BCE), Carthaginian commander famous for invading Italy with war elephants by crossing the Alps, starting the Second Punic War (218–201 BCE) and occupying Italy for fifteen years, before returning to defend Carthage from a counter-invasion unsuccessfully, later serving as a strategist at the Seleucid and Bithynian courts, with mixed results, against Rome.

[36] Archimedes: See chap. 5, n. 5.

[37] In Greek legend, Laius is the father of Oedipus, and Atreus is the father of Agamemnon; both were implicated in the mistreatment and murder of Chrysippus, for which their families bore a curse, explored in multiple plays by both authors, some lost or fragmentary. Aeschylus: See chap. 6, n. 17. Sophocles: See chap. 5, n. 22.

[38] Mithridates VI (134–63 BCE): Persian-Greek king of Pontus, waged three wars against the Roman Republic (88–63 BCE), finally defeated by Pompey. Widukind (730–808): Pagan Saxon leader in wars against Charlemagne, resisting the forcible imposition of Christianity.

[39] Aesop's fable "The Mountain in Labor": See chap. 3, n. 10.

one of the most essential elements of comedy. Therefore the actions of Metternich bear the indelible imprint of tragicomedy (tragedy for its outcome; comedy for the goals it had in mind), and this tragicomic character by definition applies to any Austrian state activity—of the Bachs, Schmerlings, Belcredis, Beusts, and Andrássys[40]—since the very existence of Austria has lost its idea and purpose.

In 1848 the fortress defended by Metternich was taken by storm; the hermetically sealed vessel, broken; the haze, dispelled. The inevitability of the downfall set in, because the awakening had begun. The peoples who had been slumbering began to ask themselves what is always the first question of the half-awake: Where are we?—In Austria.—Who are we?—Czechs, Slovaks, Serbs, Croats, Russians, Magyars, Germans, and Italians.—Then why are we not in Czechia, Serbia, Russia, Hungary, Germany, or Italy? And what exactly is Austria, if it has all of us in it? Where is this external force subduing all of us? Where is Austria itself, putting its power and its name over us, and while we slept, replacing our lives with its own? Is not the Archduchy of Austria what Austria is, Austria par excellence[41]—No, they answer themselves, glancing around—inside us there is no Austria of any sort. Austria is only the glue, the solder, the cement, or the putty they used to stick us together or blind us while we slept. It all happened by chance: by additions, by inheritances, by marital contracts; it was all done for chance purposes, which may at one time have been very good, useful, or necessary, but by now have long faded into the realm of shadows and ghosts, having nothing in common with those who feel the hopes, needs, and demands of the living, of people who have awakened. The gluing and soldering only restrict our movement, prevent us from turning to where our path lies, and make us into artificial Siamese twins, so that any movement by one of us causes pain or awkwardness to the other, and arouses mutual hatred. Our strengths are mutually canceled out and come to nothing.

And some peoples did scratch away the putty that goes by the name of Austria. Who has gone about it like the Italians, having fully awakened, with a full consciousness of what they are doing and where the liberated intend to go? Because for them, the putty proved quite weak. On the contrary, who has gone about it like the Slavs, as if drowsy or half-asleep, thinking and acting as if under a fog, overtaken with night dreams, never arguing the matter but continuing to believe in various fairy tales. Who still dreams of some idea of the Austrian state, which long ago ceased to exist, which in fact never even

---

[40] Bach and Schmerling: See n. 30 in this chapter. Count Richard Belcredi (1823–1903): Austrian prime minister and minister of state (1865–67). Count Friedrich Ferdinand von Beust (1809–86): Austrian foreign minister (1866–71). Gyula Andrássy (1823–90): Prime minister of Hungary (1867–71), foreign minister of Austria-Hungary (1871–79).

[41] *Katekzokhin*; cf. "catexochen" or "kat' exochen" in the Oxford English Dictionary; from Greek: κατ'εξοχην.

did exist, except as a temporary accidental reason for a union of peoples? Others have fallen under a new Polish-European haze, which represents the native Slavic aspect of the Russian people as a fearsome sight, with bared teeth, eager to gobble them up and absorb them into its own enormous-monstrous body.

Despite this drowsiness, the picking away continues, and both internal and external developments work at it by thoughts, words, and deeds, intentionally and unintentionally, consciously and unconsciously; the fog begins lifting, and the drowsiness turns to complete wakefulness. Austrian state officials, who never lacked understanding of their situation, see this fully well; but lacking the option of using the old, Metternich-proven sleeping potion, they began out of necessity to think up new ways of gluing what had come unglued. To date they have come up with three such means, and are hard-pressed to come up with a fourth. As is obvious, these three are centralization (that is, Germanization); dualism (or Germanization combined with Magyarization); and finally, federalism (or the pseudo-Slavicization of Austria).

Strictly speaking, there is no need to disprove the suitableness of each of these means for reconstructing the Austria that was destroyed after Metternich. It would be enough just to show that centralization cannot serve as the basis of Austrian state life, since the remaining two methods each contain an internal contradiction. As I tried to show above, the contradiction is with the idea of the state, which is the solid and harmonious form given to a nationality to increase its power to oppose the harmful external influences trying to break it down or subdue it. It is obvious then that a state must follow its own destiny, moved by a single national will, which is possible only in the following three cases: 1) when a state is composed of a single nationality; or 2) when the numerical and moral preponderance of the ruling nationality is so great that the weaker nationalities cannot show any kind of serious opposition to it as an expression of their national will, and thus, merge into a single whole with it from their own self-interest; or finally 3) when the main nationality does not have a numerical preponderance but has a single, unified national will; the others, even though numerous, constitute only material allowing the dominant nationality to rule according to its own desires. This last case can only occur when the subject nationalities are merely ethnographic entities that have never lived a historical life, or if any of them has, it has since lost its consciousness of its historical role.

In all three cases, by the very essence of things, a system of centralization will prevail within the state, even if its parts enjoy a great deal of administrative independence. When this system is unworkable, then it becomes impossible for the state to exist because it is a political entity, an indivisible political whole; but it is impossible to imagine it having two or more irreconcilable and mutually insubordinate wills, hence the internal contradiction: a divided indivisible. But to prove that centralization is impossible in Austria is also unnecessary, since the work of demonstration was taken up by history, which brought this impossibility to the attention of Austrian state officials themselves. All that remains then is simply to conclude that Austria is an impossible state, as in fact it actually is. But if this established fact has the force of proof for all, the same cannot be said of its logical conclusions. Therefore if we can be satisfied with the impossibility of centralization in Austria, proven by history, then the impossibility of any other system besides centralization as the political principle of the state, proven by logic, should be equally obvious. But people who see that something does not match their hopes and aspirations will try by all means to avoid what logical consistency leads them to, trying with all their power to get out of it—and thus it is necessary to examine in greater detail these impossibilities of dualism and federalism, to trace their lack of feasibility step by step.

The purely passive resistance of the Magyars—their refusal to participate in the general state business of Austria at its time of trial—forced the state to renounce the system of centralization and the general or individual subordination of all ethnographic elements of the monarchy to the German element. That element had turned out too weak in reality to serve as an all-uniting, all-restraining cement of the state, and the Germans had to rush to the Magyars for assistance in order, at the price of full equality of rights with themselves and governmental independence, to buy their cooperation to preserve their dominion over the Slavs and Romanians. However both ruling elements, the Cisleithanian Germans and the Transleithanian Magyars, still were almost half the size of the Slavic element, so that at the present time the Austrian state system is founded solely upon the Slavs' lack of unity, or in a manner of speaking, on their political immaturity. Does such a purely negative foundation guarantee much solidity of the state? And is it not obvious that if the Slavs mounted opposition half as energetic as the Magyars', then dualism would have to collapse for the same reason that centralization did, and just as easily? But enlisting the Magyars' help to keep the Slavic nationalities in their vassal condition will be the very reason why Slavic opposition grows stronger.

In 1848 and 1849 the Slavs invading the Hungarian Kingdom [i.e., the Serbs and Russia] saved Austria from the Hungarian Uprising, and now as a reward for that have lost the bulk of their independence and have been subjected to the Magyars. The spirit of Hungarian insolence and revolt attained all its pretenses; Slavic loyalty was sacrificed to it, "enduring all," as they say. Can it really be this lesson will turn out useless? The story is too simple not to be understood, and the lesson could hardly be lost. To make use of it required only to wait until the first such case, which for the Magyars the [Austro-Prussian] War of 1866 provided, not a long wait for anyone.

The other lesson, no less clear, consists of the fact that the Magyars attained all their goals by strictly adhering to the historical rights by which Hungary was included in the Habsburg monarchy, as an independent part, equal in rights. But the Czech kingdom has the exact same historical rights, once containing within itself the provinces of present-day Cisleithania: Bohemia, Moravia, and Silesia. The Czechs already sensed this, and demanded for themselves what the Magyars received. The martial law which this demand brought upon Bohemia could only put under wraps, but could not destroy, the Czech crown's awakening consciousness of its rights on par with the Hungarians'. And it will inevitably arise again at the first jolt from outside, wherever it should occur.

And thirdly, for all the Slavic tribes becoming part of Transleithania, subjection to the Magyar element is much more onerous and much more insulting, so to speak, than the former, general subjection of all the Austrian [subject] peoples to the German element, which could at least be justified by the German tribes' great historical and cultural significance, while the Magyars, culturally lower than the Slavs, could have no such pretenses. Contributing even more to the prevailing significance of the German element was the long tradition of German rule, which was founded upon the authority of the Holy Roman Empire. This was often considered the supreme sovereign entity, even by many essentially independent lands. Finally the primacy of the Germans coincided with the nationality of the Austrian royal house, and thus was consecrated by adherence to the Habsburg dynasty, which on the part of all the Austrian Slavs was completely sincere.

And so, on the one hand, the Austrian government's example of weakness, and the Magyar example of persistence crowned with success; and on the other hand, the elimination of the foundations (namely, the longstanding cultural-historical authority acquired by Europe and dynastic influence throughout medieval history) by which one nationality could hold sovereignty over others—both of these knocked out the legs dualism stood upon and deprived the Austrian state system's new principle [i.e., dualism] of any reasonable sense and all historical charm. It therefore offers much less guarantee of any more durable, long-lasting existence than centralization (which was already condemned by history). Therefore the only possible adherents of dualism are the Hungarians' little people-group [narodets] (which from it has gained a role to which it has no right, neither by its actual political power nor by its cultural significance) as well as a few abstract politicians like Beust, who can calculate all the mechanically-possible combinations, but are not alive to any kind of reasonable, realistic, vital principles.

Not only the Austrian Slavs but even the bulk of Austrian Germans do not sympathize with dualism and cannot forget that the elevation of the Magyars coincided with the humiliation of Austria and its division from Germany, which they could not fail to see as their true fatherland. The only ones with a positive affinity for it are the Magyars, for whom dualism was the only way to realize their most cherished hopes of predominance within the lands of the Hungarian monarchy (the same kind of accidental political conglomerate, by the way, as the whole Austrian monarchy). All of its other supporters among the Germans have a negative affinity for it, as a means of holding off the triumph of federalism, which many other peoples of Austria see as the future salvation of Austria and the realization of their cherished hopes for political equality and full political rights. In this regard, dualism is actually only a transitional stage: in a manner of speaking, the first step away from centralization toward its realization. Thus dualism must collapse under the blows of the Slavs, or even from their passive opposition, similar to the way centralization collapsed by the opposition of the Magyars.[42]

But is federalism possible? Since the sympathy of the majority of the Slavs is on the side of federalism, we must attentively examine this last hope of the Austrian state system, and also its correspondence to the true interests of Slavdom.

First of all, it may seem strange or even inexplicable that Austrian state officials, who are justly considered the most clever politicians, and who no longer believe it possible to preserve the unlimited monarchy and the exclusive sovereignty of the German nationality in Austria, still have not decided straightaway to grant the hopes and demands of the majority of their subjects, and thus to found the Austrian state upon the most sizable part of its population, the principle Belcredi ostensibly was pursuing. It appears that this, by satisfying the incomparably less radical demands of the Slavs, could even give the Austrian government the means to restrain the rebellious and separatist aspirations of the Magyars, just as to a lesser degree it restrained the Poles by patronizing the Russians in Galicia on the most modest scale. It could turn out that, although in the form of a federation, an Austria founded predominantly on the Slavs could in essence preserve much more of its state unity than under the actual dualistic form. But this only seems to be so.

The destiny of the Slavic nationality, just like the destiny of the Orthodox Church, is something peculiar: they offer the only examples of the religion and the nationality of the majority of the state's subjects that, instead of being predominant, are the most oppressed. Turkey and Austria present this kind of wonder to us. In the first case, Orthodoxy is the religion of the majority, but its followers nevertheless suffer increasing oppression; in the second case, Slavs constitute half of all the various populations of the empire, but of all its peoples they have the fewest rights and are continually sacrificed to the Germans and Magyars. If the oppressed condition of the Orthodox in Turkey can be explained by the fact that the Turks see them as their secret enemies, ready to seize any opportunity to liberate themselves from the hateful yoke, the same explanation cannot be applied to the Slavs in Austria, which, regardless of tribe, were always the most loyal subjects of Austria—not only more loyal

---

[42] [Danilevskii's marginalia, published posthumously]: *And this has already begun to come about. The desire to compensate in the East for losses in Italy and Germany forced it to flatter Slavdom by granting rights to the Czechs and Slovaks. Political paralysis started to set in; Austria still contains foreign elements, Bosnia and Herzegovina, and will have to go further down the Slavic path, and both Germans and Magyars are against this.*

than the Magyars, but even than the Germans themselves. In 1849 only they maintained loyalty to the Austrian royal house and saved Austria, aided of course by non-Austrian Slavs.

How can this be explained? In our opinion, despite these examples and the very clear feelings of the Slavs, the Austrian government with reliable tact understands that it nevertheless must not base itself upon the Slavs: that giving them equal political rights with other peoples would inevitably lead to the downfall of Austria, and that it can only exist by the Germanization (and, to this end, the Magyarization) of the Slavs. It understands and has always understood that in the East there is a magnet for the Slavs, which voluntarily or involuntarily, like a magnet itself, pulls the Slavic particles out of the embrace of Austria. Imagine the Austrian Slavs, the Turkish Slavs, and the Russian Slavs uniting in one or another political form. By their very geographic position, the Magyars, Greeks, and Romanians interspersed throughout Slavdom (like clumps or strands of completely distinct minerals within a surrounding rock layer) would have to be bundled into such a union. For the Slavs such a glorious future is opening up that it cannot fail to attract others to them. The tribe whose future holds such first-rate, world-power status cannot in simple forbearance content itself with second- or third-rate status, on par with insignificant, non-historical nationalities. But Austria, in whatever form it appears, obviously presents an obstacle to this whole future, which sooner or later by all means must be destroyed.

Both the Germans and the Magyars, on the contrary, will necessarily lose from the destruction of Austria. Their historical role will taper off, and their significance will diminish. True, the Austrian Germans can combine with the German nation, which sooner or later will have united into a single whole thanks to the persistence of the Hohenzollerns [Prussia] and the genius of Bismarck;[43] but at the same time they will lose their sovereignty over thirty million non-Germans. This would be hard for any true European, especially a German, to bear, since for them power and sovereignty are like second nature, regardless of how they conceal the fact by statements about equality and liberalism. For the Magyars, historical circumstances turned out in exactly the same way, only to a stronger degree. At the fall of Austria, this insignificant, ambitious, and power-loving little people group of some five million souls will lose any hope of power-sharing with Germans, by which it gained hegemony over a group of peoples numbering more than fifteen million. With the fall of Austria, there would be no one like the Germans for them to partner with, because among the nationalities surrounding them they are completely alone like a landless peasant; there would be nothing left for them to do but dissolve little by little into the sea of Slavs, just as the numerous Finnic clans dissolved into it long ago. Russia was preordained to topple its western neighbors—the Swedes, the Poles, and the Turks—from the historic height on

---

[43] [Danilevskii's marginalia, published posthumously]: *Which is now completed.*

which they were perched as the result of historical chance favoring them, but to which they had no right, judging by their actual internal strength. These political frogs trying to swell up to the size of bulls were popped by Russia. Without a doubt the Magyars' little people group is just another political bullfrog, and whether sooner or later, the same fate awaits it from the same hands. It feels this too, and trembles.

So from the destruction of Austria, the Slavs will be elevated to their historic role, while the Germans and Magyars are downgraded, and this is enough to show that the most numerous ethnographic element of the Austrian state cannot serve as its political foundation. By replacing centralization with dualism Austrian state officials have thus shown their customary political tact by seeking support for the Austrian empire's crumbling edifice among those nationalities whose interest requires its support, rather than its destruction.

In fact, under the system of dualism the Germans and Magyars have a very obvious interest in keeping the Slavs in the political combination with them. But imagine for a moment that federalism was adopted as the founding principle of the Austrian state system. By this the Slavs would achieve predominance within the Austrian union of peoples, while the Germans would lose their ruling position and take a subordinate position instead. Their natural aspiration to become part of the one great German nation would lose its only counterweight, which is the rule over several million non-Germans that they subject to Germanization, which they see as their historical high calling. Instead of accepting a subordinate role, would they not turn all their power toward splitting off from this union to which they no longer have any ties, and join their German brothers? And who would prevent them from doing so? Certainly not the Slavs, who characteristically have no desire to rule over foreigners, but would very happily get out of this cramped cohabitation with Germans under a single political roof, since doing so would only increase the significance and influence of the Slavic element within the union.

But whether the Germans would split off from a federative Austria or not, what would be the point of this union of peoples with a predominantly Slavic coloration? All organic, living things must have their own inherent essence, idea, or purpose—what we call the soul, for which the body serves as the shell or visible expression. Only this idea connects the parts of the body into an organic whole, gives it the ability to oppose harmful external influences, and arranges these parts according to its specific formative type. We have read Palacký's *The Idea of the Austrian State* attentively, but could not find this idea anywhere in it.[44]

A political body, whether a state or a looser confederation of peoples, can take shape and to some extent be united and unified around accidental,

---

[44] In this pamphlet, Palacký based his notion of federalism not on ethnic identity, but on traditional provinces within the Habsburg state.

temporary goals under an external threat. This type of formative principle can even be called the idea of a state, if you like, not using the word "idea" in the genuine, strict sense of the word. The Austrian state actually had this kind of idea, as was shown above. But this—its significance, its inherent purpose, its surrogate idea, at one time justifying the idea of Austria—vanished long ago. Instead of a living body we have only an accidental political aggregate, not disintegrating only by force of habit and stagnation, which there has not yet been a strong enough external jolt to overcome.

The life-giving idea of a state is not some abstract, mystical notion, but on the contrary, is something living within the consciousness of all, or at least a huge majority, of the citizens who support its life and existence independently of the state. Often they do so in spite of the most obvious, the most scandalous of its mistakes, and reveal its full might in crises when the administration or the mechanism of the state in general has broken down, or is shut down and destroyed as the result of a series of adverse circumstances. Almost any state with some degree of vitality has several examples like this in the course of its history, in which the people intentionally or just instinctively sacrifices everything for the idea living within it, and by doing so saves the state and itself. What but this kind of state idea living within them compelled the Russians to take up arms against the Poles in 1612 or to leave and burn Moscow in 1812; the French to follow Joan of Arc[45] or put up an army of thirteen hundred thousand in 1793; and the Spanish to grapple with Napoleon, who had invaded their country with his troops? Finally, what compelled the Magyars and Hungarian Slavs to rise up for Maria Theresa? In these cases and a majority of others, the principle of self-preservation acted upon millions in the same exact way as it acts upon an individual. But obviously for this principle to appear requires that the organism was living in the first place; that is, that it had within itself a life-giving idea.

Above we have tried to show the significance of nationality as the organ by means of which the progress of humanity takes place (in the only true and fruitful meaning of the word), and the significance of the state as the preserver of nationality and all the faculties of development it has, for the potentially full development of all aspects of universal human life. Therefore we do not need to show here again that by this formative, unifying, life-giving, and life-saving idea of the state, we can have only the idea of nationality in mind. At the beginning of this chapter, we also showed that the historical idea (or better to say, the surrogate idea) unifying and animating the aggregate of peoples falling by inheritance under the House of Habsburg's dominion ceased to exist more than a hundred years ago. And so

---

[45] Joan of Arc (c. 1412–31): French peasant girl claiming divine inspiration to lead the French army to several victories in the Hundred Years' War with England, subsequently captured, turned over to the English, found guilty of heresy, and burned at the stake. In posterity, she is a folk hero and patron saint of France.

it can be asked: What is the idea of the Austrian federation now? Why must precisely those peoples who were united under the scepter of the Habsburgs, form a union among themselves, for better or for worse, in life and even in death? Any community (with individual people the same as with whole tribes) certainly will place on its members different kinds of restrictions, constraints it sees fit to impose, obligations, and sacrifices, that the many must accept. In the name of what? The historical idea long ago ceased to exist, and the federation will have restored full and equal rights for all constituent nationalities of the Austrian state, and to each the freedom to manage its own fate. Any special interest not conforming with the other interests, any attraction of individual tribes to their kindred political bodies (Russians to Russia, Serbs to Serbia, Germans to Germany)—who or what will restrain them? What will be the unifying force able to counteract these separatist forces, as they are now counteracted by the old forces of habit supporting German and Magyar sovereignty? A distinct geographic character of the land, or sharply drawn natural boundaries, such as England being an island, or Scandinavia, Italy, and India being peninsulas, can sometimes serve as the unifying principle of a people. But where are the natural boundaries of Austria? Thus, all that remains is the ethnographic principle of the people, which is really the only lasting foundation of the state system; it alone gives it true meaning and significance. But where is the ethnographic basis of the Austrian aggregate of peoples? Without a doubt, the Slavic element has the predominant significance within it. But on the one hand, is its predominance sufficient to put a Slavic imprint onto several million Germans, made strong by their culture, by their long acquaintance with political sovereignty, and finally by their organic bond to the unified Germany; and also onto several million Magyars, made strong by their political experience and from having acquired the habits of rule? I will not even talk about the Romanians, who likewise have support in the Romanian Principalities. And on the other hand, why limit this federation with a predominantly Slavic character only to those Slavs who live in lands inherited by the Austrian royal house? Would that set the boundary to correspond to the living body?

So an Austrian federation would have neither historical nor ethnographic nor geographic reasons for existence. How could it hope to be able to live an actual historical life, or to be anything other than a particular stage in the decomposition of the Austrian political body, and besides that, a stage accelerating this inevitable outcome to the highest degree?

To supplement these proofs of the impossibility of Austria in a federative form, we will take a look at the practical results that would necessarily proceed from Austria's federative arrangement. In the most ideal resolution of this problem—that is, with full equality of rights for all peoples making up this federation—the heterogeneity of the Austrian union would be such that inevitably one or another tribe would end up completely wasting and exhausting its power for purposes not only foreign, but often even completely hostile, to it. For example, assume France declares war on Germany. It would be perfectly natural for the Austrian Germans to want to help their fellow tribesmen; but why involve Czechs, Serbs, or Galician Russians in this struggle? Or assume, as in 1853, that Russia goes to war against Turkey for the liberation of the Serbs and Bulgars. Barring cases of completely peculiar, temporary political combinations, in all probability Germany would oppose it.[46] But would the Austrian Slavs really go against the Russian Slavs to hinder the liberation of the Turkish Slavs? Would the Austrian Germans serve interests not correlating to the interests of Germany's Germans? Such acts by tribes and peoples within the composition of foreign states are possible, of course, under strong governmental power based on the living force of the predominant people group; but is it possible under the equality of rights of the members of a federation, and under the very absence of such predominant governmental power? The recent American civil war gives an answer to this question. As soon as the policy of the central government ceased to correspond to the interests of a few states, they considered themselves to have the right to split off from the union and raise the banner of internecine war. It is good that the idea of the American state had such vitality that it could inspire the majority of its citizens to make every possible effort and sacrifice to preserve the political unity of the union. But where would such power come from in the Austrian federation? And would it not inevitably dissolve upon the first external shock, or at the rise of the first semi-serious question producing disagreement between the members of the federation?

The absence of any inherent basis, idea, or purpose within a union or federation of the peoples of Austria would compel the many friends of Slavdom to turn toward broader ideas of federative combinations of Austrian peoples with peoples directly or indirectly under the yoke of Turkey. This course would correct much of the unnaturalness in the groupings of peoples: for example, the Serbian Principality would unite with the Serbs of Banat, and the Romanians of Moldavia and Wallachia with the Romanians of Transylvania, each under a single political roof; it would presumably offer the Christians of Turkey a brighter future. And, remarkably, plans of this sort, so pleasing to the Slavs, would not meet with the usual bitter opposition of European public opinion toward anything that could aid the liberation, prosperity, and glory of the Slavs. Even in political circles we could scarcely foresee strong opposition to the fulfillment of this plan, in its own time, of course. For instance, Mr. Beust by all accounts would not oppose strengthening the Slavic element through the annexation of Bosnia and

---

[46] [Danilevskii's marginalia, published posthumously]: *This is what happened in [the Russo-Turkish War of] 1877 and 1878. A peculiar political combination opposed it. Germany made use of the weakness of Russia's policy, but Austria would not risk a conflict with Russia, and only acted by stealth.*

Herzegovina to Austria. Also Mr. Bismarck, given the opportunity, would not be opposed to Austria directing its ambitions toward the northeast coast of the Adriatic and the lower Danube. Even Turkey-loving England would scarcely object to this.[47] Concerning the Emperor Napoleon [III], for many reasons he would welcome it. But a certain attitude in the thoughts and actions of European people toward any plan apparently favorable to the Slavs already makes it very doubtful in my eyes.

Indeed, in the absence of any historical precedent for such a combination, and also in the absence of uniting geographical conditions, only national and ethnographic demands could make up for these insufficiencies. But a national idea sufficient for this broader union of diverse tribes is just as hard to find as one for the narrower, purely-Austrian version of this federation. True, the Slavic element would be strengthened by several million Serbs and Bulgars; but to the same degree the foreign element would be strengthened by the annexation of many millions of Romanians, Greeks, and widely scattered Turks. And most importantly, the majority of Slavs would still be left outside this Slavic union. Thus this union would continue to be an accidental combination, answering various incidental, temporary demands and considerations, but having no real foundation and no inherent reason for its existence.

In essence, thus, even this combination is impossible, because it is unreasonable. If we take a more practical view of the matter, the unreasonableness and impossibility will become even clearer.

Indeed, why should the idea of strengthening Austria in the East not only find no opposition in Europe, but even enjoy almost universal sympathy there? The annexation of the Danubian Principalities or Bosnia and Herzegovina to Austria would soon lead to the complete dissolution of European Turkey, and it would be hard to limit the annexation plans of Austria. So the first step on this path would threaten the formation of a huge state with a population of 50 million, possessing some of the wealthiest lands. Such a prospect would have to be disagreeable to European political leaders; and it would have to be very disagreeable to them if such a huge state, possessing all manner of physical force, had even the slightest trace of moral force, which is the only way to invigorate it.

It takes only a careful consideration of the reasons why Turkey enjoys such sympathy at present to understand why Europe should regard the prospect of such a state with sympathy instead of fear.

Of course no one would charge us with being excessively biased toward Europe (many would sooner charge us with being ill-disposed toward it), but we cannot in good conscience claim that Europe has any sympathy with barbarism, the Turkish system, Turkish oppression, or Turkish disarray in and of themselves. This sympathy is really just fear of the Slavic. Strictly

---

[47] [Danilevskii's marginalia, published posthumously]: *And all this was proven true.*

speaking, this is completely against the natural human sympathy of the majority of people on the side of the oppressed, even in Europe; but it is overrun by political calculation, by fear of the glimmers on the horizon of the dawn of Slavic unification, and fear of the colossal rival that will arise if this unification proceeds. Turkey is a hindrance to the arousing of all-Slavic consciousness, and thus for this reason only is dear to Europe. But Europe cannot fail to see that Turkey and the Turks badly fill their role. Do my readers remember the scene from the now-forgotten novel that once made a big sensation, *The Eternal Jew* by Eugène Sue,[48] when the Jesuit Rodin reproaches the Jesuit d'Aigrigny for his handling of the order's affairs, by using force and harsh material means where the situation calls for a delicate intrigue based on moral underpinnings: not just to force the heirs to arrive late for the opening of the will but to make them voluntarily decline the incredible fortune so that it will go to the Jesuit order. In the eyes of Europe, Austria appears as a type of Rodin, the dangerous provincial superior, with its Catholic, German, Hungarian, and Polish elements. Turkey has come up empty-handed, not only in depriving the Slavs of nationality, but even in simply keeping them in a condition of dependence, so that Europe is forced to expend its own diplomatic, moral, religious, financial resources, and, occasionally, military force toward these ends. Thus they place all their hope on Austria. Will the Germans and Magyars be more successful at this than the Turks?

Until the idea of Slavic common bonds [*obshcheniia*] fades away, until Slavic peoples lose their Slavic character, here is what can be done on various fronts: either religious, political, or civilizational seduction, beginning at the upper classes and gradually working its way into the lower classes of society (as happened, for example, with the pro-Hungarians, and in general with the bulk of the so-called intelligentsia in various Slavic countries);[49] or the complete apostasy against Slavdom, as in Poland for example; or finally the complete absorption of Slavs by other nationalities, as in the lands of the Elbe and the [White and Barents] sea coast. Until then, all Europe sits under the Damoclean sword, fearing that one or another event (by the power of fact) or one or another political or moral figure (by the power of words and example) will arouse a feeling of all-Slavic common bonds [*obshcheniia*]. After all, such a

---

[48] Eugène Sue (1804–57): French Romantic novelist enjoying great popularity in the mid-1840s for his serialized novels *Les Mystères de Paris* (The Mysteries of Paris) and *Le Juif errant* (The Wandering [or Eternal] Jew), exploring themes of class exploitation and Jesuit machinations. In the latter novel, the descendants of the Rennepont family, scattered worldwide, must reconvene at an appointed date to inherit their share of a fortune, which goes to the Jesuits if none appear. The Jesuits are depicted as a spy network, conniving to acquire the money by manipulation or even murder.

[49] [Danilevskii's marginalia, published posthumously]: *And now it is appearing in Serbia.*

feeling broke out in Italy after the appearance of Cavour and Garibaldi;[50] it broke out in Germany too, despite the very strong particularism prevailing within it, bringing such daring plans into reality as only the genius Bismarck could do. There is only one sure way to guard against an explosion: Destroy the powder keg, or the general accumulation of incendiary materials, or else something will set them off—if not human carelessness or premeditation, then lightning from heaven at the predestined time.

We must not fail to realize also that the goals and intentions of Europe concerning the Slavs would be simplified in many ways by replacing Turkey with an Austro-Turkish federation. At present, having to defend Turkish barbarism and oppression often puts Europe in the most awkward position. It strips the mask of hypocrisy from its face and gives the poor Slavs a good look at the true features of the *Zmei Gorynych*[51] that cannot abide the Slavic soul and is ready to devour them all. But then the hypocrisy would get full scope and free rein; all the phrases about liberalism, humanity, and civilization could be floated out there; all the tender step-motherly concern, which is the only way to protect their beloved foster child from the greed of the Russian colossus. How many will be fooled by the wolf in sheep's clothing, if it manages to entice so many even without this disguise!

Meanwhile in complete calm Europe can conduct its experiments in the denationalization and assimilation of the Slavs by the help of an Austro-Turkish federation, because neither the formation of such a seemingly powerful political body, nor even the accumulation of such a quantity of Slavs under one state power, could disturb it in any way, since this federation could not have any internal power. Any Slavic tribe in this federation would have at least one or more internal or external enemies, and the interests of internal enemies would more closely coincide with the interests of external enemies than with the common good and benefits for the federation. So besides outside danger, any external conflict would constantly threaten to bring internal change on one side or another. In fact, let us take a look at the situation of each Slavic tribe that would be forced into this union.

We will begin with the Czechs. Without a doubt, Germany will never forget that the lands where the Czechs have settled once constituted one of the electorates of the Holy Roman Empire of the German nationality. It will never forget the blood it poured out to hinder the growth and development of independent Slavic life within it, and thus can never give up the possession of this land comprising the foremost bastion of the Slavic world, unless compelled to do so by an outside force. And so Czechs and Moravians will have a continual enemy in the Germans not included in the composition of the federation. On the other hand, will not the Germans within it, settled in

---

[50] Cavour and Garibaldi: See chap. 1, nn. 7 and 8.

[51] *Zmei Gorynych*: Slavic mythical three-headed dragon, typically depicted as green and fire-breathing.

Czechia and Moravia as well as Austro-German lands, always be trying to strengthen the German and weaken the Slavic element within these lands? Thus their goals and aspirations will coincide with the goals of the Germans of Germany. If their actions were unsuccessful and the Slavic influence gained a discernible advantage in the affairs of the federation, would they not, along with Germany, begin to aspire to unite not only themselves, but also these Slavic lands with it? Would not the Magyars start acting the same exact way toward those counties[52] settled by Slovaks included in the composition of the Kingdom of Hungary? Would not they gladly assist the annexation of Czechia and Moravia to Germany, to be given complete freedom, and even rendered assistance, in Magyarizing the Slovaks? By this they would weaken the Slavic influence on the federation's affairs, get rid of an influential rival, and at the same time receive their share of the spoils. So Czechs and Slovaks would have Germans against them on the outside, Germans and Magyars on the inside.

The situation of the Serbs, Croats, and Slovenes would be even worse. Germans included in the composition of the federation, of course, would not refrain from the gradual Germanization of the Slavs of Styria and Carniola, which of course the Germans of Germany would encourage and assist. Of course they would try to seize even the Slavic parts of these provinces should they ever separate from the union. For their part of course the Italians would not drop their claim on the Adriatic coast, receiving help in the general struggle against Slavdom from the Germans and not refusing it. Finally the Magyars, to withhold or divert the Serbian parts of the present-day Kingdom of Hungary (Vojvodenia, the Military Frontier, Slovenia, and Croatia), of course would gladly join with the internal and external enemies of the Serbs, the Italians and Germans, for the reasons indicated above in regards to the Czechs.

The Russian Galicians are in a similar situation concerning the Poles and Magyars, which of course will help each other Polonize and Magyarize them. And Russia itself would provide an example of the most ridiculous apolitical unselfishness, if under such a state of affairs it did not make use of the natural sympathies of the Russian Galicians to assert its age-old rights to its patrimony.

The Romanians, of course, from time to time begin to flatter their national vanity, trying by all means to stand in opposition to the Serbs and Bulgars. They would essentially be sacrificed to Magyarization, and would in all likelihood end up playing the same role as Poles, swallowed up by the Germans, but hostile toward the Russians.

Finally the Bulgars would have the Greeks as enemies outside, and Romanians as enemies inside, supported and stirred up by the Magyars.

---

[52] Literally, *komitatam* (comitatuses).

I will not even talk about the discord among the Slavic tribes themselves—Slovaks with Czechs, Serbs with both Croats and Bulgars—fanned by
religious differences and ambitious aspirations of predominance by some
tribes, and delicate pretensions to independence by others.[53]

And so, a Slavic federation would be constantly threatened: in time of
peace, by underground work leading to denationalization by the teaching of
liberalism, humanity, and all-human European Civilization, as well as the patronage of extreme particularism, but always to the detriment of the all-Slavic
soul and interests; in times of great international conflicts, by the seizure of
one or another territory with open or secret assistance and encouragement
from many members of the union itself. Adding to that the sympathy of Europe in general for any anti-Slavic aspirations, can there be any doubt as to
what the obvious outcome of this order of things would be?

It may be asked, why do not these fatal influences have any effect now on
the aggregate of peoples under Austrian rule? First of all, they do affect it
even now, as can be seen from the example of Austrian wars, in which one or
another of its basic constituent parts either did not take active part in the
general effort, like Hungary in 1866, or directly assisted the enemies of
Austria, like the Italian provinces in 1859. Secondly, all these elements of
disintegration cannot act with so much energy, when it is in the interests of
the ruling nationalities (German and Hungarian) not to allow the Slavic
elements to leave the composition of the state, because they hope increasingly
to turn these elements into raw materials for their state, and tools for the
pursuit of their goals. If the Slavic element threatened to become dominant, as
would have to happen in a federation of Austrian and Turkish peoples, then
the all-German sympathy of the German part of the population (not
restraining its thirst for the sovereignty it was denied) and the offended
ambition of the Magyars (whose role in the federation could only be
secondary and subordinate) certainly would not renounce their particular
views and individual goals, neither from persecution, nor from a feeling of
official patriotism toward their official homeland.

In this manner, the broader Austro-Turkish federation, just like the
narrower, purely Austrian federation, can be nothing more than a phase in
the decomposition of these unnatural political groupings, Austria and
Turkey, which have lost all meaning and all reasonable historical sense: a
phase preceding a new grouping of their constituent elements. But this phase
can become very dangerous since it can lead these elements to an
incomparably worse fate than the one under which they now suffer.[54] We
have seen that, in Europe's view, an Austro-Turkish federation can only be
the most convenient means of denationalizing the Slavs, and at the same time

---

[53] [Danilevskii's marginalia, published posthumously]: *This also was proven true.*

[54] [Danilevskii's marginalia, published posthumously]: *This also is being proven true; but
no need to lose heart if we understand that this is all just the moment of disintegration.*

a weapon against Russia, which is to say, toward the disunity of the Slavs. If the enemies of Slavdom and Russia succeed in achieving this last goal, you can be sure they will be content with it only for the time being. So long as the Slavic peoples preserve their national characteristics; so long as the consciousness of Slavdom within them has not completely died, however obscured by petty tribal rivalry, enmity, and feigned terror; however wrapped up and put away, all the same it would not lose all possibility of being enlightened and awakened, as has already happened many times with many tribes that were considered dead and buried (as was the case even with the Slavs themselves). Therefore the simplest and most evident calculation would compel Europe, while conspicuously patronizing this federation, applauding it, and aiding it in order to place it on the disastrous path of hostility toward Russia, nevertheless to try quietly to cause the weakening and dissolution of the union, by tearing away parts of it and parceling them off little by little to those that could offer a stronger guarantee than the federation (even in its anti-Russian orientation), that in its hands the Slavic spirit would not awaken.

Both Turkey and Austria have lost all meaning. Never having an internal basis or reason to exist, they have now lost the temporary and accidental significance justifying their political existence. In other words they have died, and like any carcass, they are dangerously unhygienic, producing their own kind of illness and contagion. Almost everyone agrees that Turkey has died, but a clear view of things shows that Austria is just as dead, and neither centralization nor dualism, neither simply Austrian nor Austrian-Turkish federalism will revive it. With the disappearance of the historical idea that grouped these people-elements into a political body, these elements will become free and can only be brought together again by the action of a new living principle which, according to the predominant, supreme significance of nationality in any type of political combinations (from the integral, condensed state to the entire political system) can be none other than the ethnographic principle. In the present case, this principle can only be the idea of Slavdom: not any particular idea of an Austrian, Turkish, or Austro-Turkish kind of Slavdom, but the idea of *All-Slavdom*.[55]

---

[55] *Vseslavianstvo* and *Vseslavianskii* appear dozens of times in the remaining chapters and are hereafter rendered "All-Slavdom" or "All-Slavic," a choice that may strike some as wrong since the dictionary renders these terms with the prefix "Pan-". Danilevskii used the Russian words *panslavist* and *panslavizm* only rarely, once each in chapters 12 and 13, and twice in chapter 11, as follows: "[W]e shun the charge of Pan-Slavism [*obvineniia v panslavizme*], as if any honorable Russian who understands the word could never be a Pan-Slavist [*panslavist*]...." While some embrace a term of contempt as a badge of honor (like "Gothic," "Impressionist," or "decadent"), Danilevskii clearly did not, as if he considered loaded language an unnecessary distraction from the scientific approach he was trying to articulate. Grouping all similar phenomena

The western-Slavic political essayists, who deceive by their narrow, tribal-national perspective or by other unfounded theories, do not want to recognize the centrality in the Slavic world of Russia, the true sun of the Slavs, and have become like ancient astronomers, who under the false notion of geocentrism have piled epicycles upon epicycles, in order by these artificial combinations somehow to reconcile their observations of phenomena with their false theoretical notions. These political essayists also must pile up political epicycles in the form of various federal combinations with imaginary centers of gravity to support the unnatural theory that the center of gravity for the Slavic system lies somewhere among the Austrian lands. When the famous Czech historian Palacký said that if there were no Austria, in the interests of Slavdom it would have to be created,[56] was he not affirming that Slavdom has no real foundation? And was he not offering a system of veritable epicycles (in the fullest sense of the word) with an unreal, imaginary center of gravity? Poor, pitiable Slavdom, if its interests require such a political absurdity as Austria!

The level of concentration, density, and unity a political body can and will attain depends most of all, as was shown above (in chapter 10), on two conditions: the level of similarity between the elemental people groups included in the composition of its political body, and the level of danger threatening it from other states. By ethnographic conditions, the Slavs must form a federation, but this federation must encompass all lands and peoples from the Adriatic Sea to the Pacific Ocean, from the Arctic Sea to the Archipelago [i.e., the Aegean Sea]. In compliance with these conditions, and also in accordance with the facts of history and with the political situation right next to the powerful, hostile Germanic-Roman world, this federation would have to be as closely-knit as possible, under the leadership and hegemony of a whole, united Russian state. Such an All-Slavic federation fully meeting the requirements of the ethnographic principle, like any complete answer to the question, simultaneously abolishes all other incompatibilities and hindrances that arise in our minds at every turn for the Austrian or Austro-Turkish federations.

And into this All-Slavic federation must enter, willingly or unwillingly, all those non-Slavic nationalities (Greeks, Romanians, and Magyars) crammed into the Slavic body, whose historical fate has been inseparably connected, for better or for worse, with ours. But this foreign ethnographic admixture losing itself, so to speak, in the mass of the Slavs, cannot have the same harmful, disintegrative influence for an All-Slavic union that it has had for individual Slavic unions. Not only that, but the main non-Slavic members of the Slavic federation—the Greeks and Romanians—cannot even be considered a foreign

---

together was his primary concern in both biological and historical-political realms; his preferred terms have been translated to connote that.

[56] The (in-)famous formulation of his pamphlet *Idea státu Rakouského* (The Idea of the Austrian State, 1865). See n. 44 in this chapter.

admixture within it, because whatever they lack in similarity of the blood is made up for by their similarity of spirit: though not Slavs, they are Orthodox. But even that is not all. These peoples are not so foreign to Slavs, even by blood, as some think and as many would like. They are saturated, so to speak, with Slavic elements, and as a link in the system of Slavic peoples are analogous to the Romanic peoples within the European system who, like the French, are saturated with Germanic elements. What is strictly non-Slavic in them is only the vain pretense of isolation, exaggerated within their intelligentsia by the temptations, instigations, and incitements of our Western ill-wishers. In this regard, we only have to point to Moldavia and Wallachia under Cuza[57] exchanging the Slavic alphabet for the Latin, and the replacement of a great many Slavic words in the Romanian language by French words with Slavic endings, as a consequence of which the new, literary Romanian language has become incomprehensible to the people. Concerning the Magyars, the saying applies: "Take the smooth with the rough."[58] Having encroached on Slavic lands, and having acquired the completely unjustified sovereignty over them that they have enjoyed over the course of several centuries, they must share the fate of all great tribes and exchange primacy and a ruling position for secondary, subject status. However, this tribe, like the Romanians and present-day Greeks, are thoroughly intermingled with the Slavs. Concerning the external enemies which, with the sympathy and assistance of internal enemies, could become so fearful for the Austrian or Austro-Turkish Federation, they lose their significance for the All-Slavic union, the strength of which is so great that not a single hair can fall from the Slavic head.

And so, an All-Slavic federation is the only reasonable, and thus the only possible, resolution of the Eastern Question. But before we can examine it in detail and answer all objections that could be made against it, and have been made by both friends and enemies, we must turn all our attention to one of the most essential elements of this question which we have not yet touched upon, but which can be justly considered its Gordian knot. It would be preferable not to cut this knot, but untie it: that is, to resolve it correctly (or in other words, in compliance with the inherent, essential requirements of the matter). I have in mind the question of Constantinople.

---

[57] Alexandru Ioan Cuza (1820–73): Moldavian noble, instrumental in the Moldavian Revolution of 1848, elected prince of both Moldavia and Wallachia in 1859, forming a united Romanian Kingdom under Ottoman control (eventually gaining independence in the Russo-Turkish War of 1877–78). He introduced westernizing reforms and nationalized Church lands, but was deposed in 1866 after liberal landowners rejected his land reforms.

[58] Literally, *Liubish katat'sia, liubi i sanochki vozit'* (If you like to slide down, you'd better like pulling the sled up).

⋈ 14 ⋈
Tsargrad

And the ancient vaults of Sofia
In a rechristened Byzantia
The canopy for Christ's altar reprise!
Fall before it, O Tsar of Russia,
And as the All-Slavic Tsar, arise!
—F. Tiutchev[1]

According to a popular belief spread widely among the Russian people, doubtless brought to us from the Greeks along with Christianity, Jerusalem is the center, or more colloquially, the navel, of the earth. And so it truly is in the highest spiritual point of view, as the place where the sacred Sun arose. But from a more earthly, materialist point of view, for centrality of location there is no place on the globe that can compare to Constantinople. Nowhere on earth is there another such crossroads of global pathways. There opens to the west a continuous sea-path first between Europe and Asia, then running like a canal between Europe and Africa, now widening, now narrowing, to the Western Ocean itself. To the south is a similar canal, interrupted only by a narrow portage now completely dug through, running between Asia and Africa to the Southern Ocean.[2] To the east, a once-continuous sea is now broken into three basins: the Pontos [Black], the Caspian, and the Aral Seas, divided by wide portages. But human ingenuity begins to fill in what was left unfinished, or if you will, what was ruined by nature, since even here a railroad named for the sea from Poti to Baku,[3] and perhaps in time the Amu Darya [Oxus River] returned to its ancient riverbed, will lead to the very depths of the Asian mainland. Finally, to the north, the Dnieper, the Don, joined by railroad to the Volga, and the Danube unite Constantinople with all the Slavic lands and lead to the depths of Russia and Europe.

---

[1] From the 1850 poem "Prorochestvo" (Prophecy).

[2] Danilevskii has in mind the Suez Canal, which officially opened in 1869, after this book was written; the first ship passed through in 1867, however.

[3] The construction of the Transcaucasian Railroad began in Poti, on the eastern Black Sea coast, in 1865, about the time when Danilevskii started writing this book. It reached Baku, on the western Caspian Sea coast, in 1883 (two years before Danilevskii's death).

Its advantageous world-geographic location is accompanied by local top-ographical conveniences. The Bosporus, a deep and wide saltwater river thirty-five versts long[4] with many coves or bays jutting into the coast, provides wide, safe harbors for the large vessels of world trade; cutting even more deeply into the mainland to the heart of Constantinople itself is a harbor known as the Golden Horn, offering the same convenience for vessels of the coastal trade and for deliveries of goods to various parts of the city.

Add to that a strategic position unique in all the world, as easy as it is im-portant to defend; also a lovely climate and incomparable natural beauty sur-rounding it, and, finally, a great, truly regal, world-historical memory, and with it, immense moral significance. Such singular natural advantages en-sured that Constantinople did not share the fate of the kingdom it served as capital, like other great centers of peoples that have disappeared from the face of the earth. Whereas Thebes, Memphis, Babylon, Nineveh, and Carthage are no more than archeological curiosities; whereas Athens and Alexandria live the life of secondary provincial towns, and even the eternal Rome, having twice ruled the world, has become a museum of rarities with a population of some one-hundred-and-fifty thousand, downgraded from a global city to the capital of a second-rate state; Constantinople, by which I mean all settlements along the Bosporus comprising one unbroken and continuous whole, still has up to a million and a half residents despite the complete inability of its cur-rent possessors to extract any advantage from this treasure that has fallen to them.

The peculiarity of Constantinople consists of the fact that no change of trade routes or expansion of the historical stage can diminish its historical role. On the contrary, any dissemination of culture and the means of commu-nication must only strengthen more or less its economic, political, and general cultural significance. The discovery of seaways to India sounded the death knell for Venice and other Italian trader-states; the opening of the canal from Petersburg to Novgorod and the breach of the Suez isthmus must again shift the center of trade routes back to the banks of the Mediterranean Sea, and cannot fail to diminish the economic significance of even England, which by its reliable instincts understood this itself and began to make *bonne mine à mauvais jeu*[5] when it already saw clearly it could no longer oppose the matter, destined to proceed from the realm of possibility into the realm of established fact. Rome could preserve its leading role only while the main focus of history was on the coasts of the Mediterranean Sea and eventually—after the vital movement had expanded in the eastern part of its basin due to the campaigns of Alexander, the increased significance of Alexandria, and the development of Christianity—it had to share its supremacy with Constantinople. Even if Italy had not been razed and Rome was not destroyed by barbarians, it still

---

[4] About 23 miles.

[5] French: "The best of a bad situation" or "bum deal."

would have had to forfeit its role solely due to the cultural and political development of the lands north of the Danube and east of the Rhine. If in the course of the so-called Middle Ages its significance had revived, this would have happened only thanks to the new religious element manifested in Rome. The improvement on trade routes and the development and dissemination of cultural and political life to almost the whole expanse of the Old World had to be, and were, reflected very differently in the fate of Constantinople. Being the center of the ancient world in its day, it became the center of the Muslim East, and now in its utter humiliation is the not active but passive knot at the center of European politics.

What does the future hold for it? Any increase of development in central or southern Europe, the plains of Russia, or the Caucasus; the revival of European Turkey, Asia Minor, Persia, or northern and eastern Africa; or the penetration of culture into the depths of the Asian mainland: all of this would cast a brilliant new light on the Bosporan capital. It is not only a city of the past, nor of the pitiable present but also of the future, which is destined like the phoenix to rise from the ashes in new greatness. Thus it bears four names, each of which corresponds to a particular phase in its development, a particular portion of its historical destiny.

The first name, *Byzantium*, given by the ancient Greeks, corresponds to the time when the city's importance and significance was determined solely by its topographical advantages. The first settlers were drawn by the abundance of fish in the straits connecting the two seas, which sometimes schooled in the Golden Horn, jutting into the mainland. Under this name, standing among many other scattered cities of the Bosporus, the Hellespont, and the Propontis, the city developed no more than intermediate significance as a point of trade between the Pontos [Black Sea] and the Archipelago [Aegean Sea]. The second name, *Constantinople,* although it sounds Greek, is actually a Roman name. Under this name it ruled over part of the Roman legacy and acted upon the stage bounded by coasts of the Black and Mediterranean Seas. This name befitted it while the last remnant of the Roman world breathed its last breath, and from its former significance this name has long since faded into the realm of the past, and now belongs to history. The current name, *Istanbul*, given by the Turks, is not a name but a mark of shame. It has not gained global stature, but has remained of only local importance and must disappear along with its conquerors. It has an episodic character, just as the role of the Turks themselves is only an episode inserted into the Eastern Question, just as the role of all Islam is an episode in world history. But as we have said, the Bosporan capital is not just a city of the past, but also of the future. And the Slavs, as if having a presentiment of this and its greatness, have called it *Tsargrad*. This name, both according to its meaning and because it is Slavic, is the future name of this city.

It is unsurprising that a city like Constantinople attracts all the politicians' attention, and that the question of its possession after its current possessors have inevitably left the historical stage troubles all minds that are not completely indifferent to the great interests of contemporary history. And so this particular Constantinople question alone weighs at least as much in the balance of contemporary politics as all the rest of the broader Eastern Question.

In this tangled historical dispute, the first question that comes to mind is: Who exactly has the right to Constantinople? That is, to whom must it belong if political rivalries did not insinuate themselves and cloud the truth of justice, and if political questions were resolved, like legal questions, on the basis of documents of possession? In other words, who is the legal heir, and to whom must the Bosporan capital go, after the fall and banishment of its captors, who have turned out inadequate and incapable not only of possessing such a vital historical juncture as Constantinople, but even of political life as a nation as well?

The question seems very easy to answer: The Turks took Constantinople from the Greeks, and thus to the Greeks it must be returned. But from which Greeks was it taken, and to which Greeks should it be returned? The Greeks of ancient Hellas, who missed the opportunity to merge with their Macedonian relatives and form a great eastern kingdom, fell under the Romans' power and became a constituent element in the universal Roman state, the eastern portion of which little by little took on a unique coloration and character, which was reflected in the outer political structure by the division of the Eastern Roman Empire from the Western. This eastern empire was never Greek in the ethnographic sense of the word, due to the small numbers of the Greek element within it. What was strictly Greek within it was the culture, the civilization, which did not and could not penetrate into the deep masses of the people. Put simply, even in the era of its greatness, the Eastern Roman Empire was only as Greek as the Ottoman Empire replacing it was Turkish, or to an even lesser degree.

Therefore when the northern peoples (ultimately the Slavs) occupied the greater part of the Balkan Peninsula, they preserved their Slavic nationality in their masses, while only the top part of society was Grecianized. This was not the case in Italy, for example, where the new German settlers (Goths, Heruli, and Lombards) mixed with the tribes living there previously and adopted from them not only their language but also their outward appearance. The Greeks remained only where they have been the predominant ethnographic element from time immemorial: Morea, Hellas, Thessaly, parts of Epirus, in the southwestern districts of Macedonia, and among the islands of the Aegean Sea. With the central part of the Eastern Roman Empire, the Balkan Peninsula, the same thing occurred as with its more remote provinces (Syria and Egypt), where the Arab conquest quickly erased all traces of the Greco-Roman conquest, because these traces had not penetrated the surface of society. In all these lands, as I have already said, only the culture, and the state power as well, was Greek; but there was no Greek population within the eth-

nographic makeup. Therefore, upon the destruction of the state and the erad-
ication of the culture nothing Greek remained among those who lived there,
and to establish it would require not just a revival but an actual resurrection,
which is just as impossible in the historical sense as in the physiological sense.

And so the return of Constantinople to its legal heir is impossible, because there is no heir among the living. The last of the line died when he was
stripped of his last property, which held the dead remnants of his life, and
now this property has been escheated in the full sense of the word.[6]

The rights to Constantinople that the heirs of the name the Eastern
Empire bear thus belong to the completely different kind of so-called historical rights, according to which the Poles lay claim to Belorussia, Volhynia, Podolia, Galicia, even Kiev and Smolensk; the Magyars aspire to rule over the
Slovaks, Russians, Croats, Serbs, and Romanians living within the borders of
the Kingdom of Hungary; and the Italians could, in the name of ancient
Rome, claim dominion over France, England, Spain, northern Africa, etc. According to rights of this sort, the Greeks, who already have a claim to Constantinople on the authority of one historical document, could on the same
basis lay claim by another document to all the lands from the Adriatic Sea to
the Indus River, and from the Pontos, the Caucasus, the Caspian, and the Syr
Darya [Jaxartes] River to the Indian Ocean. On the strength of such rights, any
Kalmyk, Buryat, or Mongol hordes could make legal claims to supreme authority over Russia. This historical right, over which such tears and blood
have been shed, which presently causes such pretense and falsehood, would
plunge the world into total confusion and complete chaos of absurdities, if we
took it into our heads to uphold it in a consistent manner.

All the crowns of the Arpads, Jagiellons, and Palaeologuses[7] are very re-
spectable things while they lie in museums of historical antiquities, from
which they may summon lofty reflections about bygone things and how fleeting is human greatness. These historical corpses, like all things deceased, deserve respectful memory and a kind word from the living, but only while
they lie dead in their graves. If they intend to wander in the daylight and
scare people by their appearance, like all manner of werewolves, vampires,
and zombies [oborotni, vampiry, i vukulaky], going around making their vanished claims to property long lost by the living, then according to Slavic custom there is no other way to lay them to rest than to run them through with
an aspen stake, and the sooner the better. The aspen stake is, of course, no
more than a frivolous superstition for simple corpses, since they will never

---

[6] See chap. 13, n. 1.

[7] Arpads: Hungarian ruling dynasty from the tenth to the thirteenth centuries (in Russian, *Stefanov*, from St. Stephen I of Hungary). Jagiellons: Lithuanian dynasty ruling in
Lithuania, Poland, Hungary, and Bohemia in the fourteenth to sixteenth centuries.
Paleologuses: Last ruling dynasty of the Byzantine Empire, in the thirteenth to fifteenth centuries.

get out of their graves regardless. But for historical corpses that have this incredible penchant for rising from their burial vaults and disturbing the waking hours and dreams of the living with their absurd claims—the aspen stake is a most lawful and reasonable measure serving the mutual benefit of the dead as well as the living. The aspen stake is the only rightful claim that can be recognized for the crowns of the Palaeologuses, the Jagiellons, and the Arpads. The crowns of the Suleimans and Hapsburgs are thrusting themselves onto that stake as well: even though they do not yet lie in their graves but sit among the living, yet they have long begun to stink and contaminate the political atmosphere with their putrid gases. Oh, how the Slavic heart will leap when Russia, in recognition of its historical calling, buries these corpses, builds over them a high burial mound, sharpens the aspen stake, and drives it down through the very top, to allow in its place a vast, original Slavic life to begin!

A historical right has a great significance and deserves all attention and respect when, being historical, it remains rooted in the actual needs of people in the present day and continues to be their inborn, inalienable right; when, having been a concern in days of the past, it still continues to be an urgent concern in the present. Oh, then will its voice be loud and doubly valid! Greece's aspirations for liberation, of course, gave it much power and sympathy that resonated everywhere, due to the fact that the Greeks fighting for their freedom and independence were the actual Greek people, and at the same time were restoring the freedom of the land of Miltiades and Epaminondas.[8] But these glorious recollections would have had no value if the people residing in modern Greece had lost all consciousness of their uniqueness and originality and had been assimilated by their conquerors.

Historical rights have the same properties as zero in arithmetic, which by itself means nothing, but increases tenfold the significance of the figure standing to the left of it. So the reason for equating Western Rus' with the rest of Russia is not because it all became part of Rus' in the time of the Vladimirs, Iaroslavs, and Mstislavs,[9] but because being the actual Rus' in those long past times, it always remained so—by language, by faith, and by its very essence, regardless of who ruled over it—and even now continues to be this same actual Rus' as in other times, despite the change in its upper classes. Therefore Russia has a double, or better yet, a tenfold right and a tenfold obligation to make sure that all Rus' should be Rus': a right and an obligation that is an actual, vital, traditional, tenfold-significant historical right, uninterrupted in the course of the ages inasmuch as the memory of the people consciously and unconsciously preserves it.

---

[8] Miltiades (c. 550–489 BCE): Athenian strategos credited with defeating the Persians at the Battle of Marathon (490 BCE). Epaminondas: See chap. 4, n. 14.

[9] Vladimirs, Iaroslavs, and Mstislavs: referring to rulers of Kievan Rus' and Russian cities from the tenth to thirteenth centuries.

But what of the crown of St. Stephen I and the Arpad dynasty, for example? It is nothing but the accidental conquest and subjection of the true residents of the Danube, the Slavs, by the invading Magyar horde which, despite accepting Christianity and a European outlook and manner, still could not assimilate this foreign tribe or turn it into its own flesh and blood, just as the Hellenized Romans of Byzantium could not do with the Slavs within its boundaries; nor could the invading Turks, with the Greeks, Bulgars, and Serbs; nor could the noble Livonian knights[10] (nor did they want to), with the Latvians and Estonians. Thus all these claims and all others like them are the claims of those rising from the dead, of nocturnal apparitions, specters, and midnight harpies, to which the living must pay no attention, for fear of joining the multitude of madmen and lunatics.

And so, in the strict legal sense Constantinople now constitutes a *res nullius*, a thing belonging to no one. In a broader and higher historical sense, it must belong to the one that continues to embody the idea once embodied by the Eastern Roman Empire. As a counterweight to the West, as the center of an embryonic new cultural-historical sphere, Constantinople must belong to those who were called to continue the work of Philip and Constantine,[11] consciously undertaken by Ivan, Peter, and Catherine.

But we will set aside the above considerations and be content for the present with the fact that in the strict legal sense Constantinople is *res nullius*, which no one can claim by right as the legal heir. In the absence of any legal basis, utilitarian considerations enter into legal rights, so we can and must ask: If no one has a direct right to Constantinople, who could put its possession to its true, proper use?

All the contenders can be divided in this regard into three categories: on the one hand, the great European powers; on the other hand, the smaller states, like Greece; and in the third category, Russia.

Of the great European powers, Prussia must stay completely out of this matter. Obviously the possession of Constantinople would not only be of no use, but would even be completely impossible for it. The only way Constantinople could go to Austria would be if it transformed itself into that Austro-Turkish federation we discussed in the preceding chapter, where it was shown that it would be disastrous for its constituent peoples and would only perpetuate the agony that Austria now suffers. That only leaves the two great maritime powers, France and England, for which the possession of Constantinople is at least possible due to their significant naval power. But the benefit they would get from it would be of a purely negative character. Although as we have seen Constantinople is a remarkable crossroads of world travel, it lies far from the traffic in which they, especially England, play such a primary role. The only benefit for them from the possession of Constantinople would

---

[10] Livonian Brothers of the Sword: See chap. 8, n. 25.

[11] Philip II: See chap. 10, n. 10. Constantine I: See chap. 4, n. 11.

be limited to the harm it would bring to Russia. In a manner of speaking, this would be the right to stab a knife in the body of Russia and twist it in the wound whenever they wanted to cause unbearable aggravation, extending their influence and sovereignty not only to the whole southern coast of Russia, but also deeply within the country by means of those natural and artificial lanes of transport, the rivers and railways.

The complete intolerability of such a situation would put Russia into continual hostility toward the naval power holding Constantinople, whether open or veiled. In response to any clash with one state or another, it would be assured of having Russia against it, and this fear would necessarily diminish its significance and influence in all other areas of political activity. We have seen what harm for Austria came from the possession of Venice once Italy began to unite into a single political whole: It made Italy a natural ally for any enemy of Austria. But how does the enmity of an Italy yet to unite and take shape compare to the enmity of Russia?

To hold Constantinople under continual threat of a clash with Russia, which it is now clear the Turkish Empire with all its strength cannot do, would require keeping at least an army of 150,000 or 200,000 men, and tens of squadrons of iron-clads and other forces in the outskirts of Constantinople. Since these forces would be required in addition to those that the Western power possessing Constantinople could deploy to other places, the negative significance of this possession (the harm brought to Russia) would put a strain on the state budget of at least one hundred million rubles. Although according to its state officials, France is wealthy enough to pay for glory, neither France nor England, nor any state no matter how wealthy, could permit itself such a luxury of hatred.

It must be said, however, that neither France nor England have any real claim to the possession of Constantinople. They know full well that its benefit for them would be purely negative, that the only purpose it would have for them is to keep it out of Russia's hands. Therefore even they support the dominion of Turkey as an established fact, with no need to dream it up or make any effort, great or small, to bring it about, contending with foreseeable or unforeseeable obstacles. In the event that the dominion of Turkey, despite their support, turned out inadequate, they would agree all the sooner to entrust the key to the Black Sea to a second-tier state deliberately strengthened for this purpose—Greece.

What benefit would this bring? We have seen that from the standpoint of rights, Constantinople does not belong to it [Greece] at all; from the standpoint of benefits, it would be ruinous. It would be a true Pandora's box, filled with troubles and discords, which after all is said and done must inevitably lead to its loss of political independence. *Noblesse oblige*, the French saying goes. Any high-titled personage—a count, prince, duke, marquis—grows tired under the weight of his social position which he must bear whether he wants to or not, even though the splendor of the title, which can in its own way bring a happy, calm, and untroubled existence, is not hard to bear at all. Constantinople would lay this kind of burden on a weak state. The defense of the most strategic point in the world, by fortifications, an army, and a navy against a surprise attack at least until help could arrive, would drain its weak financial means.

On the other hand, vulnerable Greece would always be caught between two fires: Russia, on the one hand, which of course would make every effort by so-called political influence to take possession of this key to the main exit from its house; and on the other hand, the European powers hostile to Russia which, in presenting this key to Greece, only intended to make themselves its true owners. Its only remaining options would be either to fall into complete dependence upon one side, preserving only the phantom and appearance of state sovereignty and freedom, or play the unenviable role of a weathervane, constantly changing from one form of dependence to another, while losing the respect and sympathy of both sides in the rivalry. Put simply, for Greece it would be a repetition of the role of Turkey, with the one difference that Turkey is, after all, a state with a population of more than thirty million, which is only weak because it has lost its vital force. But how does a fresh, hearty people and state, not to mention a dying one which could scarcely bear it, find itself in the position of having taken on a task beyond its abilities? It could not remain for long in such a state. The small Greek state would soon fall into exhaustion and senility, and the Constantinople question, not settled but glowing in the ashes, would burst into flame again with new force.

So neither the great Western powers, nor Greece, would derive any benefit from the possession of Constantinople, and not only that, but it would even be such a heavy burden that it would be hard for the first to bear, and would inevitably crush the second.

For Russia the possession of Constantinople appears in a completely different light. The advantages it would gain from it are truly priceless and innumerable.

1) Recent bitter experience[12] has shown where is the Achilles' heel of Russia, which its enemies have long sought. In contrast, the most decisive experience of many centuries, undertaken with huge means and under the leadership of the most skillful operators, had shown very clearly that from the other sides, the west and the north, it is invulnerable. The vulnerability from the east has already passed; thus all that remains is vulnerability to the south. These are not just empirical data, but facts supporting the most satisfactory explanation, since they result from the situation of Russia, the essential characteristics and particular nature of its power and strength.

Any attack from the west would be repulsed by the land forces of Russia, which always have, and always will constitute the main source of its power. Vast, impassable swamps and forests divide the expanse along the western

---

[12] Danilevskii has in mind the Crimean War (1853–56).

border of Russia into two completely separate theaters of military action. A simultaneous attack on them both is possible only in the highly unlikely event of an alliance between both our western neighbors, Prussia and Austria. Thus, in most cases Russia can be completely at peace either in the region to the south, or to the north of the woodlands and swamp system of the Pripiat' River.[13] Our weak point on that side, of course, is Poland; but our political relations with it are such that in any war with Poland, the mightiest of our neighbors, Prussia, could never be among our enemies, at least not for long. But Russia's strength consists not only in its army but in the soul of its whole people, which has always been ready to see its homes and property in the embrace of flames rather than enemy hands. And any enemy invading Russian territory would have to contend with this people.

From the Baltic Sea can only come diversions, incidental attacks at one or another point; but it cannot serve as the basis for a proper, systematically organized action, for the simple reason that any success made in summer must be left off in wintertime.

From the south, on the contrary, Russia is open to the attacks of powers with great naval means. A land defense of the coasts requires vast forces, though actually even that is not enough. To have any kind of success, enemies would have to hold it and turn it into a new point of support for further ventures. Of course, an invasion into the interior of Russia even from this side would be difficult, even impossible if you will, but there would be no need for such an invasion. Possession of the sea coasts, or even of the Crimea alone, would be enough to bring real harm to Russia and paralyze it. The possession of Constantinople and the straits would eliminate this danger and make the southern border of Russia the most safe and impregnable.

2) We have fallen into the unfortunate habit of saying that Russia is big enough, or even too big; that it needs no more conquests; that new acquisitions would be a burden to it, and already are a burden to it. Of course there are different kinds of acquisitions, but concerning general complaints about the too-vast expanse of Russia I see no grounds for complaint. England after all is bigger than Russia,[14] and it is not burdened by its far-flung possessions scattered all over the face of the earth. And concepts of size and greatness are all relative, and it seems to me a correct determination can only be made by the relationship between the size attained and the expansive force within what is growing. A big fat oak fifteen *sazhens*[15] high must not be called too big when it has only assumed its normal dimensions. Likewise a state cannot be

---

[13] [Danilevskii's marginalia, published posthumously]: *And we had the stupidity to drain these swamps!* [Translator's note: Sporadic efforts intensified in the 1870s. See R. A. French, "The Reclamation of Swamp in Pre-Revolutionary Russia," *Transactions and Papers (Institute of British Geographers)* 34 (June 1964): 175–88.]

[14] See Danilevskii's justification for this claim in chap. 2, n. 7.

[15] Thirty-five meters.

considered to have reached full size, no matter how many square miles or *versts* it is, when nearly four million of the ruling people's fellow tribesmen live outside of it. It has only reached full size when the entire people that formed it, supports it, and brings it life has united together, and when it has become the undisputed lord of the lands settled by this people; that is, it controls the access into and out of it, the mouths of the rivers that water almost its full extent, and the mouths of its inland seas. Put simply, when it has accomplished its historical purpose. Speaking of the expanse of Russia, we should not forget that, soil-wise and climate-wise, it is situated in less than ideal conditions than all the great states of Europe, Asia, and America, and thus it requires a greater expanse than they do to gather the makings of its wealth and might.

Of course the great expanse has its own disadvantages, and without a doubt the main one is the great extent of its borders. But the acquisition of Constantinople would give Russia a completely different advantage which, instead of increasing its disadvantages, would decrease them to a significant degree, condensing, so to speak, twenty-five hundred [versts] of borderlines all along the Black and Azov Seas into a single point. Therefore, if Constantinople in the hands of England or France would require a sizable army and navy to defend this point, over and above what they would need without it, in the hands of Russia it would allow a reduction of its armed forces and attending expenditures by at least the same amount.

3) The external strength of truly powerful states always comes from two elements: the army and the navy, which can never replace each other, no matter how strong one is in the absence or great weakness of the other.[16] Neither a purely-navy nor a purely-army state can be considered truly powerful, although under certain geographic and other conditions, the ratio of these two elements will change. All of history confirms this.

Carthage, Venice, and Holland were all almost exclusively based on naval predominance, and quickly lost their primacy, either being destroyed or pushed into second-rate or even lower status. England, on the contrary, besides its dominant navy having a sizable land army at its disposal, is a truly global power, the power of which in all probability will not soon end; if it should, it would be not from external, but from internal, causes. On the other hand, even Rome, the ideal of continental power, had to become for a time a mighty naval power (which was possible at the time) in order not to cede its prospects of world domination to another. How paralyzed were Louis XIV and Napoleon when their navies were routed by the English! The unsuccessful outcome of the Eastern War came from our backwardness in naval concerns, the near total lack of steamships, at least as much as our lack of functional internal support lines, and of course much more than the poor

---

[16] [Danilevskii's marginalia, published posthumously]: *The latest Turkish war proved this.*

condition of our firearms. How many times have we lost influence by the inadequacy of our navy! We will mention only the sale of our American colonies,[17] due primarily to this; the uprising in Crete,[18] of course, would have had a favorable outcome, if we could have bolstered our ambitions with a sufficient number of iron-clads and other ships. Would not our friendship with America be more fruitful, for us and even for both sides, regarding Crete as well as in other matters, if we could extend the hand of friendship to the Americans from the decks of several squadrons of battleships?

But although in the words of the poet, concerning Russia,

The endless lapping of the seven seas
Regales you with a song of highest praise[19]

six of the seas are either entirely unsuited or poorly suited to it, at least in terms of a military fleet and political power. If the Aral Sea was part of the poet's count, it belongs to the first category—perfectly unsuitable—in that it would be more beneficial if it would dry up and send the waters of the Darya on to the Caspian Sea. The Arctic Ocean, excluding the gulf of the White Sea, is one that once had, and may again acquire, great economic significance. The Caspian Sea is very important, not only in political regards, but also for fishing. The coast of the Eastern or Pacific Ocean, upon which such sanguine hopes rested after the annexation of the Amur region, if used properly could be a good base for naval guerilla actions, although not on a large scale. But despite the effect of the *Alabama* in the American Civil War,[20] or of Denis Davydov[21] in the Patriotic War [1812], still there seems no reason to believe that guerilla tactics, by land or sea, has ever had or ever will have any decisive influence on the fates of peoples or wars.

Concerning the Baltic Sea, the only one upon which we now have a navy, I must take what some consider the unpatriotic point of view, that the Baltic navy is nothing more than a means (albeit an important or even essential one)

---

[17] Russia had fur traders in coastal settlements in Alaska from the 1740s, and organized a formal colony in 1799, but sold Alaska to the United States in 1867.

[18] In 1866–69, the Greek population of Crete revolted against Ottoman rule, one of a series of uprisings throughout the nineteenth century, against the terms of the London Protocol of 1830, which specified that Crete could not join newly-independent Greece. Crete finally won its autonomy in 1898 and united with Greece in 1913.

[19] From A. S. Khomiakov, "Rossii" (To Russia; 1839).

[20] *CSS Alabama*: A British-built Confederate commerce raider that captured or destroyed sixty-five Union merchant ships, never docking at a Southern port in its two years of service (1862–64), finally sunk at Cherbourg, France.

[21] Denis Vasilievich Davydov (1784–1839), guerilla leader of 1812 turned soldier-poet, admired by Pushkin and Belinskii as a dashing Romantic figure and for his distinctively Russian voice.

of defending our Baltic shores, or maybe just assisting Kronstadt in the defense of Petersburg.

We do not control access into and out of the Baltic Sea, and there is no way we could. So we cannot of our own volition influence the course of world events with our Baltic naval fleet. After our victorious wars with Sweden[22] and the decline of that state's power, which had risen to a disproportionate height, we could think that we held dominion at least within this sea. But even this dominion was a sham, since the allied English and French navies forced us to seek shelter in a fortified harbor. As Prussia has grown stronger and Germany has become unified, preponderance in the Baltic Sea must in the natural course of things shift to Prussia, because it possesses the best unfrozen part of it, and probably will soon have its own access into and out of it by means of a canal through Holstein. Even if, through great effort on our part, we do not cede to Germany the advantage we have enjoyed until now in the Baltic, at least in time of peace between the great sea powers we will still have to share our dominion with it. It would be impossible for Germany—having a sizable merchant navy and at the same time acquiring excellent harbors along with Holstein—not to aspire to become a truly mighty naval power, and for its efforts not to be crowned with success. This is so natural that for us to oppose this trend would be strange, since it is always unwise to stand in the way of what is moving forward by the natural progression of events. To make significant efforts at sea to oppose Prussia, or Germany in general, as a rival on the Baltic Sea, would be to take the same incorrect and ill-disposed policy toward it as Europe takes in ruling the East. This policy can be called negative in the full sense of the word, since it would only bring all manner of harm to us, and to the development of sympathetic, Slavic, and Orthodox peoples, without securing any direct benefit.

However, the sacrifice of sharing sovereignty in the Baltic Sea is not so great as it seems, since we have already had to share it with such a rival as can make Prussian, German, and even English naval power seem insignificant. I have in mind the dominating power of ice. True, we have struck a defensive alliance with it, by which it protects our coast for half of each year; however, it is also an ally of our enemies should we go on the offensive, not allowing our fleets out of their harbors for fully half of the year and forcing them to return to them by a certain date, no matter what, for fear of being cut off from all retreat. Can an active, influential naval force exist under such conditions?

Only the Black Sea is able to give Russia power and influence on the seas, and moreover the kind of naval power and influence its geographic, ethnographic, and political conditions would allow. Russia cannot be powerful at sea in the same sense as England, America, and even France; it cannot be, so to speak, an oceanic naval power, whose ships are scattered the length and

---

[22] The Great Northern War (1700–21).

breadth of the seas, carrying the name and influence of the homeland to all the islands and coasts of the earthly sphere. It cannot be such a naval power, not only because it has no colonies it must defend, nor a merchant navy, requiring protection on the high seas; but also because such widespread activity is just not in the soul of Russia and the Russians. Russia moves only by friendly pressure, a wall like the wave of an ocean tide slowly, gradually, but irrepressibly flooding the coast—not like separate springs, bubbling up here and there through the soil.

In the same way, Russia cannot have naval power like that of England or America, which in a manner of speaking flow from the depths of the life of their people, and which are founded, on the one hand, upon hundreds of thousands of sailors that form a vast social class all their own, which in time of need can supply the state with a large contingent of experienced sailors; and on the other hand, upon the shipyards, the machinery, steam power, and other productive capabilities for everything a merchant navy requires, which in time of need also can furnish the state with a steady supply of new ships and unlimited quantities of naval equipment. Russia can have only a state navy that is maintained and equipped entirely by the state and by state means. Thus, due to the huge expenditures on the land army, which always is and will always have to be the main support of Russian power, the navy can never grow very large, nor be supported by reserves of people, ships, and materiel always at the ready to replace the lost.

Therefore Russia is like the clever and cautious commander of a fortified camp, having to compensate for major inadequacies in his navy with a well-chosen site and fortifications. Nature has given Russia a kind of fortified naval camp, the only one in the whole world, in the Black Sea and its defiles [narrow passes], the Dardanelles, the Bosporus, and the Kerch Strait, with a forward launch point in the Sea of Marmara, and the wide internal expanse of the Black Sea, like a parade ground in which the navy can conduct all necessary naval drills, with redoubts and citadels on the Kerch and Sevastopol harbors and reserve arsenals in the city of Nikolaev. When the occasion arises, the navy can make sorties, rout enemy squadrons at will, defend the Adriatic and Aegean coasts, dispatch cruisers to the Mediterranean and Red Seas, and threaten the Suez Canal, Malta, and Toulon. In case of failure or before superior enemy forces, it can take shelter in its inaccessible refuge, make repairs and replenish supplies in freedom, and set off on new missions under changed, more favorable circumstances, always having the option at such times.

4) Finally, in a moral sense, the possession of Constantinople, the center of Orthodoxy and repository of great historical memory, would give Russia enormous influence in all the countries of the East. It would enter its historical legacy and would appear as the restorer of the Eastern Roman Empire, just as the Frankish monarchy long ago restored the Western Roman Empire, and in this way a new Slavic era in world history would begin.

And so the defense and complete security of the border from which Russia is most vulnerable; the concentration of 2,500 versts of border lines into a single point, and along with that, the savings in military and financial outlays; the only means of acquiring significance as a strong naval power; and enormous moral influence: these are the direct, positive advantages that Russia would gain from the possession of Constantinople. For all other states, however, it would only be either harmful, as for Greece, or would give only negative advantages, the ability to continually deprive Russia while damaging itself considerably in the process.

If we look deeper into the matter, however, we will find that the direct, immediate annexation of Constantinople to Russia would not be completely harmless even for it, and could even bring disastrous consequences.

In his ode to the sculptor David, speaking of statues toppled from their pedestals, Hugo said:

Et de leur bronze auguste on ne peut faire
Que des cloches pour la prière,
Ou des canons pour le combat.

These august bronzes can only be made
Into bells for prayer or guns for war.[23]

In the same way some cities, although toppled from their pedestal of former glory, represent such a great, powerful idea and have such regal significance that through all the changes in their historical destiny they still must hold first place in whatever state possesses them, and will absolutely become or remain its capital. So Italy cannot seek its center anywhere but Rome; and so our Moscow, despite being dethroned by Peter, all the same remains its true capital and living center by its vital significance, by the idea that it united the Russian lands, and by its historical and economic role. Tsargrad is the same, and to compete with it in this regard would be dangerous not only for Petersburg, but even for Moscow itself. But on the other hand, a capital lying not just outside the center, but even outside the territory of the state, could not fail to bring chaos to the life functions of the state and the people, and produce imbalance by siphoning off the vital physical and spiritual fluids in the political organism.

To a lesser degree, Russia already went through this in the official relocation of the state center from Moscow to Petersburg. I raise this only by way of example and not to expand upon this topic, since in our society it has already been examined many times in speech, private writing, and print, and I have

---

[23] From Victor Hugo, "A Monsieur David, Statuaire" [To Mr. David, sculptor] (1828), a tribute to sculptor Pierre-Jean David D'Angers (1788–1856). The first line of the French text combines part of a preceding line in paraphrase.

nothing new to add. But despite everything done for it, all exertions on its behalf—by its topographic and climatological conditions; by its character of life, strongly tinged by the German element so unsympathetic to the Russian heart; by the stiffness, the coldness, the tenseness—simply put, by its official-ness—Petersburg has much that is repulsive to Russian people, among whom at all levels of society there are very few who would actually like it. I am not speaking of native, blood residents of Petersburg, since as everyone knows habit is second nature. Furthermore Petersburg has no kind of historical charm; not a single event happened there that would make the Russian heart clench with grief, swell with pride, or overflow with joy. If such a great mat-ter as the emancipation of the serfs were being deliberated and resolved in it, then Petersburg, being Petersburg, would take no part in it. How many times stronger is the attractive power of Constantinople! The focus of the Russian people's aspirations from the very dawn of its state existence; the ideal of en-lightenment, glory, splendor, and greatness of our ancestors; the center of Or-thodoxy; the apple of discord between us and Europe: what great historical significance it would have, for us to seize Constantinople from the hands of the Turks, in defiance of all Europe! What delight would fill our heart from the radiance of a cross placed by us on the cupola of Hagia Sophia![24] Add to this the incomparable advantages of Constantinople enumerated at the begin-ning of the chapter, its significance in world trade, the enchanting location, and all the charms of the south. Considering all that, the worry is of course justified that if Constantinople became the capital of Russia, it would draw too much of Russia's moral, mental, and material forces to itself and shatter its vital equilibrium.[25]

So Constantinople must not be the capital of Russia, must not concentrate in itself the whole life of its people and state, and thus must not directly be-come part of Russia proper. To gain all the advantages enumerated above for Russia without bringing it easily foreseeable harm, a liberated Constantinople transformed into a true Tsar-grad must in and of itself be something more than just the capital of the Russian domain, but something less than that in re-gard to Russia; it must not be too closely connected to it or take on the mater-nal significance reserved for Moscow. Simply put, Tsargrad must be the capi-tal not of Russia but of the whole All-Slavic union.

So a general view of the development of cultural-historical types, by which we have shown that it reaches the greatest fullness, power, and magni-

---

[24] Hagia Sophia: Orthodox cathedral in Constantinople, the "Church of the Holy Wis-dom of God."

[25] Danilevskii sees Russia as an organic, living body; thus to him Constantinople would not be a mere colonial possession, but an additional vital organ grafted to the outside of the body, unprotected, and siphoning the lifeblood from the other vital or-gans in the body of the state. This set him in opposition to other nationalists, like Dos-toevskii, whose reasoning did not depend on biological and anatomical analogy.

ficence in a certain relationship between the demands of unity and the diversity of the constituent elements; the investigation of the conditions of the
Slavic peoples in Austria and Turkey, their relationship to each other and to
the hostile elements surrounding them on all sides; and finally, our survey of
the fates of Constantinople: all lead us to one and the same resolution of the
Eastern Question, to the federation of the Slavic peoples and all the foreign
peoples interspersed among them.

We have seen that only for Russia can the possession of Constantinople
be of actual, positive benefit, but only comparatively in regard to European
states; to all the peoples that live in the parts of Turkey lying along the Black
Sea, as well as the basin of the upper and lower Danube, Constantinople offers many of the same advantages that Russia could gain from it. Therefore it
is a matter not only of the partial interests of these latter peoples, but also of
all propriety, that the Bosporan capital not be made directly part of the Russian state.[26] Finally, in essence, the proposed resolution of the fate of Constantinople most of all corresponds to the Greeks' true views of it. It is dear to
them as a symbol of the greatness of their ancestors; but being given into their
full and direct possession, and downgraded as the capital of an insignificant
state, it would either lose its world-historical significance, or it would place
this state under the burden of its significance, like a building crushing an inadequate foundation. Even if Constantinople was made its capital, the small
Greek people[27] could never in itself revive the Byzantine Empire. The empire
of Constantine, Theodosius, and Justinian[28] could come to life only in the
form of a Slavic-Greek federation and only in this way could Greece take part
in its glory and greatness.

So from whatever side we approach the matter, an All-Slavic federation
with Russia at the head and its capital at Tsargrad is the only reasonable, intelligent solution to the great historical puzzle passed down from ancient
times, known as the Eastern Question. We will look as well as we can into the
most essential and most salient features of this federation. From the facts of
the experience of world history, arranged according to the requirements of a
natural system, we have concluded along the way (see chapter 5) that for a
civilization characterizing an original cultural-historical type to be able to be
born and develop, the peoples belonging to it must be politically independent, and also that the civilization of the cultural type can only attain its full-

---

[26] To the organic argument against taking direct possession of Constantinople, Danilevskii adds an appeal to familial propriety among the Slavs, instead of invoking the
privileges of Russian power.

[27] *Malen'kii grecheskii narod*; compare to *narodets* (little people group), applied to
Hungarians in chapter 13. In Danilevskii's mind, the Greeks have developed as a full-
fledged, culturally-significant people or nation, but remain numerically small. He is
unwilling to grant the same status to Hungarians, by contrast.

[28] Theodosius: See chap. 4, n. 12. Justinian: See chap. 7, n. 5.

ness of diversity and richness when the various ethnographic elements comprising it are not absorbed into a single political whole. On these foundations we proposed that the soil for cultivating Slavic culture must be a federation of independent Slavic peoples. Elsewhere (see chapter 10) we expressed and tried to prove the idea that the closeness of political bonds obliging related nationalities to be united will depend not only on the closeness of their relationship, but also on the degree of danger and the force of pressure on these nationalities from outside, the defense against which will also determine the political form of the alliance uniting them. Failing to correlate the strength of the federative bond with these external circumstances could easily cause the loss of a people's independence, as happened to Greece in the Macedonian and Roman eras.

Being face to face with a West that is hostile to them is the reason that would make the Slavs wish for very close federative bonds beneath the political hegemony and leadership of Russia, which has the most legal right to it, based on its comparative strength over all the other members of the Slavic family, and based on its having maintained political independence over the course of many centuries. Despite the places where Russia swerved from the path of healthy politics, especially in the last half of the era of Catherine, still it and only it among all the Slavic states could not only preserve its independence under the most unfavorable circumstances but even unite nearly all of the Russian people and form the mightiest state in the world.

But for the political strength of the All-Slavic union, it is not enough to grant Russia undisputed hegemonic dominion over it; the secondary groups or members of the union must also provide sufficient guarantee of the power and unity of its inner structure. The divisiveness to which the Austrian Slavs are particularly inclined, from having long lived under the ruling principle of *Divide et impera*,[29] must spill over the borders of the largest linguistic and ethnographic groups into which they are divided. Dividing by minor tribal identities, each easily tempted by pretensions to political independence, would have the essential problem that each of these minor entities would have too little incentive to devote all their strength to the burdens that come with such a great political role.

In foreign affairs, the place of the minor member of a larger union of states is comparatively insignificant, so that in case of success its rightful credit completely disappears in the glory won by the dominant member of the union, but in case of failure, it alone bears the responsibility and shame; whereas if the load were correctly distributed, the material burden falling on the population of the minor state would be equally shared by the subjects of the powerful head of the union. Not only is there no moral reward of glory and influence for bearing the material burden, but their insignificant contingent even serves as an object of scorn and laughter usually directed at the

---

[29] Latin: "Divide and conquer."

various Reusses and Lippes.[30] Thus the minor members of the union take little interest in the union's foreign affairs and avoid obligations to the union as much as they can, fulfilling them only formally. In the end, the whole burden of war and the general conduct of foreign affairs fall almost exclusively upon the most powerful member. The former German Empire may serve as an example of this. Within it, the whole burden of defense fell upon the lands of Austrian inheritance. In contrast to this, while states of medium size could not challenge the pre-eminent influence of the head of the union and turn its hegemony into a fatal system of dualism, as in the former German union, they nevertheless would be conscious enough of their own power to be interested in and take an active part in the affairs of the union. These states' troops and ships have enough power to make an essential contribution to the general effort or make them feel their absence; their armies can even be major actors in side theaters of battle. Therefore a state like this bears a sufficient degree of both the glory of a general victory or the shame of general defeat, in which it made a full effort and gave full support, to attain the first or avoid the second.

Minor states present less opposition, it is true, to the head of the union's unifying plans, eagerly supporting them even if they only preserve the semblance of independence in internal affairs. Prussia, for example, can obviously expect less opposition from Braunschweig and Oldenburg than from Saxony; but from our point of view this is not an advantage or benefit, but on the contrary, a harm and detriment. The cultural significance and greatness of the Slavic family of nations requires that the form of the Slavic world is not, as Pushkin expressed it, the pouring of Slavic streams into the Russian sea, but a kind of wide ocean with independent, though unified and coordinated parts—that is, with seas and deep bays, gulfs, and harbors. Not the absorption of the Slavs by Russia, but the unification of all the Slavic peoples by the idea of All-Slavdom both politically and culturally, with the first being most important, and mainly for the possibility of accomplishing the second.

Thus we believe that only the large ethnographic and linguistic groups into which the Slavic world is divided can constitute the political units with complete independence in their internal affairs, which must enter into the All-Slavic union as independent wholes.

The supporters of independence for any minor ethnographic element will protest that the more humble nationalities would be sacrificed to some of the more ambitious nationalities, such as the Czechs and Serbs for example, while also bringing to the foreground the hard-to-reconcile historical rivalries between some tribes that prevailed over their mutual relations from time to time. This objection would be compelling if it were a question of forming entirely autocratic, supreme Slavic political entities not united by any direct

---

[30] Reuss and Lippe were small German principalities within the Holy Roman Empire, the Confederation of the Rhine, the German Confederation, and finally, the German Empire.

bonds between them upon the ruins of present-day Turkey and Austria. Then, truly, there would be a place for some kind of special Serbian ambition to strengthen itself, not only to predominate over the Slovenes and Croats, like the Magyars over the non-Magyar elements in Hungary, but even to bring the ethnographically distinct Bulgars into its state as a subject nationality. But in a close federation of Slavic peoples, any distinctly national ambitions, not only Czech or Serbian but even Russian, must be absorbed into a single, All-Slavic ambition. Such an arrangement of the political destiny of the Slavic world requires only that the secondary members of the union be strong enough to preserve their internal independence, so as not to fade into insignificance through extreme fragmentation, but to be conscious of their own active influence within the general course of union affairs. Concerning the internal order of each of the indirect members of the union, nothing should hinder granting administrative decentralization and regional independence to their constituent parts, to the full extent they are desired.

Thus, corresponding to the main ethnographic groups into which the Slavic world divides, as well as the tribes included by place of residence, but also mostly according to actual, genuine moral inclinations—the All-Slavic union must consist of the following states:

The Russian Empire with Galicia and Ugric Rus' annexed to it.

A Czecho-Moravian-Slovakian kingdom consisting, besides Czechia, of Moravia and the northwest part of Hungary settled exclusively or predominantly by Slovaks; approximately nine million in population and 1,800 square miles of territory.

A Serbo-Croat-Slovene kingdom consisting of the Serbian Principality, Montenegro, Bosnia, Herzegovina, Old Serbia, northern Albania, the Voivodeship of Serbia and Banat of Temeschwar, Croatia, Slavonia, Dalmatia, the Military Frontier [of Austria], the Duchy of Carniola, Goritzia and Gradisca, Istria, Trieste region, two-thirds of Carinthia, and one-fifth of Styria on the Drava; approximately eight million in population and 4,500 square miles of territory.

A Bulgarian kingdom with Bulgaria and most of Romania and Macedonia; approximately 6–7 million in population and more than 3,000 square miles.

A Romanian kingdom with Wallachia, Moldavia, part of Bukovina, approximately half of Transylvania along the Maros River, the western borders of Bessarabia populated predominantly by Moldavians, in exchange for which Russia must receive from it part of southern Bessarabia from the Danube delta and Dobruja. This would consist of nearly seven million in population and more than 3,000 square miles.

A Hellenic kingdom including present-day Thessaly, Epirus, the southwestern part of Macedonia, all the islands of the Archipelago [Aegean Islands], Rhodes, Crete, Cyprus, and the Aegean coast of Asia Minor; with over four million in population and 2,800 to 3,000 square miles.

A Magyar kingdom, that is, Hungary and Transylvania beyond those parts not settled by Magyar tribes, which must go to Russia, Czechia, Serbia, and Romania; approximately seven million in population and 3,000 square miles.

The Tsargrad district with the parts of Romania and Asia Minor surrounding the Bosporus, the Sea of Marmara and the Dardanelles, with the peninsula of Gallipoli and the island of Tenedos; with a population of approximately two million.

A union like this—of peoples mostly related by spirit and blood, a fresh one hundred twenty-five million in population,[31] with Tsargrad at the natural center of its moral and material unity—would give the only full, reasonable, and thus the only possible, solution to the Eastern Question. Owning only what belongs to it by right, not threatening anyone and not fearing any threat, it could withstand all storms and adversity while calmly proceeding down the path of independent development, in the fullness of its peoples' strength, and in the most harmonious coordination of the kindred elements comprising it. Corresponding to its ethnographic makeup, religious illumination, and historical background, it would form a unique cultural-historical type, strengthened by a long struggle against the hostile outside forces now separating its peoples, a struggle without which it cannot be formed.

In deliberating upon the Eastern Question we have focused on its Turkish and Austrian parts and have spoken of the primary importance of Tsargrad within it, but have not said a word about the Polish part of this complex and complicated matter. We have not done so to this point because, in our view, the Polish question cannot be finally resolved outside of a general resolution of all Slavic questions, so it seemed necessary first to explain precisely our whole idea about the destiny and goals of Slavdom, before beginning to talk about the Polish issue.

Judging by political circumstances, the character of the actions of the Russian state, their firmness and constancy, the prevailing direction of Russian public opinion, how it will directly affect Polish elements and state officials, and finally, judging by the character of the development of Polish society and the idea prevailing within it—the future of course offers very different destinies to Poland, which seem to us to come down to four possibilities. We are speaking here of Poland in the strict, true sense of the word: that is, the country settled by the Polish people. Concerning the western provinces [*guberniia*], this means that while Russia lives there can be no other possibility than a more and more complete, multifaceted integration with the remaining parts of the state.

Let us suppose, first of all, the matter takes a bad turn for Russia, and the Poles' dreams come true of being able to form an independent state of one size or another. Without a doubt it would become the center of revolutionary

---

[31] [Danilevskii's marginalia, published posthumously]: *Now 140 million.*

intrigues (as we have seen even in little Krakow, when it was a free city),[32] directed primarily against the western provinces of Russia. Obviously Russia will not stand for this, but at the first opportunity must try to destroy this harmful nest. Thus Poland would become a theater of recurring warfare and suffer horrible destruction, as it did in the last *Rzeczpospolita*.[33] But to have the ability to stand against Russia, Poland would necessarily have to live in closest harmony with its western neighbors, the Germans, who of course would not miss the chance to take this country into hand with its assets, colonization, political and cultural influence, placing it in direct dependence upon Germany. Simply put, it would not miss the chance to do what it has done under similar circumstances with eastern and western Prussia and Silesia. Independence for the Polish state would be fatal to the Polish people, through its absorption into the German nationality.

But it could be objected that the Poles, having received independence, would voluntarily side with Russia and, no longer its subjects, would become its loyal allies and supporters. But who is preventing them from acting this way, when the Kingdom of Poland was created precisely along these lines and was connected to Russia by Alexander I with all possible privileges, purely by rights of personal union? What new privileges would they attain by this path? Who prevents them even now from acting this way, which without a doubt would be the fastest way to recover those advantages which they lost, little by little, through their repeated recklessness? It is obvious that there is not the slightest probability for such an outcome, neither as a result of the character of the current Polish intelligentsia, when it has been given every opportunity to do so already; nor as a result of the continual instigations of our Western friends. On the other hand, one can point out that the Czechs, although surrounded nearly on all sides by Germans, have not however lost their nationality. But in the first place, the Czechs have no need to befriend the Germans for any kind of extraneous purposes, but they see them precisely as their main, even their only, enemies. In the second place, all the preceding history of the Czechs, all their glorious deeds in both distant and recent past, reminds them of their longstanding struggle with the Germans, and of their aspiration to return to their living roots of Slavdom, from which their spiritual, moral life derives; it reminds them of their holdings in the common treasury of Slavdom.

A second possibility is that Poland could remain, as it is now, in combination with the Russian state, but Polish society would remain incurably ill, as it has been until now, if emigrants as well as the harmful elements inside it

---

[32] Krakow was given the "free city" designation at the Congress of Vienna in 1815; an uprising in 1846 led to it being annexed by Austria, ending its status as a free city.

[33] *Rzeczpospolita* (republic): A reference either to the period of Polish history ending with the third Partition of Poland in 1795, or to the more recent *Rzeczpospolita Krakowska*, Republic of Krakow (1815–46).

maintain their influence and, by recruiting more and more new adherents in their youth, perpetuate this evil which for so long has divided the whole country. In this case, which is possible only if the Russian state and Russian public opinion is inconsistent, due to the easing of restrictions on Polish intrigues from time to time—in the general course of affairs the Russian hand more and more often would have to take up Murav'ev's[34] iron rod, and would have to wield it more and more severely. This would continue the present order of things, which is just as unhealthy for Russia as for Poland.

But if, on the contrary, the Russian state and Russian social forces remain consistent, with a proper understanding of Russia's interests, which are at the same time Polish interests properly understood; without any leniency toward Polonization of any form, whether supposedly in the name of civilization or in the name of strong land ownership or some kind of class interests, in which no truly Russian class takes any interest—then it must be expected that in Poland itself, the healthy instincts of the people will take shape over and above the harmful principles and aspirations corroding Polish society. In this regard as in many others, the greatest benefit must be expected not so much from the direct effect upon Poland itself, as upon the western provinces of Russia. If the much more numerous Russian national element were given preponderance, then the mostly falsely labeled Polish elements would be fittingly reduced to insignificance, so that Polish dreams and intentions would not find even the superficial response or sympathy that has sustained it until now; these very dreams and intentions would soon vanish, or at least become completely harmless, having no legs to stand on, not to mention grounds, which already they have none, but only a seductive mirage of the land for a reconstituted Polish state in the unlawful and unnatural boundaries of 1772. In this case the Polish people would face either a gradual merging into the kindred Russian people, or if they preserve their nationality, by sustained Russian influence it would be purified of all its harmful, distorting adulterations to become, like all the Slavs, a friendly comrade and collaborator of the Russian people in the great inter-Slavic endeavor, and in this way gradually acquire for itself a greater and greater degree of independence.

The first option is not only improbable, but even undesirable.

Improbable because a people having lived a historical life, having left its mark in extensive literature, has almost lost the ability to take on a new life or

---

[34] Count Mikhail Nikolaevich Murav'ev (1796–1866): Reactionary Russian Governor General of the Northwestern Krai after the 1863 Uprising, known for aggressive Russification and the ruthless suppression of insurgent leaders, with thousands forcibly relocated to Siberia and more than a hundred executed. Ardent Russian nationalists saw him as a hero, whereas Danilevskii sees him as a regrettable necessity, "unhealthy" in the long run, as the last sentence in the paragraph indicates. This is too fine a distinction to matter much from the Polish point of view, but it does set him apart from the most chauvinistic Russian nationalists of his day.

to change its very essence, unless it is forcibly denationalized, or most importantly, enslaved by industrial predominance and dissolved in the flow of in-
rushing elements. Concerning the Poles, this is possible for the Germans to
do, but not the Russians, since there has never been a case where industrial
power and colonization were deployed from a sparsely populated, less de-
pleted, more virgin land into a country more densely populated and more
exploited, with more intensive industrial advancement.

It is undesirable because the Russian people is already so sizable that it
does not need reinforcement from foreigners. But losing one of the constituent
parts of Slavdom would deprive it of one aspect of its diversity, which is of
essential importance for the wealth and fullness of life for cultural-historical
types. This Polish aspect in the general Slavic character presents us with a distortion of it, thus something detestable. But let us investigate where this distortion occurs. It is not in the Polish people, nor in uniquely Polish attributes
of mind, emotions, or will (in which we see much of value, much to sympathize with); we will merely point out three Poles in this regard who represent these three sides of the human spirit: Copernicus, Mickiewicz, and
Kościuszko.[35] No, this distortion consists of the so-called Polish intelligentsia,
precisely in its three sides: the Catholic-clerical side, the Szlachtist-aristocratic
side, and the democratic-revolutionary side. In harnessing together these
three sides of the Polish intelligentsia, we see that it constitutes the root distortion, the disfigurement of the Polish-Slavic nature through the European
influences foreign to it—imitative Europeanism.

By this we do not at all mean to say that all things produced by the
influence of European life were bad in and of themselves; we only affirm that
they are turned into monstrosities when transplanted onto soil that is foreign
and unsuited to them. Catholicism, while in itself one of the distortions of
Christianity, has however brought to the land where it originally developed
many grand things and fruitful advantages; but on the Polish soil it turned
into clergyism [ksenzstvo].[36] Aristocratism in Europe produced chivalry in
general; in England, the glorious institution of the peerage; in France, its illustrious nobility and its refined, if artificial, form of social life; even in Hungary,
its development of the magnate class, which did so much for the industrial
success of the country and the enlightenment of the people. But in Poland this
aristocratism turned the upper classes into distinctly lordly landowners [iasno
vel'mozhnoe panstvo] and Szlachtists [shliakhetstvo],[37] but the lower classes into
cattle. Finally democratism and revolution, which in Europe destroyed so
many evils by founding too many freedoms to enumerate or provide exam-

---

[35] Copernicus, see chap. 4, n. 6. Mickiewicz, see chap. 8, n. 8. Tadeusz Kościuszko
(1746–1817): Polish national hero, veteran of the American Revolutionary War, later
commander of the Polish army in the Kościuszko Uprising of 1794.

[36] From ksendz, "Roman Catholic (especially Polish) priest;" cf. Polish, ksiądz, "priest."

[37] Shliakhetstvo: See chap. 8, n. 38.

ples of here, in Poland produced only regional assemblies [*sejmiks*], confeder-ations, "liberum vetoes" ["*ne pozvoliam*"], the National Government [*narodnyi zhond*], "stillettists," and "hanging gendarmes."[38] And so, the triple distortion of the character of the Polish people by the foreign elements that crept into it in the course of Poland's historical life—this and only this must be what is detestable to us about the Poles.[39]

But is not the strengthening of this particular foreign influence among us in Russia what so-called Westernism in all its various forms has striven, and is striving for, from the idealism of Granovskii to the nihilism of Dobroliubov and Pisarev[40] on the one hand, to the feudalism, or if you prefer, the civilized serfdom of *Vest'* and *Nashe Vremia*[41] on the other; and the apostasy of the Jesuit Father Gagarin[42] on a third side? All of these alike draw their ideas not from within Russian life, but from outside of it. They are not trying to seek the still-preserved seed of truly Russian life and cultivate it into an original, independent whole. All these tendencies have one ideal—Europe. True, some see this ideal in forms that are already or are becoming outdated: in English aristocracy or even in the *junkers* of Mecklenburg;[43] others, the so-to-speak "normal" liberals and Westernizers, in what constitutes the present-day life of Europe: its constitutionalism, its industrial movements, the extreme develop-ment of the individual, etc. A third group, finally, sees this ideal in the events, products, and actors that have begun the decomposition of European life: in the various social systems, or in revolutionary organizations and propaganda. However different these three categories of the objects of worship may be, they are all phenomena of one and the same civilization, of one and the same cultural type, which all of them accept as the only-possible one for all human-ity. And for this reason, all these unoriginal tendencies of thought and life in Russia fall under the same generic identification: Westernism, or European-ism. Therefore there is nothing strange, for example, in the fact that [pro-

---

[38] See chap. 11, n. 17.

[39] [Danilevskii's marginalia, published posthumously]: Just as it did among us, revolu-tion and Europeanism produced nihilism and terrorist infamies.

[40] Granovskii: See chap. 6, n. 2. Nikolai Aleksandrovich Dobroliubov (1836–61) and Dmitrii Ivanovich Pisarev (1840–68): Radical literary critics at *Sovremennik* (The Con-temporary) and *Russkoe slovo* (Russian Word), respectively, in the early 1860s.

[41] *Vest'*: See chap. 6, n. 14. *Nashe* [sic; *Novoe*] *vremia* [New Time]: St. Petersburg conser-vative political and literary newspaper, founded in 1868, became more liberal after 1876.

[42] Ivan Sergeevich Gagarin (1814–82): Russian diplomat to Paris who converted to Catholicism in 1842, forfeiting his state position and family inheritance, and joined the Jesuits the following year. He wrote numerous articles in the cause of converting Rus-sians to Catholicism and reuniting the Orthodox and Catholic Churches.

[43] Mecklenberg: Pastoral, impoverished region of northern Germany, where aristo-cratic privileges remained fully in effect into the twentieth century.

aristocratic] *Vest'* can bow to [the liberal Westernizer] Granovskii, declare his name its name, burn with the same indignation against the Slavophiles, and join right along with the publishers of his biography in slandering them. It's all the same patch of berries!

Does this not explain the sympathy that all these shades of opinion have shown toward the Poles? Whether or not they all recognize it, for them the Pole (again, a Szlachtist Pole) essentially is the realization of the ideal they would like to make the Russian into, wanting to see him as a completely Europeanized Slav. Many will reject this assertion. They will say, in their opinion, the ideal is not the Pole, but a pure-blooded Frenchman, German, Englishman, or better yet, none of these in particular, but a European in general. Unfortunately, in the first place, there is no such thing as a European in general; and in the second place, however pliable the Russian may seem, he nevertheless is not shapeless soft clay from which you can make what you like, but something given, already defined by nature, which can be twisted and distorted but cannot be recreated. Likewise the Pole cannot be transformed either abstractly or concretely into some kind of European, but can only be made into a distorted or disfigured Slav. That will always be the result of rejecting one's national identity or other things given by nature in general—the rejection which, in the famous Moscow professor's [Granovskii] formulation, is the essence of the historical process.

Thus there remains only a fourth and final case, which not only is possible, but is also desirable, which we indicated above. But this happy ending can only be brought to Poland and the Poles by means of an All-Slavic federation. As an independent and self-standing member of this union, whether in the form of personal union with Russia or even without it, it would be free only for the benefit, but not the harm, of the All-Slavic endeavor. The strength of Poland would be at the union's disposal, but any action by it against Russia would not be against Russia solely, but against all of Slavdom (of which it would itself be one of the constituent parts), thus it would be a betrayal against its own self.

Thus an All-Slavic federation, in precisely this form, is the answer to the Eastern Question, giving a satisfactory answer to all the side issues of the Slavic question—the Russian, the Austrian, the Turkish, the Tsargradian, and the Polish issue -- because it alone provides the solid ground which will allow the original development of a politically independent, outwardly strong, inwardly diverse, Slavic cultural-historical type.

It only remains for me to discuss the objections which either arise naturally in the mind or have already been made against an All-Slavic federation, the idea of which, while not exactly new, it seems to me has never been so clearly and definitively expressed. My hope is that in this discussion not only the importance, but even the inevitable necessity, of this federation for all parts of the Slavic world will be brought more and more to light.

∽ 15 ∾
The All-Slavic Union

The All-Slavic union is the only solid ground on which an original Slavic culture can grow, the *sine qua non*[1] of its existence. This general idea is the main conclusion of our whole investigation. Therefore we will not present here all the evidence of the significance, benefit, and necessity of this kind of organization for the Slavic world from the cultural-historical point of view. In this chapter I intend to reveal the importance, benefit, and necessity of the unification of the Slavic family within a federative union from the more strictly political point of view.

We saw earlier, that from a general cultural-historical point of view Russia cannot be considered a constituent part of Europe by either birth or by adoption, so it has only two options: either form with the other Slavs a special, self-sustaining cultural entity, or lose all cultural-historical significance and be nothing. It is not hard to see that this applies also to the strictly political sphere. Is it possible to be and remain a member of an alliance or society that is in all ways hostile to us, only putting up with us to take advantage of us without paying us back? An alliance, society, or simply put, any bond between persons, whole peoples, and states is possible only under mutual, reciprocal service and benefits. When the first [service] is demanded only from one side, and the second [benefits] goes only to the other, then such a relationship must not be called friendship, but only the exploitation of the weak, foolish, or gullible by the strong, smart, and cunning—even if they are just fooling around. If we carefully consider the role that Russia has played in the society of European states, from the very time it became a member in the so-called political system of Europe, we will hardly find any other way to describe this role.

The entry of Russia into the European political system can be understood of course as nothing other than its assimilation of European interests, and taking active part in the factions into which Europe divides, assisting the party it sympathizes with both morally and materially and opposing the one it considers its enemy. A simple alliance with one state or another for its own advantages, or for some sort of temporary goals, is not the same as fully entering into the political group of its temporary, coincidental allies. So although in the Great Northern War [1700–21] Russia fought alongside of Poland,

---

[1] Latin: Indispensable element (literally, "without which, nothing").

Denmark, and Saxony against Sweden, it must not be said that Russia acted in this war as a member of the European political system. It fought for its own special uniquely Russian goals and used the help of other states toward that end, and to a much greater degree helped them, and that is all. In exactly the same way it might, for example, enter into an alliance with Persia and Afghanistan for a common war against Khiva, Bukhara, and Kokand,[2] but this would not at all mean that it had become a member of the political system of Central Asian states, if there were such a thing. In the past century we see yet another example: We got involved in a completely foreign, European matter in the Seven Years' War,[3] but this was completely by accident. Elizabeth's personal dislike of Frederick the Great sent our troops against the Prussian hero; Peter III's personal devotion to him put us on his side, but Catherine's keen political sense recalled our troops and ended Russia's interference.

We see something completely different with the accession of Paul,[4] who in truth did regret the political system he had undertaken in the end, as his endorsement of Rostopchin's[5] memoranda made clear, but he did not manage to change it. Only around this time did European interests begin to concern us as our own; we began to hope for the success of one or another of them, making some interest ours even though this interest was of no special concern to us. Thus, strictly speaking, Russia entered into the European political system no earlier than just before the nineteenth century, namely with Suvorov's Italian campaign, since this was the first war we undertook for interests that were completely European and foreign to us, which henceforth we have continued taking as our own, much more than our own interests, which we have continually sacrificed to the former. It may be asked, what benefit have we gotten from this? What war in which we fought as a member of the European system, what alliance or peace agreement we have concluded as a European power, has brought us any true benefits? For that matter, in which of the treaties, political relations, and wars we have undertaken for specifically Russian interests did our close relations with Europe in general not end up as an

---

[2] Khiva, Bukhara, and Kokand: Regions of present-day Uzbekistan.

[3] The Seven Year's War (1756–63) involved all the main powers of Europe, with Britain against France and Prussia against Austria. Empress Elizabeth feared the rise of Prussia and had Frederick the Great (1712–86) on the defensive, but died childless in early 1762. Her nephew reigned briefly as Peter III, long enough to make peace and even ally with Prussia, handing Frederick a victory.

[4] Tsar Paul I: See chap. 11, n. 5.

[5] Count Fedor Vasilievich Rostopchin (1763–1826): Favorite of Paul I, author of a sweeping foreign policy memorandum to the tsar, urging aggressive self-interest and proposing a partition of the Ottoman Empire, hence Danilevskii's approval; note the epigraph to chapter 16. An English translation of Rostopchin's memorandum appears in *The Great Game*, vol. 1, *Documents*, ed. Martin Ewans (London: Routledge, 2004), 38–45.

obstacle or fetters limiting our range of action? The famous Holy Alliance[6] may offer the best example. What sacrifice did Russia not make for its goals! Even though it needed a rest after the strain of the Napoleonic wars, the Spanish and Italian disturbances of the 1820s forced it to maintain a large army; the Greek uprising was left to its own devices; Krakow was given to Austria, and Hungary was pacified. But when it was time for the Holy Alliance to help us against an alliance of Western powers, when all that was required from our allies was not help but merely strict, unwavering neutrality, Austria went over to our enemies' side and the Alliance was destroyed.[7] And then, was not our influence of invaluable service to France, for having kept Germany from interfering in the Italian war? Did not Russia's friendly interference prevent a war that was ready to break out over the Luxembourg question?[8] But let us see even one such action by the European powers to the benefit of Russia. Whatever Russia has done for Germany or Austria, however selfless it has been, still it has the reputation of a roaring lion, seeking whom it may devour.

The most recent events, from the Eastern [Crimean] War to Prussia's war with Austria, have clearly shown that we cannot rely upon anyone in Europe, and its support cannot be earned by any amount of sacrifices. In serving foreign goals, Russia may have seemed the real leader of Germany, but even that delusion disappeared. Germany got its own real leader with full rights to it, and we remained alone—not in this matter only (it had been thus for a long time) but in our very concept of the political order of things. And this is how it must be.

In exploiting Russia without establishing genuine, meaningful contact with it, Europe from its own point of view is completely in the right. Not belonging in essence to Europe, Russia by its own standards is an anomaly in the Germanic-Roman world of Europe, and the natural increase in the size of its population must reinforce its position as an anomaly. By its very existence Russia throws off the whole system of European equilibrium. Not one state would dare to make war against Russia one-on-one. The Eastern War showed

---

[6] Holy Alliance: See chap. 2, n. 24.

[7] I.e., in the Crimean War (1853–56).

[8] In the Luxembourg Crisis (1867), Napoleon III of France intended to buy Luxembourg from William III (1817–90) of the Netherlands, who ruled it in personal union. Napoleon expected Prussia's acquiescence, as payback for France staying neutral in the Austro-Prussian War of the previous year. Bismarck had privately offered vague consent, but was prodded by German nationalists into public opposition, risking war. Alexander II of Russia proposed a conference to settle the matter, hosted in London and signed by Belgium, Luxembourg, Italy, Austria, Prussia, France, Great Britain, and Russia. France got no new territory, but won the removal of the Prussian garrison from Luxembourg City, and the treaty set the terms of Luxembourg's permanent neutrality.

this best of all, when four states, with the help of Austria (more than half of which took a hostile attitude toward Russia), with the most disadvantageous conditions for us and the most advantageous for them, still took a whole year to besiege a single coastal fortress [i.e., Sevastopol, in the Crimean War], without any kind of Frederick, Suvorov, or Napoleon on the Russian side, but only the immense capabilities of Russia and the unconquerable spirit of its defenders.

We must not fail to realize that Russia is too big and powerful to be only one of the great European powers, and if it could play that role for these last seventy years, it was only by contorting or crimping its own natural aspirations, not giving them free rein, and deviating from its own destiny. This self-denigration must grow progressively in proportion to its natural development of strength, since by the very essence of the matter, the expansive force of Russia is much greater than that of the states of Europe, and its disproportion with the demands of the policy of equilibrium will necessarily become more and more painfully obvious. In saying so, I am of course looking at the matter from a general point of view, but not in application to any particular case, when due to the confluence of various circumstances a weaker opponent can rule over one much stronger. Any investigations of this sort certainly presuppose the caveat expressed in the oft-used formula, "All other conditions being equal."

However, considering the proximity of Europe, considering the boundary line shared with Europe across thousands of versts, the complete separation of Russia from Europe is inconceivable. That kind of separation could not protect China and Japan,[9] separated from Europe by the earth's diameter. Russia must have some kind of direct relations with it. If it cannot and must not be in an intimate, kindred connection with Europe as a member of the European family (which the evidence of long experience proves will not accept it, but will only demand an impossible rejection of its most obvious rights, healthy interests, natural sympathies, and holy obligations); and if, on the other hand, it does not want to be in a position of submission to Europe (reconfiguring its desires accordingly and fulfilling all Europe's humiliating demands), then there is nothing left for it to do but assume its actual role, designated by ethnographic and historical conditions, and serve as a counterweight not to one or another European state, but to Europe in general, in its totality.

But however great and powerful Russia is, it is still too weak to do this. It needs to weaken the enemy, separate those who are its enemies against their will, and turn them to its side as friends. Russia's lot is a happy one: To increase its power, it does not need to conquer or oppress, like all the other powers on earth up to now (Macedonia, Rome, the Arabs, the Mongols, and

---

[9] In the nineteenth century, China and Japan were subject to violence from Europeans and Americans seeking trade.

states of the Germanic-Roman world), but to liberate and restore. And in this marvelous near-coincidence of moral conviction and obligation with political advantage and necessity, we must not fail to see the guarantee of the fulfillment of its great destiny, assuming our world is not a pitiful, accidental mess but a reflection of the highest reason, truth, and kindness.

We should not deceive ourselves. Europe's hostility is too obvious: it lies not in the accidental combinations of European policies, not in the ambitions of one or another statesman, but in its most fundamental interests. Its internal accounts are far from settled. The seeds of internal struggle have begun to germinate in recent times, but these are most likely among the last. Once they are settled, or pacified for an extended length of time, Europe will again direct all its forces and designs against Russia, which it considers its natural-born enemy. If Russia does not understand its significance, it will inevitably suffer the fate of everything outdated, superfluous, and unnecessary. With its historical role gradually diminishing, Russia will have to bow its head to the demands of Europe, which will not grant it any influence in the East, and will erect (in one form or another, depending on circumstances) strongholds against its connections with its western Slavic relatives. Not only this, but, on the one hand, with the help of its accomplices among the Turks, Germans, Magyars, Italians, Poles, Greeks, and maybe even Romanians (who are always ready to break away from disunited Slavdom), and on the other hand, by its political and civilizational temptations, Europe will so remove the very soul of Slavdom that it breaks out in the bloom of Europeanism, with Europe itself fertilizing the soil. But for Russia—having not fulfilled its calling and thus having lost the reason for its existence, its vital essence, its idea—there will be nothing left but ingloriously to live out its pitiful life, to rot through like historical rubbish lacking all sense and significance, or to turn into a lifeless mass, an inanimate body, so to speak; and also, in the best case, to dissolve into ethnographic material for new, unknown historical formations, leaving no living trace of itself.

Being foreign to the European world by its inherent constitution, and besides that, being too strong and powerful to be merely one member of the European family or just another of the great European powers, Russia can only take a place in history worthy of itself and Slavdom by being the head of its own independent political system of states, and serving as a counterbalance to Europe in general and as a whole. This is the advantage, the benefit, and the whole idea of the All-Slavic union in regard to Russia.

For the western parts of Slavdom, the union is even more important. A Russia that has not become the representative of the Slavic world would thus lack a historical purpose for its existence and would present to the world the pathetic example of a giant historical ignoramus. But if we took a lower point of view, it could still not only preserve an outward form of state independence for years and centuries, but could be a great political power even without an inherent purpose or substance. For the other Slavic tribes the question is much more pointed. Here it is not a matter of historical life or purpose, not of some great historical role, but mere survival—so to speak, the daily bread of their national life. The question "To be or not to be" is a daily thing, presented in the most fearsome, tragic form. In chapter 13 we examined this question in sufficient detail, so there is no need to rehash it now. Here I think it necessary to express only the particular, special advantages that will certainly come from All-Slavic unification for each of the parts that would have to become members of the union, individually.

We will begin with *Greece* since the idea of including it in the union would appear to belittle its historical role, while the brilliant but deceptive mirage of the restoration of Byzantium and its exclusive appropriation of Constantinople might dazzle the eyes. We have already seen what a Pandora's box this deceptive gift would be for it. We will examine, then, the actual, essential advantages it would derive from joining the union. Neither the soil nor the topography of Greece will allow it to become either an agricultural or an industrial state. Trade is the branch of activity which—due to the natural inclinations of the Greek tribe, longstanding custom, and the local conditions of the Greek mainland, the islands of the archipelago, and the western coast of Asia Minor—must serve as the most important basis of wealth and the prosperity of the Hellenic people. Not only geographic and ethnographic conditions, but even historical experience attests to this, since the most glorious times of Greece's well-being were founded on trade, and likewise in times of decline and enslavement trade was no longer the Greeks' main business. Since part of Greece regained its political independence, its people have focused their main activity in this direction.

Trade in the eastern half of the Mediterranean Sea, in the archipelago, and in the Black Sea, is to a significant degree in Greek hands and on Greek ships, to such an extent that it has and still does arouse the envy of England, as the Don Pacifico affair[10] shows. But with the opening of the Suez Canal, the trade zone of Greece must expand immeasurably, turning it from local to global trade. Beyond the bays and waterways of the eastern part of the Mediterranean Sea, the Red Sea, the Indian Ocean, and the Bay of Bengal would become like inland seas for the Greek trade fleet. They are, so to speak, right underfoot for Greece, and no one can shorten their trade routes so much as they. But far-ranging trade (especially in far-off seas) can be sustained only by relying upon a sizable military fleet to protect the flag of trade at all points

---

[10] Don Pacifico affair: In 1847, a Portuguese Jew, born in British Gibraltar (hence a British citizen), living in Athens, was attacked by an anti-Semitic mob and his house vandalized. Denied restitution, he appealed to Britain, which upheld his rights by a naval blockade of the main port of Athens for two months in 1850, until Greece agreed to pay. Independent Greece was under the joint protection of Britain, France, and Russia; the incident caused debates in the houses of Parliament and a diplomatic crisis with France and Russia.

on the globe. Without it, there is not sufficient certainty or support for trade endeavors. This is why Northern Germany feels the lack of a strong navy, and it hopes that when it joins Prussia, its trade activity will increase dramatically. The Pacifico affair clearly shows just how dependent is a country conducting sea trade without a sufficiently strong navy. But where will Greece get a strong enough navy for its seafaring trade to rely upon, with the ability to take on a global character? Besides a powerful Slavic-Greek union, the only form in which the Eastern Roman Empire could be restored, no one could provide sufficient naval might.

For *Bulgaria* a general union of Slavs with Russia at the head would have a special, essential importance. Of all the Slavic tribes, it is under the heaviest oppression, since it lives in closest proximity to its [Ottoman] subjugators. It least of all has preserved the tradition of statehood and the memory of independent political existence. It is aware of its oppression and its difference from its oppressors, and thus cannot combine with them and change its cultural principles, so of course it strives for liberation. But how should it use this freedom? How can it change from tribal to political existence, to independent statehood? True, we have seen similar examples in Greece, Serbia, and Romania,[11] but the last example is not attractive, and is precisely the rock that must be avoided to escape shipwreck. The examples of Greece and Serbia are different in many essential ways from Bulgaria. They achieved independence by means of a long struggle, in the course of which they developed leaders standing out from the rest, distinct personalities as leaders in the forefront, having lived the life of the people, having understood the people's soul and needs. The people grew accustomed to them, and in this way the elements of social structures were formed from among the people itself. Serbia even preserved the memory of popular representation in the people's assembly [*skupshchina*]. There is nothing like this in Bulgaria.

Thus in a country like this the social and state structures come from outside, amounting to a constitution by formula, borrowed from a general theory based on foreign examples. Instead of the organization of the actual essential interests in the country, it establishes the leadership of the so-called intelligentsia: The united Wallachia and Moldavia offer a pitiful example of this. If education sinks deep roots into the life of the people, and is that life taken to its its highest development, then of course those individuals produced by this education will have not only the right but the obligation to serve as leaders of the people in its political as well as in its intellectual and moral life. Such examples of the harmonious internal development and education of the people in general are not so common, and the best of them is England. Neither Russia nor any other Slavic country can claim to have this. But without these foundations in the people, the so-called intelligentsia is nothing but a more or less sizable group of people shallow enough to draw an education from

---

[11] See Cuza, chap. 13, n. 57.

abroad without digesting it or assimilating it, only mulling in their heads and bantering to each other about fashionable ideas, which for a certain amount of time run their course under the vulgar label of "up-to-date."

But however superficial our Russian education, however cut off our intelligentsia (for the most part) from the life of the people, Russia and the Russian people are not a *tabula rasa* for its civilizing experiments, but willingly or unwillingly must conform to an age-old order of things reinforced by the customs of the people. To change this order, the intelligentsia must rely upon the principles of the people, often without even realizing it. When they forget this (as often happens), then a people with a long history as a social organism expels the foreign, like pus seeping from infected wounds, or by enfolding it in scar tissue to isolate it from any living contact with the organism of the people; and although the deathly rigidity of this foreign implant obstructs the correct path of the people's life, it does not completely block it, and it flows around it and passes it by. But this is not so with completely new countries, as we can assure ourselves from the example of the Romanian state, where there was full latitude for the civilizing activity of the intelligentsia.

For Bulgaria not to end up with such a fate, it needs to get settled under the wing of Russia and under the influence of other, politically more developed members of the Slavic union, in the closest interactions and connection with them: at first as an administratively independent province, then later as an independent political body. Russia's impartial guardianship over all the Slavic nationalities is the kind of protection Bulgaria needs, for yet another reason: so that this country populated by an independent Slavic tribe could preserve its independence and not be sacrificed to the ambitions of neighboring Serbia.[12]

For *Serbia* itself, a close connection to Russia and all Slavdom is no less beneficial, to suppress its faulty ambitious instincts and guide them in the proper direction: not against Bulgaria[13] but toward the lands under the dominion of Austria settled by the Serbian, and their closely related Croatian and Slovene, tribes. The hearty and strong Serbian people must beware of the Polish tradition of eagerly embracing the foreign and letting go of what is its own. In its struggle against the Italianization, the Magyarization, and the Germanization of its land, the Serbian people can find the necessary strength and hope of success only in a political union with all of Slavdom, under the supremacy of Russia.

---

[12] [Danilevskii's marginalia, published posthumously]: *Was not everything said here literally proven true? Did not the Bulgarian intelligentsia try to sow confusion, and only thanks to the support of Russia has it until now avoided its harmful influence? But on the other hand, did not Russia make a mistake by introducing constitutionalism to Bulgaria?*

[13] [Danilevskii's marginalia, published posthumously]: *And has not everything confirmed this?*

This applies to an even greater degree to the *Czech* tribe, whose territory juts out like a bastion, the foremost fortification in the German lands, in which German settlers have had great success. This apple of discord between Germandom and Slavdom cannot forever avoid either an internal struggle with Germans or an external attack, and it will not succeed in either one without being closely united with all of Slavdom.

Romania's only hope of annexing half of Transylvania, Bukovina, and part of Bessarabia is through the consent and support of Russia, and only by its disinterested, calming influence can it resist the predations of Magyarism. Only by relying on Slavdom, which is incomparably more closely related to it, can Romania contend with the corrosive influence of Gallicism, and the imitativeness of its pitiful intelligentsia.

In the preceding chapter we saw that even *Poland* can possibly find a favorable end to its long indolence only in the depths of an All-Slavic union, in close unity and friendship with Russia.

Only for *Hungary* is the prospect of such a union, which would limit all its overly-ambitious, grandiose plans, not a happy thought. But even it can hope to satisfy all its lawful ambitions; it would only be forced to give up its unlawful lust for power.

Such are the advantages each of the peoples who can and should form independent states in a great All-Slavic federation would receive from the union that would unite them. If we add to that the great, splendid, global historical role that such a union promises for all Slavdom, then it seems it would have to be, if not the direct aspiration of all Slavs conscious of their Slavic identity, then at least the object of their hopes or their political ideal. And actually, we can name more than one famous Slavic figure for whom the idea of Slavic unification in one form or another was this kind of ideal. Some examples who more or less clearly expressed this, to name a few, are Khomiakov, Pogodin, Hanka, Kollár, and Štúr.[14] However, many Slavs, even non-Europeanized ones, do not at all regard the political unification of their tribes under the headship of Russia with the sympathy we could and should expect them to have.

The aspersions of the Poles and Europe—completely false due to their small significance and (it could even be said) complete ignorance of Russia and unfamiliarity with our ways—have penetrated so deeply that even many of the foremost Slavic thinkers who are wholeheartedly devoted to the Slavic cause, are frightened as if by specters of some kind. On the one hand, on their own behalf, they fear the specter of Russia's lust for power, which allegedly

---

[14] Khomiakov: See chap. 7, n. 2. Kollár: See chap. 3, n. 1. Pogodin: See chap. 2, n. 8. Vaclav Hanka (1791–1861): Czech philologist and fervent Pan-Slav, participant in the Prague Slavic Conference of 1848. Ľudovít Štúr (1815–56): Slovak scholar, writer, and politician, nationalist leader responsible for the formal codification of the Slovak language in the 1840s, becoming a pro-Russian Pan-Slavist in his later years.

aspires to destroy the independence of the Slavic nationalities and swallow them up, like it swallowed Poland. On the other hand, for the fate of humanity and civilization in general, they fear the specter of world domination, which is something dreadful to the Slavic heart filled with humanitarianism, even if it is the domination of none other than poor, oppressed Slavs like themselves (whose own oppression never bothered anyone, nor struck anyone as incompatible with true humanity). That Slavic independence and the development of Slavic power are repulsive to Europe is simply the way things are. It would be pointless and silly for us or anyone else to try to change its mind about this. But it is sad that Slavs themselves, even Russians themselves, can take the same opinion. As much as is within our power, we will try to disperse this haze of assumptions, starting with Russia's lust for power.

The facts themselves will provide our answer and refutation. There is nothing here to expand upon: we will only point out all the obvious examples of how Russia has dealt with the provinces under its domain. Finland, won from the Swedes, was given full separation and independence: separate troops staying within the boundaries of Finland; separate monetary, trade, and finance systems, even a constitution and parliament. A region belonging to Russia for nearly a hundred years was annexed to it;[15] Russian language was not imposed on its schools; Orthodoxy was not made the state religion; it was not turned into a market for our manufactures; not one kopeck of Finland's revenues goes to Russia. In sum, in material and moral regards, not only has Russia not exploited Finland, but completely to the contrary, it has always extended a hand of assistance to it. The Baltic region not only was not Russified, but even the strongest tool of its Germanization—the Germanized University of Dorpat[16]—was founded and is maintained by the Russian state. The Russian state not only has not Russified the region, but even erected barriers against it, to keep it from occurring even in the natural course of events—and all, once again, out of fear of getting a reputation for oppressing the nationalities under Russia's domain. The very example of Poland so often held against Russia is actually better evidence in its favor. In its annexation to Russia, Poland has enjoyed a separate state and a constitutional order. Under Russian dominion, Polish influence has spread throughout western Russia by means of the University of Vilnius, the whole system of national education, and in many other ways. Only the Poles' flagrant, crude attempts to annex western Russia to itself by force[17] opened our eyes, and even then, it seems, only for a time. Although I say all this, of course, it is hardly in praise of Rus-

---

[15] Russia acquired Finland in 1809, and incorporated Vyborg Province into it, to form the Grand Duchy of Finland within the Russian Empire.

[16] Now Tartu, Estonia.

[17] Presumably Danilevskii has in mind the border wars of the Time of Troubles (1605–18); it seems an unlikely way to refer to any of the uprisings in post-partition Poland.

sia, its government, and its public opinion. But nevertheless these things clearly show that from a state acting in such a manner toward its constituent parts, its allies have no reason to worry about their independence either politically or as a people, no reason to fear any overstepping of the bounds of purely superficial political hegemony. Any closer internal connection would of course be permitted only by that native, national sympathy that would not fail to attract the members of the Slavic family to each other, once their external barriers were broken and they took up their common historical task.

But that is not all. If Russia has often acted in this way to its own detriment, why would it act any differently when the most obvious, the most simple calculation would convince it to refrain from any interference in the internal affairs of its allies, and not to mess with the independence of either their politics or their people?

In fact, what exactly would be the immediate, tangible political benefits for Russia in the formation of an All-Slavic union? (We are not talking here of the great cultural-historical significance it would have.) Of course, it would be in the increase of its external power, in the security for itself and for its allies against attack from the hostile West, in order to develop its capacity for internal, moral, and material well-being and greatness. The simplest means of reaching these goals is the noninterference in the internal affairs of its allies and impartial, conciliatory influence over their mutual relations—in their quarrels, pretensions, and ambitious wishful thinking.

What would Russia accomplish, on the contrary, by striving to destroy the internal independence of the Slavic and other states allied to it, and make them part of its own state body, even if it could succeed in doing so? Instead of forty million loyal, well-disposed allies, it would acquire forty million unwilling subjects; as to how much they would strengthen the state, we have abundantly convincing examples in the relations of Poland to Russia, Ireland to England, and even more so, Hungary and Venice to Austria.

Disregarding differences in the moral and physical qualities of peoples (considering them all equal or at least impossible to quantify), the comparative power of states nevertheless will not be directly dependent on the number of their subjects, because of the importance here of the relations between these subjects and the state unifying them into a single political body. All other conditions being equal (education, wealth, social order, and infrastructure), they can relate to it either as: an active, involved citizenry, honoring its goals as their own, its glory as their glory, its strength as the guarantee of their well-being, and thus serving it and supporting it morally and materially; or, as passive subjects, unquestioningly obeying the ruling power, but alienated from it, not considering its affairs their own, and thus being apathetic to its fate; or finally, as hostile subjects only submitting to force, not only indifferent to the state but rejecting it, considering its goals to be diametrically opposed to theirs.

The majority of states have subjects of all these types. But the combination of these three types is most striking in the British state, which has two hundred million subjects who (due to the education, wealth, and favorable geographic position of England and the majority of its colonies) would in truth constitute immeasurable power if all these millions could be considered truly active in their support. But only the population of England itself with Wales and Scotland can be counted in this category. The native population of India and other colonies, not excluding even Canada, must be considered in the column of passive subjects from which the state can really only hope to extract some financial gains, since even Canada would hardly be able to summon much energy to defend itself in case of attack by the United States. Finally a huge majority of the Irish population is completely hostile to England, and thus does not so much bring it material benefits, as it weakens it, diverting some amount of its strength into just holding on to it.

It is the same with Russia. Besides the Russian (that is, the Great Russian, the Little Russian, and White Russian) tribes, its active population consists of the Finnish, Georgian, and even part of the Tatar tribes, while for example its Siberian savages and nomads constitute its merely passive population, and its Poles (though not a people in and of themselves, but only under the influence of its clergy and aristocrats) are its hostile population.

In a statistical calculation of the power of states, only subjects of the first category can be considered a positive quantity (which strictly speaking still must be multiplied by certain coefficients, depending on the moral and material qualities of the people); passive subjects for this would have to be taken, if not as complete zeroes, then at least as a very small, fractional quantity; and subjects of the third category, as a negative amount.

But everyone knows that for one person physically to hold another in his power, he must considerably exceed him in strength. The same ratio of strength applies to whole peoples or political bodies, which explains the success of peoples rising up against the states striving to hold them under their power, like the Dutch against Spain, the Greeks against Turkey, and so on. Therefore, counting one active subject against one hostile is not sufficient to represent numerically the weakening of state power that results from holding or, so to speak, neutralizing its hostile elements.

Taking the population of the All-Slavic union as a hundred twenty million, and the hostile Polish and Magyar elements included within it as twenty to thirty million (we are disregarding the possibility of a conciliatory outcome for the Poles, the outcome described above), then the free, active forces of the union would reach about ninety-five million. If Russia, by a disruption of the internal independence of the states and peoples of the union, managed to bring them in as subjects of whatever form, then it would acquire forty million hostile subjects, which, according to our calculation, would cut down its free, active forces to thirty million. Considering how vast its Asian border is, requiring strong protection in the Caucasus, Central Asia, and other regions, this hardly leaves more than twenty million to stand against Europe. Considering the constant readiness of Europe to take advantage of the weakness of Russia, it would of course rush to offer its hand in assistance to the peoples oppressed by Russia, making them, even if hypocritically, its best friend (as now, concerning the Poles); then instead of increasing its power as expected, Russia would be forced to collapse under its own weight.

So the freedom of the Slavs and other peoples in the union, among themselves and with Russia, would be guaranteed on the one hand by a simple political concept, Russia's instinct for self-preservation, and on the other hand, by Russia's whole past: Russian vices and Slavic virtues in general would serve as the guarantee of the fair, harmless character of the mutual relations between the head of the union and its members. From the one who has done more, less should be expected: the one who gave national and even political freedom to the constituent parts of its state—like Finland for example—and even hostile Poland (only taking it away after the most senseless repeated abuses, for self-preservation and the defense of freedom for that part of the Russian people whom the Poles had plotted against) will not infringe upon the independence of its allies.

The other bogeyman that scares people away from the idea of All-Slavdom is the danger of global monarchy, the fear of world domination. As was made clear in the explanation just given, even if such world domination were a natural and necessary consequence of the All-Slavic union, then in any case it would be not especially Russian, but All-Slavic, domination—and to the Slavs, it would seem, there is nothing to fear. The ancient Romans were not afraid of the idea of global domination; England has no fear of the idea of global domination of the seas, and the expansion of its possessions, girdling the seas and oceans with a chain of large and small British colonies; even America is not afraid of the idea of unchallenged dominion from Greenland to Tierra del Fuego. What strange kind of modesty is this: to back away from a great future and avoid it for fear of becoming too powerful and strong, applying a parody of Voltaire's idea of God (who, if not existing, would have to be invented) to Austria,[18] to prevent this unfortunate outcome?

But that is not the point. This fear itself has no basis at all. A great Slavic union guaranteeing the freedom of the Slavs and their fruitful interaction with each other could not threaten anyone's independence or anyone's legal rights. Once again, a simple statistical calculation will confirm this. The population of only those parts of Europe that at the present time play an active political role—that is, Germany (after the apportionment of all the non-German parts of Austria), France, and England, with the addition of Belgium and Holland, which willingly or not always end up following them—would equal the population of the whole Slavic union. Including Italy, Spain, Portugal, and the Scandinavian states would create an excess on the European side of at

---

[18] I.e., Palacký; see chap. 13.

least fifty million people. Thus from the outset the Slavic system of states would still be significantly weaker than the European system of states by the amount of its population, and could only be considered insuperable in terms of the defense and protection of Slavic independence and autonomy. The balance of power would be equalized somewhat by the above-cited strategic locations of Constantinople and the Czech bastion.

But considering the abundant love of humanity in the Slavic heart, which considers it a most sacred obligation to sacrifice its own Slavic goals and interests to some unknown set of all-human goals (which, due to the most absurd habit of confusing this "all-human" with "Western" and "European," goes only to the benefit of the European, which is always hostile to the Slavic), we must not limit ourselves to the preceding evidence. We need to show that not only the independence, but the political power of the Slavs is vitally necessary for the lawful and harmonious course of intra-human interactions; that the political power of Slavdom not only cannot threaten the enslavement of the whole world or world domination, but only this can put up an adequate barrier against the world domination that more and more is being acquired (and to a significant degree, already has been) by Europe.

So far we have examined the course of European history from different points of view: the development of violence as one of the fundamental mental characteristics of Germanic-Roman nationalities, and how it keeps pace with the changes in the prevailing direction of opinion; the shaping of peoples by the historical events Europe experienced, compared to those Russia experienced; and finally the political knot tying together the Germanic-Roman and Slavic cultural-historical types, which will be untangled one way or another in the near future—the knot called the Eastern Question. It is clear in and of itself that there are almost countless points of view, and the construction of a whole system of history for each cultural type (that is, the presentation of all its events, in terms of the actual, natural connections between them) would require the prior investigation of its whole complex path from all different points of view, or at least from a significant number of them. This would amount to an analytical investigation of the whole aggregate of historical events, which would be extremely complicated, at whatever chronological moment we were to attempt it.

Each aspect of life has its roots and course of development; many of them run parallel to each other, intertwine, and act reciprocally upon one another. It is obvious that tracing a chronological sequence of events in all their complexity (even if it were a careful investigation of their pragmatic connections), and untangling this complexity, is simply impossible. So before the establishment of a natural system in botany, the ingenious Michel Adanson[19] arranged the forms of the plant kingdom according to sixty different systems, based on

---

[19] Michel Adanson (1727–1806): French botanist and naturalist. He outlined his system in *Familles naturelles des plantes* (Natural Families of Plants; 1763).

all the organs of plants—or in other words, he surveyed the plant kingdom from sixty different points of view, of different levels of importance and value. Coordinating these points of view, or systems, and combining them into one, he made the first successful conscious attempt at a natural system for the plant kingdom.

It seems to me only a method like this can produce fruitful results in the construction of scientific history. True, other methods exist, like that of Jussieu[20] in botany: a physiognomic evaluation of the similarity and difference of form, grasping the relative importance and significance of forms with a genius's instinct. This method worked adequately for the plant kingdom. But the complexity of historical events is far too great, and they do not stand before the investigator in such concrete actuality and vitality as natural phenomena, so that we could hardly hope for such success taking this approach to history.

This kind of comprehensive investigation into European history would of course require much more ability and knowledge than we possess, and besides, our goal is something different. We intend only to cast a glance at one side of European life: the connection existing between the struggle establishing proper mutual relations between members of the European family, and their outward actions—that is, their political influence on countries and peoples not belonging to the Germanic-Roman cultural type. This is necessary to elucidate the question now before us: Does the formation of an All-Slavic union threaten to bring about world domination or, on the contrary, does it constitute a necessary guarantee of freedom and diversity in the living expressions of the human type, a necessary bulwark against the threat of world domination coming from somewhere else altogether?

Charlemagne's[21] monarchy was the center from which developed the European system of states. Three nationalities divided from it, playing a major role in the Middle Ages and maintaining it to present times: the German, the French, and the Italian, each of which aspired in different ways toward internal unification, which their surrounding circumstances, their national character, and internal arrangement either helped or hindered to varying degrees. Subsequently added to those, from outside of Charlemagne's domain, were: Spain, gripped during the Middle Ages by an internal struggle with Islam; and England, whose island status kept it from close involvement in all-European matters until nautical advancements gave navies much greater influence. These five peoples were, and continue to be, the leading members of the European political system. Others like the Dutch and the Swedes, while they have from time to time played a significant role, could not do so continuously due to the numeric weakness of these peoples. But the five main European nationalities (if we take into consideration not historical happenstance but the common, unchanging foundations of their power, the influence of a

---

[20] Jussieu: See chap. 4, n. 3.

[21] Charlemagne: See chap. 3, n. 4.

great people, the structure of the state, and so on) are of almost identical strength, or at least equal enough that, generally speaking, the weakest among them is strong enough to withstand attack by its neighbors.

The most numerous of these nationalities is the German, which numbers about forty-three or forty-four million, not counting the Slavs and other peoples under their dominion. But this numerical preponderance is offset by the in many ways disadvantageous geographic situation of Germany, such as: irregular borders; a considerable expanse from west to east; annexations of Slavic lands to the south and east; and a central location, permitting attack from various sides. The disadvantages are such that preserving Germany's independence from France and Turkey would have required, until very recently, the help of the Slavs it managed to include within its borders, as well as the independent states of Poland and Russia.

The French are five to six million less in number, but this is made up for by a very regular shape or the concentration, so to speak, of the lands they occupy.

England's population is seven to eight million less, but it has insurmountable defensive strength from its situation as an island, which however weakens its offensive strength. This is why, neither having been nor being able to take and hold power over any particular part of the mainland, it is all the more concerned that none of the European states should gain too much preponderance over the others.

Italy, smaller than England in terms of its population, is bounded by the Alps in the north, and by water on all other sides, which offers the best protection, considering England's concern to maintain equilibrium between European powers.

Finally, Spain's population has declined to some fifteen million only as a result of temporary, coincidental reasons and a bad state structure. It is even better protected by geographical circumstances than Italy: separated from its only neighbor, France, by the Pyrenees and, besides that, transected in various ways by high mountain ranges, which are powerful defenses for even weak nations.

From such a balance of strength among the main European nationalities it follows, as a necessary consequence, that the so-called system of political equilibrium is not some kind of artificial formula thought up by diplomats, but the natural, normal order of things, applied to Europe in the strict and only true meaning of the word "order," which not only does not contradict the principle of nationality but is precisely its only firm, solid foundation (just as in the Slavic world, by the same principle, the natural order of things can only be based on the hegemony of Russia). Thus the equilibrium of European states is the only foundation of a stable order, and whatever may disturb it, it always returns by what may be called the force of things.

But due to the stunted significance that until very recent times the principle of nationality has had in the European world, it is clear that the normal relationship between the members of the European family could not be understood and grasped from the very start, but that it became clear little by little, in the course of events and by the play of political forces, in which each strives for its fullest expression and predominance over the others. Strictly speaking, when political equilibrium was understood, in practice (even if not in the hypocritical language of diplomacy or in the naïve language of the phony science of the people's rights [*mnimaia nauka narodnogo prava*]) it never was recognized as any kind of principle of law, but was only accomplished in fact, often independent of the will of the political players involved.

This normal condition of political equilibrium for European states was disturbed both in the normal course of events (by what we call accidents of history) and by the natural striving for hegemony of various nationalities at various times, largely due to the passions and ambitious plans of those individuals in whom these nationalities' interests become concentrated. But all these attempts in the course of time proved groundless, only succeeding for a relatively short period, since from the very essence of things they were counteracted by the distribution of political power and strength resting in the very foundation of the Germanic-Roman state system.

With this natural equality of basic strengths of the leading European nationalities, the one of them that possessed the greatest internal strength and unity (from its state structure or from the character of the person ruling it), or gained particular power from the confluence of fortuitous historical accidents, would strive to achieve predominance and domination by conquering the state that, for opposite reasons, found itself weak and fragmented. If this aspiration succeeded, then by almost doubling its strength, the conquering state would [theoretically] gain such predominance that the system of political equilibrium would turn to hegemony. But this never once happened in however long a time: in part because of the opposition of other states, instinctively or consciously sensing the harm it would bring; and in part because of events that were, so to speak, extraneous, which is to say, occurring for completely different reasons.

It was natural that wars founded on the internal struggle of European states over the division of political strength and power (the category includeing all wars of pure conquest, or so-called "wars of succession," and even those of a different, moral sort, such as religious wars and revolutionary wars) would neutralize the power of Europe in other theaters of global activity and distract it from conquering and spreading European influence in other parts of the world.

After a struggle like this, of course, fatigue set in; but whenever the calm (arising either from the temporary achievement of hegemonic plans or from the establishment of equilibrium) was long enough for exhausted forces to revive, they found an outlet in external activity and went toward the occupation of countries outside of Europe. In this way the internal struggle between the main members of the European system served in a way to guarantee the independence of the countries and peoples outside of Europe. I now intend to trace, in a cursory sketch, this relationship between the gradual development and achievement of a system of political equilibrium among European states, on the one hand, and the development of the power and influence of Europe over outside countries, on the other.

In the beginning of European history, the active role in disturbances of the political equilibrium predominantly was played by Germany, then later by France. The interval of time between this change of roles, which almost co-incides with the change from medieval history to modern, was filled by the unusual successes of Spain. And on the contrary, the passive role (the object of these peoples' ambitions) was played from the beginning to most recent times predominantly by Italy. It was the main instrument by which Germany, Spain, and France hoped to achieve hegemony, because from the very fall of the Western Roman Empire until recent times, it had not once managed to achieve internal unification of any form. Temporarily filling this passive role was, from the primary states, Spain and Germany, for the same reasons of in-ternal divisiveness; and from among the secondary nationalities, the Dutch.

Induced by its idealized inheritance of the Roman imperial crown, Ger-many in the time of the Ottos[22] sought to conquer Italy, and to a great degree succeeded in this, since it encountered no opposition anywhere. Spain was then preoccupied by its struggle with the Moors; England was isolated from taking active part in the affairs of the European continent by its island posi-tion; and France, under the last Carolingians and first Capetians, was at the very height of the feudal disturbances that reduced kingly power almost to complete insignificance. Here we find the first example of counteraction by events of a completely different sort than the equilibrium of political forces: namely, by events in the moral realm, whose representatives in the Germanic-Roman territory of that time were the popes. They defended the indepen-dence of Italy and, by their spiritual influence, established the period of equi-librium that we call (see chapter 10) the period of the first harmonious devel-opment of the Germanic-Roman cultural type. This equilibrium was founded, however, not on the political balance of power among the nationalities of Europe, but on the moral hegemony of the papacy. And in the period of this equilibrium, Europe, for the first time, directed its surplus forces against the East [in the Crusades], conquering Palestine under the influence of Christian ideas, and for half a century even taking possession of the Byzantine Empire. But it could not definitively gain a foothold on the eastern coast of the Medi-terranean Sea, due to the energetic opposition of the Muslim world. Venice and Genoa won longer-lasting acquisitions in the eastern Mediterranean and the Black Sea, which, however, were likewise wrested from their hands by the Turks.

---

[22] I.e., the tenth century: Otto I (936–73), Otto II (973–83), Otto III (983–1002).

Continuous strain led to the weakening of overall strength, but on the other hand, each state was preoccupied by the struggle with feudalism, from which the first victor to emerge was France, united by the genius of its kings, particularly Louis XI [r. 1461–83]. And by the time of his son's reign it began to aspire to European hegemony by means of conquering Italy. This attempt continued under Louis XII [r. 1498–1515] and Francis I [r. 1515–47], but the alliances of the pope, Venice, and the Holy Roman Empire prevented its success.

Spain assumed the active role. The final victory over the Moors coincided fortuitously with the ability to appreciate Columbus's ingenious proposal, which gave it supremacy over America. By accident of inheritance, the wealth of the Netherlands, the battle-tested knights of Spain, and the tradition of greatness and primacy in Europe of the German empire all came into the capable hands of Charles V,[23] and his brother inherited the lands of Austria. Simply put, all of Europe except for France, England, and the Scandinavian states was consolidated under Charles V or the house of Habsburg. All the energies of France went toward maintaining its own independence. Political hegemony was asserted on a scale not seen since the time of Charlemagne.

If this order of things had continued, it is obvious that the remaining independent states would have fallen into a secondary, dependent role. But again, a force of a different order of things destroyed the power that had accumulated in certain hands. Religious wars turned little by little into a war for equilibrium,[24] and ended in a general weakening of strength, from which it took Germany a long time to recover, which Spain still has not managed to do.

The Peace of Westphalia [1648] reestablished equilibrium, and once again at that time the power of Europe expanded to other parts of the earth, predominantly in the hands of Holland, which had managed to recover earlier than others (after the efforts that won back its independence), and also England and France, establishing their first colonies in North America.

After the religious storms, the first to recover and grow internally stronger once again was France, and Louis XIV[25] articulated with full clarity its aspiration for hegemony. With reliable tact, this ruler for the first time turned the focus of activity from Italy, which all his predecessors aspired to subjugate, to one of the secondary states (in terms of the size of the people populating it), Holland, the industrial wealth, trade, navy, and colonies of which would strengthen France, if successful, to an incomparably greater degree than the acquisition of much more expansive and more populous countries. At the end of his reign, the opportunity arose for another goal—Spain.

---

[23] Charles V: See chap. 2, n. 3.

[24] Danilevskii has in mind the Thirty Years' War (1618–48).

[25] Louis XIV: See chap. 2, n. 2.

Neither one succeeded, primarily due to the opposition of England, which by the conditions of its political, state structure could not maintain a sizable land army, and by its nature opposed any unwarranted accumulation of power into single hands. At this time it began to acquire dominion over the seas and became, so to speak, the favorite sword of Europe in other parts of the world because, whereas in the hands of Spain the domination of the seas had served to strengthen its domination in Europe, in the hands of England, which did not and could not have designs on the continent of Europe, it served as the guarantee of equilibrium.

After the Peace of Utrecht [1713] there followed again a period of fatigue and balance of power, or more precisely, a balance of general weakness, during which the seeds of the future unity of Italy and Germany were formed, coming to fruition in our time. The interruption of male succession in the Habsburg Dynasty and the fragmented, disunited condition of Germany tempted France even in the time of Louis XV to bring it under its influence. Proceeding from that, as well as from the ambition of Prussia, wars[26] led to the strengthening of the latter and gave England the opportunity to seize France's, and part of Spain's, overseas possessions. These were not new acquisitions, but only changed from one European ruler to another.

The French Revolution [1789–99] sunk Europe into lethargy. And then, wars begun in order to counteract revolutionary ideas and their propaganda turned into wars to assert French superiority in Europe. Under the influence first of revolutionary enthusiasm, then the military genius of Napoleon, France achieved its goals, subsequently conquering the weak or internally divided Netherlands, Italy, and Germany.

Just as in the time of Charles V, Europe itself did not have the strength to restore equilibrium this time; but opposition from another, non-political order of things, appearing only in Spain, was insufficient to break the power of Napoleon. Help came to Europe from outside. Russia was destined to perform its servile role for the restoration of European equilibrium, regardless of its own true interests.

After the Congress of Vienna, an almost forty-year period of continuous peace set in. Europe rested and turned its efforts more successfully than at any other time toward spreading and asserting its dominion over non-European countries. Whereas during the war for equilibrium one of the warring sides (most recently, England) would only seize the colonies of its enemies, now with its forces unencumbered, not caught up in internal struggle, Europe asserted its dominion over new, formerly independent countries. France conquered Algeria, asserted its predominance in northern Africa, and acquired colonies in Australia.[27] England definitively conquered the western Indian

---

[26] The War of the Austrian Succession (1740–48) and the Seven Years' War (1756–63).

[27] A French discovery expedition to the southern coast of Australia in 1801 caused some panic among the British, but it had no political charge and no French colony in

Peninsula and crossed the Indus in the west and the Brahmaputra in the east, conquering a significant part of the Burmese Empire; assimilated the whole of the Australian mainland, Van Diemen's Land [Tasmania], and New Zealand; and even made a breach into China, which was subsequently made wider and wider with the assistance of France.

With the ascension to the throne of Napoleon III, the order established by the Congress of Vienna was destroyed. Being the heir to the name and disposition of his uncle, Napoleon could not fail to aspire to the restoration of French hegemony, but he chose a completely different path than all his predecessors to attain this goal. In accordance with his character, he wanted to gain it not by conquest of one or another country presenting the opportunity through its internal disunity, but by the smoke and mirrors[28] of European public opinion and raising consciousness of national distinctiveness.

The coronation of Napoleon in itself did not destroy the equilibrium of Europe. Internal discord did not neutralize its strength. Napoleon found the most desirable object of external activity, and intended first of all to reconcile Europe with himself and with his name, which had seemed to it like a bad omen. With the truest understanding of European public opinion, he aroused Europe as if to a Trojan campaign against Russia, with himself as Agamemnon.[29] His venture [i.e., the Crimean War] was crowned with success because on Russia's part there was no such understanding of things. Russia could not let go of the idea that it was part of the European family, and could not grasp a different notion, that it is the head of the Slavic family. It continued to consider itself the representative and defender of the legitimist, anti-revolutionary side of European life, and only later did it reluctantly give up that role, for lack of anyone to represent or defend. The Holy Alliance was destroyed at the moment when (for the first time since it was founded) it had to act on Russia's behalf. But for all that, from the very start Russia did not want to attach to the war its actual scope and actual significance, for fear of being counted among the rebels against the sultan's majesty.

In any event, success against Russia legalized and legitimized Napoleon in the eyes of Europe. Having achieved his preliminary goal, he embarked on the first step to give him hegemony in Europe, and like a majority of his predecessors—German emperors and French kings—chose Italy as the instrument. But once again he intended to follow a completely new plan. He meant not to conquer, but to free Italy, and having made of it a weak federation with the inclusion of Austria and the pope, to place it in complete dependence

---

Australia was formally declared. Another French scientific expedition produced similar rumors in the 1820s. The French colony nearest to Australia was New Caledonia, a Melanesian archipelago 1500 km from the Australian coast, which is probably what Danilevskii has in mind.

[28] *Eskamotatitsiei*; cf. French *escamotage,* "conjuring, juggling, sleight of hand," etc.

[29] Mythical king who united the Greeks to undertake the Trojan War.

upon him. But the smoke and mirrors did not succeed because Cavour was even more cunning, and with the help of the noble enthusiast Garibaldi hoodwinked Napoleon to unify Italy. He had to be content with Nice and Savoy.

Thus instead of asserting French hegemony, it turned out that European equilibrium got a broader foundation. The main motive inducing, or to put it better, seducing the ambitious man to seek predominance—the unification of Italy—was replaced by its independence and unity which, once firmly established became a new pillar of the European political system founded on the balance of powers.

Napoleon, however, did not lose heart: the Civil War in North America presented the opportunity to atone for the ambitious intentions that had been revealed to all Europe.[30] All the republicanism and freedom of the North American states is not so close to the heart of Europe as the monarchism of Russia. This became clear in the time of trial that mighty republic underwent in the first half of the 1860s [i.e., the U.S. Civil War]. Among individual people, true, sympathy for the republic on the Atlantic coast was quite high, just as in the time of Catherine, her liberal measures and plans, even her victories over the Turks inspired sympathy for Russia among the leaders of European public opinion. But just as then the foremost politicians (like Choiseul[31] and Frederick the Great) left the public opinion of Europe behind in their hostility and enmity toward Russia, so now the leading political figures have the same unfriendly regard for the North American states. Therefore the assertion of European power on the American mainland would of course be welcome and pleasing to Europe.

This undertaking, if successful, would bring European sympathies to his side. At the outset, Napoleon in fact had in mind to elevate the importance of the Latin race and stand at its head in one way or another, having reason to consider himself its predestined representative. As a matter of fact, he was Italian by descent on his father's side, Creole by descent on his mother's side, French so to speak by adoption, and through his wife he gained a connection to Spanish nationality.

---

[30] [Danilevskii's marginalia, published posthumously]: *He intended to spread European influence in America by his Mexican expedition, taking advantage of internecine strife among the North American states. But the States forced the French to withdraw, and thus power from outside of Europe saved America from European predominance. The All-Slavic Union must do the same thing.* [Translator's note: The French invaded Mexico in 1861, seized the capital in 1863, and declared the Austrian Archduke Ferdinand Maximilian of Habsburg (1832–67) Emperor Maximilian I of Mexico in 1864, all during the U.S. Civil War. The U.S. opposed the new monarchy, and after the war ended supported Mexico's republican rebels in 1866 by blockading the ports, massing troops on the border, and demanding France remove its forces, which it did over the course of the year. In 1867 Maximilian was captured and executed (despite many pleas from Europe to spare his life) as a stern warning against foreign interference.]

[31] Choiseul: See chap. 12, n. 41.

The victory of the North obviously destroyed his plans and hopes, and soon a different, more bitter misfortune befell him. In a more daring and cunning maneuver than Cavour's, Count Bismarck hypnotized or deceived him and many others, in order to lay broad and solid foundations for the unification of Germany. The seeds planted by the Peace of Utrecht (the foundation of the Sardinian and Prussian kingdoms) grew and finally brought forth its abundant fruit: Italy and Germany left their divisiveness behind.

In this manner we see that all the pretexts and temptations to destroy the system of political equilibrium of Europe (which is founded, as we have said, in the very ethnographic makeup and topographical character of the lands of its foremost tribes) one by one have disappeared, and after each new struggle, political equilibrium becomes stronger and stronger, more and more stable. What congresses could not accomplish with all the collective diplomatic wisdom of Europe emerged on its own out of these very aspirations to destroy what was for Europe the natural order of things; and today in this regard we can see it as almost completely established, since all of the five major nationalities have achieved both their unification and their independence. It is still possible and even probable for the smaller nationalities to be absorbed by the larger, for instance Portugal by Spain; a division of Belgium and Holland between France and Germany; and the unification of the Scandinavian states. But all of this would scarcely lead to a general conflict in the European world. Strictly speaking, only one essential question of equilibrium remains unresolved: Will France be reconciled to an expansion of Prussian hegemony, sooner or later, over southwestern Germany and all the German tribes in general?[32]

But whether yes or no, what is important for us now is the indisputable fact that with the unification of all the major European nationalities, and thus the near-complete elimination of the pretexts and temptations to destroy the political system of equilibrium, all the former hindrances to the spread of European dominion over other parts of the world have now fallen.

Having been a force from the very beginning of European history, strengthened by its religious fanaticism and militancy, Islam collapsed, along with the spirit of its followers. The immensity, massiveness, and/or remoteness of such political bodies as China and Japan in eastern Asia lost their defensive significance once steam power was applied to military purposes, since now it became possible to transport to the opposite hemisphere a mass of troops strong enough for a rapid and energetic suppression of any uprising that might occur, and even to take these troops deep within the country by means of rivers. Finally the truest obstacle to Europe's world domination—the internal struggles of European states to establish proper relations among themselves—has also been eliminated by the near-complete attainment of

---

[32] [Danilevskii's marginalia, published posthumously]: *Again, has this not been confirmed?*

stable equilibrium. All the ambitious activity of Europe (of which there has been no lack) is to an increasing degree directed toward what is not Europe, as was always the case during a truce in its internal struggle. The *Drang nach Osten*[33] is not long in turning from word into deed.

Fortunately, just as the old obstacles to Europe's world domination had fallen, there arose two new ones, and only they had the ability to stop it in its path, and lay the foundation of true global equilibrium. These two obstacles are the United States of America and Russia. But the first is insulated from the interference of Europe by the barriers of the New World, and because of its position is comparatively less interested in how to handle the Old World, and also cannot in and of itself have a great influence on this theater of activity. Thus the full burden of preserving the balance of powers in the Old World rests on the shoulders of Russia. But if the American states are strong enough to fulfill the task laid upon them, due to their overseas location, the same cannot be said of Russia.

The irreconcilable hostility of Europe toward Russia is proven by long experience, and from that we have every reason to believe that as soon as Europe puts the last of its affairs in order, when the new elements of its system's political equilibrium have time to settle down and get firmly established, then just as it was in the Eastern War, the first excuse will be enough for an attack on Russia. And excuses of this kind are always readily provided by the East and Poland.

But only a united Slavdom can contend with a united Europe. And so, an All-Slavic union does not threaten world domination, but on the contrary offers the necessary and at the same time only possible guarantee of preserving global equilibrium, as the only bulwark against the world domination of Europe. This union would be no threat to anyone, but a purely defensive measure not only in the particular interests of Slavdom, but for the whole world. The result of an All-Slavic union would not be world domination, but an equal and proper division of power and influence among the peoples or groups of peoples that should be considered the active agents in the present era of world history—Europe, Slavdom, and America—which are each at different stages of development.

By the position and general direction of settlement and the spread of its dominion, the power or influence of Europe is liable to be primarily in Africa, Australia, and the southern peninsulas of Asia; that of the United States is in the Americas; and that of Slavdom is western, central, and eastern Asia, or the whole continent except Arabia and both Indian peninsulas [i.e., India and Southeast Asia].

But, some might object, the world domination of Europe is nothing like global monarchy, that terrible enemy of progress, since Europe is not one state, but a collection of completely independent states. This view of the dan-

---

[33] *Der Drang nach Osten*: See chap. 3, n. 7.

gers presented by world domination is extremely shortsighted. Whether it is a world-monarchy or a world-republic, world sovereignty of one system of states or one cultural-historical type would be equally harmful and dangerous for the progressive (in the only true sense of this word) course of history. The danger consists not of the political rule of a certain state, but of the cultural sovereignty of one cultural-historical type, regardless of its internal political structure. The actual, profound danger consists of the completion of the very order of things our Westernizers hold as their ideal: the genuine, not phony, reign of the all-human civilization they so admire. This would be the same as ending the whole possibility of any further success or progress in history, such as the introduction of a new worldview, new goals, and new aspirations, which always have their roots in the particular mental framework of new ethnographic elements embarking on their creative pursuits.

For proof of this, we need only consider the collective wealth of historical experience. Imagine if the domination of Rome were worldwide, in the actual, non-hyperbolic, sense. Minus some outside shock that would hasten the disintegration and decay from internal causes of the colossal Roman cultural-historical type, and disperse the putrid vapors arising from it—where would renovation come from? Christianity itself could not pour new life into this deteriorating body, and would only manage to show its incompatibility with the Roman order of things. Did not the divine founder of Christianity himself say that new wine cannot be poured into old wineskins or they will burst and spill the wine?[34] And in this essential regard would it not be all the same whether Rome were a monarchy, a republic, or even a series of states connected (or not connected) to each other by some political bond, however it is defined? Were there not essentially the same consequences from the decomposition of the Greek historical type, even though it was fractured into many political entities independent of each other: the Kingdoms of Macedonia, Syria, and Egypt, Greek republics, and even republican federations? Do we not see, on the contrary, that where there has been the ruin of ancient cultures that outlived themselves (as in China), renovation from within did not take place? In political bodies becoming decrepit, just as in individual people, once the wellsprings of vital forces run dry, all that remains is the form they cling to like a holy Ark of the Covenant, in the preservation of which they see their salvation of whatever sort.

Neither individual people nor whole peoples can be reborn in old age and begin another kind of life, proceeding from new principles, and striving for other goals (which, as we have seen, are a necessary condition of progress). Thus, for the culture-breeding forces not to dry up in the human race in general, it is necessary for new agents, new peoples bearing these forces, to appear, with a different mental framework, different enlightening principles, a different historical upbringing. So there needs to be a place where these seeds

---

[34] Matthew 9: 17.

of the new can be born, so as not to be subordinate to the influence, not to mention the power, of the one cultural-historical type. There could be no greater restriction imposed on humanity than the realization of a single all-human civilization. World domination should thus strike fear, not so much for the political, as for the cultural, consequences. It is not a question of whether the world is controlled by a republic or a monarchy, but whether it is controlled by a single civilization, a single culture, since this would deprive the human race of one of the necessary conditions for success and perfection: the element of diversity.

So we can say with full assurance that an All-Slavic union not only would not threaten world domination, but is the only protection against it. But is it really possible for such a union to have a stable existence, or at least an existence lasting for any length of time? Does not historical experience show that most federations have been too short-lived and thus did not enjoy much political power? If we closely examine the conditions of that weakness and short duration, it will be easy to see that there were always particular reasons, not in the federative form itself, but in some kind of accidental deficiencies coming from the form not corresponding to its contents, under which, of course, no form can be long-lasting or stable, but will necessarily, so to speak, either stifle its contents or be burst by them.

We have already assessed the facts that determine the possibility and suitability of the federative structure. We will only briefly remind our readers of them, since they are not complicated and can be expressed in the following few propositions.

A single people cannot[35] constitute a federation if it is not separated from its neighbors by hard-to-surmount physical obstacles, such as wide seas, high mountain ranges, and so on.

Peoples that are not connected by tribal affinity cannot form a lasting federation.

In terms of relations existing between the ethnographic elements making up a federation, its parts must be organized by either a kind of equilibrium or a kind of hegemony.

Finally, a dualistic kind of federation is impossible—it will quickly destroy itself.

All the failures federations have encountered can be attributed to these causes. Think about it: could the German people in the German Confederation, divided only by historical chance into various kingdoms, dukedoms, and principalities, be content with a federative form having no kind of internal bases or reasons to exist, doomed to relative weakness and helplessness among the stronger, more politically-centralized neighbors surrounding it? On the other hand, could this purely artificial diplomatic structure resist the first man of ambition who senses its strength and is able to give preference to

---

[35] [Danilevskii's marginalia, published posthumously]: *And must not.*

the essence of things (however indistinct or undefined) rather than an empty form (fulfilling only an outward, conditional obligation)? This federation would have even less chance of surviving because of its dualistic form, in which Prussia would have to try to exclude Austria, while Austria would try to reduce Prussia to a second- or third-rate state, in order to acquire unchallenged hegemony.

Ancient Greece could be governed in a federative form while its geographic position and the weakness of its neighbors protected it from outside enemies. But even in this case, the main reason for the weakening of its political power and the final destruction of its independence was the dualism of Sparta and Athens. While the ethnographic composition of Greece initially required a federative arrangement of equilibrium among the parts, it later required much closer relations with Macedonia and a conscious, deliberate submission to its hegemony.

Switzerland, on the contrary, has very stably maintained its federative arrangement since the country is protected by nature [i.e., the Alps] from external attack, and its independence is assured by its widely recognized neutrality. But its arrangement by a kind of equilibrium corresponds adequately enough to the actual distribution of strength among its cantons.

A federative form suits America because its geographic position already protects its independence, but a nationality that has not yet become clear and is still in the period of its ethnographic formation leaves open the possibility of any form of state system, to which it has not yet fully adapted.

If we apply these requirements to Slavdom, we would be easily convinced that its ethnographic elements are such that no other form of political unification than the federative form could satisfy them. Besides that, the proximity of powerful and hostile Europe would force it to take the form of a close federative union. But the relative strength of the Slavic tribes as well as their historical upbringing, and the historical experience Russia has acquired as a result, obviously requires a hegemonic type of federation. On this issue, doubt could arise only in the heads of those Polish szlachtists devoid of nationality, cut off from any true soil.

In this manner all the internal and external conditions combine to lend stability and durability precisely to the federative arrangement of the Slavic world.

But for all that, suppose the political union of Slavs were short-lived; suppose it lasted only a comparatively short time, as did the late German Confederation.

This could happen without any unusual harm for Slavdom, if during this time its current enemies recognized its independence and uniqueness, and if Europe dropped its hostility toward an independent, unique Slavdom, whether accepting the fact once accomplished, or grasping its inability to overthrow it. Then suppose Slavdom were to form more extensive political bonds between its members and turn from a close federative union into a political system of states of one cultural type. Its main goal (which is not political, but cultural) would be attained: a general coordination of efforts to attain independence and uniqueness, as well as ongoing cohabitation, so to speak, under a single political roof; and the feeling and awareness of ethnic kinship uniting them will trickle through all layers of society of all the Slavic peoples.

On the other hand, an ongoing recurrent struggle with Europe, without which Slavdom cannot fulfill its destiny, will spread a saving disenchantment with what comes from enemies and foster greater value and love toward one's own, the truly-Slavic. If this regard for the foreign European and for one's own Slavic were to turn into a standard of justice, or were to turn into exclusivity and patriotic fanaticism, even that would be beneficial and healthy to the highest degree, after such a longstanding distortion of normal relations in the other direction. To straighten a tree that the wind has long bent in one direction, it is likewise necessary to bend it in the other direction by force. Therefore Slavdom's struggle with Europe—this last phase of the Eastern Question coming closer and closer, growing more and more ripe—has equal importance, in our opinion, as the triumph of Slavdom and the affirmation of its independence and uniqueness.[36]

Next, as the necessary result of the political unification of Slavdom, a common language would emerge, which could be none other than Russian; it would become predominant enough to produce a fruitful exchange of thought and mutual cultural influence among all the members of the Slavic family.

In this way essential unity would be attained, and with the attainment of internal contents, the form would lose much of its importance and meaning, but only if, I repeat, circumstances permitted this form to become the wall and stronghold its essence requires.

Many true, sincere friends of Slavdom now see this essence as the most important thing, so that their aspirations and desires are inclined only toward the attainment of spiritual unity through the introduction of the Russian language as the common language of sciences, arts, and international affairs between all Slavic peoples. Speaking off the point, we completely share this frame of mind, but would merely point out that such a view of things is completely impractical, precisely because spiritual unity is the most essential and important kind, higher than political unity, which is lower by comparison. So first of all the lower level must be attained, if we are to reach the higher level; the lower level is the foundation, which is why we must start there.

---

[36] [Danilevskii's marginalia, published posthumously]: *And this phase already began with the last Turkish war. But Russia, conducting the war poorly from the beginning, after many mistakes and a significant depletion of its financial and military resources, would not commit to this fight and accepted the shameful Treaty of Berlin, the harmful influence of which continues to this day. But its consequences inevitably will lead to this conflict.*

It seems to me that promoting Russian as the All-Slavic language while the Slavic tribes are not politically free (while they constitute parts of strange, foreign political bodies and are obliged to sustain, support, and strengthen these bodies) is on the one hand as impractical as the famous method of catching a bird by putting salt on its tail, and on the other hand, would be useless even if it were practical. Galicia can serve as proof of this latter point, where (according to the ethnic makeup of its residents) the Russian language is already the language of the people, and what? Can we be content with this kind of unity? Despite the unity of language, is there any actual unity between Russia and Galicia? And is there not constant danger threatening this language: from various distortions introduced to it and supported governmentally, or of it becoming some kind of pariah language, eliminated from the sciences, from literature, and from all higher expressions of human thought?

A few years of common struggle (in the simple, literal sense of the word) conducted for a holy cause, and a few years of political cohabitation, will do more for the spiritual unity of the Slavs and for the promotion of Russian language as the All-Slavic means of exchanging thoughts and sentiments, than a century of intense, unflagging efforts by means of special conferences and speech and print advocacy.

Under political separation there can only be a purely ideal notion of the need for a common language. In all Slavdom only a few select people can be capable of it, and from them, only those who—whether from the rare brilliance of their views, the deep national feeling burning within them, or by especially favorable circumstances of their development—do not succumb to the European influence that has divided Slavdom. But political unity, on the contrary, would turn the spread of Russian language through all Slavdom into an urgent, everyday necessity not only for the most educated and highly developed persons, not only academics and writers, but for any person engaging in practical affairs. The most simple arrangement, teaching Russian language in the schools, could within a few years accomplish the same kind of dissemination and predominance as the German language among the Austrians, Turkish among the Turks, and as Magyar doubtless will attain among the Hungarian Slavs.

How great is the significance of political unification for the dissemination of language among foreigners, even those hostilely disposed toward the language of the ruling tribe, can be seen in the example of the Poles of our western provinces and the Germans of the Baltics. Despite inadequate and even erroneous measures taken by the Russian government for the establishment of the Russian language among the upper classes of the western Russian and Baltic provinces; despite also the systematic opposition of the Poles and Germans against Russian as the language of the schools and administration—still a majority of them know it, and in any case it is disseminated among them to an incomparably greater degree than among the most amicable toward us

Slavic tribes of Austria and Turkey. How quickly the knowledge of the Russian language must spread in the Slavic lands after their liberation and union with Russia, where in place of hostility will be a friendly disposition, which doubtless will strengthen significantly when the Slavs are given a brotherly hand of assistance to win their freedom and to affirm our common greatness, glory, and prosperity!

There is still one consideration: the friends and adherents of Slavdom who would like the strengthening of Slavic common bonds [*obshcheniia*] to be confined to the purely moral realm (examples of this frame of mind were amply presented at the famous Slavic conference in Moscow and St. Petersburg [of 1867]) insist that the Slavic idea has not penetrated deeply enough, either among us or in western Slavic societies. In their opinion a scientific and literary union of Slavic hearts and souls, so to speak, constitutes a higher sphere transcending the political, and that alone is worth striving for. I know that many who have spoken and written in that vein have bridled their thoughts and words out of external considerations, for the sake of a different sort of propriety; but some sincerely think that way. Such ethereal common bonds [*obshcheniia*] and unity of hearts and souls can truly exist in one sphere of human relations, but in only one: the religious sphere, higher than all other earthly spheres. But however elevated it may be, the national interest [*interes narodnyi*], although it comes directly after the religious interest, is still completely and entirely an earthly interest, which we must attain by a more positive, earthly, and material kind of means.

They say Slavdom is still not prepared for political unification; tribal factions divide it; it has the most disturbing notions about Russia and perhaps even regards it with suspicion. But it will never be prepared, will never leave its individual quarrels and rivalries, will never recognize Russia: put simply, it will never grow up unless the force of events pushes it out of its petty setting into the world-historical arena by a great historical jolt. To think that oral and written propaganda could be substituted for the pedagogical role of history, for either the western Slavs or for us, means to misunderstand the true measure of our own power and the power of our opponents, and means taking up the struggle (which must decide our fate) in the most disadvantageous field of endeavor for us.

We must not deceive ourselves: in the realm of influence upon public opinion, in the battle of words, intrigues, and temptations, Europe is incomparably stronger and more active than us, for reasons that are entirely simple and clear. Europe is overflowing with intellectual forces in all fields of endeavor, and to survive [Europeans] must emigrate and exploit virgin lands, such as in the East. In Constantinople alone there is a vast colony of European merchants and manufacturers, and all of them are voluntary or involuntary propagandists of the European idea, even if they do not realize it. Meanwhile we lack these forces in whatever fields we have not turned our attention to. We have nothing to spare for spreading the Russian idea.

And that is not all. Europe has two accomplices in spreading its goals and plans for the East, two sorts of missionary organizations: the Catholic clergy (predominantly the Jesuits) and revolutionary emigration (of Poles in particular). How can we oppose them? Any foreign government agent is, regardless of his frame of mind or political party, also a propagandist of European influence, since however deeply divided [Europeans] are amongst themselves, it does not extend to the point of rejecting the European idea. The ultramontanist clergyman can offer his hand in this regard to the reddest democrat and socialist. Can the same be said for us? Our consuls or government agents in general (according to our own service arrangements) are official bureaucrats only, who cannot spread Russian propaganda in any way, because it would only give rise to endless rumors and scandals, and would now attract the same scrutiny as the Turkish and Austrian governments do.

Do we even need to mention that German, French, and English literatures have incomparably more influence on the Slavs than does Russian literature, due to the broad dissemination of European languages among them, with German being the official language for a majority of Slavs?

Therefore an open struggle that arouses, both among us and among the other Slavs, powerful sympathies toward a common faith and common ethnicity buried deep in the soul of the masses of the people, would quickly turn all the advantages back in our direction. Compared to such sympathies, all the avenues bringing the intrigues and temptations of Europe to the Slavic peoples would be like a babbling brook to the rising sea. We only need to figure out how to tap into them.

The struggle with the West is the only saving means of healing our Russian cultural illnesses, as well as developing all-Slavic sympathies to overtake the petty discord among the various Slavic tribes and tendencies. The already burning Eastern Question places this struggle beyond anyone's will and makes it inevitable in the not-too-distant future. The prospects for success in this struggle will have to be the subject of the next chapter, but first we consider it necessary to make this stipulation. An evaluation of the forces Russia can bring to bear at a given time, and a comparison of them to the forces of our probable enemies, cannot be part of our considerations, since it is clear that there is no way to do so, or even offer an opinion, when we are talking about a global struggle, in all likelihood coming in the near, but still indeterminate, future. We cannot be worried about the size of the Russian army and navy, their organization, arms, and the like, but should only examine the elements of hidden strength in Russia as revealed by the events of its history, and analyze the course of action that it must take to guarantee its likely success.

☙ 16 ❧
The Struggle

If not a priest, he's a preacher.
[*Kto ni pop—tot bat'ka.*]
—Russian saying[1]

The only advantage of this (the war of 1799) came from the fact that the war broke almost all Russian alliances with other lands. Your Imperial Majesty has long agreed with me that Russia must not have ties with other powers beyond trade. Frequently changing circumstances may give rise to new relations and new ties, but all of these may be incidental, temporary.
—Count F. V. Rostopchin

Holy truth!
—Emperor Paul[2]

Sooner or later, like it or not, a struggle with Europe (or at least a significant part of it) is inevitable, over the Eastern Question: that is, over the freedom and independence of Slavdom, over the possession of Tsargrad—over everything that Europe considers a matter of Russia's unruly ambition, but which every Russian worthy of the name considers a necessary requirement of its historical calling. The dreadful outbreak of the struggle may be delayed, postponed for one or another reason by us or by the Europeans, but it can only be prevented by Europe feeling the full justice of Slavic demands and voluntarily ceding them (of which there is little hope, as all can see); or by Russia actually showing itself to be, as its enemies say, "an ailing, failing colossus,"[3] weakened morally, ceasing to heed not only the voice of national honor [*narodnaia chest'*] but also the loudest summons of the instinct for self-preservation;

---

[1] Conventionally used to mean "it's all the same to me" or "it makes no difference to us," here applied to relations with Europe.

[2] Rostopchin: See chap. 15, n. 5. The second epigraph is a quote from Rostopchin's memorandum, with Tsar Paul's marginal comment.

[3] [Danilevskii's marginalia, published posthumously]: *Alas! It is beginning to turn out that way.*

ready to renounce all traditions of its history and disavow the very idea of its existence. But that is not all. Even if Russia went to such a level of self-abasement, it would be too unbelievable: they would see this as deception and a ruse, and would still not leave us in peace.

We consider the very process of this inevitable struggle, and not just certain of its desired outcomes (as we have repeatedly explained), salutary and beneficial, since only this struggle can sober our thoughts and raise in all levels of society the national spirit [*narodnyi dukh*], which is sinking into imitativeness and worship of the foreign, infected by the extremely dangerous illness we call Europeanism. Perhaps we will be accused of preaching enmity or extolling war. Such an accusation would be incorrect. We are not preaching war, if for no other reason than the fact that such a message would be only too funny from a voice as weak as ours. Yet we are affirming, and even proving, that a struggle is inevitable, and suggesting that even though war is a very great evil, there is still a greater one, something much worse than war, against which war can serve as medicine, since "man does not live by bread alone."[4]

Considering a struggle with Europe inevitable in the more or less near future, we suggest it is not out of place to take a look at what portents of success we have in this struggle; what probabilities of good fortune; what means we can count on; and what must be our course of action to ensure the likelihood of our success. Obviously we will have to survey and evaluate the state of our intrinsic moral and material forces, and also the course we must follow in our relations with Europe. But before we switch to the special subject of the present chapter, we will dwell upon a certain general historical consideration which will speak loudly on our behalf assuring us success, because this success, so to speak, lies in the general direction in which the current of historical events is moving.

The word "law" has very different meanings and value in various branches of human knowledge. In some exact sciences, it is a rule expressed very simply, from which a whole broad category of phenomena follows. And that rule is not only conceivable by the mind, but follows from necessity. Goethe's aphorism, *Was der Geist verspricht, das hält die Natur*,[5] applies to laws of this kind. One such example would be the famous law of universal gravitation. Other laws are actually hypothetical propositions, the inherent necessity of which we do not immediately recognize, perhaps because our minds are too weak to conceive of that necessity. Once accepted, however, these propositions satisfactorily explain a host of phenomena. Such for example is the chemical law of atomism, or the optical law of the wavelike movement of the ether. Both these kinds of laws not only constitute the standard by which such phenomena are organized, but they also explain them.

---

[4] Matthew 4: 4.

[5] German: "What the soul predicts, nature fulfills."

In the fields of more complex subjects, such as all the human and social sciences, "laws" simply refer to frequently recurring phenomena, for which we cannot devise even hypothetical explanations. For instance, statistics show us that the numbers of boys and girls born remains in constant ratio. Laws that manage to detect the morphology of organisms fall into this type. For example, since the time of Aristotle it has been said that animals with cloven hoofs lack upper front teeth, chew cud, and, with few exceptions, have horns on their foreheads. But why is that so? What is the internal connection for these phenomena? What could be even a hypothetical explanation for them?

In this latter, more narrow and restricted sense, we can thus use "laws" to mean those historical phenomena that repeat themselves without changing, from the very beginning of history, under very different local and temporal circumstances, revealing some kind of unknown, foreordained plan for historical movement.

We want to turn our attention now to one of these historical repetitions (or if you will, historical laws). This law, which may be called the law of preserving a store [zapas] of historical strength, can be explained as follows: at the beginning of a people's history, still in the ethnographic period of its development or having just emerged from it, it usually happens that some part of that people, located in an especially advantageous geographic location and in close direct relations with neighboring peoples who have attained a higher level of culture, finds itself in favorable conditions for precociousness, with all its advantages and disadvantages. This part of the tribe develops a native or borrowed form of enlightenment, or at least the rudiments of it. A religious, political, and cultural life begins and sometimes is even cultivated to the highest degree. But the foundation on which this development rests is unstable, since its roots are not widespread throughout the whole ethnographic body, which alone could give it strength and stability. Thus storms from outside often threaten the destruction of its first flowering. Meanwhile the remainder of the tribe, under the protective cover of mighty nature (forests, steppes, mountainous terrain) continues to lead its quiet, mostly tribal, ethnographic life, not expending but accumulating elements of future strength. Inhabiting the frontier regions of its tribal realm, this reserve part of it often pours its blood, its life, and its soul into other foreign tribes nearby, or even amongst which it lives, little by little assimilating them to itself and thus stocking up a vast store of strength, as a political and cultural reserve, which in time comes to the rescue of its forward positions, when their internal sources of life begin to dry up or when storms brew outside. This allows tribal-wide life to penetrate deeper, spread wider, and to blossom in broader measure in at least some, if not all, regards. This law has another, more general significance for the renewal of the highest, so to speak, cultured social classes by fresh strength flowing in from the lower, so to speak, ethnographic social classes. This phenomenon of social form has often attracted researchers' attention and

even constitutes a kind of ethnographic axiom. But in its strictly historical
sense, so obvious to me, it has scarcely drawn attention.

The first clear example of this oft-recurring phenomenon comes to us
from the ancient history of western Asia. The Median Empire, founded by a
people belonging to the Iranian cultural type, attained a certain level of civilization under the influence of Babylonian tutelage, and at the same time lost
its national character, thus quickly falling into the decline and decay of this
ancient Semitic culture. The warlike and half-wild tribe of Persians, still preserving the Iranian cultural type, by conquering the Medes breathed new
strength into the Iranian tribes and united them into a huge empire, constituting the golden age of the Iranian cultural-historical type, the short duration of
which yet again depended on the decadence of Babylonianism, which was all
the greater because the very centers of Babylonian culture were included in
the composition of the state.

The history of Greece presents a second example. Greek life blossomed
into its most brilliant flower in regions so hospitable for culture, the Pelopon-
nesus and Hellas, under the stimulating influence of Egypt and Phoenicia,
with which it could sustain very close relations by spanning from island to
island like a bridge. Internal discord and a general lack of political good sense
quickly ushered in a decline of Greece's good fortune, preparing it to be
mined by the first strong political body it encountered along the way. But in
the wild hill country lived a remnant of the Greek tribes, strengthening itself
internally, for the time being falling outside of the political and cultural
sphere, mixing with foreign elements which it Hellenized. Macedonia gave
Greece an anchor of salvation in Philip.[6] Had it merged with kindred Macedonia and submitted voluntarily and deliberately to its hegemony, Greece
could have in all likelihood continued to live its original existence, unthreat-
ened even by Rome.

The Parthians, also an Iranian tribe, residing in the frontiers of Scythia
and mixing with Scythian elements, outside the boundaries of the historical
life of golden-age Persia, likewise freed the eastern part of Alexander's domain from Greco-Macedonian influence, thus protecting it from Rome, and in
doing so, enabled a new rebirth of Iranian culture in the Sassanid era.

Turning to more recent times, we see in the mountains of Spain the
downtrodden Goths laying the foundation for the liberation of their homeland from the power of the Moors, and preparing the splendor and greatness
of modern Spain.

On the plains of Russia the first seeds of civil society and education
sprouted in the Dnieper valley and Carpathian foothills, under the influence
of Byzantium. Internal squabbles, the Tatar pogrom, the incursion of Lithuania, and Polish power demolished these beginnings of Russian life. But in
the remote forest country of the northeast, Russian colonization outside of

---

[6] Philip II: See chap. 10, n. 10.

active historical life formed a powerful storehouse of Russian strength, russified the Finnic tribes and, having gotten stronger, became the restorer of Russian unity, the gatherers of the Russian lands under the name of Moscow. And Peter and Catherine were perpetuators of this work.

In parts of central, southern, and northeastern Italy, in the plains and coastal areas of Lombardy there lived a multifaceted and luxurious political and cultural life, consuming itself in the process and becoming a mine for prospecting foreigners. But in the foothills of the Alps, in uncivilized Piedmont, not taking part in the advanced historical life of Italy, a moral strength and energy was preserved within the population, mixing with tribes of not purely Italian descent, and in our times Piedmont has become the reviver and unifier of Italy.

This role was played by Brandenburg in the medieval and modern eras for northeastern Germany, which was united under the auspices of the Prussian monarchy. This remote German borderland [*ukraina*], or march [*marka*], spread Germanization throughout the northwestern Slavic tribes, scarcely partaking of the medieval life percolating along the Rhine, the Weser, the northern Danube, and the Elbe. But when all political strength in these regions ran out, Brandenburg laid the foundation for the rebirth of German might in the Prussian monarchy.

In our day, what Brandenburg was for the Prussian kingdom, the Prussian monarchy has been for Germany in general.

So the ancient regions of the Persians, the Macedonians, the Parthians, Austria, Suzdal and Moscow, Piedmont, Brandenburg, and Prussia—countries storing up their tribal, ethnographic energy, in a time when the regions populated by their brethren who had blossomed and been introduced to active political and cultural fields earlier than them (the Medes, Greece, the Persian empire, Spain, southwestern Rus', Italy, central and western Germany) lost their political strength and either fell under foreign rule, or barely eked out a lethargic existence—became the renewers and restorers of the historical life of their brethren, who had started their lives before them. They were, so to speak, the preservers of their tribe's store [*zapas*] of strength.

Analogy tells us that the same relationship exists between the western Slavs, surrounded by Germanic-Roman nations, gripped voluntarily or not by the life swirling around them, and in it losing their political uniqueness and independence, and Russia, containing a vast store of Slavic strength. The voice of all history attests to us that this store is not going to die in vain, but even it is destined, as in all previous cases, to revive, restore, and renovate Slavic life in broad dimensions. This requires a law of historical economy, every bit as reasonable as a law of the economy of nature: nothing is created in vain; every outcome can be extracted from its premise. It is as impossible to move against the historical current of events as it is to swim against the tide; and from these general considerations, we draw confidence that the Russian and Slavic holy, truly world-historical and all-human [*vsechelevecheskoe*] cause will not fail.

We turn now from these general considerations to others more particular and special.

In continuing this book we constantly uphold the idea that Europe not only is something foreign to us, but even hostile to us; that its interests not only cannot be our interests, but in the majority of cases are directly opposed to ours. From this, however, it does not follow that we can or must break all ties with Europe and protect ourselves from it with a Chinese Great Wall; this is not only impossible, but even if it were possible, it would be harmful. Any kind of our relations with it must inevitably be close, but not intimate, familial, or soulful. In political relations there can be no other rule than an eye for an eye, a tooth for a tooth, measuring by the same standard by which they measure us.[7]

But if it is impossible and harmful to remove ourselves from European affairs, it is still possible, useful, and even necessary to look at these affairs always from our own Russian point of view, applying to them our only evaluative criterion: what relation can this or that event, direction of thought, or action by an influential personage have toward our own, Russo-Slavic goals? What kind of hindrance or help for them might these turn out to be? In our indifference to people and events in this regard we must remain completely unwavering, as if they lived or took place on the moon. We must fully cooperate with what can advance our goals, and must fully oppose what hinders them, not paying the slightest attention to their absolute significance—to their consequence for Europe itself, for humanity, for freedom, or for civilization. We must have our own personal understanding of all these subjects, and a firm belief that only by acting in our own interests can we facilitate them, to the extent that it depends on us; that our goal is holy and lofty; that only what leads to it lies within our duty; that only by serving it and no other can we contribute to the highest things, whatever they are called: humanity, freedom, civilization, etc.

Either this way, or not at all. All of our political wisdom is contained in the epigraphs, chosen as symbols of one of the most essential ideas of this chapter: exchanging the so-called politics of principle for the politics of circumstance (*Gelegenheitspolitik*). Without hatred or love (for in the foreign world nothing can, indeed nothing must, arouse either our sympathy or antipathy), indifferent to Red or White, to demagogy and despotism, to legitimism or revolution, to Germans, to French, to English, to Italians, to Napoleon, Bismarck, Gladstone, Garibaldi—we must be the true friend and ally to the one who desires and can assist our sole, unwavering goal. If it costs us our alliance and friendship to take a step toward the freedom and union of Slavdom, approaching Tsargrad, what do we care? Would not others pay the

---

[7] Cf. Deuteronomy 19: 21; Matthew 7: 2.

same price: France or England for Egypt; the French for the Rhine valley; the Germans for Bohemia; Napoleon for Belgium; or Bismarck for Holland?

Holding with unwavering strictness and devotion to this view and this form of action, there can be no worry about favorable combinations of political constellations. Let this be the clearly known, fully espoused, deeply loved goal, and the clear understanding of things, and then our good fortune is assured. Notice how it served Catherine until she got carried away, on the one hand, with a craving for European approval as the protector of neutral trade interests, and on the other hand, with indignation for the atrocities of the French Revolution, and maybe even a false, groundless fear of it. But after her, how many favorable constellations rose on the political horizon of Europe, what splendid horoscopes could be foretold and achieved: the European coalition against France, friendship with Napoleon in 1807, triumph over him in 1812! 1848 and 1849! A decisive course of action in 1853! So many opportunities in the recent past, were it not for glasses with lenses imprinted with the European outlook; were it not for sympathy with emigrants, legitimism, liberalism, philanthropism, especially germanophilism, unselfish care for all that does not concern us! We can boast of such unselfishness, of course, in diplomatic dispatches and circulars, although deriving from it extremely modest gain; but in the historical evaluation of events, scarcely can it deserve any kind of praise; for this unselfishness is in essence the sacrifice to thoughtless vanity, or fantastical fear, of those sacred, actual interests entrusted to us.

Many lost opportunities, so much lost time; but if only there had been some firm decisiveness, a clear understanding of the plan, some deep conviction in the greatness and the sanctity of our historical calling, in the inevitable necessity either to fulfill it or shamefully fade away and leave the field of history in disgrace—yet the opportunity will not soon reappear. The main hindrance that prevents us from catching these opportunities on the wing and making use of them consists of the idea that we (like Europe) need and benefit from a system of political equilibrium, the chivalrous, unselfish defenders of which we became, under the notion coming straight from the vainly degrading desire to worm our way into membership in the ancient and renowned family of European nations and from the pitiful self-deception that we might be accepted into it. "Vainly degrading," I say, because in the political (as well as individual) life there is nothing more degrading than vanity; there is no greater contradiction than between true, noble pride which contents itself with an evaluation of its conscience and its convictions, on the one hand, and vanity, which by its nature adapts itself to please others, on the other.

We have recently seen that the system of political equilibrium is the normal, natural order for the political relations between European states, the stable order of things for which they have striven almost from their very beginnings, which (as the conscious and unconscious operation of the factors of European life) is more and more reaffirmed in the course of time, gaining a broader and broader foundation, leading them more and more to the fear of, or at least the hope to avoid, chance disturbances of it. If Russia is not a part of Europe, neither by blood birthright, nor by adoption; and if the main goals of Europe and Russia (or more exactly Slavdom, of which it serves as the representative) are opposed to each other, mutually denying each other out of deep-rooted historical opposition, lying in the founding plan for a whole line of eras in world history (as we have already tried to show in chapter 12), then this in itself means that Russia has an interest not in the protection of, or in the restoration of, this equilibrium, but in the complete opposite.

Europe is hostile to us not by circumstance, but by essence; thus only when it is at war with itself can it be safe for us. This proposition is abundantly evident, supported as much by the most obvious considerations as by the evidence of events.

In fact, each European state finds its bulwark and defense in the system of equilibrium. Prussia surprised even itself by quickly defeating Austria;[8] the influence of France stopped Prussia, forced it to be content with moderate successes, and in doing so saved Austria, or at least was of great help. Allowed to be the victor, Austria would have reclaimed Silesia, formerly torn away by Prussia, according to its wishes and desires; the former rivalry between France and the Habsburgs would soon return, and Prussia would be protected from excessive losses, or (in the worst case) would draw support from this renewed rivalry for the return of the lost territory. Let Prussia be strengthened excessively from having formed a single united Germany, taken possession of the Rhineland (considered the Germans' national river, from source to mouth) through the return of Alsace, Lorraine, and Franche-Comté to Germany, and from the submission of Holland — and would not France be able to find help even from its archenemy England, now made uneasy by the fear of Germany's rising naval power? And England would be even more alarmed by French victories and conquests if it were to unite with Belgium and take control of the whole left bank of the Rhine. It would be exactly the same if France were to take too ambitious a view of Italy; it would find defenders and patrons in Prussia and England, maybe even in Austria itself.

All of this is too abundantly clear to require us to add any more examples or dwell longer upon it. But let the neighbors rise in arms against Russia and, having won, take complete charge of it. Let the Swedes take Finland and even Lapland to the White Sea; let Prussians, Germans as it were, take the Baltic region and part of Kovno Province to protect its connections; let a restored Poland with western Galicia be given the whole Northwestern Krai; let Austria, following the theory of a separate Ruthenian nationality, have Volhynia, Podolia, and Kiev; let the Romanian Principalities have Bessarabia, and Turkey the Crimea and Transcaucasia, the latter divided with Persia. Would even

---

[8] In the Austro-Prussian, or Seven Weeks', War in 1866; a key step toward the Prussian-led unification of Germany.

a single voice in Europe be heard to speak on Russia's behalf, in the name of the principle of broken equilibrium? Of course not! Not a one! All would find, on the contrary, that the current state of equilibrium would be upheld by this, and even those that gained nothing by it (like France and England) would find themselves comforted and compensated by the restoration of Poland, the strengthening of Sweden and Turkey, and tremendous latitude for their influence and their excursions in the East.

And so, while each European state in one way or another derives a clear benefit from the system of equilibrium, for Russia it does not and cannot have any kind of benefit. Conversely, any significant disturbance of equilibrium certainly disturbs the security of European states, damaging their influence and their freedom of action. The strengthening of Prussia threatens France, Austria, and—carried to an extreme, for instance, to the point of controlling the length of the Rhine to its mouth—even England; the strengthening of France worries Prussia, Austria, and even Italy; the strengthening of Austria (if such a thing were possible) clashes with the interests of Prussia, Italy, and, to a certain degree, even France; the strengthening of Italy is disadvantageous to Austria and France. All these powers thus have no greater interest than preserving equilibrium, except for the violator in each case.

The strengthening of any European state, on the contrary, is in no way harmful to Russia. It does no harm in itself, if it does not interfere with any of Russia's particular gains. Let France seize the left bank of the Rhine and Belgium, and gain decisive influence over the Apennine peninsula. What is the harm for Russia? For all that, France would not become strong and mighty enough to carry out a successful offensive war against us. Let Prussia expand as far as it can, i.e., unite all Germany (even the Austrian part) and seize Holland—and it would still not be strong enough to go against Russia one on one. It would be another matter if Prussia seized Slavic-Austrian lands, but that would be harmful to Russia not as a disturbance of the political equilibrium, but as a moral injury, inflicted by the subjection of the Slavic element to the German, out from under which it is just beginning to struggle. And so the system of political equilibrium that is so useful to Europe not only is completely useless for Russia, but even the disturbance of it by predominance of one sort or another, so harmful to European states, for Russia is completely harmless.

But that is not all. It takes very little to become convinced that there is direct and complete opposition between Europe and Russia, in this and in all other regards. Namely the equilibrium of European political strengths is harmful, even destructive for Russia, while its disturbance one way or another is advantageous and beneficial. In fact, let Prussia or France (the only two states capable under current circumstances) gain decisive predominance; let them realize their most vain ambitions. We have already seen that the increase of their power in and of itself would be harmless; but those injured by it, whose interests, rights, or security are violated, would turn their gaze toward Russia, and would expect it to bring their salvation. The happy victor for its part would solicit Russia's friendship, or at least neutrality, to secure its position. Both sides would be ready to buy Russia's friendship by any concession, further undermining themselves in the process.

But if everything is in a normal state, and Europe is internally secure, then its power naturally turns to foreign affairs; its natural hostility toward Russia, unrestrained by internal threats, gets free rein continually, in speech and in print; and should some energetic actor appear, word will be translated into deed. In place of both the disturber of the equilibrium and the victims of that disturbance vying with each other to offer friendship, Russia faces a general, amicable hatred and enmity. The most convincing examples of the one and the other we have seen over the course of centuries.

France, enflamed first with revolutionary enthusiasm and then vainglory, under the leadership of the great military genius [i.e., Napoleon] gained obvious predominance, increasing with each new war. Setting aside their displeasure over Catherine's seizures of territory from Turkey and even the partition of Poland, the western powers sought the favor of Russia, seeking its help. Paul gave it. Austria's egoism nullified the successes of the coalition. But was the position of Russia any worse from this? The First Consul [Napoleon] returned Russian prisoners without ransom and concluded an alliance with Paul. But even the former allies were not offended and used all measures to turn Alexander to their side.

After two unsuccessful wars [in 1805 and 1807] against Napoleon, instead of seeking some kind of reward for himself from Russia, the victor offered a whole territory [Białystok] and proposed dividing Europe, granting (as a big security deposit) the seizure, at first opportunity, of Finland, Bessarabia, Moldavia, and Wallachia.[9] But these aggrandizements did not incur envy or indignation from the others. Take them, but still, help us.

Russia took the side of the offended, defeated the unconquerable, and not content with that, wanted to overthrow him and free Europe. At its invitation, Prussia, Sweden, and eventually even Austria responded. Russia, in the person of Alexander, was the leader of Europe, while Napoleon solicited nothing but a personal audience with him. Everyone vied with one another to offer Russia friendship, and that which is more substantive than friendship. Both vanquished and victorious, Russia maintained a truly commanding position from the very beginning of the revolution to 1815, and while not entirely making skillful use of it, nevertheless gained huge advantages.

In 1815 equilibrium was established; Russia made huge material and moral sacrifices for its protection, and in reward faced a whole storm of slander, hatred, and enmity. By all appearances it played a commanding role, but that role was fruitless; it only exhausted Russia in vain. Equilibrium was at its apogee: neither the July nor the February Revolutions [1830; 1848] could

---

[9] Danilevskii here takes a rosy view of the Treaty of Tilsit (1807).

shake it; but then appeared an energetic political figure [Napoleon III] in Europe, standing at the head of the latest Trojan campaign against Russia.

A campaign against Russia in time of broken equilibrium, under the leadership of one of the greatest military geniuses commanding the forces and fates of Europe, ends in the utter defeat of all enemies. A campaign against Russia in time of equilibrium led by the most notorious mediocrities [i.e., the Crimean War], ends in their complete success, disregarding the fact that Russia had become (at least materially) twice as strong as in 1812.

Of course there were many different reasons leading to that strange, unexpected result; but indisputably one of the most important among them was forty years of uninterrupted equilibrium, during which Russia was determined to remain true to its commitment to equilibrium, while the state of European opinion everywhere turned hostile. Counting ourselves a member of the European family, we of course could not take measures to prepare for a struggle with all of Europe. Among our enemies under Napoleon I were many secret friends; under Napoleon III, those we considered friends turned out to be enemies.

So this is how the influence of political equilibrium in Europe, and its disturbance, on the fate of Russia, has been expressed in reality. It can be stated in the following formula: Under any disturbance to the equilibrium, Europe naturally is divided into two parties—the violator with its voluntary or involuntary allies, and the victims of the disturbance, striving to restore equilibrium. Both of these parties naturally try to draw to their side the single strong neighbor, situated by the essence of things (in whatever forms, words, or names) outside the family, and outside their systems. Both parties thus seek out Russia. One seeks help to shore up its predominance; the other seeks rescue from the power, influence, or danger presented by the predominant power. Russia can choose as it wants. In contrast, in a state of equilibrium, Europe's political activity is directed abroad, and its enmity toward Russia is in full swing. Here, instead of two parties vying with each other for Russia, Europe merges into one, openly or secretly hostile to Russia as a whole.

Thus we need to renounce the notion of any kind of solidarity with European interests, of any kind of connections with any political combination of European powers, and first of all return to complete freedom of action, the full capability of uniting with each European state individually, under whatever condition would make the union advantageous to us, no longer looking at whatever political principle one state or another represents to us at any given time.

Let us take a look, from this point of view, at the various possible relations Russia could have with the main representatives of European power.

First of all, we will exclude Austria, which can be no accomplice to Russia for attaining its goals, but only the object against which—like Turkey—we can and must direct our efforts.

Since the conclusion of the Napoleonic Wars, the most notorious and most constant opponent of Russia in the East is England. One of its eminent statesmen[10] famously declared that he had no intention of speaking with anyone who does not understand the importance for England of an independent Constantinople. To the present day this phrase has served as the motto for English policy in the East, sharing the fate of many aphorisms, so well characterized by the German expression *Schlagwörter*.[11]

However, put the English politician up against the wall, as they say, and demand direct arguments and evidence from him; it seems to me he would be hard-pressed, or even at a complete loss [to offer any].

If the importance of Constantinople (and Turkish independence in general) for England is presented as the economic exploitation of Turkey by English industry and trade, then its significance from this point of view, in the first case, is not so great as to prevent them from entering into a different type of mutually advantageous arrangement with Russia; in the second case, the English are too practical a people to fail to understand that, even under the most disadvantageous (for England) Russian trade policy, drawing away from the country of Turkey today, and replacing Turkish dominion with Slavic independence under Russian hegemony, would increase the benefit several times. The steppes of Novorossiisk serve as a clear proof of this, under Russian sovereignty turned from a nest of nomads into the breadbasket of England and Europe, with flourishing cities like Odessa, Berdiansk, Rostov, Taganrog, and Nikolaev.

England's other, much greater interest in the East (broadly speaking) consists of maintaining its India colony; but regarding this vital question for England, it is harder still to understand its connection to the so-called Eastern Question, in the narrow sense of the term. What actually is there in common between India and the question of whether Constantinople comes into Russian hands or not? Without thoroughly investigating the strategic ability or inability of Russians to invade India, it is safe to say that if this ability exists, then it already exists now, without the seizure of Constantinople, and if it does not exist, then the capture of Constantinople would not change this state of affairs one bit. Alexander of Macedon[12] set off on his Persian campaign, true, and made it to India, crossing the Hellespont [Dardanelles] into Asia, but it is hard to understand why Russia would choose to go this roundabout way when it has the Volga and Caspian Sea, which lead from the very center

---

[10] Danilevskii possibly has in mind Henry John Temple, 3rd Viscount Palmerston (1784–1865), British prime minister during the Crimean War and after (1855–58 and 1859–65).

[11] German: "Slogans, buzzwords," but literally "fighting words" or "words for throwing a punch."

[12] I.e., Alexander the Great. See chap. 5, n. 4.

of Russian power to Astarabad,[13] from which it is no more than half the distance to India from Constantinople.

For our part, we are convinced that an attack on India is entirely possible. If Sultan Babur[14] and many other Eastern conquerors could reach India and conquer it, it is hard to imagine why what was possible for them would be impossible for Russia, which occupies part of the very lands serving as the Muslim conquerors' departure point, could compel Persia into an alliance with it, voluntarily or by force, and has the Caucasus Army, accustomed to hot climates and mountain terrain.

The effect of such an attack, undertaken with even a few forces, even unsuccessfully, would be most disastrous for English power, just as would be, for example, a French assault, even though unsuccessful, on the English coast. In a predominantly industrial and entrepreneurial country, everything is founded on credit, on trust; and the trust of the English in the invulnerability of English territory (in the one case), like the natives' trust in the invulnerability of English rule in India (in the other), would be shaken and breached. What did not succeed the first time might, with more forces or through a favorable course of events, succeed the next time. From the moment of such an invasion, the sword of Damocles would constantly hang over England.

But on the other hand, it is obvious that Russia has not the slightest interest in seizing India, or any part of it. Such an acquisition would lay upon it such needless hard times that we can safely say that if it fell to Russia, like an inheritance from a dead uncle nabob,[15] there would be nothing to do but sell it for whatever price, and if no one will pay, then give it away as a gift. Therefore English India is protected from Russian encroachment, not so much by the physical, as by the moral, impossibility of an India campaign—with only one exception. An attack on India is Russia's sole defensive means in a war with England.

It is true, England by itself cannot bring too great harm upon Russia. However it is within its means, if not to cut off Russia's external trade, at least to greatly restrict it, by forcing it to take a land route through a blockade of Russian harbors and bombardment of Russian coastal cities.

Russia could not respond to all that: its role in a war would have to be completely passive if it did not resort to a campaign against India, which due to the few English there and the inclination of the native population, the mere start of which might have the most important consequences—just by a single rumor preceding it, embellished by the Eastern imagination.

---

[13] I.e., Gorgan, on Iran's Caspian coast.

[14] Zahir-ud-din Muhammad Babur (1483–1530): Central Asian conqueror of India, founder of the Mughal dynasty.

[15] Nabob: Mughal term for viceroy or deputy governor, adopted by the English to refer to employees of the East India Company who became rich in the colony, through legitimate or corrupt means.

But Russia's relations with England are essentially such that a war between them could arise solely because of the Eastern Question, since the existence of Turkey and its control of Constantinople not only does not at all guarantee English East Indian possessions from the possibility of Russian invasion, but actually constitutes the only reason that ever could bring this harm upon England.

On the other hand, there is a really important side to the so-called Eastern Question for England: its possession of Egypt since the construction of the Suez Canal. What Napoleon I could not do (thanks to Nelson and Sidney Smith),[16] Lesseps[17] did. A state with a powerful navy in the Mediterranean Sea, France for example, will always have an advantage over England in the delivery of troops and materiel to India, and in dispatching privateer vessels to the Red Sea, Indian Ocean, and Pacific Ocean. Therefore if the individuals directing state policy were really such cold, calculating minds, they would have already considered this; if even the direction of state policy truly depended on them as much as is typically thought, then nothing would be so easy as an agreement between Russia and England on the Eastern Question, through a mutually beneficial deal between these states. But in fact, that is not how it goes: in politics, as in any other human endeavor, passion and prejudice have tremendous influence, and those governed by them (as political axioms lay beyond all doubt) can only follow them unconditionally, either submitting voluntarily or being obligated by the force of public opinion, ever subservient to prejudice.

In any case, at present between Russia and England there lies an all-powerful prejudice, with no end of its reign in sight. Therefore in the Eastern Question we not only cannot count on England's help but must expect that, just as in the last Eastern [i.e., Crimean] War, it will be one of our absolute enemies, unless before that question is resolved, some fortunate distraction diverts a significant part of its forces—which of course we would have to use to our advantage.

The interests of Russia and France in the East are essentially in opposition no greater than that between Russia and England, except that the reward Russia could offer France for its help, or even just its noninterference in the attainment of Russian goals, is much greater. As a matter of fact, disregarding the sense of moderation and the era of peace and progress that has set in, the sincere desire that would captivate the whole French nation is to restore what

---

[16] Lord Horatio Nelson (1758–1805): British vice admiral, famous for defeating the French navy at the Battle of Trafalgar in 1805. Sir Sidney Smith (1764–1840): British admiral, famous for burning the French fleet at Toulon in 1793 and the defense of Acre in 1799, causing Napoleon to abandon his army in Egypt.

[17] Ferdinand de Lesseps (1805–94): French contractor who oversaw the fundraising for and construction of the Suez Canal (1859–69), and later led a failed attempt at building the Panama Canal.

the French call their natural boundary—that is, the Rhine, which would give to France Bavaria, the Darmstadt region, Prussian Rhineland, Belgium, Luxembourg, Limburg, and the Dutch province of northern Brabant—nearly the richest lands on the continent of Europe, in terms of population or productivity of any kind. In the East, France has long aspired to consolidate its influence in Egypt and Syria, and would not refuse to take power over not only them, but the whole northern coast of Africa, in order to make the Mediterranean Sea, not only in words but in reality, a French lake. In all of these bids for power, none of which could France attain through its own strength, its only natural accomplice could be Russia, since it is obvious that Prussia would not help it acquire its Rhine border, nor would England, with Belgium or Egypt; even Austria by reason of its German tinge could not take arms against the German fatherland, despite being excluded from it. Only Russia, from the only reasonable view of its interests, could be completely indifferent to all these French seizures of land, being neither hot nor cold as they say, since as we have seen earlier, any significant strengthening of France, just as with Prussia, starts the nations vying with each other to ingratiate themselves with Russia.

On the other hand, neither the formation of a system of Slavic states nor even the conquest of Constantinople by Russia in any way threatens the interests of France, which itself may inherit certain rich portions of Turkey. In such a state of affairs and the relations between both sides' interests, a deal would seem possible: but again, only if rational interests had complete sway over human affairs, both in the individual and in the national life.

Between Russia and France likewise stands a long line of prejudices, long preventing them from drawing closer together. From France's side, there is the Polish and Catholic prejudice; from Russia's side, the prejudice of Germanophilia and legitimism, or hatred of revolution. We must not fail to notice the strangeness in the relations between Russia and France, that these states (whose interests align in so many ways) have been hostile to one another, it is safe to say, almost from the very opening of relations between them. In the course of all this time, more than 130 years, this enmity or at least mutual ill-will has ended only for the briefest of times; alliances between these states (disregarding the obvious advantages for both) soon are broken and end up if not in open war, then at least in strained relations and mutual recriminations.

The position of Poland, beyond Germany, naturally had to attract the friendship of France, the rival of the German Empire and the House of Habsburg. The same reasons made Russia friendly toward the German states, especially the upstart Prussia, for which Poland was a complete stumbling-block in its path. It was the unquestionable right of Russia, the ambition of Prussia, justified by vital necessity, and the greed of Austria, which, as personified by Maria Theresa, shed tears but took its share, and was ultimately brought to grief by Polish disorders. The fall of Poland completely changed the political configuration of states. Russia and Germany became neighbors, but old habits and other reasons won out over the demands of healthy polit-ical interest. France, instead of seeking friendships and support from the power of Russia against its antagonist, Germany, continued with its same old dreaming about the departed, eternally weak Poland. Napoleon I, not usually known for sentimentality in politics, clearly understood the situation and turned amicable toward Russia, first in 1800, then in 1807. Russian prejudices prevented the continuation of that alliance, and when they were ready to die down at the time of the Turkish War of 1828 and 1829, they were roused once again by the Revolution of 1830, which revived Russian *legitimism-mania* and *revolution-phobia,* if the reader will pardon such barbaric words. On the other hand, the Polish Uprising of 1830–31 again roused Franco-Polish sympathies. All of this was strengthened by the Revolution of 1848 and the Eastern [Cri-mean] War. Thus a series of vain clashes, strained unfriendly relations, mar-tial comradeship of the French and Poles, Polish agitation, and sympathy for political exiles, all produced in Russia a political-diplomatic tradition, and in France a true national prejudice, that prevents them both from hearing the voice of sensible political reckoning.

Russia's natural patronage of Orthodox interests in the East, and France taking on the role of supporting the interests of Latinism (after its moral source—the Roman Catholic faith—had already dried up in the souls of the French) only increased the antagonism. What for France in the time of Saint Louis[18] would be a natural, necessary form of action now has become only a new Catholic prejudice.

So it looks, of course, only from a political point of view; from the highest historical point it acquires a completely different significance and explana-tion. France, as we have seen, is the true, or default representative of Europe, so to speak, the main practical developer of European ideas from the very be-ginning of European history to the present. Russia is the representative of Slavdom. And thus, these two states, in spite of all accounts of political wis-dom and all the reproofs of sensible political reckoning—one might even say against their will—have been constantly opposed rivals from the very begin-ning of their active reciprocal relations, and this antagonism cannot soon be expected to end.

Directed by a higher power before which all combinations of human rea-son are insignificant, circumstances turn out in such a way that relations bound by the requirements of the order of things in the lower spheres, or categories of historical events, submit to the requirements of the highest his-torical spheres and are transformed according to its norms. In the cycle of his-torical events of the Germanic-Roman cultural type, France was the constant rival and enemy of England and the House of Habsburg; but by extending the

---

[18] Louis IX (r. 1226–70): Capetian king of France, participated in the Seventh (1248) and Eighth (1270) Crusades, modeling the medieval ideal of a Christian king, and the only French monarch to be declared a saint.

historical sphere to encompass the clash of the Germanic-Roman world with the Slavic, not only are England and France reconciled and begin to act as one against Russia, but the recent wars of France with Austria, and Austria with Prussia, end up with Austria being taken under the protection of France. In this way France, being, as we have said, the true representative of Europe, stood as the main enemy of Slavdom in all theaters of action: in Turkey, Austria, and Poland. In the irresistible current of events, the country calling itself the defender of all oppressed nationalities is forced either directly to take the side of the oppressors of Slavdom—the Turks, Magyars, and Germans—or to take under its wing the Slavic nationality that changed its tribal affiliation.

And so we conclude that, in spite of all reckonings of political advantage, Russia must view France, like England, among its main enemies and opponents in the resolution of the Eastern Question.

Of the active powers of Europe, in their relations to Russia and Slavdom, there remains one more for us to examine—Prussia. The mission of this state—beginning so magnificently in the time of Frederick the Great, continuing so magnificently, but far from finished, under the leadership of Bismarck—undeniably consists of uniting Germany, and attaining political wholeness and unity for the German people. This goal is unattainable without help and action from Russia. In fact, from fear of self-destruction neither France nor Austria can allow either the expansion of Prussian predominance over southwestern Germany and the Austro-German lands or the conversion of the predominance already attained in northern Germany to full Prussian unity. The North German Confederation,[19] with the strength of thirty million subjects still not fully integrated into their new state, cannot however turn against the unfriendly seventy–eighty million of southwestern Germany, under the most unfavorable strategic conditions, with the hostility of the Danes and the possibility of being surrounded on three sides, since France's predominance on the sea opens the whole north German coast to it. It is true, Frederick the Great[20] once achieved this very thing—presumably an even greater wonder—but not without propitious circumstances. And there are not always Fredericks on hand.

Therefore, however strange this might seem to admirers of Prussian military might, which to a certain, very significant degree we would not even think to deny—Prussia and its newfangled North German Union, having won glory on the fields of Sadowá,[21] is essentially in the same political situation as

---

[19] The North German Confederation was created after the 1866 Austro-Prussian War, consisting of Prussia and twenty-one other northern German states, at first in a defensive military alliance, but then adopting a constitution in 1867 as a state that became the basis for the German Empire declared in early 1871.

[20] Frederick the Great: See chap. 1, n. 12.

[21] The Battle of Sadowá, 3 July 1866, was the decisive battle of the Austro-Prussian War.

it was at the end of the Seven Years' War [in 1763], before the campaign of 1806–07, and in 1813 during the war for German independence: that is, with not only its political power and might, but perhaps even its very existence, being dependent upon close, amicable relations with Russia. And let it be understood how pitifully mistaken are those Baltic ultra-patriots who imagine that Prussian force and German patriotism can threaten Russia into guarding their assumed privileges. These can only frighten children, who are small and unreasonable.

In affirming this, we are not trying to denigrate Prussia or deny its political might, its military power, or its ability to employ art and dexterity. We are only saying that its position (both geographically and politically) is so disadvantageous that even these great strengths are insufficient not only to extend Prussian power against France and Austria, but perhaps even to preserve what is already attained, and so it needs an alliance with Russia.[22] Of course Prussia's help is important for Russia, since it is impossible to count on any other, at least in the Old World. But the main thing is, however important for Russia is a favorable decision of the Eastern Question for it and Slavdom, it can wait a long time for it. The question about the existence of Russia, or of weakening its power in the near future, cannot seriously be asked.

Prussia—I will not say Germany—is still no more than a political combination which can be altered into a very different form, since there is no such thing as the Prussian people; but Russia is a primary, original, great historical fact, the foundation of which lies in the hidden depths of the world-historical plan for the unfolding fates of the human species. Therefore, although under the present combinations of political constellations Russia and Prussia need each other, and thus depend on each other, Prussia's needs are urgent, therefore its dependence is greater—this is important to remember.

We will add to what has been said that the interests of both states are identical in the Eastern Question, at least in the most recent phases of its development. It is advantageous for Prussia, in the first place, if Russia's main attention is turned toward the southwestern, rather than the northwestern, border. With the acquisition, or better to say, with the return to its full possession of the Black Sea, Russia can without harm grant Prussia more latitude in the Baltic Sea. With the destruction of the political combination hostile to both

---

[22] The lack of any marginal comments from Danilevskii in this passage is surprising. The German Empire was an established fact for a decade or so when Danilevskii added his other comments; it was created precisely through a successful war with France, in 1870–71. Bismarck formed the Three Emperors' League (Prussia, Austria-Hungary, and Russia) in 1873, reviving ideas of mutual self-preservation from the Holy Alliance of 1815, but the allies were wary. It dissolved over disputes leading to the Russo-Turkish War (1877–78), but was revived in 1881 and remained in force through Danilevskii's death. While his lack of comment here might indicate continued confidence in his original views, it likely suggests perplexity over how to revise his argument in light of shifting circumstances.

of them called Austria, and its conversion to a Slavic combination without its
Magyar-German character, Prussia would increase its power, since it would
have exclusive influence over all of Germany, not only in treaties but in actual
fact; and thus strengthened, it would have only one rival—France, for whom
this would be dangerous.

Again this strange historical phenomenon, this amazing combination! In
the course of European history the western Slavs and Germans have been
hostile to each other. The former were oppressed, the latter were oppressors.
But a powerful historical fate raised and is raising a representative of Germandom and Slavdom—Prussia and Russia—to help each other attain their
seemingly contradictory goals. Prussia, strictly speaking, grew up under Russia's wing, and now can rely only on it for the completion of German unity,
which in turn becomes the first stage of the separation of the Slavic from the
German. And Prussia is prompted not only by its interests, but by necessity,
to assist Russia's interests in the East.

We propose that in the current state of affairs, Russia can have no other
ally than Prussia, just as Prussia can have none other than Russia. And such
an alliance can be blessed because both have the right goal.

So the matter stands at first. What comes later is another question. Upon
attaining initial, mutually agreeable success, relations can, and truly even
must, change. But politics heeds the immediate, next worthwhile interest, not
distant, unforeseeable possibilities.

From the resources offered by external politics we turn to the incomparably more dependable source of strength and guarantee of success that Russia
can tap within itself, in that greatest task which Russia must carry out at all
costs.

As mentioned above, we have no intention of offering military and
financial statistics for Russia, not only because of our own inadequacy for that
but because of the inadequacy of any type of statistical analysis for this kind
of task, which has always been and always will be determined by moral factors that are immeasurable by ordinary statistics. History's phenomena pertain mostly to the sacred-moral sphere, which in this regard is much more
fruitful. We will attempt to investigate thoroughly the character of Russia's
internal forces and, by historical comparison, to determine somewhat the
magnitude of the force Russia might display.

For comparison, for the purpose of understanding, we turn to the subject
of the latest Russian struggle with Europe [i.e., the Crimean War], under the
most disadvantageous circumstances for us. The indecisiveness and hesitancy
of our diplomatic and military actions, the most important of which was our
false evaluation of our relations with Austria, whom we considered our
friend, turned the ground war into a naval war, which Russia had to undertake completely unprepared. And everyone knows what effort it cost the joint
forces of France, England, Sardinia, and Turkey to snatch one stronghold

[Sevastopol] from our hands. We will look at how Russia has strengthened itself since then.

Lines of communication, which were weakest on our side during the Eastern War, since then have completely changed their character, and someday soon, with the completion of the Moscow–Smolensk and the construction of the Smolensk–Brest and Sevastopol rail, the state center will be connected with the main outlying points.

The pacification of the Caucasus frees up an army of 200,000, which was swallowed up and neutralized by it, so to speak. To determine how the war in the Caucasus relates to the war in the East, it is sufficient to recall that two divisions, one of which was from the Crimea, were sent to the Caucasus in the first year of the war, and to consider their probable influence if they had been on hand at the Alme or the Inkerman.[23]

But the effect of the railroads and pacification of the Caucasus to increase Russia's means is insignificant compared to the predominant event of contemporary tsarism—the emancipation of the serfs. Under serfdom, any appeal to the national spirit to defend the fatherland produced bitter irony and thus, even in the most extreme circumstances, such as in 1812, the government could turn for help only to the privileged classes—the nobility and merchant class. The power of the people [sila narodnaia]—the peasantry—constituted not an active element of state power, but only raw material—the subject or object of contributions. The nobility thus contributed a number of souls for the defense of the fatherland, just as the merchant class contributed a sum of rubles. If 1812 was possible in Russia even under such an order of things, then we now, like the fabled bogatyr,[24] do not even know our own strength. Looking only from a purely businesslike, so to say official, point of view, we will see that in former times any rapid increase in the armed forces by means of levies caused disturbances in the general state system and confusion in government circles about what to do with the masses of people temporarily entering into state service. Restoring the former days of serfdom would mean, as it always did, stirring up powerful and justified displeasure among the people sacrificed to the life of the fatherland, the same as those who enter the ranks of the defenders through the normal recruitment process. The announcement that they are free, like soldiers going into retirement, could not only have produced disorder in the rural economy, but more importantly could have turned a hundred thousand people into homeless vagrants. [Since none of this happened,] strictly speaking, the emancipation of the serfs alone strengthened Russia's force materially and morally to an incalculable degree.

---

[23] Rivers in the Crimea.

[24] Bogatyr: Slavic term for a medieval wandering knight, the heroes of the epics (byliny) of Kievan Rus', historical personages or completely legendary, known for feats of daring, strength, and personal honor.

Regarding war, as in most other human affairs, many hold the view of the famous Austrian commander Montecuccoli,[25] who said that for war you need three things: money, money, and money. In this regard, obviously, no surplus has yet appeared. However important financial questions are in the normal course of world affairs—in time of wars to support the political equilibrium, for the acquisition or preservation of territory, for market or colonial advantages and the like—we can say that they recede to the second, third, or even lower place of importance when what is at stake is the spiritual life or death of nations, which is to say, whether or not they will fulfill their historical calling. And for nations and states the same as for individual people, omnipotent wealth loses its significance in the face of the question of life or death. We do not know—and scarcely need to know, so insignificant is the question—by what financial mechanism the Greeks repelled the Persian horde, the Romans withstood the attacks of Hannibal, or the Swiss and the Dutch won their independence. On the other hand, we know exactly all the financial combinations by which the National Convention tried to help the desperate financial situation of revolutionary France; but we also know that their influence on the course of affairs amounted to nothing, that France was saved not by one or another financial contrivance, but by the exercise of the full moral forces of the country, and the ability (without money) to field a victorious army of 1,300,000 against the internal and external enemies of the Republic. Neither by loans nor by financial mechanisms did Russia stand firm in 1812. At a crucial moment in the crisis of national life—and Russia cannot regard the struggle for Slavdom with Europe in any other way—the top priority is not money nor even one or another military organization but two moral motive-forces that are the only means of exerting the full power of the people, which vanquishes all else and cannot be vanquished by anything. These are discipline, or the gift of obedience, and enthusiasm, or the infinite readiness for self-sacrifice. Concerning the first, it is obvious to what extent the Russian people possesses this. To such a degree, we say, that by the sincere, inspired word of the Russian tsar, the head and representative of the Russian people, this first force is always ready to arouse the second.

The moral uniqueness of the Russian state system is that the Russian people in its natural form is a single organism, not merely by means of some more or less artificial state mechanism, but by a deeply rooted understanding of the people concentrated in its Sovereign [*Gosudar'*], who thus is the living embodiment of the political self-consciousness and will of the people [*volia narodnaia*], so that his thought, feeling, and will is communicated to the whole people by the same process as in the individual's self-conscious existence. This is the idea and the meaning of Russian autocracy, which must not there-

---

[25] Count Raimondo Montecuccoli (c. 1608–80): Italian general serving Austria, promoted to director of the war council and awarded various titles, author of works on military history and tactics.

fore be considered a form of rule in the usual sense of the word "form," as something external, able to be changed without changing the essence of the subject; able to be manufactured, like a sphere, cube, or pyramid, just by looking at its external requirements, corresponding to external goals. It is of course a form, but an organic form, that is, indivisible from the essence of what it bears within itself, which constitutes the necessary expression and incarnation of that essence. Any organic thing is such a form, from a plant to a person. Therefore such a form cannot be changed, or in the present case, limited. This is impossible even for the autocratic will itself which, according to its essence, that is, according to the people's inherent political ideal, cannot be subject to any kind of external limitation, but is a free, or self-determining, will. This internal, moral-political unity and wholeness of the Russian people encompasses the whole governmental side of its existence and constitutes the reason the Russian people can be induced to exert all of its moral and material strength, in a condition that we call *disciplined enthusiasm*—by the will of its Sovereign, independently of the spontaneous excitement of separate, individual persons constituting the whole people, by one or another interest, event, or excitement in general. But a people of eighty million, able by a sincere word from its head and representative, the living center of its consciousness, feeling, thought, and will, to enter the condition of disciplined enthusiasm— this is a force the world has not seen in a long time, or even ever before.

When the pope constituted the moral center of the European world, his word could ignite and arouse Europe to the Crusades, an undertaking not in the immediate interests of the sovereigns, the feudal lords, or the peoples of Europe of that day. But regardless of the fact that now it has no such living center, the Crusades themselves serve only as an example of undisciplined enthusiasm, since they proceeded under the influence of the pope and the clergy—nonpolitical actors, who therefore could not impose the character of legality and order. To that end, even this great movement of the people, strictly speaking, did not involve the whole mass of the people, but only the highest knightly class.

Another example of miracles achieved on a huge scale by the people's enthusiasm is France in the time of revolution. Under the combined influences of a reaction against the longstanding oppression of the people, the idea of freedom penetrating to the lowest levels of society, patriotism spurred by the threats of foreign invaders, and fear brought about by the Terror, an aroused France repelled and defeated Europe. In this case, it can be said that enthusiasm gripped, if not the whole people, then at least the main part of it; and although in rough and ready fashion, it was adequately disciplined by the [National] Convention, or more precisely, by the Committee of Public Safety. Thus we can take France of that time as the standard of the aroused power of the people. A population of twenty-five million—with no army, no navy, no organized finances; under the opposition of most of the aristocracy and clergy; under federal aspirations appearing in many important population centers; with the fierce resistance of Brittany and the Vendée ignited by counterrevolutionary enthusiasm—triumphed over these internal enemies and obstacles, and victoriously fought with Prussia, Austria, Germany, Spain, and England united against it. What is the eighty-million-strong population of Russia capable of, if led by the righteousness and holiness of a defensive undertaking and with the sovereign word of its tsar, exerting its moral and material forces in the same way? A simple accounting shows that, all other conditions being equal, Russia can display triple the strength of France in that terrible time of its struggle with the first European coalition. But circumstances are far from equal, since Russia possesses, over and above the enthusiasm of the people, all its normal state power and no internal source from which to expect even the slightest genuine opposition, since all that could be considered as such now would be blown away more easily than empty husks and chaff at the first gust of wind.

On the other hand, what kind of opposition can we expect? Very great, of course, from the normal state forces of Europe, or even from the coalition that will form against Russia whenever the time comes for a serious resolution of the Eastern Question, a coalition in all likelihood comprised of France, England, Austria, and maybe even Italy.[26] But history hardly presents an example of only normal state forces ever triumphing over a people mustering all of its moral and material forces in the condition of disciplined enthusiasm, if the disproportion of forces is not beyond all measure, as in the recent struggle of the *Candiotti* with the Turks.[27] A people in a state of heroism (an apt designation for the arousal of its forces) can only be beaten by the same kind of heroic agitation. But European peoples at the present state of their development lack that living, organic wholeness and unity in which all their vital energy is concentrated into a single person, or into a certain council representing their political consciousness, feeling, thought, and will, which could therefore ignite them with a sincere, authoritative word. That time has long passed for Europe. Of course, any people whose life forces have not died can be animated with enthusiasm under the direct influence of events touching on its vital interests. But for such a unanimous enthusiasm to overtake the whole people requires a powerful jolt, to shake the whole organism of the people and force all hearts to beat in unison, having overcome the all the diverse, particular, egocentric aspirations proceeding from innumerable personal motivations.

---

[26] It is worth keeping in mind that this was written in the mid-1860s and reflects more the legacy of the Crimean War than anticipation of the great wars of the twentieth century.

[27] *Candiotti* refers to the city of Candia, which was under siege from 1648 to 1669 during the Ottoman conquest of Crete (the longest siege ever recorded). Danilevskii conflates the name here with the uprising in Crete underway at the time of writing (1866–69). See chap. 14, n. 18.

Russia's good fortune and strength in this regard consists of the fact that, beyond inviolably protecting the wholeness and living unity of its organism, it can also spontaneously be aroused to the point of self-sacrifice if the matter is brought to its attention by all the channels of publicity [*glasnost'*]; then its opponents will not be able to offer anything on their own behalf but empty, meaningless words, such as a supposedly shattered political equilibrium, or the alleged threat to civilization, which do not stir the people's heart but only sound like the shrieks of street corner hawkers and gawkers. On the one side the struggle will be for all that is holy: for faith, for the freedom of oppressed brethren, for our historical calling which, even though not logically avowed by the masses, still lies in the moral foundation of any great people. On the other side, [the struggle will be] for the oppression of peoples, in contradiction to the principle declared by the opponents themselves of the equal rights of all nationalities: for actual Turkish barbarism as a dam against the flood of some kind of supposed Muscovite barbarism; for a fantastical Polish people, occupying in European minds the place of the actual Russian people oppressed by the Polish nobility—put simply , for a deceitful, false, and phony mirage.

And so the great struggle coming in the more or less near future for the Russian people, according to the rightfulness and holiness of the matter it must defend, and by the special structure of its state, can and must take on this heroic character. In order to understand what in truth we expect from the Russian people with its soul in such a state, we turn again to history to deduce from its experiences the conditions that brought us successes in battles upholding the greatness of the Russian state. We are sorry to say that this is not a pointless investigation, because the spirit of self-doubt and self-disparagement resulting from deference to everything European has reached such a point among the so-called educated classes of our society that it is often heard that our troops cannot stand against the best European armies, such as the Prussian or French. And this is considered by many to be the enlightened, impartial view, as opposed to the patriotic and state-centered.

From the beginning of the eighteenth century, that is, from the time when Russia entered into close relations with Europe in war and peace, it and only it was fated to contend with three of the greatest military geniuses of modern times, who were both commanders and sovereigns, so that they had full freedom of action and all the resources of their countries at their disposal— namely, Charles XII, Frederick II, and Napoleon I[28]—and from the struggles with all three, Russia emerged the victor.

---

[28] Charles XII of Sweden (r. 1697–1718), in the Great Northern War (1700–21); Frederick the Great of Prussia (r. 1740–86), in the War of the Austrian Succession (1740–48) and the Seven Years' War (1756–63); Napoleon I (r. 1799–1815), in the Wars of the Second, Third, and Fourth Coalitions (1798–1807) and the Wars of the Sixth and Seventh Coalitions (1812–15).

If we look at the great military exploits of other nations, we will find that to a considerable extent they depended on their opponents' comparative weakness in military talent. Only Rome defeated Hannibal, as Russia did Charles, Frederick, and Napoleon, despite much weaker commanders leading its armies.[29] This phenomenon is worth investigating. Although not a specialist in military affairs, I submit that I will raise no serious objections by saying that there are five categories by which the strength of an army can be classified: the number of troops, their tactical instruction (and when applicable, combat experience); the quality of arms; the talent of the commander; and the moral spirit animating the troops.

Evaluating the comparative force of the Russians and the Swedes in the Great Northern War by these categories, all would agree that the tactical instruction and combat experience, the quality of arms, and talent of commanders all favored the Swedes, since, although doubtless Peter the Great infinitely surpassed Charles as a sovereign and political actor in general, he ceded much to him in military talents. Considering how great the Swedes' superiority was in three significant regards, and how insignificant in this case the simple numerical advantage was, our final victory can scarcely be attributed to it.

The Seven Years' War is an even more instructive example. In that war, which could not fail to touch the Russian heart, Russians had four major clashes with the Prussians: at [Gross-]Jägersdorf, Zorndorf, Zullichau,[30] and Kunersdorf. In three of these we claimed a victory, and at Zorndorf, defeat. At Zorndorf and Kunersdorf we dealt with Frederick himself; thus we will devote our attention only to these two. Beyond all doubt, in tactical instruction the Prussian army—then the best in the world—greatly surpassed the Russian. Having participated in innumerable battles and campaigns, the battle-hardened Prussians were also incomparably more experienced and accustomed to combat than the Russians, who had long been at peace—not having occasion to measure themselves against European armies since the Treaty of Nystad.[31] In armaments also the Prussian army surpassed all others. It is well-known, for example, that Austrians attribute their defeat to the iron ramrods introduced by the Prince of Dessau.[32] Concerning the military genius of Fred-

---

[29] [Danilevskii's marginalia, published posthumously]: *The victory of the English over Napoleon at Waterloo was, in the first place, an isolated event, and secondly, they owed it over-whelmingly to chance: the timely arrival of the Prussians.*

[30] Alternately called the Battle of Kay, or Palzig.

[31] Of 1721, ending the Great Northern War with Sweden.

[32] Leopold I (1676–1747): Prince of Anhalt-Dessau, Prussian infantry officer most distinguished as a drill-master and technical innovator. He introduced iron ramrods around 1700, an improvement over wooden ramrods, which were prone to break in the heat of battle, requiring slower, more deliberate movements, and hence a slower rate of fire.

erick, one of the greatest commanders of all times and nations, our Fermor or Saltykov[33] cannot compare to him in any way. It is true that numbers again were in our favor, but this preponderance lost all significance at Zorndorf, where the Russian army was arranged in one huge square, in which one part of the army could not help another. And what happened? Frederick was so confident not only of victory, but of the complete destruction of the Russian army that in preliminary maneuvers he completely gave up his path of retreat. He broke through the square, of course, but the uncoordinated, broken parts closed up and continued to show the former level of resistance. In a sudden reversal of battle, these disconnected, uncoordinated parts turned from defense to an attack so strident that Frederick was in danger of being felled, and only his cavalry saved him. The battle was continued even by separate clusters. Here Frederick said his famous words: "The Russians are walls of flesh (*murs du chair*): It is not enough to kill them, they must be knocked down as well." Tired and weakened by the resistance of the disordered Russian army, the Prussians hurried to open the obstructed path of retreat.

At Kunersdorf numerical preponderance was also on our side, although nowhere near that of the Austrians or French in the famous battles they won against the Prussians. It is well known that Frederick was able to neutralize the numerical advantage of his enemies by his oblique combat formations. Falling upon one of the overstretched, immovable flanks of his opponent with significant force superiority at the point of attack, he rolled it up and brought disorder to the whole army. This maneuver was used at Kunersdorf, with complete success at the beginning. The poor deployment of the Russian artillery gave him the opportunity to bring the battle almost unimpeded. The Russians were overturned. But what was sufficient for others was no use with the Russians. Retreating from the onslaught of superior forces only as much as necessary, the Russians of the rolled-up flank drew near to the center, where the preponderance of Prussian forces was less and less. Like the resilience of a coiled spring increasing with compression, the resistance of the Russians increased until finally it overcame the onslaught—and the Prussians were tossed aside, their heads smashed. Prussian power would have been destroyed in its inception if Saltykov had not felt there was no reason to use his hands to pull Austria's chestnuts out of the fire. Frederick himself attributed his defeat to a shortage of bravery and courage among his battle-hardened regiments. If we consider that, in military arts, even in this case, Frederick made everything dependent upon him, we inevitably come to the conclusion that he was right. That is to say, however great the moral qualities of his troops, they proved lacking when measured against the Russians.

---

[33] William Fermor (1702–71): Imperial Russian Army officer, led the Russian forces at the Battle of Zorndorf. Count Petr Saltykov (1697–1772): Russian Field Marshall, commander-in-chief of the Russian army for the last half of the Seven Years' War, who won victories at Zullichau (Kay/Palzig) and Kunersdorf.

A comparison of the Russians with the French comes to the same result. In the struggle against Napoleon, besides France doubtless having the advantage in all other measures, even the numerical advantage was in its favor. What helped Russia finally defeat the invincible one and avoid defeat at Borodino, for example, where, tactically speaking, a whole third of the Russian army, deployed in an inherently defensive right wing, could not bring timely battle? To explain this phenomenon we can do no better than to repeat the words of Count L. N. Tolstoi,[34] pronouncing the final judgment on the results of the Battle of Borodino.

It was not Napoleon alone who had experienced that nightmare feeling of the mighty arm being stricken powerless, but all the generals and soldiers of his army whether they had taken part in the battle or not, after all their experience of previous battles—when after one-tenth of such efforts the enemy had fled—experienced a similar feeling of terror before an enemy who, after losing *half* his men, stood as threateningly at the end as at the beginning of the battle. The moral force of the attacking French army was exhausted. Not that sort of victory which is defined by the capture of pieces of material fastened to sticks, called standards, and of the ground on which the troops had stood and were standing, but a moral victory that convinces the enemy of the moral superiority of his opponent and of his own impotence was gained by the Russians at Borodino. The French invaders, like an infuriated animal that has in its onslaught received a mortal wound, felt that they were perishing, but could not stop, any more than the Russian army, weaker by one half, could help swerving. By the impetus gained, the French army was still able to roll forward to Moscow, but there, without further effort on the part of the Russians, it had to perish, bleeding from the mortal wound it had received at Borodino. The direct consequence of the battle of Borodino was Napoleon's senseless flight from Moscow, his retreat along the old Smolensk road, the destruction of the invading army of five hundred thousand men, and the downfall of Napoleonic France, on which at Borodino for the first time the hand of an opponent of stronger spirit had been laid.[35]

If four of the five categories of an army's strength favored our opponents to a significant degree, then nothing remains but to propose that the fifth ele-

---

[34] Lev Nikolaevich Tolstoi (1828–1910): Russian novelist and author of short fiction, essays, and plays, best known for the novels *Anna Karenina* (serialized 1873–77) and *War and Peace* (serialized in abbreviated form 1865–67; published full-length in 1869).

[35] Leo Tolstoy, *War and Peace,* trans. Louise and Aylmer Maude (New York: Simon and Schuster, 1942), bk. 10, chap. 39, 913–14.

ment of that force, that is, the moral spirit and selflessness, Russians possess to an incomparably greater degree than their opponents, whoever they may be—Swedes, Prussians, or French—and whoever leads them—Charles, Frederick, or Napoleon—to such a degree that this force overcomes all of their opponents' other advantages.

Russian military history tells us the same thing. Never once has any significant part of the Russian army laid down its arms, although more than once it has fallen into a desperate plight, as with the Prussians and French (no longer speaking of the Austrians), when full lines or whole divisions surrendered, or abandoned fortresses, almost failing to defend themselves.

But of the five elements of military strength, tactical instruction and the quality of arms are conditions that depend on our own circumstances, and thus can always be acquired. The number of forces depends on the whole population and its ability to answer the call of its fatherland—and the forces of the eighty-million-strong Russian people, ready for the direst circumstances, can be considered inexhaustible since the Russian tsar garnered the ability [after the emancipation of the serfs] to summon all classes of his people directly, without any intermediaries. The talent of the commander is a matter of chance or the gifts of Providence, which of course no one can foresee. The moral spirit of the troops, and of the population from which they are drawn as well, is as we have seen the most important force finally determining success in war, which history shows Russians possess in abundance, due to the permanent, fundamental quality of the people, which can be neither acquired nor replaced by any kind of substitute.

Add to this the ability to elevate these ever-present qualities of the Russian people to the level of disciplined enthusiasm or heroism, the fact that our opponents lack this ability, and the injustice and abstractness of the interests that they are expected to defend—and we will see that we are superior to them in spiritual force, which always brings victory as the final result.

In this overview of our forces, we have far from fully enumerated everything. We have outside our borders no fewer than twenty-five million loyal allies, the Greeks and Slavs of Turkey and Austria, whom we need only provide the opportunity to stand with us. Many will doubt the Slavs' dedication to Russia, judging by the literary and other (predominantly Austrian) parties that divide the Slavic tribes, or by the Czech youth movement's support of the Poles during the last revolt, and other such phenomena. But this comes only from the fact that they do not turn for sympathy and devotion where they ought to, where they have actual value and power. When even within Russian society we find confusion over Russia's interests, sympathy for Poles and Baltic Germans, and a view of our political and other relations from the hostile European perspective, why should we be surprised by these misunderstandings, the fog about the only true civilization of Europe, which alone can save, us clouding the heads of many people in our so-called "intelligentsia" and in the western Slavic countries? But there as everywhere, our support and strength is not in these eroded, surface layers, but in the very core of the people, which by living instinct lays all its hopes on Russia—all its sympathies are fixed upon it.

In the normal course of historical affairs, the power of the people [*narodnaia sila*] is mute: it does not raise its voice in brochures, magazines, in speeches on social occasions, or at meetings. Listening only to the declarations of the loudest voices, would we not think even now, as almost all thought not long ago, that the western borderlands of Russia, for instance, from Narva [Estonia] to the Dniester [River], are hostile toward Russia? Meanwhile, experience has shown that the troops sent to pacify the Polish uprising (in the Southwestern Krai, at least) were just as much protecting the Polish landowners from the people's revenge [*ot mesti narodnoi*]. In the same way, the people sided with Russia in the Northwestern and Baltic Krais. But this only became apparent in the western region as a result of the uprising. And that is not all: that test case proved that even in Poland itself—in that country of traditional Russia-fear and Russia-hatred—the people are on our side.

Let a war release us from diplomatic propriety and we will see how the Slavic peoples respond to the sincere, direct call of Russia, and this response by itself could tilt the scales in our favor in the struggle with enemy forces, which the force of circumstances will thus oblige us to undertake. The lack of such a call was the main reason for failure in the Eastern War, but it could not be done then anyway (due to the impossibility of combining liberal and national [*narodnaia*] politics before the emancipation of the serfs), as was already noted above.

The great matter of emancipation gave us a new power, and a new weapon. There was a time when France, puffed up by the fruits of freedom it had produced, threatened its opponents with so-called propaganda, which like a lever or a jack could shift the very foundations of their state structures, not founded on the famous principles of 1789. This weapon, always blunt and impotent with regard to us, long ago fell useless from France's hands even in regard to other European peoples as well. After all, could France offer other peoples what they already enjoy more of than the French themselves? Russia, on the contrary, this country of barbarism, stagnation, and absolutism, suddenly attained this kind of moral weapon, the force of which is still not clear even to us, although we already had occasion to use it with incredible success, since we not only pacified Poland, but even turned the whole mass of the population there into devoted subjects of Russia, who look solely to it for salvation and well-being. This moral force is called: the peasant allotment.[36] The

---

[36] Peasant allotment: Under the Emancipation Reform of 1861, emancipated serfs qualified for a parcel of land from their former owner's estate, the size of which varied according to the amount of quitrent they were willing to pay. Here and in the next chapter, Danilevskii refers to the *krest'ianskii nadel'* (peasant allotment), which was the standard provision for a peasant to buy about half of the land he worked, whereas the

banner on which is written "Orthodoxy, Slavdom, and the Peasant Allot-ment," expressing the moral, political, and economic ideal of the peoples of the Slavic cultural type, cannot fail to become a symbol of victory, our *In hoc signo vinces*[37] to bring the certainty of triumph to our ranks and those of our allies, and terror and confusion to the ranks of our opponents.

---

truly indigent qualified for the *bedniatskii nadel'*, or pauper's allotment, amounting to half of the half, or one-quarter of the land worked, granted without repayment.

[37] Latin: "In this sign, you will conquer"; in Russian, *Sim pobedishi*. Both expressions refer to Constantine I's legendary vision of a cross, or chi rho, with these words in Greek (subsequently explained to him by Jesus in a dream), which his soldiers added to their standards before the Battle of Milvian Bridge in 312, a key victory in his rise to sole power.

The Slavic Cultural-Historical Type: In Place of a Conclusion

The preceding chapter concluded the task I set for myself. A particular incident—the course of the Schleswig-Holstein question, compared to the course
of the Eastern Question before the Crimean War—allowed me to bring into
view Europe's hostility toward Russia and Slavdom. Then I tried to explain
the reasons for this hostility, which was merely expressed with particular
clarity and irreducibility in this matter, but which penetrates and encompasses all of Europe's relations with Slavdom, from the most particular to the
most general spheres. This investigation led to the conclusion that this hostility is rooted in the profound difference between the Slavic and Germanic-
Roman worlds: a difference that penetrates into the very foundations of the
general plan for how world history unfolds. Only a false understanding (that
is, not corresponding to the true principles of a scientific-naturalist systematization of phenomena) of the general course of history, the relationship of the
national to the universal, and so-called progress, could lead to distinctly
European or Germanic-Roman civilization being confused for inter-, or more
correctly, all-human Civilization. And it gave birth to a pernicious error
known as *Westernism* which, recognizing neither the close relations between
Russia and Slavdom, nor the historical significance of Slavdom, relegates us
and our brothers to a pitiful, insignificant historical role as imitators of Europe and deprives us of any hope of unique cultural significance, or of a great
historical future. After this general or theoretical overview, I tried to develop
and support with evidence the main aspects of the difference between the
Slavic and the Germanic-Roman cultural-historical types and the harmful
practical consequences to which this Westernism or Europeanism leads us. It
is the illness that afflicts the body of Russian society, the category under
which all our social ailments are subsumed. In our opinion, the only medicine
for this illness lies in the healing power of historical events themselves; this
alone can revive the soul of our society, which is suffering precisely from
despondency and disparagement. Recovery is possible and even probable because the illness fortunately has not penetrated any deeper than the uppermost social stratum. The event, or series of events, that we see as being
endowed with healing power is the final act of the struggle known as the
Eastern Question, the basis of which lies deep in the general course of world-
historical development, and which before long must put its imprint on a
whole historical period. The importance of this inevitable struggle compelled

us to delve into the objections raised against the only resolution of it that would be beneficial for Slavdom, consisting of the complete political liberation of all Slavic peoples and the formation of an All-Slavic union under the hegemony of Russia, which is the guarantee of our success in this struggle.

Having begun with general historical and philosophical considerations, I forayed into the realm of particular political considerations, indicating the path on which Russia and Slavdom are headed and must finally fulfill the future promise lying in their ethnographic foundation, and in the peculiarities that distinguish them from the other families of the great Aryan tribes. We would thus be able to conclude our investigation here, except we have yet to keep one promise made earlier. In one of the preceding chapters [chapter 7] we said that those who deny the uniqueness of Slavic culture pose this question: "What will this new civilization consist of? What will be the character of its science, its art, its civil and social structure?" Having rejected this demand as absurd, since a satisfactory answer to the question would make the actual development of this civilization unnecessary, I nevertheless promised to answer it generally, as well as could be done by comparing the essential character of hitherto-existing civilizations with the rudiments of the Slavic cultural-historical type that have so far managed to reveal themselves. So now the time has come to keep that promise, which compels me once again to turn to the realm of general historical considerations.

A description—even if only in most general terms—of the future direction of cultural-historical movement is an extremely difficult hypothetical matter. If we are to avoid falling into utterly pointless daydreams, we have no choice but to categorize in the most general fashion the activity of past cultural-historical types that have completed their task or at least clearly revealed their direction and tendency. In other words, they have reduced the historical results of their lives to the shortest possible, all-embracing formula. Thus we can compare these general categories of the results they have attained with the theoretical requirements of a full and multifaceted path of historical activity. In this way our historical *desiderata* can be expressed. Comparing them to the rudiments of historical life that Slavdom has already managed to reveal must show to what extent we are justified in expecting the future realization of these *desiderata* from the furthest extent of Slavic development, if it proceeds by the correct path we indicated above. The first necessary step is the attainment of complete political independence, together with Slavic unity, according to the second and fourth laws of the development of cultural-historical types.[1]

First of all we need to outline the general categories to provide a natural way of classifying all aspects of a people's activity that encompass all the various indications of historical life signified by the words "culture" and "civilization."

---

[1] See chapter 5.

The general categories of cultural activity, in the broadest sense of the word, that all have equal rank (which we must thus recognize as the highest categories of activity) number precisely four, no more, no less. They are:

Religious activity, addressing a person's relationship to God, understanding one's fate as morally indivisible from the general fate of humanity and the universe. That is, in more general terms, the worldview of a people, not as a theoretical, more or less hypothetical, structure accessible only to a few, but as a firm faith making up a living foundation of the whole moral activity of a person.

Cultural activity, in the strict sense of the word, addressing the relations of a person to the surrounding world: first, *theoretical and scientific*; second, *aesthetic and artistic* (in which, of course, the human is part of the surrounding world as a subject of scientific investigation, intellectual inquiry, and artistic reproduction); and third, *technical and industrial*, which is the procurement and production of the objects of the surrounding world, conforming to human needs and corresponding to a theoretical understanding both of these needs and the surrounding world.

Political activity, addressing the relations of persons amongst themselves as members of one people, and of that whole people with other peoples, as higher-order entities. And finally:

Social and economic activity, addressing not the direct relations between people as moral and political individuals, but the indirect relations concerning the conditions of the use of objects in the surrounding world, and thus their procurement and production.

Now we need to consider to what extent each of these cultural-historical types, the life of which makes up the content of world history, revealed its activity in the general categories of human activity, and what kind of results it attained.

The first cultures—Egyptian, Chinese, Babylonian, Indian, and Iranian—we can correctly call primary or autochthonous, because they formed themselves, or in a manner of speaking, brought the weak rays of pre-state human activity into focus at various points around the globe. They did not manifest any particular one of these aspects of human activity just enumerated, but were in a manner of speaking preparatory cultures, having the task of producing the conditions which enable life in an organized society in general.

Everything was still intertwined within them: religion, politics, culture, and social-economic organization had yet to be divided into distinct categories of activity, and for this reason these primordial civilizations—especially the Egyptian and Indian—are unfairly assigned a special religious character. Of course, in these primeval times when analytical thinking still played a very weak role in the intellectual activity of a person living under the stifling influence of the larger whole, a mystical-religious tendency permeated the whole structure of society of that day. But this only means that the religious realm, like all the others, had not yet separated or isolated itself. The astronomical pursuits of the Chaldean priests, like geometry for their Egyptian counterparts, were the same kinds of sacred duties as conducting religious ceremonies. Castes have been described and justified as people proceeding from different parts of the body of Brahma. If these examples can be seen as evidence of the interference of religion in science and socio-economic structures, then by the same token one could also confirm the interference of science and socio-economics in religion, as was actually the case. In China, where the prosaic, realistic tendencies did not grant such latitude to mystical-religious ideas, there was nevertheless the same blending of religion with other spheres of activity: namely, agriculture was a sacred rite. But science and politics were likewise muddled, so for example, since the exam was the only way of entering into service in the state hierarchy, astronomical observations became a criterion for state service. Therefore it is incorrect to call the ancient Egyptian and Indian states theocracies. In India, as is quite clear, the priestly caste or Brahmins are complete strangers to political ambition. Their ambition and pride was of another sort altogether: they considered their priestly, religious, scientific, or artistic calling to be something incomparably higher than the crude, worldly business of politics, which they left to lower castes, demanding not power, but only respect, for themselves. The Egyptian priests had the same kind of influence.

Religion became separated as something particular and higher only in Jewish civilization, and was its all-pervasive principle. Only the religious activity of the Jewish people has remained as its testament to posterity. This religion was unalloyed: it alone put its imprint on everything, and all other forms of activity remained neglected. In other areas the Jews produced nothing worthy of attention from their contemporaries or posterity. In science they did not even borrow anything from their neighbors, the Babylonians and Egyptians; in the arts, only religious poetry flourished; in other creative fields, as with technology, they were so weak that even for the construction and ornamentation of their temple to Jehovah—the very center of the life of their people—they had to look to the Phoenicians for assistance. Their political structure up to that point was so incomplete that they could not even preserve their independence, from not only mighty states like Babylon and Assyria, but even from minor Canaanite peoples. And all their political activity, the same as their socioeconomic structure, was a complete reflection of their religious views. But then the religious side of their life and activity was so perfect and sublime that this people is deservedly called God's Chosen People, since within it was produced the religious worldview [Christianity] that subordinated the highest, most advanced civilization to itself, that is destined to become the religion—its one, eternal, unchanging form—of all peoples. As we noted above, this conclusion does not change in the slightest whether we believe the old teaching and the new covenant are kinds of worldview gradually produced by this people, or divine revelation gradually revealed to it.

Thus we can call the Jewish cultural-historical type not only primarily, but even exclusively, religious.

Just as Jewish culture was exclusively religious, the Greek type was cultural, and predominantly artistic-cultural at that. All other aspects of development faded into the background before this one. It could even be said that in the very mental framework of the ancient Greeks, there was no fertile soil on which the economic, political, and religious aspects of human activity could grow. This people, so richly endowed in terms of culture, never acquired any economic, political, or religious sense. Socioeconomically, development never spread far. A people to whom slavery was not just an accidental, temporary thing (a process of preparing, so to speak, to attain other higher forms of social order) but a fundamental fact on which rested all of its political and intellectual life in all its philosophical humanitarianism and aesthetic splendor — such a people cannot contribute to the development of any socioeconomic ideas.

In political regards the Greeks could not even raise consciousness of the *political* unity of its tribes, even though they understood themselves as a distinct cultural entity, in opposition to all other peoples, or "barbarians." Only the common danger of Persian terror ignited a common Greek patriotism within them, but even then in an entirely incomplete form. The Spartans intentionally were late to the Battle of Marathon [490 BCE]; out of fear, Argos and Boeotia submitted to Xerxes I and did not take part in the struggle against him; the Peloponnesians insisted on sacrificing the Greek mainland to the enemy, and defended themselves on the Corinthian isthmus.[2] When the danger disappeared and patriotic enthusiasm passed, the political history of Greece returned to the history of internal dissensions and internecine strife for the most pitiful and insignificant reasons. Their egotistical views and their narrow ideas of predominance led the Spartans to help the Persians.[3] We should note that this occurred not under the initial crudeness and wildness of manners nor after the fall, but in the time of the Greeks' most flourishing intellectual development. Not grasping the state of affairs, and having no sense for the realization of the all-Greek idea, the famed Demosthenes used

---

[2] Danilevskii is describing the Second Persian Invasion of Greece (480–479 BCE); the First Invasion, under King Darius I, ended at the Battle of Marathon in 490. Darius died in 486, leaving his son, Xerxes I, with an army assembled for a follow-up campaign. Argos (a city of the Peloponnese) sided actively with Persia, while Boeotia (a region in central Greece) was cautiously neutral, but fell after the famous Battle of Thermopylae in 480. The isthmus of Corinth is the narrowest point of Greece between the Peloponnese and the Greek mainland; the allied Greeks dug in there, and the Persians would not attempt an assault, so the conflict shifted to the sea, where the Greek navy ultimately prevailed.

[3] This took place in the final phase of the Peloponnesian War between Athens and Sparta (and their respective allies), 415–404 BCE.

his eloquence to rally Athenians to the disastrous course of opposing Philip, and the Athenians, lacking all political sense, followed his advice rather than Phocion's.[4] And so it continued until their subjugation by the Romans.

In similar fashion the Greeks' religious teaching shows the lack of true religious sense and sentiment. Theirs is one of the most shallow and pathetic religious worldviews, utterly unbecoming a people reaching such heights in philosophical thought. Of the three aspects of religion that support the three aspects of the human soul—doctrine, ethics, and ritual worship—only the last had any significance, correspondingly to the artistic orientation of the Greeks. Their doctrine offers neither depth nor consistency; strictly speaking, it has no content, since it does not include metaphysics, cosmogony, any teaching about the spiritual side of the world, or a theory of its origins. The idea of Providence governing the world is foreign to this doctrine, and the highest idea to which the religious worldview of the Greeks could rise consists of blind and unthinking Fate and the personification of the law of physical necessity. To match this poverty of doctrinal contents, its ethical side is groundless and baseless. It does not provide us with a code of moral laws, sanctified by a higher divine authority that would serve as an indisputable guide in practical affairs. The history of the adventures of their divinities, which could offer living examples in place of a moral codex, is more like a schooling in immorality and temptation. In all these ways the religion of the Greeks cannot bear any kind of comparison with the philosophic pantheism of Brahmanism, where rough forms always conceal profound ideas, nor with the profound metaphysics of Buddhism, nor with the elevated teachings of Zoroastrianism, nor with the strict monotheism of Islam. Religion played such an insignificant role in Greek life that it never had its own holy scriptures: Hesiod's *Theogony*[5] does not deserve that name, being more a systematic collection of the people's legends than a religious codex; not a Bible but its own sort of *Lives of the Saints*, to which no kind of authority could be ascribed.

All these religious legends served only as material for the expression of the Greeks' artistic imagination, and by means of it were elevated to excellent artistic patterns without any mysterious or moral significance. This corresponds to the general significance of Greek religion and is why in the language of all other peoples it predominantly bears the name "mythology": that is, mythology does not serve as the outward form of something higher or concealed, but is in itself its full content and its own goal, or put simply, is the body without the soul. The religion of the Greeks is strictly speaking the worship of self-contained beauty, and thus from it comes Epicureanism, which is the true Greek worldview. Their national philosophy was manifested in all

---

[4] Demosthenes: See chap. 6, n. 16. Phocion: See chap. 5, n. 11. Philip II: See chap. 10, n. 10.

[5] Hesiod's *Theogony*: A poem from the seventh century BCE giving the first account of the origins of the Greek pantheon of deities and the cosmology associated with them.

aspects of their practical life both before and after it was formulized by Epicurus.[6] Their morality consisted solely of a sense of moderation, which is all that an aesthetic worldview can give. But this sense of moderation is more a fundamental principle of art—to take pleasure in life—than a moral-religious principle, the essence of which always involves self-sacrifice.

Just as one-sided as the Greek and Jewish cultural-historical types was the Roman type, developed and brought about by the success of only the political side of human activity. The political instincts of the Romans were unparalleled. The tribes of Latium crystallized around a small core and little by little, gradually, not by outbursts of conquest, but systematically, subjugated the entire Mediterranean basin and all the western fringes of the Atlantic coast. The freedom-loving Romans never lost, however, the gift of obedience, the gift of submitting one's personal will to the general will, the cultivation of which within a republic left room for a dictator, who for them was no political accident depending upon the predominance attained by the politically gifted, but a legal institution obliged to be put into effect under certain circumstances. And that is not all. In keeping with the growth of the state, they changed the form of government from a republic to an empire which became an institution entirely of that people, not guided by some external force (after all, consider how many weak and insignificant emperors there were) but by the will of the people instinctively sensing the necessity of the empire to support the expanded state in difficult and dangerous times. In an extension of the state life of Rome, the relations among citizens were defined in the most precise and thorough manner, comprising a complete codex of civil laws.

But also in Rome, just as in Greece, slavery was a basic, fundamental fact in the structure of society. Also cultural activity in the strict sense of the word was completely insignificant: in science, in philosophic thought, as in the arts (with the exception of architecture), Rome produced nothing original. Whether the reason for this lack of original productivity lies in the very moral, spiritual conditions of the Latin race or in their imitativeness, their slavish copying from the Greeks in the spheres of science and the arts, does not concern the present analysis; for us it is enough to register the fact itself.

What was said about the religion of the Greeks applies fully to the Romans as well. It was just as barren of internal content, lacking any profound doctrinal and ethical substance or sense, and likewise without any holy scriptures. Only by being so devoid of content could the Romans have such indifference toward other religious forms, so that the gods of all conquered peoples became their gods. The Romans' national divinities merged with the divinities of Greece, once they were translated, so to speak: Jupiter became a

---

[6] Epicurus (341–270 BCE): Philosopher emphasizing sensory experience as the basis for knowledge of reality, and basing ethics on seeking pleasure and avoiding pain, thus associated with hedonism; also influenced modern science by emphasizing empirical observation and rejecting speculative methods.

synonym for Zeus, Neptune for Poseidon, and so on. The only essential distinction between them lies in the fact that, whereas in accordance with the
fundamental trait of the Greeks' mental framework their religion took on an
exclusively aesthetic character, for the Romans, likewise corresponding to the
fundamental traits of their culture and worldview, their religion took on a
political character. Thus the teachings that could not submit to such a political
view of religion, the followers of which could not bow to the deified Roman
state (which itself was ready under such conditions to adopt the object of their
special reverence)—only they suffered religious persecution.

In this manner the civilizations following after the original, autochthonous cultures each developed only one aspect of cultural activity: the *Jewish*—
the *religious* side; the *Greek*—the *strictly cultural*; and the *Roman*—the *political*.
Therefore we must characterize the cultural-historical types of Jewish, Greek,
and Roman by the name of *single-foundation* [*odnoosnovnye*] *types*.

Further historical progress could and should be made in the development
of the fourth side of cultural activity—the socioeconomic—as well as the attainment of great versatility by means of combining several forms of cultural
activity that had so far appeared separately, in a single cultural type. The historical type known by the name *European* or *Germanic-Roman* entered into this
broader path or more complex phase of development and occupied the main
part of the historical stage after the fall of the Western Roman Empire.

Just as the logical process reveals thoughts in an individual sentient being, so did the logical course of world history, by means of analysis, distinguish the separate aspects of cultural activity from their original intertwined
(or undifferentiated) state, the main representatives of which were the ancient
states of Asia and Africa. But then evidently the moment arrived for the process of synthetic combination in the history of the Germanic-Roman peoples.
Religious truth in its eternal form of Christianity was revealed and assimilated with obedience and ecstasy by new peoples richly endowed with a spiritual nature, within which we must not fail to identify a fiery religious sentiment. Lying within the new religious teaching, as if in a seed, was the necessity of abolishing slavery, and this actually turned out to be only a passing
form of behavior for the Germanic-Roman peoples. It turned out these peoples were also richly endowed with political instincts and the capacity for
cultural development in science, the arts, and industry.

All these tasks were destined not to be entirely completed, however, due
to their being hindered by such things as the violence of their energetic character and the powerful influence (having fallen on fertile soil) of the Roman
lust for power and the Roman state structure. We have already seen that the
Christian truth was distorted in this way through the misrepresentation of the
essentially important doctrine of the significance of the Church, which turned
into the religious-political despotism of Catholicism. This churchly despotism, combined with feudalistic despotism rooted in the violence of the German character, and scholastic despotism rooted in the servile regard for the

patterns of ancient science, turned the whole history of Europe into a terrible struggle resulting in threefold anarchy: religious anarchy, or *Protestantism*, founding religious reliability upon the authority of the individual; philosophic anarchy, or *nihilistic materialism* that starts to take on the character of truth and little by little takes the place of religious conviction in peoples' minds; and political-social anarchy, or the ever widening *contradiction between political democracy and economic feudalism*.

Since these anarchies are the precursors and agents of decomposition, they of course cannot be considered vital contributions to the general treasury of humanity; and the Germanic-Roman cultural-historical type cannot be considered a successful representative of the religious or the social-economic forms of cultural activity.

On the other hand, from the political and the so-called strictly cultural side, the results of Europe's historical life have been tremendous. The peoples of Europe not only founded powerful states, having spread their power over all parts of the earth, but established abstract legal relations both among citizens themselves, and between citizens and the state. In other words, they managed to unite the political power of the state with freedom within it; that is, to a very satisfactory degree they fulfilled both sides of the purpose of government. If this freedom has not produced the kind of results that have been and still are expected, it is because of another sort of unresolved, or incorrectly resolved, issue: namely, the socioeconomic. Although of course the various peoples of Europe do not all have the same degree of political instincts, recent events have shown, however, that the ones that were long unable to settle their political affairs, like the Italians and Germans, have nevertheless finally attained, or at least very nearly attained, political unity, which is the first necessary condition for political power.

Even greater and more abundant are the fruits of European civilization in strictly cultural regards. The methods and results of European science are beyond comparison with all other contemporary cultural types, not excluding the Greek. It is the same with the fruit of industrial and technical activity. In the arts, although the peoples of Europe must cede the laurel wreath for first place to the Greeks in terms of the degree of perfection attained, they have however significantly expanded its domain and forged new pathways within it. For all these reasons we must adopt the term *dual-foundation political-cultural type* for the Germanic-Roman cultural-historical type, with the predominantly scientific and industrial character of its culture, in the strict sense of the word.

I turn now to the Slavic world, and predominantly to Russia as its only independent representative, in order to examine the results and tasks of the cultural-historical life it has only just begun from the four given points of view — religion, culture, politics, and socioeconomic structure — in order to explain, if only in the most general terms: What can we rightly expect and hope for from the Slavic cultural-historical type? Of what might this special Slavic civilization consist? And will it follow a unique path of development?

Religion constitutes the most essential, almost exclusively prevailing content of ancient Russian life, and in the present day it is the predominant intellectual interest of the common Russian people. And in truth, we can only be amazed at the ignorance and audacity of those who insist (according to their own imagination) upon the religious indifference of the Russian people.

On the objective-factual side, it is the historical fate of the Russian people and the majority of other Slavic peoples to be, along with the Greeks, the main keepers of the living commitment to the religious truth of Orthodoxy, and thus to be the successors of Israel and Byzantium in the great cause: to be divinely chosen peoples. On the subjective-mentality side, Russians and other Slavs are gifted with a thirst for religious truth, which is corroborated both by normal evidence as well as even the distortions of this spiritual aspiration.

We have already indicated the particular kind of Christianity Russia accepted, not by means of submission to a culturally more advanced Christian nationality, not by means of political predominance over such a nationality, not by means of active religious propaganda, but by means of internal discontent, dissatisfaction with paganism, and the free search for the truth.

The very character of Russians and Slavs in general is a stranger to violence, filled with gentleness, deference, and respect; it has the greatest resemblance to the Christian ideal. On the other hand, religious deviation is the affliction of the Russian people. The sects and the schism of the Old Believers reveal, first, the persistent conservativeness that will not allow the slightest change in the appearance or form of sacred things; second, especially the Dukhobors,[7] the capacity for religious-philosophical thought. In the other Slavic peoples we see the Hussite[8] religious movement, the most pure and ideal of all the religious reform movements. It did not have the rebellious reformer spirit of Luther's or Calvin's reforms, but a restorative, reconstructive character, striving for a return to the spiritual truth once brought by Saints Cyril and Methodius.[9] And even among the western Slavs, in the profoundly distortive influence of Latinism upon the character of the Polish people, we see evidence again that religious teaching does not skim over the surface of Slavic peoples. Rather, this amply demonstrates that in this abundant field every seed that is sown, depending on the specific circumstances, bears either good fruit or thistles and tares.

It is true that the religious activity of the Russian people was primarily defensive-conservative, and to some this is cause for complaint. But religious

[7] Dukhobors: Christian sect emerging in the eighteenth century or earlier, rejecting religious institutions from the conviction that God lies within each person, also known for resisting secular authority, and for ardent pacifism.

[8] Hussite movement: See chap. 10, n. 51.

[9] Cyril and Methodius: See chap. 8, n. 23.

activity is defensive by its very essence, coming from the very meaning of religion, which is either genuine revelation or at least is considered to be so by its adherents. In fact, or at least in the opinion of believers, religion undoubtedly comes from heaven, and thus it alone achieves its purpose—to be the firm, unshakeable basis of practical morality, the essence of which is nothing but selflessness and self-sacrifice, made possible only through the full reliability of the principles in the name of which such things are demanded. Any other kind of reliability—philosophical, metaphysical, and even positive-scientific—is not attainable. Not by the select few who are intellectually advanced, because they know that science and human thought are not complete, and have not said, and never say will their final word, and thus there will always remain some doubt over their results, with the possibility and even necessity of reconsideration and reinvestigation (the exact proportion of which remains completely uncertain besides); and not by the masses, for the simpler reason that this is beyond them.

Therefore, the moment religion loses the character of revelation, then depending on the value of its doctrinal and moral contents, it becomes either a philosophical system or a set of crude prejudices.

But if a religion is revelation, then obviously its development can consist only of discoveries of the truth contained within it from the very beginning, and their most precise formulation by directing special attention to one or another aspect, one or another area of religious teaching, at a certain time. This is the inherent reason for the strictly defensive character of the religious activity of those peoples to which religious truth was entrusted for protection and for transmission in an inviolably pure form to other peoples and to coming generations.

If this is the nature of true religious activity in general, then it is especially so for Orthodox Christianity after the split from the Western Church. According to Orthodox teaching, the infallibility of religious authority pertains only to the whole Church, and thus the discovery of the truth within Christianity can only be done by means of ecumenical councils—the only embodiments of the Church—which historical circumstances have prevented from convening since the eighth century. Thus a strictly defensive course of action was required of those to whom religious truth was entrusted; otherwise it would break the living commitment to what was ecumenical orthodoxy at that point of its development (or more correctly, of its discovery of religious truth) just before the Latin schism. It would lose the place to which anyone thirsting for truth could turn, with the full confidence that he will find the whole ecumenical truth, and nothing but it.

From this point of view, even Russian Old Believers acquire significance as the living proof of how faithfully that protective defensiveness was carried out. Where an insignificant change of ritual seems like an unwelcome innovation, troubling the conscience of millions of believers, that is where this kind

of caution has obviously been taken. And who knows how many imprudent
steps Old Belief has kept us from, after Europeanism overtook Russian life!

And so we can say that the religious side of cultural activity belongs to
the Slavic cultural type and Russia in particular, and is its inalienable heritage, both because of the mental framework of its constituent peoples and
also because the custody of religious truth has fallen to them. This is proven
by the positive, as well as the negative, side of the religious life of Russia and
Slavdom.

If we turn to the political side of the question, to what extent the Slavic
peoples show the capability for organizing a state system, what we see at first
glance is very discouraging. Namely all the Slavic peoples, with the exception
of Russia, either have failed to establish independent states or at least could
not maintain their independence and autonomy. The enemies of Slavdom will
conclude from this that they are politically bankrupt. This conclusion does not
withstand the slightest criticism, even if we ignore the reasons why the Slavs
until now have been hindered from forming independent political bodies,
and just accept how things actually are as a matter of fact. The fact is that the
huge majority of Slavic tribes (at least two-thirds of them, if not more) formed
a vast, continuous state that has already lasted a thousand years and keeps
growing and growing in power and might, despite all the storms that have
befallen it in its long historical life. This fact alone proves the first-rate political sense of the Slavs, at least of the great majority of them.

Since the Germanic [i.e., Holy Roman] Empire, after a not-too-long era of
its glory and might, turned into a political *monstrum*, would we be right to
conclude that the Germanic tribe is incapable of political life? Of course not,
since a Germanic tribe also formed the powerful British Empire, and because
of this the political dissolution of Germany [i.e., the Holy Roman Empire]
must be ascribed to disadvantageous external and internal conditions temporarily affecting this country, and not some fundamental insufficiency—as is
corroborated by the profound political sense of Prussia's course of action,
which it had from long ago (at least from the time of the Great Elector)[10] and
which has been crowned before our eyes by the actions of Bismarck.

This verdict about the Slavs' political incapability shows the same bad
faith, or at best the same optical illusion, as the verdicts about the supposed
lack of unity of the Russian state because, they say, maybe a hundred or so
different peoples of various designations have become part of it. They forget
that if we add the quantitative analysis to the qualitative, all this variety fades
before the magnitude of the Russian tribe. If all the western and southeastern
Slavic peoples were truly incapable of political life, then nevertheless it would

---

[10] Frederick Wilhelm of Brandenburg (1620–88): Elector of Brandenburg and duke of
Prussia, known as the "Great Elector" for his political instincts and military talents,
which set the course for Prussia's rise to hegemonic power over other German states.

have to be recognized that the Slavic tribes in general have advanced political instincts, if only on the basis of the Russian state.

But is this notion of the governmental incapability of the other, non-Russian Slavic peoples correct? The western Slavic tribes, which are still in the era of flexibility and pliability that characterizes the ethnographic period in the life of a people, have been under continual hostile political and cultural influence from the peoples of the Germanic-Roman cultural type that organized themselves [into states] at an earlier time.

Despite all that, the powerful state of Great Moravia was formed in the ninth century, having received the buds of an original culture in Orthodox and Slavic writings, which were subsequently nipped off by hostile German-Catholic influence. The Hungarian invasions broke the bond between the western Slavs. The southern part of them could not find its center of gravity due to the influence of Byzantium, the encroachment of the Turks, the acquisitions of Venice, the Magyar conquests, and Austrian border provinces. The northern part, having made a spiritual revival by the reforms of Hus, managed to form an especially well appointed state in the time of Poděbrad;[11] but how could that Slavic island, or outcropping, stand firm amidst the German flood, without leaning upon the full strength of a united Slavdom?

It could not, in exactly the same way that it cannot even today, without Russia's direct and active involvement in its fate.

Poland's independent existence was longer, but if Poland more than the other western Slavic countries was politically free from the direct external pressure of the Germanic-Roman world, that is only because it more than the others submitted to the moral and cultural predominance of the West, through the temptations of Latinism and feudalism acting upon its upper classes. Thus having preserved its body for the time being, it lost its Slavic soul, and to reclaim it, had to enter into close, and unfortunately involuntary, union with Russia.

If of all the Slavs only the Russian people managed to form a strong state, then it is as much due to its internal characteristics as to the situation that, by its geographic position, it was able to undergo the first stages of development in isolation from the interfering influence of foreign Western life.

In the example of Little Russia [*Malorossiia*, Ukraine], long separated from the rest of Russia and voluntarily united with it after finishing the fight for its independence, we see proof that it is not, as some think, only the Great Russian tribe that is endowed with great political instincts. Therefore we may hope that, given the occasion, other Slavs will show the same instincts and

---

[11] George of Kunštat and Poděbrady (1420–71): Moderate Hussite king of Bohemia, attempted to forge an agreement for all Western Christendom to settle religious disputes nonviolently, in the wake of the Hussite Wars (1419–34), called the *Tractatus pacis toti Christianitati fiendae* (Treaty on the Establishment of Peace throughout Christendom), but was opposed by popes and eventually excommunicated.

good sense, after winning their independence, to recognize voluntarily the hegemony of Russia in a political union (since essentially the circumstances of Little Russia in the time of Khmel'nitskii,[12] and of the western Slavs today, are very similar). The enthusiasm of the people, the favorable confluence of circumstances, the genius of the leaders who have risen at the head of the people's movement—perhaps all these can win their independence for them, as they did under Khmel'nitskii. But to defend it, and more importantly, to preserve the general Slavic way of life and culture, would be impossible without a close reciprocal combination with Russia.

Whatever can be said of the future, judging only by what the Slavs, especially the Russian branch, have shown until now in terms of political activity, we would be correct to include these tribes among the most gifted with political instincts among the whole family of humanity.

We consider it appropriate here to turn our attention to the special nature of this political activity, as revealed in the growth of the Russian state.

The Russian people does not send out swarms like bees from a hive, to form centers of new political societies, like the Greeks in the ancient world, or the English in more recent times. Russia does not have what are called "possessions," like Rome or again England. The Russian state, from the time of the first Moscow princes, is Russia itself gradually, irrepressibly expanding on all sides, settling the unsettled expanses adjoining it, and assimilating to itself those foreign settlements falling within its state boundaries. Only by misunderstanding the basic character of the Russian state's expansion—coming once again, like any other Russian "evil," from Europeanism clouding over the distinctively Russian view of things—would it be possible to think in terms of separate provincial entities, united with Russia only by an abstract state bond; or in terms of some kind of *non-Russians* within Russia, in Rosenheim's[13] apt expression; and not only being pleased with them, but to see in them some kind of political ideal, which would never recognize Russian political feelings or thoughts. We must hope that this cloud, like so many others, clears away.

For this reason, Russia has never had colonies to administer, and it is quite mistaken to consider Siberia as such, which many do. Colonists who leave their homeland, even voluntarily and not under compulsion, quickly lose their close bond with it and soon acquire their own unique center of gravity and particular interests, often opposed or even outright hostile to the interests of the mother country. The entire connection between them is limited to the patronage and protection of the mother country, which the colony draws upon from time to time, only when it sees an advantage in doing so. Colonies bring very little benefit to the original homeland, and if compelled to

---

[12] Khmel'nitskii: See chap. 11, n. 3.

[13] Mikhail Pavlovich Rosenheim (1820–87): Russian major general, didactic poet, essayist, and satirist, publisher of the satirical journal *Zanoza* (Splinter), 1863–65.

do so, they see it as oppression and strive all the more to gain their complete independence.

Besides the national character of the peoples from whom the colonies have been appropriated, geographic separation also has a great influence on their relations between the newly settled lands and their former homeland.

In the settlements of the Russian people, we see nothing of the sort. Wherever Russian people go, if circumstances of place and time allow them, or even require them, to form their own political organization (such as, for example, in Cossack societies), the center of the people's life nevertheless remains old Rus' and Moscow. The highest power in their minds continues to be embodied in the person of the Russian tsar. They are quick to swear their oath to him, to submit new lands they possess to him, and establish direct connection with the Russian state. Preserving its system, they do not cut themselves off from the Russian people, but continue to consider its interests their interests, and are ready to sacrifice everything to attain its goals. Simply put, they do not form new centers of Russian life, but only enlarge its circle, single and unbroken. Therefore the new settlements are acquired only through bordering lands that have already become an actual part of old Rus' (I speak in terms of the original settlement of people, and not of state colonization efforts). Settlement by fits and starts across the sea or great distances will not succeed, even if protected and patronized by the state. Our American colony did not succeed, nor will what we are doing in the Amur region.[14]

The manner of the Russian people's settlement, highly conducive to the unity and wholeness of the Russian state, also corresponds to the Russian people's assimilation strength, making the foreigners it comes into contact or conflict with, into its own flesh and blood—if not barred by misguided state measures, of course.

But the foundation and expansion of the state, and the securing of its durability, power, and might, all constitute only one side of political activity. There is another side: establishing lawful relations of citizens, amongst themselves and with the state; that is, establishing civil and state freedoms, without the capacity for which a people must not be considered fully endowed with healthy political instincts. So, is the Russian people capable of freedom?

It is hardly necessary to recall that our "well-wishers" would answer this in the negative: some consider slavery the Russian's natural state; others fear, or imagine they are afraid, that giving [Russians] freedom would inevitably lead to all kinds of excesses and abuses. But on the basis of the facts of Russian history and an acquaintance with the attitudes and behaviors of the Russian people, it is only possible to draw a diametrically opposite conclusion:

---

[14] Amur region: Territory in the Russian Far East, annexed from China by treaty in 1858. Its administrative center, Blagoveshchensk, was founded in 1856. Later, the construction of the Trans-Siberian Railroad (1891–1916) through the region warded off the failure Danilevskii predicted.

specifically, that rarely has there been or is there a people so capable of bearing the great burden of freedom and being less inclined to abuse it as is the Russian people.

This is based upon the following characteristics inherent in each Russian person: the ability and habit of obeying; the respect and trust of power; the absence of ambition; and the aversion for taking on what he considers himself incompetent to do. But if we delve into the reasons for all the political disturbances of various other peoples, the root of them will turn out to be not the aspiration for freedom, but precisely ambition and a vain passion for meddling in affairs that lie beyond the scope of their comprehension. The major events of Russian history as well as everyday events of Russian life equally corroborate these aspects of the Russian people's character.

In fact, take a look at the elective offices in all of our social classes, particularly the merchant class, the lower middle classes, and the peasantry. These offices, conferring power and honor, are considered not rights but duties, or to put it better, social obligations; and the only exception is really the office of the marshal [of the nobility], which confers honor but not power.

If they seek the position of magistrates, members, and chairmen of the [zemstvo] executive board mainly for the salary, which is ample enough for rural, town, or even provincial center living, what of it? Government service with an ample salary enables them to maintain their household. Would it not be interesting to see, if experimentation in such matters were allowed, how our zemstvo and court system would fare if, following the theories of *Vest'*,[15] we filled them with unpaid agents of the so-called aristocracy?

In any case these traits of the Russian people's character show that power holds little fascination for us, and even though many consider it some kind of defect, we see nothing wrong about our public figures wanting material compensation for their work for the common good. They could never go completely without compensation, since the satisfaction of ambition, vanity, and pride is the same as taking bribes.

The characteristics of the Russian people enumerated above constitute the internal reason for why Russia is almost the only state that never had (and in all likelihood never will have) a political revolution—that is, a revolution having the goal of limiting the dimensions of power, concentrating power in part or in full upon a certain social class or the full mass of citizens, and banishing the rightful tsarist dynasty and replacing it with something else.[16]

---

[15] *Vest'*: See chap. 6, n. 14.

[16] Although he clearly failed to anticipate the Russian Revolutions of 1905 and 1917, Danilevskii's observation here seems more apt if we consider the frequency and variety of attempted revolutions across Europe after 1789. Prosecuted for his participation in the Petrashevskii circle in the 1840s, he knew firsthand that groups labeled "revolutionary" in Russia paled in comparison with their European counterparts. The lack of any marginal comment here (added to previous chapters in the early 1880s) may indi-

All the disturbances in Russian history that by their strength and outward appearance could be considered popular uprisings have always had a completely unique character, not political in the strict sense of the word. The reasons for them were doubts about the rightfulness of the person on the throne; unrest over serfdom, which in practice always exceedingly oppressed the people placed under its rule; and finally, those elements of self-will and riotous conduct that inevitably take shape in Russia's borderlands in the ongoing struggle of the Cossacks with the Tatars and other nomads. These three elements simultaneously took part in the three main popular uprisings that broke out in Russia in the seventeenth and eighteenth centuries, so that each of them alternately played a predominant role.

In the disturbances of the interregnum,[17] the driving force was the impostors,[18] but also a significant part was the discontent among Cossack bandits and the peasants only just bound to the land.

The rebellion of Stenka Razin[19] [in 1670–71] was primarily the work of those bandits who had begun to fear that the introduction of stricter state regulations would limit their autonomy. But again those disturbances could spread so wide only through the discontent of the serfs over their bondage, and furthermore by the legal pretexts they used to lend all the disorders the semblance of legality in the eyes of the people.

Finally, the main force of Pugachev's[20] uprising [1773–74] was mainly serf uprisings, for which a few Ural Cossack rebellions served only as the first spark igniting the fire, so to speak. The participation of the Ural Cossacks strengthened this rebellion, but the name of Peter III was needed to lend it

---

cate that he felt this observation from the late-1860s still held up, even despite the assassination of Alexander II on 13 March 1881. It is a fair reminder that most historical events seem inevitable only after the fact.

[17] I.e., the Time of Troubles (1598–1613). See chap. 10, n. 57.

[18] Three impostors claimed to be Ivan IV's son Dmitrii during the Time of Troubles. False Dmitrii I actually ruled for nearly a year (1605–06), then was killed in a palace coup. The First False Dmitrii's widow later recognized the Second False Dmitrii as her husband, adding to the confusion.

[19] Stepan Timofeevich (Stenka) Razin (1630–71): Cossack leader of a band of marauders who acquired a popular following and led a rebellion, promising freedom from boyar rule and practicing plunder. He turned Astrakhan into a Cossack republic and proceeded up the Volga. Defeated at Simbirsk, he abandoned his armies, was anathematized by the Church, lost the Don Cossacks' support, and was captured, then executed in Red Square.

[20] Emilian Ivanovich Pugachev (1742–75): Cossack deserter turned fugitive who claimed to be Peter III and rallied supporters by promising concessions to Cossacks and Old Believers. He controlled the region from the Volga to the Urals, including the city of Kazan and its arsenal; the response of state troops was slow and ineffectual, but gradually prevailed. His own forces turned him over, and he was sent caged to Moscow for public execution.

legality in the eyes of the people, which always feels solidarity with supreme power, and expected from it the fulfillment of their cherished hopes and just demands.

Now that the rightfulness and legality of the succession to the throne is secured; now that civil society and lawful order among the Cossacks has been introduced; and finally now that the serfs have been emancipated, all the causes of former disturbances among the people have vanished. Any further—not to say revolution, but even a simple rebellion going beyond an unfortunate misunderstanding, has been made impossible in Russia, until there is a change in the Russian people's moral character, worldview, and complete frame of mind. And such changes (if they can be considered generally possible) will only happen with the passage of centuries, and thus lie beyond the scope of human foresight.[21]

In this manner all the elements of rebellion that could provoke the Russian people in former times have been removed. At the same time, the circumstances that required the continual harnessing of all the people's power under the yoke of the state, in the difficult times of the state's formation—its struggle with external enemies, its still sparse population, and the weak state of its power—have all now passed. Thus both the internal and external obstacles preventing the Russian people from enjoying all the gifts of freedom have lost their meaning, significance, and reason for existence.

The artificial creation of these obstacles in the name of precaution against completely illusory dangers would be like erecting a series of dykes and ramparts against flooding on the high ground where the water will never rise, or thick castle walls, fortifications, and bastions in a city far from any danger of hostile attack.

The moderation, equanimity, and prudence characterizing both the Russian people and Russian society have been very clearly demonstrated by the events of recent years. In the history of the human race, one could hardly find more sudden, rapid changes in the main social conditions of the people's life than those that have happened before our very eyes, in no more than twenty years, starting with the manifesto about improving the lives of manorial serfs.[22] Feudal slavery was abolished gradually in France, over centuries, so

---

[21] These changes in the people's worldview and mentality, as precursors to revolution, were not so far off as Danilevskii believed, of course. But he saw the Russian people as an organic entity, proceeding through developmental stages of a lifecycle, which justified his belief that Russia had matured through, and was safely past, a troublesome adolescent stage. The breakdown that he says is centuries away, was in his mind equated with senility and decrepitude coming only after a period of robust maturity.

[22] Presumably the Manifest o trekhdnevoi barshchine (Manifesto on the Three-Day Corvée), drafted under Paul I, in 1797, limiting serfs' labor obligations to three days per week; it was included in Nicholaevan law codes after 1833 and reissued as a circular in 1853 during the Crimean War.

that in the famous night of 4 August [1789] it only remained for the National Assembly to abolish the comparatively insignificant remnants of it;[23] meanwhile for us, serfdom remained in full force until it was abolished all at once, with all of the aftereffects of doing it thus. The transition from relations of oppressive dependence to full freedom was instantaneous: centuries concentrated into some three years, requiring committees to formulate a plan. Under the rapid implementation of the new conditions by the announcement of the Emancipation Manifesto to the people, and thus the end of the people's dependence on the landlords, the new powers of arbitrators were still not established, so that during these critical moments (as they were generally considered) the people remained for some time without direct local supervision. And yet essentially there were no disturbances anywhere, and no amount of incitement could budge it [the people] from that state of calm, full of faith in the government—neither then, nor afterward. The main agent fulfilling the sovereign's will for emancipating the serfs, Iakov Ivanovich Rostovtsev,[24] described the status of Russia during the conferences about how emancipation would be implemented by saying that Russia has fallen off its pedestal and hangs in mid-air. It really seemed that way to everyone, particularly to those who watched the reforms with malicious joy, expecting it nearly to cause the hateful colossus to topple; but in fact it turned out that even then, as always, it remained undisturbed upon its broad, unshakeable foundations.

Take another example. Preliminary censorship was weakened, then finally abolished completely. Here as well the change was so rapid and sudden, from the time when the slightest anecdote containing a hint about the awkward manner or dress of some bureaucrat in some department finding its way into print could bring severe consequences for both the author and the censor who permitted it, to the point where questions of religion, morality, and the arrangement of society and state have become commonplace themes for books, pamphlets, and magazines. The difference is huge, once again more extreme than the change in the French press from the time of Louis XV [r. 1715–74] and Louis XVI [r. 1774–92] to the revolution; after all, what could be added to what we find in the works of Diderot, Helvétius, Holbach, La

---

[23] In an extended session lasting much of the night, the National Constituent Assembly of revolutionary France abolished numerous feudal privileges in an atmosphere of heady rhetoric, grand gestures, and frequent votes by acclamation, the legacy of which was significant public confusion about the application of such laws, not to mention significant legislative remorse.

[24] Iakov Ivanovich Rostovtsev (1803–60): Russian military officer, named to the secret committee to form the plan for emancipation and author of its final report, on the strength of which he was named chair of the commission to draft the actual Emancipation Manifesto and the accompanying law statutes.

Mettrie, and Mirabeau[25] circulating under Louis XV and XVI, despite their purely nominal suppression? But here too Russian literature and Russian society showed the same good sense and moderation as the Russian people during the fundamental change to its civil and social status. Harmful teachings had already begun to circulate in part by underground press, and had great influence in part due to the public fascination with all forbidden foreign publications. They were now destroyed, deprived of significance and reliability in the eyes of the public—not by any sort of governmental measures (which in this regard were not only powerless but usually even undermined their own purposes), but by the press itself, and primarily the Moscow press.

So what do we see? The abuses and oppression that afflicted Russia before the reforms of the present tsar's reign were no less, and in many jurisdictions were more, painful than what France strove against before the revolution. The transformation (not merely in form, of course, but in essence) was no less radical than that carried out by the National Assembly. But whereas the dam that burst in France produced a catastrophic flood of harmful, antisocial elements and passions, in Russia it not only could not disrupt the calm, respect, and trust in the authorities, but even strengthened them and shored up the foundations of Russian society and the state. After that, do we not have the right to affirm that the Russian people and all layers of Russian society can accept and bear any amount of freedom? And that any advice to limit it could only have in mind the dangers arising from a morbid imagination, or even worse, under the influence of some kind of secret, bad-faith convictions and aspirations hostile to Russia?

So we conclude, both in regard to the power and might of the state, through its ability to sacrifice all personal rights to it, and in regard to its exercise of civil and social freedoms, that the Russian people is endowed with remarkable political instincts. By its [the Russian people's] trust and devotion to state interests, unpretentiousness, moderation in the use of its freedom (also shown by the Slavic peoples in Austria, and Serbia in particular), we can ap-

---

[25] Diderot: See chap. 8, n. 36. Claude Adrien Helvétius (1715–71): French philosopher and author, famous for the 1758 book *De l'esprit* (On Mind), which produced a scandal for its materialist, utilitarian, and atheistic claims, which he repeatedly retracted. Paul-Henri Thiry, Baron d'Holbach (1723–89): German-born, naturalized French philosopher and prolific atheist author, most famous for his 1770 book *Le Système de la nature* (The System of Nature), which grounded his atheism and materialism in naturalism. Julien Offray de La Mettrie (1709–51): French physician and materialist philosopher, most famous for his 1748 book *L'homme machine* (Man as Machine), which rejected the Cartesian claim that humans had souls while animals did not. He promoted sensualism in his subsequent work at the court of Frederick the Great, and died young from a lifestyle of excess. Honoré Gabriel Riqueti, comte de Mirabeau (1749–91): French politician and prominent orator, a moderate constitutional monarchist in the French Revolution. In pre-revolutionary times, he published various things, the most scandalous being several works of erotica, which Danilevskii presumably has in mind.

ply this characteristic to the other Slavs as well. If Poland in the course of its historical life has turned out an example of the absence of political sense, then even this negative example only supports our proposition by showing that any distortion of Slavic principles, having corroded its body and soul, must bear fruit correspondingly.

In regard to its socioeconomic structure, Russia is the only sizable state having firm ground beneath its feet, with no landless masses; thus the social structure is not founded on the neediness of the majority of citizens or on their lack of means, but [is founded] where there is no contradiction between the political and economic ideals. We have seen that this very contradiction threatens the poverty of European life, which, while swimming through history, has entered those dangerous waters with the Charybdis of Caesarism, or military dictatorship, on the one side, and the Scylla of social revolution on the other. What lends such superiority to the Russian social structure over the European, giving it unshakeable stability and turning those very social classes that threaten Europe with revolution into the most conservative in Russia, consists of the peasant allotment and the vast extent of its lands.

The etymological similarity of the word *obshchina* and *obshchinnyi*[26] with the word *communism* (when translated into French) gave rise to ill-intentioned dishonesty in confusing these ideas, in order to cast an unseemly shadow not only on our *obshchina* but at the same time on all actions in general of people concerned about the peasants' well-being, especially where this runs counter to Polish and German interests. What is largely forgotten in this is that our *obshchina*, whether good or not in its economic and other effects, is by historical right ours—just as sacred and inviolable as any other form of property, or as individual property itself. Thus any intention to destroy it cannot at all be called a conservative intention. European socialism, on the contrary, is a revolutionary ideology, not so much by its essence, as by the soil on which it happens to operate. If it is nothing more than an invitation to small landholders to combine their holdings into common ownership, just as factory workers are invited to combine their forces and capital by means of association, then there would be absolutely nothing criminal or harmful in that. But the issue is that in most cases the lands do not belong to those who work them, and thus European socialism, in whatever form, requires first of all the redistribution of property: the complete reorganization of land-ownership and the whole socioeconomic structure. The harm is not in socialist theories, which purport to be the medicine to treat the basic illness of European society. It may be these medicines are actually harmful and poisonous; but what is the danger in them, so long as they sit calmly on the pharmacist's shelves, unneeded for a healthy organism? Medicine may be harmful, but so is disease. There are many plans for transforming the structure, but not the material to do it, without tearing down the preexisting, longstanding, finished structure. We on the

---

[26] Noun and adjective referring to the Russian peasant village commune.

contrary have material in abundance, and all by ourselves are organically taking shape under the influence of inherent founding principles, with no need for any dreamed-up construction plans.

The health of Russia's socioeconomic structure also constitutes the reason to hope for the great socioeconomic significance of the Slavic cultural-historical type, to establish for the first time a legal, normalized character in this branch of human activity. It would encompass the relations between people, not only as moral and political agents, but also in their impact on the world of nature, as the source of human wants and needs: to establish not just abstract but real, tangible justice in relations between citizens.

We still need to examine whether we can expect the Slavic cultural-historical type to hold a prominent place in cultural matters, in the strict sense of the word.

We must not fail to recognize that what has been accomplished until now by Russian and other Slavic peoples in the sciences and arts is rather insignificant, in comparison to what has been done by the two great cultural types—the Greek and the European.

Two explanations can be offered for this unflattering fact: it is either the Slavs' basic incapacity for cultural activity, or their relative youth and recent arrival on the stage of historical activity, plus the unfavorable circumstances of their development in this regard. If it is possible to demonstrate the definite, significant influence of the latter reason, and moreover if the course of development generally requires that cultural activity follows from the political activity of the Slavs, then it will be clear that only the second explanation is most likely.

Concerning the stature of Slavic culture in general, compared to that of European culture: the amount of time elapsed from the emergence of Germanic peoples out of the ethnographic stage of life into their historical period exceeds by four centuries the historical lifespan of the Slavic states. It is exactly the same with German literature: That is, the first kernel of cultural development—the translation of the Bible into the Gothic language by Ulfilas[27]—is five centuries older than the corresponding Slavic translation by Saints Cyril and Methodius. Add to that the fact that almost all modern European peoples began their historical lives on the soil of ancient culture, thus on soil richer in nourishing substances, stimulating faster growth. This could only have a beneficial effect on them, since harmful imitativeness of the vanished peoples of the Roman world was possible only in small measure. For all that, the medieval period of the history of European peoples, which was primarily the state phase of their lives, continued for nearly a thousand years. So the Slavs have only now lived as long at the state stage of life as the Germanic

---

[27] Ulfilas (4th century): Romanized Goth, ordained bishop, practicing Arian, missionary and Bible translator, devised the Gothic alphabet in order to translate the scriptures.

peoples had lived by the beginning of modern history. But chronology alone does not have great significance for questions of this type. Above we noted that after the ethnographic stage of life, during which the peculiarities of peoples' mental frameworks, the things that make them special, unique historical subjects, are shaped and defined, they then without fail enter the period of their state existence. We do not see in history a single example in which actual cultural activity was begun any sooner than, if not the complete end of state activity (since in the life of a whole people, just as in the life of individual people, all of its functions continue until death, though diminishing in strength), then at least the completion of the urgent tasks of state administration, such as the assertion of national independence and the definition of the boundaries of the nation-state. Even if there were examples in which the cultural activity of some peoples continued after the loss of political independence, still it has never happened that culture got its start under a foreign yoke. This fact, to which there are no exceptions, we set forth as one of the laws of the development of cultural-historical types, and it is not hard to understand why it is universally true.

In fact, if a people is conquered while still in the prime of its vital strength, but before it has managed to attain cultural development, then obviously all the moral forces of the most highly-endowed individuals will strive to restore the greater good of the people—its lost independence. All the heroism of the people will take on a patriotic-militant character. But if, on the contrary, the energy of the people is dispersed—whether as the result of its actual exhaustion or as the result of the conquerors' skillful policies of suppression—and the foreign influence begins little by little to spread among the conquered people, then in the natural course of things this influence will overtake primarily the upper classes, those able to acquire an education, which will inevitably take on the character of the victorious, conquering nationality. Under such circumstances, it is from the lower classes, where nationality is generally preserved longer, that the exceptional individuals will arise due to their uncommon abilities and talents. Thus in this situation all the results of the subordinate nationality's intellectual efforts go into the victors' intellectual repository and enrich it. But this is rare. The foreign influence on education and the social milieu, not corresponding to the inner makeup of the soul of the people, cannot harmonize with its psychological needs. This would be like an eagle trying to raise a lion cub.

It is hard to teach the French or the English to think like a German, and vice versa. This is harder still for the Slav, due to the sizable ethnographic distance separating them. This means that what I say about the reasons hindering the beginnings of culture among peoples lacking political independence, also applies somewhat to the psychological subjugation of peoples from one cultural type to those of another. Only in this case the barrenness of culture is not so fatal or inevitable, since some degree of national independence is preserved in the social milieu, and the language of the people remains not only a means for everyday communication, but also as an organ of literature and enlightenment in general, and among some thinking people are glimmers of consciousness of the need for a unique, national culture. Additionally, if extraordinarily talented people appear, then with no special effort the fruit of their activity will most naturally go to the benefit of their people. And finally, other aspects of the politically independent people's historical activity have a stimulating effect on the culture itself. These considerations show that we do not need to expand much upon the reasons for the lack of an original scientific and artistic culture among the western Slavs, which do not enjoy the highest national blessing of independence, having the misfortune of losing it before the onset of the cultural period of their lives.

However, during the semi-independence that Czechia enjoyed before its inclusion among the hereditary lands of the house of Habsburg—semi-independence, because it was still part of the Germanic empire so hostile to Slavdom—some remarkable branches of culture were revealed that, if cultivated on the profoundly national religious soil of Hussitism, would have borne fruit, had that whole heroic outpouring for Slavic independence not been drenched in Slavic blood and crushed by the combined power of Latinism and Germanism.

Therefore we can focus all our attention on Russia, as the only independent Slavic state. We said the construction of the state is a people's first historical activity, derived from the circumstances of its ethnographic way of life. It must have advanced to a certain degree before it can begin its cultural activity, in the strict sense of the term. Obviously the expenditure of strength must be proportional to the difficulty of the task, but the difficulty of the governmental task for Russia was such that it is no wonder it lasted a thousand years, consuming all the strength of the people, when it took western peoples just as long to complete an incomparably easier task. Earlier I reiterated the special type of obstacles that the territory of the Russian state presented for establishing and strengthening state structures upon it: obstacles consisting primarily of the fact that its vast forests and steppes enabled its sparse population, still living in its ethnographic way of life, to shrug off the burdens laid upon it by the state and escape them without active opposition.

A territory like this, falling into the hands of a population already accustomed to life within a highly organized state (as happened in the United States of America), in no danger from outside, not needing the body of the state to have such powerful cohesion and concentration, turns the activity of the people toward the struggle with nature, and to the acquisition of wealth, the value of which the population already understands. This gave American culture a primarily technical, industrial character. In Russia, on the contrary, under threat of attack from outside enemies on all sides (first predominantly from the east, then from the west), the lack of a concentrated state inevitably led to the irrevocable loss of the people's independence because even with it the exertion of the full strength of the people was needed to repulse enemies.

From this followed the need to undertake the strongest possible approach to state-political activity, that is, autocratic or solo rule, which by its unlimited power directed individual activity toward common goals, just as the conditions of American life led to industrial activity under the weakest possible, democratic-federal approach. In both cases, scientific and artistic activity had to fade to the background; there has not yet been time enough for them.

This intense state activity during the Moscovite era was strengthened further by the Petrine reforms, the essence of which was political and state-oriented, not cultural at all. In essence, everything was sacrificed to the state, as it had to be according to the necessities of that time. For this reason, along with the completely pointless and harmful alterations of Russian life according to foreign style, it must be recognized that the reform by itself brought more hindrance than help to true cultural development. The conditions would have been more favorable for that if Russia's unique cultural forces had only gradually become acquainted with European art and science. But this is redeemed by the fact that the transformation, by shoring up the political might of Russia, preserved the main condition for the life of the people: the political independence of the state. According to the quite correct, accepted way of stating it, from the time of Peter the entire people was harnessed in the service of the state, the nobility directly, and the other classes indirectly: the merchants financially, in terms of industry; the peasants, through serfdom either to the nobility or the state.

The necessity of harnessing all the people's strength for exclusively political purposes came from the fact that the European states with which Russia had *volens-nolens* to enter into close political relations, had already managed to become densely populated, achieve a harmonious order, and amass many scientific and industrial accomplishments. The armies, not exceeding a few tens of thousands throughout the middle ages, had grown since the time of Louis XIV to number in the hundreds of thousands of soldiers, equipped with a variety of expensive armaments, the manufacture of which required significant technical development of the country. All this applied to an even greater degree to the navy.

In this regard America, to which Russia is frequently compared, stands completely opposite of it, as we have already noted. Not surrounded by enemies, it could economize where others had to spend to defend their political independence. If we take into consideration only what Russia had to spend on arms from the time of the conclusion of the peace in Europe at the Congress of Vienna [1815], this alone would run into the billions, which Russia might have used, like America, for its railroad network, a merchant fleet, and all kinds of technical advances in agriculture and industry. The recent civil war required the American people to make a massive effort to preserve its unity, and thus its strength and true independence. This effort, in financial terms, cost a few billion, and around half a million human lives. If there had been in America a standing army serving the central government, then of course the insurrection would have been put down incomparably easier and more quickly at the very start, but in general complexity, a proper military organization would still cost America more than the one-time effort it put forth. Moreover it only had to do so at the point when the long-term allocation of the country's resources (not spent on the defense of the state) had already amassed such great quantities of wealth as could not be formed without it. If however America had been in Europe's situation, then it would have had to make such extraordinary efforts all too often, and the American system would have cost even more than the European, and just simply would have been impossible.

The European states in this regard occupy a middle position between America and Russia. And although they were each surrounded from the beginning by other states from which they had to defend themselves, still, from having arisen together, they grew up and developed in a parallel, reciprocal fashion. Thus none of them could surpass the others to any significant degree in population density, productive capacity, and technical or military advances; thus none of them needed to devote all its resources toward a single side of development, in order not to fall behind its rivals. Since its political-governmental activity did not need to reach such extreme intensity, there were enough resources left free to be applied to the other fields of activity.

To explain how the intense state activity of the Russian people hindered its cultural development, we will retrace the ways that the general character of the people's activity, shaped by the force of circumstances, influences individual activity. The most crude and perhaps least valid means, in this regard, is direct compulsion by state power. Without going into the time when each had to serve [the state] for his whole life, we wonder, was not it not so long ago that avoiding state service was looked down upon, among those from the only social class that had the position and means to take up enlightened, non-physical work?

We will turn our attention to the more valid, positive means, consisting of the advantages and privileges that state service offers to any young person. Always and everywhere there are so few people with a strong enough natural inclination toward some specific vocation to overcome the attractions of such advantages, that in the general course of human affairs it is hard to place much hope on them.

But that is not all. Corresponding to state goals, in educational institutions founded by the state, the nature of education consists of preparing young people, and even children, for a certain branch of state service. Obviously, in such an order of things, parents form a certain ideal for their children's future career, for which they prepare them from childhood and, more importantly, impart to them the same view of life and its requirements from the cradle on.

We think this kind of social environment cannot fail to have an effect on the very character of intellectual and moral inclinations and the kinds of abilities, in completely distinct, purely physiological ways. In an unknown, mysterious way parents pass physical traits to their children: physical characteristics, predispositions to certain illnesses, intellectual and psychological qualities. So it would be very strange if a persistent psychological outlook were not transmitted in the same way. Only by accepting this idea can we explain the so-called "golden age" of literature, art, and science. In the second half of the fifteenth and sixteenth centuries, painting was the main interest of Italian life. It brought glory, fame, and wealth; all the somewhat-educated classes of people were enthralled by the products of this art, thinking and talking all about it; the attention of the whole society was turned toward it. As a result of all this, is it not probable that the special combination of the physical elements that produce the result we call the artistic nature have much greater chances of being fulfilled? On the other hand, the ideal of activity held up in front of Italians from childhood on certainly facilitated the development of such natures.

To all the reasons why the activity of individual persons corresponds with the outlook of the social environment in which it is done—as a consequence of which the Russian people's activity must have a political-governmental character—we must add the fact that public education has still not managed to penetrate to the masses, which explains the weakness of purely cultural results. Besides the generally beneficial effect on the level of development of the people's abilities, education is necessary for the vital purpose of enabling those with particularly gifted natures, no doubt scattered across all layers of society, to recognize their strengths and escape the limited role that fate designated for them. Finally, scientific and artistic activity may be only the fruit of leisure-time, abundance, and excess resources left over from vital historical work. Have Russians and other Slavs had much left over for this?

All these considerations, it seems to me, provide an entirely satisfactory answer why to this point Russia and the other Slavic countries have not been able to take a prominent place in terms of purely cultural activity, even if nature has given them abilities ample enough for doing so. But the indications of the abilities and spiritual resources required for brilliant activity in the field of science and art are indisputably already present in the Slavic peoples, despite all the unfavorable circumstances of their lives. Thus we can rightly expect that with a change of these conditions they will develop luxuriant flowers and fruit.

In fact, have not various Slavic peoples brought forth some famous names in various fields of science: Copernicus, Rokitansky, Purkinje, Šafárik, Ostrogradskii, and Pirogov?[28] But examples from all civilizations show not only

---

[28] Baron Carl von Rokitansky (1804–78): Czech physician and professor, pioneer of diagnostic autopsy and anatomical pathology. Jan Evangelista Purkinje (1787–1869): Czech anatomist and physiologist, credited with numerous discoveries in vision, brain

that cultural activity follows from the more or less successful completion of
the political-governmental task, but furthermore, that broad scientific development was always the last of its fruit. In other words, art precedes science.
Correspondingly, in Slavic culture the indications of original artistic development are much more abundant than indications of original scientific
development.

Having grown accustomed to looking contemptuously at everything Russian, we do not notice that in some fields of fine literature we have set forth
examples comparable to the highest works of European literature. We can
boldly state this about Russian comedy, folk tales, and lyric poetry. We cannot and will not go deeper into a comparative critical investigation of Russian
art and literature for aforementioned reasons, but so as not to leave what we
have said as an unfounded, completely unsubstantiated assertion, I will offer
at least a few examples:

To find a work on par with *Dead Souls* [1842] requires us to look as far as
Don Quixote [1605, 1615]. Gogol's declared purpose was to present in comic
form the abuse and roguery of provincial society and the crudeness of land-
lordly manners, just as Cervantes's declared purpose was to ridicule knight
errantry.[29] But for both authors, the profundity of their poetic conceptions
incomparably exceeded their stated purposes, and in all likelihood did so
completely unbeknownst to them. Don Quixote turned out as a living personification of towering heroism and the noblest spiritual qualities, which were
lacking in the fields of normal, productive activities due to the impoverished
contents of Spanish life. Only a century before, Spanish heroism could be seen
in the splendid feats of the conquistadors; in Cervantes's time there was no
practical outlet for the Spanish hero; only the realm of fantasy remained for
him. And our Chichikov is his own kind of hero, but, according to the nature

---

anatomy, pharmacology, microscopy, and fingerprinting. Pavel Josef Šafárik (1795–
1861): Slovak author, philologist, ethnologist, and academic Slavist. Mikhail Vasilievich Ostrogradskii (1801–62): Ukrainian mathematician and physicist, known for
contributions to calculus, algebra, probability theory, classical mechanics, and physics.
Nikolai Ivanovich Pirogov (1810–81): Russian physician, pioneering field surgery techniques, including the use of anesthesia and systematic triage, in the Crimean War and
later, the Russo-Turkish war of 1877–78.

[29] Nikolai Vasil'evich Gogol' (1809–52): Ukrainian-born playwright, novelist, and short
fiction writer of life in St. Petersburg and the provincial countryside, especially ethnic
Ukraine. Most famous for *Dead Souls*, an "epic poem in prose" following the rogue-
hero Chichikov through the households of various eccentric landowners. Gogol'
burned the manuscripts of his attempts to continue the story. Miguel de Cervantes
(1547–1616): Spanish novelist, playwright, and poet. His best-known work, the comic
mock-epic novel *Don Quixote*, was published in two installments, 1605 and 1615, juxta-
posing the title character's imaginary knightly adventures with the mundane world.
Danilevskii read a French translation of *Don Quixote* while in prison (see Strakhov's
introduction).

of the outlook of the times inculcated in us, a hero of practical life—smart, firm, elusive, and undeterred. He is a Ulysses of his own sort, but lacking any ideal aspiration, for where in life would he get this? He has abandoned his principles and not acquired others (since this is impossible), and at the same time is unable to apply himself to anything truly useful, likewise due to the impoverished contents of Russian life, its narrow constraints and lack of freedom. This orients people with a practical frame of mind toward goals that are purely personal and crudely egotistical, to cunning tricks of imposture, and by that imposture, connecting and correlating to the state institutions permeating all of Russian life. If the hero of the Russian tragicomic *poema* does not invoke our humane sentiments, as does the Spanish hero, it is because we better understand the reason for the perversion of his nature by the social environment, whereas the madness of Don Quixote is presented as the accidental result of his feverish hallucinations, kindled by his reading of ridiculous novels. For this reason, the entire premise of *Dead Souls* is incomparably higher than the premise of *Don Quixote,* which has in all only two real characters, the hero of La Mancha himself and his sidekick Sancho.

Gogol's "Old World Landowners" [1835] and "The Overcoat" [1842] represent the height of true humor, which fills us involuntarily with sincere, profound sympathy for the most petty, insignificant, comical personalities, based on the elements of true humanity we see within them.

Pushkin's *Boris Godunov* [1831][30] although not drama in the strict sense of the word, but dramatized in epic form, is the most complete production of its type, after the dramatic chronicles of Shakespeare. In terms of beauty of form, perfection of execution, and artistry of reproducing reality, neither *Wallenstein* nor *William Tell* by Schiller,[31] poetic works of the same sort, can compare to it.

Russian literature also presents an example of another sort of high epic work, which is Lev Tolstoi's *War and Peace*. The images of the historical background are not just the setting for the development of the novel's intrigues. On the contrary, as in an actual epic, the resources and peculiarities of the people's spirit expressed within the events constitute the main content of the work, where all the interest is focused, providing the light to illuminate the picture. Just as in real life, the fates of individual people are intertwined with these events. *War and Peace* is an epic retelling of Russia's struggle with Napo-

---

[30] Aleksandr Sergeevich Pushkin (1799–1837): Russia's greatest poet and Romantic-Classicist author of plays and short stories, most famous for his verse novel *Evgenii Onegin* (serialized 1825–32). *Boris Godunov* (1831), a play in blank verse dramatizing the title character's ill-fated reign in the Time of Troubles, was first allowed to be performed in 1866 under the relaxed censorship standards of the reform era; in 1868 it was adapted as an opera by Modest Petrovich Mussorgskii (1839–81).

[31] Friedrich von Schiller, and *Wallenstein*: See chap. 3, nn. 17 and 19. *William Tell* (1804) dramatizes the struggle of a huntsman, famed for marksmanship, caught up in a Swiss rebellion against the Holy Roman Empire in the fourteenth century.

leon. The author's hypothesis and the reflective side of his work, of course, to some extent mars the artistic, creative side of it, not so much by the error, or more precisely, the exaggeration of his views, as by their irrelevance. This flaw however does not have near the significance that the majority of our critics ascribe to it, because all these passages easily slough off, as something superficial and extraneous to the artistic structure of the great *poema*. The work of Count L. Tolstoy and its colossal success is one of the most remarkable signs of the times, since all of this shows that we are still capable of an epic understanding of our past, that it can still produce a sensation among us, and thus, that in essence we are better than we seem. Show us another comparable work anywhere in European literature!

Admittedly, Russian letters do not offer examples of true drama. But are there many in all European literature?

As a matter of fact, after Shakespeare there has not been a single true playwright, at least among those peoples whose literature is widely known. Schiller, who in the opinion of the best critics occupies first place after Shakespeare, did not produce anything capable of satisfying the requirements we rightly expect of tragedy. So even his best dramas, *William Tell* and *Wallenstein*, lack the dramatic element.

In the realm of other arts, we can point to at least one painting that stands alongside the highest artistic works, and if it does not enjoy among us the fame it deserves, it is only from our inability to appreciate it due to our habit of measuring everything by a foreign standard, due to the picture's lack of the ostentation [*effektnost*] now dominating the style in Europe, due to the depth of its content, since its primary merit is what we may call the "soul" of the work. Only truly original Russian individuals, like Gogol' and Khomiakov,[32] understood and gave Ivanov's *The Appearance of Christ to the People* [1857] its due.[33] If what is called "composition," or the expression of a profound idea by means of patterns, is one of, or even the most important quality of an artistic work, then the painting is first-rate in the highest sense of the word.

The artist's goal was to represent the variety of impressions that the idea of Christianity must have created upon the world at its first appearance: impressions that contain, as if in the seed, the whole influence that it would have in its furthest development as the fulfillment of the highest spiritual requirements, as well as all the passions and interests it would incite against itself. Simply put, the artist's intention was for his picture to serve as the frontispiece, the overture to the great event only just begun. Such a purpose had to

---

[32] Khomiakov: See chap. 7, n. 2.

[33] Aleksandr Andreevich Ivanov (1806–58): Russian Neoclassical painter, praised by the Slavophiles, but given mixed reviews from the broader public until after his death. He was friends with Gogol' in Italy, where he painted *The Appearance of Christ to the People* over twenty years; it depicts the Gospels' account of Jesus being recognized as the Christ by John the Baptist (see Matt. 3, Mark 1: 4–11, and Luke 3: 1–22).

represent in bodily forms the higher manifestations of the soul, without the help of allegory or the supernatural; thus the artist did not have at his disposal the means of conveying attributes ascribed by our imagination to the world above. The most ideal spirituality must be depicted on the basis of, and using the means of, the strictest realism. Hardly has an artist ever given himself such a difficult task. It is no wonder that the fulfillment of it took so many years and that it turned out so wonderfully profound, yet at the same time so strikingly clear, that you can read the thought of the artist as clearly in the painting as in a book.

First of all, it was necessary to convey that this is the first appearance of Christ on the field of historical activity. Still unknown to anyone, He could not in and of himself make an impression on the unprepared masses by a single appearance; he was still submerged in himself, since he had not yet stepped out of his internal preparation for his higher purpose. Therefore the artist made the figure of the Savior only an ideal center of the picture, but outside of the movement of it. To recognize Him and show him to the people requires an interpreter, gifted with the spirit of prophecy and foresight, and John the Baptist is presented to us as the archetypal severe and fiery prophet from the wilderness, in the manner of Elijah. By the truth and power of the expression, one cannot imagine anything more real and true to form than this figure, the actual center of the composition, driving and commanding everything else. If Raphael created the archetype of the Holy Virgin, then Ivanov claims the honor of having created the archetype of the Baptist. By his spirit, he recognized the Savior of the world in the form of the man approaching slowly and calmly from the hill, and the inspired look, the rapturous movement of his hands and whole body conveys to the people what he has foreseen and comprehended by the spirit. Not by themselves, but through him, do they turn to Christ, toward the great one having to fulfill his destiny, with the variety of motives, expectations, and apprehensions that have been stirred within them. The different perceptions of the great idea realized in Christ are grouped into three clusters of people in the painting. Behind John to the viewer's left are gathered the disciples and future disciples of Christ, who accept His teaching in the spirit of truth, authentically and profoundly. To the right coming down from the hill is an indifferent and hostile crowd, drawn from Jerusalem by talk of the wilderness-dweller's exploits. Within this crowd are some Roman horsemen, people from another world not at all concerned, evidently, with all that has taken place so far, or if so, only administratively, as a matter for the attention of the police—for whom the importance of these events will become clear only later. In the middle is a group of Jews with a young male child just come from the water, not yet dressed—personifying an idea toward the Savior in the middle, between his true followers and his enemies. It represents those who will shout "Hosanna" one day, and a few days later will watch the crucifixion indifferently; those who expected political power and all earthly goods from the Messiah. This crude, selfish perception of Christ's teaching is expressed with uncommon clarity in the person of a re-joicing Jew—crude, earthy joy. His young son is more indifferent; one sees in him a simple, apathetic curiosity, and while his attention is occupied, his body seems to shudder from the feeling of freshness from having just finished bathing. A slave smiles with the same kind of brutish joy; in his deep abase-ment he is still not in a condition to understand and appreciate the spiritual significance of Christianity, but only feels instinctively a coming improve-ment to his pitiful lot.

This division of the figures into three groups thus corresponds to the three main ways the teaching of Christ was received. It is not however some kind of artificially conceived gimmick, so to speak, to convey the artist's in-tentions to his viewers, but proceeds in the most natural way from the content of the subject matter. In fact, those hungering for truth first of all had to heed a call to repentance, coming from the wilderness; and here they have already accepted the baptism of John, heard his teaching, and become the Prophet's companions. Nearest of all to him is the other John who, following the direc-tion of the Baptist's gaze and hand gesture, has turned his soul toward the spiritual Sun on the horizon, and his body automatically follows the flight of his soul. Those drawn to John not by spiritual thirst but by earthly expecta-tions had to respond to the call later than the leading figures of revival. Therefore they have only just been baptized, and have only just come from the water at the moment depicted in the painting. The hostile forces from Jerusalem had to appear last of all, having come to see what the people were worked up about, what was causing the commotion; and correspondingly, they are also presented as only just reaching the Jordan. Their faces show doubt, proud disdain, and hostility toward the one capable of disrupting their power and influence.

Such is the conception of the painting, having concentrated, or focused, into itself this whole series of impressions and subsequent events proceeding from them. The details of the painting—the wonderful landscape, the hot, dusty, steppe-like atmosphere, and the freshness emanating from the Jordan; the beauty, proportion, vitality, and relief of the figures—I will not discuss, as subjects not constituting the specialties of our great master. I have elaborated on this painting by Ivanov because, in my opinion, it more clearly than any-thing else expresses the peculiarities of the Russian aesthetic gaze.

In sculpture we likewise have one artistic work standing out from the crowd: the group of the *Transfiguration* by Pimenov for St. Isaac's Cathedral,[34] where it has, however, damaged the gilding. I will devote my attention only to the sculpturally amazing figures of Elijah and Moses, depicted as flying.

---

[34] Nikolai Stepanovich Pimenov (1812–64): Russian sculptor, trained in Italy for over a decade, returned to St. Petersburg in the 1850s, when he completed his compositions for St. Isaac's Cathedral (two small iconostases, *Transfiguration* and *Resurrection*), and taught in the Academy of Arts until his death.

Since of course they must be supported by something, the folds of their robes trailing beneath provide their point of support. And here we must also note that there is the same distribution of figures in three groups as in Ivanov's painting. The flying figures are supported by sagging robes; but if technical necessity did not demand this—if the figures could suspend themselves in mid-air—their robes nevertheless still would have to fall into the same folds, by the properties of matter and the laws of gravity. The robes are not pedestals, but fulfill that purpose almost accidentally, incidentally. There is rhyme, but the poem was not written for the rhyme; if same-sounding endings were not required, those words would still have to be used, being the most precise, expressive, direct, and conveying the idea best of all. I have dwelt upon the technical challenge overcome as evidence of the strict fulfillment of the demands of aesthetics and realism, which constitutes one of the distinctive traits of Russian art, and of Russian poetry as well.

Connoisseurs of music see the same clarity of expression, artistry, and finish, combined with originality and wealth of melodies, in the musical works of Glinka.[35]

True, the other Slavic peoples, long deprived of political independence, do not present anything outstanding in the fields of art and literature. The Poles alone have a first-class poet in Mickiewicz,[36] whose works express both the originality and high lyricism of the poet, as well as the insignificance and the caricature, so to speak, that the life and customs of Polish society have become. So they are presented in *Pan Tadeusz*, in which the poet did not at all intend to satirize his fellow countrymen, but on the contrary, to show full sympathy for their way of life. But then, Slavs like the bellicose Serbs who are, or at least until recently were, at the spontaneous stage of development, offer remarkable examples of purely national creativity, but have not yet combined the parts of a national epic into a whole.

So we see that the Slavic cultural type has already shown ample instincts for artistic development, and to a lesser degree, for scientific development. In any case, from this we can draw conclusions about its ability to attain, also in this regard, a significant degree of development. Only the relative youth of the tribe and the exertion of all of its forces toward other, more urgent forms of activity fully absorbing them, have so far prevented the Slavs from attaining cultural significance in the strict sense of the word. This cannot and must not cause us embarrassment, since it shows that the path of development is correct.

---

[35] Mikhail Ivanovich Glinka (1804–57): Russian composer regarded as the "father of Russian classical music," best known for two operas, *Ivan Susanin*, retitled *A Life for the Tsar* (1836), and *Ruslan and Liudmila* (1842), the latter of which is known for incorporating Russian folk melodies, an innovation adopted by later composers in the national style.

[36] Mickiewicz: See chap. 8, n. 8.

So long as no site has been cleared and no sturdy foundation has been dug in the soil, there cannot and ought not be any thought of building a solid structure; all that can be built is a temporary dwelling, which we can rightly expect and demand to reveal the builder's talents only partially. The foundation is the political independence of the tribe, and thus, all Slavic resources must be directed toward attaining it. This is essential for two reasons: in the first place, because without the consciousness of tribal unity and wholeness set apart from other tribes (and not only without the consciousness, but without its actual accomplishment, which by itself can bring this consciousness into the general understanding of the masses of the people), cultural uniqueness is impossible. That is, strictly speaking, culture itself is impossible, since the term does not apply to what is not unique. Secondly, because without the fruitful interaction among those related to each other, freed from foreign power and the influence of the people units into which all the members of a tribe are divided, diversity and wealth of culture are impossible. We can see one example of this fertilizing influence in the mutual interaction of Great Russian [*Velikorusskii*] and Little Russian [*Malorusskii*, Ukrainian] religious outlooks.

In regard to the Slavs, this necessary prerequisite of political independence has the same particular importance, in cultural and in other regards, as the very struggle with the Germanic-Roman world, without which Slavic independence is impossible. It must serve as the medicine to eradicate the plague of imitativeness and slavish regard toward Europe which entered the body and soul of Slavdom through some unfavorable conditions of its historical development. Only now has the historical moment arrived for the beginning of this cultural development, since the emancipation of the serfs inaugurated the period of Russia's cultural life and concluded the governmental period of its life, the importance of which, we noted above, consisted precisely of leading the people from tribal rule to civil freedom by means of political discipline. But first, as the *sine qua non* of success, strong and mighty Russia was given a difficult task—to liberate its fellow tribesmen, and by this struggle to fortify itself and them with the spirit of All-Slavic self-consciousness and uniqueness.

And so, from analysis of the most essential general results of the activity of the cultural-historical types preceding us, and from comparison, partly with the particularities of the Slavic world already described, and partly with the inclinations that lie in the Slavic nature, we can nourish a well-founded hope. That is, that the Slavic cultural-historical type for the first time presents the synthesis of all aspects of cultural activity in the broadest meaning of the word, aspects that were cultivated by its predecessors on the historical field only singly, or at least nowhere near a complete combination. We can hope that the Slavic type will be the first full *quadruple-foundation cultural-historical type*. Its especially original trait must be for the first time having achieved a satisfactory resolution of the socioeconomic issue. What kind of mutual relationship do the three other aspects of cultural activity have within it? Which of them provides its predominant coloration? Will they each occupy the main role, one after the other? Finally, what qualitative character will its strictly cultural activity take on, having managed until now to be much less defined than the other forms of activity? Of course all this is impossible to foresee.

Whether this hope will be realized depends entirely on the educative influence of preparatory events under the general name of the Eastern Question, which constitutes the intersection and vital center of the future of Slavdom.

The main current of world history flows from two sources on the banks of the ancient Nile. One, heavenly and divine, flowing through Jerusalem and Tsargrad, runs in undefiled purity to Kiev and Moscow; the other, earthly and human—in turn dividing into two main channels, of culture and politics—flows through Athens, Alexandria, and Rome into the countries of Europe, occasionally drying up, but being restored again by new, more and more abundant waters. In the Russian land, a new spring has burst forth, a social and economic system that justly provides for the masses of the people. Across the broad plains of Slavdom, all these streams must flow into one vast sea.

> And I believe, it starts at once:
> The river its banks will overflow,
> Gazing at blue sky above,
> And heaven itself will all bestow.
> See how waters so widespread
> The yawning valley irrigated,
> And strangers, drawn by holy thirst,
> Upon its verdant shores are sated![37]

---

[37] From A. S. Khomiakov's 1835 poem "Kliuch" (The Key).

Appendix
Editions of Danilevskii's Works, 1991–Present

Rossiia i Evropa. Istoriko-literaturnyi arkhiv. Edited by S. A. Vaigachev. Moscow: Kniga, 1991.

Rusija i Evropa. Translated and with a foreword by Pavle D. Ivić. Notes and afterword by S. A. Vaigačev. Beograd: Dosije, 1994. [Serbian translation]

Rossiia i Evropa: Vzgliad na kul'turnye i politicheskie otnosheniia slavianskogo mira k germano-romanskomu. Literaturnoe nasledie russkikh myslitelei. St. Petersburg: Glagol, 1995.

Gore pobediteliam: Politicheskie stat'i. Moscow: Alir/Oblizdat, 1998. [Abridged reprint of the 1890 Sbornik politicheskikh i ekonomicheskikh statei, containing the articles "Stezia Nikolaia Danilevskogo" (A. V. Efremov); "Rossiia i Franko-germanskaia voina"; "Voina za Bolgariiu"; "Gore pobediteliam!"; "Neskol'ko slov po povodu konstitutsionnykh vozhdelenii nashei 'liberal'noi pressy'"; "Proiskhozhenie nashego nigilizma"; "Vladimir Solov'ev o pravoslavii i katolitsizme"]

Rossiia i Evropa. Moscow: Drevnee i sovremenee, 2002.

Rossiia i Evropa: Vzgliad na kul'turnye i politicheskie otnosheniia slavianskogo mira k germano-romanskomu. Imperskoe myshlenie. Moscow: Eksmo/Algoritm, 2003.

Rossiia i Evropa. Moscow: Izvestiia, 2003.

Rossiia i Evropa. Sotsio-Logos. Moscow: TERRA/Knizhnii Klub, 2008.

Rossiia i Evropa: Vzgliad na kul'turnye i politicheskie otnosheniia slavianskogo mira k germano-romanskomu. Russkaia tsivilizatsiia. Moscow: Institut russkoi tsivilizatsii, 2008.

Rossiia i Evropa. Vzgliad na kul'turnye i politicheskie otnosheniia slavianskogo mira k germano-romanskomu. Edited and with introduction and notes by A. V. Repnikov and M. A. Emel'ianov-Luk'ianchikov. Biblioteka otechestvennoi obshchestvennoi mysli, vol. 42. Moscow, ROSSPEN, 2010.

Politicheskaia filosofiia: Dopolneniia k knige "Rossiia i Evropa." Moscow: FIV, 2013.

Index